Internet of Things

Surya S. Durbha
Professor,
CSRE, Indian Institute of Technology Bombay (IITB)

Jyoti Joglekar
Professor,
Department of Computer Engineering
K. J. Somaiya College of Engineering (KJSCE)
Somaiya Vidyavihar University (SVU)
Mumbai

OXFORD
UNIVERSITY PRESS

OXFORD
UNIVERSITY PRESS

Oxford University Press is a department of the University of Oxford.
It furthers the University's objective of excellence in research, scholarship,
and education by publishing worldwide. Oxford is a registered trade mark of
Oxford University Press in the UK and in certain other countries.

Published in India by
Oxford University Press
22 Workspace, 2nd Floor, 1/22 Asaf Ali Road, New Delhi 110002

© Oxford University Press 2021

The moral rights of the author/s have been asserted.

First published in 2021

All rights reserved. No part of this publication may be reproduced, stored in
a retrieval system, or transmitted, in any form or by any means, without the
prior permission in writing of Oxford University Press, or as expressly permitted
by law, by licence, or under terms agreed with the appropriate reprographics
rights organization. Enquiries concerning reproduction outside the scope of the
above should be sent to the Rights Department, Oxford University Press, at the
address above.

You must not circulate this work in any other form
and you must impose this same condition on any acquirer.

ISBN-13: 978-0-19-012109-9
ISBN-10: 0-19-012109-2
eISBN-13: 978-0-19-099222-4

Typeset in Adobe Garamond Pro and Myriad Pro
by Cameo Corporate Services Limited, Chennai
Printed in India by Nutech Print Services - India

Cover image: © Chesky

Cover illustration: by Manoj Kumar

For product information and current price, please visit www.india.oup.com

Third-party website addresses mentioned in this book are provided
by Oxford University Press in good faith and for information only.
Oxford University Press disclaims any responsibility for the material contained therein.

Preface

The Internet of Things (IoT) is creating unprecedented new business and scientific opportunities that are envisaged to make giant leaps in the way humans interact with Things that were earlier mostly static in nature. The IoT technology is demonstrating the ease of making interaction with our environment more dynamically by embedding devices that host a variety of sensors and actuators capable of providing real-time actionable information.

The interdisciplinary nature of IoT is enabling many cross-domain applications providing a host of services in many areas such as smart cities, healthcare, retail, agriculture, industrial automation, etc. However, with it also comes many interoperability challenges to overcome so that the devices and applications can work without being constrained by the underlying representations and protocols. Towards this, huge efforts are underway by several organizations to develop reference models and standards at every level of the IoT stack. These standards are now gradually making their way into various IoT system implementations.

Another major reason for the widespread interest and efforts for adoption of IoT technologies is the availability of a variety of sensors that are capable of sensing a wide range of variables related to the physical environment, equipment, infrastructures, etc.

The current technologies for integration of IoT with cloud is facilitating the development of highly scalable IoT systems. Several IoT cloud solutions are also providing functionality to perform big data analytics using various approaches such as AI, machine learning, and deep learning, running on high-performance computing (HPC) systems.

Another emerging area is real-time IoT data analysis called edge analytics, which is performed at the edge of the IoT devices to provide situational awareness. This is usually integrated with IoT gateways.

Rapidly evolving electronic device technology such as microcontroller chips, nuclear batteries with large life time, etc. will open new avenues for deploying IoT solutions in inaccessible terrains in the near future. Various business models are emerging on monetization of the IoT systems and holds great promise for high return on investment.

About this Book

Internet of Things (IoT) covers a wide range of topics providing both introductory aspects of IoT as well as recent advances in IoT. A lucid treatment of the subject matter is adopted to enable the reader to easily grasp the concepts and techniques. This book strives to strike a balance between the theoretical content and hands-on material.

The IoT domain contains aspects that are related to both hardware and software, hence, there is a need to provide equal treatment on both those aspects. Various well-known hardware (sensors/actuators, microcontrollers, etc.) are described and how to use them to develop IoT-based systems is also explained. The book discusses the most relevant hardware that is available in the market for readers to purchase it and begin experimentation. It covers several examples with various hardware. The theoretical material related to the software aspects of IoT is also complemented by focused examples using well-known programming languages such as Java and Python.

The target readers of this book are undergraduate and post-graduate engineering and science students (BE/B.Tech/M.Tech/BSc/MSc), and computer applications' students (BCA/MCA). It can be adopted as a text book for the IoT courses in these degree programs. Further, software engineers, web developers, IoT product designers, educators, and beginners in IoT will find this book useful. We also recommend this book for managerial personnel who are managing IoT systems.

Features of the Book

- Approaches IoT in an application-oriented manner, connecting the foundational aspects of the subject with its relevance in real-life applications and spread with easily understandable examples throughout the book.
- Each chapter begins with a bulleted list under the heading "Chapter Objectives", listing the knowledge the readers would gain after reading it.
- This is followed by a "Recap" box that consists of a bulleted list of key concepts and the relevant sections in the book that the reader needs to be familiar with before embarking on the current chapter.
- Boxed items provided in each chapter describe a particular concept/technology/application in more detail.
- Hands-on programming exercises in Python, Java, Arduino are provided with step-by-step instructions in relevant chapters.
- Discusses use cases with fully working code in an exclusive chapter.
- A section on "Best Practices" is provided for relevant chapters at the end of each chapter, followed by the sections "Further Reading", "Exercises" and "Key References".

Organization of the Book

The book is divided into five parts and 18 chapters, listed below:

Part I: Foundational Aspects

Chapter 1: Emergence of IoT
This chapter begins with the vision and explanation of various definitions of the IoT from different perspectives and settles on one working definition forming the basis on which the rest of the concepts are explained in this book. The interdisciplinary nature of IoT, the challenges involved in its further evolution and standardization, and contribution factors across various disciplines to the widespread diffusion of IoT are also explained.

Chapter 2: Concept of Smart Things/Objects
This chapter discusses how Things are made smart through sensors, actuators, communication over network interfaces, and connection to the Internet with some motivating examples. The Machine-to-Machine (M2M) concepts are described and the key differences between IoT and M2M are explained.

Chapter 3: Wireless Sensor Networks in IoT

This chapter introduces wireless sensor networks (WSNs) and describes its basic attributes. Further, different network topologies in WSN are presented. The WSN communication patterns such as broadcast, multicast, flooding, gossiping, and other related protocols are discussed. Data aggregation approaches and various routing techniques in WSNs are described. Several real-world applications of WSNs are discussed. Finally, the evolution of wireless sensor networks towards IoT is presented.

Chapter 4: IoT Standards and Protocols

This chapter describes various wired and wireless technologies available. Various layers, protocols, packets, and services are explained. Role of IPV6 in IoT is elucidated. In addition, various low-power wide-area network (LPWAN) technologies specifically designed for low baud rate and long-range communications such as NB-IoT and LoRaWAN are discussed. Several data link layer communication protocols such as WirelessHART, Z-Wave, Bluetooth and ZigBee, DASH7 and LTE-A are introduced.

Part II: Understanding the Nuts and Bolts of IoT Hardware, Software, and Middleware

Chapter 5: Sensors and Actuators in IoT

This chapter describes the perception layer of the IoT. It covers a comprehensive description of various sensors such as those available on a mobile phone like light sensors, environment measuring sensors such as temperature and pressure, medical sensors such as heart and pulse rate sensors, flow and fluid measuring sensors, range and motion capture sensors, and touch sensors. A description is provided for different types of actuators such as servo motor, stepper motor, DC/AC motor, linear actuators such as solenoid and relay. Several application areas corresponding to the sensors and actuators are presented. The subsequent chapters provide a hands-on approach for integration of these sensors with various prototyping kits such as Arduino, Raspberry pi, pcDuino, and Beaglebone.

Chapter 6: Open Hardware in IoT

This chapter explains open hardware technologies available for making IoT applications such as Arduino, Raspberry pi, Beaglebone, pcDuino, and CubieBoardto design a customised board suitable for a specific application. Comparison of different existing open hardware platforms is provided. It discusses how to choose the right platform for a specific application based on the limitations and capabilities of the hardware and complexity of the problem. Further, cellular IoT devices discussed are Adafruit Feather 32u4 Fona, GOBLIN 2, LinkItONE, Hologram Dash, and Arduino GPRS Shield. In addition, a description of industrial microcontrollers such as PLC and RTU is given. A comparison of various hardware platforms based on several attributes such as Size, Weight, CPU, Memory, and Power, as well as Expansion Connectors, Operating System, and Programming Languages is presented.

Chapter 7: IoT Middleware

This chapter begins with the description of the function and high-level description of a middleware followed by an explanation about the fundamental features of a middleware. The need for an IoT middleware is clearly brought out and the functional and non-functional requirements are presented. Various architectures of the IoT middleware are explained with a comparison. The development of IOT services is described based on Services Oriented Architecture (SOA), and various flavours of SOA such as HTTP/REST, HTTP/SOAP, WS-I, and JMS are explained. State-of-the-art IoT Middleware

(OpenIoT, KaaIoT, Node-RED, CHOReOS, LinkSmart, CarrIoT, Oracle Fusion and Google Cloud IoT) both Commercial off the Shelf (COTS) and open source are reviewed along with the main application domains for which they were developed.

Chapter 8: IoT Software Platforms

This chapter introduces the need for developing IoT platforms, and explains the fundamental characteristics of an IoT Platform, and its benefits. A general framework for IoT platforms is presented and each component of that framework is described. Further, the IoT software platforms landscape is described in terms of Commercial IoT platforms (Amazon Web Service (AWS) IoT Platform, Bosch IoT Suite, EVRYTHNG, IBM Watson IoT Platform, Cisco Kinetic IoT, Google IoT Cloud, and Microsoft Azure IoT Suite) and open source IoT platforms (ThingsBoard, OGC SensorThings, Thinger.io, SiteWhere, and ThingSpeak). Some guidelines for choosing an IoT platform are presented. A step-by-step, hands-on exercise using an IoT platform (ThingsBoard) is given towards the end of the chapter.

Chapter 9: Prototyping IoT Applications

This chapter explains the importance of prototyping and its benefits while developing IoT projects with physical objects, software and hardware controllers, sensors, actuators, and Internet. It explains various steps of prototyping with examples in several application domains. The various stages involved in prototyping are explored such as refining IoT product idea, physical and logical design considerations, choosing a specific microcontroller, design of housing for the physical object and moving parts, and developing and enabling web services through which the IoT device shares the information or acts as a smart thing. Various online prototyping tools, APIs for real-time IoT applications, packages for IoT in Python are reviewed. The embedded code writing section explains the use of IDEs, various IoT related programming languages and efficient code writing. A real world prototype example (hands-on exercise) related to smart home is described towards the end of the chapter

Part III: IoT Big Data Science and Analytics

Chapter 10: Big IoT Data Science

This chapter introduces the foundations and principles of big data science from an IoT perspective. The steps involved in the data science process are described with examples written in Python. The concepts of artificial Intelligence (AI) and machine learning including the recently emerging Deep learning approaches are described from an IoT analytics point of view. Concepts of Data lake/Swamp are discussed and the chapter introduces the concept of Edge analytics (chapter 12 is entirely dedicated to edge analytics). Machine learning tools are explained with IoT use cases. The various forms of big IoT data analytics such as descriptive, diagnostic, predictive and prescriptive analytics are described. Further, a section on various approaches for real-time analytics such as event stream and data stream mining approaches is presented. IoT Data stream learners for classification, regression, clustering, and frequent pattern mining are explained with examples coded in Python and R. Further, currently popular machine learning and deep learning tools are reviewed.

Chapter 11: IoT in the Cloud

Elucidates the complementary aspects of cloud computing and IoT. The drivers for integration of Cloud and IoT are explained. How the Cloud IoT paradigm is evolving and various cloud computing service models are described. Emerging new services such as SaaS (Sensing as a Service), SAaaS (Sensing and Actuation as a Service), SEaaS (Sensor Event as a Service), SenaaS (Sensor as a Service), are explained. Current IoT-based cloud providers and their offerings are given.

Chapter 12: Edge Analytics: Near Real-time Sensor Stream Processing
This chapter begins with the definitions of Stream, its characteristics and Stream processing in the context of IOT, and provides a general framework for stream processing. Various existing platforms are described and compared. The concept of Fog computing, which is an extension of Cloud computing to the edge of the network is described. Edge computing and Edge analytics are described in terms of Event stream processing (ESP) and Complex event processing (CEP). Various open source stream processing tools are introduced. An example walkthrough of performing edge analytics is described. This chapter concludes with a scope for future developments and various applications, which are using the stream processing approaches.

Chapter 13: Embedded High Performance Computing (HPC) for IoT
This chapter introduces the basic elements of embedded high performance computing. It explains the need to address the data throughput requirements of high-density computing applications of IoT. Several IoT application areas, which will benefit from embedded HPC are described. A general framework for developing Embedded HPC applications is presented. Graphics processing Units (GPUs) are explained, and introduction to GPU-based cluster computing is presented. Embedded HPC development toolkits are introduced along with various software tools. IoT applications using embedded HPC are described along with a hands-on example on using an embedded HPC platform (Jetson Nano) for image analytics.

Part IV: Data Management in IoT

Chapter 14: Interoperability in the IoT Ecosystem
This chapter addresses the issues surrounding the seamless and meaningful exchange of data and services between various interconnected IoT networks that have different network and communication protocols, data representations and configurations. The IoT architecture reference model (IoT-A) and its various submodels focusing on the immutable components of IoT domain are discussed. Further, various types of IoT interoperability are described. The concept of an Ontology is introduced, and the W3C standard Web Ontology Language (OWL) for developing ontologies is presented. Semantic sensor web development efforts by various organizations are given. The concept of Web of Things is introduced and its usefulness in enabling interoperability by connecting things and applications to the internet is described. The role of W3C in developing and promoting standards related to sensor networks and IoT are also presented.

Chapter 15: CyberSecurity and Privacy
The chapter begins by describing how everyday things will pose high information security risks in an IoT context and how these risks can percolate to various levels. Subsequently, various security issues related to services, hardware resources, information, and data in IoT are presented. The key attributes; data confidentiality, privacy, and trust are described. The specific challenges encountered in IoT security are elaborated. The specific security issues involved each of the IoT layers (perception, network, and

application) are explained. Further, various forms of cyber attacks on IoT infrastructures are explained with examples. Further, various attacks on user privacy are elaborated and solutions to overcome them are presented. Need for lightweight cryptography for IoT systems is elaborated. Best practices for securing IoT devices are also explained.

Chapter 16: IoT and Business Processes Management
This chapter describes the linkages between IoT and Business Process Management (BPM). BPEL and BPMN are explained, and how they can be used for streaming data from IoT to understand optimal paths, exceptions, and business events is discussed. The BPMN extensions required to incorporate IoT processes into BPM are described with illustrative examples. The services based on Services Oriented Architecture (SOA) and BPM processes reacting to sensor-related data and events are also explained through examples. A BPM and IoT case study is described with supply chain management as the application domain.

Part V: Compelling Use Cases of IoT

Chapter 17: IoT Use Cases
This chapter describes the following applications: Smart Agriculture, Smart Healthcare, Home Automation and Smart goods transportation. The description about the targeted organizations/sectors/people are described in each use case. Further, components that are required to build a specific IoT application (based on the use case) such as sensors/actuators, prototyping boards, connections, middleware, and IoT software platforms are presented, along with the corresponding code/pseudo code to develop such an application.

Chapter 18: Future Outlook
This chapter describes the future outlook of IoT from various perspectives. It is described in terms of a roadmap for the next 5 years on different aspects of IoT such as protocols, sensors, platforms, and new applications.

Acknowledgements

Writing this book has been an interesting, challenging and rewarding experience. It took a lot of effort and time, and felt much harder than any other academic work that I have done before. It would not have been possible without the unwavering love, support and encouragement of my dear wife, Gayatri, daughter, Amruta Varshini, and son, Suryansh Prasad, who created the right ambience at home and bore extended periods of my absence while working on the book.

I am eternally grateful to my father, Dr Prasad Rao, and mother, Dr Pushpa, who both being in the academic line, instilled in me very early on the worth of books, strewing them all around the home and leaving no room without the sight of a book. To my dear sister, Dr Sitalakshmi, I express my gratitude for being there with me through thick and thin. I sincerely thank the co-author, Dr Joglekar, for making this book writing endeavour both pleasant and intellectually stimulating. Thanks to my Ph.D. students, Abhisek Potnis and Rajat Shinde, for helping in the development of some hands-on exercises.

I am highly grateful to Dr Roger King for his mentorship. He once said to me "never say never" and I kept believing it since then. My heartfelt thanks to the excellent folks at the Oxford University Press, India for their inputs, feedback and patience.

Any comments and suggestions for further improvement of the book are welcome; please send them at surya.durbha@gmail.com.

Surya Durbha

First, I would like to thank my co-author Dr Durbha, Professor, CSRE, IIT Bombay for his expert inputs throughout the journey that have culminated in the release of this book.

I appreciate my undergraduate and post-graduate interns for performing IoT experiments with me because of which we could present good use-case examples in this book. Thanks to the Oxford University Press, India team for acting as technical proof-readers and editors for compiling this book.

I want to express my gratitude to my brother, Ajit Joglekar, who helped in designing and polishing the figures and illustrations. My husband, Manmohan Soman, and daughter, Pradnya, have been the driving force to keep me motivated and focused. Many friends, especially IIT alumni from industry as well as academia, have contributed real world inputs. I owe them all my heartfelt thanks. Without all of them, this book would not have been possible.

At this moment, I cannot but remember my late mother Shakuntala Joglekar and late father Vishnu Joglekar for everything that I am today. I would like to dedicate this book to them.

Any comments and suggestions for further improvement of the book are welcome; please send them at jyotij1968@gmail.com.

Jyoti Joglekar

Every effort has been made to contact the copyright holders of the assets used in this title. We, the authors and the Oxford University Press, India, would be pleased to rectify any omissions in the subsequent editions of this title should they be drawn to our attention.

The Oxford University Press, India would like to thank all the reviewers, including:

1. J Kayalvizhi (SRMIST, Chennai)
2. Dr TT Mrinalinee (SSN, Chennai)
3. Dr Tarun Kr. Dubey (Manipal, Jaipur)
4. Mayank Deep Khare (NIET, Greater Noida)
5. Mandeep Kaur (Sharda University, Greater Noida)
6. Akshita Baisware (GHRCE, Nagpur)
7. Manisha Ingle (GHRCE, Nagpur)
8. Dr S Mallika (Kongu Engg. College, T.N.)
9. Dr J Senthil Kumar (Mepco Schlenk Engg., T.N.)
10. Dr P Yogesh (Anna University, T.N.)
11. S Jai Kumar (SRMIST, Ramapuram, Chennai)
12. Dr J Raja Sekhar (Mepco Schlenk Engg., T.N.)
13. Arumugam Umamakeswari (SASTRA, Thanjavur)

Detailed Contents

Preface   iii

Acknowledgements   ix

Part I: Foundational Aspects   1

1. **Emergence of IoT**   2
   - 1.1 Background and Vision   2
     - 1.1.1 Background   3
     - 1.1.2 Vision of IoT   11
     - 1.1.3 Various Definitions of IoT   12
     - 1.1.4 Working Definition   13
     - 1.1.5 Key Enabling Technologies   14
   - 1.2 IoT as a Disruptive Technology   18
     - 1.2.1 Motivating Scenarios   19
     - 1.2.2 Multidisciplinary Nature of IoT   22
     - 1.2.3 Challenges Involved in its Further Evolution   23
   - 1.3 Standardization   26
     - 1.3.1 Need for Standardization at Various Layers of IoT   26
     - 1.3.2 Organizations and their Efforts for Standardization   27
     - 1.3.3 Factors for Widespread Adoption of IoT   28

2. **Concept of Smart Things/Objects**   32
   - 2.1 Thing in the Context of IoT   32
     - 2.1.1 Capability to Sense the Environment   33
     - 2.1.2 Ability to Communicate   33
     - 2.1.3 Computation Capabilities   33
     - 2.1.4 Control Other Things   33
     - 2.1.5 Accessibility   34
   - 2.2 Needs of an IoT Thing   34
     - 2.2.1 Self-existence   35
     - 2.2.2 Self-expression   36
     - 2.2.3 Self-actualization   36
   - 2.3 Commonly Used Smart Things   37
     - 2.3.1 How Can Things Become Smart?   37
   - 2.4 Machine-to-Machine Technology   38
     - 2.4.1 European Telecommunication Standards Institute (ETSI) – M2M   38
     - 2.4.2 M2M Service Layer   40
     - 2.4.3 M2M Applications   40
     - 2.4.4 Key Differences Between M2M and IoT   41

3. **Wireless Sensor Networks in IoT**   43
   - 3.1 Introduction   43
     - 3.1.1 Wireless Sensor Network (WSN)   43
   - 3.2 Characteristics of Wireless Sensor Network   45
     - 3.2.1 Significant Characteristics of WSN   45
   - 3.3 Types of WSN and their Architecture   47
     - 3.3.1 Multimedia Wireless Sensor Networks   47
     - 3.3.2 Mobile Wireless Sensor Networks   48
     - 3.3.3 Terrestrial Wireless Sensor Networks   48
     - 3.3.4 Underwater Wireless Sensor Network   49
     - 3.3.5 Underground Wireless Sensor Network   49
     - 3.3.6 Architectural Design of WSN   50
   - 3.4 Network Topologies in Wireless Sensor Network   51
     - 3.4.1 Different Types of Topologies in WSN   51
   - 3.5 WSN Communication Protocols   54

- 3.5.1 Single Channel MAC Protocol 54
- 3.5.2 Asynchronous Single Channel MAC Protocol 55
- 3.5.3 Pseudorandom Asynchronous MAC Protocol 55
- 3.5.4 Medium Reservation MAC (MRMAC) 55
- 3.5.5 Multi-channel MAC Protocols 55
- 3.5.6 Routing Protocols in WSN 56
- 3.5.7 Operating Systems for WSN 57
- 3.5.8 Simulation of WSN 57
- 3.6 Security in WSN 58
- 3.7 Real World WSN Applications 58
  - 3.7.1 Applications of Wireless Sensor Network 58
- 3.8 Evolution of WSN Towards Internet of Things 60

4. IoT Standards and Protocols 63

- 4.1 An Overview of Internet Principles 63
  - 4.1.1 Transmission Control Protocol/Internet Protocol (TCP/IP) 64
  - 4.1.2 IoT Reference Framework 64
- 4.2 IoT Network Level (Addressing Protocol) 65
  - 4.2.1 IP Version 4 (IPv4) Protocol 65
  - 4.2.2 IP Version 6 (IPV6) and its Role in IoT 66
  - 4.2.3 Classification of IPv6 Addresses 67
  - 4.2.4 IoT Data Link Protocol 68
  - 4.2.5 Application Layer IoT Protocols 70
  - 4.2.6 Mobile Communication 74
- 4.3 Low-Power Wide Area Network (LPWAN) 75
  - 4.3.1 NarrowBand-Internet of Things (NB-IoT) 75
  - 4.3.2 LoRa — LoRaWAN Protocol 75
- 4.4 Wireless Technologies Supporting IoT Applications 76
  - 4.4.1 WirelessHART 76
  - 4.4.2 Z-Wave 77
  - 4.4.3 Bluetooth Low Energy 77
  - 4.4.4 ZigBee Smart Energy 77
  - 4.4.5 DASH7 77
  - 4.4.6 LTE-A 78
- 4.5 Network Layer Encapsulation Protocols 78
  - 4.5.1 6LoWPAN 78
  - 4.5.2 6TiSCH 79

Part II: Understanding the Nuts and Bolts of IoT Hardware, Software, and Middleware 83

5. Sensors and Actuators in IoT 84

- 5.1 Introduction 84
  - 5.1.1 Sensors for Different IoT Applications 85
- 5.2 Perception Layer of IoT 87
  - 5.2.1 Active Sensors vs Passive Sensors 87
- 5.3 Understanding Some Commonly Used Sensors 87
  - 5.3.1 Light Sensors 88
  - 5.3.2 Accelerometers 88
  - 5.3.3 Gyroscopes 89
  - 5.3.4 Magnetometer 89
  - 5.3.5 Global Positioning System 89
  - 5.3.6 Proximity Sensors 90
  - 5.3.7 Radio Frequency Identification (RFID) 91
- 5.4 Environmental Sensors 92
  - 5.4.1 Temperature Sensors 92
  - 5.4.2 Pressure Sensors 92
  - 5.4.3 Humidity Sensors 93

Detailed Contents   xiii

	5.4.4	Wind Speed and Wind Direction Sensors	93
	5.4.5	Soil Moisture Sensors	93
	5.4.6	Leaf Sensors	93
	5.4.7	Lysimeter	94
	5.4.8	Rain Gauge	94
	5.4.9	Chemical Sensors	94
5.5	Medical Sensors		94
	5.5.1	Heartbeat Sensor	95
	5.5.2	Pulse Sensor	95
	5.5.3	Blood Glucose Level Sensor	95
	5.5.4	Blood Pressure Sensor	95
	5.5.5	Body Temperature Sensor	96
5.6	Flow and Fluid Measuring Sensors		96
	5.6.1	Level Sensors	96
	5.6.2	Stream Gauge	96
	5.6.3	Tide Gauge	96
5.7	Range and Motion Capture Sensors		96
	5.7.1	Distance Sensors	97
	5.7.2	Touch Sensor	97
5.8	Actuators		99
	5.8.1	Servo Motor	99
	5.8.2	Stepper Motor	99
	5.8.3	DC Motor	99
	5.8.4	Linear Actuators	100
	5.8.5	Solenoid	100
	5.8.6	Relay	100
5.9	IoT Examples		102
	5.9.1	PSEUDO-CODE for the Sketch to Write an Embedded Programming Code Using Arduino IDE	103

6. Open Hardware in IoT   108

6.1	Introduction to Internet of Things (IoT) Hardware		108
	6.1.1	IoT Hardware and Technology Stack	109
	6.1.2	IoT Device Hardware Requirements	109
6.2	Prototyping Boards for IoT		111
	6.2.1	Requirement for Custom Silicon (Customized on Board Chip) in IoT	111
	6.2.2	SoC Classification based on Functionality	111
	6.2.3	Arduino Boards	112
	6.2.4	Raspberry Pi	117
	6.2.5	BeagleBone	120
	6.2.6	pcDuino	120
	6.2.7	CubieBoard Open-Source Hardware	122
6.3	Cellular IoT Hardware		123
	6.3.1	Cellular IoT Hardware	123
6.4	Industrial Microcontroller (PLC and RTU)		124
	6.4.1	Programmable Logic Controller (PLC) and Remote Terminal Unit (RTU)	124
6.5	Various Other Hardware		124
	6.5.1	Hardware to Convert Continuous Signal to Digital Signal	125
	6.5.2	Hardware for Signal Conditioning, Scaling, and Interpretation	125
6.6	Comparison of Different Hardware Platforms		125

7. IoT Middleware   129

7.1	Introduction to Middleware		130
	7.1.1	IoT Middleware	131
	7.1.2	Functional Requirements of an IoT Middleware	132
	7.1.3	Non-functional Requirements of IoT Middleware	134
7.2	Architectures of IoT Middleware		135
	7.2.1	Component-based Middleware	135

		7.2.2	Distributed Middleware	135
		7.2.3	Service-Oriented Middleware (SOM)	136
		7.2.4	Cloud-based Middleware	137
		7.2.5	Node-based Middleware	138
	7.3	State-of-the-Art IoT Middleware		139
		7.3.1	OpenIoT	139
		7.3.2	KaaIoT	139
		7.3.3	Node-RED	140
		7.3.4	CHOReOS	140
		7.3.5	Linksmart	141
		7.3.6	CarrIoT	141
		7.3.7	Oracle Fusion Middleware	141
		7.3.8	Google Cloud IoT	141
8.	**IoT Software Platforms**			**144**
	8.1	Introduction to IoT Software Platforms		144
		8.1.1	Need and Characteristics of IoT Platforms	145
	8.2	Commercial IoT Software Platforms		145
		8.2.1	Amazon Web Service (AWS) IoT Platform	146
		8.2.2	Bosch IoT Suite	146
		8.2.3	EVRYTHNG	147
		8.2.4	IBM Watson IoT Platform	147
		8.2.5	Cisco Kinetic IoT	148
		8.2.6	Google IoT Cloud	149
		8.2.7	Microsoft Azure IoT Suite	149
	8.3	Open IoT Software Platforms		150
		8.3.1	ThingsBoard	150
		8.3.2	OGC SensorThings	151
		8.3.3	Thinger.io	152
		8.3.4	SiteWhere	153
		8.3.5	ThingSpeak	153
	8.4	Choosing an IoT Platform		153
		8.4.1	Domain of Application	153
		8.4.2	Usability	153
		8.4.3	Interoperability	154
		8.4.4	Scalability	154
		8.4.5	Edge Analytics	154
		8.4.6	Security	154
		8.4.7	Recovery	154
	8.5	Hands-On Using an IoT Platform		154
9.	**Prototyping IoT Applications**			**169**
	9.1	Introduction		169
	9.2	Prototyping and its Benefits		170
		9.2.1	Prototypes and IoT Product Ideas	170
		9.2.2	Selection of Physical Devices	172
		9.2.3	Sketches and Diagrams	172
		9.2.4	Open Source versus Closed Source Technologies	172
	9.3	Physical Design Considerations		173
		9.3.1	Different Modules for IoT Prototyping	173
		9.3.2	Explore, Sketch, and Experiment	176
		9.3.3	Introduction to Mechanical Design and Methodologies	177
	9.4	Prototyping Logical Design		178
	9.5	Prototyping using API		178
		9.5.1	Application Programming Interface (API)	179
		9.5.2	API for Real-time IoT Applications	179
		9.5.3	Packages for IoT in Python	179
	9.6	Embedded Code Writing		180
		9.6.1	Writing Efficient Code	180
	9.7	Real-World Prototype Example: Smart Home Appliances (Light and Fan)		181
		9.7.1	Design Stage	181
		9.7.2	Test Cases	186
	9.8	Best Practices		187

Part III: IoT Big Data Science and Analytics — 190

10. Big IoT Data Science — 191
- 10.1 Foundations and Principles of Big Data Science — 192
  - 10.1.1 Introduction — 192
- 10.2 Concept of a Data Lake/Swamp — 210
- 10.3 Relation Between IoT and Big Data — 212
- 10.4 Big Data Analytics in IoT — 212
  - 10.4.1 Real-time Analytics — 215
  - 10.4.2 Offline Analytics/Analytics on the Cloud — 218
  - 10.4.3 Big Data Analytics Platforms for IoT — 233
- 10.5 Machine Learning and Deep Learning Tools — 234
  - 10.5.1 Tensorflow — 234
  - 10.5.2 Theano — 234
  - 10.5.3 Keras — 234
  - 10.5.4 Scikit-learn — 234

11. IoT in the Cloud — 237
- 11.1 Introduction: Cloud Computing and IoT — 237
  - 11.1.1 Evolution of Cloud-based Novel IoT Applications — 238
  - 11.1.2 Cloud Computing Service Models — 240
- 11.2 Integrating Cloud Computing with IoT — 242
  - 11.2.1 Apache Hadoop — 242
  - 11.2.2 Apache Spark — 243
- 11.3 Cloud Services — 243
  - 11.3.1 SEaaS: Sensing-as-a-Service — 243
  - 11.3.2 SAaaS: Sensing and Actuator-as-a-Service — 243
  - 11.3.3 SEaaS: Sensor Event-as-a-Service — 244
  - 11.3.4 SenaaS: Sensor-as-a-Service — 244
- 11.4 Selected Cloud Service Providers — 244
  - 11.4.1 Kaa IoT Platform — 244
  - 11.4.2 ThingSpeak IoT Platform — 245
  - 11.4.3 Google Cloud — 247
  - 11.4.4 Oracle Cloud — 248
- 11.5 REST-based Web Services for IoT — 248

12. Edge Analytics: Near Real-time Sensor Stream Processing — 252
- 12.1 Introduction — 253
  - 12.1.1 Stream Processing Workflow — 254
- 12.2 What is Streaming Data? — 255
  - 12.2.1 Bounded vs Unbounded Data — 255
  - 12.2.2 Time-bound Processing of Streaming Data — 257
- 12.3 Data Stream Management Systems — 257
  - 12.3.1 Background of DSMS Development — 259
  - 12.3.2 Stream Processing Platforms — 260
- 12.4 Edge Analytics — 261
  - 12.4.1 Event Processing — 263
  - 12.4.2 Complex Event Processing — 264
- 12.5 Edge Analytics Walkthrough — 270
  - 12.5.1 Problem Background — 271
  - 12.5.2 Steps to Develop the Air Quality Monitoring Applications — 272

13. Embedded High Performance Computing (HPC) for IoT — 282
- 13.1 Introduction to High Performance Computing — 283
  - 13.1.1 Parallel Computing — 284
- 13.2 Embedded High Performance Computing (EHPC) — 284

- 13.3 Graphics Processing Units (GPU) 285
  - 13.3.1 General Architecture of GPU 287
- 13.4 Need for Embedded HPC Edge Devices 290
- 13.5 Embedded HPC Platforms 290
  - 13.5.1 NVIDIA's Jetson TX1, TX2, and Nano Embedded HPC Platforms 290
- 13.6 IoT Applications Development using Embedded HPC 292
  - 13.6.1 Transportation 292
  - 13.6.2 Healthcare 292

Part IV: Data Management in IoT 302

14. Interoperability in the IoT Ecosystem 303

- 14.1 Need for Interoperability in IoT Systems 304
  - 14.1.1 Various Definitions of Interoperability 304
  - 14.1.2 Current IoT Systems are in Silos 305
- 14.2 Types of Interoperability 307
  - 14.2.1 Device or Technological Interoperability 307
  - 14.2.2 Syntactic Interoperability 307
  - 14.2.3 Semantic Interoperability 308
  - 14.2.4 Organizational Interoperability 308
  - 14.2.5 Approaches for Interoperability 308
- 14.3 IoT Reference Model and Architecture 309
- 14.4 Architecture Reference Model 309
  - 14.4.1 Reference Model 309
  - 14.4.2 IoT Reference Model 310
  - 14.4.3 ITU-T Reference Model 316
- 14.5 IoT Reference Architectures 318
  - 14.5.1 Need for a Reference Architecture 318
  - 14.5.2 Simplified Outline of IoT Architecture 318
  - 14.5.3 IoT-A Reference Architecture 319
- 14.6 Interoperability using Syntactic and Semantic Approaches 321
  - 14.6.1 Interoperability at Various Layers of IoT 321
  - 14.6.2 Syntactic Interoperability Approaches 323
  - 14.6.3 Semantic Interoperability Approaches 324

15. CyberSecurity and Privacy 330

- 15.1 Introduction 330
  - 15.1.1 IoT Security Challenges 332
  - 15.1.2 IoT System Security Domains 333
- 15.2 Security Issues in IoT Systems and Privacy Preservation 333
  - 15.2.1 Three-layer IoT Architecture and Security Issues in Each Layer 335
- 15.3 IoT Security Requirements Based on CIA Principles 336
  - 15.3.1 Denial of Service (DoS) Attacks in Physical Layer 336
  - 15.3.2 DoS Attacks in Link Layer 337
  - 15.3.3 DoS Attacks in Network Layer 337
  - 15.3.4 DoS Attacks in Transport Layer 338
  - 15.3.5 DoS Attacks in Application Layer 339
- 15.4 Security Technologies 339
  - 15.4.1 Network Connectivity Technologies and IoT Device Security Issues 339

15.5	IoT System Security Controls	341		15.7.9	Need for IoT Security and Privacy Certification Board	350
	15.5.1 IoT Security for Data Access, Integrity, Availability, and Data Communication	341	15.8	IoT Security with Best Practices for Home Automation Application	350
	15.5.2 Need for Lightweight Cryptography for IoT Systems	342	**16.**	**IoT and Business Process Management**	**354**
				16.1	Business Process	354
	15.5.4 Token-based Access Control	345		16.2	Business Process Management	356
	15.5.5 Device Status Monitoring	346			16.2.1 BPM Lifecycle	357
	15.5.6 User-friendly Set-up and Upgrades	346		16.3	Business Process Modeling & Notation	358
	15.5.7 Access Control for Availability	346		16.4	IoT and Business Process Management	359
	15.5.8 IoT Security Controls for Middleware Platforms	346			16.4.1 IoT-based Business Processes	362
15.6	Other Security Controls for IoT Systems	347		16.5	IoT and Business Process Execution Language	363
	15.6.1 Fault Tolerance	347		16.6	BPM and IoT Case Study: Supply Chain Management	363
	15.6.2 Privacy Preservation Methods	347	**Part V: Compelling Use Cases of IoT**	**368**
	15.6.3 Identity Management	347	**17.**	**IoT Use Cases**	**369**
	15.6.4 Trust and Governance	348		17.1	Introduction	369
15.7	Best Practices for Securing IoT Devices	348		17.2	Use Case for Home Automation Using Smart Home Appliances	370
	15.7.1 Tamper-resistant Hardware	348			17.2.1 Overview	370
	15.7.2 Firmware Updates/Patch Updates	349			17.2.2 Existing Home Automation Systems	370
	15.7.3 Dynamic Testing	349			17.2.3 Problem Statement for the Use Case Home Automation using IoT: A Novel Approach	371
	15.7.4 Strong Authentication Technique Practices	349			17.2.4 Block Diagram	372
	15.7.5 Use of Secure Protocols and Encryption	349			17.2.5 Hardware Components Used	372
	15.7.6 Network Division into Segments	349			17.2.6 Sensors	373
	15.7.7 Sensitive Information Protection	350			17.2.7 PIR Motion Sensor Module	374
	15.7.8 Encouraging Ethical Hacking and Discouraging Safe Harbour for Unethical Practices	350				

		17.2.9	Actuators	375
		17.2.10	Software Design: UML Diagrams	376
		17.2.11	Pseudocode	377
		17.2.12	Smart Door Lock System	379
		17.2.13	Component List	380
		17.2.14	Sample Source Code in Embedded C for Arduino Uno Board	382
		17.2.15	Output	383
		17.2.16	Energy Saving and Management using Smart Home Appliances	386
	17.3	Use Case: Smart Goods Transportation		386
		17.3.1	Overview	386
		17.3.2	Problem Definition	386
		17.3.3	Hardware and Software Requirements	386
		17.3.4	Block Diagram of the System Model	387
		17.3.5	Software and User Interfaces of the Smart Goods Transportation System	387
		17.3.6	Pseudocode of the Workflow	388
		17.3.7	Major Functionalities of the Back-end Server System	388
		17.3.8	Performance Requirements	389
		17.3.9	Software Design (UML Diagrams)	389
	17.4	Healthcare Use Case: IoT for Healthcare Devices and Challenges		392
		17.4.1	Teleradiology Platform for Screening Covid19 Patients and Remote Diagnosis using IoT Technologies	392
		17.4.2	A Tele-Radiology Platform Solution for Screening with X-Ray AI Module for Screening/Testing Protocol for Diagnosis and Further Treatment	393
		17.4.3	Hardware Requirements	394
		17.4.4	Software Requirements	395
		17.4.5	Methodologies	395
	17.5	Agriculture Use Case: IoT-based Smart Irrigation		396
		17.5.1	Development of IoT-based Irrigation System	396
18.	**Future Outlook**			**404**
	18.1	Future Roadmap		404
		18.1.1	Device	405
		18.1.2	Network	406
		18.1.3	Platform	408
		18.1.4	Service	408
	18.2	Expanded Opportunities for IoT Applications		409
		18.2.1	Home Automation	409
		18.2.2	Ambient-Assisted Living (AAL)	409
		18.2.3	IoT-enabled Government Services	410

About the Authors   413

Related Titles   414

PART I: FOUNDATIONAL ASPECTS

Chapter 1: Emergence of IoT

Chapter 2: Concept of Smart Things/Objects

Chapter 3: Wireless Sensor Networks in IoT

Chapter 4: IoT Standards and Protocols

Emergence of IoT

CHAPTER 1

"There are more people in the world who make things than there are people who think of things to make."

- Syd Mead

OBJECTIVES
- introduce the concept of Internet of Things (IoT)
- understand the various definitions of IoT and converge to a working definition
- recap past and current technologies that aided in the development of IoT
- describe the fundamental components of an IoT system
- present various game-changing applications that IoT is driving
- understand how technologies in various disciplines are enabling further evolution of IoT
- explain the issues in the development of disparate IoT systems based on a variety of technologies, and discuss the need for standardization of IoT systems at various levels
- overview of the role of various organizations that are actively involved in the standardization process and their activities

OUTCOMES
- understand the historical context and background of IoT and describe the IoT vision
- describe various definitions of IoT given by different organizations and able to synthesize a definition of your own
- describe key enabling technologies that converged in the development of IoT
- appreciate the interdisciplinary nature of IoT
- understand the need for standardization at various IoT layers
- name various IoT standards and the organizations that are involved in developing them

1.1 BACKGROUND AND VISION

The Internet has dramatically changed the way we conduct our daily life and has become the de facto way of communication. It has spread so deeply in our society that a lot of our routine activities are now driven by technology and are highly dependent on the Internet. By using mobile devices, we are able to conduct both personal and official businesses more efficiently. For example, with just a touch on the mobile screen, a host of services are available, such as ordering food, buying shoes, arranging meetings, keeping in touch with people, and buying tickets. Having Internet connectivity has become a way of life and will continue to percolate in many areas, which are previously unimagined.

It has revolutionized many domains and brought in many new applications to the forefront. The last decade has seen an accelerated synthesis of research in several path-breaking technologies, particularly in the areas of semiconductors, networking, and information processing. In addition, there has been a significant drop in the prices of sensors, transmitters, processors, and computing infrastructure. These have revolutionized both the information and communication technologies (ICT) and non-ICT areas. Consequently, a new paradigm has emerged called the Internet of Things (IoT), which aims to make things (physical objects) smart using sensors/actuators and digitally identifiable over the Internet so that these can be seamlessly accessed and controlled remotely. Further, these things have the ability to react in real time to the events in the environment that they exist, and send information to humans as well as other things autonomously to enable them to contextually respond for decision-making.

Gartner, a leading research and advisory company, predicts that by 2020, there will be 20.8 billion IoT devices connected around the world, overtaking the number of personal computers and smartphones. Another estimate by Cisco projects that nearly half of the devices connected to the Internet by 2023 are IoT devices (see Fig. 1.1).

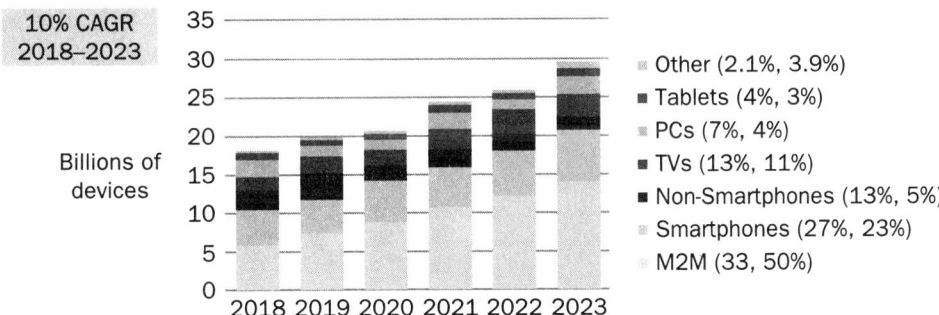

*Figures (n) refer to 2015, 2021 device share

Fig. 1.1 Number of Devices Connected to the Internet by 2023; Half (51%) of Them are IoT Devices

(Source credit: Cisco)

To understand this fast-paced development and adoption of IoT technologies in a better way, it is necessary to travel back in time and look at the key events and technologies that helped shape the current IoT. The historical context of the emergence of IoT is described in the next section.

1.1.1 Background

Although IoT has emerged recently, its roots go back to about two decades. In 1982, a Coke machine at Carnegie Mellon University (CMU), was fitted with micro-switches and was connected to a computer to show how many coke bottles were left in the machine, so that anyone can just ping to it before going to the vending machine to pick up a bottle. At that time, CMU was part of the ARPANET, so other universities were also able to find out the number of coke bottles left. Thus, it became one of the very early examples of an IoT device.

In 1991, ubiquitous computing was proposed by Mark Weiser (Weiser, 1991). In 1995, Siemens developed the first Machine-to-Machine (M2M) communication application. It was used for sales terminals. In the year 1998, the Internet protocol IPv6 was developed and launched by the Internet Engineering Task Force (IETE) to overcome the IP address exhaustion problem of IPv4. IPv4 had only 32-bits, that is, a total of 2^{32}, which are not enough to handle the huge number of IoT devices currently and for future expansion. IPv6 is 128-bits, so a total of 2^{128} addresses are theoretically possible, which are more than enough to cope with the ever expanding IoT devices in the coming years.

In the year 1999, Bill Joy wrote about Device-to-Device communication in his taxonomy of Internet (Pontin, 2005). In the same year, the Auto ID centre at MIT was working on the Radio Frequency Identification (RFID) technology for asset tracking and supply chain management, where companies will be able to track their products and reduce operating costs. The team comprising of Kevin Ashton, Sanjay Sarma and David Brock, developed a way to connect objects to Internet via a RFID tag, making

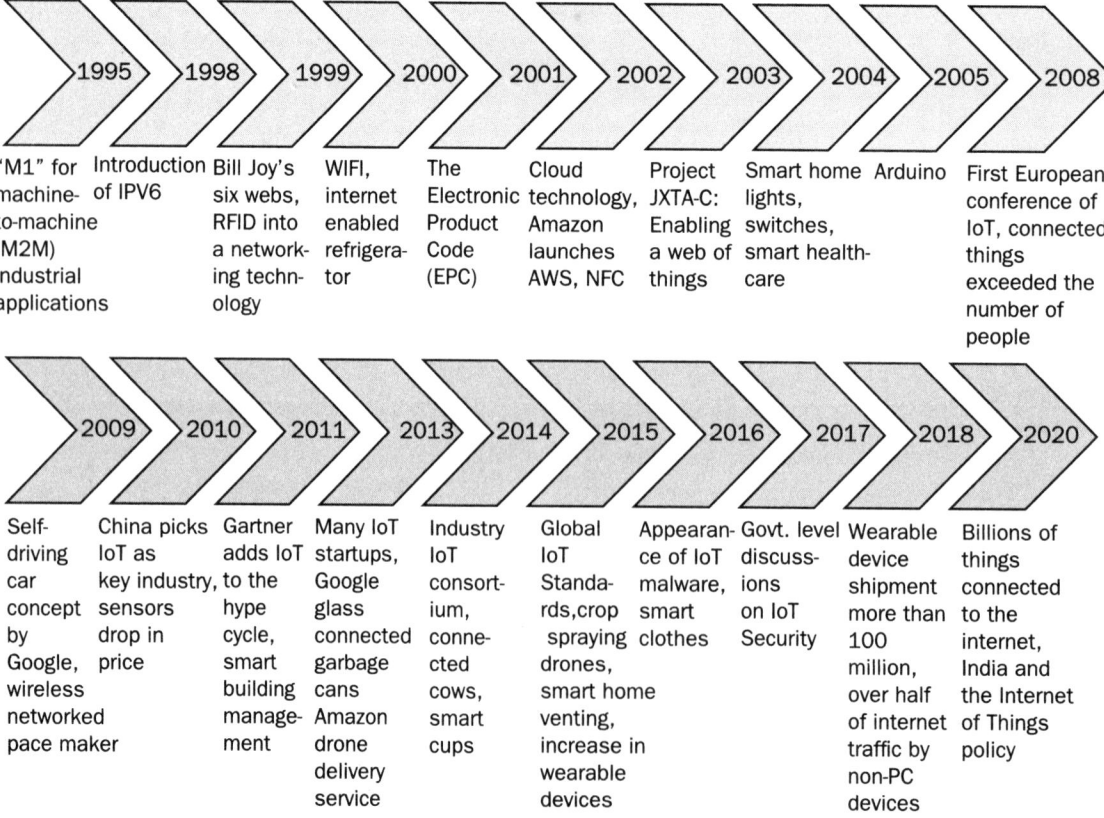

Fig. 1.2 Timeline of IoT Technology Maturity

BOX 1.1: VARIOUS AUTO-ID TECHNOLOGIES

Barcodes, RFIDs, QR Codes, and NFC

Barcodes, QR Codes, RFID, and NFC are all systems for conveying large amounts of data in a small format.

Barcodes These are limited to 20 alphanumeric characters and data is stored only in the horizontal direction. UPC consists of 12 numeric digits that are uniquely assigned to each item at the point of sale. The bars represent numbers. These are inexpensive as they can be printed on paper or plastic. The data on the barcodes cannot be rewritten. Barcodes help to identify the type of the item, but not an individual item. The line of sight is important to scan the code properly. Reading items using a barcode could be time consuming as it can only read one item at a time.

Standard UPC-A barcode

Radio Frequency Identification (RFID) It uses electromagnetic fields to read and capture information stored of an object by reading a unique tag attached to it. It can be used for identification, authentication and tracking of items. It can store 1000s of characters.

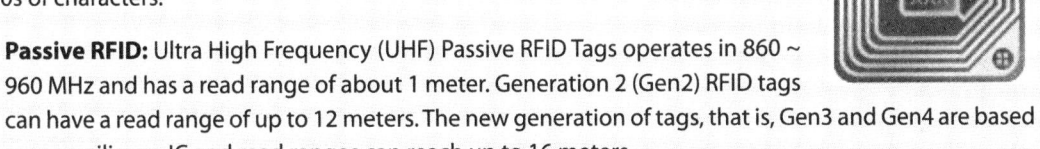

1. **Passive RFID:** Ultra High Frequency (UHF) Passive RFID Tags operates in 860 ~ 960 MHz and has a read range of about 1 meter. Generation 2 (Gen2) RFID tags can have a read range of up to 12 meters. The new generation of tags, that is, Gen3 and Gen4 are based on new silicone IC and read ranges can reach up to 16 meters.

2. **Active RFID:** It operates in the Ultra high frequency at 433 MHz. These can have a read range of up to 500 meters. Another variant of the active RFID is the 2.45 GHz. Super High Frequency tags. These can have a read range of up to 100 meters. The advantages of the active RFID are: (1) ability to obtain real-time location information, which is useful in any location and tracking applications (2) data on the RFID tags can be rewritten and reused (3) identification of individual item rather than only the item type is possible with it, that is, it gives a count of the number of items that are present in a particular product. An RFID can read potentially 100s or even 1000s of tags simultaneously. Currently, many quick payment systems, anti-car theft devices use 13.56 MHz RFID systems.

Quick Response (QR) codes It is a type of two-dimensional barcode first designed for the automotive industry. The code consists of black modules embedded in a square pattern on white background. It can work both in horizontal and vertical directions and can hold up to 300 times the information that could be encoded in a UPC barcode. QR codes can be quickly read and scanned from any direction.

Near Field Communication (NFC) NFC technology has its roots in RFID. When two electronic devices are brought close (within 4 cm) to each other, a communication is established and data can be exchanged. Normally a 'Tap' is done with the item and the required information is transferred. These are used in many applications such as identity/key cards and credit cards. An NFC-enabled smartphone can be used to make several types of transactions such as payments in a retail store. NFC tags are inexpensive and are becoming quite popular currently.

it a networking technology (Roberti, 2005). A majority of sources attribute Kevin Ashton for coining the term 'Internet of Things' in a presentation he made for Proctor and Gamble (P&G), in which he emphasized the need for a standardized way to make computers understand the real world. The important aspect of this endeavour is connecting the Internet to the physical world (objects connection using RFID) through wireless sensing networks (WSNs). It was a pioneering solution at that time because there was no widespread usage of Internet Protocol (IP) configurations by mobile networks then. See Box 1.1 for more details on various Auto-ID technologies.

In the year 2000 (Fig. 1.2), the Internet-enabled refrigerator was launched by LG. The consumer could get the information about the temperature, freshness of the food, and nutrition information on a LCD screen attached to the refrigerator.

In 2001, David Brook, proposed the Electronic Product code (EPC) to address the issue of tracking a product throughout its lifecycle. He suggested a unified product directory for this purpose. The EPC provides a unique identity to any object. It is designed to be stored on a RFID tag. Bernard Traversat in 2003 (Traversat et al., 2003) published the paper 'project JXTA-C: Enabling the web of things' in which a standard and open source set of protocols for ad hoc, pervasive, peer-to-peer computing were proposed for the Web of Things.

By the year 2004, major transition for smart things has gained and many publications were describing various smart devices in areas such as healthcare, smart bulbs/switches, and transportation. For the first time, Walmart deployed RFIDs on a large scale to keep track of its inventory.

The open hardware-based microcontroller Arduino appeared in 2005. It was developed by faculty members at the Interaction Design Institute (IVREA), Italy. It brought with it a revolutionary change in the embedded computing arena. With its intuitive interface and ease of programming, it enabled non-domain (e.g. non-electronics background) people also to venture into smart devices development. The product ideas were limited only by the resourcefulness and imagination of developer. Several online web portals sprung up offering various sensors, electronic components, and PCB shields that could be easily put together to prototype quickly. Further, several community-based online forums were formed to help developers ideate, implement, and exchange information about innovative IoT devices. In the same year, Ubiquitous Network Societies emerged, almost 15 years after the Ubiquitous term coined by Mark Weiser, who described it as:

(i) A new era in which small non-traditional computing devices will be embedded in everyday objects invisibly at work in the environment around us.
(ii) The applications that are built on the concepts of ubiquitous computing will use these non-traditional computing devices in a large number.
(iii) The computing devices will have sensors to measure various environmental parameters and be able to act independently based on certain predefined conditions.
(iv) The computing devices are mobile and have geographical location and usually the devices in a neighbourhood are often used for a particular task. Hence, communication networks should connect these devices together in an ad hoc and spontaneous manner, and form temporary networks to facilitate anywhere, anytime, always-on communications.

The year 2008 marked the first European conference, which took place in Zurich, Switzerland. During that time, several key industry players such as those from semiconductors, communications, networking, and Internet providers, have made vital contributions to further promote the growth of IoT.

Google launched the ambitious self-driven cars project in 2009, it has heralded a new era in autonomous vehicles area. It is significant from an IoT perspective as it combines the major components of an IoT system, ranging from sensors/actuators that are deployed on various parts of a car (e.g., wheels, bonnet, bumper, and seats) and also those that allow measuring the surroundings around it. These inputs are fed through various models and are continuously learned and used to trigger responses to various events happening inside and outside of the car (e.g., seat belts, temperature, detecting pedestrians, and lanes). Another device that made its entry in the same year was the wireless networked pacemaker that is inserted directly into the heart without surgery and can deliver electric pulses to the heart for its proper functioning.

The fast-paced developments happening in the IoT area prompted China to declare IoT a key industry and included it in its 12th 5-year plan. A national IoT centre was established in Shanghai in the same year. Across the country several initiatives begun on developing a range of standards, industry chains, and applications, which aimed at creating an industry worth more than CNY 500 billion over the coming decade.

Gartner, a leading research and advisory company added the IoT to its hype cycle in 2011. It tracks specific technologies and their advancement through a life cycle from 'technology trigger' to 'plateau of productivity'.

The year 2011 also saw the emergence of the smart building concepts. McGlinn et al., 2010, define Smart Buildings as an environment, which is "able to acquire and apply knowledge about the environment and its inhabitants in order to improve their experience in that environment" (Cook and Das, 2007). Smart buildings are characterized by real-time measurement and monitoring of various building management infrastructure [e.g., Heating, Ventilation, and Air Conditioning (HVAC)], external environment such as weather, noise, light, people movement, and energy pricing, and optimize energy consumption and ambience in the building. This can be achieved by IoT devices measuring various parameters in and outside the building. Such real-time data can be used to perform smart analytics (e.g., Edge analytics) and trigger intelligent control mechanisms.

Buoyed by the great potential of IoT and its wide commercial applications, several start-ups began to emerge in the year 2013. Google glass also appeared in the same year. However, it was discontinued in 2015 due to privacy and safety concerns (a new version of Google glass is launched for enterprise applications in 2018). Amazon's Drone-based delivery prototype was announced in 2013 and named it 'Prime Air'. Due to restrictions by Federal Aviation Administration (FAA), the project could not take off immediately. The first delivery happened in UK in 2016 as a proof of concept. IoT application for garbage management was also demonstrated in the same year called the connected cans that can send an alert when the garbage can is full so that the pickup can be planned by the garbage-collecting trucks. The industrial Internet Consortium (IIC) was founded in 2014 to "accelerate the development, adoption and widespread use of interconnected machines and devices and intelligent analytics" (IIC, 2018). Several industries in areas of Energy, Healthcare, Manufacturing, Mining, Retail, Transportation, and Smart Cities are involved in IIC.

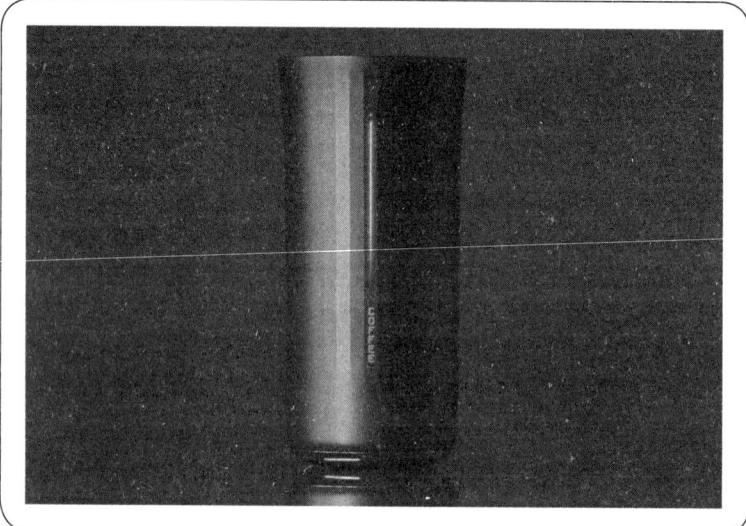

Fig. 1.3 IoT-based Smart Cup Capable of Sending Nutritional Information to a Smart Phone

Connected cow was an interesting application that appeared in the same year. It has transformed the dairy industry by enabling the dairy companies to monitor individual cows by tagging with RFID and other health monitoring sensors and transmit the information in real time to help monitor health and other location specific attributes. This led to more focussed treatment for diseases (if any), and also provide optimal nutrition, thus boosting the milk yield. Currently, many companies including Microsoft, Huawei, and Fujitsu are involved in providing IoT-based solutions for this purpose. A 13-ounce smart cup named 'Vessyl' made its first appearance around this time (see Fig. 1.3). Any beverage poured into it is recognized and the related nutritional value is displayed on the smartphone. Further, it can also keep track of the drinking habits of the user and provide that information via a smartphone.

The year 2015 saw the emergence of global IoT standards with a meeting in Geneva, Switzerland. A group called the IoT global standards initiative (IoT-GSI), which is part of International Telecommunication Union (ITU) was formed whose aim is to promote a unified approach for developing standards for IoT to enable it to scale at the global level.

The year 2015 also saw the emergence of drones in agriculture. Drone-based sensing was demonstrated in the areas of crop health monitoring, irrigation equipment monitoring, and weed detection. The ability to monitor at high temporal frequency made this technology very attractive to the farmers. Another area that saw the use of IoT is the smart home venting systems that allows adding room-by-room smart vents that can control the central air conditioning installations. This enables to distribute the airflow from rooms that are over conditioned to those rooms that need more air. All these can be achieved by IoT devices and smartphone applications. The wearable devices market also emerged in the year 2015 (see Box 1.2).

BOX 1.2: WEARABLE DEVICES

Wearable technology is related to the development of devices that are worn directly on body or on the user's clothing, which helps to track a user's data related to health and fitness, location, emotions, gestures, and other reflexes of the human body. The wearable technology can help the user to continuously record, monitor, and analyse internal and external stimuli and react based on certain preset controls.

Head
Navigation, AR, photography
web browsing, gesture,
eye tracking, sound

Neck, chest, back
Pedometer, heart rate, BP,
calories, radiation, posture

Wrist
Fitness, photography, phone calls,
location, SOS, notifications

Waist, arms
Pregnancy, weight loss, sports

Smart garments
Speakers, musical instruments,
socks, diapers, ECG

Legs, ankles
Workout, location, baby
monitors, activity, power
generation

A wearable device can have sensors, computing architecture and display. Depending upon the parameter (e.g., pulse, gesture, etc.) that is being tracked, the wearable may use the computing on its device (very limited) or delegate an external device such as a smart phone to do the computing. Similarly, the display on a wearable depends on the amount of information that needs to be shown. If it is limited, then it is displayed on the wearable itself (e.g., smartwatches); otherwise, it is shown on a smartphone, nearby display, or ear buds (verbal communication).

Due to increasing adoption of wearables, the global wearables shipment is expected to reach 2.5 billions in 2023. Currently it is in the early phases, and mainly dominated by healthcare, activity, and fitness wearables.

In 2016, IoT reached the peak of inflated expectations. It is expected that it will take another 5 to 10 years for the technology to mature and reach a stage where it could be widely adopted. Similarly, several key components of it, such as IoT platforms, IoT architectures, and wide-area IoT networks, have not peaked (i.e., reached a high level of expectations yet) and are also expected to reach the plateau of productivity in another 5 to 10 years. Whereas, other components such as IoT services, IoT edge architecture, IoT for customer service, and messaging platforms such as MQTT are expected to quickly reach wide adaptability in a span of another 2 to 5 years. Another key component for real-time decision-making in IoT systems is the event stream processing (although developed independently of IoT) has reached high expectation levels for its application in IoT edge analytics. Many event stream processing engines are emerging, but it is expected to take another 5 to 10 years, for it to be completely adopted and integrated with IoT edge analytics. Another, closely related innovation are the low-cost development boards (e.g., Arduino, Raspberry Pi, etc.), which have played an important role in enabling users from diverse disciplines to work in IoT. These low-cost development boards and related programming interfaces have reduced the complexity of developing certain class of electronic products, particularly those that are useful for IoT.

In August 2016, the Mirai malware appeared and targeted under-secured networked devices running Linux OS systems into bots and recruited them to be part of a larger botnet network that can trigger large-scale attacks. The devices that were affected by this malware were mostly IP cameras and home routers (see Box 1.3). Smart clothes that monitor the wearer's physical condition began to appear in the wearable segment of IoT in 2016 (see Box 1.2).

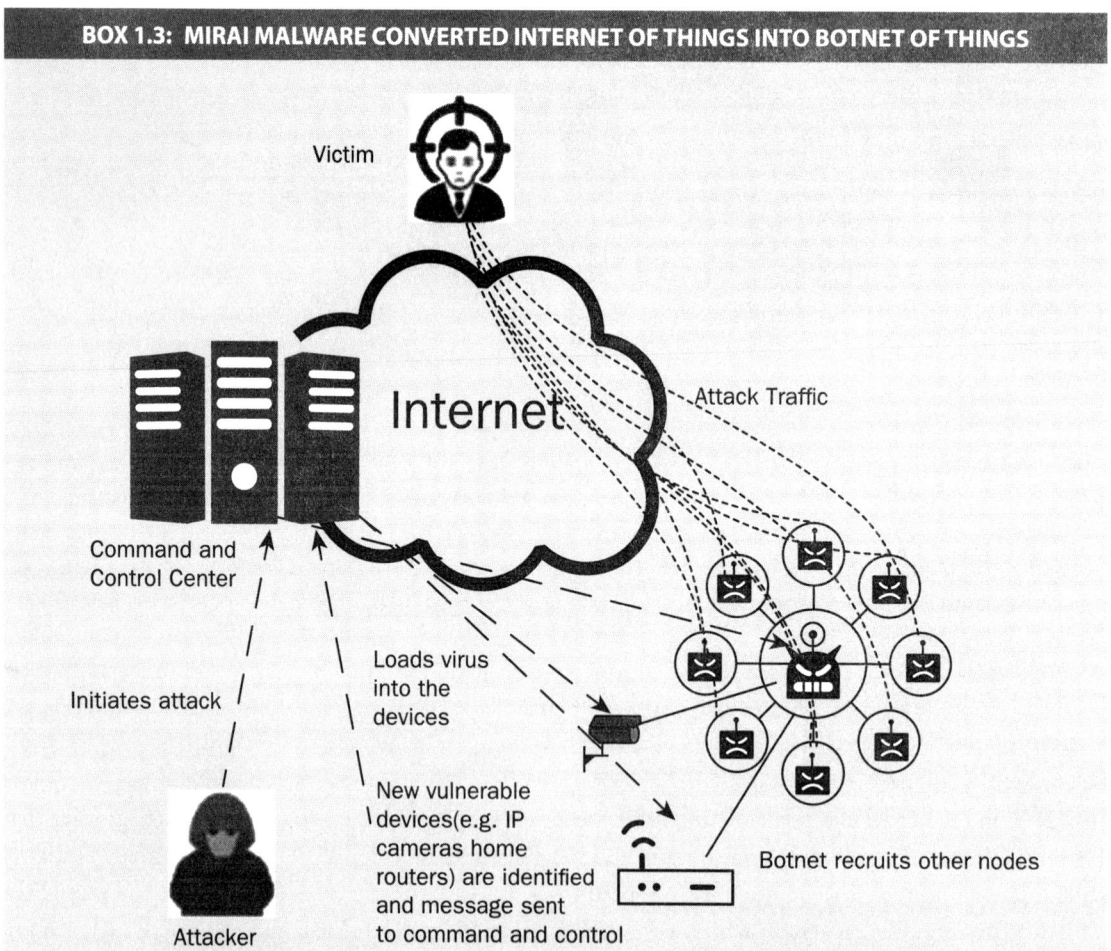

BOX 1.3: MIRAI MALWARE CONVERTED INTERNET OF THINGS INTO BOTNET OF THINGS

In October, 2016, Paras Jha, Josiah White, and Dalton Norman used their Mirai botnet, which is a piece of malware that gets installed on under-secured IoT devices such as IP Cameras, home routers. These then become bots and are recruited by other bots and form a network known as a botnet. The attacker then initiates a Distributed Denial of Service (DDoS) attack. In this case, they attacked the domain name server (DNS) Dyn causing the shut down of a number of major websites including Twitter, Reddit, and the New York Times. Subsequently they were indicted by a court in Alaska and have pleaded guilty to charges that carry a sentence of up to 5 years in prison.

(Contd)

Box 1.3 *(Contd)*

> The main functionality of the Mirai malware was to search for under-secured IoT devices by scanning wide-ranging IP addresses and finding those devices, which can be easily accessed based on a dictionary of username/passwords (usually the default factory set credentials). Subsequently install the virus and make it as a part of a bigger network. Next, based on the instructions received from the command and control centre, use this network of bots to launch DDoS attacks on specified targets.

The security aspects of IoT received wide attention in 2017 owing to the large-scale attacks that happened in the preceding years. The US government enacted a bill called the 'Internet of Things Cybersecurity Improvement Act 2017', which basically mandates all the IoT devices that are sold to the government to have security measures and these include wearables, sensors, IoT tools, etc. Further, compliance in terms of including industry standard protocols, passwords that can be changed (controlled) by the users and do not have any known vulnerabilities (as defined by the National Institute of Standards (NIST)) (NIST, 2018).

In 2018, the number of wearables that were shipped crossed 100 million units. IoT is providing a great market opportunity for companies involved in IoT hardware manufacturing, Internet service providers, and application developers. The global IoT market is expected to have a compound annual growth rate (CAGR) of nearly 27 per cent from 2018 to 2024.

The IoT market is fast gaining ground and many industry leaders such as Google, Amazon, IBM, CISCO, Samsung, Intel, and Apple have announced new products in the IoT landscape. Along with these, a plethora of start-ups are testing ground. The industry is investing mainly in the areas of manufacturing, healthcare, transportation, consumer electronics, smart cars/fleets, home automation, and utilities.

By the year 2020, billions of things are expected to be connected to the Internet.

1.1.2 Vision of IoT

The vision of IoT can be perceived from four major perspectives (Fig. 1.4):

Things perspective The persistent and reliable availability of anything that is of interest to the user, which could be connected in anyway using a variety of technologies. Further, these connected things should be available to be accessed at anytime and from any location. This is similar to the ubiquitous computing concept that was there much earlier before the advent of the IoT.

Standards and semantics perspective Access of the things should be seamless, which is possible only if well-defined standards are adhered to by the providers of these things as they are highly heterogeneous in nature. In addition, the things should be interoperable, that is, the ability to integrate data from heterogeneous IoT devices is a must, otherwise, many IoT applications will be very specific to a particular application domain and cross-domain integration becomes highly challenging. Hence, standards are necessary in every component of the IoT architecture.

Internet perspective The aforementioned two are possible only if the things are able to communicate with people and people with things (people 2 things, i.e., P2T), and further, among things themselves (things 2 things, i.e., T2T), so that certain level of autonomous decision making is achieved. Hence, the web enablement or web addressability is one of the prime goals of IoT.

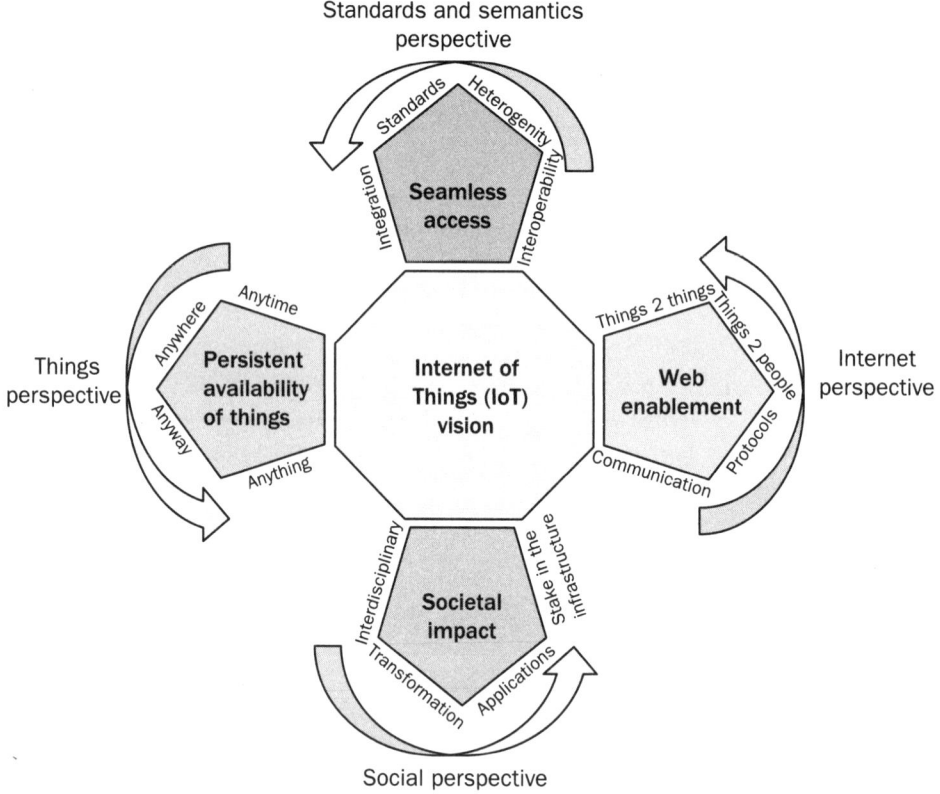

Fig. 1.4 The Vision of IoT from Four Different Perspectives

Social perspective The societal impact of the IoT is primarily driven by the acceptance of the users and their perceived value that it would bring to their lives. It is envisioned that the IoT infrastructure will be owned by the stakeholders in some form of democratic process, who will develop, maintain, and take in directions that are congenial for their growth. The society will be benefited by a spectacular transformation of traditional services into IoT-based smart services that provides applications that are much easier to use and provides far-reaching benefits. These IoT services also operate in an interdisciplinary mode, where they can be easily integrated and a common set of services will come together and cooperate in real time to address a particular problem. Several applications such as monitoring air pollution, improved water conservation, and increased production of food grains.

1.1.3 Various Definitions of IoT

The understanding of IoT is being approached from various perspectives and based upon a particular domain and its view of the components involved in the IoT systems. There may be specific emphasis on particular modules that are important in that domain. Hence, there is no global consensus on an overarching IoT definition. Indeed, there have been efforts by organizations such as IEEE to lead an initiative for developing a definition of IoT. Following are some selected definitions of IoT.

1.1.3.1 IEEE Definition

IEEE led an initiative in 2015 on developing a definition for IoT. In the special issue of IEEE on Internet of Things, IoT is defined as:

"A network of items, each embedded with sensors, which are connected to the internet."

1.1.3.2 ITU Definition

The international Telecom Union (ITU) defines IoT as:

"A global infrastructure for the information society, enabling advanced services by interconnecting (physical and virtual) things based on, existing and evolving, interoperable information and communication technologies."

1.1.3.3 IETF Definition

The Internet Engineering Task Force (IETF) is playing a crucial role in the development of several standards for IoT. They define IoT as:

"IoT will connect objects around us (electronic, electrical, non-electrical) to provide seamless communication and contextual services provided by them. Development of RFID tags, sensors, actuators, mobile phones make it possible to materialize IoT which interact and cooperate each other to make the service better and accessible anytime, from anywhere."

1.1.3.4 OASIS

Organization for the Advancement of Structured Information Standards (OASIS) is a non-profit consortium that drives the development, convergence, and adoption of open standards for the global information society. It describes IoT as:

"System where the Internet is connected to the physical world via ubiquitous sensors."

In addition to standard bodies such as IEEE, IETF, and ITU, there are several projects that have also given definitions of IoT such as:

1.1.3.5 IoT-A

Internet of Things Architecture (IoT-A) developed an *Architecture Reference Model (ARM),* which addresses the issues of heterogeneity in IoT-related technologies. IoT-A defines it as:

"It can be seen as an umbrella term for interconnected technologies, devices, objects and services."

1.1.3.6 Texas Instruments

Texas instruments in its paper on evolution of Internet of Things defines IoT as:

"The IoT creates an intelligent, invisible network fabric that can be sensed, controlled and programmed. IoT-enabled products employ embedded technology that allows them to communicate, directly or indirectly, with each other or the Internet."

1.1.3.7 Gartner

"The Internet of Things (IoT) is the network of physical objects that contain embedded technology to communicate and sense or interact with their internal states or the external environment."

1.1.4 Working Definition

Based on the aforementioned definitions, it is useful to have a working definition whose spirit will be used as the foundation for the rest of the contents of this book.

$$IoT = Sensing + Communication + Computation + Web Application$$

"Making things (objects) to sense the environment in which they exist, communicate, access, actuate, and process data autonomously with other things in a network, and also with humans via web applications."

1.1.5 Key Enabling Technologies

The enabling technologies of IoT are distributed in several layers of the IoT systems. The technologies at each of these layers are specialized and serves some key purposes for the functioning of that layer. These can be categorised into four major categories (Fig. 1.5).

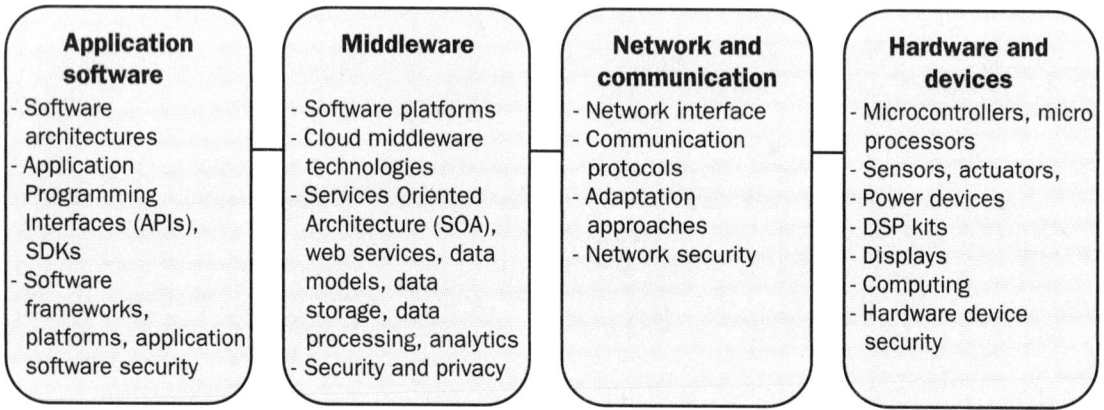

Fig. 1.5 Major Categories of Enabling Technologies for IoT

1.1.5.1 Applications and Software

Currently, the IoT technology is being applied in a variety of fields due to its immense potential to create more smarter ways of performing various tasks in those domains. IoT applications have emerged in many domains such as healthcare, transportation, smart cities, industry, and energy management. Most of the traditional approaches in these domains are getting transformed by using the new IoT system functions to build practical applications. The main enabling technologies for IoT in this layer are:

Application Programming Interfaces (APIs) The application programming interface, or API enables to integrate the 'things' of IoT and act as a glue between the IoT devices and the network (e.g., Internet). It provides an interface for other applications to interact with your application without having direct access. From an IoT perspective, device level APIs can be used to enable applications to communicate with devices. For example, Google IoT product NEST is a smart Thermostat that can control via a mobile phone the temperature in a home/office setting. While the manufacturer of NEST has provided the core applications to interact with the NEST device, they also provided an API. Using the API, developers can connect and use the NEST data in their own applications and sell them. Development of APIs that allow to securely expose connected IoT devices to users are one of the key enabling technologies for IoT. Many IoT-based APIs are available.

Software Development Kits (SDKs) Software development kits have pre-built functionality to make them easier to work than an API thus making them easier to integrate in an application. For example, the amazon IoT SDK allows hardware devices to connect device gateway and device shadow. Similarly, the Azure IoT has three main IoT SDKs including device SDKs, service SDKs, and Gateway SDK.

1.1.5.2 Middleware

The purpose of an IoT middleware is to function as a mediator between the hardware (IoT devices) and the application layers. Its primary tasks include collection, aggregation, filtering, and processing of data from heterogeneous devices over a variety of protocols and network topologies. Some examples of IoT middleware are Google Fit and Apple's HealthKit, which allows users to access and control their fitness data generated by variety of devices (e.g., wearables) and mobile applications. Xively is another IoT-based middleware that allows sensors to connect to its platform easily and store the data persistently, so that it can be seamlessly retrieved anytime. Node-RED is an open-source IoT middleware platform from IBM, which provides a visual tool to compose an IoT application by simply dragging and dropping its various components.

Some of the enabling technologies in these areas are:

IoT platforms An IoT platform is designed to seamlessly manage any kind of connected device, irrespective of the underlying protocols. The IoT platform can:

- Connect various components of the IoT system such as IoT sensors and devices
- Enable communication between different hardware (e.g., edge hardware) and software irrespective of the underlying protocols
- Handle authentication, security, and privacy
- Device management functions such as monitoring, troubleshooting and administration
- Enable aggregation, analysis and visualization of data

These IoT platforms are in between the data collected at the IoT gateways and the end application. It is estimated that the IoT platform market share will cross over $22 billion by 2023.

Data storage Cloud-based data storage is the most common form in IoT rather than storing it on the premise of where the data is collected. Although, it increases the cost, the main advantage is the connectivity it provides to the users. Users can access the data from the device, anytime and from anywhere.

Data processing One of the key functions of an IoT middleware is the ability to manage the huge data that is being generated by the IoT devices. This kind of data can be considered as big data. The attributes of big data such as Velocity, Volume, Variety, Value, and Veracity are present in the data generated by the IoT systems. Various IoT Middleware provides the ability to do analytics on both continuous streaming data as well as data that is stored. A publish/subscribe kind of middleware can provide functionality for continuously processing of the data using various data processing functions such as preprocessing, filtering and data mining approaches.

Edge/Fog computing Various other forms of computing technologies are becoming key enablers in the middleware domain such as Edge computing, which facilitates the computation to be performed on computing infrastructure available close to the devices and sending the result directly to the relevant application. There is a no collection point or cloud in this type of computing. Fog computing is another emerging approach, where the computation is placed at the edge of a network.

Security and privacy Due to the vast amounts of data stored and managed by the IoT middleware, the main concern is of security and privacy. Many cloud middleware systems provide authentication and authorization services. Recently, new security algorithms and tools have been developed to address the requirements of low powered IoT devices.

16 Internet of Things

1.1.5.3 Ubiquitous Connectivity

It is expected that billions of devices are going to be connected to the Internet in the near future. In addition to this connectivity, the devices themselves need to communicate with other devices as well as various other forms of computer systems (e.g., Gateway). As these devices are energy constrained, the optimization of energy during wireless communication is of utmost importance. These communication technologies can also be distinguished in terms of the system performance, frequencies, Medium Access Control (MAC) scheme, and standardization process (i.e., open vs proprietary).

The key enabling technologies in this area can be classified into proximal range, short range, short/medium range, medium range, and long range.

Proximity Each IoT application has its own requirement depending upon the environment in which the IoT system is deployed. The communication protocols such as Radio Frequency Identification (RFID), Near Field Communication (NFC) work in the proximity range, that is, 0 to 10 meters. Several applications particularly in the retail sectors uses NFC for bill payment at checkout by just such as payment at retail checkout by tapping a credit card with an item having an NFC tag.

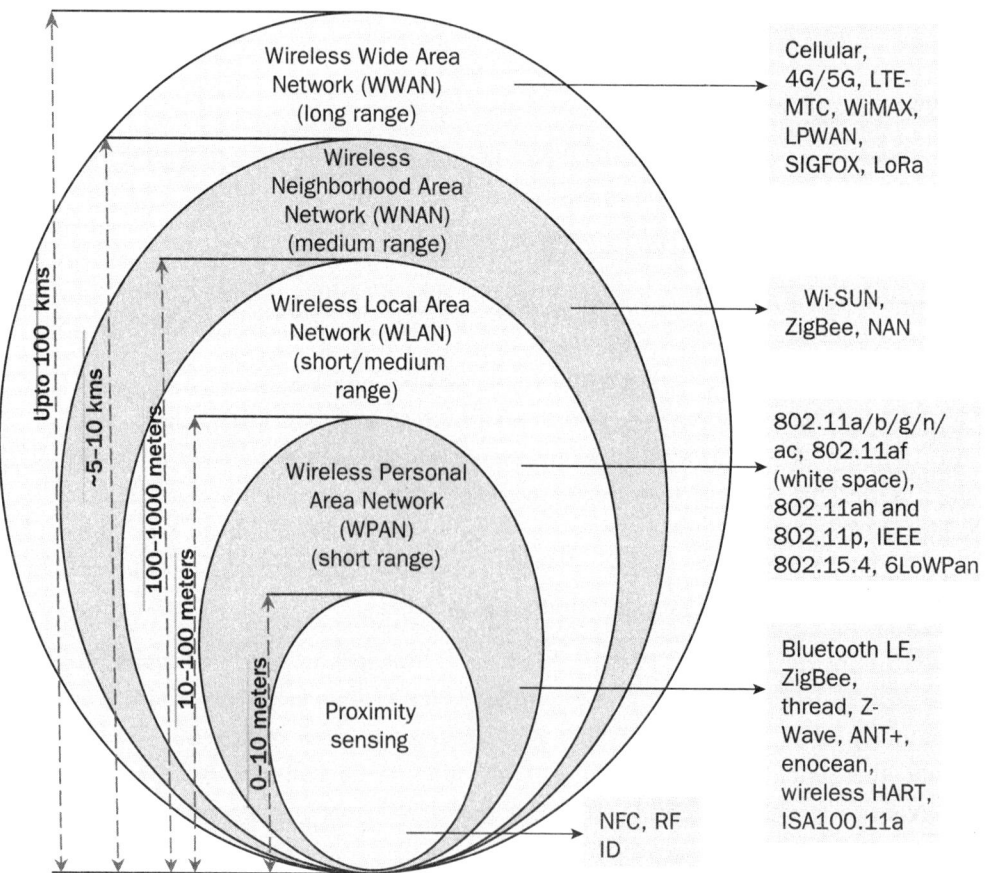

Fig. 1.6 Various Types of Short-, Medium-, and Long-range Connectivity in IoT

Short range In the short-range communication space, applications such as Wearables, Home automation, and Healthcare are popular. Key enabling technologies for this type of communication are Wi-Fi, Z-Wave, ZigBee, IrDA, Bluetooth, Bluetooth Low Energy, and Radio Frequency Identification (RFID) (see Fig. 1.6).

Short-to-medium range In this range of communications, Wi-Fi is a popular technology for many years now. IEEE developed a set of five (designated as a, b, g, n, and ac) media access control (MAC) and physical Layer (PHY) specification for wireless local area network (WLAN) called the IEEE 802.11. These are abbreviated as BGN, ABGN, and A/B/G/N/AC in the specifications for wireless routers, Wi-Fi access points, and Wi-Fi in portable devices. However, since these Wi-Fi protocols have fairly large energy consumption, they are not very useful for IoT devices due to their low-power requirement. To overcome this issue, duty cycling (i.e., keeping the chips in sleep mode for most of the time) and other energy-harvesting methods are being developed. A low power Wi-Fi standard emerged called IEEE 802.11ah. Another enabling technology that is specifically developed by IETF for IoT is the 6LoWPAN, which defines the mechanisms for transmitting IPv6 (128-bit Internet scheme that offers about 3.4×10^{38} unique addresses to accommodate the requirements of the IoT) packets on top of IEEE 802.15.4 networks which defines low-data-rate, low-power, and short-range radio frequency transmissions for wireless personal area networks (WPANs).

Long range There are two main options available for IoT system developers to enable long-range communication in their systems.

Cellular These technologies operate in the licensed spectrum. The key technologies in this space are GSM, WCDMA, 3G/4G/5G, LTE-MTC, and WiMAX providing high-quality voice and data services. The 3rd Generation Partnership Project (3GPP) is a collaboration between groups of telecommunications standards associations that developed Narrowband IoT (NB-IoT), which is a Low Power Wide Area Network (LPWAN) radio technology standard.

Unlicensed low power wide area network The technology in this area uses the unlicensed spectrum and mostly proprietary in nature. Technologies such as SIGFOX and LoRA are popular for machine-type communication (MTC) applications addressing the ultra-low-end sensor segment.

1.1.5.4 Hardware and Devices

Miniaturization and composability Novel hardware developments are enabling the development of ultra-compact wireless. Advancements in the miniaturization of the hardware mainly through the use of the microelectromechanical systems (MEMS) technology is enabling the development of a new generation of devices that are ultra-compact and have high computing ability. Further, nano-electromechanical systems (NEMS)-based sensors are miniaturizing the sensors to nanometres size. Wearable medical devices that are almost invisible to other individuals are currently available. The Moore's law states that the density of transistors on silicon chips doubles every 2 years. This is evident from the fact that today's devices (e.g., smartphones) have the computing power of yesteryears high end computing systems and even supercomputers. Further, the increased ability to put together complex systems from simpler components is enabling the development of revolutionary products in many areas.

High durability The IoT sensors are expected to work in harsh situations. In many field-based applications, these sensors are deployed in open environments, exposing them to the elements of weather for years. Some of these sensors are explicitly required to withstand harsh extreme environments such as extreme temperatures, vibration ratings, and dust and liquid resistance. Hence, durability of these sensors is of great concern.

Improvements in System on Chip (SOC) architectures Some key advancements happened in the area of SOC architectures specifically designed for IoT devices such as application processors (high end) (are usually based on technologies adapted from mobile phone/tablet architectures) microcontrollers (low end), and smart analogue.

Lower costs One trend that is driving greater adoption of IoT is the lowering of the cost of the sensors. It is estimated that the average cost of the sensors will drop to $0.38 by 2020, down by $0.92 as compared to 2004. This is helping to sense and acquire more data from a variety of environments and develop more data-driven intelligent applications than before.

1.2 IOT AS A DISRUPTIVE TECHNOLOGY

The term disruptive technology was first coined by Harvard professor Clayton Christensen, he later named it as disruptive innovation. The reason it is called as disruptive is due to its impact on an existing business model and the current system/society.

A disruptive technology (a hardware, software, networking, etc.) has the potential to replace an existing technology or a well working system that is already in place. From a product perspective, it could be something that begins small and steadily moves up the market and eventually becomes a threatening competitor to the existing products, and may eventually replace them.

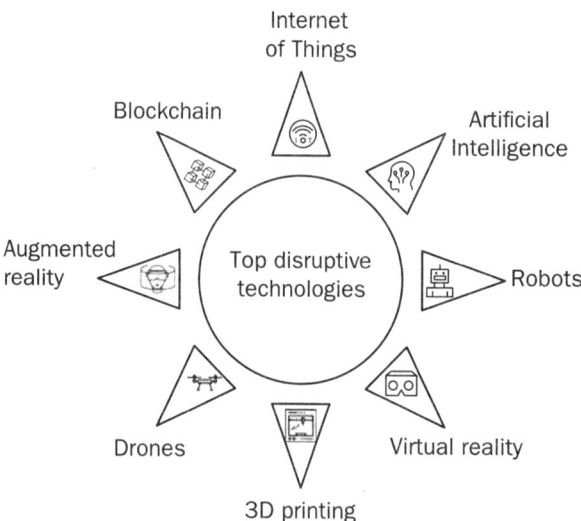

Fig. 1.7 Internet of Things (IoT) Along with Other Disruptive Technologies (Projection for the Year 2020)

Currently, IoT is considered as one of the top disruptive technology along with other technologies such as artificial intelligence, robotics, and virtual reality (see Fig. 1.7). Section 1.2.1 discusses some selected areas that IoT is already playing a crucial role and acting as disruptive technology.

1.2.1 Motivating Scenarios

1.2.1.1 Home and Personal Space

The personal space IoT centres on a person's space. It includes all objects implanted or wearable by the person such as implanted sensors, smartwatches, Google glasses, ECG sensors, and smartphones. It also includes all fixed or mobile objects and devices that come into contact (or reachable) with wearable objects on the person. Devices are reachable when they are within the wireless transmission radius of one another.

Smart buildings IBM is building a solution with the Watson IoT platform and IoT-enabled sensors for tracking every asset in the building using that information in their IoT platform. This will facilitate the owners of the building to understand, monitor, and control of installations such as Heating, Ventilation, Air Conditioning (HVAC) systems, to enable to monitor remotely. The burden of facility management is overtaken by smart sensors that capture every pulse of this infrastructure and to enable remote diagnostics and analysis.

Smart elevators KONE, the elevator company, is trying to understand how people are using the elevators. By using sensors, they are assessing how people move through buildings and estimating how much time can be reduced for the elevator wait. They conclude that even 2 or 3 minutes reduction in the waiting time will make a huge difference in moving people to their relevant floor.

1.2.1.2 Social

Food security In February 2018, a meeting at Rome was organized by the Food and Agriculture Organization (FAO) of the United Nations (UN). During that meeting Vicente Muñoz, Chief Internet of Things Officer, Telefónica said "The future of agriculture hinges on the adoption of technologies such as the Internet of Things (IoT), Big Data and Artificial Intelligence". Further, FAO's director General José Graziano da Silva was of the opinion that the greatest challenges currently faced by humanity is in their fight against hunger, poverty, and effects of climate changes in agriculture, further he said:

"Access to reliable information, including that related to changing weather patterns, is essential to empower farmers, especially those who live in developing countries."

To address the above issues, investment and integration of new technologies such as IoT that will enable farmers to connect with real-time information (e.g., Agro-meteorological) about their farms and facilitate the use of simple and intuitive tools that are data driven to decrease uncertainty and mitigate risk. IoT's contribution is this sector is gaining wider acceptance. Several areas are currently getting transformed by the use of smart sensing systems for monitoring and management of various field tasks and parameters such as soil health, irrigation scheduling, nutrients, and early pest and disease prediction and warning.

Reducing food wastage A Chicago-based tech start-up, Ovie, developed a smart food storage system based on the IoT concept that will eliminate waste and change the way people eat, save, and shop for food. The system tracks the food items in the fridge and sends reminders to eat those before getting spoiled.

Water ATM Piramal Sarvajal, a mission-driven social enterprise, is committed to leveraging technology to bring community-level safe drinking water to the underserved. The organization has developed and implemented innovative market-based drinking water solutions in 16 states in India. Their infrastructure includes remotely monitored water purification units and solar powered, cloud connected water kiosks called water ATMs (see Box 1.4).

> **BOX 1.4: WATER ATM FOR DISPENSING SAFE DRINKING WATER**
>
> Peeth is a village in the heart of the Aravallis in Rajasthan. It is one of the most backward districts of the country and faces a serious water shortage. In Peeth, 84% of the population gets its drinking water from the local well, polluted with dangerously high levels of fluoride and other heavy minerals. Surveys showed that although the locals were aware of hazards of drinking polluted water, but the only alternative was a single private drinking water supplier, who charged ₹2 per litre and only catered to 40 families. Thus, the villagers welcomed the Sarvajal Kendra, as a much-needed solution. Today, the facility serves more than 200 families daily, ensuring they get safe water delivered at their doorstep.
>
> *Adapted from* www.sarvajal.com; www.downtoearth.com; www.thehindu.com

1.2.1.3 Healthcare

Currently, IoT in Healthcare is being adopted in many areas. It can not only improve the existing healthcare systems, but also enable transformative ways (see Box 1.5) in which the patient gets treatment and care. It is estimated that the global IoT healthcare market to reach over USD 160 billion by 2020. The concept of 'Connected medical devices' is ushering new era in personal fitness and wellness area. Some of the use cases are:

- Remote diagnosis and follow up monitoring
- Memory disabilities monitoring
- Early intervention for detection of critical signs
- Monitoring patient fall
- Timely medicine alerts and enhanced drug management
- Healthcare assets monitoring and tracking

> **BOX 1.5: OPEN ARTIFICIAL PANCREAS SYSTEM DEVELOPMENT**
>
> Dana Lewis and her husband Scott Leibrand have hacked Dana's CGM (continuous glucose monitor) and her insulin pump. Using the data feed from the CGM and a Raspberry Pi computer, their own software completes the loop and continuously alters the amount of insulin Dana's pump delivers. Its success led to the unveiling of the open artificial pancreas system project. "The Open Artificial Pancreas System project (#OpenAPS) is an open and transparent effort to make safe and effective basic Artificial Pancreas System

(Contd)

Box 1.5 *(Contd)*

(APS) technology widely available to more quickly improve and save as many lives as possible and reduce the burden of Type 1 diabetes."

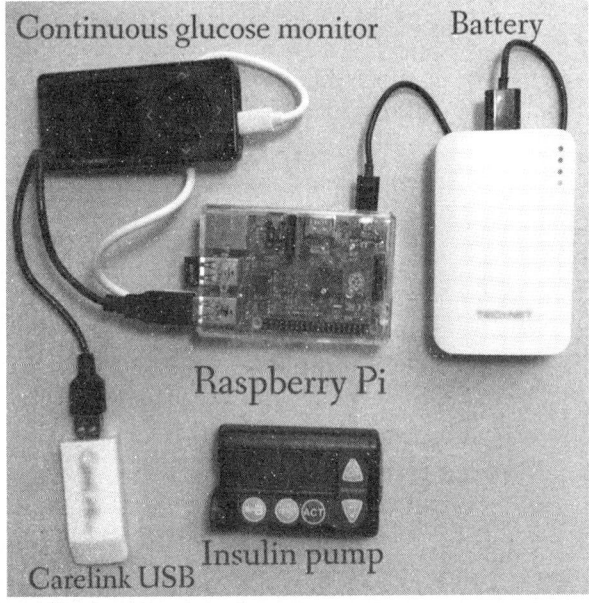

Adapted from www.diyps.org; www.healthline.com; www.itas.kit.edu; www.openaps.org

1.2.1.4 Environmental

Saving critical species The International Union for the Conservation of Nature (IUCN) maintains a database of the extinction risk of animal species called the IUCN red list. It reveals that the number of threatened species rose globally from roughly 10,000 in 2000 to over 25,000 in 2018. In the wake of such a revelation, it is necessary to take urgent action to protect these animals from extinction. Many organizations around the world are adopting IoT-based technologies to help identify, track, and protect them. The ruggedness of the terrain, remoteness, and real-time information gathering are some of the aspects of the problem that IoT is able to address. For example, in South Africa, IoT devices enabled collars are sending location and heart rate of Rhinos, which is helping the authorities to monitor them and immediately send rescue teams if they find the animal in distress.

Monitoring and reducing air pollution The effects of air pollution are causing serious problems worldwide. At the individual level, poor air quality is leading to several debilitating conditions in humans such as asthma, attacks, lung cancer, heart diseases, and chronic bronchitis. According to the American Association for the Advancement of Science (AAAS), it is the world's fourth reason for deaths. IoT-based air quality monitoring devices are highly capable of measuring various air quality parameters such as surface ozone, NO_2, SO_2, and particulate matter (PM2.5/PM10), and relay this information in real-time to the authorities to help track the zones of high pollution. Low power wide area network (LPWAN) technologies such as LoRA are enabling the development of dense air quality monitoring networks due to its ability for long-range connectivity and low-power consumption. An urban sensing project called the 'Array of Things (AoT)' is being carried out in Chicago to collect real-time data on the city's environment for a more healthier, more efficient, and more livable city. The list of sensors includes environmental sensors, air quality sensors, and light and infrared sensors.

Improving water conservation Water conservation and management is essential in many facets of human lives. The various current practices are time consuming and lack real-time tracking and alerts for timely intervention to reduce wastage of water. Out of many applications of IoT in this area, two applications are described as follows:

- Smart water meters that can be used to detect leakage of pipes in the water delivery infrastructure (e.g., water grid). It also can help to precisely understand the water consumption behaviour of the users through data analytics and make and send alerts in real time. Further, by analysing the requirement of water in an area, adjustments to the optimal supply of water can be achieved.
- Water quality aspects can be studied by the deployment of IoT sensors in the water supply network to measure various water quality parameters to quickly react to those conditions when the water quality is deemed below the safe level.

For more compelling use cases, the reader is referred to Chapter 17.

1.2.2 Multidisciplinary Nature of IoT

IoT is driven not only by people who have specific background in Information and communication technologies (ICTs), but also by non-IT people who are showing significant interest in understanding the IoT ecosystem and contributing to its development using their own domain specific expertise. Institutions are increasingly feeling the need to have personnel particularly those who are involved in systems development to understand a host of disciplines to help them design complex IoT systems. Hence, multi-domain research and development teams are currently preferred in the development of IoT system. As shown in Fig. 1.8, there are a multitude of disciplines that are involved in IoT, each of them have their own set of requirements and goals. However, the domain expert in any of these areas, for example, a person with Transportation systems development, has to work with a person who knows about sensors and their deployment, and in turn need to work with an Information Technology (IT) person to help develop the software and integrate with the system. Similarly, doctors and electronics and communication technology engineers have to work hand in hand to develop new IoT devices for healthcare. In addition, social scientists are required to understand about the societal aspects of the developed technology. This line of thought can be extended to many sectors such as defence, environmental monitoring, energy, and industries, who are currently building transformative IoT solutions Therefore, it can be seen that for any of the technology that is being developed in IoT, there are multidisciplinary teams (members with varied but complimentary experience) involved to make the idea take shape and finally come out with tangible product.

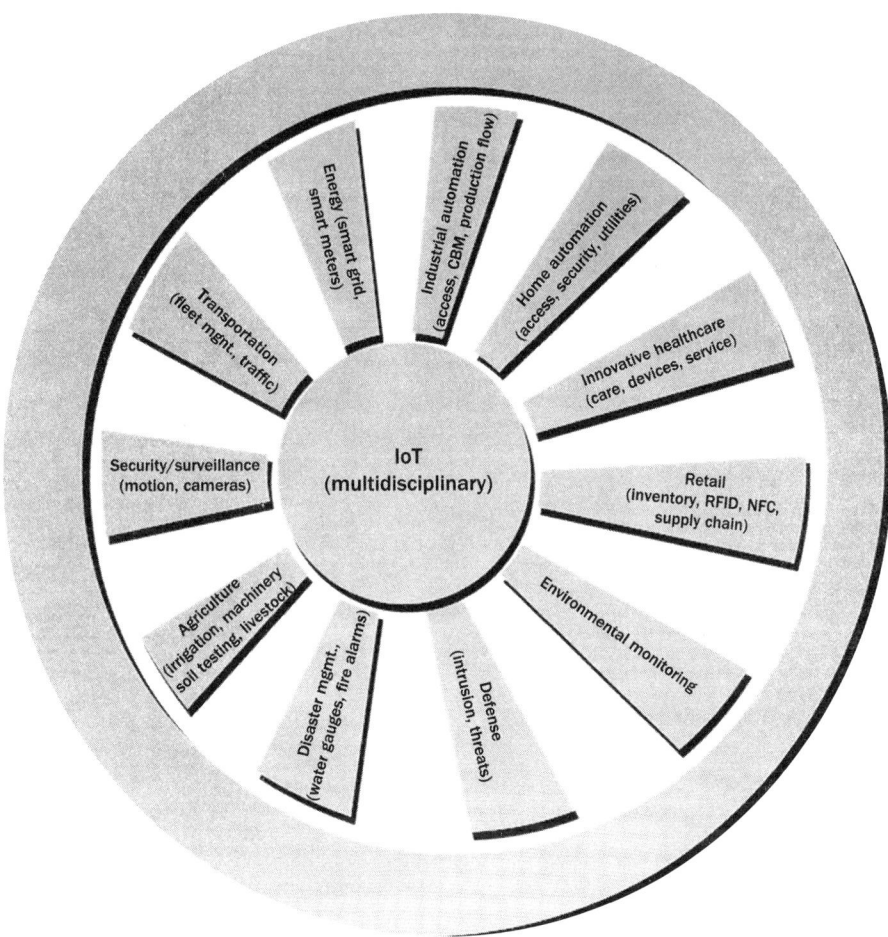

Fig. 1.8 Interdisciplinary Nature of IoT Encompasses a Variety of Domains

1.2.3 Challenges Involved in Its Further Evolution

The main challenges involved in the further evolution of IoT are as follows:

1.2.3.1 Technological Challenges

The technological challenges that could impede the future evolution of IoT include the following:

IoT system design considerations Currently, there are a variety of protocols (network, communication, data protocols, etc.) that are being used by various organizations/entities to design, develop and implement IoT systems in diverse domains. This is leading to non-interoperable systems, whose integration and access is becoming very challenging. Unless, standards are implemented in every step of the IoT systems development process, there will be many systems that could become unusable and obsolete. For example, users will end up with an IoT system (e.g., home automation), which will become highly vendor dependant and is no longer able to integrate with other systems implemented by a different vendor.

Maturity and integration with existing technology Currently, most of the IoT technologies have not reached a matured phase where they are guaranteed to continue to grow in a particular direction. Hence, an IoT solution provided using a particular technology may soon be abandoned and a new technology used for the same functionality. Therefore, products that the user is using may no longer be useful, since the technology is no longer supported by the vendor. Integration with existing technologies and overhead due to constant requirement for upgradation of existing the hardware infrastructure is another barrier that needs to be crossed for greater adoption of IoT.

Standard operating procedures (SOPs) The lack of well understood and standard operating procedures for IoT devices maintenance, response, and incident management are aspects that need to be strengthened to streamline the processes involved in the IoT systems. Since, it is a rapidly evolving cluster of technologies, the best practices are scattered and few. Hence, there is a need to document and guide developers on the best approaches.

Security The security aspects of IoT are a major concern to its widespread proliferation in the future. It is considered as crucial barrier for widespread acceptance of IoT. Malicious attacks and hacking of IoT devices (e.g., baby monitors, smart fridges, thermostats, health and medical machines, cameras, etc.) can pose significant security nightmare. The main challenges include (ACE-OAuth, 2018):

(i) Authentication and authorization for secure communication Authentication allows establishing the identity of an entity. Whereas authorization determines whether an entity (a device or a user) has access rights to resources and to what extent (i.e., level of permissions, e.g., read/write). In the case of IoT, authentication enables to establish the identity of various IoT devices deployed in a shared environment, hence maintain the integrity of the IoT device and data. Trust is the backbone for ascertaining the identity of an entity. In computer-networked environments, passwords are the most common way of authentication of human users. However, in a machine-to-machine interaction, cryptography-based authentication and authorization mechanisms are useful, where cryptographic keys are commonly used. A digital certificate issued and digitally signed by a certificate authority (CA) contains a public key and identity of the owner. The IoT devices can use these digital certificates for authentication and create the required Trust for all parties in the network. However, such CAs are non-existent at present for the IoT domains. Hence, efficient ways to deploy the keys and manage them is an ongoing effort. Further, current security protocols and cryptography approaches require good amount of memory space, which is difficult to implement on low-powered IoT devices. Therefore, the challenge is to develop approaches for deploying and managing the keys that can adapt without causing additional overheard on the IoT node (Yang, et al., 2016). In addition, the authorization and access control should be customized based on the type of the IoT Node (Li, et al., 2017). Recently, IETF proposed the authentication and authorization in constrained environments (ACE-OAuth) framework for IoT devices. It is based on OAuth 2.0 (OAuth is a widely used open standard for delegation) and Constrained Open access Protocol (CoAP).

(ii) Privacy IoT devices that collect sensitive user's data are posing an immense threat to an individual's privacy. For example, data gathered by sensors related to health, home appliances usage, tracking devices for phones, work habits, etc. could be transmitted to a cloud service or a third party without the user being aware of it. Existing privacy approaches are user-centric, that is, it is based on individual's preference to the content and quantum of data that he/she deems to be sharable and what remains private. The data-collection entities are obligated to inform the users about the intended usage of the acquired information. However, in the case of IoT nodes that are collecting private information, there is a threat to privacy at (i) endpoints where each IoT node emits the data, and (ii) data obtained from networked IoT nodes, which are collected, combined, and analysed to reveal a pattern and thus giving out more sensitive information. In addition to data privacy issues, IoT device deployment at sensitive areas and across socio-cultural borders requires a new way to understand the implications of privacy invasion.

1.2.3.2 Connectivity

Huge challenges need to be overcome for ensuring connectivity of billions of devices in IoT. Many technologies are available for enabling connectivity in IoT such as those in the unlicensed spectrum, low-power wide area networks (LPWAN), cellular, and satellite-based technologies. These are at various stages of maturity and continuously evolving in terms of the core technologies and applications to IoT. The future of these connectivity solutions depend on the adaptability to the vast array of diverse IoT devices and applications, as the requirements vary in terms of data capture rate, data transmission rate, latency, storage, etc. Hence, connectivity needs are based on the device and its particular characteristics. Therefore, no single technology will be able to cater to all the needs of the IoT systems. Integration and interoperability of various connectivity solutions will be a key factor for seamlessly switching between various IoT devices implementing varied connectivity technologies.

1.2.3.3 Societal Drivers

Issues of privacy and trust are going to be the main drivers for the wide acceptance of IoT. There is a need for various institutions (public and private) to implement mutually agreed and standardized privacy procedures into their systems and the core IoT system architecture is built on the foundations of privacy, trust, and data protection. For example, an IoT device could capture the location of the user to give location-based services, but does not use that data for any other purpose, such as tracking the individual. Similarly, the data captured by the device may send only the summary and does not transmit the original raw data, or the data lives only for a short period or anonymised so that it cannot be identified with any particular user. Such kind of approaches will make the user to feel protected when using privacy friendly IoT applications. Currently, such things are not fully implemented in the IoT ecosystem. The current focus is more on giving better functionality and user experience rather than focusing on implementing the principle of *Privacy by Design*. According to it, starting from the fundamental building blocks in the IoT system development, privacy is given utmost importance and embedded in each and every process of the system development. Such systems are robust and have better chances of gaining the trust of the consumer.

1.2.3.4 Uncertain Returns on Investment

The investment in IoT according to the market reports is very high (see Box 1.3). However, businesses are struggling to understand and make an estimate of the return on investment (ROI) due to the emerging nature of the IoT technology and lack of historical data or business cases (World Economic Forum report, 2015) that could be used as a benchmark or point of reference to estimate the ROI.

1.3 STANDARDIZATION

The massive scale of IoT comprises billions of devices and subsystems. To be able to interconnect them and derive meaningful information requires that these heterogeneous systems need to be interoperable, that is, the ability to work with any underlying protocols, data models, and content types. Since, there are many public and private stakeholders involved in IoT, there will be many proprietary and open solutions in various domains with each solution providing its own IoT infrastructure, devices, APIs, and data formats due to which it becomes challenging to integrate them. To achieve interoperability and enable scaling up of IoT, standards are required.

1.3.1 Need for Standardization at Various Layers of IoT

As IoT is a multi-layered system comprising of various layers related to sensing, networking, communication, session, etc., standardization is required at each of these layers (the architecture reference model of IoT is explained in Chapter 14). Considering this need, several standards have been proposed with a focus on specific requirement in the development of an IoT system. For example, the data link layer connects two things or thing and gateway device that connects a group of things to the Internet. Various short-, medium-, and long-range protocols have been developed for connectivity (see Figs 1.6 and 1.9). Specialized routing protocols were developed to enable several IoT devices to communicate and aggregate information and then send it on to the Internet. Further, in the network layer, among other protocols such as UDP, 6TiSCH, and THREAD, the 6LoWPAN is developed for power constrained devices, standardizes a way to carry packet data in the form of IPv6 over IEEE 802.15.4. The messaging among various components of the communication subsystem is addressed in the session layer. Among them, the Constrained open Access protocol (CoAP) was developed by IETF Constrained RESTful Environments Working Group (CoRE). It works on UDP or UDP analogue. The Message Queuing Telemetry Transport (MQTT) originally developed by IBM works on the TCP/IP. More details on the IoT standards and protocols are discussed in Chapter 4.

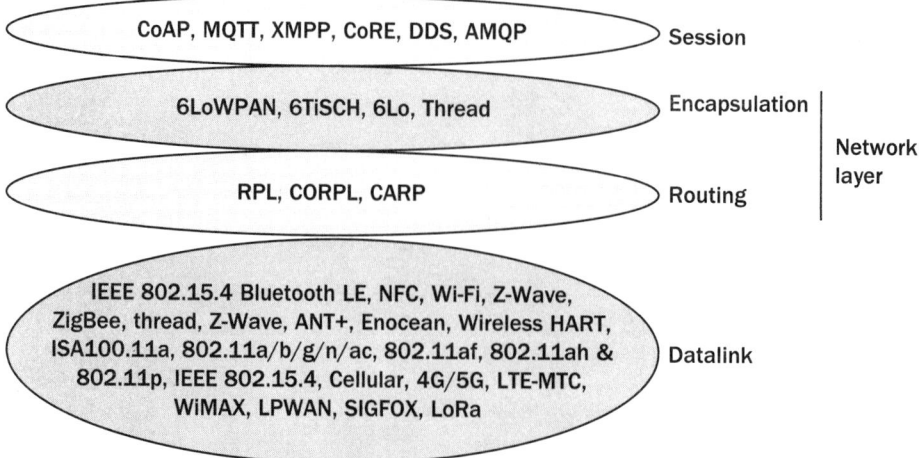

Fig. 1.9 Variety of Standard Protocols Currently Available for IoT

1.3.2 Organizations and Their Efforts for Standardization

Various organizations are involved in the IoT standardization efforts. Following are some key institutions and their contributions:

Institute of Electrical and Electronics Engineers (IEEE) IEEE is a global, professional engineering organization whose mission is to foster technological innovation and excellence for the benefit of humanity. The standards body of IEEE called the IEEE standards association is involved in developing standards, specifications, and best practices for IoT. The IEEE P2413 defines an architectural framework for the IoT, including descriptions of various IoT domains, definitions of IoT domain abstractions, and identification of commonalities between different IoT domains.

ETSI (European Telecommunications Standards Institute) ETSI develops standards for information and communications technologies (ICT), including fixed, mobile, radio, converged, broadcast, and Internet technologies. In the IoT space, it works with ONE M2M (another standards body) to provide standardized M2M interfaces. The goal is to enable IoT devices to connect seamlessly and to ensure that they are network agnostic. From an M2M standpoint, various M2M technologies are supported by ETSI such as smart appliances, smart metering, smart cities, smart grids, e-health, and intelligent transportation systems. Further, specific to IoT, ETSI is working in the areas of: security for the IoT, low power supplies in the IoT, radio spectrum requirements, and embedded communications modules.

OneM2M It is a Global standards initiative for M2M and IoT. It has over 200 member organizations. It works in a partnership mode with various standards organizations and provides a detailed standard for M2M/IoT in the areas of architecture, interfaces, security, communication protocols, etc. The oneM2M-layered model consists of network layer, common services layer, and the applications layer. The goal is to have applications to share common infrastructure, environments, and network elements to enable interoperability. The common services layer can be readily embedded within various hardware and software and provides functions that M2M applications across different domains commonly need (e.g., data transport, management, discovery and policy enforcement, security/encryption, etc.). The Representational State Transfer (REST)-based architecture of oneM2M allows the use of multiple protocols such as HTTP, CoAP, MQTT, or WebSocket to work with oneM2M application servers worldwide.

Internet Engineering Task Force (IETF) It is an open, international community of network designers, operators, vendors, and researchers concerned with the evolution of the Internet architecture and the smooth operation of the Internet. Its mission is to "make the Internet work better by producing high quality, relevant technical documents that influence the way people design, use, and manage the Internet." Within IETF, specific IoT-based focus is towards:

6LoWPAN 6LoWPAN is IPv6 adaptation layer and header compression mechanism that is suitable for low power constrained IoT devices and networks.

Routing Over Low power and Lossy networks (ROLL) ROLL establishes routing protocols for constrained-node networks.

Constrained RESTful Environments (CoRE) CORE extends the Web architecture to most constrained networks and embedded devices.

International Telecommunications Union (ITU) It released the ITU report on The Internet of Things in 2005, which describes the various visions of IoT, and terms IoT as an 'ubiquitous network'. It published recommendations in the areas of tag-based identification services, ubiquitous sensor networks (USN), and ubiquitous applications in next-generation networks. Specifically for IoT, this organization contributed towards IoT terminology, common requirements and capabilities, APIs and protocols for IoT, IoT testing, network, security, and privacy protection aspects of IoT. Further, various focus groups were formed for several application areas such as e-health, smart grids, home networks, smart sustainable cities, and smart water management.

Object Management Group (OMG) It developed the Data Distribution Service (DDS) for IoT. It is a middleware protocol and API standard for data-centric connectivity. It is pub/sub standard, which enables scalable, real-time, reliable, high performance, and interoperable data exchanges between publishers and subscribers. In a data-centric system, the focus is on user-defined data (the data model). The middleware understands the context of the data and ensures that all interested subscribers have a correct and consistent view of the data.

OASIS It is a standards body that is responsible for providing a lightweight publish/subscribe reliable messaging transport protocol suitable for communication in M2M/IoT contexts where a small code footprint is required and/or network bandwidth is at a premium.

1.3.3 Factors for Widespread Adoption of IoT

IoT-based technologies are driving a wide range of application areas that have stagnated and lacking much innovation in the preceding years of IoT. It has already permeated in various walks of life. The various factors that led to the widespread adoption are mainly due to the technological advancements and economic viability in the areas of the following.

1.3.3.1 Technology Viewpoint

Communication and network Connectivity is one of the key pillars of IoT. There are a host of technologies that are being developed (some of them have already reached mature levels) and in multiple ranges (short, medium range) which are enabling the IoT revolution gain widespread acceptance. Customized versions of Internet protocols for low-powered devices such as the 6LoWPAN, which is based on the IPV6 Competing wireless technologies such Cellular (4G/5G) and LPWAN (e.g., LoRA) technologies are giving the IoT system developers options to develop IoT networks that can be deployed in remote challenging areas. More details are presented in Chapter 4.

Computing A computing revolution has happened in the last decade, with new paradigms of computing emerging such as the cloud computing. It has completely changed the way in which data is stored, processed, analysed, and disseminated. The low-cost nature and always available kind of computing resources is an attractive alternative to the user as compared to in-house computing infrastructure.

The IoT has considerably gained by cloud-based infrastructure, since there is a need to process data from a very high number of sensors, which requires considerable computing power. Organizations and individuals working in deploying IoT-based solutions can now subscribe to a cloud-provider for a considerably low rate and quickly deploy the IoT solutions. Various cloud providers (e.g., Amazon Web Services (AWS) IoT, IBM Watson IoT, etc.) are providing off the shelf IoT platforms to enable end-to-end management of the IoT resources. Further, the emergence of 'Data Science' area has ushered in new ways for analytics, both at the edge of the IoT network through streaming data processing analytics and also batch-processing/offline approaches that includes machine learning-based techniques.

Low-cost devices Sensors and their integration with IoT is becoming affordable. Due to it, an ever-increasing number of domains are able to use IoT sensors to drive their processes; these solutions are contributing towards developing automation in several sectors.

1.3.3.2 Consumer Viewpoint

From a consumer perspective, usefulness, price, connectivity, security, and privacy are the main enablers for high adoption of IoT products. The IoT products such as wearables in the fitness and wellness area have already showed high promise due to the practical use and affordable pricing. As the consumers get more educated in the value that IoT products bring to their daily lives, greater will be the adoption. Companies have already embarked on targeted campaigns to create consumer awareness and change their perception of this new technology.

REVIEW QUESTIONS

1. Describe the historical context that led to the emergence of IoT.
2. Describe various Auto-ID technologies.
3. What is the vision of IoT? Explain the different perspectives from which IoT's vision can be understood.
4. Various organizations have defined IoT. Describe in what aspects these are similar (if any). What components or parts of these definitions are similar?
5. Give your own definition of IoT. How is it different from other definitions?
6. What is an enabling technology? Describe the key enabling technologies of IoT.
7. Explain the evolution of a disruptive technology.
8. Why is IoT considered as a disruptive technology?
9. Give some motivating scenarios where IoT has been a disruptive technology.
10. What is the need for IoT standardization?
11. Give an overview of IoT Standards and mention the organizations that are involved in IoT Standardization and their specific roles.
12. What is leading to the widespread adoption of IoT?

REFERENCES

1. ACE-OAUTH [ONLINE]. Available at: https://tools.ietf.org/pdf/draft-ietf-ace-oauth-authz-13.pdf [Accessed 2/10/2018]
2. Array of Things [ONLINE]. Available at: https://arrayofthings.github.io/ [Accessed 2 Oct 2018]

3. Blowers, M., Iribarne, J., Colbert, E., Kott, A. (2016). The future Internet of Things and security of its control systems. arXiv preprint arXiv:1610.01953.
4. Buckman, A. H., Mayfield, M., Beck, S. B. M. (2014), What is a Smart Building? *Smart and Sustainable Built Environment*, 3(2): 92–109.
5. Christensen, C. (2013), The innovator's dilemma: when new technologies cause great firms to fail. Harvard Business Review Press.
6. Coke Machine, The Only Coke Machine on the Internet, Carnegie Mellon University, School of Computer Science [ONLINE]. Available at: https://www.cs.cmu.edu/~coke/history_long.txt [Accessed 2/10/2018]
7. Cook, D. J., Das, S. K. (2007), How smart are our environments? An updated look at the state of the art, *Pervasive and Mobile Computing*, 3(2): 53–73.
8. Gartner. (2018), Gartner worldwide IT spending forecast for 2018, 2018. Available at: https://www.gartner.com/newsroom/id/3845563 [Accessed 2/10/2018]
9. IIC: Industrial Internet Consortium. Available at: https://www.iiconsortium.org/
10. IEEE. (2015), Towards a definition of Internet of Things. Available at: https://iot.ieee.org/images/files/pdf/IEEE_IoT_Towards_Definition_Internet_of_Things_Issue1_14MAY15.pdf [Accessed 2/10/2018]
11. IoT-A, Internet of Things – Architecture IoT-A Deliverable D1.5 – Final architectural reference model for the IoT v3.0.
12. ITU, International Telecom Union (ITU) [ONLINE]. Available at: https://www.itu.int/en/Pages/default.aspx [Accessed 2/10/2018]
13. IETF [ONLINE]. Available at: https://www.ietfjournal.org/internet-of-things-standards-and-guidance-from-the-ietf/ [Accessed 2/10/2018]
14. IIC (2018) [ONLINE]. Available at: https://www.iiconsortium.org/index.htm [Accessed 2/10/2018]
15. Kim, H. Lee, E. A. (2017), Authentication and authorization for the Internet of Things, *IT Professional*, 19(5): 27–33.
16. Li, F., Hong, J., Omala, A. A. (2017), Efficient certificateless access control for industrial Internet of Things, *Future Gener Comput Syst*.
17. Ma, H. D. (2011), Internet of things: objectives and scientific challenge, *Journal of Computer Science and Technology*, 26 (6): 919–924.
18. McGlinn, K., O'Neill, E., Gibney, A., O'Sullivan, D., Lewis, D. (2010), SimCon: a tool to support rapid evaluation of smart building application design using context simulation and virtual reality, *Journal of Universal Computer Science*, 16(15): 1992–2018.
19. McKinsey. (2015), The Internet of Things: mapping the value beyond the hype, June, 2015.
20. Montori, F., Bedogni, L., Felice, M.D., Bononi, L. (2018), Machine-to-machine wireless communication technologies for the Internet of Things: taxonomy, comparison and open issues, *Pervasive and Mobile Computing*, 50: 56–81.
21. Mauro, C., Ali, D., Franke, K., Watson, S. (2018), Internet of Things security and forensics: challenges and opportunities, *Future Generation Computer Systems*, 78: 544–546.
22. Nguyen, H. H, Mirza, F, Asif N. M., Nguyen, M. (21017). A review on IoT healthcare monitoring applications and a vision for transforming sensor data into real-time clinical feedback. *2017 IEEE 21st International Conference on Computer Supported Cooperative Work in Design (CSCWD)*, Wellington, pp. 257–262.
23. NIST. (2018) [ONLINE]. Available at: https://www.nist.gov/ [Accessed 2/10/2018]
24. OASIS [ONLINE]. Available at: https://www.oasis-open.org/orgf [Accessed 2/10/2018]
25. Pontin J. (2005). ETC: Bill Joy's Six Webs. *MIT Technology Review* [Retrieved 17/11/2013]
26. Roberti, M. (2005), The History of RFID Technology - RFID Journal [ONLINE]. Available at: http://www.rfidjournal.com/articles/view?1338. [Accessed 2/10/2018]

27. Texas Instruments [ONLINE]. Available at: http://www.ti.com/lit/ml/swrb028/swrb028.pdf [Accessed 2/10/2018]
28. Traversat, B., Abdelaziz, M., Doolin, D., Duigou, M., Hugly, J-C., Pouyoul, E. (2003), Project JXTA-C: enabling a Web of Things. *HICSS*, 2003: 282.
29. The Societal Impact of the Internet of Things [ONLINE]. Available at: https://www.bcs.org/upload/pdf/societal-impact-report-feb13.pdf [Accessed 2/10/2018]
30. World Economic Forum (2015). Industrial Internet of Things: unleashing the potential of connected products and services, 2015 [ONLINE]. Available at: http://www3.weforum.org/docs/WEFUSA_IndustrialInternet_Report2015.pdf [Accessed 2/10/2018]
31. Weiser, M. (1991), The Computer of the 21st Century, *Scientific American*, 265: 94–104.
32. Yang, Y., Cai, H., Wei, Z., Lu, H., Choo, K.-K. R. (2016), *Towards Lightweight Anonymous Entity Authentication for IoT Applications*, Springer, Cham, pp. 265–280.
33. Yu, T., Sekar, V., Seshan, S., Agarwal, Y., Xu, C. (2015), Handling a trillion (unfixable) flaws on a billion devices: rethinking network security for the internet-of-things, *Proceedings of the 14th ACM workshop on hot topics in networks*, ACM, p. 5.

Concept of Smart Things/Objects

CHAPTER 2

"There's no such thing as simple. Simple is hard."
                                                              -Martin Scorsese

OBJECTIVES
- introduce the fundamental concept of a Thing
- explore the nature of a Thing
- understand the needs of a Thing
- identify various domains where commonly used Things are becoming smart
- understand what is making Things smart
- introduce Machine-to-Machine (M2M) technology
- key differences between M2M and IoT

OUTCOMES
- describe a Thing from an IoT standpoint
- think about a Thing from its needs perspective
- gain ability to visualize how commonly used things turn into Internet of Things
- explain the core components of an M2M architecture
- tell how IoT is quickly gaining ground and set to influence the M2M technology

REVISION

Chapter 1 introduced the emergence of IoT. Several definitions of IoT were given and converged on a working definition. The basic building blocks of IoT are explained. Further, various IoT domains and motivating examples where IoT is making an impact are described in that chapter. This will form the necessary background for this chapter, which is focused on understanding the concept of a Thing in much more depth.

2.1 THING IN THE CONTEXT OF IOT

A Thing in the context of IoT is an entity or physical object that is a unique identifier, an embedded system, having the ability to transfer data over a network. It has some distinct characteristics as shown in Fig. 2.1.

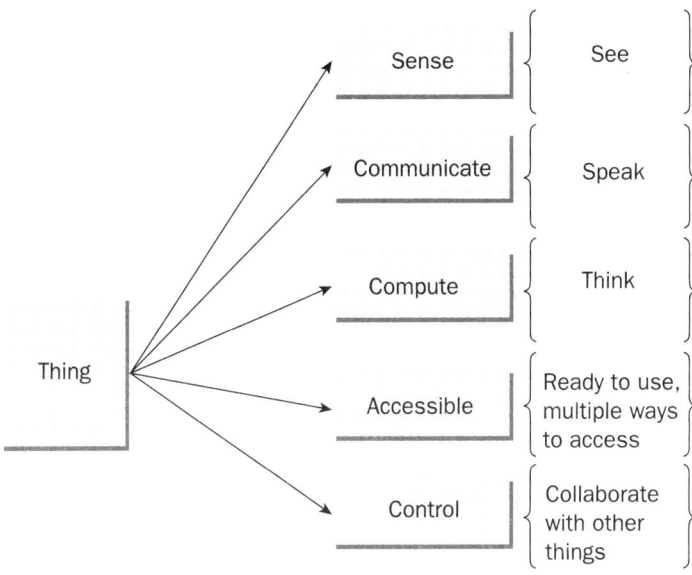

Fig. 2.1 Attributes of a Thing

2.1.1 Capability to Sense the Environment

Things can see, hear, and feel the environment around it through the embedding of sensors, which can make a dumb thing smart.

2.1.2 Ability to Communicate

Things can communicate with humans as well as other Things and collaborate with them so as to solve a bigger problem. It can be a main actor or just one node out of many that will come together dynamically to accomplish a task.

2.1.3 Computation Capabilities

A Thing is capable of thinking and analysing what it sensed; although the extent of this capability depends on the characteristics of the computing hardware that is available on the Thing. Normally, the computations at the Thing level are not too intensive or complex; it basically captures the change of a particular variable and uses in-built and pre-configured processes to output the observation value.

2.1.4 Control Other Things

An IoT Thing can remotely access other Thing(s) to affect a change in its state. It can trigger certain functionality in a remote Thing by commanding it to make some data acquisition by changing the state of an actuator to begin the process.

2.1.5 Accessibility

The Thing's availability via internet enables it to be integrated in a variety of ways. It can have a unique address/code that can be used to identify it uniquely out of millions of Things that are available via Internet. This characteristic of unique identification makes it discoverable and used in many different ways.

2.2 NEEDS OF AN IOT THING

Considering an IoT thing as an entity that can perform many actions and having some ability to think, analyse, and react to external stimuli just like a human, it is pertinent to understand its needs as well. Maslow's hierarchy of needs is a theory that describes the behavioural motivation of a human. The hierarchy as shown in Fig. 2.2 moves from basic needs to psychological needs and then self-fulfilment. The bottom level needs in the pyramid have to be satisfied first before moving up to the next level of needs. This is natural for a human being to first address his or her psychological needs and then move on to the next level. However, recent work by sociologists suggests that these levels are somewhat overlapping and lower levels and strict hierarchy need not be enforced.

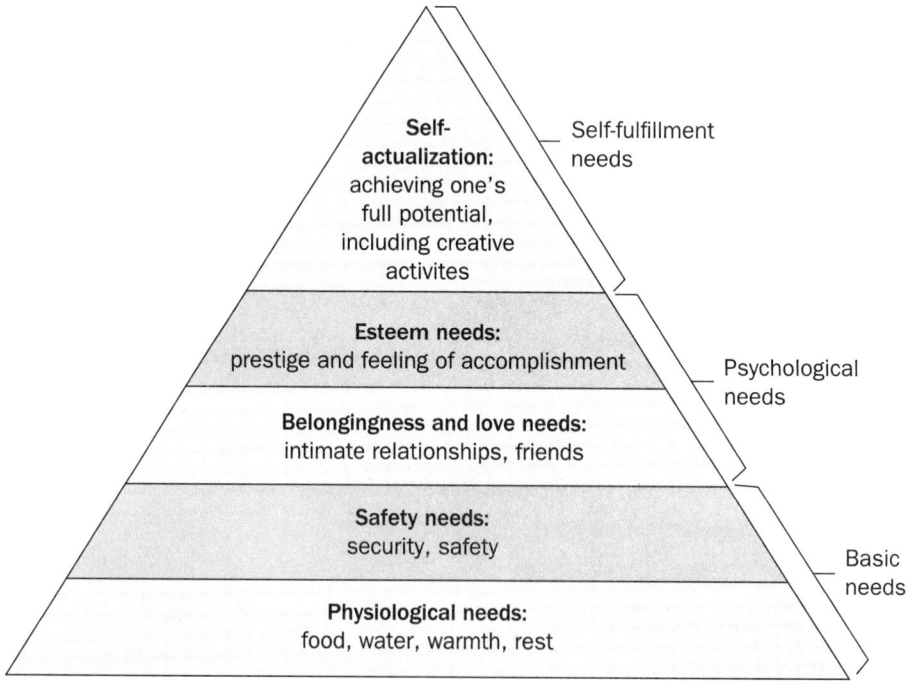

Fig. 2.2 Maslow's 'Theory of Human Motivation' Describes a Hierarchy of Needs

The Maslow's theory has been found useful to be applied in many domains in addition to IoT. A few are listed below:

- Data science
- Choosing a right data center
- Employee needs

- Market analysis
- Retail
- Technology integration

This perspective of an IoT Thing helps to have a more in-depth look at the various ways in which a Thing can express itself and how the technology is aiding in this aspect. Treating a Thing as a living being and a human, Fig. 2.3 shows a hierarchy of needs of a Thing.

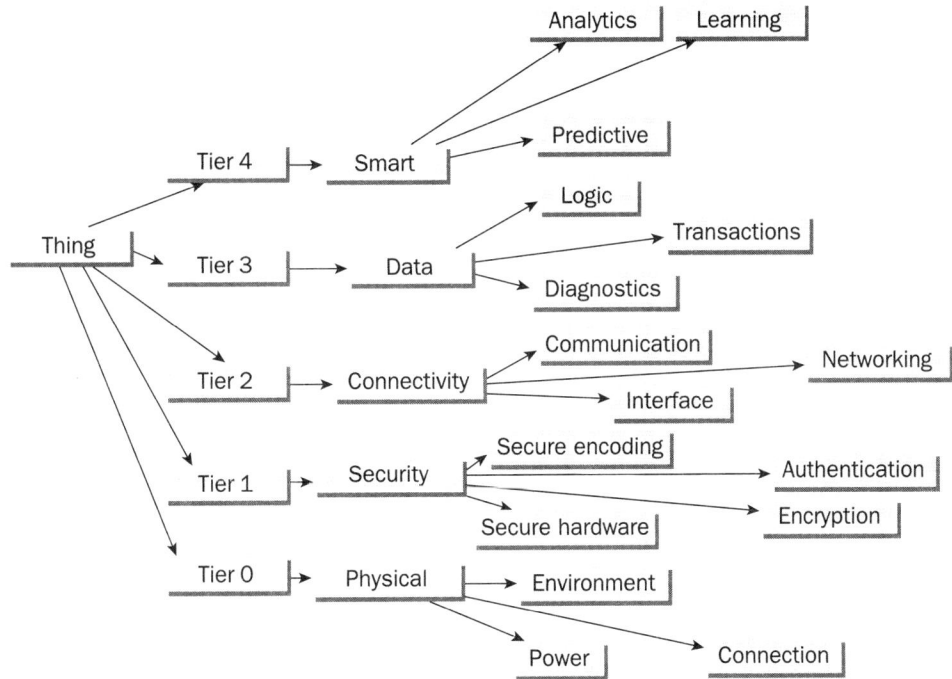

Fig. 2.3 Hierarchy of Needs of a Thing in Various Tiers Based on Maslow's Hierarchy of Needs Theory in Psychology (Needs lower down in the hierarchy must be satisfied before Things can fulfil needs higher up).

2.2.1 Self-existence

These needs are very basic in the sense that they are more physiological in nature and determine the very existence or survival of the Thing. Hence, these are at the bottom, that is, Tier 0 of the hierarchy.

2.2.1.1 Physical Needs

The physical needs are its core of existence, which points to the basic necessity of having power to be "on" and having the ability to sense the environment around it. A connection so that the values of the sensed environment variable are broadcasted/transmitted, so some radio equipment is needed. Furthermore, the Thing needs physical protection from damage/accident for being in the open external environment. Hence, various Things need different kinds of physical enclosures to protect against the elements of both natural and human interaction. This is the Tier 0 at the bottom of the hierarchy. According to Maslow, if the needs at this level are not fulfilled, the Thing will not feel the need for higher level tiers to exist.

2.2.1.2 Security Needs

The Thing needs to feel secure. In addition to having a protective casing or shield (at Tier 1 level), it also needs to be able to distinguish between a genuine user asking for its attributes or sensed readings, and a rogue (hacker or a bot) trying to extract information from it through fraudulent means. Hence, the Thing needs some form of security built into it so that it can allow or disallow access to it. Therefore, protection in the form of encryption, authentication, and authorization are necessary to enable the Thing to feel protected and exist without succumbing to threats.

2.2.2 Self-expression

The psychological needs come next in the hierarchy. Once the basic needs are met, the Thing is now looking for a way to connect with other things and feel the belongingness. The connectivity needs have to be met to satisfy this requirement. It also needs to feel important and useful. Therefore, the data that the Thing gathers should be useful and shareable, so that many other Things feel the need for its data.

2.2.2.1 Connectivity Needs

The ability of a Thing to reach out and express about its form and function, that is, self-expression is fundamental to its existence (shown in Tier 2 of the hierarchy). The addressable nature of the 'Thing', for example, an IP address gives it a unique identity among billions of other Things, similar to humans. This unique identity allows it be recognized and enable it to communicate with other fellow Things as well as other entities. Having multiple ways of connectivity makes the Thing more flexible and can seamlessly merge with other Things having a different set of communication pather ways. Hence, the transport and network protocols come into play to fulfil the connectivity needs of a Thing.

2.2.2.2 Data Needs

In Tier 3, a Thing's data needs come into focus as it determines, what, where, how, and quantity of data the Thing is going to acquire. It is entirely based on the need of that particular Thing, for which it has come into existence. Therefore, the kind of environment that it will collect the data, at what locations this data would be acquired, the modalities of acquisitions, and the frequency of the data collection are all programmed and placed into the brain of the Thing. Further, the Thing needs a way to pre-process and store the data in a way to make it available for higher-level processing.

2.2.3 Self-actualization

This level reflects the ability of the Thing to reach its full potential in all the dimensions for which it was born to accomplish. It is able to display intelligent and learned behaviour.

2.2.3.1 Smart Needs

This forms the top of the Tier, that is, Tier 4, where the Thing finally is able to realize itself, and get the feeling of self-fulfilment, that is, it is able to perform the function(s) it is made for. It is also now a part of a bigger goal or a system to provide a collective solution. The Thing can have several attributes at this stage such as predictivity, self-configuration, and learned behaviour, and has reached its full potential.

2.3 COMMONLY USED SMART THINGS

There are a variety of applications that benefit from IoT including smart cities, smart metering, smart retails, smart logistics, smart industrial control, smart environment, etc. However, in this section, commonly used Things are described to give a flavour of how ordinary things are made smart by IoT technology:

Home   Many things around the home can become smart such as power outlets, lighting and switches, door knobs, door bells, water taps, doors, windows, garage, door locks, and thermostats. Through IoT-based technology, these things can become part of home-automation strategies. Many such products are already available in the market such as the IoT products line from Samsung (https://www.smartthings.com/products).

Kitchen   Bluetooth-enabled cutlery, connected refrigerator, remotely controllable crock-pot, cooker, and cook tops that can automatically adjust to temperature, smart plates that know what you are eating, forks that can monitor eating habits.

Office   Office IoT products include smart products such as badges for security, lighting, window shading, chairs, meeting, scheduling, etc. These can help to increase the office productivity and also reduce wastage of energy, time, etc.

2.3.1 How Can Things Become Smart?

Adding smartness to things implies making them react and do tasks that they are already performing in an easier way (less energy spent to perform that task and also quicker) or adding a new functionality for novel applications (e.g., an eating fork's ability to count the calories of food intake) that the Thing is not originally intended to do. As can be seen from the aforementioned examples (Section 2.3), there are several things that are performing multiple tasks and allowing the user to gain more insights and feedback in his or her daily routine. To enable this smartness, certain technological integration is necessary. Following are some major approaches to make things smart.

2.3.1.1 Sensors and Actuators

Sensors enable things to sense their surroundings and obtain certain information, which can be converted to perform tasks. On the other hand, an actuator is not only a sensor, but is also able to perform a certain action based on the change of state of a certain parameter. In IoT, a Thing can command another Thing to perform a certain action; an actuator comes into picture at this juncture and plays the role of an intermediary to make the Thing perform that action. An actuator is able to move and control a mechanism (e.g., open a valve) after it receives a signal either from the same Thing or an external Thing of a Thing such as a tap. Chapter 5 on sensors and actuators gives more details on these concepts.

2.3.1.2 Communication over Network Interfaces

The ability of a Thing to interconnect with other Things is a central part of IoT and requires communication protocols that are specifically tailored for such type of interaction. Some of the earlier technologies such as HTTP, TCP, and IP stack are being transformed to specifically suit (e.g., IPV6 is preferred over IPV4 for IoT devices) IoT devices communication. Because the IoT devices are deployed in diverse ways (e.g. wearables, connected homes, factories, transportation, etc.), there are several communication protocols such as Wi-Fi and low-power technologies such as LPWAN and IEEE 802.15.4 that are chosen based on specific requirements, for example, if the communication is required only between Things that are in local network or there is a need to communicate remotely. More details on the IoT protocols are described in Chapter 4 on IoT standards and protocols.

2.3.1.3 Connecting to the Internet

Things usually connect to other things via a local network in situations where only local communication is necessary, for example, connected home. However, the main feature of IoT is the ability to remotely control Things and transmit data measured by Things over the Internet, which is possible by connecting to an IP network. One of the recommended ways is to use 6LoWPAN (IPv6 over Low-power Wireless Personal Area Networks), thus enabling global communication. Another, indirect way to make Things visible on the Internet is to use a gateway, which acts as an intermediary between the Things on a local network and the Internet. Multiple Things can connect to a gateway, which is further connected to the Internet.

2.4 MACHINE-TO-MACHINE TECHNOLOGY

Machine-to-Machine (M2M) technology mainly resides in the non-consumer world. It is mostly a business solution for automation and instrumentation, where machines of same type or function are usually connected either by wired and wireless means. It helps in the remote monitoring and management of equipment. However, the remote access is achieved by point-to-point communication through hardware integrated with the machine. These are commonly proprietary solutions tied to a particular solution provider's cellular or wired networks to access and exchange data. Some examples where M2M technology is prevalent are: supply chain, traffic control systems, logistic services, telemedicine, etc.

2.4.1 European Telecommunication Standards Institute (ETSI) – M2M

European Telecommunications Standards Institute (ETSI) developed a set of M2M specifications based on Representational State Transfer (RESTful) (a distributed Service Oriented Architecture [SOA] that uses web protocols) architecture to (Swetina et al., 2014) the way heterogeneous devices can offer services and access to them seamlessly. The core components of an M2M are shown in Fig. 2.4. These components form the major building block of any M2M system. Following is a brief description of each of these components.

2.4.1.1 M2M Device

The M2M devices consist of sensors and communication equipment that are at the lowest end of the M2M system; they are usually connected to an operator's own network or can connect based on existing standards such as Zigbee, bluetooth, Device Language Message Specification (DLMS),

European Committee for Standardization (CEN), Meter-Bus (M-Bus), etc. In this case, the gateways play a major role in ensuring that the data is further moved for processing. For example, sensors placed at selected locations around a water body that can detect contaminants for water-quality monitoring, the data can be sent to a gateway for real-time analysis, aggregation, and further processing. In this case, the gateways are responsible for the proper addressing and routing of the devices. It is outside the scope of the network operator for management purposes. On the other hand, the devices that are connected to a fixed network (embedded SIM, radio stack or fixed line access, etc.), form the end points of the network and hence are managed by the network operator itself.

2.4.1.2 M2M Area Network Layer

This is the connection between the M2M device and the gateways, which is possible via various area networks, such as WBAN and WPAN using technologies such as IEEE 802.15.6 Zigbee/IEEE 802.15.4, Bluetooth, Bluetooth Low Energy (BLE), wireless USB, and proprietary solutions such as ANT, Sensium, Z-wave, and Zarlin.

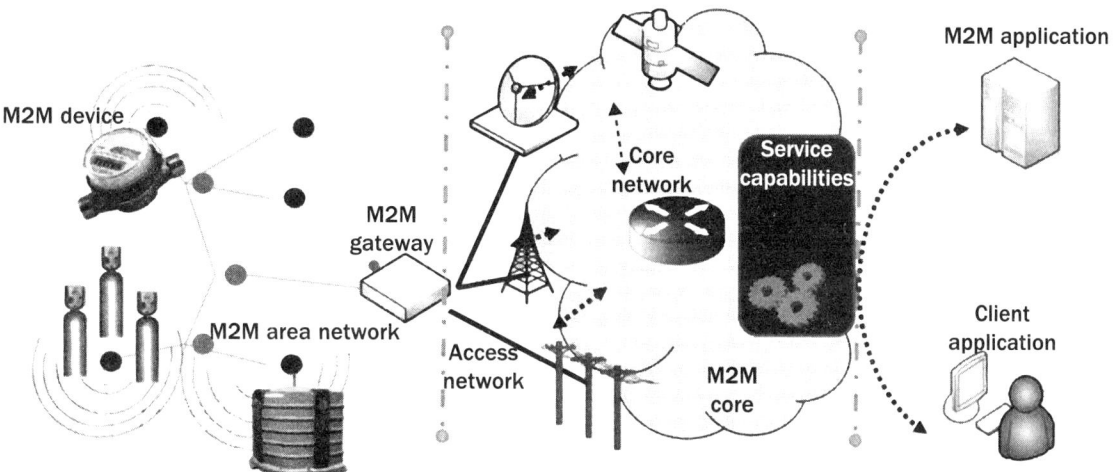

Fig. 2.4 Core Components of ETSI M2M Architecture

2.4.1.3 M2M Gateway

Gateways along with routers are equipment that ensure the connection of the M2M devices to communicate with M2M applications via a communication network. As shown in Fig. 2.5, the M2M gateway acts as a conduit between the communication and data transmission functions of an M2M system. If the M2M devices are not connecting directly to the network, then the gateways act as end point to the operators network. This means that the accessibility of an M2M device from an M2M application or an operator-specific interface is mainly dependent on the gateway, which needs to ensure the proper access with suitable authentication and other security features.

2.4.1.4 M2M Communication Network

During the formative years of M2M technology, the communication aspects of the M2M applications (e.g., monitoring and control of machines, alarms, etc.) relied on specialized communication networks.

40 Internet of Things

However, this has changed over a period of time with M2M technology being widely applied to a wide variety of communication networks. It is mainly the communications between the M2M gateway(s) and M2M application(s). Technologies such as GSM, UMTS, xDSL, LTE, LTE-A, WiMAX, WLAN satellite, etc. are being used for this purpose.

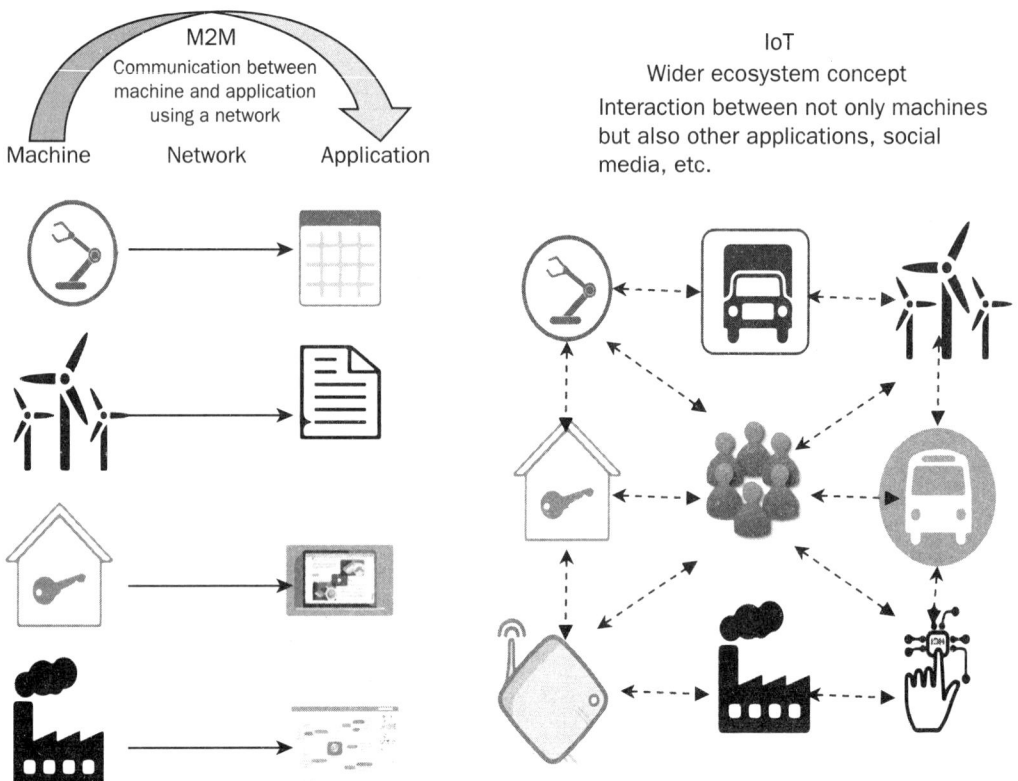

Fig. 2.5 Distinction between M2M and IoT

2.4.2 M2M Service Layer

This layer is one of the core M2M layers which provides M2M standardized device and data related functionalities such as data transport and device management. Irrespective of the communication technologies used, the M2M service layer enables to seamlessly connect various M2M devices and applications across various application domains, thus ensuring interoperability. oneM2M is a global initiative to standardize a common M2M service layer platform.

2.4.3 M2M Applications

The application layer is at the top of the M2M system. Usually, a middleware layer sits between the communication layer and the applications. It is a software that enables making the connection between diverse components and applications, which otherwise are unable to talk with each other by providing services to ensure effective communication. More details on IoT middleware is provided in Chapter 7: IoT middleware. Some typical M2M applications are as follows:

- Health monitoring
- Remote access, control, and monitoring of equipment such as pumps and remote diagnostics of vehicles
- Smart grid applications, smart meters, and industrial meters
- Tracking and monitoring of assets
- Monitoring production chain in a manufacturing unit

2.4.4 Key Differences Between M2M and IoT

M2M and IoT are technologies that offer similar functionality in terms of communication, monitoring, data acquisition, and exchange, to enable automation. Hence, it is quite possible to assume that they are synonymous with each other. However, there are some key differences between them in terms of connectivity, scalability, and data usage and sharing. M2M is now thought as a subset of IoT as it offers more advanced device connectivity, and services and incorporates many new communication, network, data protocols and standards, and in various application domains (Fig. 2.5).

Table 2.1 provides a comparison of M2M and IoT, based on connection type, communication protocols, interoperability, targeted business type, and scalability. It can be seen that IoT is forging ahead with many focused developments happening in many areas and it is envisaged that current M2M systems will slowly transform into IoT systems in the near future.

Table 2.1 Comparison of M2M and IoT

Machine-to-Machine (M2M)	Internet of Things (IoT)
M2M uses point-to-point connections between machines/devices of similar types using wireless or wired connections	IoT is based on IP network connections
M2M is all about machines	IoT is about Things
Older protocols and communication techniques	Varying new protocols specifically developed for IoT protocols such as 6LoWPAN for lower-powered IoT devices
Mainly hardware-based, i.e., the M2M technology is integrated into the hardware	IoT is both hardware and software based. Emphasis is on integration of a variety of Things
M2M has less built-in intelligence	More intelligent form of machine communications, cloud, context, collaboration, and insights
Ability for Integration and interoperability are limited due to lack of well-recognized standards and more proprietary systems are in vogue. Data is usually not shared	High levels of integration is possible. Plethora of standards has emerged for low-powered IoT devices. Data sharing from multiple assets is highly recommended for developing cross-domain applications
Business-to-Business (B2B)	Business-to-Business (B2B), Business-to-Consumer (B2C)
In majority of M2M systems, Internet connection is not required	Internet connection is required for majority of IoT systems
Limited scalability	Potential for high scalability due to Internet enablement and cloud services

SUMMARY

The IoT revolution has ushered in new ways of interacting with everyday things by adding smartness using various sensors/actuators, communication, network, and cloud technologies. The life of a Thing is now analogous to a human and has its needs to be fulfilled to realize its full potential. This perspective of Things is put in terms of Maslow's theory on human motivation to understand the various needs such as psychological, safety, belongingness, esteem, and self-actualization. Further, M2M is introduced in terms of its core components and areas in which M2M systems are prevalent. The key differences between IoT and M2M are discussed to show the various strengths of each of these systems. It can be concluded that IoT has potential for developing systems that have far-reaching impact and applicable in a variety of domains.

REVIEW QUESTIONS

1. Explain the distinct characteristics of a Thing.
2. Describe Maslow's theory of human motivation.
3. Describe the connection between Maslow's theory and a Thing.
4. What additional needs do you think a Thing requires over and above those that were described using Maslow's Theory?
5. It now believed that there is a somewhat overlap of layers in the Maslow's Pyramid of human motivation. Where you think these overlap can happen from a Thing perspective?
6. What makes commonly used things to become smart? Explain with real-world examples.
7. What is M2M?
8. Explain the core components of M2M.
9. How is M2M different from IoT?

REFERENCES

1. Maslow, A. H. (1943), A theory of human motivation. *Psychological Review* 50(4): 370–96.
2. Needs of a Thing. Available at: https://techcrunch.com/2015/09/05/the-hierarchy-of-iot-thing-needs/ [Accessed: 10/22/2019]
3. Swetina, J., Lu G., Jacobs P., Ennesser F. and Song J., (2014, June), Toward a standardized common M2M service layer platform: Introduction to oneM2M, *IEEE Wireless Communications,* 21(3):20-26, DOI: 10.1109/MWC.2014.6845045.

Wireless Sensor Networks in IoT

CHAPTER 3

"When wireless is perfectly applied, the whole earth will be converted into a huge brain, which in fact it is, where all things being particles of a real and rhythmic whole."

— *Nikola Tesla*

OBJECTIVES
- learn about wireless sensor network (WSN)
- understand challenges of WSN technology
- list various characteristics of WSN
- gain knowledge of different types of WSN and their architecture
- Study WSN communication patterns and data integration approaches
- gain insight into various applications of WSN and best practices

OUTCOMES
- understand the challenges while designing WSN
- describe the desired characteristics of WSN
- gain the ability to select a particular type of WSN for an application
- select communication protocol based on domain requirements.
- comprehensive understanding of WSN application areas

REVISION

In Chapters 1 and 2, an introduction and an overview and comprehension of important technologies, required for Internet of Things are covered.

Wireless sensor network as one of the most important technologies in IoT and a core base of IoT is explored in this chapter.

3.1 INTRODUCTION

Recent advances in efficient and affordable integrated electronic devices have a great impact on the state of Wireless Sensor Networks (WSN). WSNs are enabling applications in a variety of domains and paving the way to new market opportunities. However, there are significant challenges in their design, deployment, and maintenance, which cannot be ignored. The development of WSNs requires knowledge of software, hardware, as well as embedded engineering.

3.1.1 Wireless Sensor Network (WSN)

A WSN consists of a group of sensors that are deployed in an area with the purpose of collecting information about the surrounding environment. The WSN can be a small network consisting of a few nodes or hundreds of nodes forming a large scale network that can monitor vast areas (and in terrains that are hostile in nature) without much human intervention. A node in a WSN is a self contained unit consisting of sensor(s), trans-receiver, power source, and microcontroller. All these are encased in a compact form, which can be easily placed in the field for acquiring the data.

In a WSN, the data obtained by the node is transmitted to a base station by routing it through the other connected sensors in a multi-hop fashion. It also depends on the topology of the WSN, which is elaborated in section 3.4. A bidirectional WSN is useful to remotely interact and control the nodes and is particularly helpful for custom data acquisition (e.g., increase the frequency of data collection from 1 hour to 15 minutes).

The cost and size of a sensor node depends on the application for which it is designed, and also factors such as on-board memory requirement to store the data, computing efficiency, power requirements based on the frequency of data collection and transmission, etc.

Various sensors (e.g., seismic, magnetic, thermal, infrared, acoustic, visual, and radar) used in a WSN can have resource constraints such as computation capabilities, energy consumption, memory, communication speed, etc. The major WSN functionalities include sensing, computing and data transfer.

The ability to self-organise is an important characteristic of WSN, which enables the nodes to configure the self's based on the requirements of a particular application such as surveillance, disaster monitoring, health monitoring, etc., where human intervention may not be possible either due to accessibility or safety reasons. Figure 3.1 shows the important modules of WSN namely data acquisition, data processing, and data distribution.

The wireless nature of WSN results in some unique challenges such as power limitations, communication network constraints, loss of connectivity of nodes, limited memory, no GUI/display, etc.

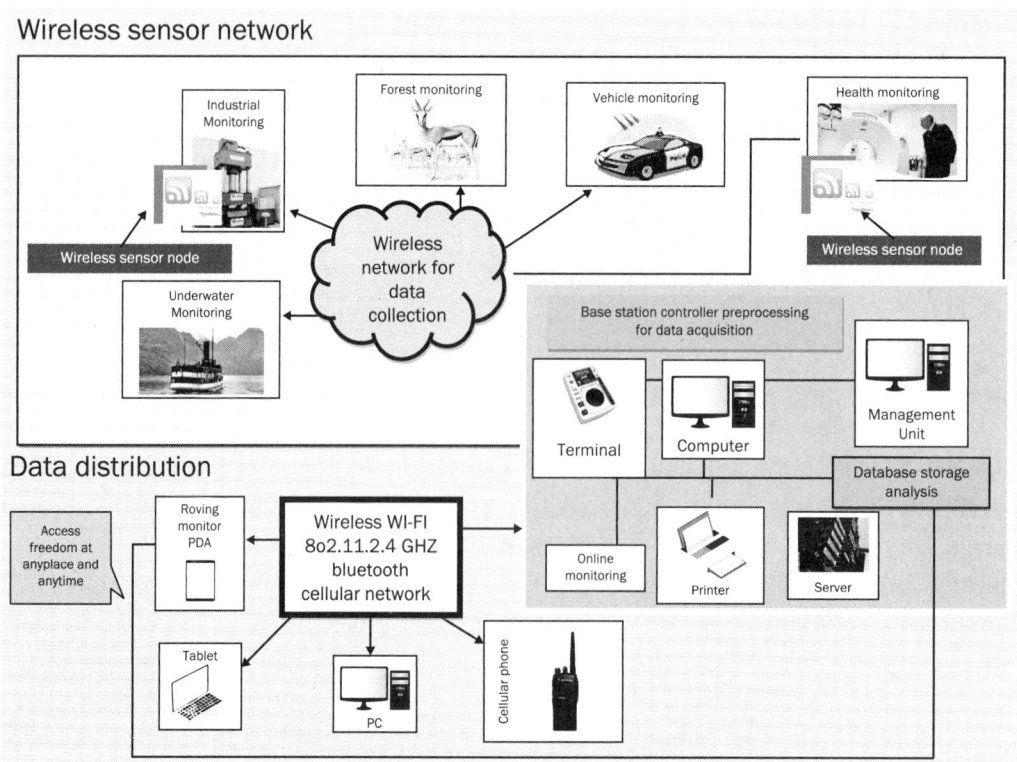

Fig. 3.1 Wireless Sensor Network

3.1.1.1 Categories of WSN Services

Wireless sensor networks are categorized into four major categories based on the services offered:

Monitoring WSNs can be deployed to acquire information about surrounding environment for monitoring purposes. For example, a WSN deployed for precision agriculture can monitor the meteorological conditions such as temperature, humidity, wind speed, etc. and send this information on an hourly basis. Similarly, a WSN for water quality information on a water body can make measurements of various parameters such as turbidity, dissolved oxygen, etc., and send this information twice a day. Such monitoring examples are ample in various domains and WSNs have proven to provide accurate, consistent and timely information which can be used for decision making purposes.

Alerting A WSN can be deployed in remote or in accessible terrains or disaster prone areas. The WSN nodes can be subscribed to send alerts when the measured parameter crosses certain threshold, for example water level above 10 meters for water level sensor nodes in flood a monitoring WSN. Similarly, alerts can be issued from a Tsunami monitoring WSN consisting of sensor nodes on Buoys deployed on the oceans. A WSN deployed for monitoring landslides can send advance alerts to avoid accidents and loss of life and property.

Information on Demand The network can be queried about the actual values of certain features of interest and it responds by providing information accordingly. For example, soil moisture values can be queried at a particular location, or soil moisture values in the last two days. Further, subsetting of WSN archived data based on current time instant, arithmetic, boolean, logical operators can also be performed.

Actuating Based on the context of the environment in which the WSN is monitoring, the sensor nodes can send a signal and change the behaviour of an external system. Some examples of actuations are (i) sensing weather conditions by a WSN node may trigger a sensor node to capture GPS location of the mobile entity on which it is deployed, (ii) activating a sensor such as a camera to acquire data for specific monitoring purposes.

3.2 CHARACTERISTICS OF WIRELESS SENSOR NETWORK

WSN is deployed to gather information from unattended physical environment. Hence, for efficient design and deployment of WSN, it is necessary to take into consideration some unique characteristics of WSN.

3.2.1 Significant Characteristics of WSN

Energy efficient In WSN, energy is used for various tasks such as sensing, communication, computation, and storage. If the sensor nodes run out of power they cannot be recharged at a remote location, and consequently, can fail to sense the surrounding physical environment. Hence, to reduce the power consumption of a sensor node, efficient protocols and algorithms are used while designing a WSN.

While designing energy efficient WSN, the following should be kept in mind:

- All remotely deployed sensors are generally battery operated.
- Lifetime of the sensor node depends on the battery lifetime. Sometimes a nearby power source may be available for charging the battery.

- Lifetime of the sensor is an important factor while designing a WSN for its optimal use and high efficiency.
- The power is utilized mainly for sensing, computation, and communication.

Low cost Generally, for measuring the physical environment, a large number of sensor nodes are employed in a WSN. It is desirable to have the cost of the individual sensor nodes as low as possible and consequently reduce the overall cost of the network. Further, deployment cost also needs to be taken into account while using a large WSN.

Computational power Typically, the sensor node has limited computational capabilities and is usually decided by cost, size, and energy of the node.

Communication capabilities Generally, radio waves are used for communication in WSN. The communication channel can be unidirectional or bidirectional. Sometimes, WSN is used in a remote and inaccessible terrain environment; hence, it must be robust and resilient enough to quickly recover in case of failure of some of the nodes of WSN.

Cross-layer design This type of design is recent emerging in wireless communication as it improves WSN performance in terms of energy efficiency, datarate, Quality of Service (QoS), etc. The traditional layered approach faces problems such as:

- In traditional layered approach, network optimality cannot be ensured as there is no data communication to share information among different layers leading to incomplete information at each layer.
- Dynamically changing environment cannot be adapted by traditional layered approach of WSN.
- Other limitations include interference between different users, access conflict, fading, etc.

Distributed sensing and processing To enable robustness and resilience, the sensor nodes in a WSN are distributed randomly and uniformly. A sensor node sends the data to a sink node which is capable of collecting, processing, sorting, aggregating, and sending the data.

Security and privacy Sufficient security must be provided to each sensor node to protect from unauthorized access, unintentional damage, and malicious attacks to damage the information inside the node.

Dynamic network topology A sensor node can fail due to battery exhaustion or physical or sensor data tampering. To overcome such issues, WSN nodes must have the capabilities to dynamically reconfigure and adjust itself under various conditions such as addition of new nodes or replacement of existing ones.

Multi-hop communication In case a node requires to communicate with another node or a base station beyond its radio frequency range, then to reach to the sink node, a multi-hop route is needed.

Self-organization Sensor nodes should have the capability to self-organize themselves in a collaborative fashion to fit in a distributed topology to form a self-adjusted network for optimal performance. For example, if some sensor nodes fail, replacement with new nodes becomes necessary and has to be carried out autonomously. These new sensor nodes need to have self-configuring capability to adjust with the current network topology of other sensor nodes, and able to support the communication regardless of energy constraints.

Robust operation WSN nodes are left unattended most of the time and are prone to physical damage, battery drainage, communication failures, and impact of harsh environment. Therefore, it is necessary to have sensor nodes with capabilities of fault and error which is a measure of its reliability. The sensor nodes must have the capability of self-testing, self-configuring, and self-repairing for robust use.

Small physical size A wireless sensor node has four main units: sensing, processing, communication, and energy/power. All these factors have to be considered while designing a sensor mode and it in turn determines the size of the node. Future sensor nodes are envisaged to be as small as the grain of sand.

Application oriented WSN is highly dependent on the specific application (e.g., military, health, environmental, etc.) for which it is designed.

3.3 TYPES OF WSN AND THEIR ARCHITECTURE

Depending on the application environment, the type of WSNs are chosen. Broadly, the various types of WSNs are:

- Multimedia WSNs
- Mobile WSNs
- Terrestrial WSNs
- Underwater WSNs
- Underground WSNs

3.3.1 Multimedia Wireless Sensor Networks

Multimedia WSN is used in situations where tracking and monitoring of the events is performed using multimedia (images, audio, and video). These WSNs consist of low cost sensor nodes with devices such as camera and microphone. The sensor nodes are connected to form a network using wireless connections to collaborate with each other for performing data pre-processing operations such as data retrieval, correction, and compression. However, these are challenging to perform as they require high bandwidth and energy (see Fig. 3.2).

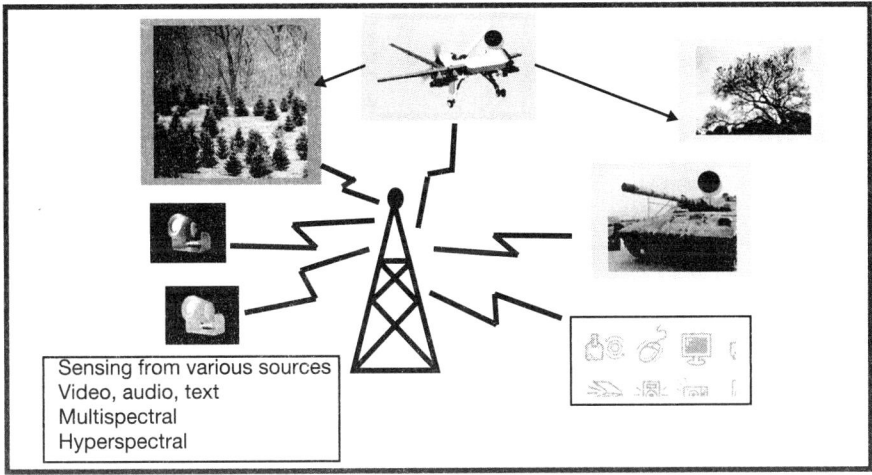

Fig. 3.2 Multimedia Wireless Sensor Network

3.3.2 Mobile Wireless Sensor Networks

A collection of sensor nodes that can move on their own and interact with the surrounding physical environment forms a mobile WSN. The mobile sensor nodes have computing and communication capabilities (see Fig. 3.3).

As the sensor nodes can move, mobile WSNs have wide versatile applications than static sensor networks as these WSNs have improved coverage of the surrounding environment, better energy efficiency, and channel capacity.

3.3.3 Terrestrial Wireless Sensor Networks

Terrestrial WSN is capable of communicating efficiently with the base station. It can have a very large number of sensor nodes, which are randomly distributed for covering the required terrain for effective mapping. These nodes are deployed in a structured or unstructured way in a target area to optimally acquire data for a specific application. The deployment of a structured WSN requires considering various optional models such as 2D, 3D, or grid placement to gain maximum efficiency (see Fig. 3.4).

Further, in this type of WSN, the sensor nodes have limited power and solar panels are usually used as additional sources of power. The energy is managed by approaches such as optimal routing, minimizing delays, low duty cycle operations, repeaters etc.

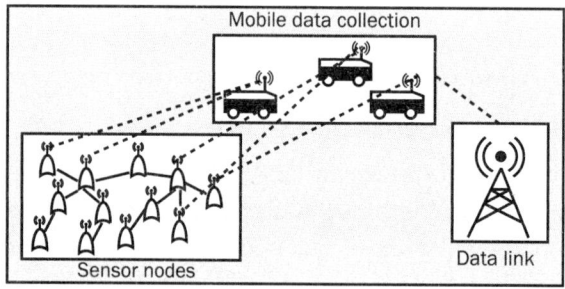

Fig. 3.3 Mobile Wireless Sensor Network

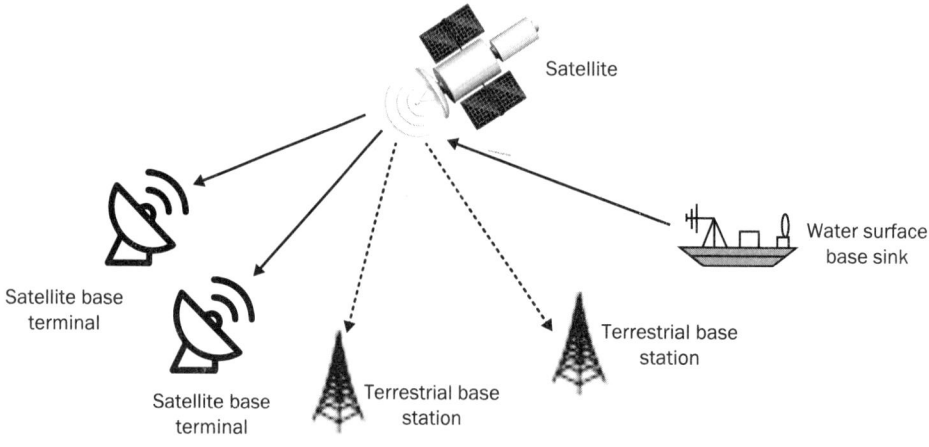

Fig. 3.4 Terrestrial Wireless Sensor Network

3.3.4 Underwater Wireless Sensor Network

Although more than 70% of the earth is covered by water, its monitoring is not as advanced as that of the terrestrial land mass. This is due to the huge challenges involved in deploying sensors underwater. A WSN where the sensor nodes are deployed under water is called an underwater WSN (see Fig. 3.5). Specific challenges of underwater WSN are long propagation delay, bandwidth limitations, and sensor node failure. For designing and developing underwater WSN, the major issue is energy conservation. The data is gathered from these sensor nodes by using autonomous underwater vehicles. For example, in the ocean observing systems, both drifting as well as moored buoys are used to measure various marine, biological, and water parameters.

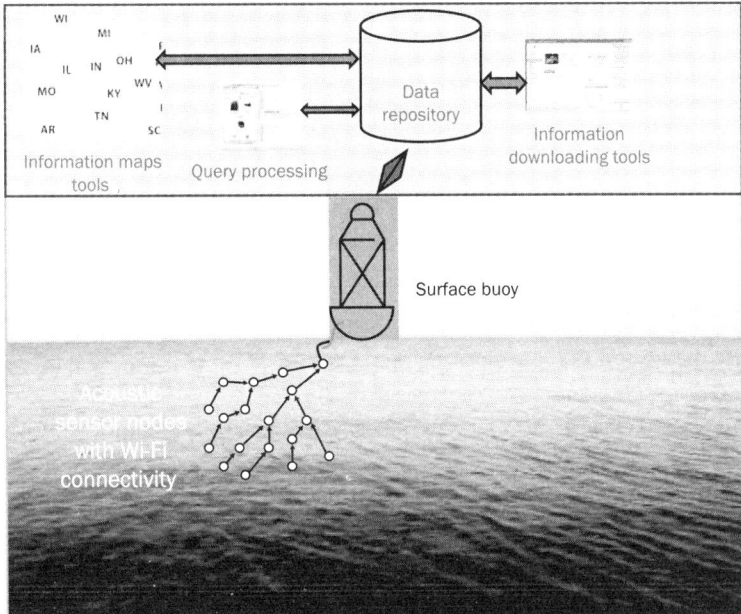

Fig. 3.5 Underwater Wireless Sensor Network

3.3.5 Underground Wireless Sensor Network

Underground wireless sensor network (UWSN) is specifically designed for subsurface region. Potential applications include monitoring precision agriculture, landslides, earthquakes, environmental, infrastructure, etc. The cost of underground WSN is high due to the need for special infrastructure for developing underground WSN such as equipment cost, careful planning, and maintenance (see Fig. 3.6).

For data transfer from underground sensor nodes to the base station, deployment of additional sink nodes is required over ground and it also secures resilience of the WSN. Since the sensor nodes are underground, it is difficult to recharge them, also the communication signal from the sensor nodes gets attenuated.

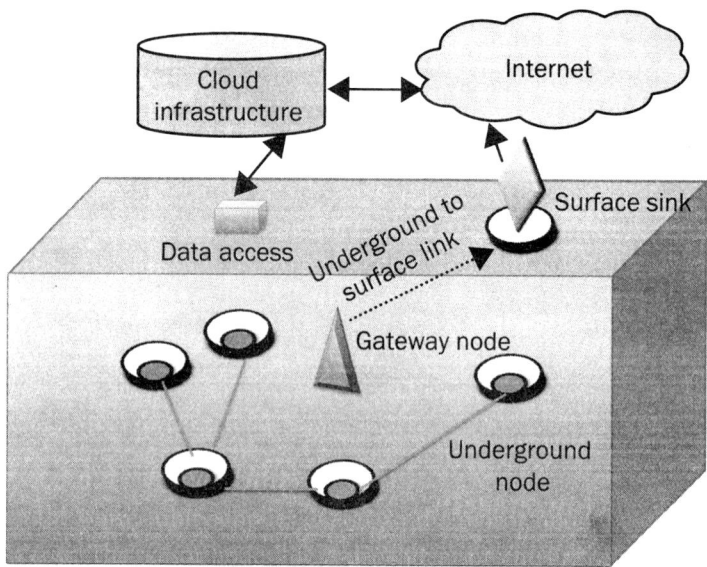

Fig. 3.6 Underground Wireless Sensor Network

3.3.6 Architectural Design of WSN

WSN architecture is different than conventional communication architecture because of the resource limitations that are imposed on it, yet it has to deliver maximum efficiency with less overhead. Hence, WSN does not strictly follow the layered architecture of Open Systems Interconnection model. However, for categorizing protocols and adding security features for reliable communication, the layered model is very useful. Figure 3.7 below shows the communication protocol model for WSN.

The structure of a sensor node has a sensing unit (with/without analogue-to-digital converter), processing unit (processor and storage), communication unit, and a power supply unit. The attributes such as low cost, fault tolerance and low energy consumption should be considered while designing a sensor node. The block diagram for sensor node structure is shown in Fig. 3.8.

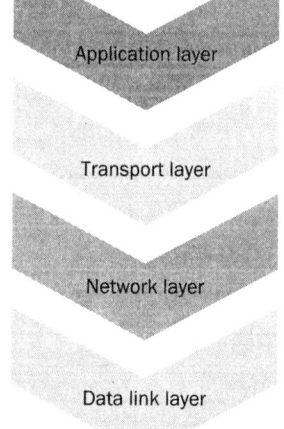

Fig. 3.7 Communication Protocol Stack for WSN

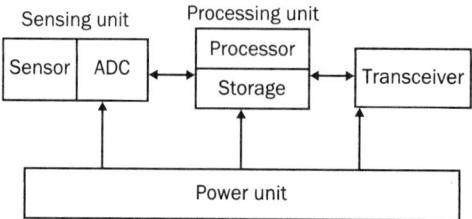

Fig. 3.8 Structure of a Sensor Node

3.3.6.1 Sensor Device Unit
The sensor unit consists of an analogue or/and a digital sensor and optionally an analogue-to-digital converter unit (ADC). A suitable sensor is selected as per the need of the application by thoroughly studying the constraints of the working environment.

3.3.6.2 Communication Unit
A transceiver unit is made up of a transmitter and a receiver. Communication of information is performed using network protocols. A suitable communication method is selected (such as radio, infrared, optical, etc.) based on the requirements of the application.

3.3.6.3 Processing Unit (A Microcontroller Unit and Storage)
It also has an operating system and a timer. The microcontroller unit collects data from many sources and then processes and stores the data.

3.3.6.4 Power Unit
The power unit supplies energy to the sensor node for monitoring the physical environment at a low cost. The sensor nodes life is dependent on the life of the battery.

Some important goals to be considered while designing WSN architecture are:

- requirements analysis of the specific application/domain for which the WSN is to be designed
- quantitative analysis of the needs of the application
- understanding and selecting latest and relevant technologies that can suit the intended application, and achieving optimal configuration by selection of hardware and software recommended best practices.
- developing a best fit solution that takes into consideration various parameters and alternatives (design costs and other WSN constraints) in a complex and heterogeneous WSN deployment scenario.
- employing power optimisation strategies that are tailored to the needs of a particular application

3.4 NETWORK TOPOLOGIES IN WIRELESS SENSOR NETWORK
Wireless sensor networks are classified into four basic network topologies categories based on communication pattern: one-way, bi-directional, star, and mesh.

3.4.1 Different Types of Topologies in WSN
Traditional topologies in network have been adapted with modification wherever required for development and deployment of WSNs. Different topologies in WSN are: Bus, Tree, Ring, Star, Mesh, Circular, and Grid.

3.4.1.1 Bus Topology
In bus topology, a sensor node sends a broadcast message to the nodes on the network and only the intended recipient accepts the message. Bus topology is easy to design and install but not good to take care of traffic and congestion. When limited nodes are used in the WSN, bus topology works best (see Fig. 3.9).

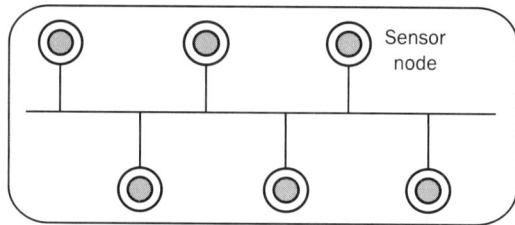

Fig. 3.9 Bus Topology

3.4.1.2 Tree Topology

In this network topology, there is a central hub as a root node and it acts as the main router. The tree network is a combination of star and peer-to-peer network topologies. In distributed implementation, tree topology is more suitable. However, load-balancing problem is faced in fat trees while communicating between sensor nodes (see Fig. 3.10).

The intermediate nodes need to work more (depending on the number of sub nodes) to forward the information and may gradually loose power and have to be replaced. The leaf nodes do not participate in routing. The root node acts as a sink/ base station.

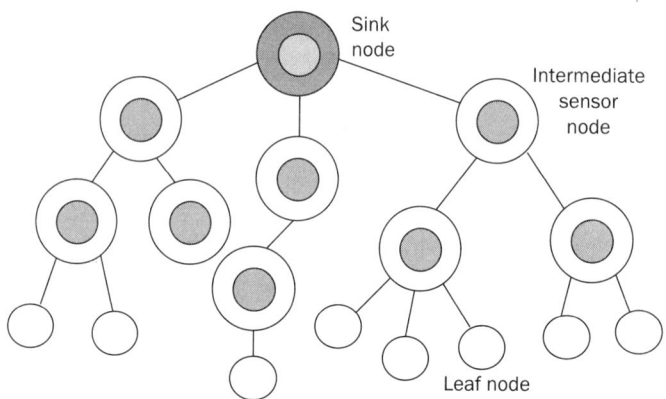

Fig. 3.10 Tree Topology

3.4.1.3 Star Topology

The star network is connected to a centralized hub also called as sink. In this network, the nodes cannot communicate with each other directly as the entire communication is routed through the central communication hub. In this topology, each sensor node acts as a client and the sink node acts as a server (see Fig. 3.11).

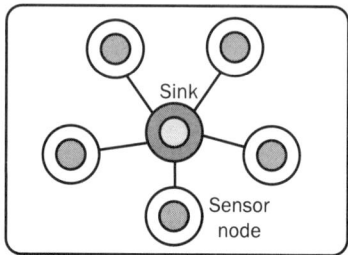

Fig. 3.11 Star Topology

3.1.4.4 Ring Topology

In a ring network, every node has exactly two neighbours for communication (see Fig. 3.12). All messages travel through the ring in a single direction (clockwise or anti-clockwise). A failure in a node breaks the loop. Congestion of traffic is taken care by a variant of ring network as a double path communication (clockwise as well as anti-clockwise).

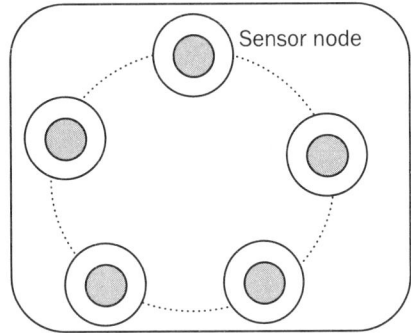

Fig. 3.12 Ring Topology

3.1.4.5 Mesh Topology

In a Mesh network, the message can take multiple paths from source to destination. A mesh in which every node is connected to every other node is known as a full mesh. Mesh network is useful for load balancing, reliable data transmission, and minimizing energy consumption (see Fig. 3.13).

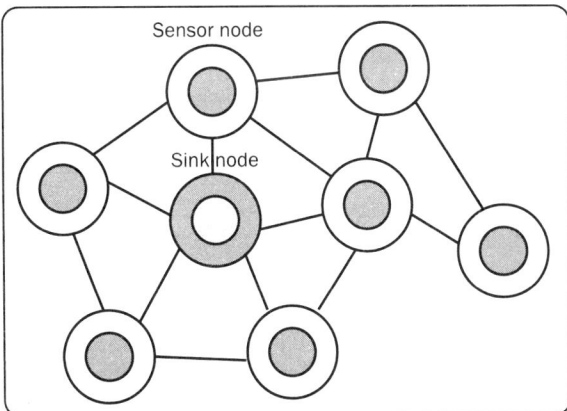

Fig. 3.13 Mesh Topology

3.1.4.6 Circular Topology

In a circular network, there is circular sensing area and every such sensing area has a sink node. The event information is captured by sensor node and sent to the sink node. Distribution of the nodes is random and uniform. This topology is easy to install and maintain. It is an energy-efficient topology. Short beacon messages are sent to the nodes to check the location of the node (see Fig. 3.14).

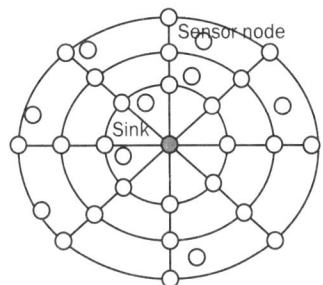

Fig. 3.14 Circular Topology

3.1.4.7 Grid Topology

In the grid network, the sensor network field is divided into non-overlapping square grids of same size. In each grid, at least one node should be in active state. To increase life span of the network and to make it energy efficient the nodes of the grid become active in turns. In grid topology, a node called as head node is responsible for routing the information and transmitting the data packets. Grid-based multi-path routing algorithm is efficient to avoid congestion due to traffic and also good for fast packet transfer (see Fig. 3.15) (Sharma et al., 2013).

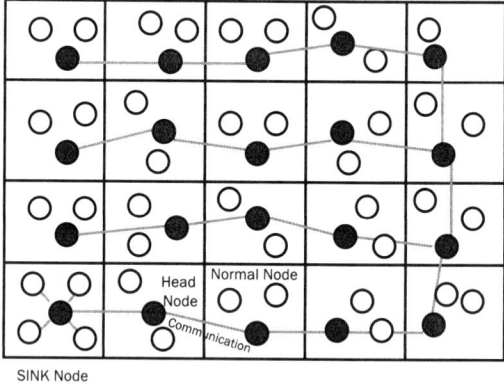

Fig. 3.15 Grid Topology

3.5 WSN COMMUNICATION PROTOCOLS

The primary goal of communication is to optimize the network to work in an energy efficient way so that WSN lifetime is increased. The physical layer of WSN is about the communication hardware. The physical layer is responsible for signal detection, carrier frequency generation, modulation, frequency selection, and data encryption. Medium Access Control (MAC) protocols are applied in data link layer. Routing of data coming from transport layer is managed by network layer. The transport layer is responsible for the data flow to the WSN application. Various kinds of applications and functionalities are supported by application layer depending upon the type of sensing required.

3.5.1 Single Channel MAC Protocol

Single channel MAC protocol is divided into two categories:

- Synchronous Single Channel MAC Protocol
- Asynchronous Single Channel MAC Protocol

The *synchronized single channel* approach is based on synchronization between nodes. Several synchronized MAC protocols are proposed such as S-MAC, T-MAC, RMAC, and DW-MAC (demand wake up MAC). In these protocols, wireless sensor nodes are synchronized to schedule the active and sleeping period of nodes to make the WSN, energy efficient. The exchange of data happens only in the active time of the sensor node. This approach saves energy by reducing idle listening time of each node. The overhead of implementing synchronous protocol is substantial.

In *asynchronous* approach, each sensor node wakes up independently as per its duty cycle. A sender transmits a preamble for a period of sleeping of the receiver node before transmitting data. If receiver senses the preamble, it remains active and becomes ready to receive the data. In receiver initiated asynchronous MAC protocol, a receiver starts a transmission by sending a control message. Thus, energy efficiency is achieved in asynchronous MAC protocol without synchronization.

3.5.2 Asynchronous Single Channel MAC Protocol

Each sensor node in a network periodically checks the availability of the wireless medium according to its own schedule. If the medium is busy, it waits further until it becomes idle or a data packet arrives from the sender. The sender assumes that in such a case the receiver is not ready to receive the data even after receiving long preamble, due to network errors. This problem consumes energy. WiseMAC protocol utilizes the preamble sampling method to overcome this problem. In this method, dynamic length preambles are utilized to reduce idle listening time. In dynamic length preamble, the sensor nodes keep a track of sleep-live schedule of their neighbours. The drawback of WiseMAC is buffering time of the packet increases in a sender buffer. While broadcasting, the sender sends the packets to all its neighbours and that causes waste of energy.

3.5.3 Pseudorandom Asynchronous MAC Protocol

This protocol uses a hash function to decide the next wake up time. The next wake up time decided by the hash function is non-periodic and this way the pseudorandom asynchronous MAC protocol saves energy wasted in idle listening and even collision is reduced.

3.5.4 Medium Reservation MAC (MRMAC)

In this protocol, additional information about next packet arrival time (NPAT) and medium reservation information (MRI) is there in the beacon message to reduce the end-to-end latency in delivery of message. Due to this additional information in the beacon message, every node in WSN knows when the wireless medium is idle, so each node decides its own flexible schedule of transmission and reception, hence idle listening and collision is reduced. MRMAC shows better performance than RI-MAC if the network has periodic traffic pattern.

3.5.5 Multi-channel MAC Protocols

As single channel–based communication uses only one channel, capacity and throughput of the network is less. The multi-channel radio uses several orthogonal channels and divides the bandwidth into multiple channels. Adjacent nodes use different channels to send the packets. Thus, multi-channel MAC protocol improves network throughput and reduces collision. The multi-channel MAC protocol is efficiently designed for WSN by considering following points.

Multi-channel networks are orthogonal and do not interfere with each other. The nodes cannot communicate with each other when they belong to different channels, the nodes should be assigned same channel for communication. There are three methods for channel assignment: fixed, semi-dynamic, and dynamic. In the *fixed* assignment, approach is based on cluster approach. The sensor nodes are divided into several clusters. The cluster communicates through the assigned channel. This approach prevents interference between clusters. In *semi-dynamic* assignment approach, each node is assigned to a certain channel for transmission and reception. While in *dynamic* channel assignment approach, each node is assigned different channel after every wake up schedule of the node. The main advantage of multi-channel protocol is that there is less interference and collision while transmitting and receiving the data. However, in semi-dynamic and dynamic approach, due to switching between channels, there is energy overhead.

3.5.5.1 Flooding

It is a robust algorithm that delivers data packet delivery from source to destination in a network. In flooding, the WSN node that receives the message broadcasts it to all its neighbours. That causes unnecessary retransmission of messages and increased collisions causing waste of limited battery power of sensors. Hence, for dense WSN, flooding algorithms are not useful.

3.5.5.2 Gossiping

Some critical problems of WSN are handled by the gossip protocol. The main goal of gossip protocol is to reduce retransmissions. In gossip protocols, some of the nodes discard messages and do not forward all messages received by it. Gossip protocols are of two kinds: nondeterministic and probabilistic.

In *nondeterministic* behaviour, any probabilistic distribution is not followed for scheduling the wait time, before retransmitting the packet, if the sink node is not active. On the contrary, in *probabilistic* behaviour, based on pre-specific gossip probability p_{gsp}, the packets are forwarded by a node. When a node receives a message rather than forwarding it immediately as in *flooding*, it gives the decision control to p_{gsp}, whether to forward the packet or not. The main advantage of *gossiping* protocol is that it is easy to implement and reduces energy loss overhead due to unnecessary retransmissions. Gossiping protocol suffers from latency, propagation delays. Hence, based on specific application requirement a suitable choice of protocol is used.

3.5.6 Routing Protocols in WSN

Many routing protocols have been developed for WSN. Various challenges and constraints are to be taken into consideration while designing routing protocols. Wireless links are unreliable; consequently, failure of a sensor node may be possible. All major routing protocols are listed in Table 3.1 and the design issues in all these protocols are listed in Box 3.1. They are classified into seven categories.

Table 3.1 Routing Protocols for WSNs

Category	Representative protocols
Location-based protocols	MECN, SMECN, GAF, GEAR, Span, TBF, BVGF, GeRaF
Data-centric protocols	SPIN, directed diffusion, rumour routing, COUGAR, ACQUIRE, EAD, information-directed routing, gradient-based routing, energy-aware routing, information-directed routing, quorum-based information dissemination, home agent based information dissemination
Hierarchical protocols	LEACH, PEGASIS, HEED, TEEN, APTEEN
Mobility-based protocols	SEAD, TTDD, joint mobility and routing, Data MULES, dynamic proxy tree-base data dissemination
Multipath-based protocols	sensor-disjoint multipath, braided multipath, n-to-1, multipath discovery
Heterogeneity-based protocols	IDSQ, CADR, CHR
QoS-based protocols	SAR, SPEED, energy-aware routing

(Source credit: International Journal of Computer Science and Engineering Survey (IJCSES))

3.5.7 Operating Systems for WSN

Operating systems of WSN are less complex as compared to any general purpose OS. WSN OS are like embedded system OS.

- **TinyOS** is an operating system specially designed for WSN. TinyOS software has event handlers and tasks with run-to-completion semantics based on event-driven-programming model.
- **LiteOS** is another newly developed OS for WSN. It has UNIX like environment and uses C programming language.
- **Contiki** is an OS that supports advanced technology such as 6LoWPAN and Prothreads.
- **RIOT** is a state-of-the-art, real-time OS with functionality same as Contiki.
- **PreonVM** OS supports Java programming language specifically designed for WSN and provides 6LoWPAN based on Contiki.

3.5.8 Simulation of WSN

Simulation of WSN is possible by some simulators such as NS, Opnet, and Tetcos NetSim. Refer to Box 3.1 for WSN simulation design steps in NS2 simulator for a sensor network.

BOX 3.1: WSN SIMULATION DESIGN STEPS IN NS2 SIMULATOR FOR A SENSOR NETWORK

1. ENERGY MODEL
   Creation of multiple nodes
2. **Communication model using UDP (User Datagram Protocol) and CBR (Constant Bit Rate)**
3. **Simulator instance creation**
   Fixing the coordinate of simulation area
   Define options
   Channel type, Radio-propagation model, Network interface type, MAC type
   Interface queue type, Link layer type, Antenna model, Max packet length
   Number of mobile nodes, Routing protocol,
   X dimension of topography, Y dimension of topography
   Time of simulation, Energy set up
   Setup topography object
   General operational descriptor for storing the hop details in the network
4. **Set up transmission range**
5. **Set up Antenna**
6. **Set up communication and sensing range**
   Default communication range
   Initialize the shared Media interface with parameters
   Sensing range, Communication range
7. **Configure the number of nodes with transmission range**
   Node creation
8. **Configure the remaining nodes with lesser transmission range**

3.6 SECURITY IN WSN

Several threats are encountered by WSN such as eavesdropping, node outrage, message corruption node malfunction, denial of service, and false node. WSN are prone to threats due to infrastructure-less architecture and flaws due to unattended working environment. Hence, security is a primary concern when WSN is to be deployed for special and critical applications. Mitigation methods are needed to avoid attacks due to intrusion and other threats.

Sensor nodes, when deployed in a hostile environment are prone to different malicious attacks. Hence, to ensure security to the sensor network, key management is applied.

Since WSN sensor nodes are distributed, trust in WSN is an important issue. It solves the problems of access control, secure routing, privacy, and reliable communication. Figure 3.16 shows major trust computation steps for WSN.

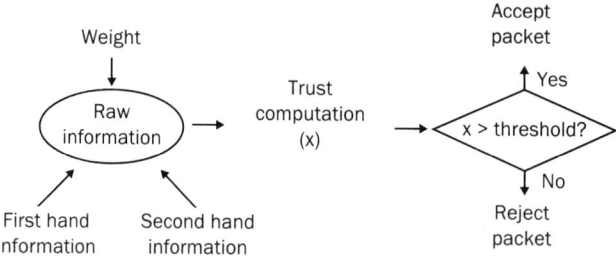

Fig. 3.16 Trust Computation in WSN

3.7 REAL WORLD WSN APPLICATIONS

Wireless sensors are used for measuring various environmental conditions such as temperature, humidity, pressure, and wind speed. Such networks were built initially for military applications and now-a-days they are used for many industrial and consumer applications.

3.7.1 Applications of Wireless Sensor Network

Wireless sensor networks have a wide domain of applications. Some of the major areas are explored below.

3.7.1.1 Healthcare Monitoring

Many types of sensor networks can be used for health care solutions such as wearable, implanted, and environment-embedded devices. The wearable devices are used on the human body surface or placed in close proximity of a human. Implanted devices are inserted in the human body. The sensors contained in the environment are the environment-embedded system sensors. The application areas are body position measurement, finding location of a person, and monitoring of patients in hospital and ill people at home. Environment-embedded system has application such as tracking of a person for continuous health diagnosis. Authenticity and privacy of data are important concerns in health care applications.

Area monitoring It is a common application of WSN where wireless sensor network is deployed over a specified region as per the application, for example, geo-fencing of gas and oil pipelines.

Earth/Environmental sensing For monitoring physical environment around is required in many applications. Some additional constraints as harsh environment and limited power are to be taken care. Some examples are listed as follows:

- **Detection of forest fires:** A network of sensor nodes is installed in a forest area to sense the outbreak of the forest fire. The sensor nodes can also sense temperature, humidity, dryness, solar index, etc., to predict any possibility of the fire based on these climatic conditions and type of vegetation.
- **Air pollution monitoring:** At several cities, concentration of dangerous gases is to be monitored constantly with a certain frequency to decide the air pollution level. This can be done by ad hoc wireless links instead of wired network. This ad hoc wireless network can be made mobile to cover different areas.
- **Water quality monitoring:** Properties of water in rivers, dams, lakes, and oceans are monitored for various reasons. Distributed wireless sensor node network is useful for sensing different parameters to decide water quality. The water samples from unreachable remote places even can be checked with such sensor network.
- **Natural disaster prevention:** Natural disasters such as floods and earthquakes can be predicted from the information collected by sensor nodes. WSN installed in the disaster prone areas for taking precautionary measures that can save loss of different kinds.
- **Landslide detection:** WSN sensor nodes can detect even a slight movement of soil and changes in other environmental parameters to detect a possibility of landslide well before it may happen.

3.7.1.2 Industrial Monitoring

Data centre monitoring In data centre with plenty of server racks cabling, IP addresses become a critical issue. To overcome this problem, wireless temperature sensors are fitted on, as many racks as possible to monitor intake and outtake temperature of racks. Wireless sensor with Mesh network is useful to address this issue effectively.

Data logging The live data feed from different sensors and its logging for statistical analysis is useful to show how systems have been working. This analysis is useful when design changes are needed to evolve the system in future.

Machine health monitoring Maintenance of machinery can be easily planned for best performance and long life of machinery by using the parameters checked by sensor network to decide the machine health.

Wastewater monitoring Wastewater is produced by industrial processes. Quality of such water is required to be monitored before recycling this water for any use.

Structural health monitoring Condition of any civil infrastructure can be monitored by WSN by monitoring different geophysical processes in real time and over long time by logging the data using appropriate sensors.

Wine production Wine production processes can be monitored using WSN for maintaining the desired quality of wine.

3.8 EVOLUTION OF WSN TOWARDS INTERNET OF THINGS

Wireless sensor networks are playing an important role in many applications from various domains such as healthcare, agriculture, smart metering, etc. Furthermore, high heterogeneity is present in WSNs because there are many proprietary and non-proprietary solutions for different applications. Current trend is heading towards IP-based sensor networks using the emerging standard 6LoWPAN/IPv6 instead of proprietary and closed standards. Native connectivity between WSN and Internet enables every day things to become smart to participate in IoT.

Recent research activities are aimed at creating networks of things web technologies such as AJAX, Javascript, Ruby, and PHP can be used to build applications with network of things and can be shared using Web mechanisms. Applications based on RESTful principles are already contributing towards the success of IoT.

THOUGHT EXERCISES

1. Design a suitable Wireless Sensor Network architecture for a Home Automation application using ZigBee communication protocol over mesh topology and mention the advantage and disadvantages of it over Wi-Fi communication.
2. Design a suitable WSN with MAC protocol for broadcast transmission for any suitable application. Choose the suitable routing algorithm for this WSN model and justify the selection.
3. Device the security measures to be taken for data confidentiality and integrity in any WSN based healthcare applications.
4. Suggest two WSN based applications, one using Broadcast protocol and another using Gossip protocol. Justify your selection of the protocol for that application.

SUMMARY

WSN is a backbone of IoT-based applications; hence in this chapter, several characteristics of WSN are explored. While designing the WSN, architecture, the characteristics especially those which are useful for energy efficient and reliable data communication are given prime importance. Various challenges are to be overcome while designing and deploying WSN, useful for different kinds of applications. Hence, different WSN topologies are listed. WSN MAC layer protocols are covered and network layer routing protocols are visited. WSN can be deployed in a wide variety of domains some of which are discussed in this chapter. The importance of data aggregation for energy efficient WSN is described. Finally the evolution of of WSNs towards IoT is presented.

KEYWORDS

Wireless sensor network, WSN topology, MAC protocols, routing protocols, sensor node, base station data aggregation, WSN applications

FURTHER READING

1. Singh, S., Sharma, S. (2015), A survey on cluster based routing protocols in wireless sensor networks. Procedia Computer Science 45: 687–695.
2. Kiran, M., Kant, K., Gupta, N. (2011), Efficient cluster head selection scheme for data aggregation in wireless sensor network. International Journal of Computer Applications 23(9): 10–18.
3. Kong, D., Kong, J., Chen, W., Niu, L. (2014), A design on improved GAF algorithm by wireless sensor network. Microelectronics and Computer 31: 147–152.
4. Chen, Y., Ye, Q. (2014), Summary on security authentication scheme for wireless sensor networks. Journal of Computer and Digital Engineering 42: 261–266.

REVIEW QUESTIONS

1. What are the major challenges while designing WSN?
2. Describe classes of WSN based on the service offered by them.
3. Explain the characteristics of wireless sensor network and their role in design and development of WSN.
4. Explain requirements for designing and developing energy-efficient WSN.
5. What are the objectives of WSN architecture?
6. What are the different WSN topologies? Explain their major strengths and weaknesses.
7. Explain different network layer routing protocols for WSN. Describe their advantages and disadvantages based on specific application.
8. Explain the MAC protocols used in WSN and classify them according to their application areas.
9. Explain duty-cycling technique of MAC protocol for designing energy optimized WSN.
10. Compare the Flooding and Gossiping protocols.
11. Explain any application area for WSN in detail with its requirements.
12. Explain the important goals to be achieved by a good WSN architecture.
13. If data aggregation is applied in WSN then what are the security issues surfaced?
14. What are the major security issues while sending or receiving the data?
15. What are the different applications of mobile WSN?
16. Explain the energy loss happening during idle listening. What are the methods that can reduce this energy loss?

REFERENCES

1. Toor, A., Jain, A. K. (2015), A review on wireless sensor network. *Journal of Mobile Computing Communications & Mobile Networks* 2(2): 10–13.
2. New frontier for wireless sensor networks [ONLINE]. Available at: http://www.networkworld.com/news/2004/0607sensors.html
3. Wireless sensor networks: a survey [ONLINE]. Available at: http://www.ece.gatech.edu/research/labs/bwn/sensornets.pdf
4. Suri, P., Bedi, R., Gupta, S. (2012), Review paper on various clustering protocols used in Wireless Sensor Network (WSN). In Networks (ICON), 2012 18th IEEE International Conference on Electrical, Electronics, Signals, Communication and protocols in Wireless Sensor Networks, pp. 86–91.
5. Akkaya, K., Younis, M. (2005), A survey on routing protocols for wireless sensor networks. *Ad Hoc Networks* 3(3): 325349.

7. Ganashree, K. C. (2013), Evaluation of routing protocols for wireless sensor networks. IJRCCT 2(6): 322–328.
8. Khalid, L., Jaffar, M., Javaid, N., Saqib, M. N., Qasim, U., Khan, Z. A. (2012), Performance analysis of hierarchical routing protocols in wireless sensor networks. Seventh International Conference on Broadband, Wireless Computing, Communication and Applications (BWCCA), pp. 620–625.
9. Sujee, R., Kannammal, K. E. (2015), Behavior of LEACH protocol in heterogeneous and homogeneous environment. International Conference on Computer Communication and Informatics (ICCCI), pp. 1–8.
10. Wireless bands [ONLINE]. Available at: http://www.beagle-ears.com/lars/engineer/wireless/bands.html
11. Sensor network [ONLINE]. Available at: http://en.wikipedia.org/wiki/Sensor_network
12. Manap, Z., Borhanuddin, M. A., Chee K. N., Noordin, N. K., Sali, A. (2013), A review on hierarchical routing protocols for wireless sensor networks. Wireless Personal Communications 72(2): 1077–1104.
13. Toor, A. S., Jain, A. K. (2016), A survey of routing protocols in wireless sensor networks: hierarchical routing. IEEE International Conference on Recent Advances and Innovations in Engineering. December 23–25, Jaipur, India Amanjot Singh Toor PhD Scholar.
14. Lindsey, S., Cauligi, S. R. (2002), PEGASIS: power efficient gathering in sensor information systems. In Aerospace Conference Proceedings, IEEE, vol. 3, pp. 3–1125.
15. Wireless Networking Tutorial [ONLINE]. Available at: http://www.tutorial-reports.com/wireless/
16. Ehlali, S., Awatif, S. (2014), Efficient lifetime maximization data gathering technique for routing in wireless sensor networks. *Applied Mathematical Sciences* 8(28): 13811389.
17. Yang, X., Deng, D., Liu, M. (2015), An overview of routing protocols on wireless sensor network. Fourth International Conference on Computer Science and Network Technology.
18. Singh, S., Singh, M. P., Singh, D. K. (2010), Routing protocols in wireless sensor networks – a survey. International Journal of Computer Science & Engineering Survey (IJCSES) 1(2).
19. World Academy of Science. (2012), Engineering and technology. International Journal of Information and Communication Engineering 6(12).
20. Fahmy, H. M. A. (2016), Chapter 2, Wireless Sensor Networks, Signals and *Communication Technology*. Protocol Springer Science + Business Media Singapore.
21. Introduction to Wireless Networks [ONLINE]. Available at: http://www.csie.nctu.edu.tw/~yctseng/WirelessNet05-02/contents.html
22. Kothapalli, K., Scheideler, C., Onus, M., Richa, A. W. (2005), Constant density spanners for wireless ad-hoc networks. *SPAA* 116–125.
23. Wong, E. L., Balasubramanian, P., Alvisi, L., Gouda, M. G., Shmatikov, V. (2007), Truth in advertising: lightweight verification of route integrity. *PODC* 147–156.
24. Canetti, R., Adrian, P., Dawn, S., Doug, T. (2002), The TESLA Broadcast Authentication Protocol RSA Cryptobytes.
25. Intanagonwiwat, C., Govindan, R., Estrin, D., John, S., Heidemann, F. S. (2003), Directed diffusion for wireless sensor networking. *IEEE/ACM Trans Netw* 11(1): 2–16.
26. Sharma, D., Verma, S., Sharma, K. (2013), Network topologies in wireless sensor networks: a review. *IJECT* 4(3), April–June.
27. Saha, M. K., Gupta, D. K., Rani. (2015), Energy efficient routing protocols for wireless sensor networks. *Second International Conference on Advances in Computing and Communication Engineering*.
29. Sachidananda, V., Khelil, A., Suri, N. (2010), Quality of Information in wireless sensor networks: a survey. *ICIQ*.
30. Arnborg, S., Artman, H., Wallenius, K. (2000), Information awareness in command and control: precision, quality, utility. *Proceedings of FUSION*.

IoT Standards and Protocols

CHAPTER 4

"The protocol of science fiction and the protocol of science are not separate- they're woven together."

—Ellen Galagher

OBJECTIVES
- introduce Internet principles and overview of IPv4 TCP/ IP protocol stack
- explain the role of IPv6 in Internet of Things (IoT) applications
- describe low-power wide area network (LPWAN)
- overview of various wireless technologies for IoT

OUTCOMES
- describe IPv4 address mechanism
- explain the contribution of IPv6 in IoT
- explain the developments in low-power wide area network
- elaborate wireless technologies for IoT

REVISION

Chapter 3 covered wireless sensor network and its various types and application domains as it plays major role in industrial Internet of Things (IoT) applications. In Chapter 4, the focus is to explore the Internet principles and various protocol standards suitable for IoT applications.

4.1 AN OVERVIEW OF INTERNET PRINCIPLES

Internet of Things (IoT) focuses on developing suitable network technologies for widespread deployment of smart devices through Internet connectivity using various technologies such as RFID, short-range wireless communication, and sensor networks. IPv6 Internet protocol with its address space expansion can cope with the requirement of huge number of addresses, which will support the increasing demand of the IP addresses. In IoT paradigm, network technologies must be capable of connecting anything to the network. Hence, security, scalability, and compatibility with heterogeneous platforms are essential requirements. Mission critical applications can be managed with reliable and secure wireless communication protocol and ubiquitous sensor networks.

All data networks are based on Open Systems Interconnection (OSI) network standards. Reliable and efficient data communication is the major goal of the network. The OSI model conceptualizes and standardizes the network functions.

The OSI model architecture is of seven layers, physical, data link, network, transport, session, presentation, and application. Provision of each layer is for some network services. The Transmission Control Protocol/Internet Protocol (TCP/IP) model is based on packet switching. The sender sends a packet without any dedicated connection. The message data packets follow different best available routes in any order while reaching to the destination address. The higher layer protocol arranges the packets in order again.

4.1.1 Transmission Control Protocol/Internet Protocol (TCP/IP)

Transmission Control Protocol/Internet Protocol (TCP/IP) is a connection-oriented protocol which sends the data in packets (streams of bytes). The packet header information has sequence number of the packet and acknowledgment messages ensure packet delivery. TCP can retransmit the data packets if the packets have been lost, until reaching the timeout condition. TCP layer flow control mechanism reduces data transfer rate. Packet delivery information is transmitted to the application layer protocols by TCP layer. TCP detects duplicate messages and discards them properly. Due to these properties TCP is a reliable end-to-end protocol.

The TCP/IP model is different from OSI model. OSI model has seven protocol layers while TCP/IP is five-layered standard: application layer, transport layer, network layer, data-link layer, and physical layer. In TCP/IP model the application, presentation, and session layers are presented as application layer. In transport layer of TCP/IP model, the main protocols are TCP and User Datagram Protocol (UDP). This protocol defines the level of service and connection status while transmission of data. The Internet layer of TCP/IP protocol suite divides the messages into packets known as datagrams. The packet contains information of source and destination address to forward the packets to the destination. The Internet layer is responsible for routing packets. The main protocols at Internet layer are IP, Internet Control Message Protocol (ICMP), Address Resolution Protocol (ARP), Reverse Address Resolution Protocol (RARP), and Internet Group Management Protocol (IGMP).

Routers which is the main device of TCP/IP layer hascomponents such as CPU, RAM, flash memory, ROM, and interfaces.

4.1.2 IoT Reference Framework

The IoT reference framework consists of four main levels:

- Device level
- Network level
- Application service platform level
- Application level

IoT network level protocols are mapped with TCP/IP protocol layers as shown in Fig. 4.1. Data packets are formed and routed by IoT Network layer. The Internet layer address protocols such as IP version 4 (IPv4), IP version 6 (IPv6) are explored in section 4.2.1 and in section 4.2.2, respectively.

4.2 IOT NETWORK LEVEL (ADDRESSING PROTOCOL)

Internet Protocol (IP) is responsible for packet routing. In case of erroneous delivery of the packets, IP ensures error reporting, fragmentation and reassembly of data packets called datagrams for transmission over heterogeneous networks. IP addresses are globally unique numbers assigned by Internet Engineering Task Force (IETF).

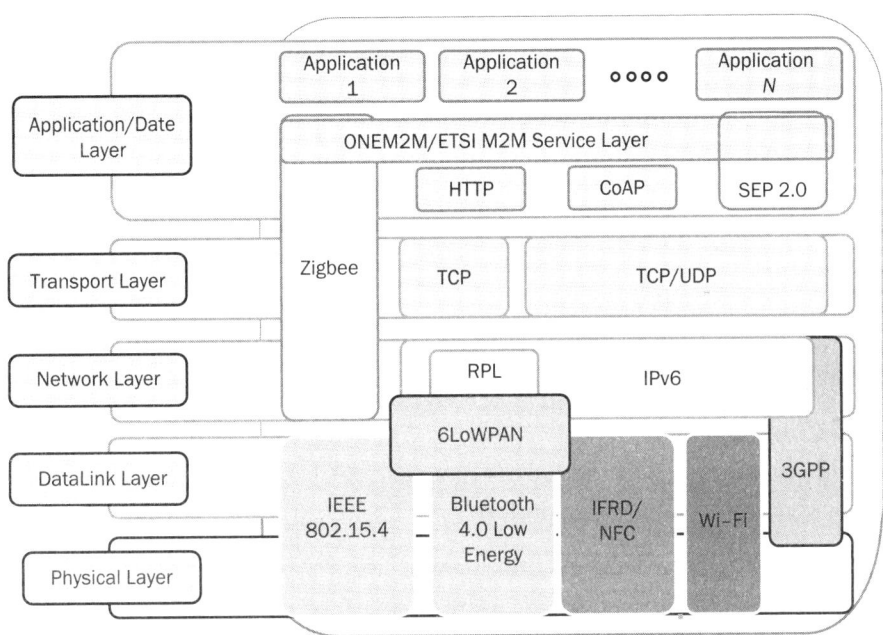

Fig. 4.1 IoT Layers and its Mapping to TCP/IP Layers

4.2.1 IP Version 4 (IPv4) Protocol

IPv4 addresses are represented in dotted-decimal format, for example 192.168.11.15 is a 4-octet (32-bit) IP address. This number uniquely identifies the destination whether it is a host (router, computer, printer, internet-enabled sensor or an output device using a network interface card (NIC) or any other TCP/IP network.

IPv4 addresses are made up of two parts namely network address and host address. A subnet mask extracts an IP address as a host or a network. This subnet mask helps the TCP/IP protocol to identify whether the host is in the local subnet or on a remote network. Because of IPv4 Subnet Mask in TCP/IP networks, routers passing packets from one network to another are unaware of the exact location of the destination address of the host. Routers have only information of the network of which the host is a member and the best possible route is assigned to the packet by checking routing table so that the packet can reach to the destination host in efficient way.

4.2.1.1 IPv4 Addressing

The packet is delivered to the destination network, and then the packet is delivered to the appropriate destination host. To identify network and host on that network, an IP address is made up of two parts namely network address and host address. The IP address such as 192.163.11.10 is represented in binary format as a 32 bit number 11000000.10100011.00001011.00001010. The first three binary octets represent an IP address and used as a network address, in Class C IPv4 addressing and the last octet shows the host address. If in this given IP address example 192.163.11.10 and if you will divide it into two parts two parts you get 192.163.11 as network address part and 10 as host address part host or 192:163:11:0 as Network Address and 0:0:0:10 as Host Address

The subnet mask is useful to separate the destination network address and the destination host address. 255 is represented in binary as 11111111. The subnet mask is a 32-bit number, for example, the subnet mask is 255.255.255.0. Hence, the subnet mask is given as: 11111111:11111111:111111 11:0000000. With this subnet mask the network and host address is separated as 11000000:101001 1:00001011:10001010 is the IP address 192:163:11:10. 11111111:11111111:11111111:00000000 is the subnet mask 255:255:255:0. The first 24 bits (the number of ones in the subnet mask) are used to identify the network address, and the last 8 bits. The host mask as 0.0.0.255 in the subnet mask is useful to identify the host address.

4.2.1.2 IPv4 Classes

The network address and the host address parts are determined by the class structure of the IPv4. Five classes are established in IPv4 addressing protocol (A, B, C, D, and E).

Classes A, B, and C identify actual networks. Multicasting is done using Class D structure. Class E is reserved class for experiment purpose.

The class structure is useful when a large number of hosts are present in the network. As the first bit of the octet is zero always, the octet value ranges from 1 to 127. Class A addresses are ranging from 1.x.x.x to 126.x.x.x and loopback IP addresses are in the range 127.x.x.x. 8-bit address is used in Class A networks for the network address purpose and the remaining 24 bits are used to represent host address. 255.0.0.0 is a default subnet mask for Class A IP address.

In Class B, two octets are for the network addresses and two octets are for host addresses. Hence, the default subnet mask for Class B addresses is 255.255.0.0. Class C allocates three octets for network address field and one octet for host addresses. The default subnet mask of Class C is 255.255.255.0.

4.2.2 IP Version 6 (IPV6) and its Role in IoT

With the advent of IPv6 protocol and gradual replacement of IPv4 with IPv6 protocol, it will have an impact on the future internet communications. IPv6 is an important protocol for IoT as interconnected products have huge demand of IP addresses and could not be met by IPv4.

Security Security is an important issue for smart IoT technology-based products. Also, due to their wide range of applications, privacy is a great concern. IPv6 offers better security solutions than its predecessor IPv4. With IPv6 end-to-end encryption is possible and the attacks such as man in the middle attack and cyber trap are made significantly difficult. IPv6 uses secure name resolution. the SEcure Neighbor Discovery (SEND) protocol is useful for authentication for a host which is secured with cryptography. In IPv4, it is easy to redirect traffic between legitimate users and manipulate the data or at least eavesdrop. However, IPv6 protocol deters such attacks.

Scalability   As there is exponential growth expected for IoT objects in next 5 years, IPv6 protocol will become a need for meeting the demand of addresses. A unique identifier is assured for IoT and high scalability in the future.

Connectability   The capacity of IPv4 is about 4.3 million addresses which cannot cater to the growing number of IoT devices. Hence, IETF worked on the successor IP protocol IPv6. It is a 128-bit address IP protocol with huge addressing capacity of 340 trillion trillion addresses. A large number of IP addresses will be available per square meter area with IPv6 protocol. The transition from IPv4 to IPv6 is challenging due to interoperability issues as they were designed separately. However, transition mechanisms such as multicast addressing (with simplified way such as hierarchical address allocation) and optimized delivery service are devised for communication between IPv6 and IPv4. Further, issues related to device security, mobility, and configuration, are considered while designing IPv6.

4.2.3 Classification of IPv6 Addresses

IPv6 addresses are classified mainly into three categories: Unicast, Multicast, and Anycast.

Unicast Addresses   Unicast address identifies a single address for a single interface.

Multicast   IPv6 packet with multicast address is delivered to multiple interfaces. Multicast address identifies a group of address interfaces belonging to different nodes.

Anycast   The IPv6 Anycast address delivers the packet to one of the interfaces identified by Anycast address.

Address notation for IPv6: 128-bit-long address of IPv6 with eight blocks of 16 bits each. These 16 bits are converted to four digit hexadecimal number, separated by colons, unlike IPv4 address where the separator is a dot.

4.2.3.1 IPV6 Address Example

Generally IPv6 address is represented in its final form by removing leading zeros. An example of 128 bit IPv6 address in final form is as below:

Final form (simplified by removing the leading zeros):
83DA:D3:0:3F3B:3AA:FF:FE28:9C58

Binary form:
1000001111011010000000001101001100000000000000001111110011101100000011101010 10000000011111111111111110001010001001110001011000

16-bit boundaries form:
1000001111011010   0000000011010011   0000000000000000   0011111100111011 0000001110101010 0000000011111111 1111111000101000 1001110001011000

16-bit block hexadecimal form delimited with colons:
83DA:00D3:0000:3F3B:03AA:00FF:FE28:9C58

4.2.4 IoT Data Link Protocol

In this section, different data link protocols are presented in brief including Ethernet and 802.3 as well as different protocol standards used in IoT and their use in IoT systems. The standards in IoT such as 'Bluetooth' and 'ZigBee' are used very frequently. IEEE 802.11ah uses existing infrastructure of IEEE 802.11, which is widely available.

4.2.4.1 Ethernet and IEEE 802.3

The term Ethernet refers to all Carrier SenseMultiple Access/Collision Detection (CSMA/CD) LANs that conform to Ethernet specifications, including IEEE 802.3. IEEE 802.3 specification is based on Ethernet technology, which was introduced in 1980. Ethernet and IEEE 802.3 maintain the largest market currently for any local area network (LAN) protocol. Both Ethernet and IEEE 802.3 LANs are broadcast networks.

CSMA/CD nodes listen to the network to find if it is in use or free, before sending data. If the network is free, the node transmits the data. In case of collision, both transmissions are corrupted/damaged. CSMA/CD nodes can detect collision and they must retransmit the data again after some wait time. 'Exponential-back-off' algorithm is used to determine the retransmission time to avoid collision.

4.2.4.2 ContikiMAC

ContikiMAC is a protocol that proposes enhancement over X-MAC protocol. ContikiMAC is based on asynchronous mechanisms with no signalling messages and no additional packet headers. ContikiMAC is a radio duty cycling protocol that uses periodical wake-ups to listen for packet transmissions from neighbours. When there is no activity the nodes go to sleep mode for duration of a period of duty-cycle. Channel check rate is an important parameter of this protocol that is to be tracked. This parameter defines the frequency with which the nodes will listen to the medium for receiving the data from neighbours.
ContikiMAC packets are ordinary link-layer messages. When the packet is successfully received, the receiver sends a link-layer acknowledgment. For transmitting a data packet, a sender repeatedly sends the packet until it receives a link-layer acknowledgment from the receiver. If a packet transmission is detected during a wake-up, the receiver is kept 'on' to be able to receive the packet. ContikiMAC uses a fast sleep optimization approach to allow receivers to detect quickly false-positive wake-ups and a transmission phase-lock optimization to allow run-time energy-efficiency of transmissions.

4.2.4.3 IEEE 802.15.4

One of the commonly used protocols IEEE 802.15.4 is used as IoT standard for MAC layer. The formats for and source, destination addresses are as per this standard. The frame formats used for traditional networks are not suitable for most of the resource constrained IoT networks. Hence, low power multi-hop networking protocols are needed for IoT.

IEEE802.15.4e was designed and developed in 2008. For IoT communications time synchronization is one of the requirements. This protocol also supports the feature channel hopping and provides high reliability and low cost solutions. IEEE802.15.4e also supports low power communication.

Slot frame structure For sending and receiving information, scheduling of various activities in a node is needed. The frame structure of the standard IEEE 802.15.4e is designed to satisfy this need. In the sleep mode, radio signalling of the node is turned off as this saves the power. During the turned off period, the node stores the messages that are to be sent in the next transmission. After data transmission it waits for an acknowledgment. In the receiving mode, radio signalling is turned on just before the scheduled receiving time to receive the data and to send the acknowledgement for the received data. Again it turns off its radio signalling while delivering the data to the upper network layers and sleep mode is activated.

Node activity scheduling The protocol standard is not meant for scheduling the nodes for their activities, but mobility issues of the node are handled by this protocol. The central manager node handles the activity scheduling and informs other nodes the schedule so that the nodes can follow for effective synchronization.

Synchronization of nodes Connectivity of nodes with the neighbouring nodes in a network is established by synchronization. Mainly two synchronization methods are used namely: 'acknowledgment-based' and 'frame-based'. Acknowledgement-based synchronization is basically used for guaranteed reliable communication and it is also to maintain connectivity. In frame-based synchronization an empty frame is sent at a pre-defined interval typically of 30 seconds.

Frequency channel hopping The frequency channel hopping is done with a pre-determined random sequence. IEEE802.15.4e has an in-built feature of channel hopping to access the wireless medium in time slots. Thus, frequency diversity is introduced which reduces interference effect. It also takes care of multi-path fading.

Network formation Network formation of nodes is based on advertising and joining by the node to the network. A new device node listens for advertisement command and after receiving such a command, the node sends a join request to the advertising node. Then a join request is sent to the manger node for an action in a centralized system approach. In distributed system approach, the node request for joining is processed locally in a distributed fashion. The 'network formation mode' of a node is deactivated when a device node joins the network. The node now becomes functional for that network, and its network formation node is activated again after receiving any other join request.

4.2.4.4 IEEE 802.11 AH (Wi-Fi)

IEEE 802.11 standards are also known as WiFi. The original WiFi standards have drawbacks such as frame overhead and substantial power consumption. Hence, the original Wi-Fi protocol is not suitable for most of the IoT applications. A low energy version of Wireless Medium Access protocol standard 'IEEE 802.11' is known as 'IEEE 802.11ah'. It is for less overhead requirements that are suitable for IoT. This protocol is used widely for all digital device applications such as digital TVs, mobiles, laptops and tablets. 802.11ah task group standards support low overhead and low power consumption communication suitable to effectively manage sensor network.

Main features of 802.11ah MAC layer are as follows:

Frame synchronization Valid medium information is used by the node to collect the information of the medium and the node uses this information to stop packet exchange by other nodes using the shared media for synchronizing the frame exchange. With the duration field packet, it can gain such information.

Bidirectional packet exchange It saves the power consumption of a sensor device as it communicates both ways between the access point and the sensor, using uplink and downlink. It switches to sleep mode after communication to save power.

Short length MAC frame The frame size is reduced in 802.11ah protocol as it is made shorter than 30 bytes to make it suitable for IoT applications. About 12 bytes frame is used in IEEE 802.11ah to remove the constraints due to large frame size length.

Preamble as a very small signal is used to avoid the overhead due to Acknowledgment (ACK) frames. The sleep time is increased in 802.11ah protocol as this protocol is designed for low-power sensors.

4.2.4.5 IEEE 802.16

IEEE 802.16 is a latest series of wireless broadband standards from the Institute of Electrical and Electronics Engineers (IEEE). The commercially recognized name for this standard is WiMax (Worldwide Interoperability for Microwave Access). The 802.16 family of standards is officially called WirelessMA by IEEE.

4.2.5 Application Layer IoT Protocols

Many Application layer protocols are designed to address the constraints of IoT applications. Various Application Layer data transfer IoT protocols such as traditional HTTP and other data transfer protocols such as File Transfer Protocol (FTP) and Message Transfer Protocols, MQTT, XMPP and AMQP are introduced in this section.

Table 4.1 shows the evolution of application layer IoT protocols.

Table 4.1 Evolution of Protocols

Protocols	Year
FTP	1971
UDP	1980
TCP	1983
HTTP	1989
HTTPS	1994
COAP	1997
MQTT	1999
XMPP	1999
AMQP	2003
LORA (LoRaWAN Protocol)	2009

4.2.5.1 HTTP

The application layer protocol Hypertext Text Transfer protocol (HTTP) is for hypermedia information both for distributed as well as collaborative systems. Initially HTTPS was supported by SSL protocol. After further evolution of Secure Sockets Layer (SSL), Transport Layer Security (TLS) is introduced. The current version of HTTPS is available in RFC 2818.

4.2.5.2 File Transfer Protocol

File transfer protocols such as FTP and SFTP (SSH FTP) are suitable for web applications and messaging protocols are a good option for IoT to reduce chunks of data in a message.

4.2.5.3 Messaging Protocols

Many messaging technologies are emerging to support IoT applications. IoT devices in a distributed network are using these next generation IoT technologies. Message Queue Telemetry Transfer (MQTT) and Constrained Application Protocol (CoAP) enable message management with small message sizes (to reduce message overhead).

CoAP

Constrained Application Protocol (CoAP) is an application protocol of a synchronous request/response type. Low-power small devices are using this lightweight protocol that also supports computation and communication capabilities for RESTful communication. This protocol supports the devices with constrained resources with web service functionalities. CoAP is a HTTP-like web transfer protocol, which enables REpresentational State Transfer (REST) architecture to LoWPANs. The binary nature of COAP is useful for IoT applications and supports integration of devices easily. This protocol runs over connectionless UDP. A thin control layer as messaging sublayer that detects duplicate messages is present in CoAP. An optional, simple stop-and-wait mechanism is used for retransmission for reliable delivery of the messages. Though CoAP is a lightweight protocol for IoT applications, it is not equipped with security features. CoAP protocol architecture has two sublayers, namely messaging and request/response. The request/response sublayer is responsible for communication. CoAP has four messaging modes namely: confirmable (reliable communication), non-confirmable (unreliable communication), piggyback, and separate.

MQTT

IBM introduced Message Queue Telemetry Transport (MQTT) in 1999. In this protocol middleware and application layer connectivity is provided. MQTT was released by IBM for lightweight machine-to-machine communications. The MQTT protocol is a messaging protocol ideal for IoT and Mobile-to-Mobile (M2M) applications and wireless sensor network. In IoT applications, where sensor node and processing node communication is required, MQTT is a suitable lightweight protocol. It is an asynchronous publish/subscribe protocol which runs on TCP protocol stack. MQTT is used to connect embedded devices such as IoT boards and networks.

For transition flexibility, MQTT utilizes publish/subscribe pattern. It is a suitable protocol for networks with low bandwidth for routing low-power and low-memory devices which are vulnerable to different attacks. In MQTT protocol architecture, there is a broker that works as a server for the topics and a subscriber that receives messages automatically when there is some update on the topic for which it has subscribed. The subscriber receives the update messages about the topic for which it has subscribed. MQTT protocol was designed for remote telemetry applications.

MQTT enables the transfer of data which is originally in the telemetry style to the form of messages to a message broker or server from devices with constrained networks and/or high latency. Different kinds of devices such as sensors, mobile phones, embedded systems, and actuators, are used for M2M communication using MQTT. One of such example is sensors on patient collecting his physical parameters by monitoring equipment.

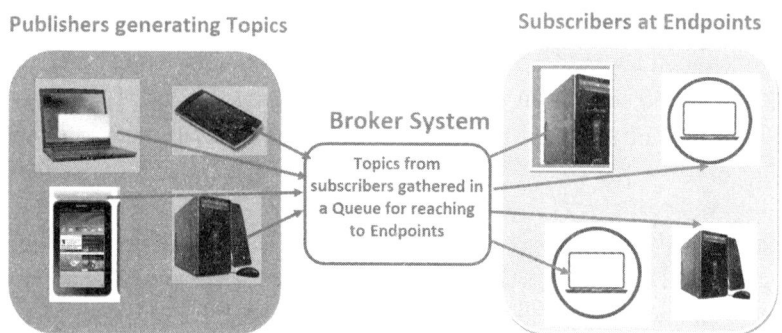

Fig. 4.2 MQTT Architecture

Figure 4.2 shows the MQTT architecture with three main components: publishers, subscribers, and a broker [25]. In IoT applications for low power consumption, the publishers are typically lightweight sensor nodes that connect to the broker to send the data to the subscriber. After data transmission is over it switches to sleep mode to save battery power. Sensor data is subscribed by some applications through the brokers, so that subscribers will receive the information when new data of interest arrives. Quality of service levels offered by MQTT are Level 0: At most one (best effort no acknowledgment), Level 1: At least one (acknowledged and retransmitted if acknowledgment is not received), Level 2: Exactly once (request to send (publish), clear to send (pubrec), message (reply to publish), ack (pubcomp).

SMQTT

Secure MQTT (SMQTT) is an extension of MQTT which is based on lightweight attribute-based encryption technique. The major advantage of this encryption scheme is that, after encrypting one message it can be delivered to multiple nodes. This scenario is very typical in IoT applications. This protocol works in four stages namely: setup, encryption, publish, and decryption. The data to be published is encrypted. This encrypted data is then published by the broker and sent to the subscribers. SMQTT provides enhanced security features as compared to MQTT.

XMPP

Extensible Messaging and Presence Protocol (XMPP) is a messaging protocol that was designed originally for messaging and chatting applications. It is a well-proven protocol, standardized by IETF and used widely all over the Internet. In contrast to CoAP's request/response approach, XMPP supports publish/subscribe as well as request/response architecture which is a favourable feature for IoT applications. It runs over a variety of Internet-based platforms in a decentralized fashion.

Quality of service is not ensured by this protocol, thus it is not suitable for M2M communication. Header and tag formats of XML messages put overhead which is a negative feature that increases power consumption in critical IoT applications. Hence, XMPP is not preferred in IoT applications.

AMQP

Advanced Message Queuing Protocol (AMQP) is a protocol that is designed and developed for applications of financial industry. AMQP uses a reliable transport protocol such as TCP to exchange messages. AMQP provides asynchronous publish/subscribe communication with messaging. Reliable communication is achieved by this protocol by message delivery guarantee primitives namely: at-most-once, at-least-once, and exactly-once delivery. AMQP implementations are interoperable with each other by defining a wire-level protocol.

It runs over TCP and has similar architecture as that of MQTT providing a publish/subscribe architecture. However in this protocol, broker works as an exchange or queues unlike in MQTT as shown in Fig. 4.3.

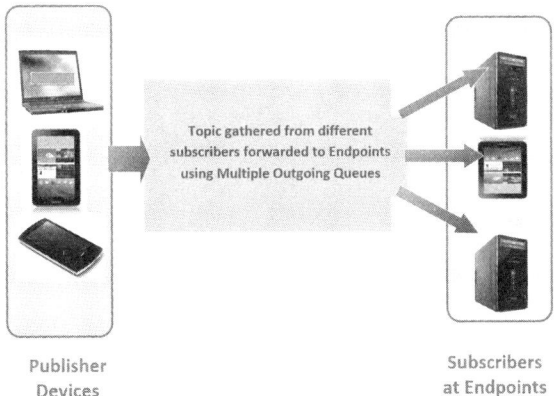

Fig. 4.3 AMQP Architecture

Queues represent topics subscribed by subscribers when messages are available in the queue.

4.2.5.4 DDS

Data Distribution Service (DDS) is also a publish/subscribe protocol. 23 types of quality service levels are offered by this protocol based on the criteria such as priority, security, urgency, reliability, and durability. DDS protocol structure has two sublayers namely data-centric publish-subscribe and data-local reconstruction. Sensor data distribution is carried out by Publisher layer. Subscribers receive the sensor data and supply it to the IoT application as per its requirements. Guaranteed delivery of the message is the most important benefit of this protocol as it follows a broker-less architecture, which is suitable for IoT.

4.2.6 Mobile Communication

Continuous evolution from 1G to 5G is happening in the last three decades in mobile communication. First generation of wireless cellular technology is called as 1G. The second generation technology is named as 2G and so on. 1G was introduced in 1980s. New features are added in the next generations as they are faster than their predecessors. New generation of wireless mobile technology is released after every 10 years. Most wireless carriers support 3G and 4G. Next generation 5G is released in 2020.

4.2.6.1 1G: Voice Only

In 1980s, the 1G technology is introduced for the cell phones. The maximum speed of 1G technology is 2.4 Kbps and this technology supports voice only calls. 1G also supports analog technology with high power consumption.

4.2.6.2 2G: SMS and MMS

Cell phones technology is evolved from 1G to 2G in 1991. GSM networks switched cell phones from analog to digital communications. The maximum speed is increased from 2G speed of 50 Kbps of General Packet Radio Service (GPRS) is to the speed is 1 Mbps with Enhanced Data Rates (EDGE) with the evolution of GSM. The 2G telephone technology has security features such as call and text encryption and data services such as SMS, MMS and picture messages.

4.2.6.3 3G: Faster Data Transmission

Faster data transmission speeds were achieved with the introduction of 3G networks in 1998. High speed was obtained with 3G to fulfil data-demanding needs such as internet access through mobile and video calling. The maximum speed of 3G is around 2 Mbps for nonmoving devices and 384 Kbps in moving mode. 3G cellular technology used the term 'mobile broadband'. 3G also evolved further with additional features to bring about 4G.

4.2.4.4 4G: The Present Standard

4G, the fourth generation of networking was introduced in 2008. Mobile web access and higher speed than the 3G service are the main enhanced features of 4G communication. A 4G network can provide maximum speed of 100 Mbps when the device is moving and the speed is increased to 1 Gbps for low-mobility communication such as when the user is stationary or walking. Video conferencing, gaming services, HD mobile TV, 3D TV are the added features with 4G. Latest smart phone models support both 4G and 3G technologies.

Fifth generation (5G) will be the future wireless technology after 4G, to improve data rates significantly, much lower latency, low energy consumption and higher connection density. The maximum speed of 5G connections is 20 Gbps.

> **BOX 4.1: COMPARISON OF MESSAGING PROTOCOLS**
>
> Table 4.2 summarizes three messaging protocols, MQTT, COAP, and XMPP with respect to mode, transport, and security. Cryptographic protocols such as Transport Layer Security (TLS) and Secure Sockets Layer (SSL) work on the principle of handshaking and use TCP as transport protocol. To encrypt the whole MQTT communication, TLS is used instead of plain TCP. Datagram Transport Layer Security (DTLS) as a security protocol for communication uses CoAP for protecting confidential information. DTLS is also used for authentication of communicating devices.
>
> **Table 4.2** Messaging Protocols
>
> | | MQTT | COAP | XMPP |
> |---|---|---|---|
> | **Mode** | Publish/Subscribe | Client/Server | Client/Server |
> | **Transport** | TCP or UDP | UDP | TCP or HTTP |
> | **Security** | SSL/TLS | DTLS | SSL/TLS |

4.3 LOW-POWER WIDE AREA NETWORK (LPWAN)

A low-power wide-area network (LPWAN) is designed for low baud rate and long-range communications between connected objects. The objects/things connected to LPWAN such as sensor and actuators are generally powered by battery at remote places, where power supply by traditional way is not possible.

4.3.1 NarrowBand-Internet of Things (NB-IoT)

NarrowBand-IoT (NB-IoT) is a standards-based Low-Power Wide Area Network (LPWAN) technology. This protocol is useful for a wide range of new IoT systems. NB-IoT attains low power consumption of devices and also enhances system capacity and spectrum efficiency in applications which need deep coverage systems. Battery life is improved by 10 years due to low power consumption feature for the applications using NB-IoT protocol. Due to large demand for extended coverage and for ultra-low device complexity, new channels are developed for physical layer. NB-IoT technology is simpler than GSM/GPRS and hence its cost will be decreased as the demand will increase.

Goals of NB-IoT are to reduce cost, increase battery life, better indoor coverage and provide high density connections.

4.3.2 LoRa — LoRaWAN Protocol

Long Range (LoRa) is a low-power, low-bitrate, long-range, and wireless communication system, for the applications of IoT. This system is useful where long battery life and low powered devices are needed. This protocol aims for low energy consumption. For smart sensing technology applications such as environment monitoring and smart metering, LoRa is the best option due to its long range and low-power consumption nature and it is also useful for industrial application. LoRa is a specification based on Chirp Spread Spectrum (CSS) for the physical layer. It is integrated with Forward Error Correction (FEC). Other useful properties of LoRa are high robustness, multipath resistance and Doppler resistance. Also, very long distance communication is achievable with LoRa infrastructure.

LoRa radio in a sensor network having following benefits:

- Relatively large range (maximum 10 km), hence LoRa enabled networks can span large areas with less number of hops. Node to the sink one hop solution is possible in many cases.
- Different spreading factor orthogonal to each other, are used for transmission on the same carrier frequency. Based on this channel division, virtual sub channels are created.
- When multiple transmissions occur at the same time with the same parameters then the high probable transmission is considered as strongest.

This wireless technology is used nowadays in smart home appliances, cars, street lights, and manufacturing equipment.

4.4 WIRELESS TECHNOLOGIES SUPPORTING IOT APPLICATIONS

In IoT applications multiple objects/things are connected in distributed locations. Hence some data link protocols are designed to provide connectivity with low cost and in energy efficient manner. Few protocols such as WirelessHART, Z-Wave, Bluetooth and ZigBee, DASH7 and LTE-A are introduced in this section.

4.4.1 WirelessHART

Wireless Highway Addressable Remote Transfer Protocol (WirelessHART) is a data link protocol which operates in the physical layer. Time Division Multiple Access (TDMA) is used in MAC layer to obtain a secure and reliable MAC protocol. TDMA protocol provides advanced encryption features for data security and integrity while data in transit. It enables different security mechanisms such as per hop, end to end and peer to peer. End to end security mechanisms ensures security from source to destination. In per-hop mechanisms data security is guaranteed only till next hop location.

The WirelessHART architecture is shown in Fig. 4.4. Its different modules such as network manager and gateway connect the wireless network to the wired networks.

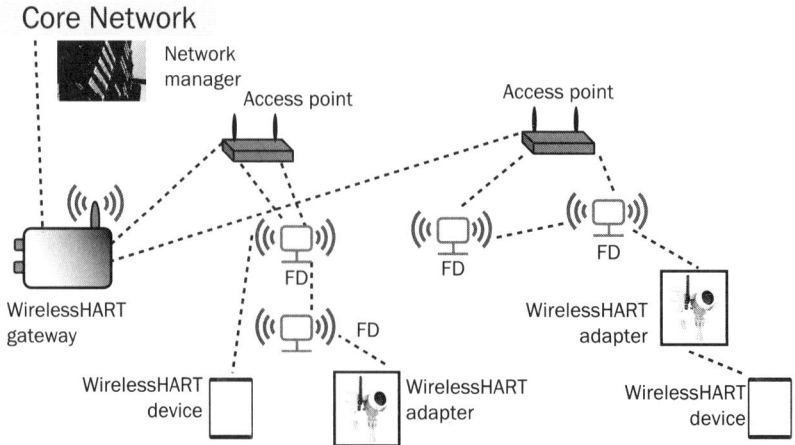

Fig. 4.4 WirelessHART Architecture

4.4.2 Z-Wave

Z-Wave is a MAC layer protocol with low-power consumption with its applications predominantly in home automation. It is frequently used in many application domains as well as in small commercial applications. Master/slave architecture used by Z-Wave where by handling scheduling of the whole network, the master controls the slaves by sending commands. CSMA/CA technology is used for collision detection and ACK messages guarantee reliable transmission. Small messages in IoT applications are efficiently managed by this technology and used in applications such as wearable devices in healthcare control, energy control, etc. Point-to-point communication in a range of 30 m is achievable by this protocol.

4.4.3 Bluetooth Low Energy

Bluetooth low energy also known as Bluetooth smart is a short range MAC layer communication protocol. It is also used in Physical layer. Its major application area is for in-vehicle networking. Contentionless MAC is used by access control with low latency and fast speed transmission. It takes 10 times less time for data communication and improved latency by 15 times. The master/slave architecture follows architecture of two types of frames namely adverting and data frames. Advertising frame is sent by slaves on dedicated channels to discover master node. Master nodes sense these advertisement channels to locate the slave nodes and connect to those nodes. After connection, the wake up cycle schedule is informed to the slave node by the master. For low power consumption, when the nodes are communicating, only for that duration they are in 'awake mode', otherwise they switch to 'sleep mode'.

4.4.4 ZigBee Smart Energy

IoT applications such as smart home, healthcare systems and remote controls use ZigBee smart energy protocol. ZigBee standard has two stack profile: ZigBee and ZigBee Pro. This standard's two stack structure supports full mesh networking for the applications with low memory and low processing power constraints. It also supports many other network topologies such as cluster-tree, star, peer-to-peer etc. The central node of the star topology, works as a coordinator and controls the network. ZigBee Pro stack profile offers features such as symmetric-key exchange based security, scalability and performs better with many-to-one routing mechanisms.

4.4.5 DASH7

DASH7 is a wireless communication protocol suitable for IoT applications which works on active RFID that uses Industrial Scientific Medical (ISM) band. It follows master/slave architecture. It is also useful for applications having asynchronous and transitive traffic and need lightweight technology. The low-cost solution of this protocol supports encryption as well as IPv6 addressing. This protocol is useful to make the application scalable which need a higher data rate as compared to the ZigBee protocol and long range coverage.

Its MAC layer features are as below:

- Filtering of incoming frames
- Validation with Cyclic redundancy check (CRC)
- Link quality assessment using 4-bit subnet mask

The frames are processed further only after passing all the above three checks.

4.4.6 LTE-A

Long-Term Evolution Advanced (LTE-A) is a set of standards developed for M2M and IoT applications. The MAC layer access technology used by LTE-A is OFDMA (Orthogonal Frequency Division Multiple Access) that uses multiple bands for frequency division and each band is then used separately.

Figure 4.5 shows LTE-A architecture which consists of Core network (CN) that controls mobile devices, Radio access network (RAN) for managing and controlling wireless connectivity through radio-access control and mobile nodes. LTE-A protocol is a low cost, scalable protocol. NodeB is a telecommunication node. eNodeB (evolved NodeB) is an element of the LTE network. Two eNodeBs are connected using X2 interface. X2 interface supports control plane and user plane.

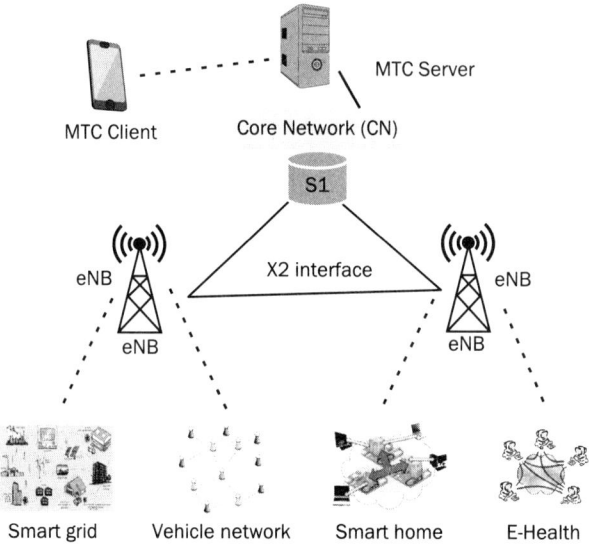

Fig. 4.5 LTE-A Architecture

4.5 NETWORK LAYER ENCAPSULATION PROTOCOLS

IPv6 addresses are very long and are not suitable for most of the IoT data link frames which need smaller frames. IETF is developing a set of standards suitable for data link layer, especially for IoT applications. These standards are briefly introduced below.

4.5.1 6LoWPAN

In Low power wireless Personal Area Network(6LoWPAN), the IPv6 long header is broken efficiently to small packets to avoid long headers of more than 128 byte size. This protocol supports variable length addresses and different topologies such as star and mesh and multi-hop delivery. Applications that requiring low power consumption, low cost, scalable networks and are benefitted by it. Further, transmission overheads are reduced by header compression.

Different types of frames in 6LoWPAN and their use:

- Unless the frame adheres to the 6LoWPAN specification, frame forwarding is not allowed.
- IPv6 header header compression of dispatch header is used for multicast messages.
- Due to frame length limit of 128-bytes of this protocol, frame fragmentation mechanism which is available in IEEE802.15.4 is used for this purpose.

4.5.2 6TiSCH

This standard is developed by IETF working group for IPv6. It integrates various other standards such as IEEE802.15.4 TSCH, 6LoWPAN, RPL and CoAP. The main focus area of 6TiSCH (Time Slotted Channel Hopping standardised in IEEE 802.15.4e) is industrial Internet of Things (IIoT) where it has proven reliability of 99.99% similar to wired technologies. TiSCH is adopted by IEEE as MAC technique which is integrated with IEEE 802.15.4. TiSCH works on the concept of timeslots by partitioning time into slots (10 ms in general) which are used by nodes to communicate (maximum size of 127 B frame) while synchronising with the network. A slotframe is used to group a number of timeslots. A node knows to transmit, whom to transmit, receive or sleep in a timeslot in a slotframe based on a pre-defined schedule.

THOUGHT EXERCISES

- Design the IPv6 class encapsulation mask for a wireless personal area network.
- Design an IPv6 address in binary and 16-bit block hexadecimal and 16-bit block hexadecimal

---

SUMMARY

The quality of the life is envisaged to improve by fast emerging Internet of Things (IoT), by connecting smart devices, using IoT technologies. The 'Internet' is a backbone of the "Internet of Things." is a focus of this chapter. An overview of the Open Systems Interconnection (OSI) model is presented at the beginning. Followed by the description of TCP/IP model, the basic model for the Internet. This chapter also explains and compares IP version 4 with IP version 6. It showed the limitation of IPv4, especially in the scenario when 20 billion devices for IoT are expected. IPv4 has room for about 4.3 billion addresses, whereas IPv6, with a 128-bit address, has huge number of addresses (340 trillion trillion trillion).

The standards are categorized based on the network layer of operation and the network model for example data link layer, network routing standards, network encapsulation layer. For each layer, some recommended standards and some draft standards are presented. The fast evolving IoT technologies would allow for the automation of almost everything around us. Comparison of data transfer protocol for instant messaging is presented with respect to mode of transport medium and required security.

Network encapsulation protocols IPv6 in IoT MAC frame is explored in this chapter. Many session layer protocols for IoT applications are discussed. MQTT is most frequently used in IoT due to its lightweight nature in low power consumption and low transmission overheads. Other protocols such as XMPP, CoAP, RPL, CORPL, 6LoWPAN are also discussed.

KEY TERMS

IPv4, IPv6, IoT network layer protocols, IoT application layer protocols, LoRA, LoWPAN

FURTHER READING

1. http://tools.ietf.org/html/rfc768
2. http://tools.ietf.org/html/rfc4347
3. https://datatracker.ietf.org/wg/roll/RPL
4. http://www.ccnx.org/releases/latest/doc/technical/CCNxProtocol.html
5. http://mqtt.org/
6. http://portals.omg.org/dds/
7. http://openkontrol.org/llap/index.php
8. http://www.bluetooth.com/Pages/Bluetooth-Home.aspx
9. http://www.zigbee.org/
10. https://www.ericsson.com/news/1987789
11. https://www.lora-alliance.org/What-Is-LoRa/Technology
12. http://postscapes2.webhook.org/internet-of-things-technologies
13. http://raml.org/
14. https://tools.ietf.org/html/draft-jennings-senml-senml-08
15. http://www.ipso-alliance.org/wp-content/media/draft-ipso-appframework-04.pdf

REVIEW EXERCISES

1. Why does the Internet require both TCP and IP?
2. How many total IPv4 addresses are available? Explain.
3. Find the ratio of the number of addresses in IPv6 to IPv4. Explain its usefulness in the evolutionary expansion of IoT based applications.
4. IPv6 uses a 128-bit address. Explain, how many IPv6 addresses exist?
5. Are IPv4 and IPv6 protocols interoperable? Which constraints will be faced by an enterprise in transition from IPv4 to IPv6?
6. How many IPv6 address will be available on each square meter of earth?
7. What is a low-power/lossy network? How does that relate to IoT?
8. What is RPL and how does it work (high level)?
9. Explain the application of Z-Wave for home automation.
10. What is the advantage of Bluetooth smart energy over the Bluetooth technology?

REFERENCES

1. Kaukalias, T. Chatzimisios, P. (2014), Internet of Things (IoT) enabling technologies, applications and open issues, Encyclopedia of Information Science and Technology, 3rd Ed., IGI Global Press, USA, 134–136.
2. Colitti, W., Steenhaut, K., De Caro, N., Buta, B., Dobrota, V. (2011). Evaluation of constrained application protocol for wireless sensor networks in Local Metropolitan Area Networks (LANMAN). 18th IEEE Workshop, January, pp. 1–6.
3. Fielding, R., Gettys, J., Mogul, J., Frystyk, H., Masinter, L., Leach, P., Berners-Lee, T. (1999), Hypertext Transfer Protocol HTTP, IEEE International Conference on Pervasive Computing and Communications Workshops (PERCOM Workshops), June, pp. 45–46.
4. Sye, K., Kumar, S. S., Hannes, T. (2014), Securing the Internet of Things: A standardization perspective. IEEE Internet of Things Journal, 1(3): 265–275.

5. Shinho, L., Hyeonwoo, K., Dong-kweon, H., Hongtaek, J. (2013). Correlation analysis of MQTT loss and delay according to QoS level. International Conference on Information Networking (ICOIN), 28–30, January, pp. 714–717.
6. Chen, M., Wan, J., Gonzalez, S., Liao, X., Leung, V.C.M. (2014), A survey of recent developments in home M2M networks. IEEE Communications Surveys and Tutorials, 16(1): 98–114.
7. Kirsche, M., Klauck, R. (2012), Unify to bridge gaps, bringing XMPP into the Internet of Things, IEEE International Conference on Pervasive Computing and Communications Workshops (PERCOM Workshops), 19–23 March, pp. 455–458.
8. Saint-Andre, P. (2011), Extensible messaging and presence protocol (XMPP): Core. Internet Engineering Task Force (IETF), and Request for Comments, IEEE International Conference on Distributed Computing in Sensor Systems, March, pp. 230–234.
9. Johnsen, F.T., Bloebaum, T.H., Avlesen, M., Spjelkavik, S., Bjrn, V. (2013), Evaluation of transport protocols for web services, Military Communications and Information Systems Conference (MCC), 7–9 October, pp. 54–56.
10. Hausenblas, M. (2014), Smart phones and Internet of Things, Chief Engineer, EMEA, MapR, Popular Blog on IoT, pp. 1–4.
11. Lee, G., Kong, N., Crespi, N., Chong, I. (2012), The IoT-concept and problem statement, IETF Standard draft-lee-iot-problem-statement-05, July 30, pp. 67–68.
12. Atzori, L., Iera, A., Morabito, G. (2010), The Internet of Things: A survey, Comput. Newt, 54(15): 2787–2805.
13. Miorandi, D., Sicari, S., De Pellegrini, F., Chlamtac, I. (2012), Internet of Things: Vision, applications and research challenges, Ad Hoc Netw., 10(7): 1497–1516.
14. Giusto, D., Iera, A., Morabito, G., Atzori, L. (2010), The Internet of Things, Springer-Verlag Berlin/Heidelberg, Germany, 67–71.
15. Zhang, Y., Yu, R., Xie, S., Yao, W., Xiao, Y., Guizani, M. (2011), Home M2M networks: Architectures, standards, and QoS improvement, IEEE Conference, May, pp. 44–52.
16. Hussein, D., Han, S., Han, X., Lee, G., Crespi, N. (2013), A framework for social device networking proceedings, 9th IEEE International Conference on Distributed Computing in Sensor Systems, Cambridge, May, pp. 45–48.
17. Odom, W. (2013), CCNA Routing and Switching 200-120 Official Cert Guide Library Book. ISBN: 978-1587143878.
18. Rayes A., Salam S. (2017), Internet of Things. From Hype to Reality, Springer International Publishing AG.
19. Browning P., Tafa F., Gheorghe D., Barinic D. (2014), Cisco CCNA in 60 Days. Reality Press Ltd., U.K., ISBN: 0956989292.
20. Inter NIC (InterNIC is a registered service mark of the U.S. Department of Commerce. It is licensed to the Internet Corporation for Assigned Names and Numbers, which operates this web site)—Public Information Regarding Internet Domain Name Registration Services. Online: http://www.internic.net. [Accessed: 20/10/2018]
21. Understanding TCP/IP addressing and subnetting basics. Online: https://support.microsoft.com/en-us/kb/164015 [Accessed: 20/10/2018]
22. Tutorials Point, IPv4—Address Classes. Online: http://www.tutorialspoint.com/ipv4/ipv4_address_classes.htm [Accessed: 4/11/2018]
23. Data Transfer Protocols in IoT-An Overview, (2018), International Journal of Pure and Applied Mathematics, 118(16), 121–138. ISSN: 1311-8080 (printed version); ISSN: 1314-3395 (on-line version) url: http://www.ijpam.eu [Accessed: 4/11/2018]
24. Online: https://msdn.microsoft.com/en-us/library/aa921042.aspx. [Accessed: 20/10/2018]
25. Tara, S. Network Protocol and Standards. Online at: https://www.cse.wustl.edu/~jain/cse570-15/ftp/iot_prot/index.html.[Accessed: 4/11/2018]
26. Colitti, W., Steenhaut, K., De Caro, N., Buta, B., Dobrota, V., (2011), Evaluation of constrained application protocol for wireless sensor networks in Local Metropolitan Area Networks (LANMAN), 18th IEEE Workshop, January, pp. 1–6.

27. Dunkels A. (2011), The ContikiMAC Radio Duty Cycling Protocol. Technical Report T2011:13 ISSN 1100-3154.
28. Fielding, R., Gettys, J., Mogul, J., Frystyk, H., Masinter, L., Leach, P. (1999), Berners-Lee, T., Hypertext Transfer Protocol HTTP, IEEE International Conference on Pervasive Computing and Communications Workshops (PERCOM Workshops), pp. 45–46.
29. Keoh, S.L., Kumar, S.S., Tschofenig, H. (2014), Securing the Internet of Things: A standardization perspective, IEEE Internet of Things Journal, 1(3): 265–275.
30. Lee, S., Kim, H., Hong, D.-k., Ju, H. (2013), Correlation analysis of MQTT loss and delay according to QoS level, International Conference on Information Networking (ICOIN), January, 28–30, pp. 714–717.
31. Online: https://cse.wustl.edu/ [Accessed on 4/11/2018]
32. Online: https://link.springer.com/ [Accessed on 4/11/2018]
33. Xavier Vilajosana, Thomas Watteyne, Malisa Vucinic, Tengfei Chang, Kristofer Pister. 6TiSCH: Industrial Performance for IPv6 Internet of Things Networks. Proceedings of the IEEE, Institute of Electrical and Electronics Engineers, 2019, 107 (6), pp.1153 - 1165. 10.1109/JPROC.2019.2906404. hal-02266569

PART II: UNDERSTANDING THE NUTS AND BOLTS OF IOT HARDWARE, SOFTWARE, AND MIDDLEWARE

Chapter 5: Sensors and Actuators in IoT

Chapter 6: Open Hardware in IoT

Chapter 7: IoT Middleware

Chapter 8: IoT Software Platforms

Chapter 9: Prototyping IoT Applications

Sensors and Actuators in IoT

CHAPTER 5

"Accelerating technology innovations such as ubiquitous sensors, cheap computing power, and 5G networks will open entirely new opportunities and challenges."

— Cathy Engelbert

OBJECTIVES
- understand perception layer of Internet of Things (IoT) architecture
- gain knowledge of various sensors for IoT applications
- conceptualize functions of various commonly used sensors
- understand various actuators for IoT applications
- gain knowledge of environmental sensors

OUTCOMES
- comprehend the concept and importance of perception layer in IoT
- understand the role of various sensors in IoT applications
- acquire knowledge about the functionality of various commonly used sensors
- gain knowledge of various actuators and environmental sensors for IoT applications

REVISION

In Chapter 4, network protocols and standards for IoT applications are discussed. Network is the backbone of an IoT application. Various protocols suitable for IoT applications are designed and developed by considering various constraints such as low power devices and low computing power.

This chapter also presents edge nodes and their network for sensing physical environment as well as actuator devices through which controlling action is carried out.

5.1 INTRODUCTION

Though the concept of Internet of Things (IoT) was introduced in the early 1990s, as the cost of IoT devices is reducing, the practical and economical implementation of IoT applications is possible now. The end device of any IoT system is either a sensing device (sensor) on one end or an actuator at the other end that triggers control action as an output. Hence, it is also known as the edge device and on some occasions can be both a sensor and an actuator.

The edge device/node is connected to the network by wireless or wired network. Data integrity is a major issue as the data is collected from signals from many sensors for intelligent decision making. The device at edge is capable of sensing, pre-processing, measuring, interpreting, and connecting to the cloud through the gateway for providing intelligence. Large IoT applications need a large array of edge nodes to make an array of network of edge devices. For the purpose of such a sensor network, each edge device must be identified with a unique identifier in order to communicate with them as well as for being recognized effectively.

Local intelligence is obtained by edge nodes with processing unit such as one or more microcontroller, hybrid circuit. Edge nodes with a processing unit are larger in size as compared to end nodes. Some examples of edge devices (nodes) – sensors are: light, sound, pressure, temperature, humidity, vibrations, motion, gas, Radio Frequency IDentification (RFID), Near Field Communication (NFC), ultrasonics, altitude, colour fluid, flow meter, cameras, etc. Typical examples of actuators are: switch, relays, PLCs, motors, light, sound, etc.

In IoT systems, a Sensor is an important hardware component and as sensors' prices have decreased over the years, development of IoT applications has gained momentum. Sensors are also described as physical objects that interpret the environmental changes and convert those changes to an electrical signal output. Real-time environmental information is sensed by the sensor devices and this data is converted further into machine-understandable information. Sensors must be uniquely identified with an IP address to identify them easily over a large network of sensors. Interfacing of a sensor with the microcontroller board is relatively easy and the entire unit of both things together makes a smart sensor. Sensors need to be active in nature as to collect real-time data. The sensor nodes are autonomous or made to work by the user depending on the need of a specific application (user controlled). The growth as well as cost effective smart sensors are giving a boost for IoT applications in various domains.

5.1.1 Sensors for Different IoT Applications

Sensors play an important role in almost all IoT applications. Often, IoT applications need things that can react and collect real-time data, using some hardware such as communication modules, to communicate and process the sensed data and some nodes for data collection, sharing, and storage.

The most important aspect of various IoT application domains is the smart sensor (with microcontroller boards). Figure 5.1 shows sensors used for IoT applications such as transportation, industrial, agricultural or environmental home automation, retail and logistics, health care. The domain-wise sensors are listed in Fig. 5.2, for real-time access of data as described below:

Healthcare Various healthcare applications use sensors for developing IoT applications such as smart wearables for monitoring blood pressure and sugar level and also for monitoring conditions of patients inside the hospital. Light sensors, biosensors, motion sensors, and acoustic sensors are commonly used in healthcare applications.

Building automation Building automation applications of IoT are smart lighting, smart waste management, smart parking, energy and water management, etc. A sensor is selected based on specific requirement of the application. Some sensor examples are ultrasonic sensor for smart parking and PIR sensor for smart waste management, and temperature sensor for room temperature monitoring.

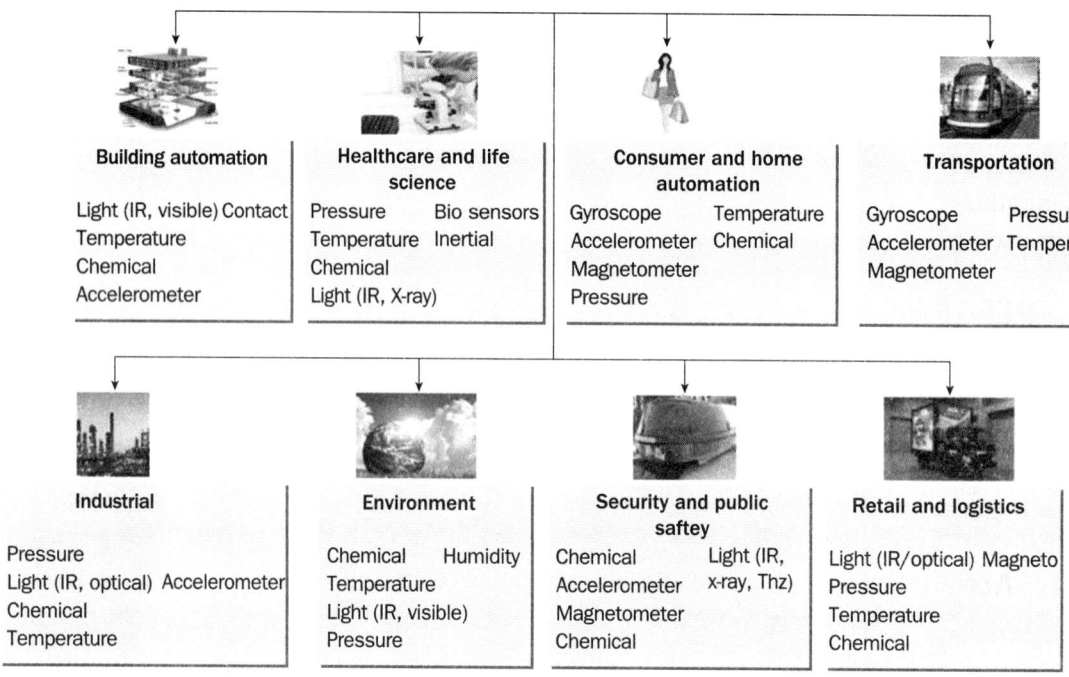

Fig. 5.1 Examples of Sensors

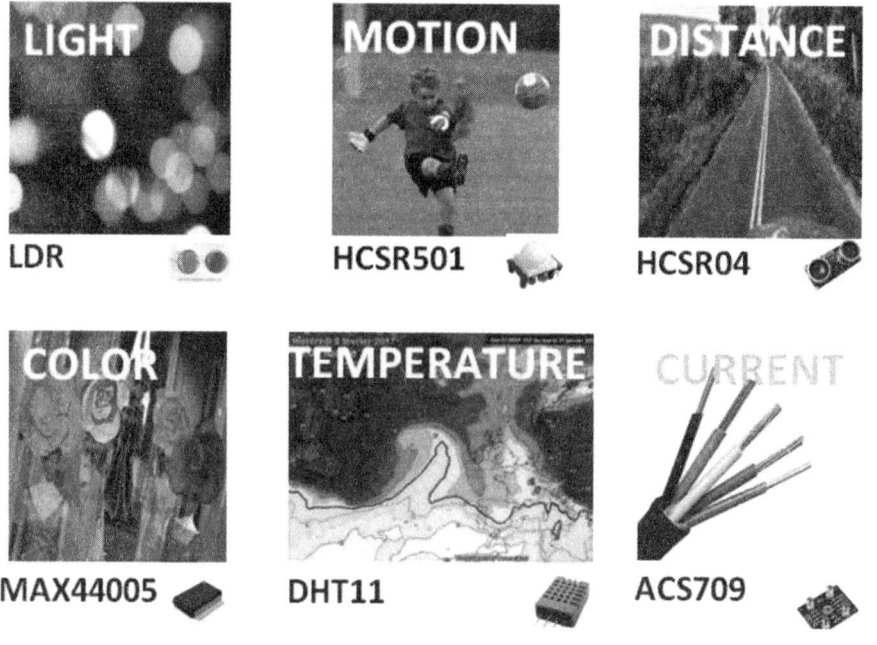

Fig. 5.2 Sensors and IoT Applications
(Note: HCSR501, DT11, etc., are products available in the market)

Agriculture Smart agriculture applications of IoT are soil moisture level detection for best utilization and management of water resources, crop farming management to maximize agricultural production management of green house, controlling micro-climate, etc. Some commonly used sensors for smart agriculture are soil moisture, PH sensor, solar radiation, soil nutrients, leaf wetness, and weather sensors such as temperature, relative humidity, wind speed/direction, and barometric pressure.

Many other IoT application domains (as shown in Fig. 5.2) are transportation, industry, environment, security, etc. some of which are covered in more details in Chapter 17.

5.2 PERCEPTION LAYER OF IOT

The basic IoT architecture is of three layers namely, perception, network, and application. In the IoT architecture, physical layer is also known as perception layer which consists of sensor devices for sensing and collecting information from the environment. Physical parameters are sensed by these sensors. The task of perception layer is to identify other smart objects in the environment. The discussion in this chapter is mainly focused on the perception layer.

5.2.1 Active Sensors vs Passive Sensors

Sensors detect and respond to the physical environment around them. The sensor which requires external source of energy for its operation is called as active sensor while passive sensor does not need external energy source for its operation. The external energy input for an active sensor can be mechanical, electrical, or any other type. Active sensors are widely used in networking and manufacturing applications and many data centres for the purpose of anomalies detection.

Other sensor-based technologies are GPS, LiDAR, scanning electron microscope, x-ray, sonar, seismic, infrared, etc. Seismic as well as infrared light sensors are both active and passive. Remotely sensed data is used for many applications such as resource exploration, cartography, atmospheric and chemical measurements. In IoT applications, remote sensing is needed so that almost every physical or logical entity can be equipped with a unique identifier and automatic data transfer over a network is possible.

Active sensor is a device with a transmitter, which sends a signal that bounces back from the target. This reflected data is gathered by the sensor. For making observations and measurements from a large distance, remote sensing technology is used in active as well as passive forms. Sensors are also used in hostile environments with extreme conditions and at inaccessible places. Various sensors are to be mounted at different places such as satellite, airplane, boat, submarine, UAV, or a building top based on what is being sensed.

Sensors such as accelerometers, magnetometer, barometer, are passive sensors because they are able to extract a measurement without interacting with the surrounding environment by sending some form of a signal.

5.3 UNDERSTANDING SOME COMMONLY USED SENSORS

In the following subsection, some commonly used sensors are explained.

5.3.1 Light Sensors

Light sensors that convert light energy (photons) into electronic signals are also known as photoelectric devices or photo sensors. The light sensor is a passive device. In a photo sensor, a beam of light is used to detect presence or absence of an object. Visible or infrared light beam is emitted from its light-emitting element. For detecting the light beam reflected from a target, a reflective-type photoelectric sensor is used. The emitted beam of light from the light-emitting element is received by the light receiving element. In a single housing, both the light-emitting and light-receiving elements are installed.

Some common type of light intensity sensors are photoresistors, phototransistors, and photodiodes. When this interfaced circuit, is balanced with potentiometer, the change in light intensity is interpreted as change in voltage. Bright light allows a larger amount of current flow. These sensors are widely used for measuring light intensity as they are simple, cheap, and reliable.

5.3.2 Accelerometers

There are two common types of accelerometers namely piezoelectric accelerometers and seismic mass type accelerometers (Fig. 5.3). For high frequency applications, the piezoelectric accelerometer is preferred due to its compact size. The seismic mass type accelerometer is based on the relative motion between a mass and the supporting, and is used for low- to medium-frequency applications.

Accelerometer is an electromechanical device. The forces are measured by an accelerometer. These forces may be static such as the constant force of gravity pulling some object or they could be dynamic which is caused by moving or vibrating the accelerometer. An accelerometer produces analog or digital outputs. Analog accelerometer's output is a continuous voltage that is proportional to acceleration with some specific calibration. Digital accelerometers commonly use pulse width modulation (PWM) for output. In some accelerometers, piezoelectric effect is used in which microscopic crystal structures get stressed by accelerative forces, which cause a voltage to be generated. Another way is by sensing changes in capacitance. Two microstructures side by side have a certain capacitance between them. If an accelerative force moves one of the structures, then the capacitance will change. Using accelerometer this change in capacitance is measured to convert from capacitance to voltage.

Fig. 5.3 Various Kind of Accelerometers

5.3.3 Gyroscopes

A gyroscope consists of a rotor (rotating disk) mounted at the centre of a larger spinning axis. Angular velocity (change in rotational angle per unit time and expressed in degrees per second) is sensed by gyrosensors. A gyroscope device uses Earth's gravity to determine orientation based on the principles of angular momentum.

There are three basic types of gyroscopes, namely rotary, vibrating structure and optical. Various kinds of gyroscopes can measure rotational velocity in three directions and also tilt and lateral orientation. Gyroscopes are generally implemented with a three-axis accelerometer to provide complete six degrees-of-freedom, which is useful for motion tracking systems that are used in aircrafts, autonomous vehicles, robots, etc.

5.3.4 Magnetometer

Magnetometer measures the strength, direction, or relative change of a magnetic field. Some applications of magnetometers include mobile devices using it as a compass, detecting metal objects under water (for example submarines), various surveys for minerals and oil exploration, locating underground buried objects, equipments that need to maintain precise direction, etc.

5.3.5 Global Positioning System

Satellite-based Global Positioning System (GPS) uses satellites and ground stations to decide and compute a position on earth. GPS receiver collects data from at least four satellites for accurate GPS computation. GPS receivers are used in applications such as smartphones, military applications, fleet management system, etc. for finding or tracking location of a physical entity.

5.3.5.1 Working Principle of GPS

Global positioning system on the satellites transmits information signal to receiver over radio frequency range 1.1–1.5 GHz. With this received information, a ground station or GPS module can compute its own position and time. Accurate location of a system is computed by a GPS receiver on the system, using constellation of satellites and ground stations (refer to Fig. 5.4).

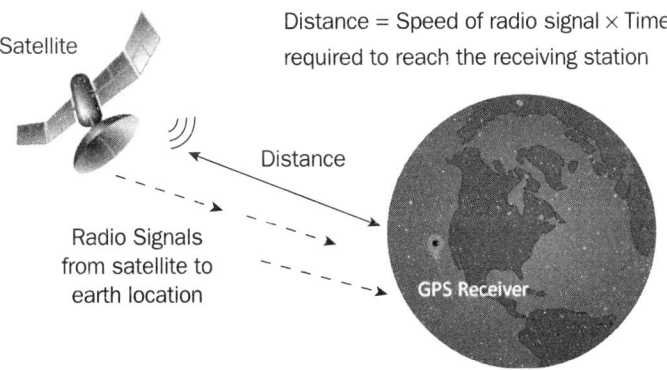

Fig. 5.4 GPS Communication

5.3.5.2 GPS Distance Calculation

Global positioning system calculates its distance from satellites using the time required for the signal to reach to the receiver. To calculate the distance both, satellite and GPS receiver (refer to Box 5.1) generate a synchronized pseudocode signal. The pseudocode signal received from the GPS receiver is transmitted by the satellite. These two signals are compared and the difference between the signals is computed. The receiver computes the distance from the information signals received from three or more satellites and then it can calculate its location by using Trilateration method.

BOX 5.1: GPS RECEIVER

Global positioning system receiver module gives output in standard National Marine Electronics Association (NMEA) string format. Output is received serially on Tx pin with default baud rate of 9600.

GPS receiver module

VCC: Power supply 3.3–6 V

GND: Ground

TX: Information about location, time, etc. is transmitted by TX

RX: Receive data serially

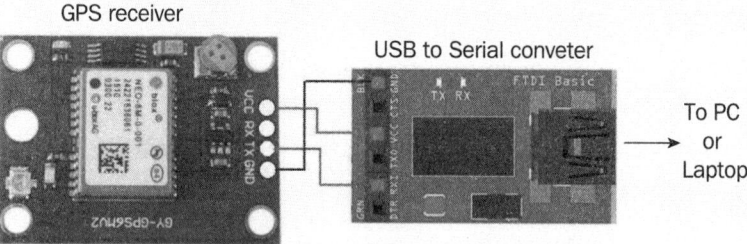

Fig. 5.5 Global Position System (GPS) Receiver Module

5.3.6 Proximity Sensors

A proximity sensor emits a beam of electromagnetic radiation and any change in the field results in a return signal. These sensors have the capability to detect the presence of objects in their vicinity without any physical contact. Proximity sensors are of four types:

- capacitive proximity sensor
- inductive proximity sensor
- photoelectric or optoelectronic sensor
- ultrasonic proximity sensor

Some of the common application areas include detection, position, inspection, and counting on automated machines and in manufacturing systems.

Any change in the dielectric medium surrounding the active face is responded by the capacitive sensor mostly without making physical contact. They can be configured to sense almost any substance. Capacitive sensors can also sense any object beyond a layer of thin carton, glass, or plastic.

Inductive proximity sensors can sense and respond to ferrous and non-ferrous metal objects also. These sensors can detect metal covered in a layer of non-metallic material. Inductive proximity sensors are made of a coil wound around a soft iron core. When a ferrous object is nearby, the change in inductance of the sensor takes place. The change in inductance is then converted to voltage to operate a switch. This concept is used in mobile phones to detect accidental touch when held close to the ear.

5.3.7 Radio Frequency Identification (RFID)

RFID identification technology uses RFID tag (a small chip with an antenna) to embed data in it with an RFID reader. This technology is similar to the bar code technology. Unlike a traditional bar code, line of sight communication is not required between the tag and the reader and RFID tag can be identified from a distance. Radio waves are used to transmit the data stored in the tag. The range of RFID can be varied with the frequency variation and can be extended up to hundreds of meters.

Two types of RFID technologies are used often, namely near and far. In near RFID reader, there is a coil through which alternating current (AC) is passed and a magnetic field is generated. The ambient change in the magnetic field is registered by the tag with a small coil, which generates a potential difference. This voltage is then coupled with a capacitor, that powers up the tag chip. The charge is accumulated by producing a small magnetic field which encodes the signal to be transmitted and it is read by the RFID reader.

Radio frequency identification tags are also classified as active and passive. An external power/energy source is associated with active tags and passive tags do not need any such external power source. Passive can sense the electromagnetic waves emitted by the reader without any external power source and are hence a cheaper option with a long lifetime. The raw data collected from the RFID tags is then pre-processed to make it suitable for IoT applications. Many available user level tools can process the data collected by particular RFID readers and the raw data from RFID tags is then processed and managed. This processed data can be further analysed and inferences are drawn from this analysis for some control action.

A dipole antenna is present in far RFID reader, which is used for propagating EM waves and for sensing the alternating potential difference. The object to be tracked is attached with the RFID tag and the reader detects its presence when the object passes across it. Thus, object motion can be tracked with RFID technology for searching smart things.

Authorized object with RFID tag is useful for access control. For example, small RFID chips are attached in front of vehicles and when the car reaches a (for example a toll plaza) on which an RFID reader is present, the tag data is read for car authorization. If authenticated successfully, it opens automatically. RFID technology is being used in many other applications such as object tracking, supply chain management, identity authentication, and access control.

5.4 ENVIRONMENTAL SENSORS

Various parameters related to the understanding of the physical environment (temperature, humidity, and pressure, etc) are sensed by environmental sensors. For example, to decode the air quality of a particular location, the presence of gases and other particles in the air can be measured using various sensors. Below is a description of a few environmental sensors.

5.4.1 Temperature Sensors

The amount of heat or coldness that is generated by an object is measured by temperature sensors or systems. Sensing or detecting any physical change to temperature is done either by an analog or digital output.

There are two basic physical types of temperature sensors namely contact temperature sensors and non-contact temperature sensors. Contact temperature sensors require physical contact with the object to be sensed and use conduction principle of heat to monitor changes in temperature. Non-contact temperature sensors use convection and radiation heat principles to monitor changes in temperature.

The most common devices used to measure temperature are thermistors, Resistance Temperature Detectors (RTDs), infrared, and thermocouples (refer to Fig. 5.6). Thermistors are semiconductor devices which change the resistance with temperature change. Thermistors are useful for measuring temperature in a limited range of up to 100°C with high sensitivity. The RTDs are based on principle that the resistance of a metal changes with temperature. Radiation heat is used by infrared type sensors to sense the temperature from a distance. These non-contact sensors are used to sense and generate a thermal map of a surface.

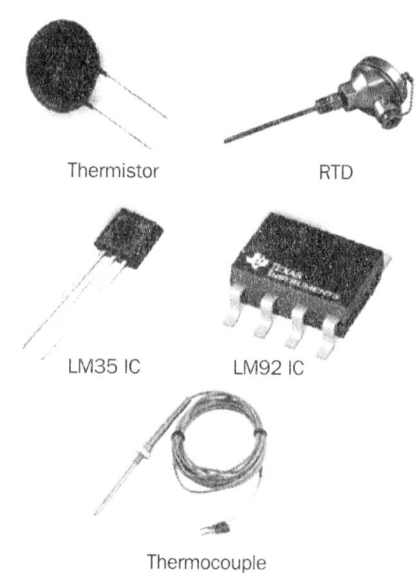

Fig. 5.6 Various Temperature Sensors

5.4.2 Pressure Sensors

In many applications, pressure sensors are used for control and monitoring. Pressure sensors are also useful to indirectly measure many other variables such as water level, fluid/gas flow, altitude, and speed.

Some pressure sensors work as pressure switches to turn on or off a particular pressure value. For example, a water pump is controlled by a pressure switch using which the water is released from the system to start the pump. Very high pressure changes occurring in dynamic mode are captured by some specially designed pressure sensors, for example, a pressure sensor measuring combustion pressure in a gas turbine. These sensors are manufactured using piezoelectric materials such as quartz. Further applications include altitude sensing (aircraft, rockets, satellites, weather balloons, etc), flow sensing (flow/ depth measurement), and leak testing.

5.4.3 Humidity Sensors

The term 'humidity' refers to the presence of water vapour in air or other gases. Presence of water vapour in air is measured by the humidity sensor (refer to Fig. 5.7). Measurement of water vapour content in the air is important to understand various physical, chemical, biological processes and also has profound affect on certain manufacturing processes.

There are three main types of humidity sensors, namely thermal, capacitive, and resistive. These three types of sensors can monitor minute changes in the atmosphere to calculate the humidity in the air. Based on the humidity of the surrounding air, two thermal sensors conduct electricity. One sensor is encased in dry nitrogen while the other is open in ambient air. Relative humidity is measured by placing a thin strip of metal oxide between two electrodes. Electrical capacity of the metal oxide changes with the relative humidity of atmosphere. Resistive humidity sensors work on ions in salts to measure the electrical impedance of atoms that changes with change in humidity.

Fig. 5.7 HPP801A031 Humidity Sensor

Application areas of humidity sensing include, building and construction, health monitoring and medical applications, fuels, aerospace, indoor, etc.

5.4.3.1 Relative Humidity

The Relative Humidity Sensor (RHS) is used for monitoring Agriculture, weather studies, discharges, etc. RHS is encased with an integrated circuit which is used to monitor relative humidity over the range 0–95% (±5%).

5.4.4 Wind Speed and Wind Direction Sensors

Wind vanes measure wind direction and wind speed is measured by anemometers. The manufacturer Campbell Scientific offers variety of anemometer designs such as propeller, cup, ultrasonic, lidar, and sonic.

5.4.5 Soil Moisture Sensors

The water content in the soil is measured by soil moisture sensors indirectly by measuring some properties of soil.

Some soil sensors measure moisture in soil as water potential. Such sensors include tensiometers and gypsum blocks and this property is called as soil water potential. Soil moisture affects reflected microwave radiation. This measure is useful for drawing inferences in remote sensing hydrology and agricultural applications.

5.4.6 Leaf Sensors

Leaf sensors are commonly known as phytometric devices that are mounted on randomly selected leaves on the plant. Generally, the sensor records measurements at 5-min intervals throughout the day.

The sensors determine from these records whether the plant is with enough water content or is water-stressed.

Farmers get correct information and can avoid over-watering or under-watering a crop. Even unnecessary water wastage can be avoided using such sensors, especially in areas of the world where irrigation water-shortage problem is faced.

5.4.7 Lysimeter

A lysimeter is a device which measures the amount of actual evapotranspiration which is released by plants. Record of the amount of precipitation that an area receives, the amount lost through the soil, and the amount of water lost to evapotranspiration can be calculated. Two types of lysimeters are available, weighing and non-weighing.

5.4.8 Rain Gauge

The amount of rainfall of any area in a given time period is measured by the rain gauge. No need to rely on local weather reports if such data is collected using rain gauge. It is like a transparent cylinder with markings on it. The rainfall is measured in inches or millimetres.

Based on the collected information, intelligent decision making is possible about the land and crops.

5.4.9 Chemical Sensors

Chemical and biochemical substances are detected by chemical sensors. Monitoring pollution level in smart cities, testing food, agricultural products, and checking food quality in smart kitchens, medical, automotive, detection of harmful gases indoor such as carbon monoxide are some of the applications of chemical sensors.

These sensors are made of a transducer and a recognition element. Recently, technologies such as electronic tongue (e-tongue) and electronic nose (e-nose) are being developed to sense taste and odour, respectively, and are being integrated with innovative IoT products. Pattern recognition software analyses to identify the stimulus.

5.5 MEDICAL SENSORS

The IoT technology is very useful for healthcare applications. A patient's health can be monitored remotely when they are not in hospital or when they are alone. Many medical parameters in the human body can be measured and monitored using medical sensors for providing real-time feedback to the doctor, patient, or relatives. Currently, a plethora of wearable sensing devices are available in the market such as wristbands, smart watches, monitoring patches, etc. Various parameters such as blood pressure, blood glucose levels, body temperature,etc, are sensed by these wearable sensing devices.

Monitoring patches that are attached on the skin are devices which are stretchable, disposable, and cheap. Such patches when worn by a patient are useful to monitor health parameters more frequently. Companies such as Apple, Samsung, and Sony have brought IoT devices with innovative features such as smart watches and fitness trackers in the market. These devices help to integrate contextual information (such as brisk walking to heart rate) with health parameters to enable correct inferences regarding an underlying condition in a person.

5.5.1 Heartbeat Sensor

Heart rate is defined as the sound of the valves in a person's heart while contracting or expanding to pump the blood from one region to another. Heartbeat rate is the number of times the heart beats per minute (BPM). There are two methods to measure a heartbeat:

Manual way Manually, heartbeat can be measured by checking a person's pulse in the wrist (radial pulse) and the neck (carotid pulse).

Sensor use for heartbeat measurement Heartbeat can be measured using the optical power variation as light is scattered during its path through the blood when there is change in the heartbeat.

5.5.2 Pulse Sensor

Pulse sensor captures the heart beat or heart rate of a person. The flat side of the sensor is placed on top of the vein and a slight pressure is applied on top of it using a fastening band clip to attain this pressure.

5.5.2.1 Applications

Pulse sensors are used in the following devices:

- Health bands
- Advanced gaming consoles
- Sleep tracking
- Remote patient monitoring/alarm system
- Anxiety monitoring

5.5.3 Blood Glucose Level Sensor

The concentration of blood glucose is measured and monitored using blood glucose level sensor. This is a monitoring device for diabetes patients which can be easily used at home.

Continuous glucose monitoring system The finger-prick test is inconvenient and the chance of contaminating a blood sample is heightened. Alternatively, blood sugar levels can be continuously monitored by a transmitter implanted in the body. The approximate concentration of glucose in the blood is measured by the sensor device, making it simple. The patient is alerted frequently by an alarm system about the fluctuations in the blood sugar level.

5.5.4 Blood Pressure Sensor

For measuring human blood pressure, the blood pressure sensor is used which is a non-invasive sensor. The systolic, diastolic, and mean arterial pressure is measured by the oscillometric technique. Even the pulse rate is also measured by such a device. The common risk factor for heart attacks is high blood pressure. Hence, diagnosing and monitoring high blood pressure is important.

The new breed of monitoring devices to be worn around wrist and the index finger are similar to traditional cuff devices but simple to use. Such devices are useful to monitor hypertension as well as sleep apnea, which cause breathing to stop many times throughout the night.

5.5.5 Body Temperature Sensor

Body temperature is measured by such sensor devices. The reason is that a number of diseases are accompanied by characteristic changes in body temperature. By measuring body temperature certain diseases can be monitored.

5.6 FLOW AND FLUID MEASURING SENSORS

This section discusses level sensors, stream gauge, and tide guage.

5.6.1 Level Sensors

A level sensor detects the level of a liquid (or semi-solid materials such as slurries) in either an enclosed space or free-flowing (e.g. river).

The level sensing measurement can either be point measurements made at specific locations or continuous, where a range of measurements are recorded. Point-level sensors indicate whether the substance is above or below the sensing level to detect the level above or below the decided threshold.

The selection of a particular method such as acoustic, vibration, mechanical, etc., for level monitoring depends on the application and the domain (industrial, commercial, hydrology, etc.) in which it is used.

5.6.2 Stream Gauge

Terrestrial bodies of water are tested and monitored by stream gauging station also known as stream gauge or gauging station by hydrologists. These network of stations along a river basin are usually shown on a map. The data from these stations are made accessible remotely and are used in various hydrological models.

5.6.3 Tide Gauge

A tide gauge also known as a mareograph is a device for measuring the change in sea level relative to a vertical datum. Tide gauges enable to determine the mean sea level by obtaining hourly measurements at geographically distributed locations for 19 years and averaging them. This mean sea level is usually used as a vertical datum against which height measurements are made. Also, tide gauges are useful in measuring the tide heights during Tsunamis and other ocean related events used in climate modeling.

5.7 RANGE AND MOTION CAPTURE SENSORS

Motion sensors are primarily used to detect movement of objects. Whereas range sensors enable to measure distance of an object. Some sensors combine both these functionality and can do both motion and range sensing.

A Passive Infrared (PIR) sensor (see Fig. 5.8) can sense motion upto 12 metres. It is a pyroelectric device capable of detecting naturally emitted infrared radiation from objects (temperature above absolute zero). The field of view of the sensor is generally around 110° and use a Fresnel lens (Fig. 5.8) to achieve such wide breadth of sensing.

PIR sensors have a wide variety of applications such as

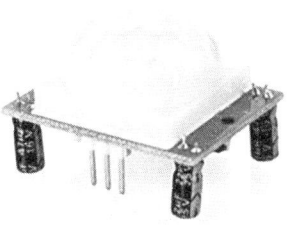

- Motion detection of Humans in indoor spaces such as homes, malls, hotels, etc.
- Vehicles movement detection in parking lots and basements
- Smart automated lighting, AC (indoors), street lights to conserve electricity
- Capture movement of animals in remote areas by integrating with a camera module

Fig. 5.8 PIR Motion Sensor

5.7.1 Distance Sensors

Distance sensors are of two types, namely ultrasonic and laser, which are explained below:

5.7.1.1 Ultrasonic Distance Sensors

Ultrasonic sensors measure distance from ojbects with high accuracy. These sensors come in various sizes to fit into the measuring environment such as small containers, openings, etc. The range of Ultra sonic sensors varies between different manufacturers. The popular low-cost version HC-SR04 distance sensor has a range of 2cm to 400 cm with a measure angle of 15 degrees and accuracy of approximately 3 mm. Some commercially available sensors have a high range of upto 21 meters.

Applications of Ultrasonic sensors include object/people detection, liquid level measurements, monitoring garbage level in trash cans, industrial production lines (objects on conveyor belts).

5.7.1.2 Laser Distance Sensors

Laser sensors are a highly efficient way of object detection as well as measuring distance from an object even under varying lighting conditions and material characteristics of the object. These sensors have many applications in the areas of building and construction, oil and gas, mining, transportation, electronics, etc. In general, it can be used in situations requiring precise contactless measurements of length, width, height, diameter, etc. of objects.

5.7.2 Touch Sensor

A touch sensor is a device that captures and records physical touch on an and sends it to a processing unit or software that processes these records.

Touch sensors are very commonly used on displays of smartphones and tablets. Two types of touch sensors/screens are normally used namely, capacitive and resistive.

5.7.2.1 Capacitive Touch Sensors

A capacitive touch sensor works on the principle of capacitive coupling to sense anything whose dielectric (non-conductors of electricity) is different from the surrounding air. In a touch sensor, the electrical charge conductor is a human body, when the finger comes in contact with the sensor surface. The exact coordinates (location) is sensed by the change in the electrostatic field around that region (see Fig. 5.9).

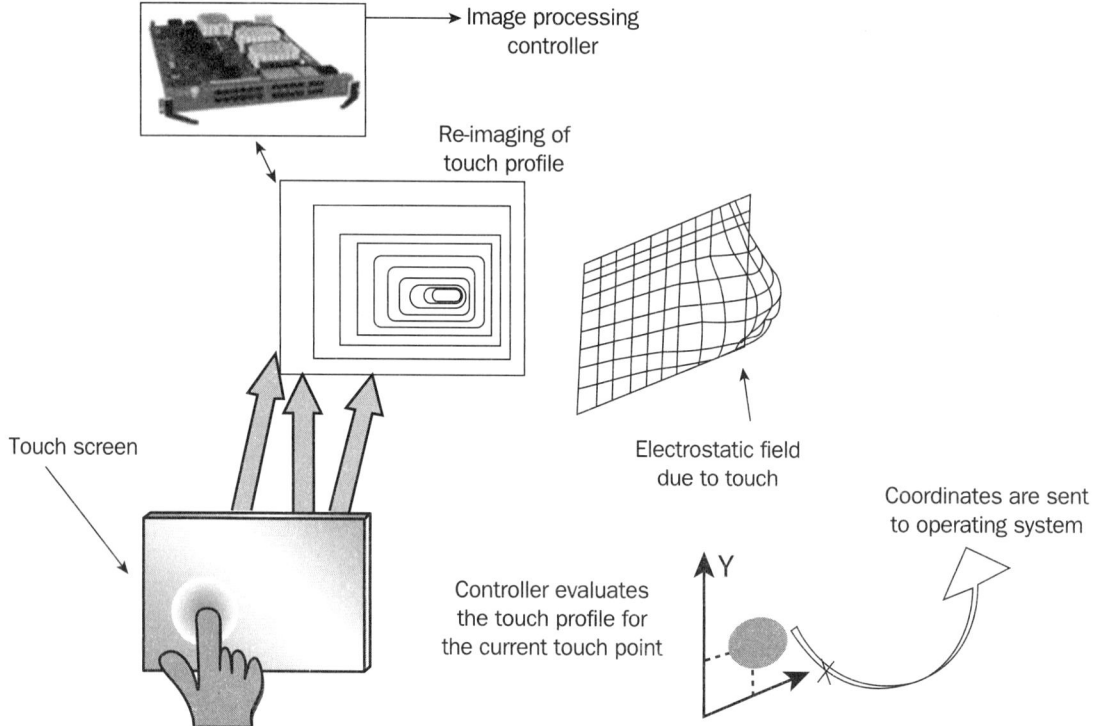

Fig. 5.9 The Image Processing Controller that Evaluates Touch Points

5.7.2.2 *Resistive Touch Sensors*

Resistive touch sensors are usually of two varieties. First type is based on glass (insulating material) as the base support material with film based electrically conductive and resistive layers. The second type is similar to the above, except that the support material is made of polycarbonate. Both the support material and the film are coated with ITO (Indium-Tin-Oxide), which is transparent to light and has high electrical conductivity. An air gap is introduced between these film and support material (glass or polycarbonate) (see Fig. 5.10).

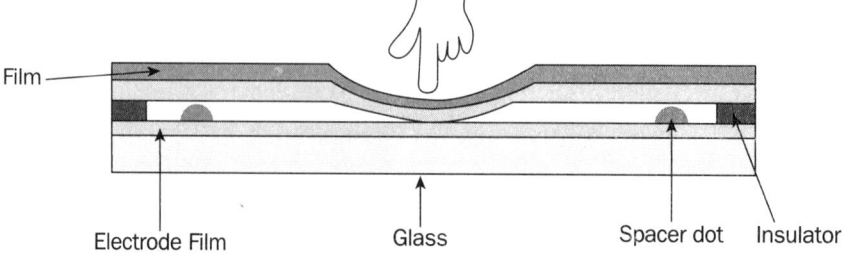

Fig. 5.10 Resistive Touchscreen and its Layers

5.8 ACTUATORS

An actuator is a device that converts the effective change in the environment sensed in the form of electrical energy into some other form of energy. Based on their operation, these are classified into electrical, hydraulic, and pneumatic actuators. Lights, displays, motors, heating or cooling elements, and speakers are some of the examples of electrical actuators. Another example is a smart home system that uses many sensors and actuators.

Pressure of compressed air is used in pneumatic actuators and hydraulic power is used in hydraulic actuators. Actuators are used in home applications such as locking and unlocking doors, switching lights on and off, etc. In this section, some examples of actuators are presented which are useful in IoT applications.

5.8.1 Servo Motor

To push or rotate an object with precision, a servo motor is used. It is an electrical device which can rotate an object at some specific angles or distance. It is a simple motor which uses servo mechanism for its operation. If motor operates on DC power, then it is known as DC servo motor and if it is an AC powered motor, then it is known as AC servo motor. Servo motor is available in small and light weight packages with high torque. Hence, such motors can be used in many applications such as Robotics, RC helicopters and planes, machine toy cars, etc.

5.8.2 Stepper Motor

A stepper motor is an electromechanical device which converts electrical power into mechanical power. It is a brushless, synchronous electric motor and divides its full rotation into an expansive number of steps. If the motor is carefully sized to the application, the motor's position can be controlled accurately without any feedback mechanism.

There are three main types of stepper motors:

- Permanent magnet stepper
- Hybrid synchronous stepper
- Variable reluctance stepper

Stepper motors are used in various applications such as:

- Actuators in fluid pumps, medical scanners, samplers, blood analysis machinery, respirators, etc.
- Focus and zoom functions in digital cameras
- Machine tooling equipment, automotive gauges, and surveillance systems for security industry

5.8.3 DC Motor

Electric machines are used for converting energy. Electrical energy is converted by motors to produce mechanical energy. Many day-to-day applications use electric motors. There are two main classes of electric motors:

- Direct Current (DC) motor
- Alternating Current (AC) motor

A direct current power motor is known as DC motor. Field windings of DC motor are used to provide the magnetic flux and the armature of DC motor acts as the conductor. Its working principle is that when a current carrying conductor is placed in a magnetic field, it experiences a force which causes rotation with respect to its original position.

DC motor mainly consists of two parts. The rotating part is called the rotor and the stationary part is called as the stator. The rotor rotates with respect to the stator.

5.8.4 Linear Actuators

The type of actuator is useful when motion in a straight line (linear motion) between two points is required. These could be mechanical or electro-mechanical (also known has electric linear actuators) devices. The rotation of the electric motor is converted to linear motion by using gears and lead screw in the electric linear actuators.

Applications include valves, automatic windows/doors, agriculture implements, robotics, machine design, material management, industrial equipment, etc.

5.8.5 Solenoid

A coiled wire around a cylinder is called as a solenoid. When current runs through a solenoid, a strong magnet is generated because the magnetic field is concentrated inside the coil. Unlike regular magnets, an electromagnet is particularly useful as it can be switched on and off, and its strength increases by increasing the amount of current flowing through it. This phenomenon is useful in many applications.

5.8.5.1 *Electromagnet Solenoid and its Use*

Solenoids have a wide range of applications such as valves (air compressors, metres), pistons, home automation devices (door bells, auto locks, AC, heating equipment), automobiles (engine starter), drinks, coffee dispensers, sprinkler system, etc.

5.8.6 Relay

The relay device receives input signal from one side and controls the switching operation on the other side.

Many types of relays are present. A commonly used relay is made of electromagnets and operates as a switch. Relay is a switch that controls the circuit electromechanically. A high-powered circuit is controlled by a relay switch with a low power signal. Generally, a DC signal is used to control a circuit that drives high voltage appliances such as smart home appliances that operate on AC power supply.

5.8.6.1 *Different Mechanical Parts of a Relay*

- Electromagnet
- Movable armature
- Contacts
- Spring (optional)
- Yoke

Figure 5.11 shows how a relay is internally connected.

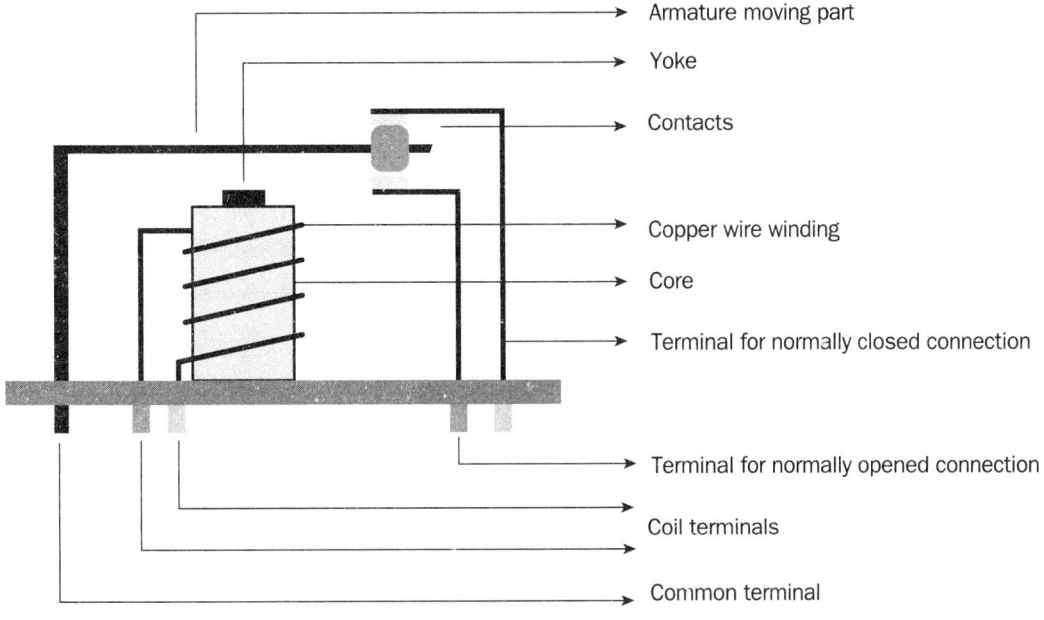

Fig. 5.11 Electromagnetic Relay

When the relay is on, the armature moves and connects the normally opened contact pin of the relay. The circuit is closed and the current flows through the coil and comes back to the original position after it is de-energized.

The circuit representation of the relay is as shown in Fig. 5.12.

5.8.6.2 Different Types of Relay
There are many types of relay other than the electromagnetic relay which works on different principles. The classification of relay is as follows:

5.8.6.3 Based on the Principle of Operation
- Solid state relay
- Hybrid relay
- Electrothermal relay
- Electromechanical relay

5.8.6.4 Based on the Polarity
- Polarized relay
- Non-polarized relay

102 Internet of Things

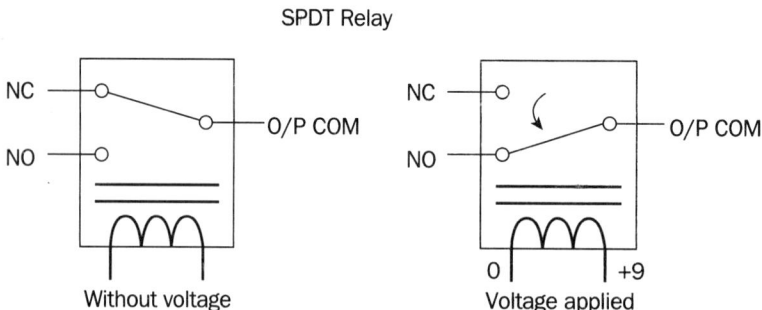

NC: Normally closed
NO: Normally opened
SPDT relay: Single Pole Double Throw replay

Fig. 5.12 Circuit of a Relay

5.8.6.5 *Applications of Relay*

Applications of relay include home appliances, home/office automation (temperature-based control of heating/cooling, lighting), traffic signals control, industrial applications, precision agriculture, automotive applications, etc.

5.9 IOT EXAMPLES

Figure 5.13 shows the circuit diagram for the sensor as Light-Dependent Resistor (LDR) and actuators as LED and buzzer.

The text below explains the process for connecting the sensor – LDR and actuators – LED and buzzer:

- Connect the LED, buzzer, and the LDR to the breadboard
- Connect the +ve, that is, VCC of the LDR to 5 V on the Arduino board
- Connect the +ve, that is, VCC of the buzzer to 5 V
- Connect the -ve, that is, GND of the LDR buzzer and LED to the GND on the Arduino board
- Connect resistors of 270 ohms to the +ve of LED and then connect it to pin 13, and resistor of 10 kilo-ohm to the A0 pin of the LDR
- Connect A0 pin of the LDR to the analog pin A0
- Connect I/O pin of buzzer to the digital pin 12
- Push the code into the Arduino board using the Arduino IDE

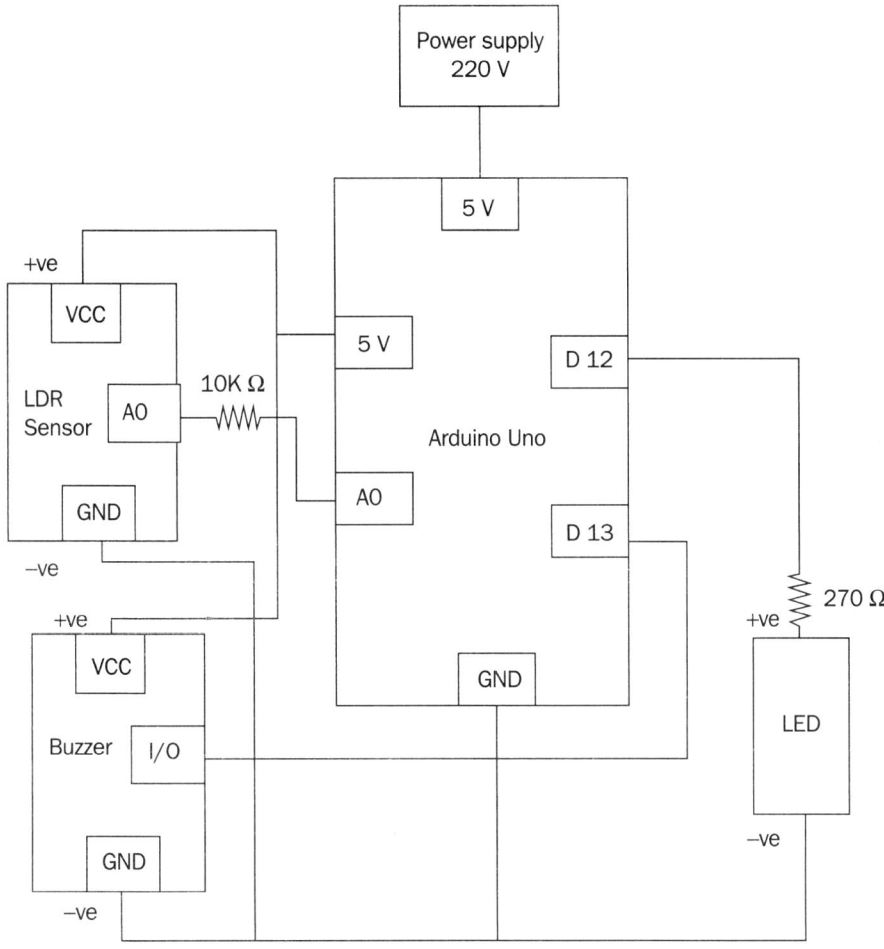

Fig. 5.13 Circuit Diagram for Sensor as Light Dependent Resistor (LDR) and Actuators as LED and Buzzer

5.9.1 PSEUDO-CODE for the Sketch to Write an Embedded Programming Code Using Arduino IDE

- In the function void setup(), we initialize analog pin A0, as the input, pin 12 and 13 as the output
- We read the input A0, and print it on the serial monitor
- If the ldrStatus is greater than 100. LED blinks and the buzzer beeps or the alarm is deactivated and our LED stops blinking

Box 5.1 shows LDR as sensor and buzzer as an actuator.

BOX 5.1: LDR AS SENSOR AND BUZZER AS AN ACTUATOR

LDR configuration with Arduino Uno board

Buzzer configuration with Arduino Uno board

THOUGHT EXERCISES

- Design a sensor and actuating circuit for temperature and humidity sensor.
- Write a code in Python or Embedded C for collecting the information from a temperature and humidity sensor.
- Write a Python code for generating an output for actuating a fan using a relay.

SUMMARY

In this chapter, various kind of sensors and actuators are explored. Initially, the difference between passive and active sensor is introduced. Various environmental sensors and their applications are explained in detail. Medical sensors and their use in IoT applications are also explained. Different actuators such as servo motor, DC motor, linear actuators, and relays are explained along with their application areas.

KEYWORDS

Environmental sensors, medical sensors, linear actuators, servo motor, solenoid, DC motor, relay

REVIEW QUESTIONS

1. What is the difference between passive and active sensors?
2. Write a note on the importance of sensor communication interface.
3. Explain the commonly-used sensor GPS and list its applications.
4. State and explain IoT application of a temperature sensor.
5. Design an IoT application using a humidity sensor.
6. Explain the use of pressure sensor with an example.
7. Design an application using a distance sensor.
8. Write a note on soil moisture sensor and its applications.
9. Explain capacitive touch sensor and its applications.
10. Explain the use of solenoid as an actuator with an example.
11. Write a note on servo motor as an actuator.
12. State some applications of electromechanical actuators.
13. Explain the use of DC motor as an actuator.
14. Write a note on relay as an actuator.
15. Explain the working principle of an RFID sensor and give an example of the same.

REFERENCES

1. Lakowicz, J.R., Geddes, C.D. (2006), In: *Glucose Sensing: Topics in Fluorescence Spectroscopy*. Volume 11, Springer Science and Business Media, Inc., USA.
2. Gault, V., McClenaghan, N. (2009), In: *Understanding Bioanalytical Chemistry. Principles and Applications*, John Wiley & Sons, Ltd, Oxford, UK.
3. McMahon, G. (2007), In: *Analytical Instrumentation: A Guide to Laboratory, Portable and Miniaturized Instruments*, John Wiley & Sons Ltd, West Sussex.
4. Zhang, X., Ju, H., Vang, J. (2008), In: *Electrochemical Sensors, Biosensors and Their Biomedical Applications*, Elsevier Inc., New York.
5. Munden, J., Foley, M. (2007), In: *Diabetes Mellitus: A Guide to Patient Care*, Lippincott Williams & Wilkins, Ambler, Pennsylvania.
6. Porth, C.M. (2011), In: *Essentials of Pathophysiology: Concepts of Altered Health States*, Wolters Kluwer Health, Lippincott Williams & Wilkins, China.
7. http://www.who.int/mediacentre/factsheets/fs312/en/index.html [Last accessed: 30/10/2018]
8. Poretsky, L. (2010), In: *Principles of Diabetes Mellitus*. 2nd Edition. Springer Science and Business Media, LLC, New York, USA.
9. Baura, G. (2012), In: *Medical Device Technologies: A Systems Based Overview Using Engineering Standards*, Elsevier Inc., Oxford, UK.

10. Obtaining Tide Gauge Data. *Permanent Service for Mean Sea Level. PSMSL*. Retrieved 2016-03-07.
11. Other Long Records not in the PSMSL Data Set. *PSMSL*. Retrieved 2015-05-11.
12. Tide gauge history UK National Oceanographic Centre Archived 2015-08-24 at the Wayback Machine.
13. History of tide gauges. *Tide Observation*. Geospatial Information Authority of Japan. Retrieved 2014-04-19.
14. Sclater, N. (2007), In: Mechanisms and Mechanical Devices Source Book, 4th Edition, p. 25, McGraw-Hill, USA.
15. Jafarzadeh, M.,Gans, N., Tadesse, Y. (2018), Control of TCP muscles using Takagi–Sugeno–Kang fuzzy inference system, *Mechatronics* 53: 124–139. doi:10.1016/j.mechatronics.2018.06.007.
16. https://www.electronicwings.com/sensors-modules/gps-receiver-module [Last accessed: 07/08/2020]
17. https://circuitdigest.com/article/relay-working-types-operation-applications [Last accessed: 07/08/2020]
18. https://www.arrow.com/en/research-and-events/articles/how-touch-sensors-work

FURTHER READING

1. https://www.ti.com/lit/wp/snia011/snia011.pdf?lCID=I-CT-TP-resources-955 : Temperature sensor solutions for low-voltage systems [Last Accessed: 05/08/2020]
2. https://www.ti.com/lit/an/sbva048/sbva048.pdf?lCID=I-CT-TP-resources-960 : Low-Power Battery Temperature Monitoring [Last Accessed: 05/08/2020]
3. https://www.st.com/resource/en/application_note/cd00174666-increasing-the-resolution-of-analog-temperature-sensors-stmicroelectronics.pdf : AN2648 Increasing the resolution of analogue temperature sensors [Last Accessed: 05/08/2020]
4. https://pdfserv.maximintegrated.com/en/an/AN4679.pdf?lCID=I-CT-TP-resources-963 : Thermal Management Handbook [Last Accessed: 05/08/2020]
5. https://pdfserv.maximintegrated.com/en/an/AN4699.pdf?lCID=I-CT-TP-resources-964 : Overview of Sensor Signal Paths [Last Accessed: 05/08/2020]
6. https://www.st.com/resource/en/technical_note/dm00208005-hts221-digital-humidity-sensor-reference-design-implementation-stmicroelectronics.pdf: Digital Humidity Sensor: Reference Design Implementation [Last Accessed: 05/08/2020]
7. https://www.st.com/content/ccc/resource/technical/document/technical_note/c1/d1/80/37/c3/ad/4b/56/DM00208005.pdf/files/DM00208005.pdf/jcr:content/translations/en.DM00208005.pdf: HTS221 Digital Humidity Sensor: Reference Design Implementation [Last Accessed: 05/08/2020]
8. https://sensing.honeywell.com/white-paper-do-you-know-when-your-proximity-sensor-is-sick.pdf: Healthy Sensing: Do You Know When Your Proximity Sensor is Sick? [Last Accessed: 05/08/2020]
9. https://www.ti.com/lit/an/snoa926a/snoa926a.pdf?lCID=I-CT-TP-resources-926: Capacitive Sensing: Ins and Outs of Active Shielding (Rev. A) [Last Accessed: 05/08/2020]
10. https://www.ti.com/lit/an/snoa927/snoa927.pdf?ts=1596731989011: FDC1004: Basics of Capacitive Sensing and Applications [Last Accessed: 05/08/2020]
11. https://www.ti.com/lit/an/snoa928a/snoa928a.pdf?lCID=I-CT-TP-resources-928: Capacitive Proximity Sensing Using the FDC1004 (Rev. A) [Last Accessed: 05/08/2020]

12. https://www.ti.com/lit/an/snoa943/snoa943.pdf?ICID=I-CT-TP-resources-929: Power Consumption Analysis for Low Power Capacitive Sensing Applications [Last Accessed: 05/08/2020]
13. https://www.st.com/resource/en/technical_note/dm00127867-a3g4250d-supplementary-data-related-to-the-3-axis-digital-output-gyroscope-stmicroelectronics.pdf: TN1189 A3G4250D: Supplementary Data Related to the three-axis Digital Output Gyroscope [Last Accessed: 05/08/2020]
14. https://www.st.com/content/ccc/resource/technical/document/white_paper/c9/a6/fd/e4/e6/4e/48/60/ois_white_paper.pdf/files/ois_white_paper.pdf/jcr:content/translations/en.ois_white_paper.pdf: Optical Image Stabilization (OIS) White Paper [Last Accessed: 05/08/2020]

Open Hardware in IoT

CHAPTER 6

"You don't need anyone's permission to create something great."
—Massimo Banzi—Cofounder of Arduino

OBJECTIVES
- discuss popular Internet of Things (IoT) platforms such as Arduino, Raspberry Pi, Beaglebone, pcDuino, and CubieBoard
- understand hardware configuration of various microcontroller boards and their parameters
- get started with various boards and software installations
- learn interface hardware peripheral devices and perform experiments

OUTCOMES
- comprehend the popular Internet of Things (IoT) platforms and their hardware configuration
- conceptualize the software compatibility of the popular IoT platforms and the interfacing capabilities of various microcontroller boards with hardware and peripherals
- compare popular boards and select a board for a suitable application
- ability to design and develop prototypes with sensors and actuators

REVISION
In Chapters 3 and 4, the middleware technology hardware for wireless sensor network and low power consumption networking protocols are explored, and in Chapter 5, the topics related to sensors and actuators as input and output hardware for the applications of Internet of Things (IoT) are covered. In this chapter, various open electronics hardware boards and devices are explained which can be used for developing IoT applications.

6.1 INTRODUCTION TO INTERNET OF THINGS (IOT) HARDWARE

In the present technology evolution, three fields are are gaining importance namely electronics, data processing, and cloud computing. Their significance from an IoT perspective are:

Electronics Various innovative sensors are being designed and manufactured for capturing information in many of these areas, and is a major contributor to the development of new innovative products surrounding environment, infrastructures, manufacturing sector, supply chain, automotive, etc. A variety of open source embedded development boards are currently available for prototyping in many of these areas, and is a major contributor to the development of new innovative products.

Data Processing Massive Data processing technologies such as those running on various distributed/cluster computing platforms are resulting in gaining new insights from data analytics on real-time as well as archived data.

Cloud Computing Cloud computing Infrastructures such as SaaS, PaaS, IaaS are providing on demand access to hardware, software tools, storage, networking, etc. IT infrastructure and business solutions can be easily configured in cloud using these systems.

The developments in the above mentioned areas are immensely driving the IoT technology in several dimensions and producing many new scientific and business opportunities. In this chapter, the main hardware components of IoT are elaborated.

6.1.1 IoT Hardware and Technology Stack

IoT hardware is a critical component of a system that can have an impact on the cost, functionality, usability, etc. unless it is managed efficiently. The IoT technology stack consists of both the hardware and software. Fig. 6.1 presents the technology stack for an IoT application.

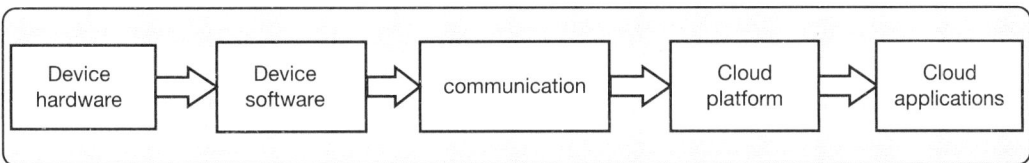

Fig. 6.1 IoT Technology Stack

In this chapter hardware requirements of an IoT application is explored.

6.1.2 IoT Device Hardware Requirements

IoT device framework is explained in four modules as shown in Fig. 6.2.

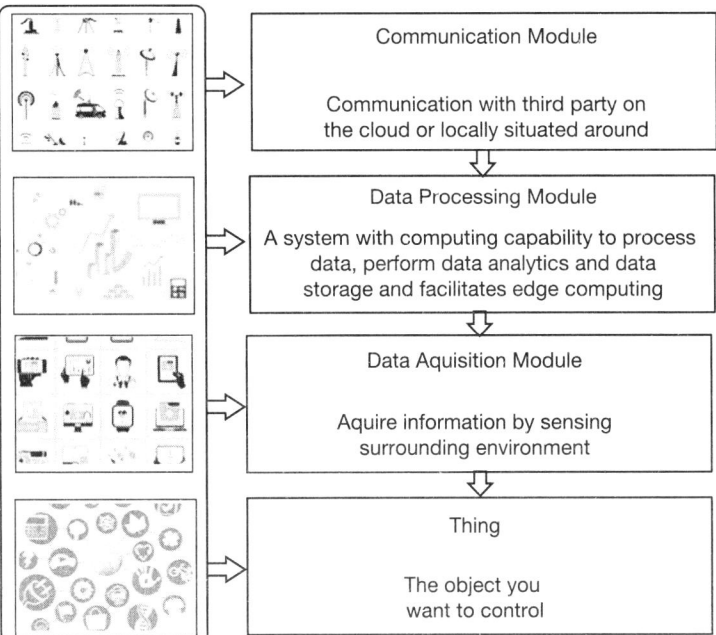

Fig. 6.2 IoT Device Framework

6.1.2.1 Smart Thing Ideation

A smart thing provides some service for controlling some functionality or for monitoring some environmental parameters of an application. Smart IoT device framework constitutes of four modules as shown in Fig. 6.2.

Smart device model functionality is also based on business needs. Sometimes the existing system is modified or sometimes a completely innovative product is required for development, for example smart door lock, autonomous vehicle, etc.

6.1.2.2 Data Acquisition Requirement

While acquiring data from surroundings, necessary hardware is required to sense and acquire the data. Even some additional hardware units such as ADC to convert analog sensor information to digital information.

Major consideration while data collection is right hardware for sensing the physical signal, frequency of generated information from the sensor, information accuracy requirement while collecting it, different sensor requirements specific to the application.

In the data acquisition process, some additional connected hardware are required, such as analog to digital converter (ADC), digital to analog converter (DAC), voltage amplifier for signal boosting, edge hardware for performing preprocessing of the sensor signal before sending the signal to the nearby server or to cloud server.

6.1.2.3 Data Processing Requirements

In data processing stage of IoT framework, end point processing capacity and processed data storage capacity is to be considered while designing and developing the necessary hardware for a specific application. The selection of hardware to fulfill such requirements decides the size, precision, life and cost. The processing power requirement of edge IoT devices for real time application is significantly higher as the number of connected sensors increase. Hence, substantial provision for additional requirement of processing power is needed.

Storage capacity of the end device depends also on off-line time for the IoT device, that is time for which data buffering is needed and frequency of data collection. (volume of the data per unit time).

Many System on Chip (SoC) boards are available such as raspberry Pi, Arduino, Atmel. Choosing the right board is application specific as the processing power and storage capacity of the edge device varies as per the requirements of the application. The network connectivity hardware is supported by SoCs.

6.1.2.4 Communications Requirements

Data transmission capacity is best utilized when interleaving of the frames from different data packets is done. As the data is received from various sensors, by multiplexing the data frames the network bandwidth use can be optimized.

Communication devices and cloud platforms useful for IoT applications are explored in chapter 11.

6.2 PROTOTYPING BOARDS FOR IOT

System on Chip is a mini computer without display monitor and keyboard. It has all functionalities of a CPU such as RAM, input /output ports, limited storage and processing capacity. It also has hardware devices such as ADC and DAC. SoC integrates a programmable micro-controller unit MCU where the application specific program software (firmware) is embedded in a permanent memory space known as SDRAM. Many commercial manufacturers are providing SoCs, for example Raspberry Pi, Beaglebone, Arduino etc.

Arduino board supports programming language known as Embedded C while Raspberry Pi, Beaglebone SoCs support popular programming languages such as Python and Java.

6.2.1 Requirement for Custom Silicon (Customized on Board Chip) in IoT

The semiconductor industry has evolved from emerging technology to enabling technologies in the last few decades. Semiconductor evolution plays major role in the growth of IoT. Devices are usually designed around standard computing components. However, the following factors are driving the change for custom silicon for IoT:

- Ultra-low power
- Increased computing power for better edge analytics
- Hardware level product differentiation
- Customized security features
- Lower BoM (bill of material cost for reducing customized silicon chip cost)

Open-silicon is one of the pioneers and its focus is on custom silicon for IoT applications.

6.2.2 SoC Classification based on Functionality

IoT SoCs are broadly classified in the following categories:

- Edge SoCs
- Gateway SoCs
- Cloud side SoCs

Figure 6.3 represents SoCs at different levels for an IoT application, from endpoint to cloud.

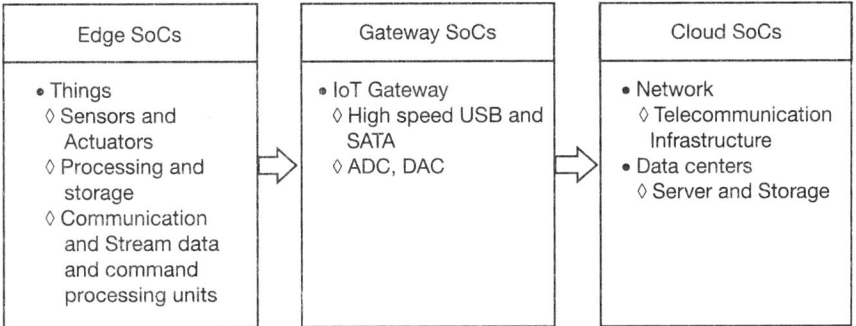

Fig. 6.3 Different Types of SoCs for IoT Applications

6.2.2.1 IoT Edge SoCs

Edge SoCs sense and/or actuate and mainly belong to microcontroller class (CPU based). It has analog and digital interfaces to connect to sensors and actuators and wired or wireless connectivity.

An edge device is an endpoint device, which is a remotely manageable secured device with the ability to manage the following:

- Sensors and actuators
- Local processing of real-time streaming data and local and /or cloud-based
- Send and receive commands for communication with the devices

6.2.2.2 Gateway SoCs

These are built using application class CPUs and wired or wireless connectivity on both sides. These SoCs have high-speed interfaces such as USB and sufficient computing power given by CPUs and DSPs (Digital Signal Processing hardware units such as ADC, DAC) as well as hardware engines.

6.2.2.3 Cloud SoCs

Traditional Application Specific Integrated Circuits (ASICs) are used for cloud SoCs in many networking applications. Cloud side SoCs are LTE (Long-Term Evolution) base stations, satellite modems, networking switches etc.

6.2.2.4 Single-Board Computer (SBC)

A computer built on a single circuit board with a microprocessor(s), memory, input/output (I/O), and other features required for a complete functional computer is known as Single-Board Computer (SBC). Single-board computers are generally without peripheral functions. The first single-board computer was developed in 1976 using Intel C8080A. Other early single-board computers are KIM-1.

Currently, Raspberry Pi and Onion Omega are two most popular SBC families. The Raspberry Pi SBC was developed by the Raspberry Pi Foundation for promoting the basic level computer science in the schools and also in developing countries. Many generations of Raspberry Pi are available. These models have a Broadcom SoC and a CPU compatible with ARM and also have a graphics processing unit (GPU).

The Omega SBC is developed by a start-up company called Onion. This system combines the power efficiency and tiny form factor of Arduino and flexibility of Raspberry Pi. The D-Link routers are powered by SBC Onion Omega.

6.2.3 Arduino Boards

Arduino is a popular open-source electronics platform with hardware and software. Arduino boards support functionalities such as reading input from sensors, or an electronic message, turning such inputs into outputs by processing and publishing locally or online. To perform a specific task, the Arduino programming language and Arduino software (IDE) are used to write instructions to the microcontroller on the board. This open source platform is the brain of thousands of projects over the years, and useful to make things smart ranging from everyday objects to complex scientific instruments.

Arduino is an easy tool for prototyping, which is useful for students from various engineering and non-engineering disciplines. Arduino boards are completely open-source, and can be easily adapted for a particular IoT application. The software supporting the Arduino boards is also open source.

Arduino software is user friendly for beginners and also flexible for advanced users. This software is compatible with different operating systems (OS) such as Mac, Windows, and Linux. Arduino simplifies working with microcontrollers as compared to many other competing platforms.
There are different kinds of Arduino boards:

- Arduino Uno (R3)
- Arduino Mega (R3)
- Arduino Leonardo

More details about these and other Arduino boards are at reference [27].
Advantages of Arduino platform:

- Low cost
- Open-source as well as extensible software and hardware
- Simple and easy-to-use programming environment
- Compatibility with many OS

Figure 6.4 shows the popular Arduino Uno board used for IoT applications and by other DIY products.

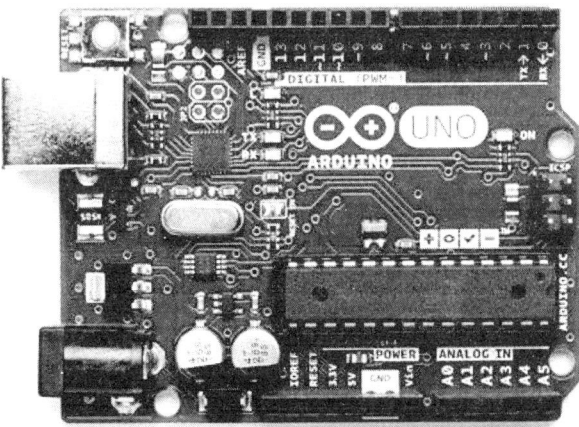

Fig. 6.4 Arduino Uno Board

6.2.3.1 Arduino Board Pin Layout

As shown in Fig. 6.5, power supply can be given to Arduino Uno either by an external source (at X1) or by a USB connection. External power source can be through AC to DC adapter and the Arduino board operates on an external supply of 6 –20 V. To supply 5 V, the board power supply should not be less than 7 V. To avoid overheating, voltage-regulator power supply of more than 12 V is avoided. Hence, the recommended voltage range is 7 to –12 V.

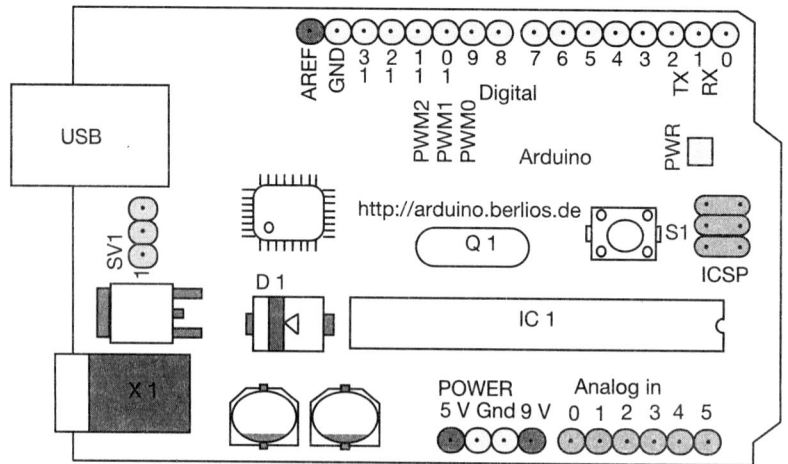

Fig. 6.5 Arduino Board Pin Layout [19]

The power pins are explained as follows:

VIN It represents the input voltage to the Arduino board when the power is supplied from the external source. Other way to supply the power to the Arduino board is using USB connection or any other regulated power supply. The power supply is given through this pin. If the voltage is supplied through power jack then voltage access is through this pin.

5 V The Arduino microcontroller on its board is powered by regulated power supply. This power supply is either given through the VIN pin on the board or by on-board regulator or it is supplied using USB or any other regulated supply.

3V3 3.3 V supply is generated by the on-board voltage regulator with maximum current limit of 50 mA.

GND These are Ground pins.

Memory 32 KB of flash memory is provided in the ATMega328 microcontroller chip for storing the code. 0.5 KB is used for bootloader. The board also has 2 KB of SRAM and 1 KB of EEPROM.

Input output pins Fourteen digital pins on the Arduino Uno board can be used as an I/O using different functions such as pinMode(), digitalWrite(), and digitalRead(). All these pins need 5 V power supply. The maximum current provided or received by each pin is 40 mA.

Some pins that have specialized functions are listed below:

Serial 0 (RX) for receiving and 1 (TX) for transmitting

TTL Series Data These pins are connected to the corresponding pins of ATmega8U2 USB to TTL serial chip.

External interrupts Pin numbers 2 and 3 can be configured to trigger an interrupt on some event such as low value, a rising or falling edge, and change in a value. The function *attachInterrupt()* can be used for this purpose.

PWM   Pins 3, 5, 6, 9, 10, and 11 provide 8-bit PWM output with the *analogWrite()* function.

SPI   Pin numbers 10 (SS), 12 (MISO), 12 (MISO), and 13 (SCK). These pins are used for Serial Port Interface (SPI) communications, which are facilitated by the microcontroller hardware.

LED   The in-built LED is connected to digital pin 13. When the pin is HIGH value the LED is on and for LOW value it is off.

I2C   4(SDA) and 5 (SCL). Support I2C (TWI) communication using the wired library [20].

Reset   To reset the microcontroller.

Arduino Uno board has six analog inputs, each of which has 10-bit resolution which means it can take values between 0 and 1023. The value measured will ground means 0–5 V.

6.2.3.2 Arduino Communication

Arduino board has many facilities to communicate with other Arduino boards or computers or other microcontrollers. The serial communication of ATmega328 microcontroller chip is with UART TTL (5 V), with pins 0 (RX) and 1 (TX).

An ATmega8U2 on board channels is for serial communication over USB and works as a virtual communication port to software on the computer. Standard USB COM drivers are used by 8U2 firmware and no external driver is needed. Windows systems require *.inf file for installation of drivers for external devices.

6.2.3.3 Programming

The Arduino Uno can be programmed using the Arduino software. To access the software, select "Arduino Uno w/ATmega328" from the Tools > "Board menu" (with the microcontroller on the board) [21].

The bootloader is preburned on the chip ATmega328 on the Arduino. Hence, new code can be uploaded to the microcontroller chip without the use of external hardware programmer. Even new code can be uploaded using In-Circuit Serial Programming (ICSP) header.

6.2.3.4 Automatic Software Reset

The Arduino software allows uploading of the code just by pressing the upload button in the Arduino environment. A sketch may run on the board to receive one-time configuration or other data when it first starts. It must be taken to ensure that the software with which it communicates waits for a second after opening the connection and before sending the data.

To disable the auto-reset, the UNO contains a trace that can be cut. The pads on either side of the trace can be soldered together to re-enable it. It is labelled as "RESET-EN." An example sketch in embedded programming is in Box 6.1 to represent how to access A5 analog pin on Arduino Uno board to sense temperature sensor output.

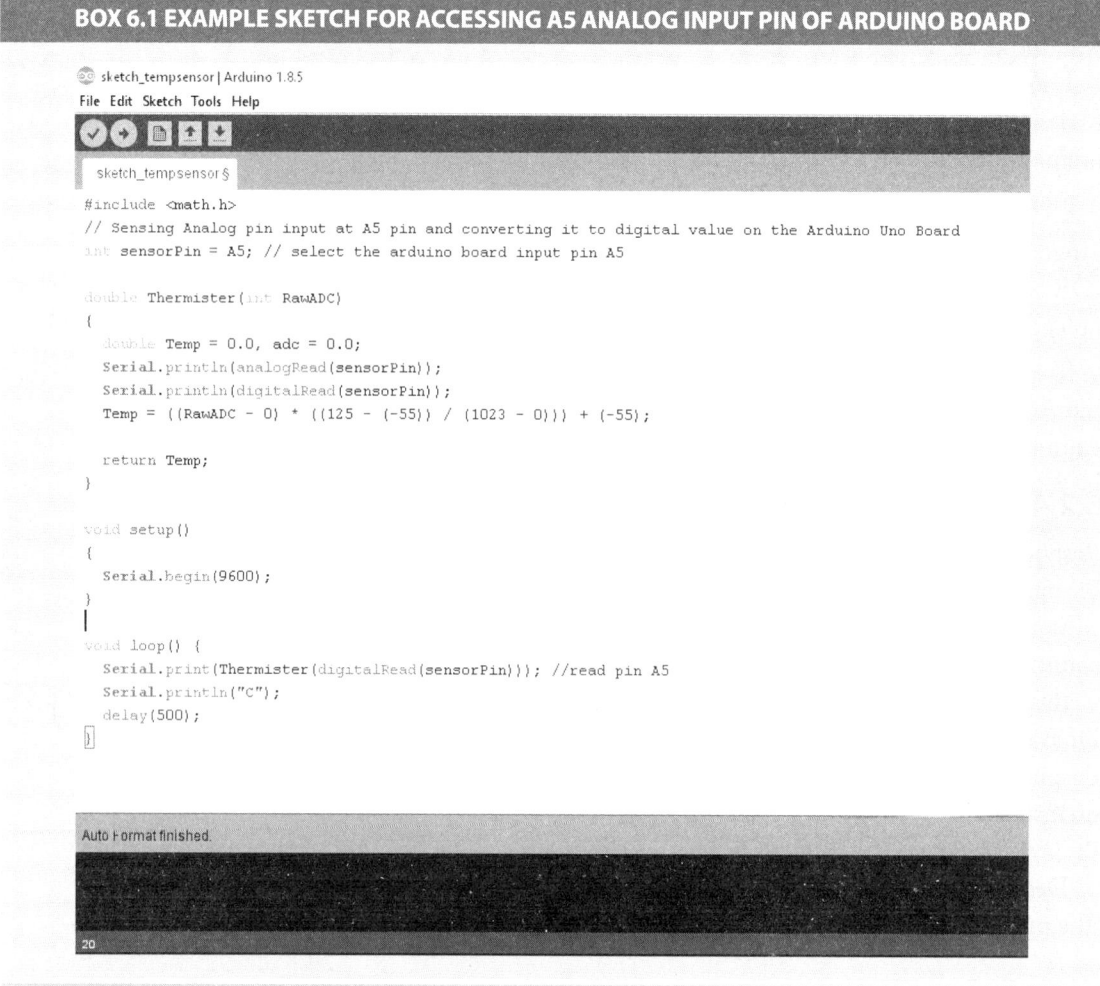

6.2.3.5 Arduino Board Other Parameters

USB overcurrent protection The computer's USB ports are protected from short and overcurrent by the resettable poly-fuse of Arduino Uno.

Physical characteristics The UNO PCB is of size 2.7-inch length and 2.1-inch width.

6.2.3.6 Functionality of Arduino

The environment can be sensed by Arduino using various sensors. These sensor inputs are used to control the output devices such as lights, motors, and other actuators. The microcontroller chip is programmed using the Arduino development environment using one of the programming languages supported by Arduino board microcontroller. The Arduino official website is useful for the latest instructions [22]. From this site Arduino IDE can be downloaded and unzipped. The IDE is installed on PC and then you can plug the Arduino board to PC using USB cable.

6.2.3.7 Getting Started with Arduino

Arduino is an open-source hardware and software, platform for making interactive projects. Arduino technology is used to teach and learn the innovative multidisciplinary studies. It is a very good platform to design and develop applications in engineering, IoT, Robotics, and art fields. Arduino technology is useful to develop building skills and problem-solving skills.

6.2.3.7.1 Software (IDE) setup on Arduino board Two options are available to upload the programming Arduino software (IDE). If you have a reliable Internet connection, then even online IDE can be used (Arduino web editor). The Arduino software allows you to write the programs and upload them to the board. If you are working offline, then a latest version of desktop IDE is needed.

There are many retired Arduino boards listed and instructions for retired boards are available on the Arduino website. The instructions for different example shields are on the links provided on the Arduino official website [17].

6.2.4 Raspberry Pi

Raspberry Pi foundation developed first two models of Raspberry Pi. After the first two models of Pi, model B and subsequently several models such as B+, Zero, etc. released. The foundation is an educational charity to promote teaching of the basic computer science in schools and in developing countries.

Raspbian is the official OS of the foundation. The OS can be installed with NOOBS (New Out Of Box software for easy OS installation manager for Raspberry Pi) or by downloading the image Raspbian. The installation guide is available on the Raspberry Pi official website [23]. Raspbian comes preinstalled with plenty of software for education and general use. It supports Python, Scratch, sonic Pi, Java, Mathematica, etc.

Desktop image for Raspbian OS is contained in a ZIP archive and is of a size more than 4 GB. The pin layout for raspberry Pi board is shown in Fig. 6.6.

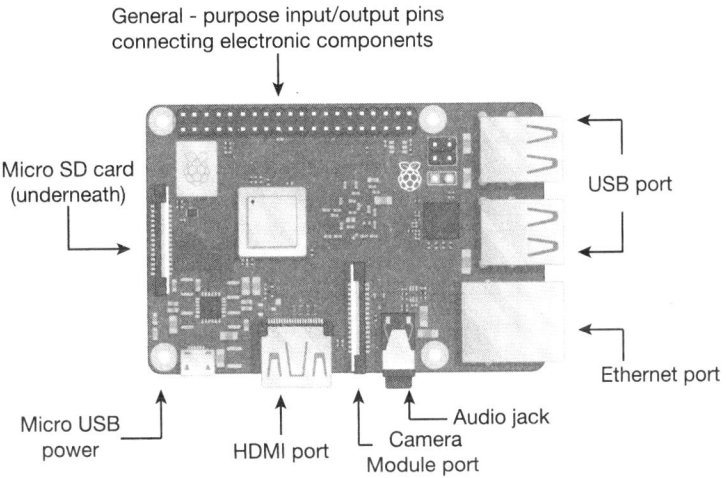

Fig. 6.6 Pin Layout for Raspberry Pi Board

(Source: Copyright © the Raspberry Pi Foundation)

The latest model of Raspberry Pi board

Raspberry Pi 4 Model B+ Model is using the Broadcom chip BCM2711 and a large memory variant up to 16 GB. This chip architecture also has quad-core design. But it has more powerful ARM A72 core for upgrading SoCs. This architecture is capable of addressing more memory and has attached Ethernet controller. Default operating system image is a 32-bit LPAE kernel. Many other options are available for OS such as gentoo-on-rpi-64bit Gentoo. Even the 64 bit beta version OS is released. Both 32 and 64 bit OS images are called as Raspberry Pi OS. This model is 50% faster than Raspberry Pi 3B+ model. Its new 32 bit unit, VideoCore runs at 500 Mhz as additional memory unit. The VideoCore is 32-bit, and has a new Memory Management Unit, which means it can access more memory than previous versions.

6.2.4.1 Set up Procedure for Raspberry Pi

Essential requirements for the setup of Raspberry Pi board are at reference [27]:

SD card

- 8 GB Class 4 SD card (ideally with NOOBS preinstalled)

Connectivity cables and display

- Any DDMI or DVI monitor and any TV can be used as a display device for Raspberry Pi.
- HDMI input will give best result but even other connections are available for compatibility with the older versions.

Keyboard and mouse

- Any standard USB keyboard and mouse
- With wireless pairing, wireless mouse and keyboard can be used
- Keyboard layout and configuration details are available at link raspi-config[32]

Power supply

- USB micro power supply (used for most standard mobile phone chargers)
- A good-quality power supply with current specification at least 2 A at 5 V for 3B model or 700 mA at 5 V for earlier models (Low current power supply works for basic usage but are likely to cause Pi to reboot if too much power is drawn)

Optional (network) cable (model B, B+, 2, 3 only)

- Local network can be connected to Raspberry Pi using Ethernet cable.
- USB wireless dongle can be used to connect Pi to wireless network, which needs configuration.
- Audio lead
    o If HDMI cable is not there, then audio lead is needed to produce sound
    o Audio can be played through speakers and headphones with standard jack of 3.5 mm
    o With HDMI cable, audio can be played by connecting to monitor with speakers. If any other speakers are to be used to play, the audio configuration is required.

Troubleshooting   For any setup issues, Raspberry Pi forum can be used to post the query with proper details of the problem.

Raspberry Pi OS image installation steps are available on Raspberry Pi official website at [23].

For more advanced steps, use the system-specific guide for different OS such as Linux, Mac OS, and MS Windows.

Some examples for getting started with software Raspbian are available at [29] for the functionalities as listed below:

- Scratch: Programming tool to create animation
- Python: A general purpose programming language
- Sonic Pi: For writing code to play music with Pi
- Terminal: Linux terminal for using command prompt
- GPIO: General purpose I/O pins for interaction with the surrounding environment
- Minecraft: Programming interface using Python code to access the world around through GPIO
- Python games: Some readymade Python games to play on Raspberry Pi
- WordPress: A content management and blogging system
- Mathemaica: Industry leading computational platform
- Camera module: Raspberry Pi camera
- Webcam: Use of any standard USB webcam
- Codi: Media center software for Raspberry Pi
- Playing audio
- Playing video
- Demo programs: To explore Pi capabilities

Basic guide for Raspberry Pi configuration is available at [28] and they are useful for configuration of Raspberry Pi. Some of the configuration tasks are mentioned in the Box 6.2. If you want your Raspberry Pi to access the internet via a proxy server of a workplace, then you will need to configure your Pi to use the server before you can get online.

For configuring proxy server, you need:

- The IP address or hostname and port of your proxy server
- A username and password for your proxy (if required)

BOX 6.2 RASPBERRY PI SOFTWARE CONFIGURATION TOOLS (RASPI-CONFIG)
1. Change user password for the current user
2. Configure network settings
3. Boot Configure options for start-up
4. Localization options to set up language and regional settings to match your location
5. Interfacing options for configuration of connections to peripherals
6. Overclock option for configuration of overclocking for your Pi
7. Advanced options to configure advanced settings
8. Updation of this tool to the latest version is needed frequently
9. About raspi-config tool more information is available at source mentioned at link below

(Source: Copyright © the Raspberry Pi Foundation)

6.2.5 BeagleBone

Beagle family offers tiny and affordable open-source boards called Beagels with high performance and low-power. Beagels support Android, Ubuntu, and other Linux flavours with flexible peripheral interfaces and a proven ecosystem of "Cape," plug in boards.

6.2.5.1 BeagleBone Black

BeagleBone Black is an open hardware with Linux OS and boots the OS in few seconds. Its microcontroller chip is with 1 GHz AM335x ARM Cortex-A8 processor (refer to Fig. 6.7).

Fig. 6.7 BeagleBone Black Board [24]

6.2.5.2 BeagleBone Board Features

These boards are open software tiny computers. Beagle supports much functionality through small software packages just like a mini-computer. These boards are very user friendly for any DIY project or developing any IoT product.

This board can be connected to USB client for power and communication, USB host, HDMI, Ethernet, and 2 × 46 pin headers. It has software compatibility Ubuntu, Debian, Cloud 9 IDE on node.js, Android, and many other software. BeagleBone Black comes with in-built wireless networking capability with on-board 802.11 b/g/n 2.4 GHz Wi-Fi and Bluetooth.

Pocket BeagleBone is an ultra-tiny yet a complete Linux enabled with scalability, open-source computer. It is low cost with slick design and an ideal development board for DIY projects. You can get its more information on the website https://beagleboard.org/pocket.

6.2.6 pcDuino

pcDuino as shown in Fig 6.8 is a mini PC platform. It runs an OS such as Ubuntu Linux. Any HDMI-enabled TV or monitor screen can be connected to it as an output device. This platform can easily run an OS such as a full-blown OS for a PC. It can also run Android 4.0 ICS.

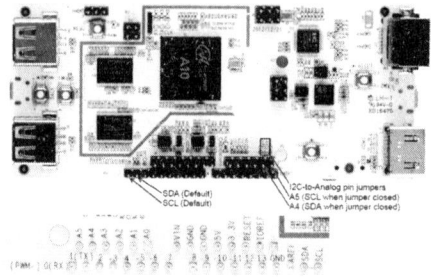

Fig. 6.8 pcDuino Board Source: SparkFun Electronics and Juan Peña

(Source: SparkFun Electronics and Juan Peña)

6.2.6.1 Hardware and Software for pcDuino

Hardware specification Components of pcDuino are CPU All Winner A10 SoC, 1 GHz ARM Cortex A8, GPU OpenGL ES2.0, OpenVG 1.1 Mali 400 core DRAM 1GB, Onboard Storage 2 GB Flash, Micro-SD card slot for up to 32 GB, Video Output HDMI, OS Linux3.0 + Ubuntu12.04, Android ICS 4.0, Extension Interface Arduino Headers, Network interface USB Wi-Fi extension (not included), Ethernet 10/100 Mbps, and accessories required are power adaptor with Micro USB port, cable of Micro USB with 2 A current carrying capacity.

The pcDuino boards have very well-exposed hardware peripherals. The tutorial "Getting started with pcDuino" helps to know basics about pcDuino [26]. A fully functional Linux OS makes pcDuino a microcomputer. SPI, a serial peripheral interface, with synchronous clock for communication between chips is at board level. It requires minimum four wires as clock, master-in-slave-out data, master-out-slave-in data, and slave chip select. Each additional chip needs one extra chip select line. IIC or I²C (interintegrated circuit) TWI (two-wire-interface), SMBus, is used for communication with multiple devices. Serial communication is an asynchronous data interface with minimum two wires (data transmit and data receive). Sometimes, additional signals are added to indicate whether the device is available for sending or receiving the data.

The pcDuino has 18 GPIO pins. The GPIO pins can be accessed easily by opening the file associated with the pin you wish to access and can read and write the file. These files are located at the location: /sys/devices/virtual/misc/gpio/pin/. Each pin has its own file out of the 20 files available and 18 of them are mapped to GPIOs. Some pins can be used for multiple purposes such as serial, SPI, input, and output. "0," "1," and "8" makes the pin "INPUT," "OUTPUT," and "INPUT with pull-up register," respectively. The logic on these pins is 3.3 V and use of 5V devices may cause damage to the pcDuino board. The output current capacity is not as high as Arduino boards though it is sufficient to drive a small output actuator such as LED.

Unlike Raspberry Pi boards, pcDuino has some analog I/O pins. Analog I/O is accomplished using six pins labelled A0–A5 on Arduino-ish headers. The high output of all the pins is limited to maximum 3.3 V. A0 and A1 are 6-bit inputs returning a value between 0 and 63 with a voltage range 0–2 V. A2–A5 are 12-bit inputs operating in the range 0–3.3 V. Using pulse width modulation analog output of pcDuino is accomplished in the Arduino-ish header, 6 PWM enabled pins are given, numbered 3, 5, 6, 9, 10, and 11, same pins like on Arduino boards. Pin numbers 5 and 6 are 520 Hz 8-bit PWM while other pins are having range 0–20 at 5 Hz. The pin configuration details are at the link [30] GPIO read and write example in C++ programming language is at [31].

Serial communications Several built-in serial ports are there on pcDuino board. The A10 processor on the pcDuino board has eight serial ports. Two ports map to the Linux device: /dev/ttyS0 as debugging port and /dev/ttyS1 as the UART, a pinned out on the Arduino-ish header. The mode registers for each pin control the functionality of that pin. For serial I/O for pins 0 and 1, you may need to write "3" to the mode files.

I2C communications There are several I2C bus devices but easily available one is at location /dev/i2c-2. The I2C bus speed is fixed with clock 200 kHz, hence some devices may not work on the I2C bus of pcDuino. Users cannot change the bus speed as it is compiled with driver software. A set of tools allows to work with I2C bus without writing the code. These tools can be installed at the command prompt: >>COPY CODEsudo apt-get installs i2c-tools.

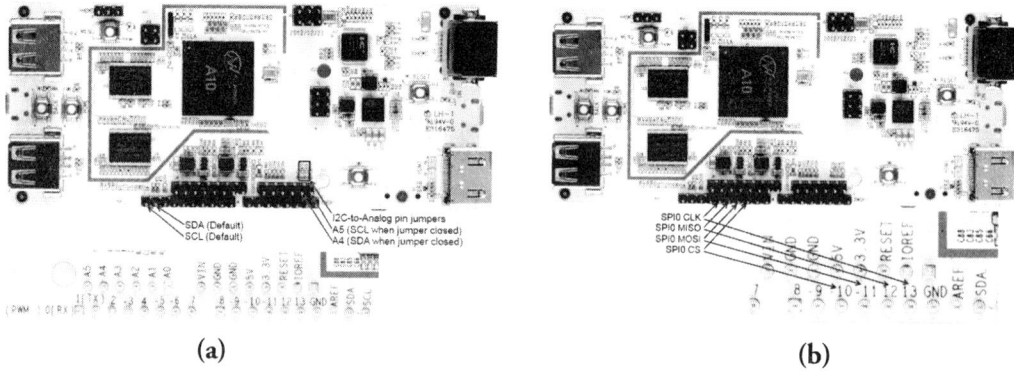

Fig. 6.9 pcDuino (a) I2C Pin to Analog Pin Jumper Layout and (b) SPI Pin Layout

(Source: SparkFun Electronics and Juan Peña)

SPI communications By using pcDuino headers, two different SPI buses are used. At a time, only one device is supported on the bus. SPI peripheral SPI0 can be accessed with the Arduino compatible headers using four pins MOSI, MISO, SCK, and CS from the processor to provide hardware support for SPI communications.

6.2.7 CubieBoard Open-Source Hardware

Cubieboard is a single-board computer made in Zhuai, Guangdong, China. It can run Android 4 ICS, Ubuntu 12.04 desktop, Fedora 19 ARM Remix desktop, Armbian, Arch Linux ARM, Debian-based Cubian distribution, or OpenBSD. It uses ALLWinner A10 SoC and is compatible with media PCs and chip tablets. It can run Apache Hadoop computer clustering Lubuntu Linux distribution. The little motherboard uses AllWinner A10 SoC capabilities.

CubieBoard2 CubieBoard2 is released by CubieTech, few months after the release of CubieBoard1. In 2013, the board is upgraded with 2 ARM Cortex-A7 MPCore CPUs. This board also has dual core Mali400 GPU.

CubieTruck (CubieBoard3) The third version is with a larger PCB layout. The Network Interface Card (NIC) RTL8211E achieves a transfer sending rate up to 630–638 Mbit/s (Idle for 5–10%) and receiving rate 850–860 Mbit/s (0–2% Idle). 3.5-inch HDD add-on package can be used to power CubieBoard and to supply necessary 12 V to 3.5-inch HDD. Even LiPo batteries are used as another option to power the CubieTruck.

CubieBoard3/CubieTruck is suitable to make real products. CubieTruck is the third board of Cubieteam. So also named as Cubieboard3. It is with AllWinner A20 main chip but having enhanced features such as 2 GB RAM, on board VGA display interface, on board WiFi, and Bluetooth. It supports Li battery and RTC, SPDIF audio interface.

6.3 CELLULAR IOT HARDWARE

In this section, the cellular IoT devices discussed are Adafruit Feather 32u4 Fona, GOBLIN 2, LinkIt ONE, Hologram Dash, and Arduino GPRS Shield.

6.3.1 Cellular IoT Hardware

Ubiquitous cellular networks are expanding day by day. Leading IoT providers Twilio, Hologram, and Particle have allowed to go beyond the local area network for getting affordable IoT applications. Following are some top cellular enabled hardware devices:

Adafruit Feather 32u4 FONA The all-in-one Adafruit Feather 32u4 FONA is Arduino compatible as well as is a cellular board capable to support audio, SMS, data. The Feather has a Lipo battery that can be used in mobility and micro USB port for powering while stationary. As the name suggests, the feathers are flexible, lightweight, and portable. The GSM module of this board is trusted and tested FONA module.

Particle Electron Full stack of IoT device platform including the device, connectivity hardware, cellular products, SIMs, and cloud is called a particle. Particle Electron is a device solution that integrates hardware, network, and cloud using a global SIM data plan, which has worldwide coverage. The Electron complies with any cellular standard and is certified by FCC/PTCRB/CE/IC.

Hologram Dash Hologram.io It is a cellular connection platform. This platform lets you interact with devices and can easily do routing of incoming and outgoing messages with a secure API.

Hologram also offers the 'Hollogram Dash', a cellular board with Arduino IDE compatible and pre-certified for secure end use. It is also equipped with a networking firmware OTA (over the air) code updates.

Arduino GPRS Shield For cellular IoT application, you need to connect Arduino to the Internet using the GPRS wireless network. This shield is compatible with all the Arduino boards, which have the same pinout and form factor as that of the standard Arduino board. By plugging the GPRS module onto the Arduino board and plug in a SIM card from a service provider that offers GPRS service, the IoT application will be ready to connect to Internet. The GPRS shield acts as human machine interface.

The GPRS shield uses UART and with simple AT commands, the shield is configured and controlled. The IoT application can make or receive calls using the onboard audio or microphone jack. The application can even send or receive SMS messages. The GPRS Shield also has 12 GPIOs, 2 PWMS, and 1 ADC.

Linkit ONE Design and prototype of IoT devices are enabled by Linkit One development platform. It uses hardware and API similar to Arduino boards. Linkit One development kit includes a development board, a WiFi and Bluetooth antenna, and a GSM antenna and a GPS antenna. These modules are powered by Li-battery. This board has all-in-one connectivity.

GOBLIN 2 The GOBLIN 2 are autonomous IoT boards with a module to control the charge of Li-Po battery of 3.7–4.2 V. This board is compatible with Arduino and ATMEL Studio. It has simple connectivity and versatile setup for remote communication.

Important guidelines for getting started with cellular IoT devices is available at the websites in references [34-39].

6.4 INDUSTRIAL MICROCONTROLLER (PLC AND RTU)

Robust and rugged digital computers are required in the applications such as robotic devices, assembly lines, and for any process where high reliability, process fault diagnosis, and easy programming are needed.

6.4.1 Programmable Logic Controller (PLC) and Remote Terminal Unit (RTU)

A gigantic microcontroller is used as a Programmable Logic Controller (PLC) in the last few decades. It does the same thing as a microcontroller can do with higher speed, better performance, and higher reliability.

Many functions of RTUs and PLCs are similar in terms of usage. RTUs are better options for wide area applications while PLCs are best options suited for local area network. Various PLC and RTU units used in last two decades are shown in Fig. 6.10.

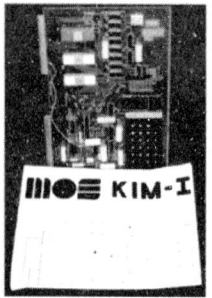

Fig. 6.10 Programmable Logic Controller (PLC) and Remote Terminal Unit (RTU)

6.5 VARIOUS OTHER HARDWARE

IoT hardware includes many devices such as ADC, PWM, PDM, amplifiers, and filters as peripheral devices I/O may not be suitable as a control output or input without conditioning.

6.5.1 Hardware to Convert Continuous Signal to Digital Signal

Hardware ADC is an analog-to-digital converter useful for converting analog voltage received as an input on a pin to a digital number. This digital number is useful for writing a programming logic to perform some function.

The ratiometric value is reported by ADC in a given normalized range. ADC is dependent on the system voltage. Generally, 10-bit ADC is used by IoT Arduino boards.

Pulse-width modulation (PWM) or pulse-duration modulation (PDM) is a way to convert digital signal to analog signal. Modulation encodes the digital information to a pulsing signal.

6.5.2 Hardware for Signal Conditioning, Scaling, and Interpretation

Signal conditioning includes amplification, filtering, converting, range matching, isolation, etc.
Amplifying Amplifying increases the resolution of a signal and its signal-to-noise ratio.
Filtering It is a common signal conditioning function for bandpass limiting the given signal to preserve only desired frequency range of the signal.
Excitation External power is needed for an active sensor. The stability and precision of excitation signal is important.

6.6 COMPARISON OF DIFFERENT HARDWARE PLATFORMS

Various popular hardware microcontroller boards such as Arduino Uno, Raspberry Pi, BeagleBone Black, pcDuino, and CubieBoard are compared for several hardware and software parameters in Tables 6.1 and 6.2.

Table 6.1 Comparison of IoT Platforms: Size, Weight, CPU, Memory, and Power

IoT platform name	Size (mm)	Weight (g)	Processor	RAM and FLASH	Power	LAN (Mbit)	WiFi Module
Arduino (Uno) B Model	75 × 53 × 15	~30	ATMEGA328,	RAM: 2 KB FLASH 32 KB EEPROM 1 KB	7–12 V /USB	–	–
Raspberry Pi R3	85.6 × 53.98 × 17	45	ARM BCM2835	RAM: 256–512 MB SDRAM FLASH: SD card	5 V/ USB	10/100	–
Beagle-Bone Black Rev A5	86.3 × 53.3	39.68	AM335x 1GHz ARM® CortexA8	RAM: 512 MB DDR3 FLASH:	5 V	10/100	–
pcDuino3	121 × 65		CPU:1GHz ARM Cortex A8 GPU: OpenGL ES2.0, OpenVG 1.1 Mali 400 core	RAM: 1 GB On Board FLASH: 2 GB	5 V	10/100	b/g/n (RTL8188)
Cubie-Board3	86.4 × 53.3	40	CPU: ARM Cortex-A7 GPU;	RAM; 1 GB FLASH: 8 GB	5V	GbE	a/b/g/n (BCM4329)

Table 6.2 Comparison of IoT Platforms: Expansion Connectors, Operating System, and Programming Languages

IoT platform name	Analog inputs	Digital I/O pins	Min power	Clock speed	USB ports	Board operating system	Programming language supported
Arduino (Uno)	6	14	42 mA 0.3 W	16 MHz	1	–	Arduino
Raspberry Pi	0	14	700 mA 3.5 W	700 MHz	1–2	Raspbian, Ubuntu, Android, ArchLinux, FreeBSD, Fedora, RISC OS	C, C++, Java, Python
BeagleBone Black	6	14	170 mA 0.85 W	700 MHz	1	Linux Angstrom, Android	Arduino,
pcDuino		14		1 GHz	1–2	Ubuntu Linux, Android	C, C++, Python

HANDS-ON EXERCISES

1. Design and develop a circuit using Arduino Uno board to sense LDR sensor using analog pin input and display the output by writing a sketch using embedded programming using Arduino IDE.
2. Install Raspbian OS on Raspberry Pi board using NOOBS and configure WiFi connectivity.
3. Write a Python program using Raspberry Pi IDE to read input from a digital pin and send it to a remote system using WiFi connectivity.

BEST PRACTICES

- For the beginners, Arduino boards are recommended as tutorials, sample projects are available on the website https://www.arduino.cc/. This board is simplest to interface to external hardware and a wide variety of sensors and actuators.
- For application where minimum board size is needed, Arduino board is recommended as it is a very small, inexpensive, and embedded system on a chip microprocessor of Atmel.
- For applications using the Internet, Raspberry Pi or BeagleBone is recommended. Both the devices are Linux mini computers.
- For applications that use external sensor interface, Arduino is recommended.
- For battery-powered applications, Arduino is recommended as Arduino works on uses least-power consumption. But Arduino cannot work with wide range of input voltages and in terms of computer power per watt BeagleBone performance is much better.
- For applications that use Graphical User Interface (GUI), Raspberry Pi is recommended. Raspberry Pi is an ideal choice when a low-cost web-browsing IoT smart object is to be prepared. It is a small and affordable computer that you can use to learn programming.
- The pcDuino board is similar to the Raspberry Pi board. It has all the features of Raspberry Pi and also some enhanced features such as 2 GB of flash memory and more storage capacity, which makes this board little expensive than Raspberry Pi.
- PcDuino, Beaglebone Black, and CubieBoard have expansion connectors equipped with GPIO and other devices. When power affordability is a major concern, then Cubieboard can be a good choice.

SUMMARY

The Arduino platform is flexible and has great ability for interfacing with hardware peripheral devices. This is usually a better choice for performing mini projects and experiments with best price/performance ratio.

Raspberry Pi used when the applications demand higher computing power and GUI interface. It is a popular board with small computer capability to learn programming and design and develop projects slightly complex IoT applications.

The BeagleBone is a great combination to provide best of Arduino interfacing flexibility and full Linux environment as Raspberry Pi.

pcDuino is a mini PC platform that combines the benefit of an ARM-based mini PC and Arduino ecosystem. Hence, pcDuino is a bridging platform powered with open software Linux and open hardware.

Various other platforms are also available for developing IoT applications such as Cubieboard, Particle Photon, Intel Edison, and Tessel. The selection of the board based on the desired application to be developed is a major design decision to make the product with optimum functionality and for making it cost effective.

KEY TERMS

IoT Platforms, Prototyping boards, microcontroller, System on Chip (SoC), Arduino, Raspberry Pi, Beaglebone, pCDuino, Cubieboard.

FURTHER READING

1. Arduino Board. [ONLINE]. Available at: http://arduino.cc/en/Guide/HomePage
2. Raspberry Pi Board. [ONLINE]. Available at: http://www.raspberrypi.org
3. pcDuino. [ONLINE]. Available at: https://s3.amazonaws.com/pcduino/book/Introduction+to+pcDuino.pdf
4. pcDuino User Guide. [ONLINE]. Available at: https://strawberry-linux.com/pub/pcDuino_UserGuide_Rev02.pdf

REVIEW EXERCISES

1. Explain with a diagram the analog and digital pins of Arduino Uno board useful for interfacing input and output.
2. Which programming language is supported by Arduino boards? Explain with its advantages and disadvantages.
3. Explain with a diagram the interfacing pins for input and output on Raspberry Pi board.
4. Describe the steps to write Raspbian OS on the Raspberry pi board using NOOBS.
5. Explain Internet connectivity configuration for Arduino board through WiFi as well as through proxy server of a workplace.
6. Describe steps for WiFi Internet connectivity configuration for Raspberry Pi board.
7. Compare the boards Arduino Uno and Raspberry Pi with respect to its support to speed, memory, and storage.
8. Write a note on Beaglebone board and what are its advantages and disadvantages when compared with Raspberry Pi board?
9. Write a note on pcDuino board and its enhanced features as compared to Arduino board.
10. Compare the boards Beaglebone and pcDuino for their different features.

REFERENCES

1. Arduino vs Raspberry Pi vs Beaglebone vs pcDuino. [ONLINE]. Available at:https://randomnerdtutorials.com/arduino-vs-raspberry-pi-vs-beaglebone-vs-pcduino/
2. Exploring Beaglebone. [ONLINE]. Available at:http://exploringbeaglebone.com/chapter10/
3. Turn your pcDuino into an Apple TV. [ONLINE]. Available at: http://www.linksprite.com/
4. Automate your garage with pcDuino. [ONLINE]. Available at: http://www.pcDuino.com/
5. Single Board Computer. [ONLINE]. Available at: https://www.allaboutcircuits.com/news/single-board-computer-beaglebone-black-raspberry-pi-3-asus-tinker-board/
6. How To Choose Right Platform. [ONLINE}. Available at: https://makezine.com/2014/02/25/how-to-choose-the-right-platform-raspberry-pi-or-beaglebone-black/
7. Adafruit. [ONLINE]. Available at: https://www.adafruit.com/index.php?main_page=category&cPath=17
8. Arduino Final Hand-out. [ONLINE]. Available at: https://dlnmh9ip6v2uc.cloudfront.net/learn/materials/1/Arduino_final_handout.pdf
9. IoT Solutions. [ONLINE]. Available at: https://www.open-silicon.com/solutions/iot-asics/
10. IoT Edge SoC Platforms. [ONLINE]. Available at:https://www.open-silicon.com/iot-edge-soc-platform/
11. IoT Gateway Platform. [ONLINE]. Available at: https://www.open-silicon.com/iot-gateway-platform/
12. Adafruit Feather 32u4 Fona. [ONLINE]. Available at: https://cdn-learn.adafruit.com/downloads/pdf/adafruit-feather-32u4-fona.pdf
13. Hologram.[ONLINE]. Available at: http://hologram.io/dash/
14. Cellular electron datasheet. [ONLINE]. Available at: https://docs.particle.io/datasheets/cellular/electron-datasheet
15. Goblin2. [ONLINE]. Available at: http://verse-technology.com/goblin2/
16. Linkit Documentation. [ONLINE]. Available at: https://docs.labs.mediatek.com/resource/linkit-one/en/documentation
17. GPRS SIM900. [ONLINE]. Available at: https://github.com/Seeed-Studio/GPRS_SIM900
18. https://www.arduino.cc/
19. https://www.arduino.cc/en/Reference/Board
20. https://arduino-esp8266.readthedocs.io/en/latest/libraries.html
21. https://www.arduino.cc/en/Tutorial/HomePage
22. http://arduino.cc/en/Guide/HomePage
23. https://www.raspberrypi.org/
24. http://beagleboard.org/static/ti/
25. https://cdn.sparkfun.com/assets/e/e/f/8/d
26. https://www.generationrobots.com/en/content/84-pcduino-tutorial-getting-started-with-the-pcduino
27. https://www.arduino.cc/en/Main/Productshttps://projects.raspberrypi.org/en/projects/raspberry-pi-setting-up
28. https://www.raspberrypi.org/documentation/configuration
29. https://www.raspberrypi.org/documentation/usage/
30. https://strawberry-linux.com/pub/pcDuino_UserGuide_Rev02.pdf/
31. https://learn.sparkfun.com/tutorials/programming-the-pcduino/all
32. https://pimylifeup.com/raspi-config-tool/
33. https://elinux.org/RPi_raspi-config
34. Connect your Particle devices with Ubidots
35. Connect the Adafruit FONA to Ubidots
36. Hologram and Ubidots cloud-to-cloud integration
37. Connect you Linkit One to Ubidots over GPRS
38. Connect the Arduino UNO with Ubidots using the Arduino-GPRS shield
39. Connect the GOBLIN 2 to Ubidots

IoT Middleware

CHAPTER 7

"In computing terms, children are the 'front end', Mothers are the 'backend' while fathers are the 'middleware."

-Austin Ben

OBJECTIVES
- explain the concept of a middleware
- explain middleware from an Internet of Things (IoT) perspective
- evaluate the need for an IoT middleware
- classify IoT middleware
- discuss various middleware architectures
- outline various existing IoT middleware

OUTCOMES
- identify a middleware and understand its various components
- analyze different IoT middleware architectures
- obtain a broad understanding of various middlewares that are currently popular in IoT

REVISION

Chapter 1 introduced the emergence of Internet of Things (IoT). The basic building blocks of IoT are explained. Further, the highly heterogeneous nature of the IoT systems was highlighted, and specifically the diverse types of device, network, communication, data protocols, storage systems, analytics platforms, etc. were mentioned. To be able to use all these in a unified and standardized way, so that applications can be developed easily on top of these components there is a requirement for a layer of software called the middleware. It can handle these complex interactions between the various system components and provide a uniform way for the application developers to use the underlying infrastructure without having to know their complexity. These concepts will form the background of this chapter and is focused on understanding the need for an IoT middleware, the various requirements of such a middleware, their architectures, and overview of popular middleware platforms.

7.1 INTRODUCTION TO MIDDLEWARE

The function of a middleware is to provide a connection between the applications, the network communications, and the operating system (OS). This is crucial for the proper functioning of the overall system. The primary goal of the system software (OS, system utilities, and drivers) (see Fig. 7.1) is to perform system-related tasks, while the application software is focused on a domain-specific application; its functionality; and the user interfaces. The OS interacts with the hardware through the device drivers.

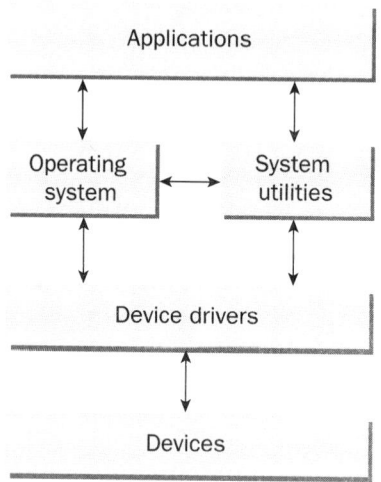

Fig. 7.1 Components of System Software

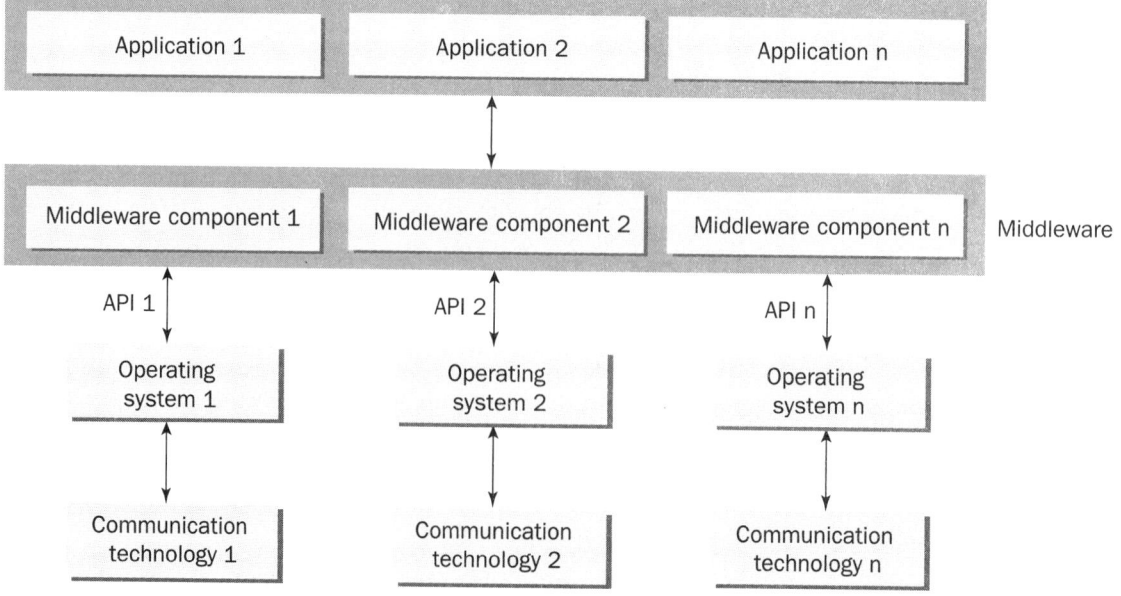

Fig. 7.2 High-level Depiction of Middleware

A middleware layer sits in between the system software and the application software (see Fig. 7.2). There are a number of technologies for communication and several OS's system utilities, device drivers, etc., which makes it hard for the applications to work with the underlying devices (i.e., hardware) in a consistent and uniform way. The middleware layer is precisely meant to address this issue. More specifically, a middleware is a software layer that has the following features:

Transparency Middleware hides from the application, the diverse hardware, OS, and communication protocols. This makes it easier for the application to have a homogeneous way to interact with the various components of the system, without the need to have a separate way to access each one of them. The middleware is designed to hide this complexity.

Flexibility, reusability, and portability The developers of the application do not need to worry about the underlying heterogeneity of the system components, but can instead focus on the application functionality, reusability (ability to change and customize specific components of the Internet of Things (IoT) system and assets to meet specific needs), and portability. This is possible because the middleware is capable of handling various conflicts between applications and things, and provides uniform, standard, and high-level interfaces that can be directly used by the software developers. Further, portability is an important issue that needs to be considered when using commercial off the shelf software, which should be capable of working with any device and in any kind of connectivity environment. Hence, platform-independent software tools have high portability.

Interoperability Various applications built for the same underlying devices (hardware) are expected to have access to a group of common services that perform various common and routine functions to reduce duplication of efforts, and also enable collaboration and interoperability between various applications. Interoperability approaches are also required to overcome the diversity of protocols, data models, configurations, etc. Interoperability is usually achieved by standards at syntactic and semantic levels (see Chapter 14).

Maintainability This characteristic reflects the level of resiliency of the various components (devices, applications, and system processes) of the IoT system. The more resilient it is, the better it will recover from failures and return to normal functioning rapidly. The middleware should be able to identify and isolate the failures and quickly be able to take remedial measures and parallely maintaining the stability of the system.

7.1.1 IoT Middleware

The middleware can be specifically developed for a particular category of applications or it can be very general in nature providing a uniform way to interact with the system. The highly heterogeneous nature of components involved in IoT applications makes it a very complex system. One of the solutions to tackle it is to use standards in each and every component of the IoT system. However, given the extreme variety of devices, manufacturers, vendors, and application domains involved in IoT, enforcing standards is difficult. Hence, there is a need for middleware that is focused on addressing various IoT specific challenges. It should provide a layer of integrating software (aka software glue) for performing all the required tasks rather than having a variety of tools from different vendors. The IoT specific needs for a middleware are described further.

7.1.1.1 Need for Middleware in IoT

IoT consists of a plethora of devices, communication protocols, transport requirements, data types, etc., which makes it extremely difficult to design and maintain a robust IoT system. There is an immense need for middleware that can aid in various functions of IoT systems such as:

Device management An IoT device should have the capability to be self-addressable, that is, making itself identifiable, so that its capabilities can be understood before it can be connected and used for a particular task. This is possible by incorporating information about the device (device name, vendor details, hardware description, software description, etc.) in metadata standard, which makes the device to announce its presence to every other device in the network. In addition, the middleware needed to provide mechanisms for registering the various devices, that is, a device registry and is used to search (syntactic and semantic approaches; refer Chapter 14 for more details) for appropriate devices and retrieve their functions and services.

Analytics The data obtained from IoT devices is highly intensive. This data needs to be analysed in two modes, that is, online and offline. The online module contains capturing, processing, and analysing data streams emanating from the device. This process is accomplished in the IoT edge computing framework (i.e., computing infrastructure at the edge of the network), where various real-time techniques for events detection and processing are provided. Methods such as complex event processing (CEP) and stream data mining techniques (see Chapter 12 for more details) are usually available on this online analytics module either on the gateways or on the cloud. The offline analytics modules are generally made available via a cloud infrastructure where services for data storage (massive repositories), machine learning-based big data analytics are provided. To achieve these functions, an IoT middleware is necessary to bridge the gap between the physical devices layer and the cloud computational infrastructure at a massive scale.

Cloud services Cloud services have emerged as the backbone for deployment of IoT systems. Currently, a variety of cloud offerings for IoT are available such as Google IoT cloud, IBM cloud, AWS IoT, and Azure IoT. Hence, the middleware is required to be flexible and be able to adapt to different cloud platforms by providing a uniform way to work with them.

Security Security and privacy play a crucial role in IoT as these systems are constantly being integrated into our daily lives. As explained in Section 7.1.2.6, it is one of the core functional requirements of the middleware as the security and privacy aspects are integrated in each and every component of the IoT system. The middleware should provide the necessary security modules for authentication and management of access to the IoT system.

The basic functional and non-functional requirements of IoT (Razzaque et al., 2016) are described in the following sections.

7.1.2 Functional Requirements of an IoT Middleware

The functional requirements are related to specific functions or behaviors of the middleware. Some of the core functions of a middleware are described in the sections below.

7.1.2.1 Resource Discovery

The intent of this requirement is to enable automatic discovery of resources based on a given context with minimal human intervention. The IoT middleware service should provide services to detect the various connections of the components and their status in real time. To make this happen, the devices should be made self-descriptive, that is, the ability to announce their presence, capabilities, and the resources it can offer.

7.1.2.2 Resource Management

Resource optimization is a prime need in IoT. Hence, the IoT middleware is required to provide services that can manage the resources and provide some crucial information about the resources such as current availability, how long a particular resource is in use, receive notification when it is released from another task and is available. Resource allocation systems should be provided, for example, a queuing system to manage the demand for a particular resource. The middleware is also responsible to resolve any conflicts that may arise for task that are competing for the same resource.

7.1.2.3 Data Management

The IoT middleware is designed to provide data level management functions such as data acquisition from devices and sensors, data related to network, and system health. Further, the middleware provides interoperability between diverse datasets generated from a variety of devices including gateways having different data protocols. Some middleware are specialized to provide data harmonization capabilities to resolve conflicts in syntactic and semantic representations of various data. The data management middleware is also expected to provide several data processing tools for filtering, aggregation of data from multiple sensor streams and also time-series data, data compression, etc.

7.1.2.4 Event Management

This component of the middleware is required to capture events from the data stream of sensors, that is, the ability to process and capture events that can be used for a particular purpose. For example, a particular pattern of the data in a given time window might represent unusual characteristics of that data and a warning may be sent to application/user for further investigation. These kind of events can be captured either in real time or on archived data based on actual values of the data as well as capturing various patterns (e.g., using CEP) from the streams of data coming from sensors in real time. Chapter 12 (Edge Analytics: Near Real-time Sensor Stream Processing) provides more details on various ways to capture and process events.

7.1.2.5 Code Management

Code management is required for accomplishing a certain pre-defined task by allowing applications and users to command a set of devices/nodes by injecting relevant codes so that they can execute the required task. It also can migrate the code to other devices/nodes and reprogram them.

7.1.2.6 Security and Privacy

The security aspects of IoT need to be incorporated in all the components of IoT system. It is extremely important to ensure that the IoT system is not compromised in any way. At the middleware level, the security- and privacy-related functions ensure that the data reaches only to those that are designated to receive it and ensure that the privacy of individuals and ownership of devices is protected. The middleware should deny access to devices and related services to all external malicious applications.

7.1.3 Non-functional Requirements of IoT Middleware

The middleware should be capable of supporting certain non-functional requirements which can help to evaluate the operation and performance of the middleware. These requirements are discussed in the following sections.

7.1.3.1 Scalability

The IoT system is said to be scalable if it can support the increasing number of devices that are added to an existing system. The middleware should be able to seamlessly integrate the new devices into the existing IoT setup and continue generating the data so that users/applications can use this data without any interruption or loss of the Quality of Service (QoS). This is achieved by loose coupling of hardware and services, so that the middleware can hide the underlying complexity and provide to the users/applications only high-level methods for interaction with it.

7.1.3.2 Reliability

Ensuring reliability implies that all the components and services from various layers of the IoT system (e.g., sensors, communication, data, etc.) are performing their designated functions in a reliable way. The middleware is expected to be resilient and continue to perform in a reliable fashion despite intermittent failures of components in the IoT system.

7.1.3.3 Availability

This requirement is tied with reliability to ensure that at all times the IoT system is available, especially for mission critical applications. It is expected that any failure is quickly recovered (i.e., resilient) and the system comes back to its original state and continues to perform its functions. The uptime of the IoT system is required to be very high and expected to be that way indefinitely.

7.1.3.4 Real-Time/Timeliness

Many IoT systems are designed for real-time dynamic applications (e.g., traffic monitoring, ambulance routing, disaster response activities, healthcare, industrial automation tasks, security, etc.). Hence, timely delivery of data is utmost important to ensure quick response to events.

7.2 ARCHITECTURES OF IOT MIDDLEWARE

The architecture of the IoT middleware is classified into different types based on the functionality and technologies used for its development. The existing middleware architectures were suitably modified to incorporate IoT's specific needs.

7.2.1 Component-based Middleware

The component-based middleware is based on Component-Based Software Engineering (CBSE). In this approach, the software is developed as a set of independent components that can communicate with each other using interfaces. This modeling approach is standardized into a component model, some of the well-known component models are: component object model (COM), COM+, .NET, Enterprise JavaBeans, etc. The main characteristics of the component-based architecture are reusability and loose coupling of the software components. These attributes make it more useful for developing systems that can be modified or extended in the future.

7.2.2 Distributed Middleware

The distributed systems are composed of software and hardware components in a networked environment, that is, these components are independent and interconnected. The middleware architecture is designed to provide distributed computing capabilities and interfaces to access these components and their functionality, but makes it look like a single coherent system (Fig. 7.3).

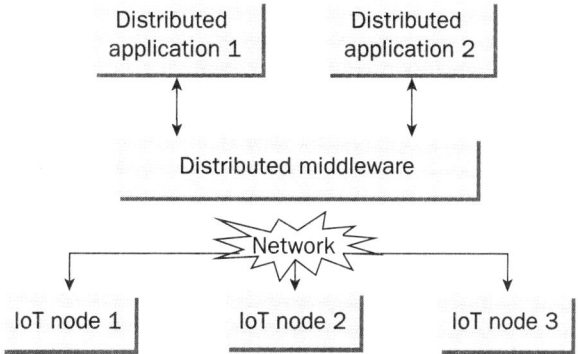

Fig. 7.3 Architecture of Distributed Middleware

This is achieved by developing higher-level programming abstractions (i.e., higher than low-level components such as sockets used for reading and writing data) and paradigms, that characterize the core principles of distributed systems. The Java Remote Method Invocation (RMI—an API that provides a mechanism to create distributed application in java) and the Common Object Request Broker Architecture (CORBA—provides interoperability among distributed objects) are the two most widely used distributed object systems.

7.2.3 Service-Oriented Middleware (SOM)

Service-Oriented Middleware (SOM) is built on the principles of Service-Oriented Architecture (SOA). SOA is a type of software architecture and development model that enables to design the software components in the form of services for interaction with each other's components, and also with external interfaces through communication calls.

Service-oriented architecture

The main characteristics of SOA are:

Loose coupling The services are designed such that they are independent and have minimal dependency on other services, that is, they are self-contained.

Independent of implementation technology The implementation of the components of the services can be done using any technology as long as the communication (request/response, pre-defined contracts) between the components is in a standard form. Also, the person using the service does not need to know the logic or implementation details, but can simply use the service by knowing how to send a request and understand the response from the service.

Service reusability The services can be developed once and used many times in several contexts. Because they are built as components, a software developer can pick and choose a service suitable for a particular task, thus reducing the development time and cost.

Service composability Several related services can be composed together to solve a bigger task. The services can be chained in a workflow kind of environment and triggered based on some other event(s) happening in the system.

Service discoverability Services are described using metadata that encodes several characteristics of that service such as identification, function, provider, request/access methods and their parameters, and response formats. This metadata describes the capabilities of the service, using which the right kind of service for a particular task can be discovered from a registry of services.

As shown in Fig. 7.4, the SOM has a three-layered architecture consisting of the sensing layer (sensors, actuators, tags, etc.), middleware components, and end-user services-based applications. This is a popular middleware architecture but requires high computational resources, and hence is not integrated with

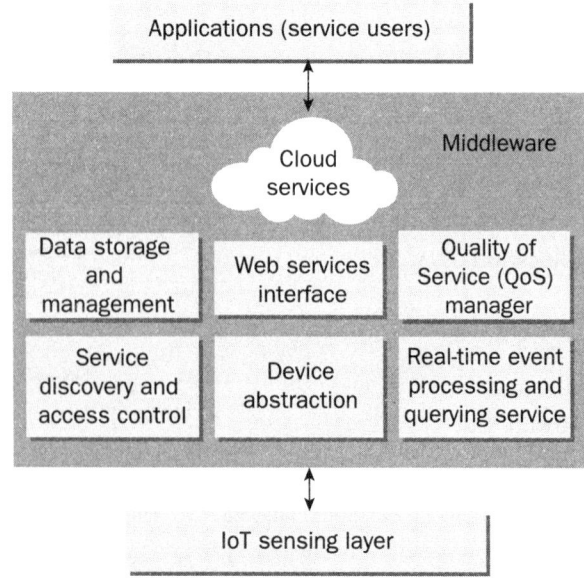

Fig. 7.4 Service-oriented Middleware

devices, but rather deployed on multiple high-end server nodes on cloud infrastructure or on gateways having sufficient computational capacity. Several core services provided by the service-oriented IoT middleware are discussed further.

7.2.3.1 Data Storage and Management

The core functionality of the data storage and management involves data generation, aggregation, preprocessing, filtering and storage, and archival. The data is generated from the sensing devices and sent in a pre-defined time interval for further aggregation. This data may need pre-processing as there can be a variety of formats and data models in which it is generated by various IoT systems. The data may have missing values or outliers due to the malfunctioning of IoT devices. There may be a need to fuse data from multiple devices to generate a new value. All these require a good amount of pre-processing on the raw data. Also, specific applications may require certain filtered data, for example, a traffic monitoring application may require data where the traffic density is above a particular threshold. So filtering techniques and approaches such as CEP (refer Chapter 12) are required. Finally, this data needs to be efficiently stored and organized, so that further querying and analysis can be performed. The difference between normal database management systems and IoT data management systems is that the IoT data management system needs to manage (i) real-time streaming data from sensors, (ii) dynamic queries on streaming data have to be handled to enable edge analytics, and (iii) massive storage and archival of IoT data for offline in-depth and intensive big data analytics.

7.2.3.2 Service Discovery and Access Control

Developing effective service discovery mechanisms in IoT is challenging because of highly heterogeneous nature of devices, communication and computation resources, data and information models, etc. Thus, one of the basic requirements to make services discoverable is to provision them with self-descriptive information, that is, a rich set of metadata. These services are often registered with a registry service, which can be based on either centralized, distributed, or decentralized registry architectures. Further, mechanisms for restricting unauthorized discovery or access to restricted services are expected to be provided by the middleware.

7.2.3.3 Quality of Service (QoS)

The middleware should ensure QoS by providing proper monitoring of the resources that are being used by various components of the IoT system. It should provide mechanisms for proper and fair allocation of resources, resolve conflicts in resource access and usage.

7.2.3.4 Real-Time Event Processing and Querying

The middleware provides data processing and analysis services at the edge of the network where real-time stream data processing is performed. The stream data processing engine can capture and analyse patterns from the streaming data and provide useful insights in real time, which is critical for many dynamic applications. See Chapter 12 for more comprehensive information on real-time event processing methods.

7.2.4 Cloud-based Middleware

The cloud middleware provides various functionalities as shown in Fig. 7.5. The cloud middleware provides a set of APIs that can be used to develop powerful cloud-based applications. The APIs that will be available on the cloud middleware are vendor specific. Each of them will have an array of offerings ranging from database, storage infrastructure, high-performance computing nodes, powerful analytical engines, security and privacy modules, and other ancillary components. Thus, cloud-based middleware acts as a go-between the actual IoT devices and client applications that require to access them. The cloud enablement of these devices makes them accessible only through the middleware, which provides a uniform way of access and control through web services based on RESTful principles or highly specialized vendor applications (IoT cloud platforms).

7.2.5 Node-based Middleware

Service-based architecture for IoT is not meant for software components that are embedded in the device. This is due to the low-power constraint of these IoT devices. However, the attractiveness of the service-based architecture lies in its ability to enable the development of big systems by decomposing into logically smaller independent components that are loosely coupled with each other. Therefore, in order to carry these features forward and make them work on mobile and embedded devices such as those that are frequently used in IoT system development is a challenge. Node-based architecture provides a middleware architecture that takes the best of the services-based architecture principles and combines with the

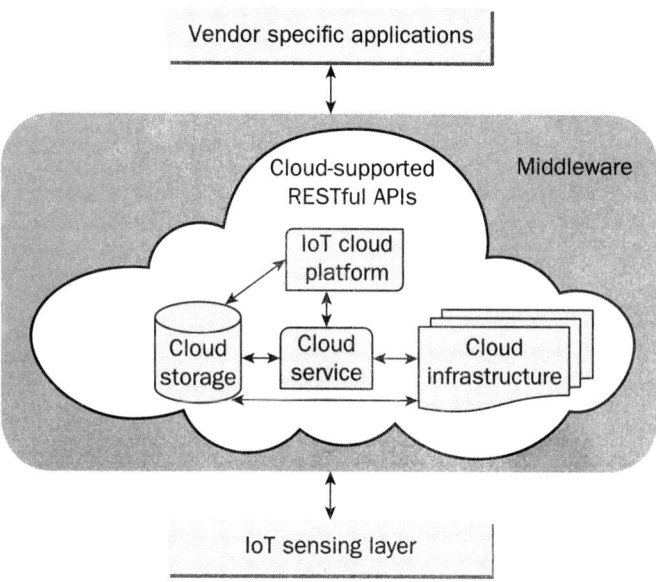

Fig. 7.5 Cloud-based Middleware Architecture

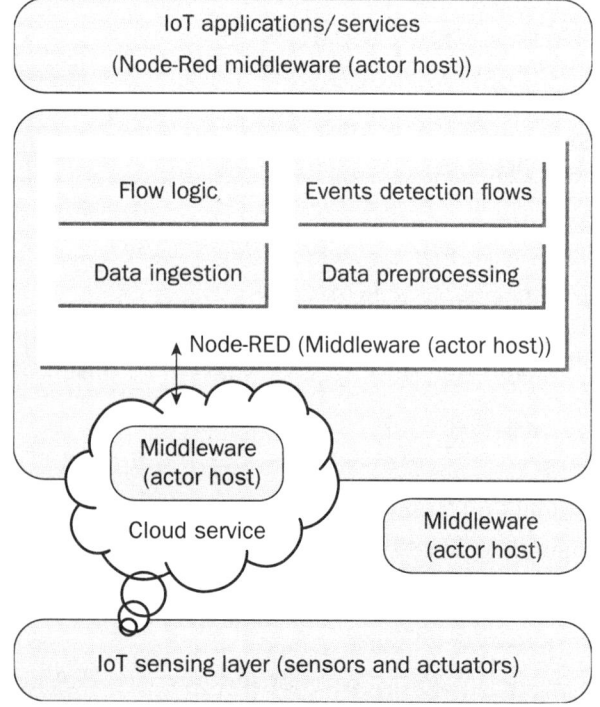

Fig. 7.6 Architecture of a Node-based Middleware. Node-based Middleware called Node-Red (refer to section 7.3.3) is Illustrated as an Example

requirements of the software in mobile/embedded devices. This type of middleware is also called as actor-based middleware. The actor host (i.e., the middleware) can be embedded at the sensing layer, cloud layer, as well as at the application layer. Only those components that are relevant to that particular layer are used in that middleware. Hence, the middleware remains light weight but is able to provide the necessary functionality (see Fig. 7.6). The main characteristics of such a middleware are simplicity (can be easily used by developers), loose coupling, flexibility, lightweight, and dynamic. The main components of the node-based architecture are:

Nodes It is a fundamental component, which can perform some fixed set of operations and can be controlled using an interface. For example, it could be a temperature-measuring node, which can make temperature measurements every 5 min and output the average temperature every 1 h. A node could be a piece of hardware such as a device in IoT or a software component in the middleware and can either reside locally or in a networked environment.

Streams The function of a stream is to act as a conduit for moving data between nodes. The node produces the stream based on some other operations in the middleware which triggers the data stream. It is the responsibility of the middleware to ensure this connection between the nodes via streams. It also determines which node produces the data stream and which consumes it.

7.3 STATE-OF-THE-ART IOT MIDDLEWARE

IoT middleware is a crucial component of IoT systems. Several commercial as well as open source entities are offering sophisticated IoT middleware solutions. Some popular IoT middleware are discussed below.

7.3.1 OpenIoT

OpenIoT is a middleware designed and maintained by the OpenIoT consortium. The middleware is developed to make it easy for deploying IoT solutions, by hiding the complexities of the various IoT system processes and allowing the user/application to connect, acquire, and process data from IoT devices easily. It provides services in a SOA-based architecture on the cloud platform to manage the various components of the IoT system. This middleware is offered as Sensing-as-a-Service (SaaS).

7.3.2 KaaIoT

Kaa is an enterprise-grade IoT platform for device management, data collection, analytics and visualization, remote control, software updates, etc. Kaa middleware is based on SOA for developing IoT solutions. The core modules of KaaIoT are:

Connectivity The popular MQTT and CoAP protocols are supported for connectivity between the platform and devices. Based on these two protocols the Kaa protocol is developed, which is open, asynchronous and has flexibility to process many kinds of messaging formats.

Device management Device management is made easy in Kaa by providing a registry for things, devices, and other components that the Kaa platform supports. The other important feature is the ability to obtain more information about any device, so that it can be used for specific purposes. This is achieved by storing attributes (metadata) of the devices and enabling to query it. Kaa also allows storing device attributes, which provide more detailed information about any characteristic of the device. The Kaa credential management provides facilities to provision, suspend, or revoke access to devices.

Data collection Kaa has its own protocol optimized for minimal network usage for obtaining data from devices and providing information about the status of the data delivery. It also provides an easy to use protocol for collecting data from connected devices. Functionalities such as batch processing, data buffering, are also available.

Data processing and analytics Kaa provides adapters to facilitate the uploading of data to database engines or analytics systems for further processing. This connection to external systems is made easy in Kaa.

Data visualization Both real-time and historical data can be used for visualization. Kaa provides a number of widgets (charts, maps, tables, etc.) to enable the visualization of a variety of data sets from different domains.

Configuration management Modules are available for setting the parameters for device, data processing, analytics, etc. so that they can be fine-tuned.

7.3.3 Node-RED

According to node-red.org, 'Node-RED is a flow-based programming tool, originally developed by IBM's Emerging Technology Services team and now a part of the JS Foundation. It is a programming tool for wiring together hardware devices, APIs, and online services in new and interesting ways, like for the Internet of Things.' It is developed on node-based middleware architecture that incorporates streams and nodes as explained in Section 7.1.2.3. It can also be used for rapid prototyping. It supports IoT network protocols such as TCP and MQTT. The light-weight programming model of node-red is based on Node.js, which is an asynchronous event driven, non-blocking javascript runtime environment that is highly scalable. Hence, Node-RED is suited for IoT edge applications which run on the device hardware and support concurrent connections. It is also useful for cloud applications, for example, Node-RED is available on IBM cloud platform, amazon web services, etc.

7.3.4 CHOReOS

The CHOReOS middleware provides the ability to easily compose and execute complex large scale web services to solve a particular task. There are several components that CHOReOS middleware provides. Their main characteristics are:

- Facilitate the composition and execution of various services (each meant to do a different task) to solve a complex task. This is called as Xecutable Service Composition (XSC).
- Access and selection of service using the eXtensible Service Access (XSA) component of the middleware. Further, services that were developed for a particular task may be adapted for a different context. For example, a weather monitoring service originally used for precision agriculture can also be adapted for air quality monitoring (i.e., in a different context).

- Integrate heterogeneous services which are offered using different technologies such as client/server, publish/subscribe, and tuple space.
- Discover required services via a service lookup modules termed as eXtensible Service Discovery (XSD).
- Manage the large number of things involved in the IoT system and be able to discover specific things and the corresponding service.
- Provision of high-end computing service to perform intensive big data analytics.

7.3.5 Linksmart

The Linksmart IoT middleware (known earlier as Hydra) is based on the Linksmart historical data store (HDS) middleware platform which is built on REST-based architecture for communication with server. This middleware is completely based on well-known standards for services and systems such as OGC SensorThings, MQTT, REST, TLS, etc. and features such as pub/sub, device abstraction, data storage, live data management, stream mining at the edge or in the cloud, online machine learning, fast built-in visualizations, etc.

7.3.6 CarrIoT

It is an IoT middleware for primarily supporting M2M communication systems. It is designed as a Platform as a Service (PaaS) on the cloud in a SOM architecture. It provides end-to-end functionality ranging from device access and management, data collection, storage, data management, and security. It provides specific methods for development of user interface of a custom application. This middleware enables the exchange of data with other data storage and management systems and APIs (e.g., ERP, Dropbox, etc.). However, the security aspects are not built into this product at the storage level, and also lack data standardization and interoperability.

7.3.7 Oracle Fusion Middleware

It is a middleware stack which provides a highly scalable IoT services infrastructure having the ability to integrate various functions such as monitoring, management, analytics, and security into IoT applications. The cloud middleware also provides the capabilities for mediating and managing the interactions between various applications. In addition, the middleware allows the integration with Business Process Management (BPM) tools to manage business processes that includes devices, applications, and humans in the loop. The Oracle business activity monitoring dashboard provides the visualization of real-time data from devices and event patterns captured by the Oracle event processing engine. The middleware also provides support for authentication, authorization, and identity management to ensure that the communication between devices, gateways, various services, and applications can communicate with each other in a secure way.

7.3.8 Google Cloud IoT

It is based on the SOM architecture and runs as a PaaS on the cloud. It provides functionality for connecting to the devices, acquiring data from the devices and storing it. In addition, the archived data can be used to perform analytics (e.g., machine learning) in the offline mode on the cloud. The online component of this middleware platform allows capturing and analysing data in real-time using edge analytics. It can be easily integrated with Google Maps to build location aware IoT applications such as logistics and supply chain management, Smart cities, etc. The Xively middleware that was separately developed for IoT was acquired and integrated with Google Cloud IoT platform.

SUMMARY

This chapter introduced the concept of a middleware and put it in the context of IoT. The need for an IoT middleware is presented. The middleware forms an important module in the overall IoT system. The basic functional requirements of the middleware such as resource discovery, resource management, data management, event management, and code management are described. These give an overview of the required characteristics that a middleware architecture should ideally possess. Further, the IoT middleware should also address non-functional requirements such as scalability, reliability, availability, timeliness, security, and privacy. Having understood the requirements of the middleware, an overview of various middleware architectures are described highlighting their core technology aspects. Finally, the currently popular middleware platforms (both open source and commercial) are presented.

REVIEW QUESTIONS

1. Define a middleware.
2. What are the main features of a middleware?
3. What is IoT middleware?
4. Explain the need for a middleware in IoT.
5. Describe the functional requirements for IoT middleware.
6. Describe the non-functional requirements of IoT middleware.
7. Explain component, distributed, service-based, cloud-based, node-based architectures of IoT middleware.
8. Describe the various state-of-the-art IoT middleware.
9. Write a comparison between all three types of middleware architectures.

REFERENCES

1. Amaral, L.A., de Matos, E., Tiburski, R.T., Hessel, F., Lunardi, W.T., Marczak, S. (2016), Middleware technology for IoT systems: Challenges and perspectives toward 5G. In: Mavromoustakis C., Mastorakis G., Batalla J. (Eds.) *Internet of Things (IoT) in 5G Mobile Technologies. Modeling and Optimization in Science and Technologies*, vol. 8, Springer, Cham.

2. Ngu, A.H., Gutierrez, M., Metsis, V., Nepal, S., Sheng, Q.Z. (2017), "IoT middleware: A survey on issues and enabling technologies," *IEEE Internet of Things Journal*, 4(1): 1–20.

3. Razzaque, M.A., Milojevic-Jevric, M., Palade, A., Clarke, S. (2016), "Middleware for Internet of Things: A survey," *IEEE Internet of Things Journal*, 3(1): 70–95.

4. Oliveira, A.M., Melo, D.F., Silva, G.M., Gregório, T. (2016), "Comparing IoT platforms under middleware requirements in an IoT perspective an fulfillment analysis of IoT middleware requirements in IoT platforms that uses REST to communicate

with external applications", In: *UBICOMM 2016: The Tenth International Conference on Mobile Ubiquitous Computing, Systems, Services and Technologies*.

5. Spiess, P., Karnouskos, S., Guinard, D., Savio, D., Baecker, O., Souza, L., Trifa, V. (2009), "SOA-based integration of the internet of things in enterprise services". In: *IEEE International Conference on Web Services (ICWS)*, pp. 968–975, Los Angeles.

6. Abu-Elkheir, M., Hayajneh, M., Ali, N.A. (2013), "Data management for the internet of things: Design primitives and solution", *Sensors*, 13(11): 15582–15612.

7. Google IoT cloud: https://cloud.google.com/solutions/iot/ [last accessed: 28/08/2019]

8. Linksmart: https://linksmart.eu/ [last accessed: 28/08/2019]

9. Satyadevan, S., Kalarickal, B., Jinesh, M. (2015), Security, trust and implementation limitations of prominent IoT platforms, *Proc. Front. Intell. Comput. Theory Appl. (FICTA'14)*, 328: 85–95.

10. Oracle Fusion Middleware: http://www.oracle.com/us/solutions/machine-to-machine/iot-wp-2190408.pdf [last accessed on 28/08/2019]

11. Da Cruz, M.A.A., Rodrigues, J.J.P.C., Sangaiah, A.K., Al-Muhtadi, J., Korotaev, V. (2018), "Performance evaluation of IoT middleware", *Journal of Network and Computer Applications*, 109: 53–65.

12. OpenIoT Consortium. OpenIoT—Open Source Cloud Solution for the Internet of Things. [Online]. Available: http://www.openiot.eu/ [last accessed: 28/08/2019]

13. CHOReOS: Integrated CHOReOS middleware—Enabling large-scale, QoS-aware adaptive choreographies [https://hal.inria.fr/hal-00912882/document]

14. Perera, C., Zaslavsky, A., Christen, P., Georgakopoulos, D. (2014), "Context Aware Computing for the Internet of Things: A Survey", *IEEE Communications Surveys & Tutorials*, 16(1): 414–454.

15. Hartikainen, V.-M, Vulli, M, Järvinen, H.-M. (2009), "Node based architecture for lightweight middleware", *Annales Universitatis Scientiarum Budapestinensis de Rolando Eötvös Nominatae. Sectio Computatorica*. 30.

16. Criado, J., Asensio, J.A., Padilla, N., Iribarne, L. (2018), "Integrating cyber-physical systems in a component-based approach for smart home," *Sensors*, 18: 2156.

17. Cruz-Piris, L., Rivera, D., Marsa-Maestre, I., de la Hoz, E., Velasco, J.R. (2018), "Access control mechanism for IoT environments based on modelling communication procedures as resources". *Sensors*, 18: 917.

18. Rambold, M., Kasinger, H., Lautenbacher, F., Bauer, B. (2009), "Towards autonomic service discovery: A survey and comparison", In: *2009 IEEE International Conference on Services Computing, Bangalore*, pp. 192–201.

19. Farahzadi, A., Shams, P., Rezazadeh, J., Farahbakhsh, R. (2017), "Middleware technologies for cloud of things—A survey". *Digit. Commun. Networks*.

20. Da Cruz, M.A., Rodrigues, J.J., Sangaiah, A.K., Al-Muhtadi, J., Korotaev, V. (2018), "Performance evaluation of IoT middleware", *Journal of Network and Computer Applications*, 109: 53–65.

21. Al-Jaroodi, J., Mohamed, N., Jiang, H., (2003), "Distributed systems middleware architecture from a software engineering perspective", In: *Proceedings Fifth IEEE Workshop on Mobile Computing Systems and Applications, Las Vegas, NV, USA*, pp. 572–579.

22. Marques, G., Garcia, N., Pombo, N. (2017), "A survey on IoT: Architectures, elements, applications, QoS, platforms and security concepts". In: Mavromoustakis, C., Mastorakis, G., Dobre, C. (Eds.), *Advances in Mobile Cloud Computing and Big Data in the 5G Era. Studies in Big Data*, vol. 22, Springer, Cham. https://nodered.org/ [last accessed: 28/08/2019]

IoT Software Platforms

CHAPTER 8

"Open platforms historically undergo a lot of scrutiny, but there are a lot of advantages to having a open source platform from a security stand point."

— Sundar Pichai

OBJECTIVES
- explain the need for an IoT platform
- outline the fundamental characteristics of IoT platforms
- explain the various functionalities of the IoT platform
- summarize the usefulness of the IoT platform from various perspectives
- outline most popular commercial IoT platforms and their applications
- explain selected open source IoT platforms
- show with an example how open source IoT platform can be used
- explain the selection of an IoT platform for a given goal

OUTCOMES
- justify why an IoT platform is required
- evaluate the characteristics, usefulness, and core functions of an IoT platform
- compare various commercial and open source IoT platforms
- choose the right IoT platform for a specific application

REVISION

Chapter 7 introduced the concept of IoT middleware that can handle complex interactions between the various IoT system components and provide a uniform way for the application developers to use the underlying infrastructure without having to know their complexity. This chapter extends these concepts and introduces the IoT platforms that are currently popular both commercial and open source. The challenges involved in choosing of appropriate platform are discussed. A hands-on tutorial on using an open source IoT platform is presented.

8.1 INTRODUCTION TO IOT SOFTWARE PLATFORMS

The IoT software platforms are designed to ease the deployment and management of IoT applications in various domains. Using these platforms, an IoT solutions' provider can build faster, cheaper, and stable IoT systems.

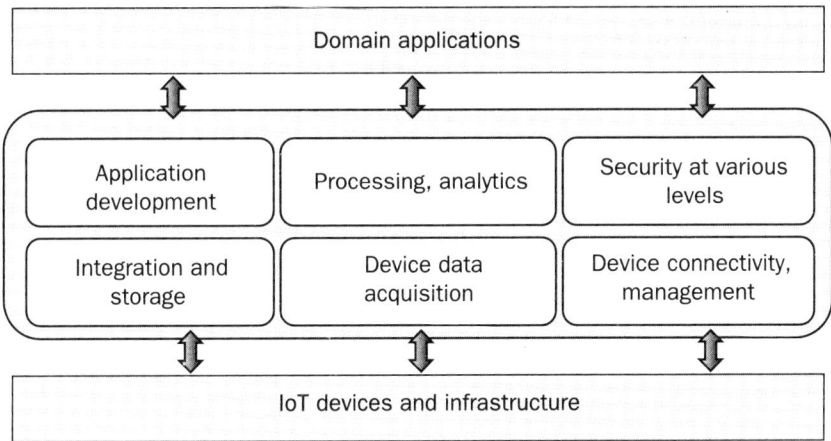

Fig. 8.1 Components of an IoT Platform

8.1.1 Need and Characteristics of IoT Platforms

An IoT platform is a suite of components as shown in Fig. 8.1. Each of these components addresses a particular need for the development of IoT systems. Hence, the essential characteristics of IoT platforms are:

- Device connectivity and management, which involves various functions such as management of large number of diverse types of devices, device registration to a centralized registry service, ability to make and sustain connections on a large scale in a variety of communication and network protocols, management of security and privacy aspects (e.g., access, credentials, certificates, policies, etc.).
- Acquiring the data from a wide range of devices requires some fundamental understanding and transformations, for instance acquisition of physical/analog signal from a sensor and converting it into a digital form, and setting of various acquisition parameters such as sampling rate and resolution.
- Integration of data from devices of various types (data sources) by implementing standards at various layers of the IoT system thus enabling interoperable systems development.
- Requirement of data in the stream mode for real-time analytics. Reading and writing large volumes of data. Storage of data in various data models, databases (e.g., NOSQL), cloud-based storage, etc. (see Chapter 7 for more details), indexing and archiving for offline analytics.
- Data preprocessing, data cleansing to address uncertain and incomplete data, resampling, data transformations, quality of the data.
- Real-time and offline analytics to extract meaningful information and knowledge from the data.
- Support for enabling the development of domain-specific applications, client-user interfaces, visualization environments, etc.

8.2 COMMERCIAL IOT SOFTWARE PLATFORMS

'The IoT software platform market is highly competitive, with many commercial vendors offering products that provide sophisticated tools for end-to-end deployment and management of the IoT systems. It is projected that it will grow at a compound annual growth rate (CAGR) of 28.8% between 2019 and 2024. (Reuters, 2019)

8.2.1 Amazon Web Service (AWS) IoT Platform

Amazon IoT platform is a cloud-based platform that enables efficient management of devices remotely. Device metadata such as name, type, manufacturer, access policies, and certificates, can be added quickly and made available as service due to its tight integration with amazon web services (AWS). AWS IoT provides complete end-to-end solutions ranging from:

Device level software Such as IoT operating system for microcontrollers and software for edge connectivity.

Control services These enable device management, connecting devices with web services to develop IoT applications, and security.

Data services Edge processing to capture and process events in real-time, cloud storage, and machine learning-based analytics.

8.2.2 Bosch IoT Suite

The Bosch IoT platform consists of a suite of tools that are offered in the form of Platform-as-a-Service (PaaS). It is built on the eclipse IoT components. The Bosch IoT suite is a comprehensive toolbox for IoT developers, which enables the development of end-to-end IoT solutions in residential, mobility, and industrial domains (Fig. 8.2). The foundation of the Bosch platform is based on the open source technology, which enables it to support easy integration of other platforms and services.

The core components of the Bosch IoT suite are:

Device connectivity The Bosch IoT provides the necessary tools for connecting devices to the cloud in a secured manner. It provides device-to-cloud and cloud-to-device communications such as telemetry, events capture, and command and control of the devices. Further, support for gateways, multiple protocols (MQTT, HTTP, LoRaWAN), identity management, and security are provided.

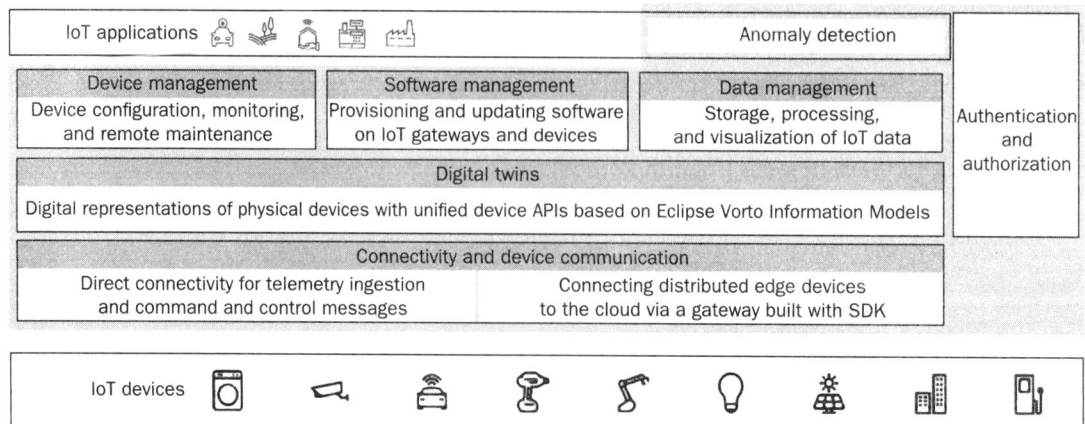

Fig. 8.2 Core Components of Bosch IoT Suite

(Source credit: "Picture: © Bosch.IO")

Digital representations of physical things   Digital twins are the digital representation of the things so that they can interact with each other. The applications will easily be able to manage the device assets using this approach.

Device management   The IoT remote manager, which is available as a cloud service, provides multiple device protocols and complete management of the devices throughout its lifecycle. Remote configuration, firmware updates, monitoring, diagnostics, backup, etc. are some of the functionalities of the device management component of the platform.

Software provisioning   Bosch IoT rollouts provide the necessary functionality both at small and large scales for updating of the software on devices, controllers, and gateways.

Data management and analytics   This is supported on the cloud by the Bosch IoT insights component. It provides support for data storage, preprocessing, analytics, and visualization. Third-party analytical tools such as Matlab, Excel, and Tableau can be easily connected.

User and permissions management   User management, authorization management, etc. are handled by the Bosch IoT permissions module.

8.2.3 EVRYTHNG

EVRYTHNG is an IoT Software-as-a-Service (SaaS) platform for consumer products. The concept of active digital identities is introduced by this product, which give products digital identity that can be used for developing applications that are driven by the products.

The adaptive analytics component provides machine learning tools that can be applied on real-time product data, thus enabling real-time services. The block-chain integration gives these services robust integrity. Further, the ability to easily integrate with Customer Relationship Management (CRM) and Data Management Platform (DMP) products, makes it easy for businesses to operate and give custom service to the consumers. The digital identity is managed by GS1 link support (standard for web-enabling barcodes) in addition to securing product data.

8.2.4 IBM Watson IoT Platform

The IBM Watson IoT platform built on the IBM cloud enables to communicate and acquire data from connected devices and gateways (Fig. 8.3). The device management component provides functions such as device registration, rebooting or updating firmware, receive device diagnostics and metadata, or perform bulk device addition and removal. The connectivity between devices and applications is provided by the standard MQTT protocol, which is highly efficient for real-time exchanging of data between the devices. In addition, it uses TLS to secure all communication between devices and services. Further, the platform provides cloud-based storage, analytics, and rapid visualization.

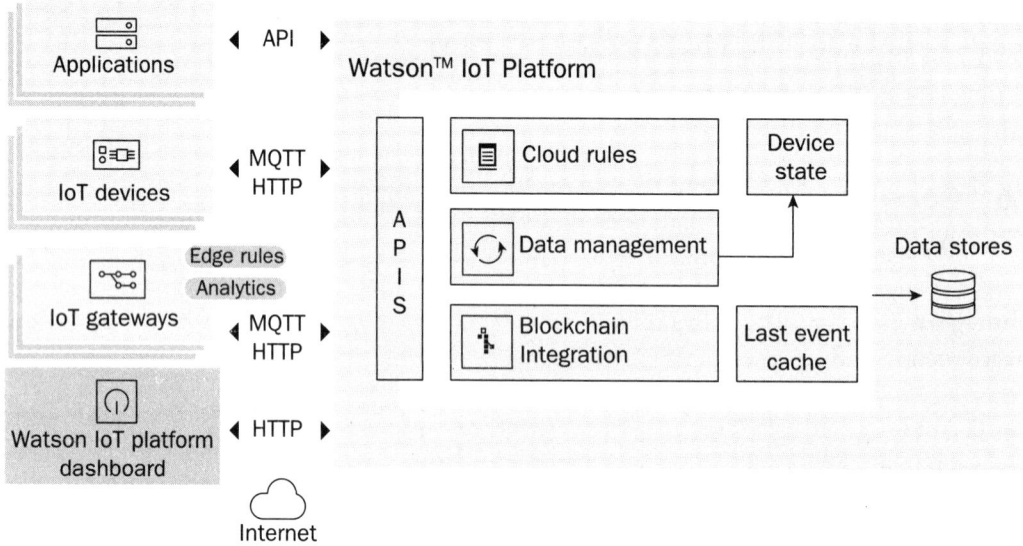

Fig. 8.3 IBM Watson IoT Platform

(Source credit: Courtesy of International Business Machines Corporation, © International Business Machines Corporation)

8.2.5 Cisco Kinetic IoT

The Cisco Kinetic IoT platform is built on three major components (see Fig. 8.4):

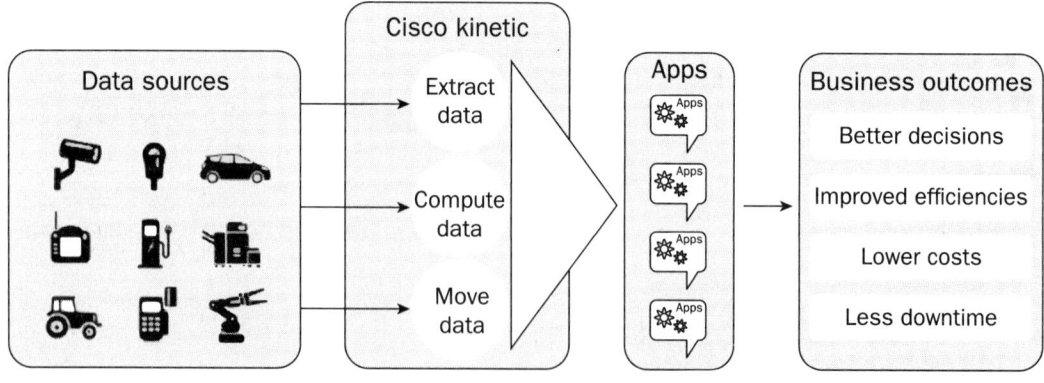

Fig. 8.4 Cisco Kinetic IoT Platform

(Source credit: Cisco)

Extract data This component of the platform can extract data from a variety of devices and is independent of the underlying protocol that the device uses. The data is further processed in a form that is readily usable by applications.

Compute data This component is for making computations at the edge/fog where real-time capture of streaming data and processing for capturing interesting events is performed. This is achieved by running complex rules on streaming data to reduce, compress, normalize, and transmit data in optimal ways. The analytics can also be performed on stored/archived data and on the cloud.

Move data   This component facilitates cloud-based applications to consume data when required in a timely and secure manner, programmatically to get the right data to the right applications at the right time. The data can be moved across multiple cloud platforms, locations, etc. at the same time the security of it is not compromised.

8.2.6   Google IoT Cloud

The Google IoT cloud has a set of core IoT components for various functions of the IoT system (see Fig. 8.5).

Through the device manager tool, the configuration of the devices can be performed and also managed securely. The device identity management, role-level access control, etc. are also handled by this component. Further, massive deployment of devices automatically is enabled by REST APIs.

The heterogeneity of the protocols is handled by the protocol bridge component of the platform that allows secure connection of various standardized protocols such as MQTT and HTPP and makes it as a unified system. The publish/subscribe model allows the data to be easily used by other applications in the pipeline.

The platform provides tools for edge processing on both edge devices as well as gateways. These are Machine learning-based tools for developing models that can do real-time predictions on the stored data. In addition, various analytical tools such as Google Big Data Analytics, Dataflow, BigQuery, Bigtable, ML, Data Studio, etc. are available.

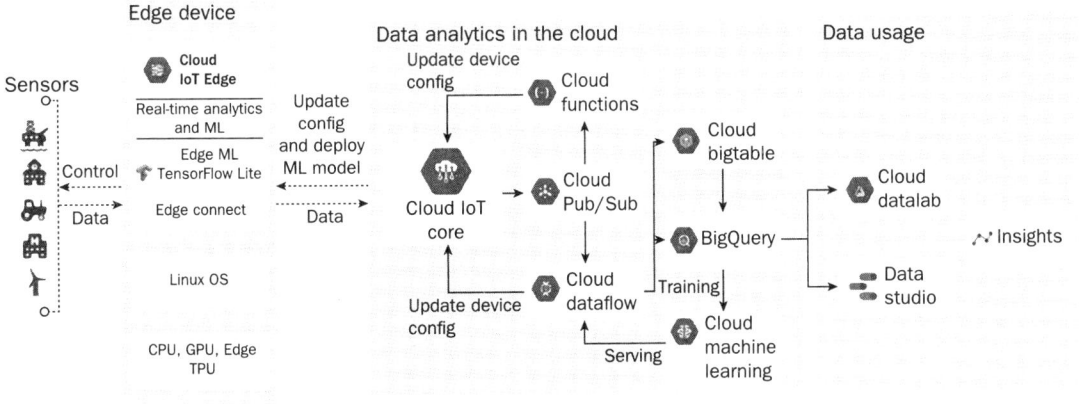

Fig. 8.5   Architecture of Google IoT Cloud

8.2.7   Microsoft Azure IoT Suite

The Microsoft Azure IoT suite consists of a set of Azure services for connecting 'Things' (device connectivity), performing streaming analytics, efficient storage, device metadata management, etc.

As shown in Fig. 8.6, the IoT hub can translate multiple protocols such as HTTP and AMPQ, as well as MQTT via a free, open source MQTT protocol gateway. It also provides security on per device basis.

The stream analytics components support writing queries in a simple SQL-like language so that the data can be analyzed in real time. The various windowing operations are supported to enable capture of specific portion of the data stream and run some logic/rules on it and consequently capture events from data coming from multiple devices.

A web application is provided to interact with the devices and manage the response to events captured by stream analytics by sending text messages based on some preset threshold values on the device measurements.

A logic app is provided to enable the development of workflows. This allows automating a series of steps involved in existing business process (i.e., end-to-end) by connectors that can execute certain rules and perform some actions.

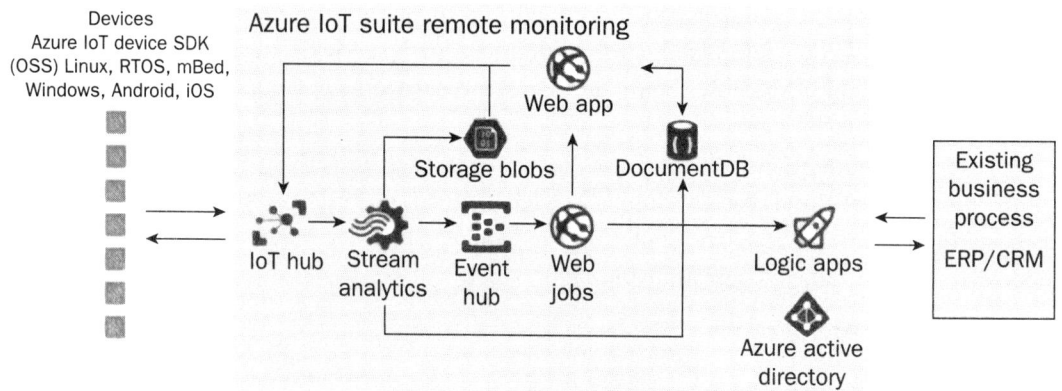

Fig. 8.6 Microsoft AZURE IoT Suite

8.3 OPEN IOT SOFTWARE PLATFORMS

In addition to several commercial IoT platforms that are currently available, the open source community is also actively involved in the development of IoT platforms. These open source IoT platforms are also being widely adopted for developing large scale IoT systems.

8.3.1 ThingsBoard

ThingsBoard is an open source IoT platform for device management, data collection, processing, and visualization. It provides various functionalities as mentioned below:

Device provisioning and management All kinds of IoT entities can be deployed, monitored, and managed using the server side tools available in the component of the platform. Security is ensured in all these processes. Remote Procedure Calls (RPC) are supported, which allow commands to be sent to devices and receive the results. Further, a novel way of connecting device, assets, customers, etc. is available such that a hierarchical arrangement of these based on their relationships can be developed. For example (see Fig. 8.7), air quality and traffic monitoring stations are deployed in five different zones (assets) of a city, and in each zone (asset), between four and eight stations of each are deployed. Further, each station (device) has some sensors associated with it.

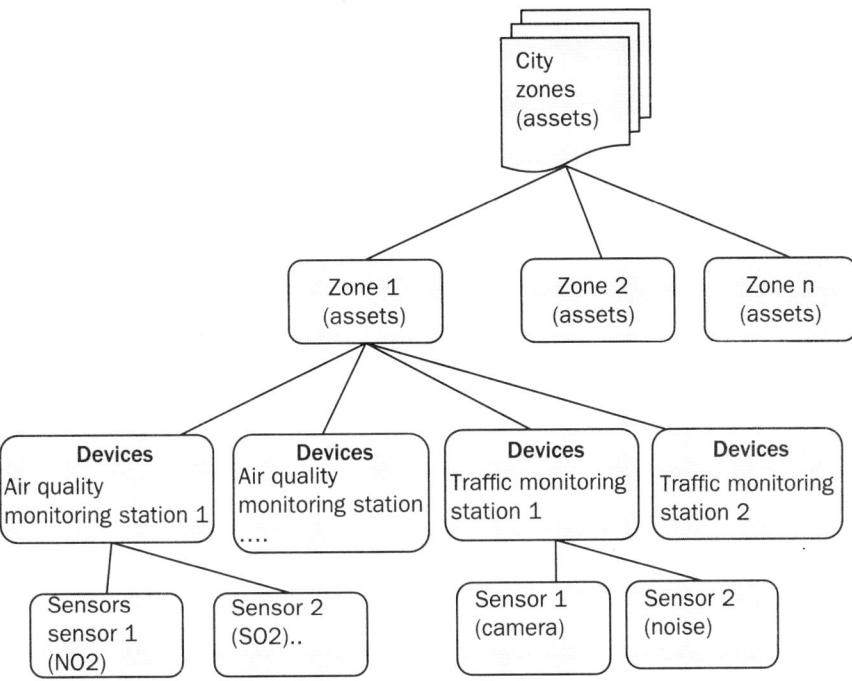

Fig. 8.7 Hierarchy of Assets and Devices in ThingsBoard

Data acquisition and visualization Data from the devices can be acquired in such a way that its integrity is maintained and in a fault-tolerant way. An API is provided for acquiring time-series data from the devices. Several IoT dashboard templates are available, using which the users can quickly create a dashboard having custom widgets (selecting from the provided widget library) that suit their requirements.

Rules engine It consists of three main components: the first is the message, which is any incoming data from various devices, events, REST-based web service-generated event, RPC request, etc. The second component is the rule node that allows the processing of an incoming message by a function. Various types of nodes are provided each of which can execute a specific function (filter, transform, etc.) on the message.

8.3.2 OGC SensorThings

The OGC SensorThings is a REST-based API that provides 'an open, geospatial-enabled, and unified way to interconnect the Internet of Things (IoT) devices, data, and applications over the Web (OGC SensorThings, 2019).' It is a standardization done at the data and interface of IoT and Web of Things (WoT). The core benefits of such a standardized approach are:

(1) it permits the proliferation of new high value services with lower overhead of development and wider reach, (2) it lowers the risks, time, and cost across a full IoT product cycle, and (3) it simplifies the connections between devices-to-devices and devices-to-applications.

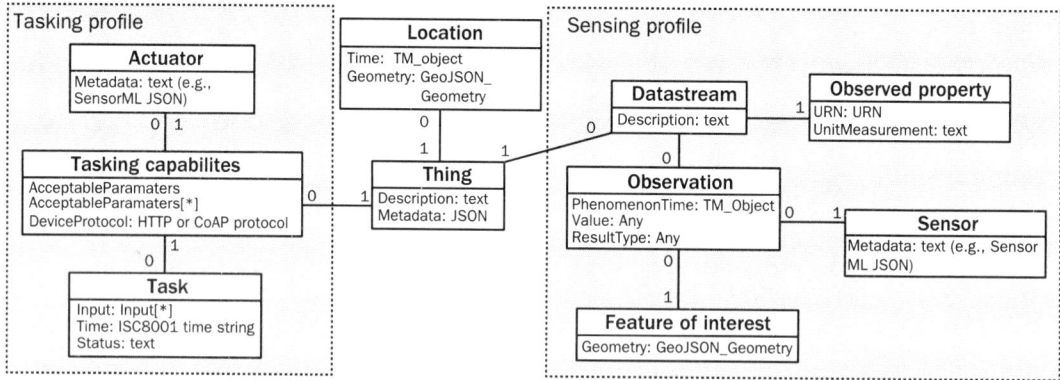

Fig. 8.8 Tasking and Sensing Profile of OGC SensorThings API

(Source credit: Open Geospatial Consortium)

8.3.2.1 Sensing

A shown in Fig. 8.8, a thing has a property called *location* that can be defined in terms of space and time. It can also have *data stream(s)* that are understood in terms of *observation* (having a time of observation, value of observation, etc.) of a certain observed property (i.e., sensing environment) such as temperature of a feature of interest (e.g., room). The actual observation is obtained by a sensor (e.g., thermometer). Basically, the goal of the sensing profile is to provide a standardized way to manage and retrieve observations and metadata from heterogeneous IoT sensor systems.

8.3.2.2 Tasking

The goal of the tasking profile is to provide multiple tasking capabilities that can be executed by an actuator. The applications can get full control of the IoT devices using which, remote control of sensors is possible. For example, custom acquisition of data can be tasked to sensors remotely based on certain triggers or new requirements/on demand. Before sending a request to execute a particular task on the sensor, it is possible to request for the tasking capabilities of that particular sensor and also the way to request for tasking. This is achieved through the *TaskingCapabilities* component (see Fig. 8.8).

8.3.3 Thinger.io

It provides scalable cloud infrastructure to connect, use, and manage large number of devices and also a REST API for integrating with users' own applications (e.g., WebServices, mobile phones, or desktop applications). Many hardware platforms such as Arduino compatible hardware (Arduino + Ethernet, Arduino + WiFi, ESP8266, NodeMCU, TI CC3200, etc.), Raspberry PI, Sigfox, ARM MBED, can be programmed to connect and use the Thinger.io platform. It provides a mobile app to manage different elements of the Thinger.io platform using a smartphone.

8.3.4 SiteWhere

SiteWhere is an industrial strength open-source application enablement platform for IoT. It provides a multitenant microservice-based infrastructure that includes the key features required to build and deploy IoT applications.

It uses Kubernetes (open-source system for automating deployment, scaling, and management of containerized applications) as the infrastructure platform, allowing it to be deployed in any cloud service platforms such as Google cloud and AWS. The core concept of SiteWhere is microservice, which is a specialized service for each core component (e.g., event ingestion, big-data event persistence, device state management, etc.) of the IoT system. Further, each microservice is a Spring Boot (create stand-alone, production-grade spring-based applications) application wrapped as a Docker (container software) container.

8.3.5 ThingSpeak

It is an Open IoT platform with Matlab analytics. It is a free web service that lets you collect and store sensor data in the cloud. It also provides apps using which various analytics on the sensors data can be performed using Matlab and also perform visualization. It supports data acquisition from several hardware platforms such as Arduino, Raspberry Pi, and BeagleBone Black. The platform uses REST and MQTT APIs for data management functions. Alerts can be obtained based on the events, for example, if the data is not received continuously within a certain time period (preset), an alert is generated and sent to the user called as a *ThingTweet*. Also, using the *TalkBack* function, commands can be sent to the sensors to perform certain task based on the events that are generated.

8.4 CHOOSING AN IOT PLATFORM

Given the availability of IoT platforms both commercial and open source, choosing an IoT platform is rather challenging. Following are some general guidelines for selecting an IoT platform.

8.4.1 Domain of Application

The application in which the intended IoT platform will be deployed is crucial to consider. It is possible that some of the IoT platforms are not general enough to be applicable in any domain, they may be designed specifically for certain application areas, for example, industrial, healthcare, etc. Hence, it is suggested to look at the capabilities in terms of acquisition of data from a large variety of device types, communication, network, and data protocols. The specific needs of the application domain have to be identified and matched with the functionality offerings or the scope of the use cases that the IoT platform supports.

8.4.2 Usability

The ease of use of an IoT platform needs to be assessed beforehand. The user-friendliness of the IoT platform helps in performing essential tasks, using interfaces and functions for various protocols, visualization, decision-making, etc. Further, considerations are in terms of ease of provisioning and management of devices.

8.4.3 Interoperability

The ability of the IoT platform to integrate third-party solutions, ability to assimilate data coming via heterogeneous communication, network and data protocols, open source tools, ERP tools, existing business processes, work flows, etc., makes it a highly interoperable IoT solution.

8.4.4 Scalability

It is the ability to handle a large number of IoT devices/end points. A truly scalable IoT solution can handle an unlimited number of devices and their connections seamlessly by approaches such as load balancing and distributed processing. Hence, it is important to check for the number of IoT devices that can be handled, not only in terms of connectivity, but also further processing at the edge, storage, and subsequent deep analytics and visualization capabilities.

8.4.5 Edge Analytics

It is necessary to find out if the IoT platform supports edge analytics, if your intended application is all about providing real-time information to the customers. For example, real-time traffic updates, energy estimations in a building, industrial processes, retail, etc. which need stream data processing capabilities. Hence, choose an IoT platform that provides these capabilities, particularly those that can be set to trigger alerts/warnings based on predefined rules/criteria that run on a subset of the incoming stream using various windowing techniques.

8.4.6 Security

The capability of ensuring high-level of security end-to-end (all levels of the IoT stack) by the IoT platform plays a major role in its selection. The IoT platform needs to be assessed for comprehensive security tools for secure authentication, certification, encryption, identity-based authentication for devices, Cloud-based gateways offering SSL or DTLS encryption, etc.

8.4.7 Recovery

In the event of instability or a crash of the IoT system, how resilient is the system to come back to its original condition is an aspect that needs to be given importance while selecting an IoT platform. The IoT platform needs to provide the ability to have enough redundancy such that failures can be handled smoothly. The data recovery ability is another attribute to pay close attention. The IoT platform should be able to take periodic backups and restore the data on demand.

8.5 HANDS-ON USING AN IOT PLATFORM

In this section, the ThingsBoard IoT platform that is described in Section 8.3.1 is used to demonstrate the usefulness of an IoT platform. Refer to Box 8.1 for step-by-step instructions.

Goal The goal of the hands-on exercise is to be able to connect a soil moisture and soil temperature sensor to a microcontroller (NodeMCU) and use the ThingsBoard IoT platform to send information via Wi-Fi on to the ThingsBoard dashboard for visualization of the live readings from the sensors.

BOX 8.1: SENSORS AND THEIR CONNECTIONS TO A MICROCONTROLLER AND THINGSBOARD IOT PLATFORM

Connecting Soil Moisture and Soil Temperature Sensors to NODEMCU and ThingsBoard Platform

Soil moisture sensor: The DFRobot soil moisture sensor measures soil moisture levels by capacitive sensing. It is made of corrosion resistant material which gives it an excellent service life (Fig. 8.9).

Fig. 8.9 Soil Moisture Sensor

(Source credit: DFRobot)

Soil temperature sensor: The soil temperature sensor that is used in this exercise is Dallas Semiconductor DS18B20 which is a digital thermometer providing 9- to 12-bit (configurable) temperature readings which indicate the temperature of the device (Fig. 8.10).

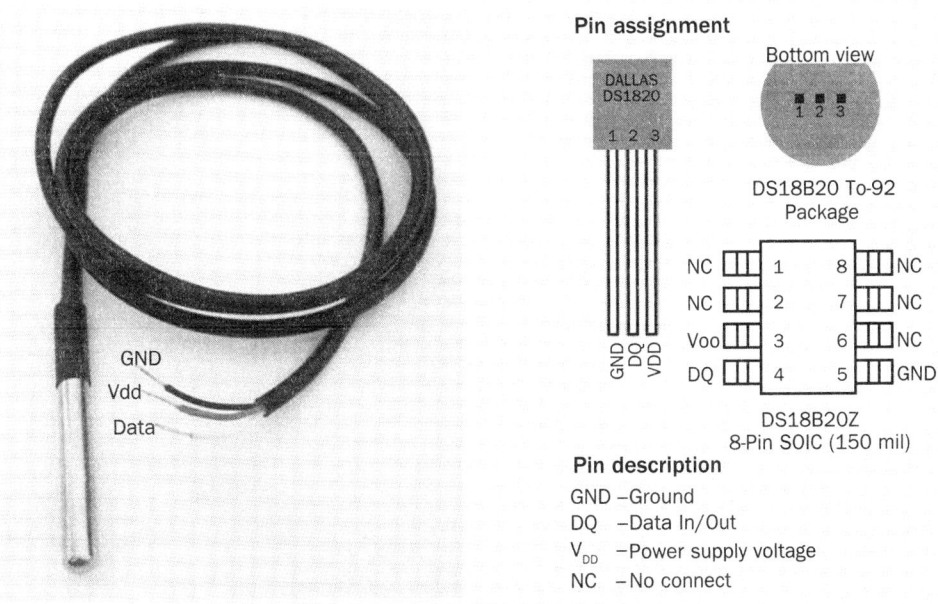

Fig. 8.10 Soil Temperature Sensor

NodeMCU: NodeMCU is an open source LUA-based firmware developed for ESP8266 Wi-Fi chip. It can be programmed directly through USB port using LUA programming or Arduino IDE. NodeMCU has a programmable Wi-Fi module (Fig. 8.11).

(Contd)

Box 8.1 *(Contd)*

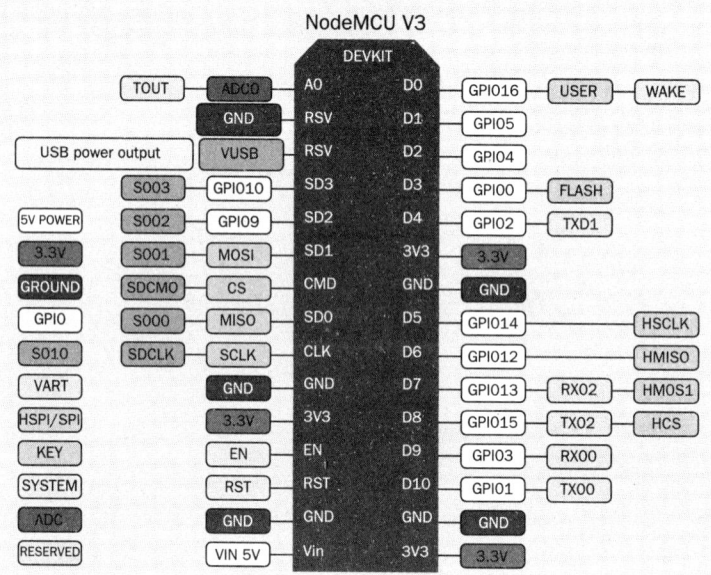

Fig. 8.11 Pinout Diagram of NodeMCU

Wiring schemes: Figures 8.12(a) and (b) show the initial and final wiring schemes of soil moisture and soil temperature sensors with NodeMCU.

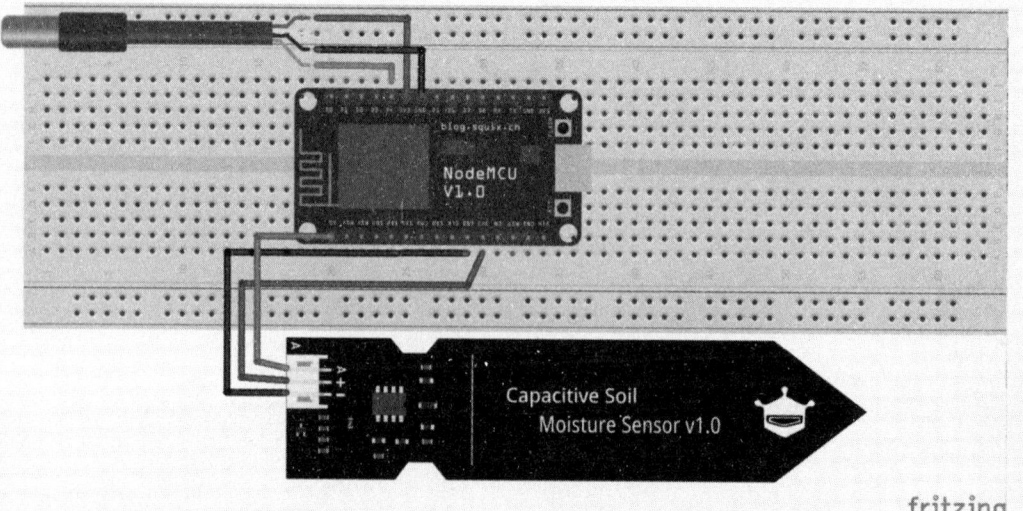

Fig. 8.12(a) Programming/Flashing Schema (Initial)
(Source credit: This image was created by Fritzing)

(Contd)

Box 8.1 *(Contd)*

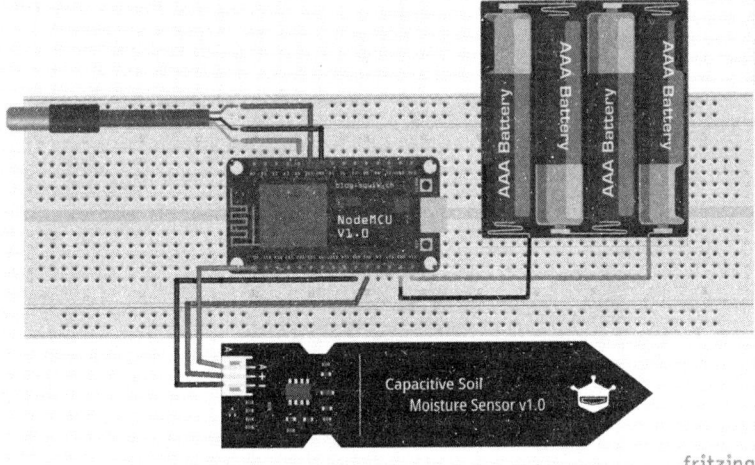

Fig. 8.12(b) Final Schema (Battery Powered)

(Source credit: This image was created by Fritzing)

Step 1: Refer to Section 8.3.1 for a review of the ThingsBoard IoT platform.
Step 2: Complete the setup of the soil moisture and soil temperature using NODEMCU.

Thingsboard Configuration

Provision your device: Using ThingsBoard public server: https://demo.thingsboard.io
- Enter login username and password

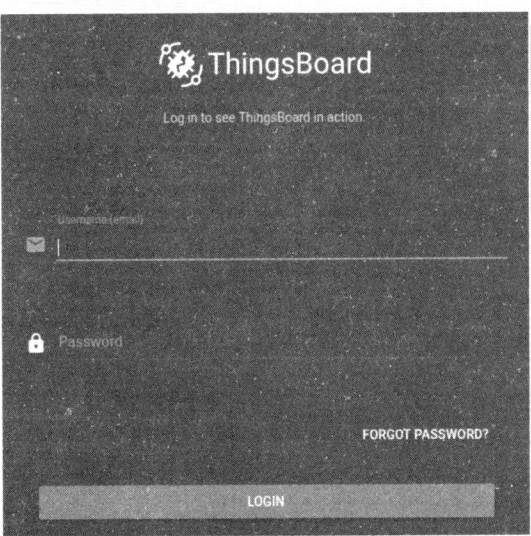

- After logging in, enter 'Devices' section

(Contd)

Box 8.1 *(Contd)*

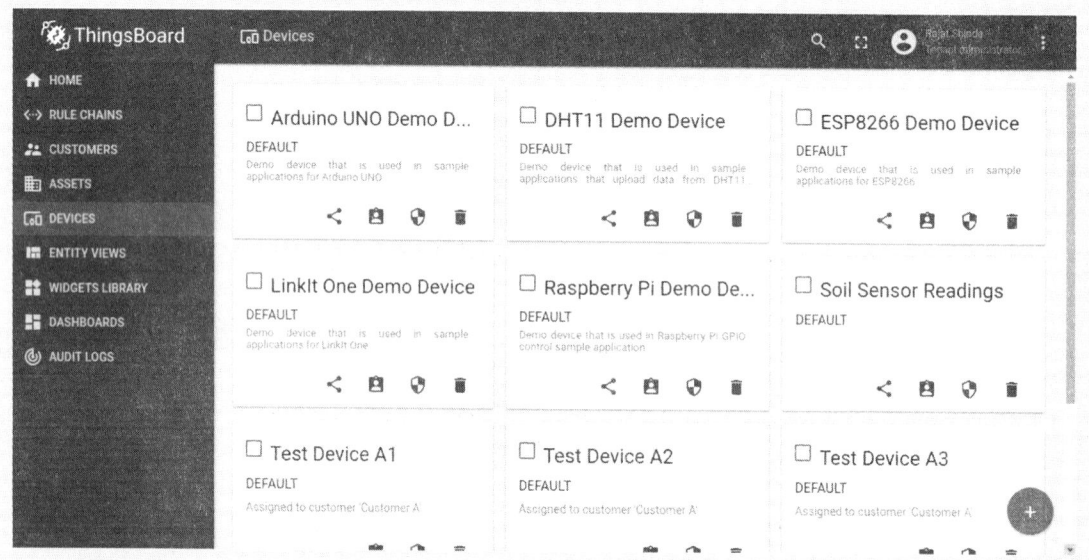

- Click '+' button and create a device with the name 'SoilTempAndMoisture.' Select device type as 'default'

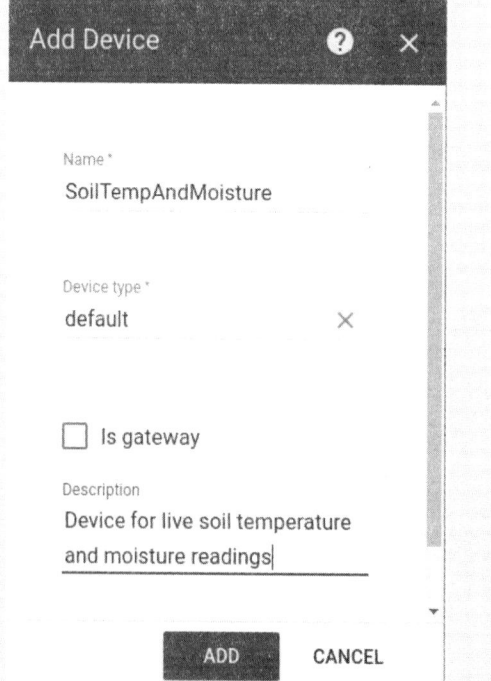

- Once device is created, open its details and click 'Manage credentials'
- Copy the auto-generated access token from the 'Access token' field. Please save this device token. It will be referred to later as $ACCESS_TOKEN

(Contd)

Box 8.1 *(Contd)*

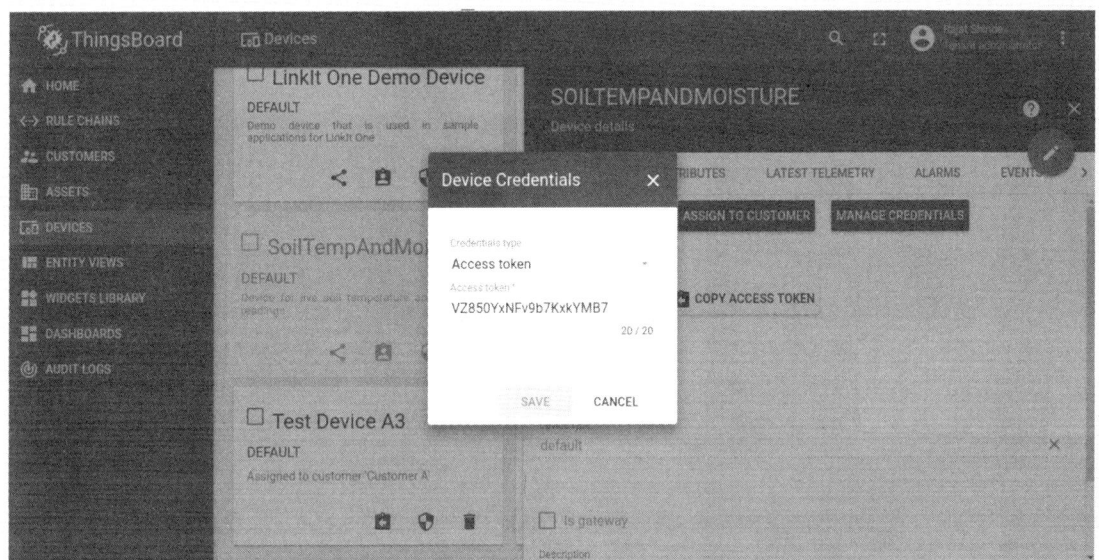

- Click 'Copy Device ID' in device details to copy your device id to the clipboard
- Paste your device id to some place; this value will be used in further steps

Provision your dashboard:

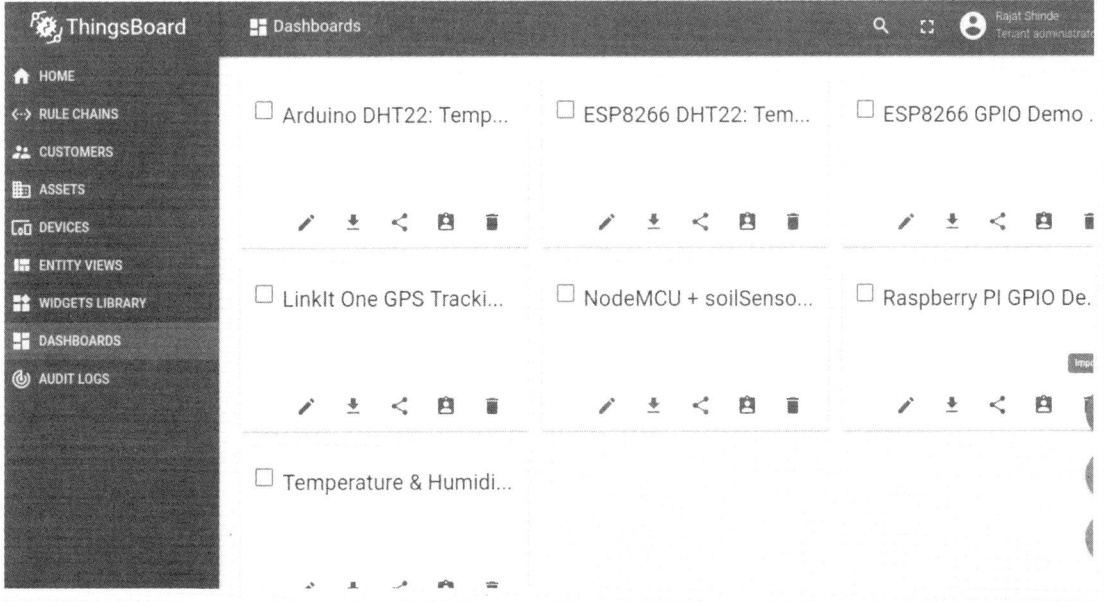

- Use import/export instructions to import the dashboard to your ThingsBoard instance

(Contd)

Box 8.1 *(Contd)*

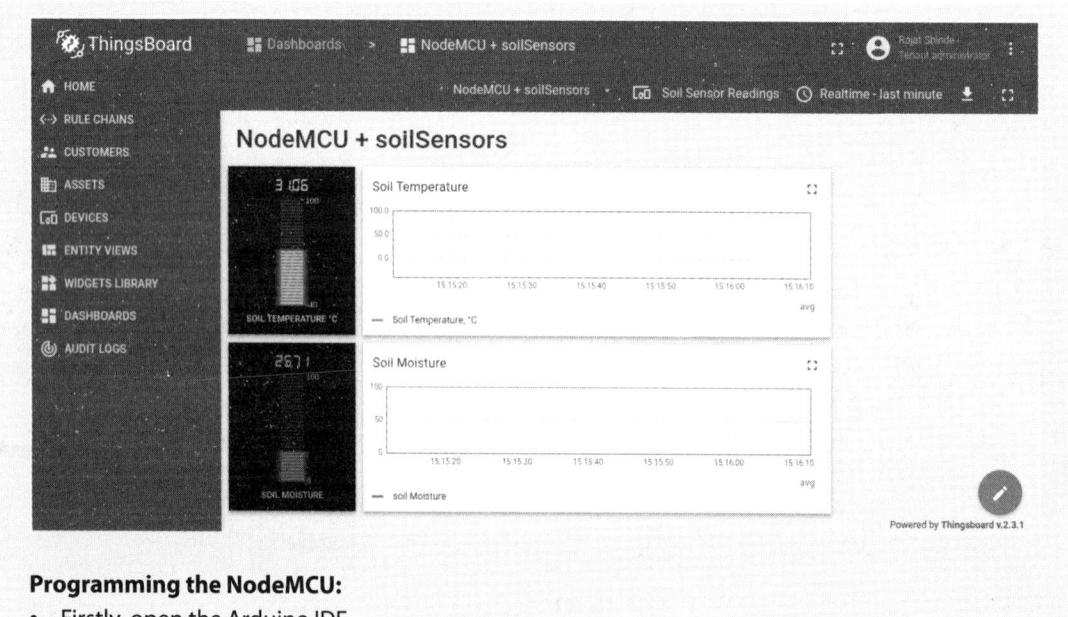

Programming the NodeMCU:
- Firstly, open the Arduino IDE
- Go to files and click on the preference in the Arduino IDE

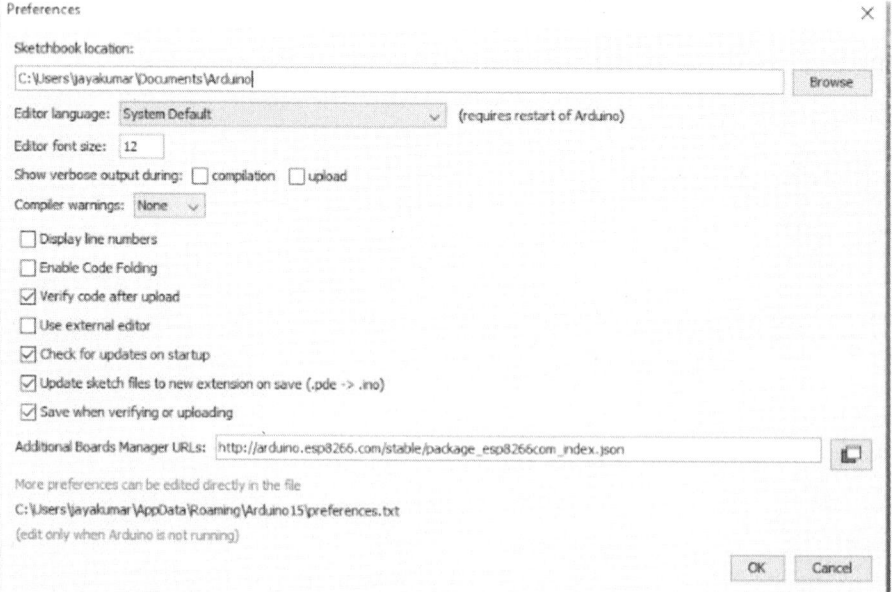

- Copy the URL http://arduino.esp8266.com/stable/package_esp8266com_index.json in the Additional Boards Manager
- Click OK to close the preference tab

(Contd)

Box 8.1 *(Contd)*

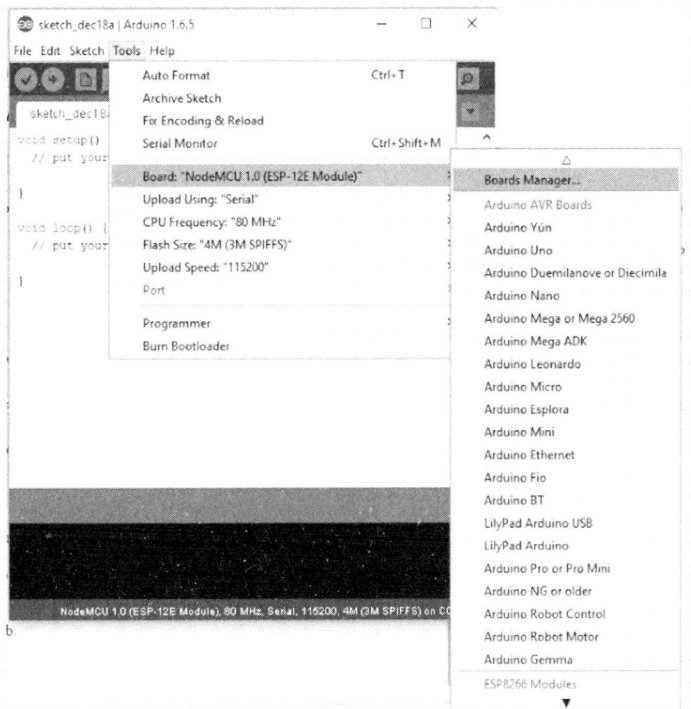

After completing the above steps, go to **Tools** and **Board**, and then select **Boards Manager**.

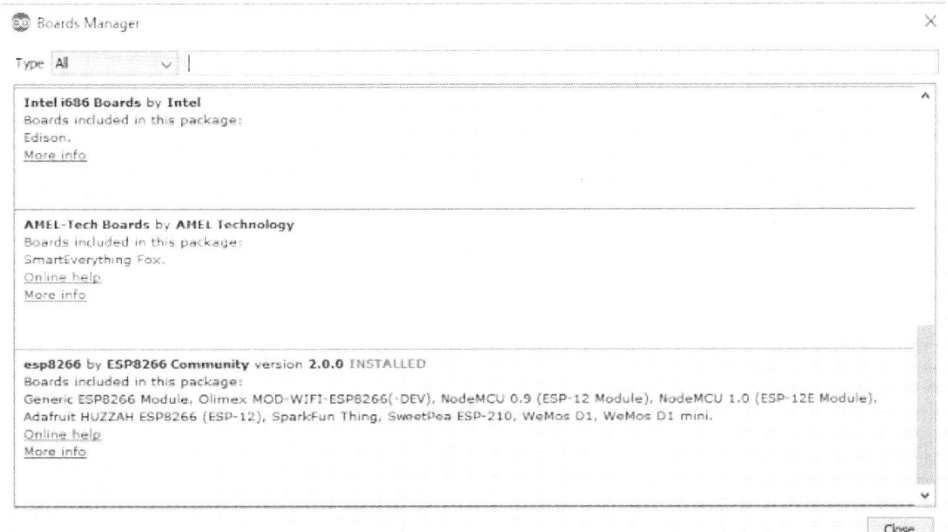

Navigate to **esp8266 by esp8266** community and install the software for Arduino.

Once all the above process has been completed, we are ready to program our **esp8266 with Arduino IDE**.

(Contd)

Box 8.1 *(Contd)*

Step 1:
- In the Tools menu 'Board,' some new boards are added after performing the above steps
- Select 'NodeMCU x.y (ESP12 module)'
- Prepare your hardware according to the programming/flashing schema as shown earlier
- Connect USB-TTL adapter with PC
- In the Tools menu, select the corresponding port of the USB-TTL adapter. Open the serial monitor (by pressing CTRL-Shift-M or from the Tools menu). Set the key emulation to 'Both NL & CR' and the speed to 115200 baud. This can be set in the bottom of terminal screen

Step 2: Install libraries

- Open Arduino IDE and go to Sketch → Include Library → Manage Libraries. Find and install the following libraries:
    - PubSubClient by Nick O'Leary (http://pubsubclient.knolleary.net/)
    - Adafruit Unified Sensor by Adafruit (https://github.com/adafruit/Adafruit_Sensor)
    - DHT sensor library by Adafruit (https://github.com/adafruit/DHT-sensor-library)
    - One Wire by Paul Stoffregen et al. (https://github.com/adafruit/DHT-sensor-library)
    - Dallas Temperature (https://github.com/milesburton/Arduino-Temperature-Control-Library)

Note: This hands-on tutorial was tested with the following versions of the libraries: PubSubClient 2.7.0, Adafruit Unified Sensor 1.0.2, DHT sensor library 1.3.4, One Wire Library 2.3.4, and Dallas Temperature 3.8.0.

Step 3:
Note: For the soil moisture sensor to send proper readings, it has to be calibrated first in air and water. Use the sketch (Code listing shown in Box 8.2) before proceeding with the next steps.

- Copy and paste the soilSensorThingsboard.ino sketch (Code listing as shown in Box 8.3)
- Edit following constants and variables in the sketch:
  WIFI_AP—name of your access point
  WIFI_PASSWORD—access point password
  TOKEN—the $ACCESS_TOKEN from ThingsBoard configuration step
  ThingsboardServer—ThingsBoard HOST/IP address that is accessible within your Wi-Fi network. Specify "demo.thingsboard.io" (if you are using live demo server)
- Connect NodeMCU to PC via a debug cable and select the corresponding port in Arduino IDE
- Compile and upload your sketch to the device using 'Upload' button

After application will be uploaded and started, it will try to connect to ThingsBoard node using MQTT client and upload 'soil Temperature' and 'soil Moisture' time series data once per second.

Autonomous operation: When you have uploaded the sketch, you may remove debug cable required for uploading and connect your NodeMCU, soil moisture and soil temperature sensor directly to the power source according to the final wiring schema as shown above.

Data visualization: Open ThingsBoard Web UI. You can access this dashboard by logging in as a tenant administrator using:

- Local ThingsBoard installation
    - login: tenant@thingsboard.org
    - password: tenant

(Contd)

Box 8.1 *(Contd)*

- ThingsBoard Demo Server
  - login: <your ThingsBoard login>
  - password: <your password>

Go to 'Devices' section and locate 'SoilTempAndMoisture,' open device details and switch to 'Latest telemetry' tab. If all is configured correctly, you should be able to see latest values of 'soil Temperature' and 'soil Moisture' in the table.

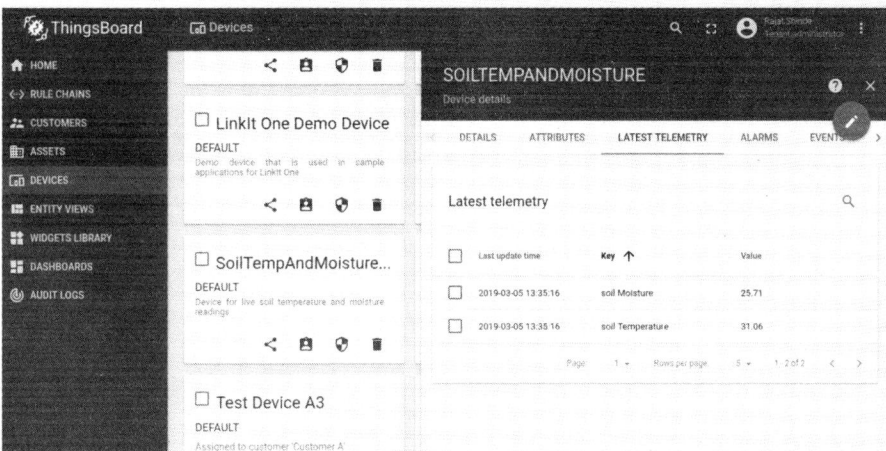

Note: The key values (soil Moisture and soil Temperature) shown in the above image are directly called from the Device attributes stored in 'Device' menu. These key values are defined in the payload of the MQTT message which is sent to the ThingsBoard instance by the NodeMCU.

Open 'Dashboards' section, then locate and open 'SOILTEMPANDMOISTURE' dashboard. As a result, you will see two digital gauges and two time series charts displaying soil temperature and soil moisture.

BOX 8.2: CALIBRATION OF DFROBOT SOIL MOISTURE SENSOR

Code Listing: Calibration of DFRobot Soil Moisture Sensor
(Source credit: DFRobot)

```
void setup() {
Serial.begin(9600); // open serial port, set the baud rate as 9600 bps
}
void loop() {
int val;
val = analogRead(0); //connect sensor to Analog 0
Serial.println(val); //print the value to serial port
delay(100);
}
```

Note: Run the above code first in Arduino IDE makes sure the soil moisture sensor is calibrated using the above code and also putting it in water and air and noting the readings are correct.

BOX 8.3: CONNECTING A SOIL MOISTURE AND SOIL TEMPERATURE SENSOR TO NODEMCU

Code Listing: Connecting a Soil Moisture and Soil Temperature Sensors to NODEMCU (Arduino Sketch)

```
#include "DHT.h"
#include <PubSubClient.h>
#include <ESP8266WiFi.h>
#include <OneWire.h>
#include <DallasTemperature.h>
// Data wire is plugged into pin 2 on the Arduino
// #define ONE_WIRE_BUS 2
// Data wire is plugged into pin 2........ on the Arduino
#define ONE_WIRE_BUS 2
OneWire oneWire(ONE_WIRE_BUS);

#define WIFI_AP "USERNAME"
#define WIFI_PASSWORD "PASSWORD"

#define TOKEN "9FcooE0NbneIeSZ68ai5"
// DHT
#define DHTPIN 2 //D4 for NodeMCU
#define DHTTYPE DHT11
DallasTemperature sensors(&oneWire);

char thingsboardServer[] = "demo.thingsboard.io";

WiFiClient wifiClient;
```

(Contd)

Box 8.3 *(Contd)*

```
// Initialize DHT sensor.
DHT dht(DHTPIN, DHTTYPE);

PubSubClient client(wifiClient);

int status = WL_IDLE_STATUS;
unsigned long lastSend;

void setup()
{
Serial.begin(115200);
sensors.begin();
delay(10);
InitWiFi();
client.setServer( thingsboardServer, 1883 );
lastSend = 0;
}

float SMpin = A0;
float Po;
double PoY;
float VMC;
float temp;

void loop()
{
if ( !client.connected() ) {
reconnect();
}

if ( millis() - lastSend > 1000 ) { // Update and send only after 1 seconds
getAndSendSoilTemperatureAndMoistureData();
lastSend = millis();
}

client.loop();
}

void getAndSendSoilTemperatureAndMoistureData()
{
Serial.println("Collecting temperature data.");

// Po = analogRead(SMpin);
// PoY = (1.39*0.001*Po*Po)-(1.413*Po)+471.23;
```

(Contd)

Box 8.3 (Contd)

```
// VMC = (1.17*0.0000001*PoY*PoY*PoY)-(3.95*0.0001*PoY*PoY)+(4.90*0.001*PoY)-1.9;
float moisture_percentage;
moisture_percentage = ( 100.00 - ( (analogRead(SMpin)/1023.00) * 100.00 ) );
float m = moisture_percentage;

// Read temperature as Celsius (the default)
sensors.requestTemperatures();
temp = sensors.getTempCByIndex(0);
float t = temp;

// Check if any reads failed and exit early (to try again).
if (isnan(m) || isnan(t)) {
Serial.println("Failed to read from Soil sensors!");
return;
}

Serial.print("Soil Moisture: ");
Serial.print(m);
Serial.print(" %\t");
Serial.print("Soil Temperature: ");
Serial.print(t);
Serial.print(" *C ");

String soilTemperature = String(t);
String soilMoisture = String(m);


// Just debug messages
Serial.print( "Sending temperature and humidity : [" );
Serial.print( soilTemperature ); Serial.print( "," );
Serial.print( soilMoisture );
Serial.print( "] -> " );

// Prepare a JSON payload string
String payload = "{";
payload += "\"soil Temperature\":"; payload += soilTemperature; payload += ",";
payload += "\"soil Moisture\":"; payload += soilMoisture;
payload += "}";

// Send payload
char attributes[100];
payload.toCharArray( attributes, 100 );
client.publish( "v1/devices/me/telemetry", attributes );
```

(Contd)

Box 8.3 *(Contd)*

```
Serial.println( attributes );

}

void InitWiFi()
{
Serial.println("Connecting to AP ...");
// attempt to connect to WiFi network

WiFi.begin(WIFI_AP, WIFI_PASSWORD);
while (WiFi.status() != WL_CONNECTED) {
delay(500);
Serial.print(".");
}
Serial.println("Connected to AP");
}


void reconnect() {
// Loop until we're reconnected
while (!client.connected()) {
status = WiFi.status();
if ( status != WL_CONNECTED) {
WiFi.begin(WIFI_AP, WIFI_PASSWORD);
while (WiFi.status() != WL_CONNECTED) {
delay(500);
Serial.print(".");
}
Serial.println("Connected to AP");
}
Serial.print("Connecting to ThingsBoard node ...");
// Attempt to connect (clientId, username, password)
if ( client.connect("ESP8266 Device", TOKEN, NULL) ) {
Serial.println( "[DONE]" );
} else {
Serial.print( "[FAILED] [ rc = " );
Serial.print( client.state() );
Serial.println( " : retrying in 5 seconds]" );
// Wait 5 seconds before retrying
delay( 5000 );

}
}
```

SUMMARY

This chapter began with defining an IoT platform and identifying the need for such a platform. The basic characteristics of the IoT platforms are described with examples. Further, various commercial and open source IoT platforms were described in terms of their unique offerings. Some guidelines were identified in terms of usability, domain application, scalability, and security for optimal selection of an IoT platform. To get a feel of an IoT platform, a hands-on tutorial is presented that describes end-to-end steps to make devices enabled via an IoT software platform.

REVIEW QUESTIONS

1. What is an IoT platform?
2. What is the need of an IoT platform?
3. Describe the core characteristics of an IoT platform?
4. Describe various commercial IoT platforms?
5. What is device provisioning and management?
6. Describe open source IoT platforms.
7. What are the important considerations while selecting an IoT platform?
8. What is NodeMCU?
9. Describe the steps involved in connecting ThingsBoard IoT platform with soil moisture sensor and visualize its data.

REFERENCES

1. [Arduino] https://www.arduino.cc/ [last accessed: 09/04/2020]
2. [AWS IoT platform] https://d1.awsstatic.com/IoT/ [last accessed: 09/04/2020]
3. [EVRYTHNG] https://evrythng.com/ [last accessed: 09/04/2020]
4. [Google IoT Cloud] https://cloud.google.com/solutions/iot/ [last accessed: 09/04/2020]
5. [IBM IOT platform] https://www.ibm.com/support/knowledgecenter/en/SSQP8H/iot/platform/iotplatform_overview.html [last accessed: 09/04/2020]
6. [Bosch IoT Suite] https://www.bosch-iot-suite.com/capabilities-bosch-iot-suite/ [last accessed: 09/04/2020]
7. https://developer.cisco.com/docs/kinetic/#!overview/overview [last accessed: 09/04/2020]
8. [OGC SensorThings] http://www.opengeospatial.org/standards/sensorthings [last accessed: 09/04/2020]
9. [ThingsBoard] https://thingsboard.io/ [last accessed: 09/04/2020]
10. [OGC SensorThings Sensing] http://docs.opengeospatial.org/is/15-078r6/15-078r6.html [last accessed: 09/04/2020]
11. [Thinger] https://thinger.io/ [last accessed: 09/04/2020]
12. [ThingSpeak] https://thingspeak.com/ [last accessed: 09/04/2020]
13. [SpringBoot] https://spring.io/projects/spring-boot [last accessed: 09/04/2020]
14. [SiteWhere] https://sitewhere.io [last accessed: 09/04/2020]
15. [NodeMCU] https://www.nodemcu.com/index_en.html [last accessed: 09/04/2020]
16. [Microsoft Azure IoT Suite] https://azure.microsoft.com/en-gb/blog/microsoft-azure-iot-suite-connecting-your-things-to-the-cloud [last accessed: 09/04/2020]
17. https://www.dfrobot.com/wiki/index.php/Capacitive_Soil_Moisture_Sensor_SKU:SEN0193 [last accessed: 09/04/2020]
18. https://cdn.sparkfun.com/datasheets/Sensors/Temp/DS18B20.pdf [last accessed: 09/04/2020]
19. https://thingsboard.io/docs/user-guide/ui/dashboards/#dashboard" [last accessed: 09/04/2020]

Prototyping IoT Applications

CHAPTER 9

"To take the jobs of tomorrow, students must become more than good test takers. They need to become makers who design, build, test and prototype."
—Charles Best

OBJECTIVES

- introduce the concepts of prototyping and its importance and benefits
- explain prototyping from an IoT perspective
- describe the concepts of Logical design
- understand prototyping with API
- explain embedded coding and memory management techniques

OUTCOMES

- ability to prototype an IoT product idea product idea
- use online API for prototyping
- develop a working physical prototype

REVISION

Internet of Things (IoT) open hardware for IoT boards, sensors, and actuators are covered in Chapters 5 and 6. IoT middleware technology and different IoT platforms are explored in Chapters 7 and 8. These chapters give the necessary foundational material to start designing and developing IoT prototype for a new product idea.

9.1 INTRODUCTION

A new product idea usually takes a preliminary shape in the form of a prototype. While building an Internet of Things (IoT) prototype the following points are important:

- What is unique and novel in this device that you have set out to develop?
- How is it different from similar existing devices? What are its major functions?
- How do you interact with it ?

This information helps in deciding different layers in the prototype device to be made, though the IoT device is complex. The full stack prototype of IoT is shown in Fig. 9.1.

Some examples for showing goals of different prototype devices are given as follows:

- Purpose of the physical device
- Functionality of the device
- Device communication interface (as a web application or a mobile app)

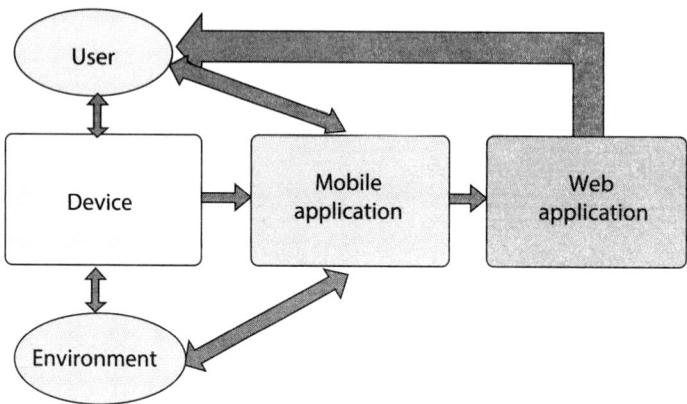

Fig. 9.1 Full Stack Prototype

Understanding and setting proper goals for the new product helps to decide the steps to be followed to implement the proper information flow of the chosen prototype.

9.2 PROTOTYPING AND ITS BENEFITS

Goal setting before prototype design is a very important step as the constraints for the prototyping process can be well understood. Various constraints such as size of the product, specialized/customized hardware, power need, cost, functionality, memory, and security (shown in Fig. 9.2)

Additionally, many other constraints, which are specific to the product to be prototyped, can be determined by asking some questions related to goals of design, need for field testing, extended scope of the product, funding and investors interest.

Understanding primary and secondary constraints for the prototype gives clarity for the design of the prototype.

9.2.1 Prototypes and IoT Product Ideas

A large number of possible applications can be developed using technologies of IoT, such as home automation and security, industrial asset tracking, chronic disease monitoring, and agricultural parameter monitoring. Some IoT products are complementary for the existing business products while others are new business opportunities.

Dimensions:
Are the prototype dimensions flexible to support possible changes in the future driven by market needs and technology?

In-built Memory:
Is the available device memory sufficient to support all the functions envisaged in the prototype?

Hardware Customization:
Is there any requirement to add additional hardware to support specific functionality of the product?

Power Requirements:
Is power consumption addressed in the prototype for the required time availabillity of the battery power?

Expenditure:
How much budget is allowed on the prototype development?

Security:
Testing the prototype may require certain security protocols to be followed, thus adding additional constraints.

Fig. 9.2 Common Constraints for Prototyping IoT Product

Step 1: Ideation Basically, every IoT product starts with an idea. It is suggested to continue with the components originally conceived for the prototype at the early stage instead of trying to optimize one particular component very early in the prototype development process. For example, to get better battery life, a lower powered processor is selected, but it may not support a particular sensor that you want to include in the prototype.

Step 2: Prototype At early stage, proof of concept creation becomes an expensive task. Rapid prototyping has become easier and cheaper now. It enables to develop an early product and verify its feasibility with minimal time and cost. Also, flexible enough to allow changes and adjustments as the development process evolves.

Step 3: Iterate In this step, various processes, vendors/ suppliers of components used in the product and other essential supporting services are finalised. However, certain components may change at a later point of time due to the evolving nature of technology, for example network connectivity, security, etc. Hence, those aspects have to borne in mind at this step.

Step 4: Deploy In this step, the conditions of the geographical area to be deployed are considered. For example, if the product is to be deployed for long durations and under harsh conditions, then durability of the device is important. Also, the battery life and connectivity issues have to be taken into account. Remote management and frequency of upgrades of the device needs due consideration. Any specific, socio-cultural aspects have also to be kept in mind.

Step 5: Scale Scaling IoT prototypes on a massive scale such as industrial, commercial, residential, etc. requires considerations such as connectivity and interfacing with external systems, tweaking the functionality of the application for specific segments of the market, ensuring high performance, ability to capture feedback from the consumers, frequent upgradation of the product, etc. These require the selection of right hardware, software components early on keeping in mind the scalability of the product. Examples of scaling includes increasing the number of devices to cover more geographical area, gateways to support and manage the increased sensors, support for massive volumes of data storage, maintaining connectivity, version control, global vs local needs, etc. All these require several iterations in order to obtain optimal solutions.

9.2.2 Selection of Physical Devices

While building your prototype, keep in mind the key components listed further. You must take into consideration other objects that the prototype will be using such as for a specific task if the users will be wearing masks, gloves, eye protection, or have their hands engaged or gestures. The prototype to be tested should be subjected to the natural environment for which it is defined as close as possible, such as the targeted consumers, similar geographical area or location of its intended use, the entities with which it is going to interact either static or interactive, mode of interaction such as online, offline, real-time, etc.

9.2.3 Sketches and Diagrams

It is one of the oldest methods of prototyping. With very little efforts and without any artistic skills these sketches can be drawn. With such sketches, your ideas can be shared with others to take inputs from team mates.

A system, process, or the structure of your ideas can be illustrated by sketches. Sketches are useful to understand complex use cases, where many factors are interacting with each other. Behaviour maps, journey maps, system flow diagrams, and many other mapping methods are used for understanding complex situations.

9.2.4 Open Source Versus Closed Source Technologies

When deciding software hardware requirements, IoT product developers encounter the dilemma of selecting open versus closed technologies for the development as each choice will have some positive features and some drawbacks.

Open source software (OSS) uses freely available code for any kind of software (system or application). The hardware that supports such software is called open hardware. A product developer can customize the available open source code by modifying and improving to make it suitable for their product idea.

However, most open source software licenses require that such modified software is open to the public for download, modification, update, and improvement.

Closed source software (CSS) means the software developed is proprietary. It can be accessed by the original developers for any kind of changes that are to be done. Any changes to the software are prohibited.

Some basic aspects to be considered while choosing the technology:

Prototype cost and price Open source is often free of cost but it is challenging to integrate it in commercial products. Careful study of the open source licensing is required as different open sources licenses (e.g. GPL, LGPL, BSD, Apache, CC, etc.) provide varying levels of restrictions for use in commercial products. Usually, CSS is a paid software. Its cost depends on the complexity of the software. However, for the higher cost of the paid software, you get full support for the product and better readily available functionality. Even some free trials for limited time period are given by the companies for promoting their software-hardware technologies.

Continuous quality support Between open source and closed source software, CSS provide better support as they are charging you for that service also. The responses from customers are documented and analyzed for improving the services and the product. However for OSS, support options are limited to hired experts, forums, and useful articles.

Source code availability OSS code is available for any kind of change and customization, without any restrictions. CSS is restricted than OSS because the source code cannot be changed or altered.

Security In OSS, bugs are fixed quickly as the code can be modified or updated by anybody. Due to availability of the open source code to anyone, hackers can find the vulnerabilities for the attacks in such OSS. In CSS, the code is not openly available and hence, security threats are less. Good support teams are available for quickly fixing the problems and bugs that a customer faces.

Usability In OSS, user guides are written for developers rather than for novice users. Usability is a major benefit of CSS. It is well documented and also well written with detailed instructions.

OSS is more flexible while CSS provides ease of use and learning is usually more faster.

9.3 PHYSICAL DESIGN CONSIDERATIONS

Once the objectives and constraints to achieve those objectives in a product prototype are identified, then relevant functional modules can be designed for the same. This step provides a better clarity for selection of right tools and technologies. Following discussion is for choosing the right module for a specific prototype.

9.3.1 Different Modules for IoT Prototyping

At least some of the following elements are there in an IoT product. (refer to Fig. 9.3):

Processor modules For executing the device firmware

Sensory modules Sense the surrounding environment for information collection

174 Internet of Things

Power module   To supply the power

Input/output module   These modules facilitate users to interact with the product physically for providing input or accessing output.

Communication module   For device communication, to facilitate the device with the Internet

Action modules   Modules to control surrounding objects using the device

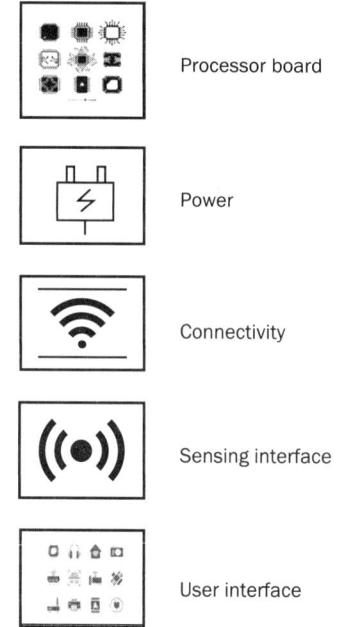

Fig. 9.3   Modules Required in an IoT Device

9.3.1.1 Selection of Embedded Platform: Microcontroller, System on Chips (SOC)

Processor modules: The processor board is the main part of a prototype of any IoT device. An IoT device processor is generally a low-power microcontroller board.

Main things to consider while selecting the processor:

- User-friendly development environment: It should be easy to use and support wide range of software
- Hardware capabilities of the selected processor: It should have suitable communication interfaces
- Memory: Memory size of the processor and its suitability for your design should also be considered

9.3.1.2 Common Open Source Microcontroller Boards for IoT Prototypes

Various microcontroller boards are explained in detail in Chapter 6 (considering various parameters such as memory, requirement, size, weight, I/O analog and digital pins, input/output current, etc).

Popular open source microcontroller boards with their application area are listed in Box 9.1.

BOX 9.1: POPULAR OPEN SOURCE MICROCONTROLLER BOARDS

Raspberry Pi:

- Compatible with Android
- Used for smartphone/tablet applications
- Many models and varying in cost
- A Broadcom chip with 700MHz CPU
- Supports at least one HDMI port
- Low cost and wide variety of capabilities

Arduino Board:

- Largest open source platform
- Easy to understand and affordable for small applications Microcontroller ATmega328 chip
- Operating voltage varies as per the models, Flash memory, SRAM, EEPROM
- Analog input pins, digital I/O pins
- Different Clock speed with different models

BeagleBoard:

- ARM Cortex-A8 processor, 512MB of DDR3 RAM, 2GB of on-board storage
- 3D graphics accelerator
- USB port and HDMI
- List of common applications of the board
  - Wi-Fi radio alarm clocks
  - Solar powered controllers
  - Retro gaming computers
  - Educational tool
  - Industrial robotics
  - Flying drones
  - 3D printers

Intel:

- Intel's Open Source Hardware namely Edison and Galileo
- Edison board is good for entry level inventors and for entrepreneurs going for mass production
- Galileo board is good for advanced user developing commercial products
- Running the code on an emulator

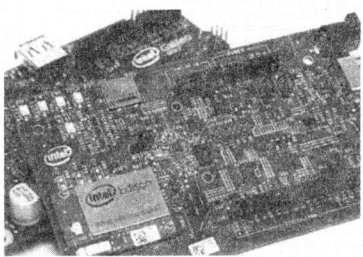

9.3.1.3 Selection of Sensors and Actuators

Sensor modules Choosing a sensor (for example, a temperature sensor) for an IoT application looks like a simple and straightforward decision. However, selecting the right sensor involves considering many factors into account such as availability, accuracy and precision, measurement range, power consumption, cost, and supplier. Some examples of environmental sensors are accelerometer, temperature, humidity, camera, etc.

More details on sensors are covered in Chapter 5.

Action modules (actuators) There are several action modules (actuators) that allow the device to control the surroundings. Some examples are: servo motor controllers, DC motor controllers, sound amplifiers, and relays. These and many other actuators are covered in detail in Chapter 5.

9.3.1.4 Communication Modules

Information is to be communicated from the IoT device to the Internet. This is achieved by wireless or wired connectivity.

Commonly used wireless communication modules:

Wi-Fi Wherever coverage is available, internet connectivity is possible of a device. Wi-Fi configuration on an IoT device is somewhat complicated but once set up, it offers very high data rates.

Bluetooth LE (BLE) BLE is low power as compared to Wi-Fi. It allows direct communication with mobile devices. BLE can provide limited distance range of approximately 100 feet and limited bandwidth of less than 100kbps. However, the range issue can often be solved using BLE-Wi-Fi or BLE-Cell wireless gateway hub.

Cellular Cellular connectivity allows a wider range of network connectivity than BLE or Wi-Fi. Hence, the IoT prototype can communicate with the Internet. However, for cellular connectivity data subscription to the network carrier is required. 4G, and now upcoming 5G are IoT focused.

Other communication modules that are generally in some specific applications are: USB (wired), Ethernet (wired), Zigbee, LoRa, Z-Wave, and Thread.

9.3.1.5 Power Modules

An IoT device usually works on low energy but still it needs to be powered. Many power options are available and selection of appropriate option for your prototype depends on the device characteristics such as battery operated or plugged in, life of the battery, and rechargeable or not.

Commonly used power modules for IoT devices are: USB powered, 9 V battery, AA/AAA batteries, rechargeable LiPo (lithium polymer) batteries, rechargeable/replaceable coin cells, and PoE (Power over Ethernet).

9.3.1.6 Input/Output Modules

Many kinds of Input/Output modules such as LEDs switches, touch- pads, LCD displays, etc.

9.3.2 Explore, Sketch, AND EXPERIMENT

The development of a prototype begins with exploratory analysis of the domain knowledge and then choosing the necessary set of tools and experimenting with them and thus give a basic shape to the idea. The next step is the selection of relevant prototyping tools that can support teams to iteratively work on the design in various stages such as preliminary testing of the idea, layout, device interaction, visualisation, etc. There is no single best tool that can be suggested because it all depends on what you need for a specific IoT application.

9.3.3 Introduction to Mechanical Design and Methodologies

This section presents an overview of different physical prototyping stages.

9.3.3.1 Rapid Prototyping Techniques

The manufacturing of the prototype requires certain experience to decide on the right option. This knowledge could be built over a period of time. Also, the cost of manufacturing and time required to do it could play a major role. Also, the specific properties of the material and number of pieces to be manufactured determines the selection of a particular method. It is suggested that for the initial prototype manufacturing less complicated methods may be used. Below are some approaches:

3D printing A reduced setup can be used for quicker outputs. If specific look and feel are required then it will be more costly and time consuming. For low volumes, it is significantly faster and cheaper than other techniques.

Computerized Numerical Control (CNC) machining Setup time plays a major role in deciding cost. Hence, it is good to make many units for return on investment.

CNC machining technology includes:

Turning The work piece is put into high-speed rotation and a moving cutting tool removes the material.

Milling The cutting tool itself is put into rotation to bring cutting edges to the work piece.

Drilling Holes are drilled by rotating a cutter on the work piece.

Casting Multiple models are created from a first master model that will be used as a reference.

9.3.3.2 Prototype Stage to Production Stage

9.3.3.2.1 Sourcing

Sourcing team checks the availability of required components to build the prototype and the available components are replaced for the specific components in a prototype.

9.3.3.2.2 NPR Release with Tooling and Sampling

After sourcing and quoting stage when the components are available the product goes through a stage named as Non Production Release (NPR). Continuously evolving quality procedure is documented for product specification and then certification by a third party audit. This is an iterative process till the right changes are made in the product.

9.3.3.3 Production Launch

In the product launch stage, various goals are achieved such as making the product available to customer as quickly as possible, improving the production quality by monitoring and obtaining enough sample quantity for the product to assess the quality of the product.

After completion of production phase the final product is inspected for quality control and issues are fixed and reported.

9.4 PROTOTYPING LOGICAL DESIGN

Some important points while developing IoT products and systems for different kinds of clients in consumer and industrial applications are listed as follows:

Unambiguous business strategy Performance/cost trade-off for the device to be developed and value addition by taking inputs from target customers for their expectations is important for business model clarity.

Optimising design Depends on the scale of data transfer as well as the cloud server or other system where the raw data of the sensor is processed. Further, the data capture and actual processing timestamps are to be captured to understand latency in the processing and consider it while improving the design accuracy.

Selecting application specific power model An IoT application determines the kind of battery to be used. Applications that track slowly changing features such as infrastructure, assets, bridges, tunnels, etc. require the IoT device to have long battery duration generally few years. Other applications such as wearables, health monitoring devices, etc. require devices that monitor for shorter duration so the battery maybe used accordingly. Hence, the power model has large variations and needs to be carefully understood.

Device security aspects Protecting user's data for security reasons, for preserving privacy and for properly recording critical data (for example, medical condition of a serious patient) and fixing bugs in the device with patches, security practices are needed.

Adapting to network technology evolution It is important to be ready for the fast changing communication technology landscape. As the communication technology is evolving (2G, 3G, 4G, and now 5G), adapting new technology and balancing with existing technologies is needed for the long life of an individual device.

Support for multiple platforms Decision about device compatibility and connectivity to various platforms needs to be thoroughly assessed. For example, which OS (s) will be fully supported by the device software and version control mechanism has to be put in place.

Adopt well proven technologies Many existing large-scale IoT platforms (e.g. Microsoft, Apple, Google, Samsung, Amazon, etc.) are providing a bouquet of services. Hence, it is not necessary to build the infrastructure from scratch as reuse of well proven current technologies is always a good choice.

9.5 PROTOTYPING USING API

Prototyping is an important stage of the design process as it is useful for reviewing concepts and obtaining feedback in the early stages of a project. A prototype helps to identify the drawbacks of the developed product and the limitations can be resolved before mass production. Some of the interactive tools to develop such mockup of your prototype are available, for example InVision, Framer, Marvel,

Origami Studio, Proto.io, etc. InVision is a web based interactive prototyping tool. Framer is a screen design tool for macOS which supports animated and interactive prototypes with your customized code. Marvel is a web based and mobile based tool for simplifying prototyping process. It supports different image formats for uploading such as GIF, TIFF, PSD. Facebook has made available the tool named as Origami Studio for prototyping. Proto.io is also a web based interactive prototype designing tool.

9.5.1 Application Programming Interface (API)

Sometimes a software application needs to send data to or receive data from another software application. Integration between two separate applications built with separate development languages is required in some cases. An Application Programming Interface (API) is a set of routines for providing such an interface. Software components' communication with one another is specified with an API. The applications of APIs are in wide areas. Software applications need not operate in isolation when API is used and the application can use functionalities that already exist in other applications using API calls.

For example, functionalities of YouTube and Twitter can be embedded into other websites with the use of APIs. An API works as a broker that sends messages from one system to another.

9.5.2 API for Real-time IoT Applications

IoT devices can be brought up to speed and scale with real time in different ways. Sensors connected with other IoT objects can provide immediate information to multiple IoT devices on that sensor network. Thus, excellent real-time services can be provided by IoT applications. Real-time data needs to be pushed to multiple devices often. Talend is one such platform where you can stream connected devices with external data such as the weather. Many real-time services for data streaming in medical data on online payment transaction data are benefited with theft or corruption of data with real-time transfer. In addition, the data can be transmitted in real time to multiple devices.

Polling Polling is a mechanism to fetch fresh data. Instead of manually refreshing or reloading a webpage, the new data is refreshed by a web application from the server. It is a synchronous operation. Due to the frequent fetching of data packets, the CPU could be over utilised, leading to higher battery usage. On the other hand if fetching is less frequent, it could lead to higher latency and the application may exhibit lagging. Hence, proper optimisation of polling is recommended using a spooling method.

Push For pushing the data to a browser, when browser is not requesting the data, HTTP requests are used. Web sockets and Server Sent events (SSE) technologies enable a client to receive automatic updates from a server via HTTP.

9.5.3 Packages for IoT in Python

IoT has wide area of applications such as in wireless sensor networks, big data and machine learning, data analytics, and real-time analytics. For such diversified fields, a programming language is needed which spans these diverse fields and is lightweight and scalable. Over the last decade, Python programming language is a popular choice of developers. Some major advantages of Python over other languages are:

- It is a very simple language for programming and for deployment
- It is embeddable, portable, and scalable, irrespective of the operating system
- It provides a good support and libraries for the language

The popular Python packages are mraa (GPIO), opencv (signal, video and image processing) numpy (scientific computing) tensorflow (numerical calculation, machine learning, deep learning) mysqldb (relation database) sockets (networking), pandas (data science), pano-Mqtt (MQTT protocol), matplotlib (data visualisation) tkinter (GUI development).

9.6 EMBEDDED CODE WRITING

Survey of IoT developers shows four preferred languages are used for embedded code writing:

- Java
- C/C++
- Python
- JavaScript

These languages are also preferred for developing desktop applications, mobile apps, and for server applications. In IoT also these languages are used predominantly. IoT applications need some additional functionalities and support.

Three broad areas to be focused when designing IoT architecture for an application are sensors to collect environmental information, local gateway to organize data hubs and centralized server to gather, process and analyze data.

If the sensor has basic construct, it is probably using C so that direct connectivity to RAM can be accomplished. For the rest, developers generally choose the language that best suits them to build the application.

There are many other languages used by developers to build some innovative and interesting smart such as: B#, Go, PHP, parasail, etc.

More than one language may be necessary for providing the required functionality. These days in IoT, the languages listed above are used in a combination to make the things smarter.

9.6.1 Writing Efficient Code

Most IoT devices need careful embedded programming as the nodes need to be managed efficiently due to reasons such as exponential growth of the nodes as the IoT system scales up, need to ensure uptime of the sensors, smart power management of the nodes to ensure longer runtimes and managing other resource constraints of gateways, memory, etc.

9.6.1.1 Memory Management

Memory management in IoT has high requirement due to the limits in memory in the devices, gateways and other resources. Hence, embeddded software has to be written by considering memory handling techniques for reliability and long run time.

From an IoT perspective if the memory issues (arising due to unpredictable usage patterns of the device) are not properly taken care of, it could lead to errors such as fragmentation (due to issues in heap usage, allocation and freeing of memory) mainly due to limited onboard memory and heap failures due to the inability to supply allocated memory even if it is available because of memory leaks and fragmentation. Hence, careful consideration should be given during the testing phase to include as many usage patterns of the device as possible and test the memory aspects.

9.6.1.2 Debugging Syntax

After following the necessary steps of design, testing, iteration, and physical working prototype, you bring up a great, perfectly functioning device and you can move confidently toward your first production run. However, a production run is filled with many bugs and errors. With proper debugging, you can get through.

Different validation tests such as preproduction validation, market requirement validation, Design for Manufacturing (DFM) validation are needed for removing flaws.

9.7 REAL-WORLD PROTOTYPE EXAMPLE: SMART HOME APPLIANCES (LIGHT AND FAN)

The product idea of smart fan and smart tube is as below:
Smart light and fan can be turned on and off automatically depending on the motion of a person and room light (Fig. 9.4).

- The bidirectional visit count is evaluated for each time a person is entering and coming out of the room
- This helps in automatic turning off the light and fan when nobody is present in the room
- This helps in saving energy consumption instantly

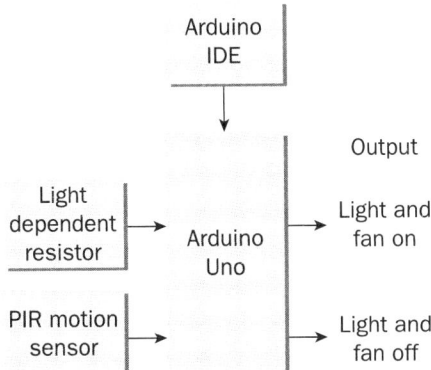

Fig. 9.4 Block Diagram of Automation of Smart Light and Smart Fan

9.7.1 Design Stage

Design stage is comprised of gaining domain knowledge, sketching the prototype design, and iterations of the previous two steps.

9.7.1.1 Functions of a Smart Light

- On/Off operation based on environment light and motion of the body
- If there is enough light of the environment and body motion is detected, then the light will remain OFF
- If there is darkness in the room and motion is detected, then the light will be switched ON automatically
- If there is no motion, then light will be OFF whether there is brightness or darkness in the room

Software and hardware requirements

Software: Arduino IDE, Raspbian OS, Python IDE, Arduino Uno and other sensors and actuators, Raspberry Pi, computer system, Embedded C programming, Python programming

Hardware: Arduino Uno and other sensors and actuators, Raspberry Pi, computer system

9.7.1.2 List of Components, Model Name, and Specifications

Table 9.1 represents various components and their specifications.

Table 9.1 Components and their Specifications

S. no.	Component name	Description, model name, and specifications	Component image
1.	Arduino Uno	It is an open source microcontroller board It is based on microchip ATmega 328P microcontroller	
2.	Connector cable	It is USB A to USB B connector cable It is used to connect Arduino Uno to Laptop	
3.	Breadboard	It is a solderless device It is used for building the prototype of an electronic circuit	
4.	Jumper wires	These are electronic wires that are used to interconnect the components within a circuit In this project, male to male, female to female, and female to male jumper wires are used	
5.	Resistors	It is a passive electronic component It controls the flow of current in the electronic circuit	
6.	LED	It is an electric light source It is a semiconductor light that emits light when the current flows through it	
7.	Relay module	It is an electrically operated switch It can control the flow of current flowing through the appliance	

(Contd)

Table 9.1 *(Contd)*

S. no.	Component name	Description, model name, and specifications	Component image
8.	Bulb	It is a night lamp and is 0.5 W Less maintenance Light weight and simple design	
9.	Fan	It is a 12 V DC fan Maximum air flow: 49.7 CFM Voltage: 12 V Rated speed: 4000–5000 rpm	
10.	LDR sensor module	LDR light sensor Working voltage: 3.3–5 V LM393 chip is used On board sensitivity adjustment	
11.	PIR motion sensor	Big Dome PIR Input voltage: 5 V DC Sensing angle: 110° Range: 3–5 m	
12.	IR module	IR sensor Input voltage: 5 V Two on-board LEDs	
13.	DHT11 temperature and humidity sensor module	DHT11 humidity + temp Input voltage: 3.3–5 V DC Output: digital Humidity: 20–90% RH Temperature: 0–50°C	

9.7.1.3 Development Stage: Experimentation, Iterations, and Testing

The circuit diagram for Arduino uno showing all the connections with sensors, actuators, and different modules is represented in Fig. 9.5.

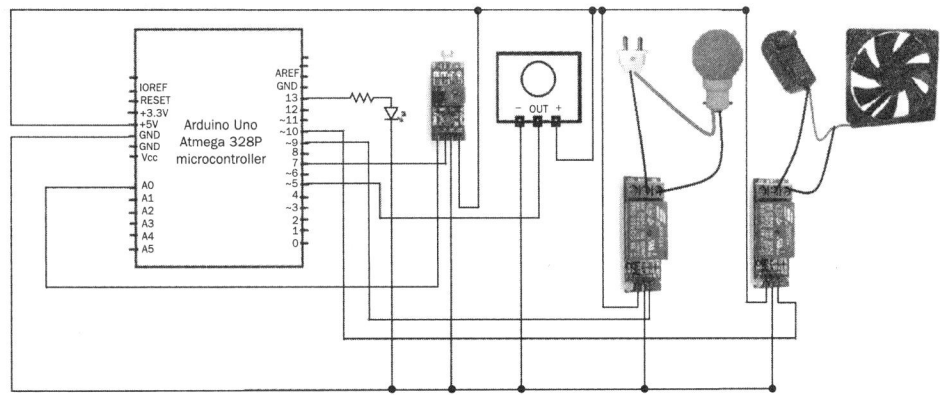

Fig. 9.5 Circuit Diagram for Arduino Uno Connectivity with Sensors, Actuators, and Different Modules

Connections for LDR sensor module

- Connect A0 pin of LDR module to the A0 pin of Arduino Uno
- Connect D0 pin of LDR module to the digital pin 7 of Arduino Uno
- Connect Vcc pin of LDR module to the 5 V pin of Arduino Uno
- Connect GND pin of LDR module to the GND pin of Arduino Uno

Connections for PIR sensor

- Connect Vcc pin of PIR sensor to the 5 V pin Arduino Uno
- Connect OUT pin of PIR sensor to the digital pin 5 of Arduino Uno
- Connect GND pin of PIR sensor to the GND pin of Arduino Uno

Connections for LED

- Connect positive end of LED to the resistor and another end of the resistor is connected to the digital pin 13 of Arduino Uno
- Connect negative end of LED to the GND pin of Arduino Uno

Connections for relay module 1 (Bulb)

- Connect IN pin of relay module 1 to the digital pin 9 of Arduino Uno
- Connect GND pin of relay module to the GND pin of Arduino Uno
- Connect Vcc pin of relay module to the 5 V pin of Arduino Uno
- Connect bulb and its supply pin to the NC and COM connection port of relay module

Connections for relay module 2 (Fan)

- Connect IN pin of relay module 2 to the digital pin 10 of Arduino Uno
- Connect GND pin of relay module to the GND pin of Arduino Uno
- Connect Vcc pin of relay module to the 5 V pin of Arduino Uno
- Connect fan and its supply pin to the NC and COM connection port of relay module

Box 9.1 shows the pseudocode for smart light and fan.

BOX 9.1: PSEUDOCODE: SMART LIGHT AND FAN

```
1. define ldrpin = 7
2. define pirpin = 5
3. define ledpin = 13
4. define relaypin1 = 9
5. define relaypin2 = 10
6. initialize the count = 0
7. setup( )
        i. set the pin mode of ldrpin as INPUT
       ii. set the pin mode of pirpin as INPUT
      iii. set the pin mode of ledpin as OUTPUT
```

(Contd)

Box 9.1 *(Contd)*

```
      iv. set the pin mode of relaypin1 as OUTPUT
       v. set the pin mode of relaypin2 as OUTPUT
8. loop()
   1. if pirpin is HIGH
         if ldrpin is HIGH
            1. set ledpin HIGH // darkness in the room
            2. set relaypin1 LOW // Bulb ON
            3. set relaypin2 LOW // Fan ON
         else
            1. set ledpin LOW // brightness in the room
            2. set relaypin1 HIGH // Bulb OFF
            3. set relaypin2 LOW // Fan ON
   2. else
         set ledpin LOW
         set relaypin1 HIGH // Bulb OFF
         set relaypin2 HIGH // Fan OFF
```

Steps for loading the code and working of smart light

- Compile the sketch code in the Arduino IDE
- Download software from the website https://www.arduino.cc/en/Main/Software
- Upload sketch from the Arduino to the Arduino Uno microcontroller
- **Case 1:** If brightness is present in the room and motion is detected
- **Case 2:** If brightness is not present in the room and motion is detected
- **Case 3:** If brightness is not present in the room and motion is not detected

9.7.1.4 Embedded Programming using Arduino IDE
Sketch snapshot of the code is shown in Fig. 9.6.

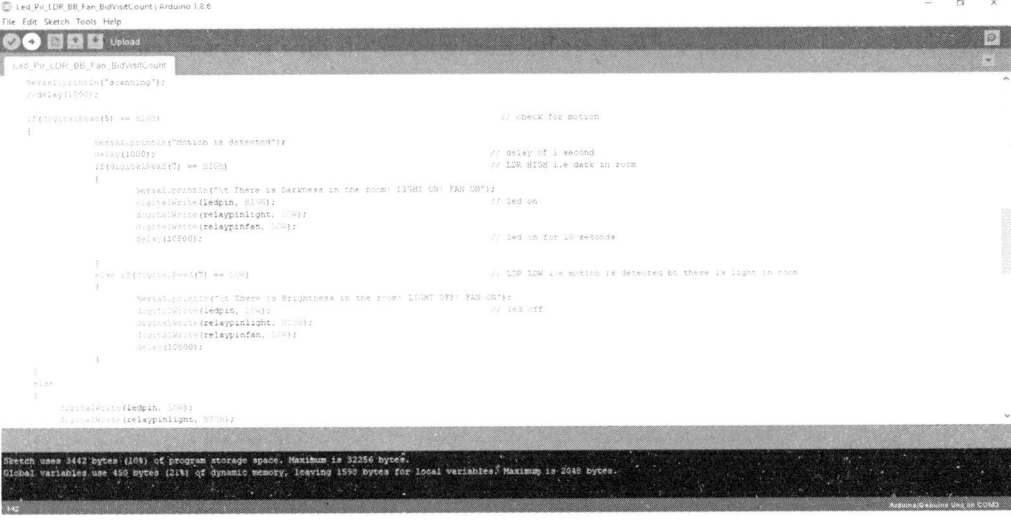

Output sketch

Fig. 9.6 Snapshot of the Code

9.7.2 Test Cases

Test case 1 If motion is detected and brightness is present in the room, then light remains OFF and the fan is turned ON. Figure 9.7 below shows the circuit and output of the connection for test case 1.

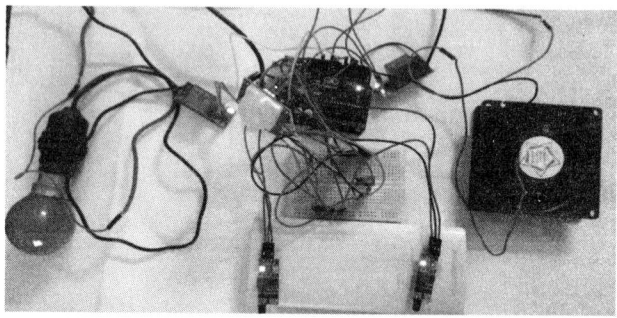

Fig. 9.7 Circuit and Output

Test case 2 If motion is detected and enough brightness is not present in the room, then light and the fan are turned ON. Figure 9.8 below shows the circuit and output of the connection for test case 2.

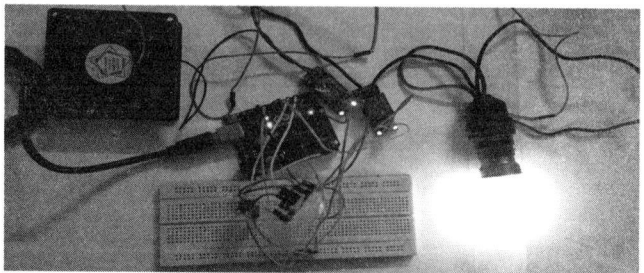

Fig. 9.8 Circuit and Output

Test case 3 If motion is not detected, whether there is brightness or darkness, light and fan are turned OFF. Figure 9.9 below shows the circuit and output of the connection for test case 3.

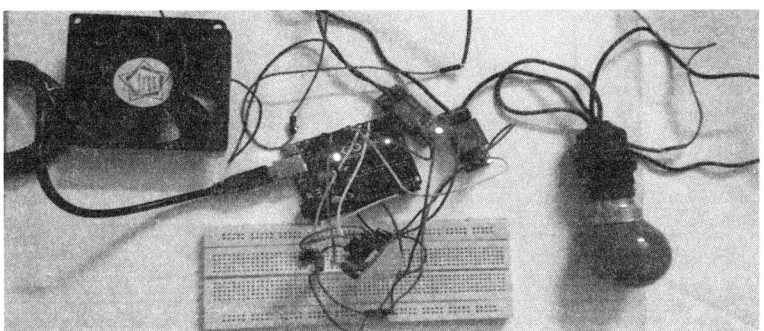

Fig. 9.9 Circuit and Output

THOUGHT EXERCISES

Write prototyping step for a smart house appliance for water sprinkling system for the garden with idea statement, design stage (knowledge, sketch, and experiment stage) with testing and with iterations in design.

9.8 BEST PRACTICES

IoT product should be built around four key elements that is people, objects, location and interactions.

As range of choices is wide, with the right prototype you can take a big step towards ultimately realizing your idea in the form of a user-friendly design.

Some recommendations to help create an excellent prototype are:

Fix right set of goals Based on a clear problem statement, fix a set of unambiguous goals. Ensure proper testing of the goals so that they fully satisfy the stated functionality of the prototype.

Select the right prototyping approach While creating a prototype, consider the stage of the design process, available resources, and the time limit to complete the task.

Explore and select right set of prototyping tools Do an exploratory analysis of the existing tools, by installing and getting familiar with the GUI and tools provided by software. It makes it lot easier to use this knowledge later when actually working on the prototype.

SUMMARY

Selection of right tools, platforms, and hardware makes the prototyping process smooth and fast with less number of iterations. It is possible to build and iterate network-connected IoT devices very quickly with electronic hardware using high-level software packages and libraries and good debugging tools. Many commercial web services can provide storage, communication, and computation for web-based IoT applications.

IoT applications often work with heterogeneous devices, services and protocols. Considering such high heterogeneity it is necessary to realise the importance of design space and prototyping using various tools.

KEY TERMS

IoT prototyping, prototyping modules, rapid prototyping, embedded programming, memory management, representational state transfer (REST), APIs for IoT prototyping

REVIEW EXERCISES

1. Explain what are the benefits of prototyping and its importance.
2. Explain prototype framework with its feasibility considering different parameters such as cost, time, and availability based on geographical area.
3. Compare open source vs closed source technology usage in context to IoT application areas.
4. What are the selection parameters for choosing embedded platforms for IoT device?
5. List popular open source embedded platforms and compare their advantages and disadvantages.
6. Explain mechanical design methodologies while prototyping the physical device.
7. Write a note on use of IDE while writing the embedded code.
8. What are the popular programming languages for IoT applications?
9. Write a note on Python packages useful for IoT applications?
10. Explain the importance and benefits of API?
11. Write a note on real-time API.
12. Explain how to write efficient code with memory management in IoT scenario of constrained memory.

REFERENCES

1. Massimo, B., O'Reilly. 2008. Getting Started with Arduino. ISBN: 978-0-596-15551-3
2. Pollie B. et al. Al.2012. Telematic Dinner Party: Designing for Togetherness through Play and Performance. In Proceedings of Designing Interactive Systems. DIS 2012.
3. Casaleggio A. 2011. The Evolution of Internet of Things. Online at: http://www.casaleggio.it/pubblicazioni/Focus_internet_of_things_v1.81%20-%20eng.pdf [last accessed 30/6/2019]
4. John, G. 2009. The Embedded Internet: Methodology and Findings. IDC.
5. Steve, H., et al. 2013. NET Gadgeteer: Experiences with a new platform for K-12 computer science education. Proceedings of the 44th SIGCSE Technical Symposium on Computer Science Education.
6. Tomas, L., Damith C., Ranasinghe, Mark H., Duncan M., Adding sense to the Internet of Things, An architecture framework for Smart Object systems.
7. Hideaki, K., Saul, G. 1999. Mediating awareness and communication through digital but physical surrogates. In CHI'99 extended abstracts. pp. 11–12.
8. Leonard Richardson and Sam Ruby, RESTful Web Services, O'Reilly, 2007.
9. Constantine A. Valhouli, "The Internet of things: Networked objects and smart devices," The Hammersmith Group Research Report, February 2010.
10. Villar, N., Scott, J., Hodges, S. 2011. Prototyping with Microsoft .NET Gadgeteer. In Proceedings of the fifth International Conference on Tangible, Embedded and Embodied Interaction, TEI.
11. OpenIoT Summit, 3/6/2016 Embedded Programming for IoT. Online at: https://events.static.linuxfound.org/sites/events/files/slides/Embedded%20Programming%20for%20IoT.pdf [last accessed: 30/6/2019]
12. Jakob, N. 2003. Paper Prototyping: Getting User Data Before You Code. Online at: https://www.nngroup.com/articles/paper-prototyping/ [last accessed: 30/6/2019]
13. Whitney, Q., Kevin, B. 2010.Storytelling for User Experience: Crafting Stories for Better Design.

14. Tim, B. 2009. Change by Design: How Design Thinking Transforms Organizations and Inspires Innovation.
15. IDEO, Determine What to Prototype. 2016. Online at: http://www.designkit.org/methods/ 34memory issues in some detail: https://01.org/blogs/2016/heap-allocation-iot [last accessed: 30/6/2019]
16. Rise of the Embedded Internet. Intel embedded processors white paper. 2009. Online at: http://download.intel.com/ embedded/15billion/applications/pdf/322202.pdf. [last accessed: 30/6/2019]
17. Casaleggio, A. 2011.The Evolution of Internet of Things. Online at: http://www.casaleggio.it/pubblicazioni/Focus_internet_of_things_v1.81%20-%20eng.pdf. [last accessed: 30/6/2019]
18. Valhouli, C. A. 2010. The Internet of Things: Networked Objects and Smart Devices. The Hammersmith Group Research Report. Online at: http://thehammersmithgroup.com/ images/reports/networked_objects.pdf [last accessed: 30/6/2019]
19. Richardson, L., Ruby, S. 2007. RESTful Web Services, O'Reilly.
20. Kuzuoka, H., Greenberg, S. 1999. Mediating Awareness and Communication through Digital but Physical Surrogates. Proc. Conf. Human Factors in Computing Systems (CHI 99). ACM. pp. 11–12.
21. P. Barden et al., "Telematic Dinner Party: Designing for Togetherness through Play and Performance," Proc. Designing Interactive Systems Conf. (DIS 12), ACM, 2012, pp. 38–47.
22. S. Hodges et al., ".NET Gadgeteer: Experiences with a New Platform for K-12 Computer Science Education," Proc. 44th SIGCSE Tech. Symp. Computer Science Education, ACM, 2013 (to appear).
23. G. Korteum et al., "Educating the Internet-of-Things Generation," Computer, Feb. 2013, pp. 53–61.
24. Jamal Hadi Salim; Robert Olsson; Alexey Kuznetsov (2001-11-10). Beyond softnet (PDF). 5th Annual Linux Showcase & Conference (ALS '01). pp. 165–172. Retrieved 2011-03-06. The classical NAPI paper.
25. http://arduino.cc/[last accessed 30/6/2019]
26. http://shieldlist.org/ [last accessed 30/6/2019]
27. http://mbed.org/[last accessed 30/6/2019]
28. http://nodejs.org/ [last accessed 30/6/2019]
29. http://www.raspberrypi.org/[last accessed 30/6/2019]
30. http://beagleboard.org/bone [last accessed: 30/6/2019]
31. http://sense.open.ac.uk/[last accessed: 30/6/2019]
32. http://www.iobridge.com/[last accessed: 30/6/2019]
33. http://electricimp.com/[last accessed: 30/6/2019]
34. https://iot.intersog.com/ [last accessed: 30/6/2019]
35. https://www.element14.com/[last accessed: 30/6/2019]
36. https://breadware.com/[last accessed: 30/6/2019]

FURTHER READING

1. Picking The Best Prototyping Software For Your Project: online at: https://www.smashingmagazine.com/2016/06/picking-the-best-prototyping-software-for-your-project/
2. 12 Factors In Selecting A Mobile Prototyping Tool: online at: https://www.smashingmagazine.com/2016/04/factors -selecting -mobile -prototyping -tool/
3. The Skeptic's Guide To Low-Fidelity Prototyping: online at: https://www.smashingmagazine.com/2014/10/the -skeptics -guide -to -low- fidelity-prototyping/
4. Lego Serious Play: online at: http://www.lego.com/en-us/seriousplay
5. d.school, Wizard of Oz Prototyping: online at: http://futureofstuffchallenge.org/download/prototype/bootleg-wizardofoz.pdf

PART III: IOT BIG DATA SCIENCE AND ANALYTICS

Chapter 10: Big IoT Data Science

Chapter 11: IoT in the Cloud

Chapter 12: Edge Analytics: Near Real-time Sensor Stream Processing

Chapter 13: Embedded High Performance Computing (HPC) for IoT

Big IoT Data Science

CHAPTER 10

"You have got to think about the big things while you're doing the small things, so that all the small things go in the right direction."

– Alvin Toffler

OBJECTIVES

- define and expand on the concept of data science
- explore the applicability of AI, machine learning, deep learning for Internet of Things (IoT)
- introduce big data with reference to IoT
- explain the concepts of data swamp/lake
- discuss various IoT specific requirements for analytics
- explain IoT analytics in terms of real-time and offline analytics
- discuss various methods for IoT data analytics
- introduce commercial and open source analytics platforms that are relevant to IoT

OUTCOMES

- gain insight into the unique data science aspects of IoT
- relate big data concepts with IoT
- understand various methods used to perform IoT analytics
- get an overview of IoT data analytics platforms and their applicability in various application domains

REVISION

Chapters 1 and 2 introduced the fundamental concepts of Internet of Things (IoT) and highlighted the huge data generation potential of IoT from multiple devices. Chapters 7 and 8 described middleware and software platforms that enable to quickly get an IoT system up and running and also emphasized IoT analytics as an important component of the middleware. The concept of real-time streaming analytics and also cloud-based offline analytics were also introduced. Building on these concepts, this chapter focuses on analytics in IoT, by first introducing data science and its components. The discussion will focus on IoT specific needs for analytics and unique challenges that it poses for performing real-time streaming analytics. Further, currently popular analytics platforms are explained and how they are actually applicable on power-constrained devices. Hands on exercises for performing IoT analytics are also given.

10.1 FOUNDATIONS AND PRINCIPLES OF BIG DATA SCIENCE

The heterogenous and huge volume of data (having varying characteristics) coming from IoT devices forms the fundamental reason for studying and exploring the area of data science. Data science is the study of data in a scientific manner, which comprises integrating several disciplines (statistics, computer science, linguistics, econometrics, sociology, etc.). This section focuses on the background of data science and its relevance to IoT.

10.1.1 Introduction

Data science as defined by Jeffrey Stanton 'Data Science refers to an emerging area of work concerned with the collection, preparation, analysis, visualization, management and preservation of large collections of information.'

The word 'science' is the key term in data science, and 'data' is like a raw material that is used to perform scientific analysis focused on extraction of knowledge, which is general enough to be applicable on new data.

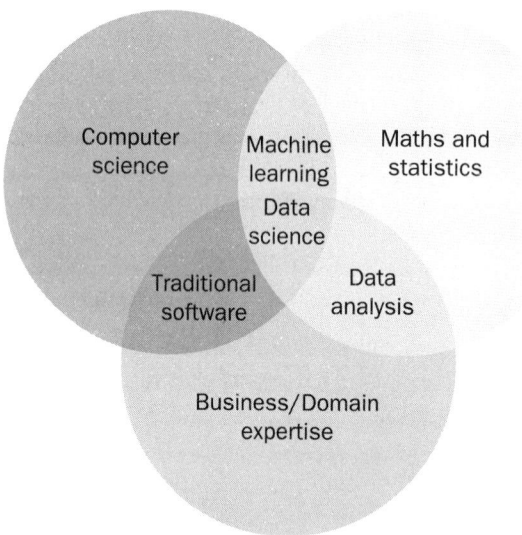

Fig. 10.1 Interdisciplinary Nature of Data Science

As shown in Fig. 10.1, data science includes techniques derived from several scientific disciplines such as mathematics, statistics, machine learning, artificial intelligence, computer science, databases, and optimization and combined with the understanding of the domain in which it is applied. Hence, any problem-solving exercise in data science requires:

- Data scientists, who understand the science of data and know how to formulate the problem that is domain specific; whose main goal is to extract hidden insights from data.
- Domain experts, who can explain the nature of the problem to the data scientists, and also interpret the validity of the results in the context of the domain.

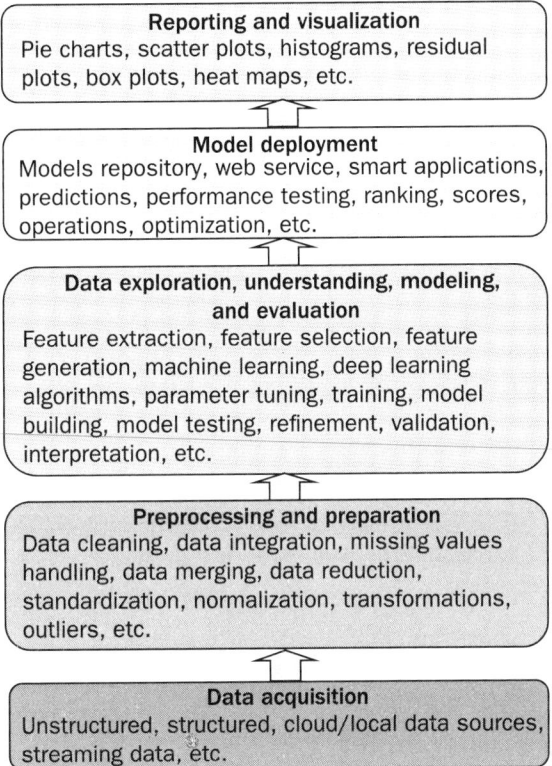

Fig. 10.2 Data Science Process

10.1.1.1 Data Science Process

The data science process involves several steps including (see Fig. 10.2):

Data acquisition The data can be obtained from a variety of IoT devices (such as sensors, actuators, etc.) and ancillary sources (other supporting data such as device health, etc.) either in online mode or data that is acquired from these devices and stored, secured, and managed in local (on premises) or cloud repository or both. The data generated by the IoT devices is highly heterogeneous in nature and can be in several forms such as:

Unstructured This form of data does not fit into a row/column format, which is the standard way of representation in a relational database. There is no predefined data model, schema associated with the data. It can be text, images, videos, discrete sensor readings, time-series data, etc. Due to differing requirements for storage of each of these types of data, data storage is a challenge. Unstructured databases such as NoSQL are usually preferred for this type of data. However, the type of storage is usually determined by the kind of end analytics that will carried out on that data.

Structured This form of data has a predefined record length and associated data model. Rarely, IoT data is directly available in structured form. It goes through a number of preprocessing steps to make it ready for further downstream analytics.

Further, the data can be classified based on its state such as:

Static data This type of data from IoT devices is usually high in volume and communicated using communication protocols such as MQTT or CoAP, and then ingested by IoT services for further processing and storage. Various IoT platforms (as discussed in Chapters 8, 9, and 11) have their own way of storing and managing the data.

Streaming data This type of data is usually captured at the gateways and in some cases on the device (having sufficient memory) to perform edge analytics. Since, this data is in motion, the analytics are tuned to work on a subset (window) of data at a time. This real-time processing is useful to send warnings, alerts, etc. and also trigger other IoT devices. Section 10.4.1 discusses analytics that can be performed on streaming data. In addition, Chapter 12 provides a more comprehensive material on edge analytics.

Data understanding, preprocessing, and preparation This process involves various operations such as:

Importing data Various ways to import the data include reading from tables, excel sheets, clipboard, comma separated values, fixed width formatted data, etc. Listing 10.1 shows an example of reading a CSV file in Python.

LISTING 10.1: IMPORTING DATA

 # Import the `pandas` library as `pd`
import pandas **as** pd
 # Load in the data with `read_csv()`
PData = pd.read_csv("**/Users/user1/datasets/pdata/pollutiondata.csv**",
    header=0)
 # set the width of the display in the output
pd.set_option('**display.width**', 300)
 # set the number of columns to show in the output
pd.set_option('**display.max_columns**', 10)
#print the first 10 rows of the data
print(PData.head(10))

OUTPUT

	ozone	particullate_matter	carbon_monoxide	sulfure_dioxide	nitrogen_dioxide	longitude	latitude	timestamp
0	44	69	57	67	83	10.189355	56.182102	8/1/14 0:05
1	41	66	54	67	78	10.189355	56.182102	8/1/14 0:10
2	46	62	59	68	80	10.189355	56.182102	8/1/14 0:15
3	44	58	58	64	80	10.189355	56.182102	8/1/14 0:20
4	48	55	63	59	82	10.189355	56.182102	8/1/14 0:25
5	47	60	60	62	80	10.189355	56.182102	8/1/14 0:30
6	48	55	55	61	82	10.189355	56.182102	8/1/14 0:35
7	52	52	54	65	86	10.189355	56.182102	8/1/14 0:40
8	56	54	50	67	90	10.189355	56.182102	8/1/14 0:45
9	56	53	54	70	87	10.189355	56.182102	8/1/14 0:50

(Contd)

Listing 10.1 *(Contd)*

Exercise: Practise importing data from other formats. Check Pandas library (https://pandas.pydata.org/) for corresponding functions.

Data cleaning This is a major step in the preprocessing operations. The data cleaning process helps to make the data in a form that is usable for further processing. It involves rectifying improper data having missing values, formatting issues, malformed records, outliers, etc. Listing 10.2 shows ways to perform data cleaning using various operations. The missing values can be filled using data imputation techniques as shown in Listing 10.3.

LISTING 10.2: MISSING VALUES IDENTIFICATION AND FILLING

Missing values

```python
# Import the `pandas` library as `pd`
import pandas as pd
# Load in the data with `read_csv()`
PData = pd.read_csv("/Users/user1/datasets/pdata/pollutiondata_missing.csv",
    header=0)
# set the width of the display in the output
pd.set_option('display.width', 300)
# set the number of columns to show in the output
pd.set_option('display.max_columns', 10)
#print the first 10 rows of the data
print(PData.head(10))
```

OUTPUT

```
   ozone  particullate_matter  carbon_monoxide  sulfure_dioxide  nitrogen_dioxide  longitude   latitude   timestamp
0   44.0                 69.0             57.0             67.0              83.0  10.189355  56.182102  8/1/14 0:05
1   41.0                 66.0             54.0             67.0              78.0  10.189355  56.182102  8/1/14 0:10
2   46.0                 62.0             59.0             68.0              80.0  10.189355  56.182102  8/1/14 0:15
3   44.0                 58.0              NaN             64.0              80.0  10.189355  56.182102  8/1/14 0:20
4    NaN                 55.0             63.0              NaN              82.0  10.189355  56.182102  8/1/14 0:25
5   47.0                 60.0             60.0             62.0               NaN  10.189355  56.182102  8/1/14 0:30
6   48.0                  NaN             55.0             61.0              82.0  10.189355  56.182102  8/1/14 0:35
7   52.0                 52.0              NaN             65.0              86.0  10.189355  56.182102  8/1/14 0:40
8   56.0                 54.0             50.0             67.0              90.0  10.189355  56.182102  8/1/14 0:45
9   56.0                 53.0             54.0             70.0              87.0  10.189355  56.182102  8/1/14 0:50
```

Note: Notice the NaN values in the output. Some data is missing.

LISTING 10.3: DATA IMPUTATION APPROACH TO FILL MISSING DATA

```
# Imputation is the process of replacing missing data with substituted values. You can either fill #in
the mean, the mode or the median or choose an interpolation technique using the #interpolate()
function to perform interpolation which gives an approximate value based on #neighborhood values.
```

(Contd)

Listing 10.3 (*Contd*)

```python
# Import the `pandas` library as `pd`
import pandas as pd
import numpy as np
# Load in the data with `read_csv()`
PData = pd.read_csv("/Users/user1/datasets/pdata/pollutiondata_missing.csv",
    header=0)
# set the width of the display in the output
pd.set_option('display.width', 300)
# set the number of columns to show in the output
pd.set_option('display.max_columns', 10)
#print the first 10 rows of the data
print(PData.head(10))
# Identify missing values
s=PData.isnull()
# Prints True or False depending on whether there is data value present or not
print(s)
# calculate Mean
mean_ozone=np.mean(PData.ozone)
# Replace missing values with the mean
filled_data = PData.ozone.fillna(mean_ozone)
print(filled_data)
```

OUTPUT

	ozone	particullate_matter	carbon_monoxide	sulfure_dioxide	nitrogen_dioxide	longitude	latitude	timestamp
0	False	False	False	False	False	False	False	False
1	False	False	False	False	False	False	False	False
2	False	False	False	False	False	False	False	False
3	False	False	True	False	False	False	False	False
4	True	False	False	True	False	False	False	False
5	False	False	False	False	True	False	False	False
6	False	True	False	False	False	False	False	False
7	False	False	True	False	False	False	False	False
8	False	False	False	False	False	False	False	False
9	False	False	False	False	False	False	False	False
10	False	False	False	False	False	False	False	False

```
0     44.000000
1     41.000000
2     46.000000
3     44.000000
4     51.229167
5     47.000000
6     48.000000
7     52.000000
8     56.000000
9     56.000000
10    57.000000
```

(*Contd*)

Listing 10.3 (*Contd*)

Note: Notice that the value in the fourth row (see output of listing 10.2), which was originally 'NaN', is replaced with the values 51.229.

Exercise: Modify the above code so that the missing values in all the columns are replaced at once.

Data merging This involves combining datasets from different sources to create a unified dataset which is further used for processing. This process is useful for data integration purposes when there is heterogeneity in the datasets in terms of data models, formats, etc. The merging technique is demonstrated in Listing 10.4 where data from two sensors is merged based on the timestamp of their acquisition.

LISTING 10.4: DATA MERGING TECHNIQUE USING PANDAS IN PYTHON

Data merging

```python
# Import the `pandas` library as `pd`
import pandas as pd
import numpy as np
# Load in the data with `read_csv()`
ozonedata = pd.read_csv("/Users/user1/datasets/pdata/ozone.csv",
    header=0)
patriculatedata = pd.read_csv("/Users/user1/datasets/pdata/particulate_matter.csv",
    header=0)
# set the width of the display in the output
pd.set_option('display.width', 300)
# set the number of columns to show in the output
pd.set_option('display.max_columns', 10)
#print the first 10 rows of the data
print(ozonedata.head(10))
print(patriculatedata.head(10))
mergeddata=pd.merge(ozonedata,patriculatedata)
print(mergeddata)
```

OUTPUT

```
   timestamp     ozone
0  8/1/14 0:05    44
1  8/1/14 0:10    41
2  8/1/14 0:15    46
3  8/1/14 0:20    44
4  8/1/14 0:25    48
5  8/1/14 0:30    47
6  8/1/14 0:35    48
7  8/1/14 0:40    52
8  8/1/14 0:45    56
9  8/1/14 0:50    56
```

(*Contd*)

Listing 10.4 (*Contd*)

```
    timestamp  particullate_matter
0  8/1/14 0:05                   69
1  8/1/14 0:10                   66
2  8/1/14 0:15                   62
3  8/1/14 0:20                   58
4  8/1/14 0:25                   55
5  8/1/14 0:30                   60
6  8/1/14 0:35                   55
7  8/1/14 0:40                   52
8  8/1/14 0:45                   54
9  8/1/14 0:50                   53
```

Merged data:

```
    timestamp  ozone  particullate_matter
0  8/1/14 0:05     44                   69
1  8/1/14 0:10     41                   66
2  8/1/14 0:15     46                   62
3  8/1/14 0:20     44                   58
4  8/1/14 0:25     48                   55
5  8/1/14 0:30     47                   60
6  8/1/14 0:35     48                   55
7  8/1/14 0:40     52                   52
8  8/1/14 0:45     56                   54
9  8/1/14 0:50     56                   53
```

Data standardization Data standardization is required because the variables are measured at different scales, for example, in Listing 10.5, the data is measured by different sensors (light, temperature, humidity, etc.) at different scales; hence, it is possible that the analysis can be skewed. Hence, there is a need to standardize these sensor observations. It is also a general requirement for many machine learning algorithms. The common way to do standardization is to bring the data into a normal distribution, that is, Gaussian with zero mean and unit variance.

LISTING 10.5: DATA STANDARDIZATION BY A NORMAL DISTRIBUTION

from sklearn import preprocessing
import numpy as np
import pandas as pd
 # set the width of the display in the output
pd.set_option('display.width', 300)

(*Contd*)

Listing 10.5 (*Contd*)

```
# set the number of columns to show in the output
pd.set_option('display.max_columns', 10)

# Read the CSV training and testing data using pandas
dataset=pd.read_csv("/Users/user1/datasets/Occupancy_data/datatraining.txt")

print(dataset.head(10))

# convert to numpy arrays and select the first 10 rows of data
Xtrain=np.array(dataset.head(10))

X_train=Xtrain[:,1:6]

print(X_train)

X_scaled = preprocessing.scale(X_train)
print(X_scaled)

xscaledmean=X_scaled.mean(axis=0)
print(xscaledmean)

# standard deviation tells you how much the individual numbers tend to differ from the mean
xscaledstd=X_scaled.std(axis=0)
print(xscaledstd)
```

OUTPUT

Snippet of raw data:

```
                  date  Temperature  Humidity  Light         CO2  HumidityRatio  Occupancy
1   2015-02-04 17:51:00       23.180   27.2720    426  721.250000       0.004793          1
2   2015-02-04 17:51:59       23.150   27.2675  429.5  714.000000       0.004783          1
3   2015-02-04 17:53:00       23.150   27.2450    426  713.500000       0.004779          1
4   2015-02-04 17:54:00       23.150   27.2000    426  708.250000       0.004772          1
5   2015-02-04 17:55:00       23.100   27.2000    426  704.500000       0.004757          1
6   2015-02-04 17:55:59       23.100   27.2000    419  701.000000       0.004757          1
7   2015-02-04 17:57:00       23.100   27.2000    419  701.666667       0.004757          1
8   2015-02-04 17:57:59       23.100   27.2000    419  699.000000       0.004757          1
9   2015-02-04 17:58:59       23.100   27.2000    419  689.333333       0.004757          1
10  2015-02-04 18:00:00       23.075   27.1750    419  688.000000       0.004745          1
```

Scaled:

```
[[ 1.8519298   1.78624382  0.79240582  1.7058527   1.88909147]
 [ 0.91818368  1.64283441  1.67285672  0.98681595  1.22642022]
 [ 0.91818368  0.92578739  0.79240582  0.93722721  0.95034791]
 [ 0.91818368 -0.50830667  0.79240582  0.41654543  0.3982138 ]
 [-0.63805985 -0.50830667  0.79240582  0.04462987 -0.60933159]
 [-0.63805985 -0.50830667 -0.968496   -0.30249132 -0.60933159]
 [-0.63805985 -0.50830667 -0.968496   -0.236373   -0.60933159]
 [-0.63805985 -0.50830667 -0.968496   -0.50084629 -0.60933159]
 [-0.63805985 -0.50830667 -0.968496   -1.45956195 -0.60933159]
 [-1.41618161 -1.30502559 -0.968496   -1.5917986  -1.41741545]]
```

(*Contd*)

Listing 10.5 (*Contd*)

> **Zero mean:**
> [1.10134124e-14 -4.44089210e-17 -5.79536419e-15 4.48530102e-15
> -6.06181771e-15]
>
> **Unit variance:**
> [1. 1. 1. 1. 1.]

Data scaling It is the process of scaling the features (e.g., temperature, humidity, light, etc.) between a predefined maximum and minimum. In Listing 10.6, the data is scaled between 0 and 1, which is a very common way of scaling.

An alternative standardization is scaling features to lie between a given minimum and maximum value, often between 0 and 1, so that the maximum absolute value of each feature is scaled to unit size.

LISTING 10.6: SCALING DATA IN A GIVEN RANGE OF VALUES

```
from sklearn import preprocessing
import numpy as np
import pandas as pd
# set the width of the display in the output
pd.set_option('display.width', 300)
# set the number of columns to show in the output
pd.set_option('display.max_columns', 10)

# Read the CSV training and testing data using pandas
dataset=pd.read_csv("/Users/datasets/Occupancy/Occupancy_data/datatraining.txt")
print(dataset.head(10))
# convert to numpy arrays and select the top 10 rows
Xtrain=np.array(dataset.head(10))
X_train=Xtrain[:,1:6]
print(X_train)
min_max_scaling = preprocessing.MinMaxScaler()
X_train_minmax = min_max_scaling.fit_transform(X_train)
print(X_train_minmax )
```

(*Contd*)

Listing 10.6 (*Contd*)

OUTPUT

```
[[1.         1.         0.66666667 1.         1.        ]
 [0.71428571 0.95360825 1.         0.78195489 0.79958571]
 [0.71428571 0.72164948 0.66666667 0.76691729 0.71609206]
 [0.71428571 0.25773196 0.66666667 0.60902256 0.54910795]
 [0.23809524 0.25773196 0.66666667 0.4962406  0.24439201]
 [0.23809524 0.25773196 0.         0.39097744 0.24439201]
 [0.23809524 0.25773196 0.         0.41102757 0.24439201]
 [0.23809524 0.25773196 0.         0.33082707 0.24439201]
 [0.23809524 0.25773196 0.         0.04010025 0.24439201]
 [0.         0.         0.         0.         0.        ]]
```

Data normalization It is the used for scaling the sample data values so that it has unit norm. The normalization is usually performed using either L1 or L2 norm. Listing 10.7 shows the Python code for normalization.

LISTING 10.7: NORMALIZATION USING L2 NORM

```
from sklearn import preprocessing
import numpy as np
import pandas as pd
# set the width of the display in the output
pd.set_option('display.width', 300)
# set the number of columns to show in the output
pd.set_option('display.max_columns', 10)

# Read the CSV training and testing data using pandas
dataset=pd.read_csv("/Users/user1/datasets/Occupancy/Occupancy_data/datatraining.txt")

print(dataset.head(10))
# convert to numpy arrays
Xtrain=np.array(dataset.head(10))
X_train=Xtrain[:,1:6]

print(X_train)
# Normalization using L2 norm
X_normalized = preprocessing.normalize(X_train,norm='l2')
print("Normalized data(L2 Norm):",X_normalized )
```

(*Contd*)

Listing 10.7 (*Contd*)

OUTPUT

```
Normalized data( L2 Norm): [[2.76470340e-02 3.25276061e-02 5.08094757e-01 8.60242590e-01
   5.71664827e-06]
 [2.77579995e-02 3.26950865e-02 5.14991827e-01 8.56121454e-01
   5.73558322e-06]
 [2.78323112e-02 3.27555645e-02 5.12162616e-01 8.57812270e-01
   5.74615621e-06]
 [2.79837279e-02 3.28793693e-02 5.14948945e-01 8.56132841e-01
   5.76780149e-06]
```

Data exploration, modeling, and evaluation

Exploratory data analysis (EDA) It is performed to gain a basic intuition and understanding of the data and prepare it for further modeling and analysis. The core tasks involved in EDA are:

Data description Describe the data and understand its various characteristics, so that you get a feel of the data. This is achieved by extracting summary statistics from the data such as count, mean, standard deviation, minimum and maximum values (see Listing 10.8).

LISTING 10.8: EXTRACTING SUMMARY STATISTICS FROM THE DATA

Exploratory data analysis: Extracting summary statistics from the dataset

```python
# Import the `pandas` library as `pd`
import pandas as pd
import numpy as np
# Load in the data with `read_csv()`
PData = pd.read_csv("/Users/user1/datasets/pdata/pollutiondata.csv",
   header=0)
# set the width of the display in the output
pd.set_option('display.width', 300)
# set the number of columns to show in the output
pd.set_option('display.max_columns', 10)
#print the first 10 rows of the data
five_variables=np.array(PData)
print(PData.head(10))
# Put the data in a DataFrame using Pandas and Convert the data array to numpy float type
df=pd.DataFrame(five_variables[:,0:5].astype(float))
# use the describe function to show the summary statistics of the data
print(df.describe(include=[np.number]))
```

(*Contd*)

Listing 10.8 (*Contd*)

OUTPUT

```
              0          1          2          3          4
count  49.000000  49.000000  49.000000  49.000000  49.000000
mean   51.163265  53.428571  46.877551  66.040816  79.714286
std     4.579606   4.699291   6.978039   6.928080   5.078550
min    41.000000  45.000000  31.000000  47.000000  68.000000
25%    48.000000  50.000000  42.000000  64.000000  76.000000
50%    50.000000  53.000000  47.000000  67.000000  79.000000
75%    54.000000  55.000000  51.000000  70.000000  84.000000
max    63.000000  69.000000  63.000000  80.000000  90.000000
```

Sampling the data This is useful for quickly seeing the data samples. Random sample rows or columns can be extracted from the dataset as shown in Listing 10.9.

LISTING 10.9: RANDOM SAMPLING OF THE DATASET

Data sampling

```python
# Import the `pandas` library as `pd`
import pandas as pd
import numpy as np
# Load in the data with `read_csv()`
PData = pd.read_csv("/Users/user1/datasets/pdata/pollutiondata.csv",
    header=0)
# set the width of the display in the output
pd.set_option('display.width', 300)
# set the number of columns to show in the output
pd.set_option('display.max_columns', 10)
#print the first 10 rows of the data
print("Sampled Data:")
# Sample 10 rows from the total 50 rows of data
print(PData.sample(10))
```

OUTPUT

```
Sampled Data:
    ozone  particullate_matter  carbon_monoxide  sulfure_dioxide  nitrogen_dioxide  longitude   latitude   timestamp
35   50                   50               44               69                72  10.189355  56.182102  8/1/14 3:00
19   55                   54               46               76                74  10.189355  56.182102  8/1/14 1:40
25   50                   53               36               75                84  10.189355  56.182102  8/1/14 2:10
21   52                   53               40               73                74  10.189355  56.182102  8/1/14 1:50
16   47                   59               48               73                77  10.189355  56.182102  8/1/14 1:25
28   50                   49               40               69                84  10.189355  56.182102  8/1/14 2:25
33   46                   56               47               64                68  10.189355  56.182102  8/1/14 2:50
38   50                   50               48               66                76  10.189355  56.182102  8/1/14 3:15
29   55                   51               43               67                81  10.189355  56.182102  8/1/14 2:30
46   57                   47               40               53                84  10.189355  56.182102  8/1/14 3:55
```

Further, it is possible to extract a predefined percentage of random sample data from the dataset.

Listing 10.10 shows how a predefined percentage of sample data can be extracted from the dataset.

LISTING 10.10: SAMPLING BASED ON A PREDEFINED QUANTITY OF SAMPLES

```python
# Import the `pandas` library as `pd`
import pandas as pd
import numpy as np
# Load in the data with `read_csv()`
PData = pd.read_csv("/Users/user1/datasets/pdata/pollutiondata.csv",
    header=0)
# set the width of the display in the output
pd.set_option('display.width', 300)
# set the number of columns to show in the output
pd.set_option('display.max_columns', 10)
#print the first 10 rows of the data
print("25% Sampled Data:")
samples=PData.sample(frac=.25)
print(samples)
```

OUTPUT

```
25% Sampled Data:
    ozone  particullate_matter  carbon_monoxide  sulfure_dioxide  nitrogen_dioxide  longitude   latitude    timestamp
11    55                   54               51               68                88  10.189355  56.182102  8/1/14 1:00
17    50                   57               47               77                78  10.189355  56.182102  8/1/14 1:30
6     48                   55               55               61                82  10.189355  56.182102  8/1/14 0:35
48    63                   48               44               47                81  10.189355  56.182102  8/1/14 4:05
26    48                   50               40               70                88  10.189355  56.182102  8/1/14 2:15
10    57                   54               54               69                87  10.189355  56.182102  8/1/14 0:55
4     48                   55               63               59                82  10.189355  56.182102  8/1/14 0:25
27    46                   50               42               69                89  10.189355  56.182102  8/1/14 2:20
35    50                   50               44               69                72  10.189355  56.182102  8/1/14 3:00
18    51                   57               45               80                79  10.189355  56.182102  8/1/14 1:35
0     44                   69               57               67                83  10.189355  56.182102  8/1/14 0:05
28    50                   49               40               69                84  10.189355  56.182102  8/1/14 2:25
```

Data querying The data can be further explored by making specific queries. It enables to make selections of the data based on some conditions. This is also a filtering technique to select specific subsets of the data (see Listing 10.11).

LISTING 10.11: QUERYING AND RETRIEVING SPECIFIC SUBSETS OF THE DATA

```python
# Import the `pandas` library as `pd`
import pandas as pd
import numpy as np
# Load in the data with `read_csv()`
```

(Contd)

Listing 10.11 (*Contd*)

```
PData = pd.read_csv("/Users/user1/datasets/pdata/pollutiondata.csv",
    header=0)
```
 # set the width of the display in the output
pd.set_option('**display.width**', 300)
 # set the number of columns to show in the output
pd.set_option('**display.max_columns**', 10)
#Query the data and show only those rows where the values of ozone are greater than sulfurdioxide
print(PData.query('**ozone > sulfure_dioxide**'))

```
    ozone  particullate_matter  carbon_monoxide  sulfure_dioxide  nitrogen_dioxide  longitude   latitude   timestamp
43   56           49                   46               54                81        10.189355  56.182102  8/1/14 3:40
44   59           46                   41               50                84        10.189355  56.182102  8/1/14 3:45
46   57           47                   40               53                84        10.189355  56.182102  8/1/14 3:55
47   62           45                   40               52                86        10.189355  56.182102  8/1/14 4:00
48   63           48                   44               47                81        10.189355  56.182102  8/1/14 4:05
```

Data reduction The data reduction approach is used when the dataset has high dimensionality. It would be easier to reduce the number of dimensions using a transformation, which extracts a new reduced set of features from the original dataset. This process can also be termed as feature extraction through transformations. Approaches such as principal component analysis, kernel principal component analysis, linear discriminant analysis (LDA), and multidimensional scaling transform the original features in the dataset and create new set of features based on their combinations, which can aid in creating better predictive models by increasing the information content in the features. Listing 10.12 shows the PCA analysis on a data having a dimensionality of 562. It is reduced to five components, which can be further used for various other analyses such as classification.

LISTING 10.12: DATA REDUCTION USING FEATURE TRANSFORMATION

Dimensionality reduction using principal component analysis

 # Import the `pandas` library as `pd`
import pandas **as** pd
import numpy **as** np
from sklearn.decomposition **import** PCA
from sklearn.preprocessing **import** StandardScaler
 # set the width of the display in the output
pd.set_option('**display.width**', 300)
 # set the number of columns to show in the output
pd.set_option('**display.max_columns**', 10)
 # Read the CSV training and testing data using pandas
train_data = pd.read_csv("**/Users/User1/datasets/activity/train.csv**", header=0)

(*Contd*)

Listing 10.12 (*Contd*)

```
test_data=pd.read_csv("Users/User1/datasets/activity/test.csv", header=0)
print(train_data.head(10))
# convert to numpy arrays
Xtrain=np.array(train_data)
Xtest=np.array(test_data)
# subset the data so that features and labels are assigned to X_train and y_train
X_train=Xtrain[:,0:561]
y_train=Xtrain[:,562]
print(y_train)
# test data
X_test = Xtest[:,0:561]
# true values of the test labels
y_test=Xtest[:,562]
#preprocess the data
# Standardize the data
X_standardized_data=StandardScaler().fit_transform(X_train.astype(float))
#print("Standardized Data:",X_standardized_data)
# PCA projection
pca=PCA(n_components=5)
# Do the PCA Transformation
PrincipalComponents=pca.fit_transform(X_standardized_data)
pcomponents_df=pd.DataFrame(data=PrincipalComponents,columns=['Principal Component 1','Principal Component 2','Principal Component 3','Principal Component 4','Principal Component 5'])
#pcomponents_df=pd.DataFrame(data=PrincipalComponents,columns=['Principal Component 1','Principal Component 2','Principal Component 3'])
# display the variance explained by each component
print("Explained Variance: ",pca.explained_variance_ratio_)
# Concatenate the labels with the principal components and display
finalDf = pd.concat([pcomponents_df, pd.DataFrame(y_train)], axis = 1)
print(finalDf)
```

```
Explained Variance:    [0.50781172 0.0658068  0.02806437 0.02503953 0.01888285]
    Principal Component 1  Principal Component 2  Principal Component 3  Principal Component 4  Principal Component 5         0
0             -16.138544               2.152024               3.144729              -0.272487               6.799680   STANDING
1             -15.296194               1.387144              -0.682232               2.813658               4.266437   STANDING
2             -15.137019               2.473351              -1.756667               3.717915               4.181649   STANDING
3             -15.350884               3.915681              -1.790296               2.567528               3.205163   STANDING
4             -15.544814               4.598737              -2.188562               2.897649               3.080099   STANDING
5             -15.359102               4.725042              -2.434422               2.527150               2.232916   STANDING
6             -14.900628               3.157020              -1.960183               2.529063               3.416565   STANDING
7             -15.228728               2.080484              -0.419245               2.002432               4.014655   STANDING
```

Feature selection   The goal of this approach is to select those features (attributes) that contribute maximum to the estimators' (e.g., classification algorithms) accuracy. Feature selection is a preprocessing technique, which is useful for building robust predictive models. The main contribution of feature selection process is:

- Dimensionality reduction and at the same time increasing the performance of the estimators. This is due to the reason that high dimensional data is complex, increases the training time in the model building process and can also sometimes lead to overfitting.
- Speeding up the learning process of the classification/regression algorithms.
- Reduce the model complexity and make it easy to understand as the number of features is reduced.
- It can result in models with higher accuracy than those without feature selection as only those subset of the features that are relevant to the problem are used in the model and thus have the highest impact on the overall accuracy of the model.

Approaches for feature selection

The main approaches for feature selection are filter-based, wrapper-based, and embedded.

Filter-based methods These methods filter/select the features based on a predefined performance criteria or metric. The subset of features that result from the selection can then be used for further analysis such as classification and regression (see Listing 10.13). The features that are selected by these filter methods can be ranked based on their relevance. Some of the performance metrics that are used by the filtering methods for feature subset selection include information gain, gain ratio, variance threshold, chi-square, correlation, fisher score, etc.

Wrapper-based methods These feature selection methods are called wrapper-based because they consider the actual induction or modeling algorithm that will be actually used for the final modeling task as the performance metric. This is in contrast to the filter-based methods, which do not care about where the selected subset of the features will be used. Examples of wrapper-based approach are using a classifier such as Naive bayes and SVM, which will be used every time a subset of features are selected by the feature selection algorithm (e.g., Genetic algorithm) and tested with the classifier to see if its accuracy has improved for that subset selection. Similarly for feature subset selection for clustering a clustering algorithm (e.g., K-means) will be used as the performance criterion and for a regression task a regression algorithm (e.g., support vector regression, logistic regression, etc.) will be used. High accuracy can be achieved using these methods. See Listing 10.14 for an example of wrapper-based feature selection.

Embedded methods These are the methods where the feature selection is embedded in the model construction process itself. Hence, no separate feature selection process is required. It combines the advantages of the filter- and wrapper-based approaches. Examples of such methods include CART, C4.5, random forests, multinomial logistic regression, etc. Both high accuracy and efficiency can be achieved using these methods as it performs the filtering operation first to obtain several potential subsets of features and then a wrapper-based approach is employed to actually select the most relevant features for the task at hand.

LISTING 10.13: FEATURE SELECTION USING A FILTERING TECHNIQUE

Feature selection (Filter-based approach using Chi-squared test)

```
# importing necessary libraries
import pandas as pd
import numpy as np
from sklearn.feature_selection import SelectKBest
from sklearn.feature_selection import chi2
# set the width of the display in the output
pd.set_option('display.width', 300)
# set the number of columns to show in the output
pd.set_option('display.max_columns', 10)
# Read the CSV training and testing data using pandas
dataset=pd.read_csv("/Users/user1/datasets/Occupancy/Occupancy_data/datatraining.txt")
# convert to numpy arrays and select the top 10 rows
Xtrain=np.array(dataset)
X_train=Xtrain[:,1:6].astype(float)
Y_train=Xtrain[:,6].astype(int)
print("X_Train:",X_train)
print("Y_Train:",Y_train)
## Select three features with highest chi-squared statistics
kbest=SelectKBest(score_func=chi2,k=3).fit(X_train,Y_train)

#summarize the scores
np.set_printoptions(precision=3)
features=kbest.transform(X_train)
scores=kbest.scores_
# summarize Selected Features
print("Scores:",scores)
print("Selected Features:")
print (features)
```

OUTPUT

```
Scores: [1.183e+02 1.711e+02 2.127e+06 6.728e+05 1.381e-01]
Selected Features:
[[ 27.272 426.    721.25 ]
 [ 27.267 429.5  714.   ]
 [ 27.245 426.    713.5  ]
 ...
 [ 36.095 433.    798.5  ]
 [ 36.26  433.    820.333]
 [ 36.2   447.    821.   ]]
```

Note: The score indicates the strength of a particular feature out of the five features (temperature, humidity, light, CO_2, and humidity ratio and in the same order). The selected features (3) and their values are displayed for the whole dataset.

LISTING 10.14: FEATURE SELECTION USING A WRAPPER-BASED TECHNIQUE

Feature selection using recursive feature elimination and logistic regression

```
# importing necessary libraries
import pandas as pd
import numpy as np
from sklearn.feature_selection import RFE
from sklearn.linear_model import LogisticRegression
```

```
# set the width of the display in the output
pd.set_option('display.width', 300)
# set the number of columns to show in the output
pd.set_option('display.max_columns', 10)
```

```
# Read the CSV training and testing data using pandas
dataset=pd.read_csv("/Users/user1/datasets/Occupancy/Occupancy_data/datatraining.txt")
```

print(dataset)

```
# convert to numpy arrays and select the top 10 rows
Xtrain=np.array(dataset)
```

```
X_train=Xtrain[:,1:6].astype(float)
Y_train=Xtrain[:,6].astype(int)
```

```
print("X_Train:",X_train)
print("Y_Train:",Y_train)
```

```
RModel=LogisticRegression()
## Select the features using recursive feature elimination with the logistic regression model as the decision function.
rfe=RFE(RModel,4)
fit= rfe.fit(X_train,Y_train)
```

```
print("No. of Features:", fit.n_features_)
print("Selected Features:", fit.support_)
print("Feature Ranking:", fit.ranking_)
```

OUTPUT

```
No. of Features: 4
Selected Features: [ True  True  True  True False]
Feature Ranking: [1 1 1 1 2]
```

Note: Out of the five features, that is, temperature, humidity, light, CO_2, and humidity ratio, the wrapper-based algorithm chose the first four features.

The clustering and classification approaches, and their evaluation methods, which also come under the modeling and evaluation component of the data science process (refer Fig. 10.2) are explained in Section 10.4.

Model deployment The models that were developed by the processing steps as outlined in Fig. 10.2 and described in the above sections are now ready to be deployed into the production environment. This is the last mile task after which these models will be used for real-world tasks or address a business problem and are expected to perform well and highly scalable. The process of deployment of the models is often related to the cloud infrastructure and the tools and environment that it provides.

The machine learning models and other related tools and computational requirements are all integrated in a platform called the DataOps (Data operations). It provides automation, data access, integration modules and model deployment, and management functionality.

Reporting and visualization Reporting is of three types, that is, static or canned reports, dashboards, and alerts. These are based on the purpose of the report and its reach or coverage of the topic. The canned reports are those that can be generated by analysis tool itself, and extracted by the users of the tools by themselves on a regular basis and sent to other end users based on their requirements. These reports generally have the same structure and could be routine for some people, while, they are specifically useful for certain set of users. The dashboards on the other hand are more focused and can have a very specific set of information shown to a specialized group of people. These dashboards can have several different views and each view can show a different perspective of the analysis for different people, that is, company top management, operational staff, etc. Various visualization tools are built into these dashboards for enhanced understanding of the information. The real-time information is usually reported in the form of warnings, alerts, etc. These are normally brief and are triggered based on a set of predefined criteria. The alerts are usually graded to provide the level of urgency for response activities. For example, during flood disasters, the IoT sensors can be used to capture the water levels and based on the predefined thresholds, warnings and alerts can be sent on a regular basis.

10.2 CONCEPT OF A DATA LAKE/SWAMP

A data lake consists of data that is in its raw and unprocessed form and the data is gathered irrespective of its quality, that is, it retains all the data (both current and historical). The reason behind this is to enable the use of data in ways that were not originally intended or perceived, that is, to go beyond traditional ways of looking at data. The big data approaches usually are aligned with data lake concept and go further than the traditional relational database, which is the foundation of data warehouse (a central repository that integrates business data from heterogeneous sources and optimized for performing analytics). Hadoop, NoSQL kind of approaches are more relevant in this context. The main characteristics of a data lake are:

- Retaining all data to ensure that in some future time, it may be necessary to use that data to gain some unforeseen insights. It also helps to rewind and go back in time to perform analysis.
- Support for various data types/formats, data in the form of web logs, images, videos, sensor data, social network data, etc. is all supported by data lakes. Some of the above kinds of data were

usually not stored in traditional transactional type of data repositories earlier, but the recent acknowledgement of usefulness of such data and the understanding that can be obtained from them resulted in their acquisition, storage in their raw forms, and transformation into a usable format whenever it is necessary.

- Support for various kinds of users, that is, (i) those that just need structured data, (ii) those that go beyond the already transformed data and seek the raw data and combine with data from other sources, and (iii) those that perform more in-depth analysis by integrating various types of data from a variety of relevant sources and creating a new data source and then performing analytics on top it.
- Adaptability to the changing conditions that require a different way of answering questions than it was originally designed for. Since, the data lakes store raw, untransformed data, new novel ways of extracting information from it can be done easily without the need for major rewriting of the analysis tools. This provides the opportunity to obtain more useful insights than was possible earlier using data warehouses, which are more structured and were built for specific end goals in mind.

BOX 10.1: SOME KEY DIFFERENCES BETWEEN DATA WAREHOUSE AND DATA LAKE

Data Warehouse vs Data Lake

Feature	Data warehouse	Data lake
Data storage	Preprocessed data is stored for predefined uses. Takes less storage, but more costly storage infrastructure.	All the data is stored, no specific use is preconceived. Needs a lot more storage, but available at low-cost (i.e., commodity off-the-shelf servers and cheap storage).
Data model	Structured data with well-defined data models and methodology.	Data is stored as it comes in raw form, unstructured, structured, nontraditional data, etc.
Types of users	Applicable to users that have been trained to work with specific data sources and data structures. Cannot go beyond what is offered by the warehouse. Usually, business professional are typical users.	Since data is available in raw form, it is up to the user to curate it to their needs. Hence, more flexibility in transforming data based on the need. Data scientists are typical users.
Accessibility	Because the data is preprocessed, it is easier to understand readily by users, but is limited to using the data for specific purposes only. Changes to the data are not permitted.	Data is in raw form, hence certain level of processing before it can be put to use. Data repositories are more easily accessible due to its unstructured nature, so changes can be made quickly, that is, configured and reconfigured as necessary.
Purpose and adaptability	Well defined purpose for using the data. Cannot go beyond what it was intended to do. Adaptability to new situations, use cases is limited.	No predefined purpose. Can be moulded for use with any tool, application, etc. High adaptability.
Security	The security aspects are more mature and sophisticated in data warehouses.	Security aspects are still evolving. Recently, many robust approaches are in operation.

However, the data lakes over a period of time can become data swamps and unmanageable if care is not taken to ensure data quality and good data governance practices (See Box 10.1).

10.3 RELATION BETWEEN IOT AND BIG DATA

IoT systems in various application domains are generating tremendous amounts of data at a rate that is unprecedented. This data has characteristics of big data in terms of:

Volume/Scale: Millions of devices are being connected to the Internet, connecting people, devices, and applications in a way that is massive in scale.

Velocity: The extremely high rate at which the data is being generated by the IoT devices.

Variety: The data from diverse types of IoT devices is generated in a variety of data models: structured, unstructured, semistructured, etc.

Heterogeneity: The data used for IoT-based solutions is usually gathered from heterogeneous data sources having multiple characteristics and structures.

In addition, other requirements such as big data storage, big data security, and big data analytics are required to efficiently process and manage IoT data. Hence, big data technologies combined with IoT specific technologies related to devices and connectivity are emerging as the solutions for developing IoT applications. In this chapter, the analytics for IoT are specifically discussed from a big data viewpoint.

10.4 BIG DATA ANALYTICS IN IOT

Big data analytics provides a means for analyzing and visualizing data from IoT sensors, actuators, devices, and other connected components of the IoT system. The analytics are useful to understand, summarize, and obtain useful insights from large volumes of data coming at very high speed in the form of streams.

IoT data analytics are useful for:

- Automating many decision-making processes so that human intervention is minimized and IoT devices and applications can autonomously perform actions.
- Increasing the efficiency with which processes can be executed. For example, supply chain operations can be made highly efficient by deploying IoT-based solutions.
- Condition-based monitoring and predictive maintenance of equipment, which is critical in many areas such as industries, manufacturing, healthcare, and transportation.
- Service efficiency that encompasses remote management, service chain, material management, etc.
- Analysis of the product usage by customers and accordingly customize the product thus enabling competitive advantage in the market.
- Reducing overall operational expenditure and increasing revenue.

The data from IoT can take various forms such as structured/semistructured/unstructured, time-series, spatiotemporal (e.g., mobile sensors), etc. Due to such high diversity and having the prime attributes of big data such as volume, velocity, variety, and veracity, the data from IoT requires a different way of processing as compared to traditional data, which is primarily seen as a transactions database and is static to a certain extent. Several data analysis methods that are traditionally used such as preprocessing, transforming, and filtering, are still applicable on the IoT data albeit the data in the continuous streaming form requires some adaptation of these methods. The analytics can be in the form of:

Descriptive analytics Descriptive analytics provides summaries in the forms of reports, charts, figures, etc. The data from the IoT devices is continuously monitored for providing feedback and enabling situational awareness. It can answer questions such as: What is the current status? What happened earlier or from x days till now? These analytics are based on descriptive statistics that are techniques for summarizing and organizing the information of the data.

Diagnostic analytics Diagnostic analytics can provide the causative factors for a particular problem. The IoT data is deeply examined to extract the reasons for the occurrence of unexpected events, anomalies, etc. In general, it can answer questions such as: Why is it happening that way? What processes led this event to happen?

Predictive analytics Predictive analytics are developed based on the models that are generated using IoT data in conjunction with various methods for building predictive models using AI, machine learning, and deep learning techniques (see Box 10.2) that take into consideration the historical data and can provide future projections. In real-time systems, these analytics can quickly trigger automated reconfigurations, start processes that can recover the system from failure, reduce risk, etc. It can answer 'what if' kind of questions, that is, what will happen in X amount of time, steps, etc.

Prescriptive analytics Prescriptive analytics provides the steps or rules for action so that a particular task can be accomplished in a more efficient manner. It assists in the process of decision making. It can answer questions such as: What are my options? What steps do I need to take? What actions will address this issue?

BOX 10.2: AI, MACHINE LEARNING, AND DEEP LEARNING

Artificial intelligence (AI): According to John McCarthy who first coined the term Artificial Intelligence, it is 'the science and engineering of making intelligent machines, especially intelligent computer programs.'

The goal is to make a computer-controlled system think and possess intelligence similar to a human being. AI techniques have proven to be successful in many domains such as natural language processing (NLP), computer vision systems, robotics, medical domain, industrial applications, intelligent transportation systems, etc.

Machine learning: Machine learning is a field of study that applies the principles of computer science and statistics to create statistical models, which are used for future predictions (based on past data or big data) and identifying (discovering) patterns in data. Machine learning is itself a type of artificial intelligence (Fig. 10.3) that allows software applications to become more accurate in predicting outcomes without being explicitly programmed.

(Contd)

Box 10.2 (*Contd*)

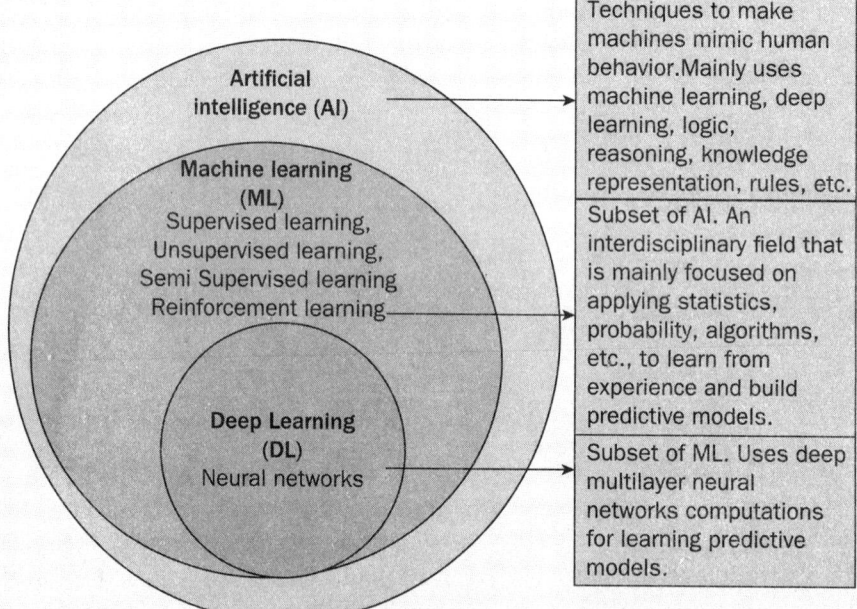

Fig. 10.3   AI, Machine Learning, and Deep Learning

Deep learning: Deep learning is a form of machine learning that is used for supervised, unsupervised, and reinforcement learning. These algorithms are based on deep artificial neural networks and are showing unprecedented new levels of classification accuracy in many domains such multimedia image recognition, audio/video processing, medical images, etc. It is also used commonly for feature extraction and data visualization.

A neural network is a system that tries to mimic the human brain by using layers of connected units (called neurons) to learn relationships based on training data (Fig. 10.4). When there are many hidden layers (deep) with increasing complexity in the network hierarchy, the approach is called deep learning.

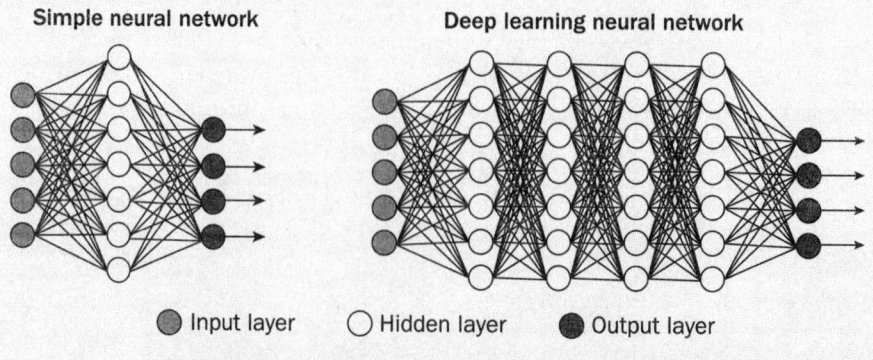

Fig. 10.4   Neural Network Versus Deep Learning

Several deep learning methods are available as shown in Fig. 10.5.

(*Contd*)

Box 10.2 (*Contd*)

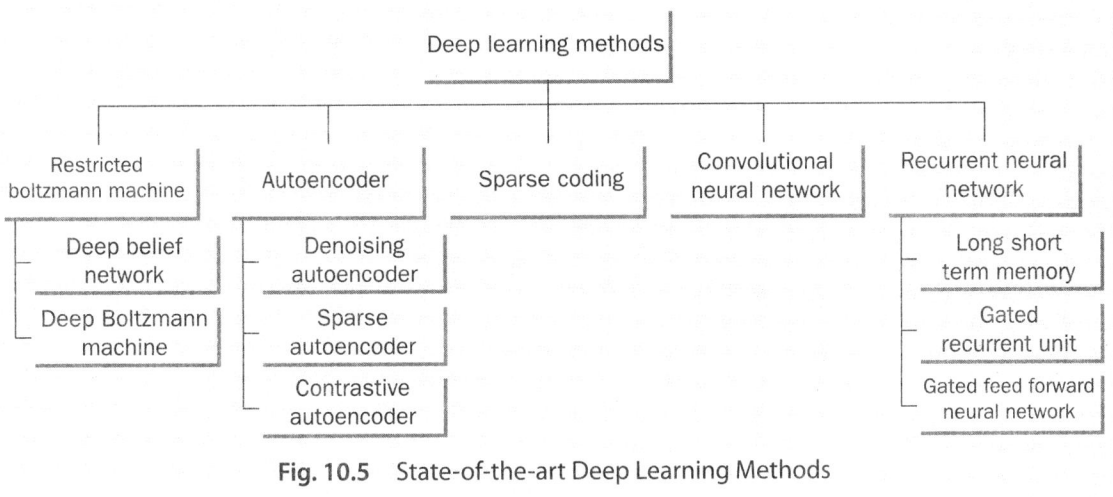

Fig. 10.5 State-of-the-art Deep Learning Methods

The broad classification of analytics in IoT based on the mode of IoT data acquisition (i.e., streaming or static mode) is: (i) real-time/edge analytics and (ii) offline analytics or analytics on the cloud. These are discussed below.

10.4.1 Real-time Analytics

This main characteristic of this type of analytics is its application on continuous streaming data, that is, data that is in motion. The approaches for doing analytics on this type of data can be mainly divided into:

10.4.1.1 Event Processing-based Approaches

These are based on methods such as event stream processing (ESP) and complex event stream processing (CEP). The goal is to capture interesting patterns from data coming from a single or multiple IoT devices and able to send alerts, warnings, etc. in real time. This requires understanding several filters that operate on streaming data using various kinds of predetermined window sizes and their configurations. The reader is referred to Chapter 12 for more in-depth information into these topics.

10.4.1.2 Data Stream Mining Approaches

In this approach, hidden knowledge/patterns are extracted from streaming data. This is different from classical data-mining techniques, where the dataset is static and the algorithm can iterate through the data many number of times to build the model. However, the stream mining approaches cannot do that due to the huge volume and continuously changing nature of the data. The key challenges of data stream mining as compared to traditional data mining are (Fig. 10.6):

Memory bounded The streaming data is continuous and can arrive indefinitely; therefore, the system cannot store the entire stream, but only a small fraction, in some form of summary (using data reduction approaches such as random sampling, histograms, and wavelets) may be stored and the rest discarded. The computations need to be performed (i.e., running the main algorithm) using limited amount of memory; due to this limitation, approximate answers/results are allowed.

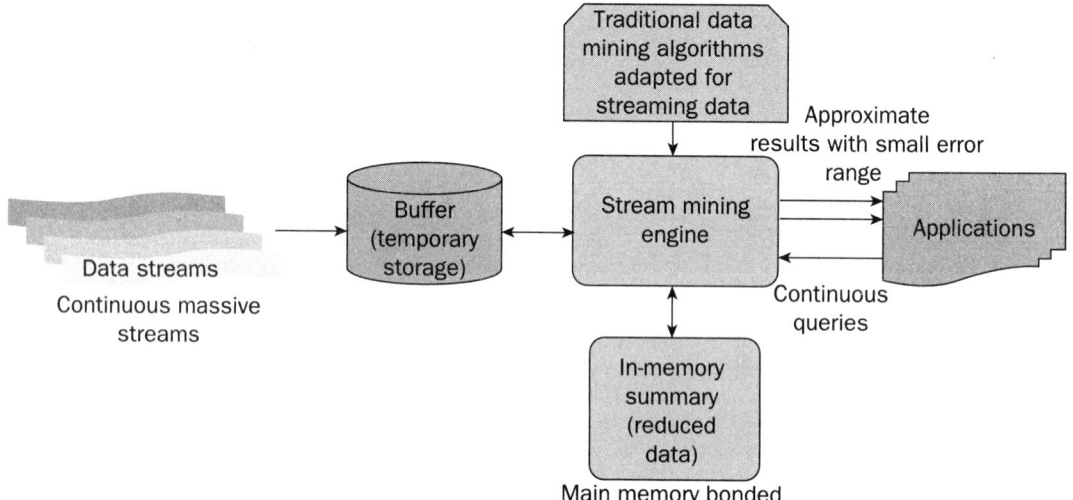

Fig. 10.6 Data Stream Mining Process

Single pass Each record (tuple) is examined only once. Since, it cannot be stored, the possibility of rewinding and looking back at the same data is not possible.

Real-time response The time taken for processing each record should be minimum, that is, rapid processing is a requirement.

Concept drift The patterns that were modeled using the data stream mining algorithms may not remain consistent over a period of time due to the arrival of new data and the possibility of underlying data distribution of that data is different than the previous data stream that was used to build the model. This phenomenon is termed as concept drift, so the stream data-mining algorithms need to be adaptable to these changing conditions and have the capability for anytime predictions.

Stream data-mining applications There are several stream data-mining applications from an IoT viewpoint. In general, any application that requires real-time information obtained from IoT device data streams is a candidate for data stream mining. A few examples are listed below.

- Industrial processes particularly in manufacturing; industrial IoT (IIoT) is an example for the application of data stream mining
- Real-time security monitoring using IoT devices (e.g., video streams)
- Traffic monitoring (continuous traffic-related data transmitted by IoT sensors)
- Real-time disaster monitoring using IoT sensors
- Real-time weather monitoring applications
- Streaming data from sensor networks/social networks
- Live stream monitoring of Smart Agriculture devices

Algorithms for stream data mining

Stream frequent pattern analysis This is a form of stream mining focused on capturing frequently occurring patterns (set of items, subsequences, substructures, etc.) in various types of data (i.e., structured, unstructured, semistructured, etc.). Windowing is a technique that is most common for frequent pattern analysis. Several kinds of windows are available such as:

Landmark window It captures the frequent item sets from a given starting point to the current point of time.

Sliding window The length of the window is kept constant. At a current time point, the frequent pattern time is captured and moved along with the current time point. Only those patterns are captured that arrived from the current time points are retained.

Damped window This type of window is useful to capture more recently arrived data and is given more weight than the historical data.

Stream clustering The objective of clustering of the streaming data is to find groups of data items that are similar in some way and separate them from other dissimilar data items. These groups or clusters are homogeneous and have distinct characteristics. The clustering algorithms have been developed outside the stream data-mining domain a few decades back and many are being developed currently. Some of these algorithms are being extended/adapted to the streaming data in such a way that they address the challenges as outlined in Section 10.4.1.2. They are classified into (i) partitioning methods, (ii) hierarchical methods, (iii) density-based methods, and (iv) grid-based methods. Figure 10.7 shows some of the currently available stream clustering algorithms.

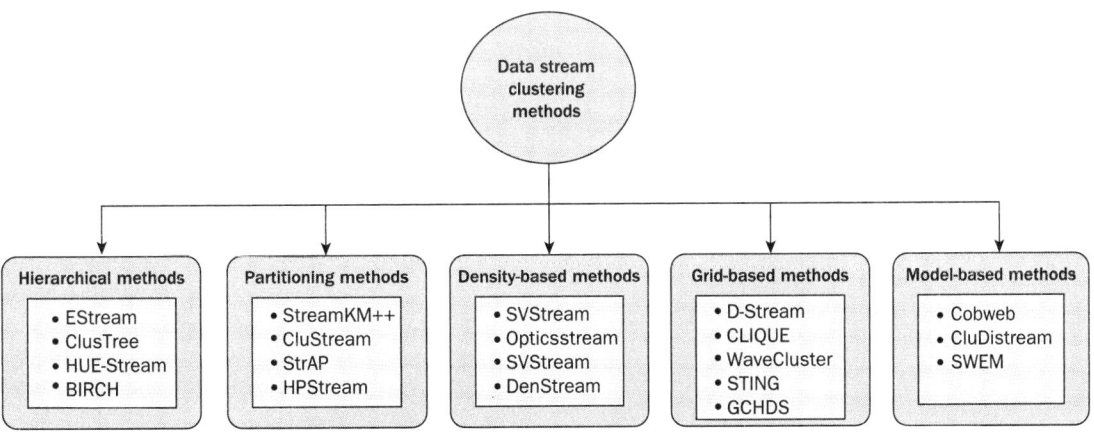

Fig. 10.7 Selected Stream Clustering Algorithms

Stream classification The objective of classification is to assign data to distinct predefined categories called classes. This is achieved by developing a model based on data with known classes (also called class labels) and applying it on new data to automatically assign class labels. This process is basically divided into two steps, that is, training and testing.

In normal data, that is, data that is persistent and residing in a repository, the classification models are built by creating a training dataset, which is used by the classification algorithm to learn the class labels (also termed as batch learning). This learned model is then applied on a test dataset, which assigns a class label for the unlabeled data.

As described earlier in Section 10.4.1.2, several constraints of stream data mining such as memory boundedness, single pass, real-time response, and concept drift makes the development of stream classification challenging. The need for processing huge volumes of streaming data sequentially, the need for high-speed computationally-intensive processing capability, and the restriction on access of the data items only once due to the sequential nature and inability to store the huge volume of data in memory, makes stream classification a unique process. Figure 10.8 lists some state-of-the-art data stream classification algorithms.

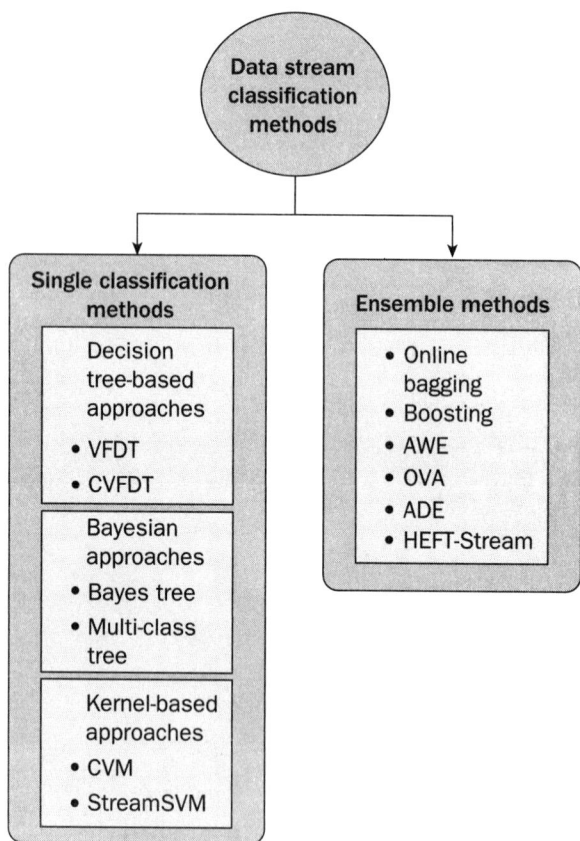

Fig. 10.8 Selected Data Stream Classification Methods

10.4.2 Offline Analytics/Analytics on the Cloud

Offline analytics are those that usually performed on highly scalable computing infrastructures such as cloud computing platforms. These are required for processing large volume of data, which is mainly stored in a repository on the cloud. The various cloud computing platforms that are currently popular are described in Chapter 11. This section is focused on the various analytics that can be performed on the big data obtained from IoT systems and is stored on the cloud. Hence, the assumption is that the data is static and is at rest (the next section describes the analytics on data in motion). The main classes of algorithms for offline analytics which are normally performed on the cloud are described in the subsequent sections :

10.4.2.1 Clustering

Clustering is an unsupervised classification technique (see Fig. 10.9 and Box 10.3) that separates an unlabeled dataset into a number of distinct groups. The clustering techniques can be categorized based on the principle on which the cluster model is built i.e. the way they form clusters or groups.

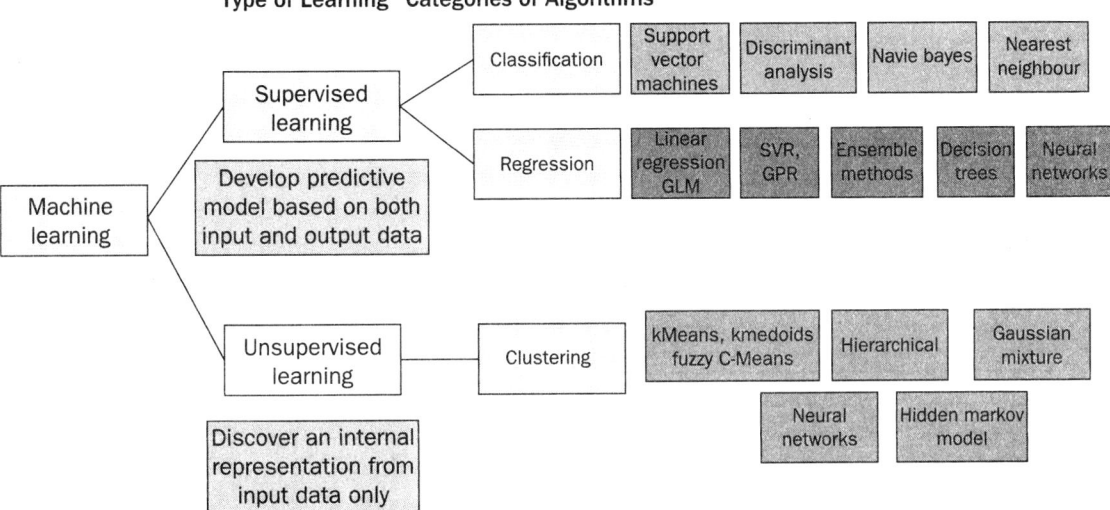

Fig. 10.9 Main Classes of Algorithms for Supervised and Unsupervised Learning

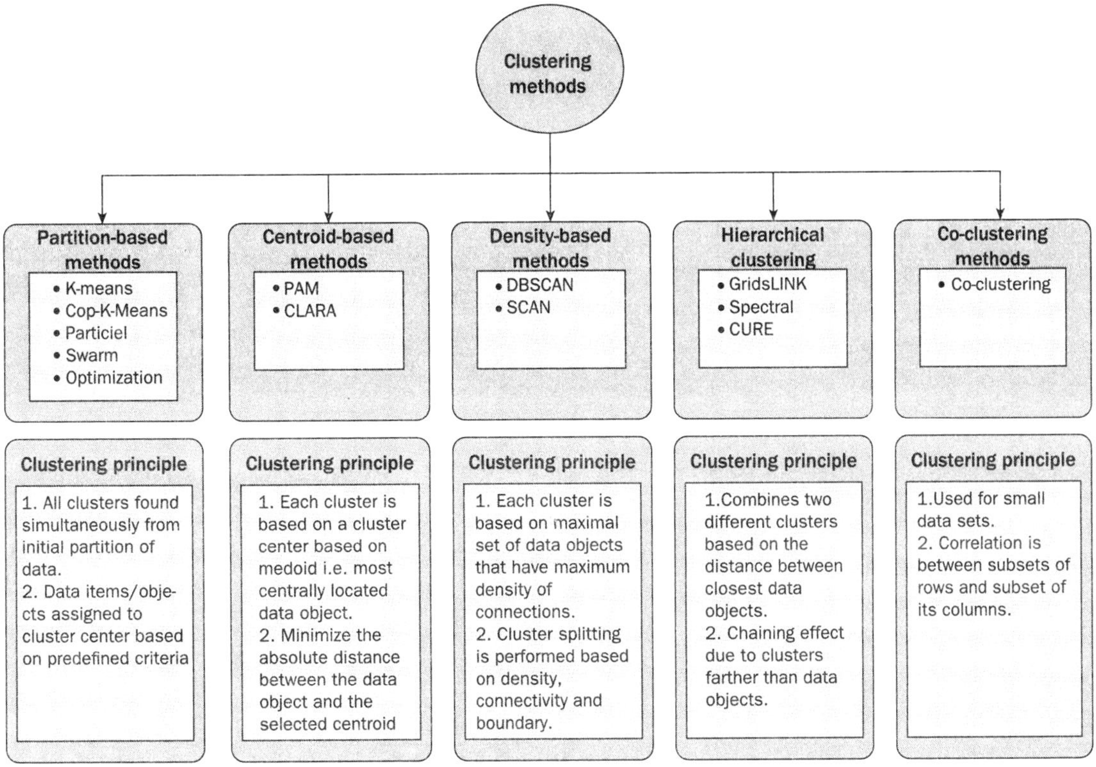

Fig. 10.10 Various State-of-the-Art Clustering Techniques

Clustering methods

Partition-based methods
- K-means
- Cop-K-Means
- Particiel
- Swarm
- Optimization

Clustering principle
1. All clusters found simultaneously from initial partition of data.
2. Data items/objects assigned to cluster center based on predefined criteria

Centroid-based methods
- PAM
- CLARA

Clustering principle
1. Each cluster is based on a cluster center based on medoid i.e. most centrally located data object.
2. Minimize the absolute distance between the data object and the selected centroid

Density-based methods
- DBSCAN
- SCAN

Clustering principle
1. Each cluster is based on maximal set of data objects that have maximum density of connections.
2. Cluster splitting is performed based on density, connectivity and boundary.

Hierarchical clustering
- GridsLINK
- Spectral
- CURE

Clustering principle
1. Combines two different clusters based on the distance between closest data objects.
2. Chaining effect due to clusters farther than data objects.

Co-clustering methods
- Co-clustering

Clustering principle
1. Used for small data sets.
2. Correlation is between subsets of rows and subset of its columns.

The K-means algorithm is one of the popular techniques for clustering. Figure 10.10 gives a list of various clustering algorithms and their main principle of clustering.

> **BOX 10.3: UNSUPERVISED LEARNING**
>
> In unsupervised learning, the training data does not have any labels or classes, which tell what that training sample is about. It can be raw data or data with features extracted. The main goal of unsupervised learning is to find some interesting structure and pattern in the data, which is not readily apparent by just looking at the data in its unprocessed form. The unsupervised learning algorithm is designed to find clusters in data that exhibit some form of homogeneity and are separable from each other. It is an approach most commonly employed for visualization of high-dimensional data by projecting it into a lower dimension. It can also be used for assigning unknown data points to existing cluster so that its characteristics can be better understood. Figure 10.11 shows three clusters from the air-quality variables particulate matter and ozone. It can be seen that the clusters are not well defined but rather have a partial overlap.
>
>
>
> **Fig. 10.11** Clustering of Two Air-quality Variables

In IoT, clustering is typically done for data coming from various sensors and there is a requirement to capture some form or structure of the data in terms of their natural groupings. For example, sensor data from various air-quality monitoring sensors is clustered using the K-means algorithm (see Figs 10.12, 10.13) as shown in Listing 10.15.

> **LISTING 10.15: CLUSTERING AIR-QUALITY DATA**
>
> **K-means clustering using R**
>
> **Install packages:**
>
> Download and install R:
> The R project for statistical computing
> https://www.r-project.org/

(Contd)

Listing 10.15 (*Contd*)

Install factoextra package as follow:

if(!require(devtools)) install.packages("devtools")
devtools::install_github("kassambara/factoextra")
The remaining packages can be installed using the code below:
pkgs <- c("cluster", "fpc", "NbClust")
install.packages(pkgs)

# Read the data
citypulse <- read.csv(file="/Users/user1/data/pollutionData204273.csv", header=TRUE, sep=",")
str(citypulse)
summary (citypulse)
# Show the top few columns of the variables
head(citypulse)
citypulse_new <- citypulse[,c(1,2,3,4,5)]
#citypulse_new<-scale(citypulse_new)
result <- kmeans(citypulse_new,3)
result$size
result$centers
result$cluster
# prepare for plotting
par(mfrow=c(3,3), mar=c(5,4,2,2))
# Plot 2 variables at a time
plot(citypulse_new[c(1,2)], col=result$cluster)
plot(citypulse_new[c(2,3)], col=result$cluster)
#plot cluster centers
plot(citypulse_new[c(1,2)], col=result$centers)
# plot all possible combinations of the variables
plot(citypulse_new[,], col=result$cluster)

OUTPUT

```
> result$centers
    ozone particullate_matter carbon_monoxide sulfure_dioxide nitrogen_dioxide
1 151.78810           168.44307        130.94273       122.76009        119.2661
2  88.56335            77.68161         43.69736        83.72753        147.8420
3  76.14906            80.56786        123.31419       144.81624         62.1788
```

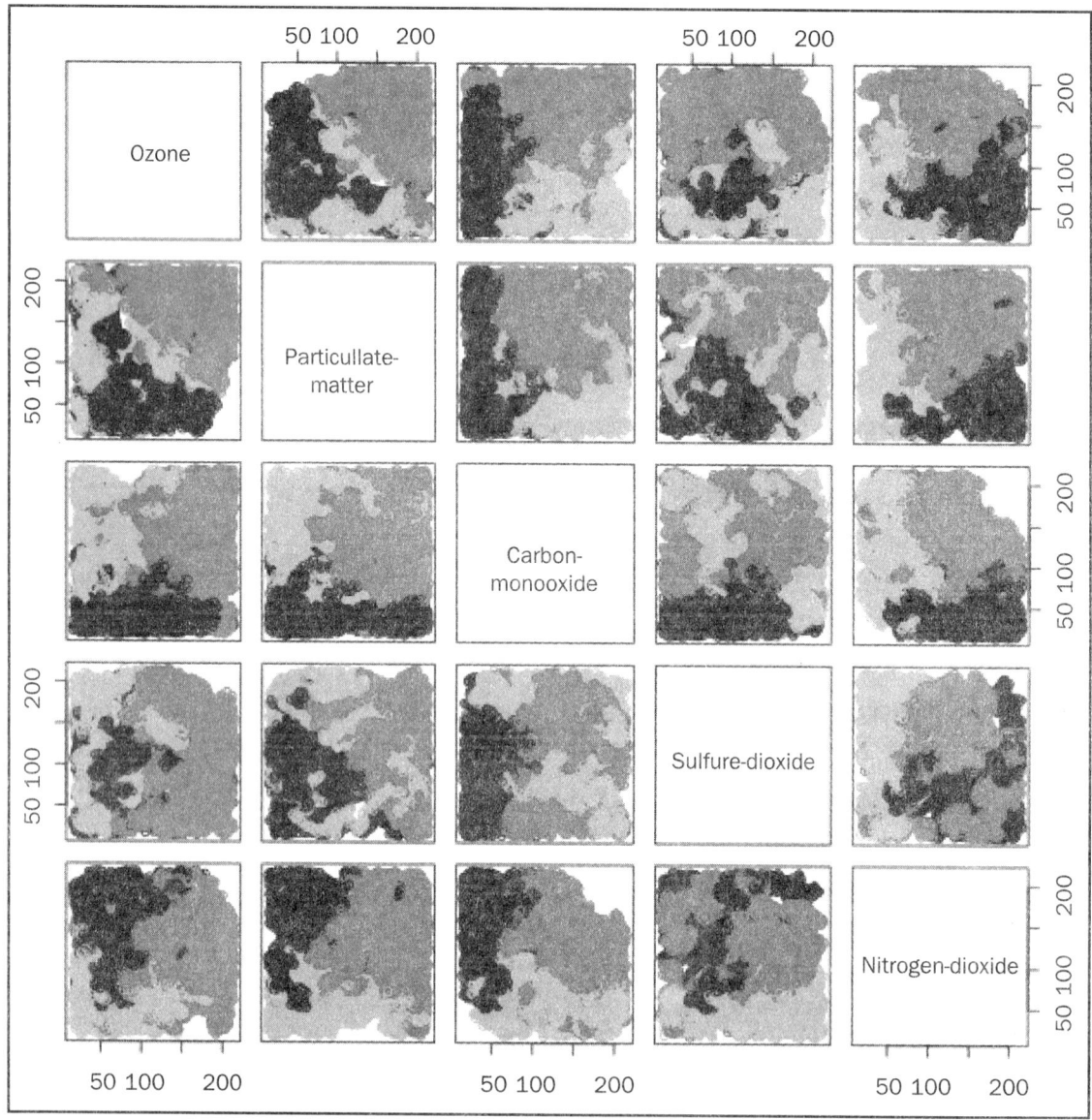

Fig. 10.12 K-means Clustering with $K = 3$

10.4.2.2 Classification

Classification is a supervised learning approach (see Box 10.4) in which a set of labeled data also called as training data is used to learn (by a learning algorithm) a model (hypothesis), which has the capability to predict the class label(s) of unlabeled data.

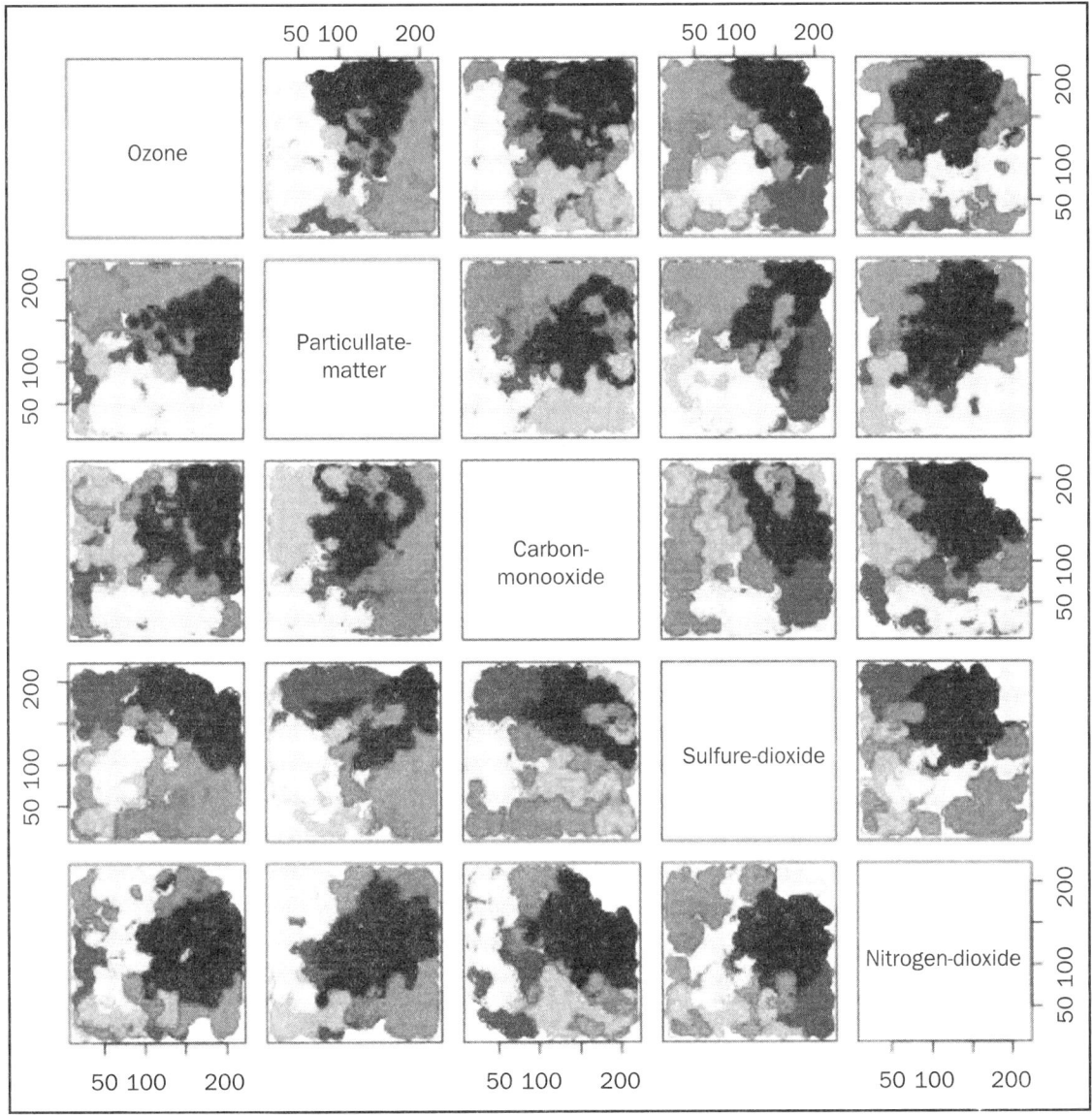

Fig. 10.13 K-means Clustering with $K = 6$

BOX 10.4: CONCEPT OF SUPERVISED LEARNING

Supervised learning: Supervised learning is based on making the learning algorithm learn by giving examples. Once it has seen sufficient number of samples, the algorithm is able to form a hypothesis and is ready to make predictions on data samples that are unlabeled and drawn from similar distribution.

Given a set of input variables (x), an output variable (Y), a learning algorithm is used to learn the mapping function from the input to the output $Y = f(x)$. Once the mapping function is obtained with sufficient accuracy, new input data (x), can be used to predict the output variables (Y) for that data.

Training sample A training sample is a training dataset that can be used in the predictive modeling task. For example, if we are interested in classifying occupancy of a room based on the attributes temperature, humidity, CO_2, the dataset will contain several rows of such data, and the corresponding outcome or class label. Each row in such a training data is called a training sample or training instance or training example. Table 10.1 shows an example of a training data. The goal is to predict the occupancy of the room.

Table 10.1 Sample Training Data Obtained Using Various Sensors in a Room. Each Row is a Training Sample

Temperature	Humidity	CO_2	Room Occupancy (Class Label)
21.1	36.2	821	Yes
20.9	35.68	712.6	Yes
21.84	35.95	1513	Yes
23	27.2	681.5	No
20.2	33.06	448	No

There are many classification algorithms that are available such as naive bayes classifier, support vector machines, decision trees, boosted trees, random forest, neural networks, nearest neighbors, etc. Listings 10.16–10.18 show the application of three classification algorithms (support vector classification, naive bayes, and decision trees) on human activity dataset.

LISTING 10.16: CLASSIFICATION USING SUPPORT VECTOR CLASSIFICATION (SVC)

Classification of human activity using data from mobile phone

Data set description: The Human Activity Recognition database was put up from the recordings of 30 study applicants performing activities of daily living (ADL) while carrying a waist-mounted smartphone with embedded inertial sensors. The objective is to classify activities into one of the six activities (WALKING, WALKING_UPSTAIRS, WALKING_DOWNSTAIRS, SITTING, STANDING, LAYING) performed.

Python code for performing classification using support vector classification (SVC) method

```
# importing necessary libraries
from sklearn.metrics import confusion_matrix
import pandas as pd
import numpy as np
# importing necessary libraries
from sklearn.metrics import confusion_matrix
import pandas as pd
```

(Contd)

Listing 10.16 (*Contd*)

```python
import numpy as np
from sklearn.metrics import average_precision_score, auc, roc_curve, precision_recall_curve

# Read the CSV training and testing data using pandas
train_data = pd.read_csv("/Users/user1/datasets/activity/train.csv", header=0)
test_data=pd.read_csv("/Users/user1/datasets/activity/test.csv", header=0)

# convert to numpy arrays
Xtrain=np.array(train_data)
Xtest=np.array(test_data)

# subset the data so that features and labels are assigned to X_train and y_train
X_train=Xtrain[:,0:561]
y_train=Xtrain[:,562]

# test data
X_test = Xtest[:,0:561]
# true values of the test labels
y_test=Xtest[:,562]

# training a linear SVM classifier
from sklearn.svm import SVC
# learn the model with a linear kernel, hyperparamter C=1
svm_model_linear = SVC(kernel='linear', C=1).fit(X_train, y_train)

#predictions
svm_predictions = svm_model_linear.predict(X_test)
y_pred = svm_model_linear.predict(X_test)

# model accuracy for X_test
accuracy = svm_model_linear.score(X_test, y_test)
print("Accuracy:",accuracy)

# Set width and number of columns to display in the output
desired_width = 500
pd.set_option('display.width', desired_width)
pd.set_option('display.max_columns', 10)

# Select the true labels that are unique from the test data
unique_label = np.unique(y_test)

# creating a confusion matrix
print(pd.DataFrame(confusion_matrix(y_test, y_pred, labels=unique_label),
    index=['true:{:}'.format(x) for x in unique_label],
    columns=['pred:{:}'.format(x) for x in unique_label]))
```

(*Contd*)

Listing 10.16 (*Contd*)

OUTPUT

```
Accuracy: 0.9640312181879878
                    LAYING  SITTING  STANDING  WALKING  WALKING_DOWNSTAIRS  WALKING_UPSTAIRS
LAYING              537     0        0         0        0                   0
SITTING             0       435      54        0        0                   2
STANDING            0       16       516       0        0                   0
WALKING             0       0        0         492      3                   1
WALKING_DOWNSTAIRS  0       0        0         4        410                 6
WALKING_UPSTAIRS    0       0        0         18       2                   451
```

Note: You can experiment with other kernels such as 'poly' and 'rbf'. Below is an example of using a 'rbf' kernel.
svm_model_l=rbf = SVC(kernel='rbf',gamma=0.2, C=1).fit(X_train, y_train)
Data sourced from UCI machine learning repository : http://archive.ics.uci.edu/ml/datasets.php

---

LISTING 10.17: NAIVE BAYES CLASSIFICATION

Classification using Naive Bayes

 # importing necessary libraries
from sklearn.metrics **import** confusion_matrix
import pandas **as** pd
import numpy **as** np
from sklearn.metrics **import** average_precision_score, auc, roc_curve, precision_recall_curve

 # Read the CSV training and testing data using pandas
train_data = pd.read_csv(**"/Users/user1/datasets/activity/train.csv"**, header=0)
test_data=pd.read_csv(**"/Users/user1/datasets/activity/test.csv"**, header=0)
 # convert to numpy arrays
Xtrain=np.array(train_data)
Xtest=np.array(test_data)
 # subset the data so that features and labels are assigned to X_train and y_train
X_train=Xtrain[:,0:561]
y_train=Xtrain[:,562]
 # test data
X_test = Xtest[:,0:561]
 # true values of the test labels
y_test=Xtest[:,562]
 # training a Naive Bayes classifier
from sklearn.naive_bayes **import** GaussianNB
gaussianNB = GaussianNB().fit(X_train, y_train)
gnb_predictions = gaussianNB.predict(X_test)

(*Contd*)

Listing 10.17 (*Contd*)

```
#predictions
y_pred = gaussianNB.predict(X_test)
# model accuracy for X_test
accuracy = gaussianNB.score(X_test, y_test)
print("Accuracy:",accuracy)
# Set width and number of columns to display in the output
desired_width = 500
pd.set_option('display.width', desired_width)
pd.set_option('display.max_columns', 10)
# Select the true labels that are unique from the test data
unique_label = np.unique(y_test)
# creating a confusion matrix
print(pd.DataFrame(confusion_matrix(y_test, y_pred, labels=unique_label),
    index=[format(x) for x in unique_label],
    columns=[format(x) for x in unique_label]))
```

OUTPUT

```
Accuracy: 0.7702748557855447
                    LAYING  SITTING  STANDING  WALKING  WALKING_DOWNSTAIRS  WALKING_UPSTAIRS
LAYING                 323      211         0        0                   0                 3
SITTING                  5      368       111        0                   0                 7
STANDING                 8       54       455        0                   0                15
WALKING                  0        0         0      416                  42                38
WALKING_DOWNSTAIRS       0        0         0       80                 257                83
WALKING_UPSTAIRS         0        0         0        9                  11               451
```

Data sourced from www.kaggle.com; www.github.com; www.nbviewer.jupyter.org; www.datacamp.com

LISTING 10.18: DECISION TREE-BASED CLASSIFICATION

Classification using decision tree

```
# importing necessary libraries
from sklearn.metrics import confusion_matrix
import pandas as pd
import numpy as np
from sklearn.metrics import average_precision_score, auc, roc_curve, precision_recall_curve

# Read the CSV training and testing data using pandas
train_data = pd.read_csv("/Users/user1/datasets/activity/train.csv", header=0)
test_data=pd.read_csv("/Users/user1/datasets/activity/test.csv", header=0)
# convert to numpy arrays
```

(*Contd*)

Listing 10.18 (*Contd*)

```
Xtrain=np.array(train_data)
Xtest=np.array(test_data)
# subset the data so that features and labels are assigned to X_train and y_train
X_train=Xtrain[:,0:561]
y_train=Xtrain[:,562]
# test data
X_test = Xtest[:,0:561]
# true values of the test labels
y_test=Xtest[:,562]

# training Decision Tree Classifier
from sklearn.tree import DecisionTreeClassifier
decisiontree_model = DecisionTreeClassifier(max_depth = 8).fit(X_train, y_train)
decisiontree_predictions = decisiontree_model.predict(X_test)

#predictions
y_pred = decisiontree_model.predict(X_test)

# model accuracy for X_test
accuracy = decisiontree_model.score(X_test, y_test)
print("Accuracy:",accuracy)

# Set width and number of columns to display in the output
desired_width = 500
pd.set_option('display.width', desired_width)
pd.set_option('display.max_columns', 10)

# Select the true labels that are unique from the test data
unique_label = np.unique(y_test)

# creating a confusion matrix
print(pd.DataFrame(confusion_matrix(y_test, y_pred, labels=unique_label),
    index=[format(x) for x in unique_label],
    columns=[format(x) for x in unique_label]))
```

OUTPUT

```
Accuracy: 0.8741092636579573
                    LAYING  SITTING  STANDING  WALKING  WALKING_DOWNSTAIRS  WALKING_UPSTAIRS
LAYING              537     0        0         0        0                   0
SITTING             0       372      119       0        0                   0
STANDING            0       55       477       0        0                   0
WALKING             0       0        0         469      17                  10
WALKING_DOWNSTAIRS  0       0        0         13       349                 58
WALKING_UPSTAIRS    0       0        0         70       29                  372
```

Data sourced from UCI machine learning repository : http://archive.ics.uci.edu/ml/datasets.php

10.4.2.3 Regression

The regression problem is similar to the classification problem, where given a set of input variables (*x*) and an output variable (*Y*). A learning algorithm is used to learn the mapping function from the input to the output $Y = f(X)$ except the output variable (*Y*) is a real or continuous value, *S*. The target value *S* is usually predicted based on a set of independent variables. A linear regression is the most common form of regression where there is one independent and one dependent variable as shown in equation below.

$$Y = mX + c + e$$

Where *X* is the independent variable and *Y* is the dependent variable. As shown in Fig. 10.14, the relationship between *X* and *Y* is established by a best-fit straight line also called the regression line or regression model. The slope and intercept, that is, *m* and *c* are found such that the error is minimum between the observed and the predicted values. This approach is called the least-squares approach used for fitting the best-fit line for the observed data by minimizing the sum of the squares of the vertical deviations from each data point to the line.

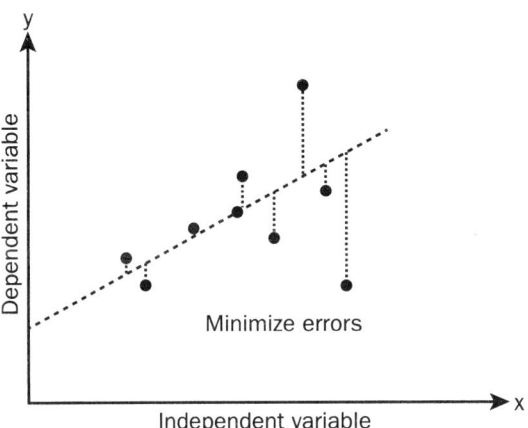

Fig. 10.14 Linear Regression

Various other forms of regression techniques are: logistic regression, polynomial regression, stepwise regression, ridge regression, lasso regression, support vector regression, etc. The regression technique is mainly useful for time-series data from IoT sensors such as air-quality data over a period of time, weather monitoring data, traffic monitoring, and infrastructure monitoring. In all these cases, the output to be predicted is a continuous value and not a categorical variable.

10.4.2.4 Correlation and Pattern Analysis

This type of analytics is often exploratory in nature and mainly focused on the identification of patterns in the data. Correlation analysis is a frequently used approach that gives an understanding about the relationships between various variables (data attributes). The correlation coefficient is a metric that quantifies/measures the strength of the relationship between pairs of attributes. This is obtained by the statistical measure called covariance (see Listing 10.19) that explains the association between two variables *X* and *Y*. There are some well-known approaches for correlation analysis such as Pearson's correlation coefficient, Spearman's correlation coefficient, and Kendall's Tau coefficient. Listing and 10.20 provides examples of measuring the strength of the relationship between air pollution variables using the above-mentioned correlation measures.

LISTING 10.19: COVARIANCE MATRIX

```python
#The covariance and covariance matrix are used to characterize the relationships between two or more variables.

# Import the `pandas` library as `pd`
import pandas as pd
import numpy as np

# Load in the data with `read_csv()`
PData = pd.read_csv("/Users/user1/datasets/pdata/pollutiondata.csv",
    header=0)
# set the width of the display in the output
pd.set_option('display.width', 300)
# set the number of columns to show in the output
pd.set_option('display.max_columns', 10)
#print the first 10 rows of the data
five_variables=np.array(PData)
print(PData.head(10))
#print(five_variables[:,0:5])
ozone=five_variables[:,0:1].astype(float)
print("Ozone:",ozone)
particulate=five_variables[:,1:2].astype(float)
print("Particulate:",particulate)
co=five_variables[:,2:3]
print("CO:",co)
so2=five_variables[:,3:4]
print("SO2:",so2)
no2=five_variables[:,4:5]
print("NO2:",no2)

cov_oz_no2 = np.cov(ozone.astype(float).T, no2.astype(float).T,bias=True)
print("Covariance (Ozone,NO2:",cov_oz_no2)

cov_oz_particulate = np.cov(ozone.astype(float).T, particulate.astype(float).T,bias=True)
print("Covariance (Ozone,Particulate:",cov_oz_particulate)
```

(Contd)

Listing 10.19 (Contd)

OUTPUT

```
Covariance (Ozone,NO2: [[20.54477301  6.74052478]
 [ 6.74052478 25.26530612]]
Covariance (Ozone,Particulate: [[ 20.54477301 -13.33527697]
 [-13.33527697  21.63265306]]
```

Note: Ozone and NO2 show positive correlation but Ozone and particulates show negative correlation.

Exercise: One important assumption in generating the covariance matrix is that the data is normally distributed. To make the data distributed use the function preprocessing.PowerTransformer (method='box-cox', standardize=False) in 'sklearn'. Perform it on each of the variables and then do the covariance matrix estimation.

Pearson's correlation coefficient measures the linear association between continuous variables. In other words, this coefficient quantifies the degree to which a relationship between two variables can be described by a line commonly used in linear regression and has been used to measure the strength of relationships between the four air pollutants. Spearman's correlation coefficient can be used to find the strength between two data variables when they have a nonlinear relationship and also non-gaussian Gaussian distribution (See Listing 10.20).

LISTING 10.20: PEARSON'S AND SPEARMAN'S CORRELATION COEFFICIENTS

Pearson's correlation coefficient

```python
#Pearson's correlation coefficient = covariance (X, Y) / (std(X) * std(Y))
#Provides the strength of the linear relationship between two data samples.
# Import the `pandas` library as `pd`
import pandas as pd
import numpy as np
from scipy.stats import pearsonr
# Load in the data with `read_csv()`
PData = pd.read_csv("/Users/user1/datasets/pdata/pollutiondata.csv",
    header=0)
# set the width of the display in the output
pd.set_option('display.width', 300)
# set the number of columns to show in the output
pd.set_option('display.max_columns', 10)
#print the first 10 rows of the data
five_variables=np.array(PData)
print(PData.head(10))
```

(Contd)

Listing 10.20 (*Contd*)

```
#print(five_variables[:,0:5])
ozone=five_variables[:,0:1].astype(float)
print("Ozone:",ozone)
particulate=five_variables[:,1:2].astype(float)
print("Particulate:",particulate)
co=five_variables[:,2:3].astype(float)
print("CO:",co)
so2=five_variables[:,3:4].astype(float)
print("SO2:",so2)
no2=five_variables[:,4:5].astype(float)
print("NO2:",no2)
# Calcluate the Pearson's Correlation Coefficient
corr, _ = pearsonr(ozone, particulate)
print('Pearsons correlation (Ozone,Particulate Matter): %.3f' % corr)
corr, _ = pearsonr(ozone, no2)
print('Pearsons correlation(Ozone,NO2): %.3f' % corr)
```

OUTPUT

```
Pearsons correlation (Ozone,Particulate Matter): -0.633
Pearsons correlation(Ozone,NO2): 0.296
```

Note: There is a positive correlation between ozone and NO2 but it is very weak as it is 0.296. Any value above 0.5 can be considered as having some significant linear relationship.

Spearman's correlation coefficient

```
#Spearman's correlation coefficient = covariance(rank(X), rank(Y)) / (std(rank(X)) * std(rank(Y)))
# Import the `pandas` library as `pd`
import pandas as pd
import numpy as np
from scipy.stats import pearsonr
from scipy.stats import spearmanr
# Load in the data with `read_csv()`
PData = pd.read_csv("/Users/user1/datasets/pdata/pollutiondata.csv",
    header=0)
# set the width of the display in the output
pd.set_option('display.width', 300)
# set the number of columns to show in the output
pd.set_option('display.max_columns', 10)
```

(*Contd*)

Listing 10.20 (*Contd*)

```
#print the first 10 rows of the data
five_variables=np.array(PData)
print(PData.head(10))
#print(five_variables[:,0:5])
ozone=five_variables[:,0:1].astype(float)
print("Ozone:",ozone)
particulate=five_variables[:,1:2].astype(float)
print("Particulate:",particulate)
co=five_variables[:,2:3].astype(float)
print("CO:",co)
so2=five_variables[:,3:4].astype(float)
print("SO2:",so2)
no2=five_variables[:,4:5].astype(float)
print("NO2:",no2)
# Calcluate the Pearson's Correlation Coefficient
corr, _ = pearsonr(ozone, particulate)
print('Pearsons correlation (Ozone,Particulate Matter): %.3f' % corr)
corr, _ = pearsonr(ozone, no2)
print('Pearsons correlation(Ozone,NO2): %.3f' % corr)
# Calculate Spearmans correlation coefficient
corr, _ = spearmanr(ozone, particulate)
print('Spearmans correlation(Ozone,Particulate Matter): %.3f' % corr)
corr, _ = spearmanr(ozone, no2)
print('Spearmans correlation(Ozone,NO2): %.3f' % corr)
```

OUTPUT

```
Spearmans correlation(Ozone,Particulate Matter): -0.517
Spearmans correlation(Ozone,NO2): 0.277
```

10.4.3 Big Data Analytics Platforms for IoT

The most popular analytics platforms that are currently available are:

- Microsoft Azure Stream Analytics
- AWS IoT Analytics
- IBM Watson Analytics
- Cisco Data Analytics

- Oracle Stream Analytics and Oracle Edge Analytics
- Google Cloud IoT

For more information on these platforms please refer to Chapter 8 on IoT Software Platforms.

10.5 MACHINE LEARNING AND DEEP LEARNING TOOLS

IoT data analytics can be performed using many ready-to-use tools that are freely available. The most popular among them are described below.

10.5.1 Tensorflow

TensorFlow is an open source software library for numerical computation using data flow graphs. Graph nodes represent mathematical operations, while graph edges represent the multidimensional data arrays (tensors) that flow between them. This flexible architecture enables you to deploy computation to one or more CPUs or GPUs in a desktop, server, or mobile device without rewriting code. TensorFlow also includes TensorBoard, a data visualization toolkit.

10.5.2 Theano

Theano is a Python library that allows defining, optimizing, and evaluating mathematical expressions involving multidimensional arrays efficiently. It can use GPUs and perform efficient symbolic differentiation. It is tightly integrated with the Python package NumPy and can use GPU for significantly speeding up computations than on a CPU.

10.5.3 Keras

Keras is a high-level neural networks API, written in Python and capable of running on top of TensorFlow, CNTK, or Theano. It was developed with a focus on enabling fast experimentation. Keras is highly modular, that is, the various components (neural layers, cost functions, cost function, etc.) are available as stand-alone modules and it is up to the user to select those that are required and connect them together to create new models. It supports convolutional networks as well as recurrent networks.

10.5.4 Scikit-learn

It is a machine learning library written in Python programming language. It provides various classification, regression, and clustering algorithms. It is tightly integrated with the Python numerical and scientific libraries NumPy and SciPy.

SUMMARY

The IoT analytics forms one of the most important modules of the IoT solution. It enables to gain insights and enables to solve a business problem. IoT analytics are based on the big data paradigm since the data generated by IoT has similar characteristics. The whole data analytics comes under the umbrella of data science; hence, this chapter focused on introducing the data science and the end to processes involved in it.

Several Python code examples are provided that uses real-world data sets from sensors to demonstrate each step of the data science process. Further, the chapter described the need for online and offline analytics of IoT data and the various approaches involved in them are explained in detail.

REVIEW QUESTIONS

1. Define data science.
2. Explain the interdisciplinary nature of data science.
3. Describe the data science process.
4. What is a data lake/swamp?
5. What are the main characteristics of a data lake?
6. How is a data lake different from a data warehouse?
7. How are big data and IoT related?
8. What are the uses of IoT data analytics?
9. Explain descriptive, diagnostic, predictive, and prescriptive analytics.
10. Write a note on real-time analytics.
11. What are the key challenges of data stream mining as compared to traditional data mining?
12. Explain the data stream mining process with a diagram.
13. Describe stream-frequent pattern analysis.
14. Describe stream clustering and classification methods.
15. Give some real-world applications of data stream mining.
16. Describe data reduction approach.
17. Explain standardization and normalization of data.
18. What is dimensionality reduction?
19. Why do we need to do feature selection?
20. Explain filter-based, wrapper-based, and embedded feature selection techniques.
21. Describe clustering and classification methods with IoT examples.
22. What is correlation and pattern analysis?

REFERENCES

1. Nguyen, H.-L., Woon, Y.-K., Ng, W.-K. (2015), A survey on data stream clustering and classification. *Knowl Inf Syst* 45: 535–569. DOI 10.1007/s10115-014-0808-1.
2. Bifet, A., Holmes, G., Kirkby, R. (2012), Moa: massive online analysis. *J Mach Learn Res* 11: 1601–1604.
3. Gama, J. (2013), Data stream mining: the bounded rationality. *Informatica (Slovenia)* 37(1): 21–25.
4. Nguyen, H. L., Woon, Y. K., Ng, W. K. (2015), *Knowl Inf Syst* 45: 535. https://doi.org/10.1007/s10115-014-0808-1
5. Jin, R., Aggarwal, G. (2007), Frequent pattern mining in data streams, In: *Data Streams: Models and Algorithms*, Springer, US Boston, MA.
6. Siow, E., Tiropanis, T., Hall, W. (2018), Analytics for the Internet of Things: a survey. *ACM Comput. Surv.* 1(1): 35. https://doi.org/10.1145/3204947
7. Tomas, J. J., Cook, K. (Eds.), In: *Illuminating the Path: eResearch and Development Agenda for Visual Analytics*, IEEE Computer Society Press, 2005. ISBN: 0-7695-2323-4.
8. Anguita, D., Ghio, A., Oneto, L., Parra, X., Reyes-Ortiz, J. L. (2013), A public domain dataset for human activity recognition using smartphones. *21st European Symposium on Artificial Neural Networks, Computational Intelligence and Machine Learning*, ESANN 2013, Bruges, Belgium 24–26 April 2013.
9. Stanton, J. M. (2012), Introduction to data science, Third Edition. *iTunes Open Source eBook*. Available: https://itunes.apple.com/us/book/introduction-to-data-science/id529088127?mt=11
10. Jović, A., Brkić, K., Bogunović, N. (2015), A review of feature selection methods with applications, *MIPRO 2015*, 25–29 May 2015, Opatija, Croatia.
11. Pandas Python Data Analysis Library: https://pandas.pydata.org/

12. Sci-KiT Learn Python Machine Learning Library: https://scikit-learn.org/stable/
13. R Project for Statistical Computing: https://www.r-project.org/
14. TensorFlow: An open source machine learning library for research and production. https://www.tensorflow.org/
15. https://github.com/Theano/Theano
16. https://scikit-learn.org
17. https://keras.io
18. Y. LeCun, L. Bottou, Y. Bengio and P. Haffner: Gradient-Based Learning Applied to Document Recognition, Proceedings of the IEEE, 86(11):2278-2324, November 1998,
19. Krizhevsky, A., Sutskever, I., & Hinton, G. E. (2012). Imagenet classification with deep convolutional neural networks. In Advances in neural information processing systems (pp. 1097-1105)
20. Simonyan, K., & Zisserman, A. (2014). Very deep convolutional networks for large-scale image recognition. arXiv preprint arXiv:1409.1556.
21. He, K., Zhang, X., Ren, S., & Sun, J. (2016). Deep residual learning for image recognition. In Proceedings of the IEEE conference on computer vision and pattern recognition (pp. 770-778).
22. Szegedy, C., Ioffe, S., Vanhoucke, V., & Alemi, A. A. (2017, February). Inception-v4, inception-resnet and the impact of residual connections on learning. In Thirty-first AAAI conference on artificial intelligence.
23. Xie, S., Girshick, R., Dollár, P., Tu, Z., & He, K. (2017). Aggregated residual transformations for deep neural networks. In Proceedings of the IEEE conference on computer vision and pattern recognition (pp. 1492-1500).
24. Reyes-Ortiz, J. L, Oneto, L., Sam, A., Parra, X., Anguita. D. Transition-Aware Human Activity Recognition Using Smartphones. Neurocomputing. Springer 2015.

IoT in the Cloud

CHAPTER **11**

"Cloud is about how you do computing, not where to do computing."
—Paul Martiz

OBJECTIVES
- discuss the background of cloud computing and Internet of Things (IoT)
- explain the integration of cloud computing and IoT
- study the cloud services for IoT
- review selected cloud service providers for IoT applications
- learn about open source cloud platform ThingSpeak for IoT

OUTCOMES
- gain knowledge about cloud services for Internet of Things (IoT)
- explain the integration of cloud computing and IoT
- list various cloud services useful for IoT applications
- outline popular cloud platforms and how to integrate with complex IoT applications
- describe RESTful APIs useful for real-time IoT analytics

REVISION

In Chapters 8, 9, and 10, different Internet of Things (IoT) platforms, programming concepts, and prototyping concepts are explained. Further in this chapter, we will explore the use of different cloud services and communication models required for large and complex IoT applications.

11.1 INTRODUCTION: CLOUD COMPUTING AND IOT

The computing power required these days has increased considerably for processing large volumes of data. Earlier, mainframe computers were rented by businesses and organisations for their computing needs, but with the advent of the PCs, the way people/ organisations/ businesses have used computers for various needs has drastically changed. However, the recent big data era has ushered in new requirements for computing to cater to the needs of processing high volume, velocity and variety of data. It led to the shifting of the computing infrastructure from desktop to remote services that can provide highly scalable computing infrastructure and can be charged by a subscription plan.

Majority of IoT applications produce high frequency and volume of data. These data are processed at various levels such as:

- Edge/fog computing, where streaming raw data from IoT sensors is processed for real/ near real-time applications. These computations usually happen on an specialised edge device integrated with an IoT gateway or on nearby available servers.
- Cloud comma after computing where the data is further sent to a remote location hosting a large network of servers and capable of providing various services such as hardware, software, storage, processing, security, etc.

Chapter 12 provides more details about edge computing for IoT. This chapter is focused on the second approach (cloud) for IoT data processing.

Some major advantages of using cloud for IoT includes:

- On demand processing of high volumes of data
- Availability of latest computing hardware and software that enables more efficient processing
- High scalability and availability that allows aggregation and processing of data from multiple IoT applications and distributed IoT sensors
- Payment of the cloud services such as data storage, processing, etc. on the basis of "pay as you go" approach
- No maintenance is required at the user end for the computing infrastructure as it is managed by the cloud service provider
- Several options for choosing off-the-shelf (commercial and open source) IoT platforms to quickly setup the required infrastructures for integrating the IoT sensors with the processing hardware/software and begin gaining useful insights in a particular domain.

All the above is possible assuming that sufficient internet bandwidth is available with the IoT data producers. Also, some latency and occasional disruption of services is expected in the cloud service.

11.1.1 Evolution of Cloud-based Novel IoT Applications

IoT is used for developing objects such as physical devices, vehicles, etc. with embedded hardware, software, sensors, and network connection to collect, send, and receive data.

The market expansion for IoT applications is displayed in Fig. 11.1.

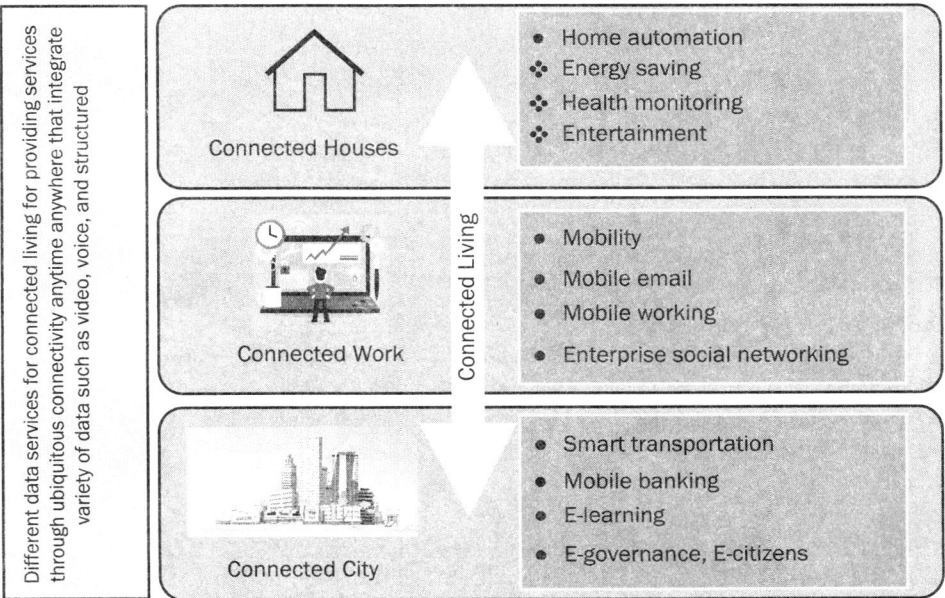

Fig. 11.1 Connected Living with Smart Things

High volumes of data generated by various IoT applications can cause heavy stress to the local computing and internet infrastructure. Consequently, several organisations are migrating their data to the cloud to reduce the load on the local devices, thus enabling secure storage and for availing various functionalities offered by cloud services. Generally, cloud providers allow for data transfer by the Internet or by a dedicated data link for secure transmission of the data, thus providing high quality of service.

Cloud computing provides on-demand service for computing power, data storage, software and applications, and other IT resources. Using the various resources in such a way on the cloud organisations resembles and works like a virtual machine, reducing significant investment on the infrastructure. In general, organisations decide on the need for a cloud service based on the application's computing and data requirements. Based on it, the organisation can decide on a subscription plan.

"Pay as you grow (PAYG)" is another model that is relevant to small and medium enterprises (SMEs). As the business grows and more IoT system deployments and aggregation of data from multiple domains is required, the need perceived for more computing resources can be easily scalable by the PAYG cloud service model.

Cloud computing plays an important role in IoT as it allows massive data generated by IoT to be handled efficiently without the need for expensive local infrastructure. Hence, cloud computing and IoT are inseparable. IoT has gradually changed the way daily tasks are performed. In smart home applications, people can start their cooling devices through their mobile phones from a remote place before reaching home. Cost-effective solutions are possible due to cloud integration which enables cities to host these data and applications. In a smart city, many IoT applications are likely to be deployed, such as applications for smart transport management, smart energy management, urban mobility of the citizens, smart water management, and more (refer to Fig.11.2).

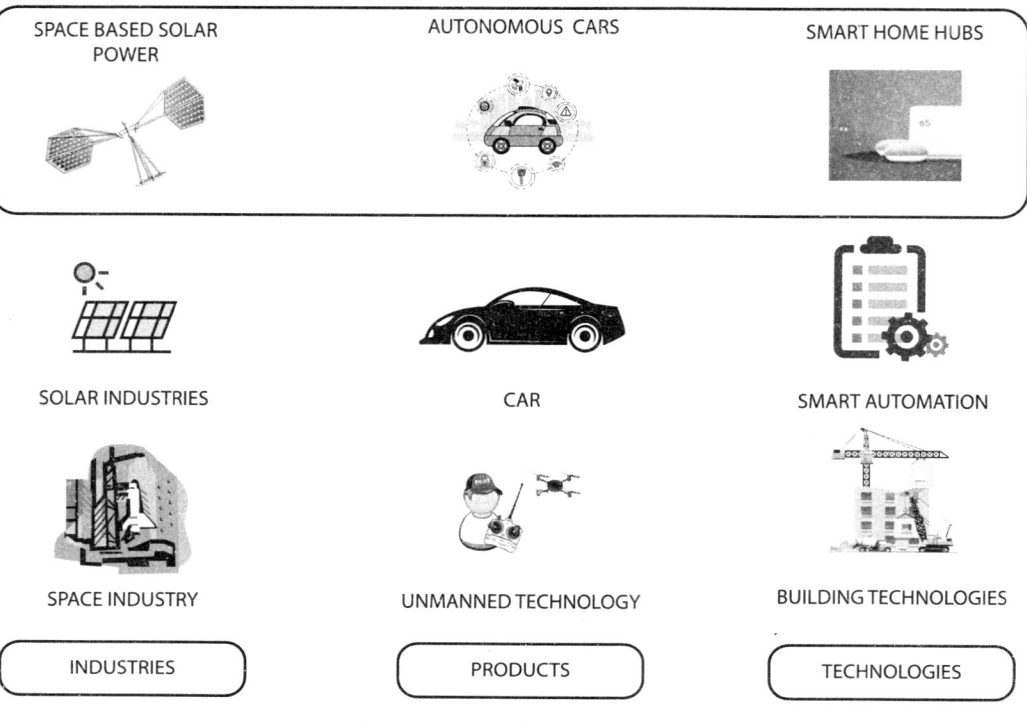

Fig. 11.2 IoT Application Domains

11.1.2 Cloud Computing Service Models

For many applications, cloud computing needs to be integrated with another platform of the cloud or even another cloud provider as shown in Fig. 11.3. Cloud computing services are categorized by different levels at which they are provided and by underlying APIs. Following are some of the common services.

IaaS APIs (Infrastructure-level) Infrastructure-as-a-Service (IaaS) help in management of cloud resources and their distribution. Infrastructure APIs are useful for provisioning or de-provisioning of cloud resources. In addition, network configurations as well as workload management are provided by these APIs. Examples of IaaS include AWS EC2, Google compute engine, etc.

PaaS APIs (Service-level) Platform-as-a-Service (PaaS) provide access and functionality in a cloud environment. Storage, database integration, portals, messaging systems, and many other components are available through these APIs. Examples of PaaS include Google App engine, AWS elastic, Azure, Apache Stratos, etc.

SaaS APIs (Application-level) SaaS consists of cloud-hosted applications which can support multiple users simultaneously. Software-as-a-Service APIs are useful to connect the application layer with the cloud Infrastructure. Examples of Saas include Google Apps, DropBox, etc.

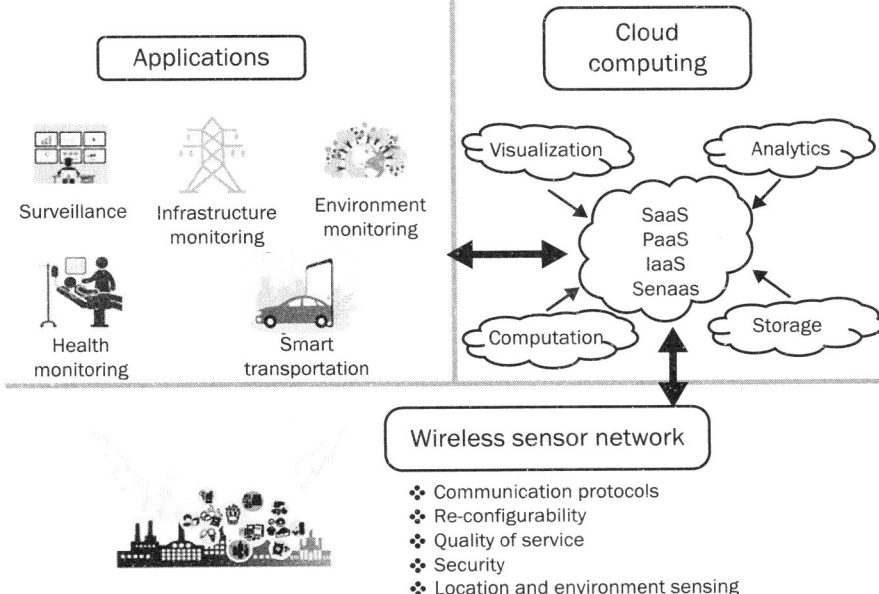

Fig. 11.3 Cloud Computing Service Model

Cloud provider and cross-platform APIs   Many cloud providers are providing services to a variety of environments. Hence, cross-platform compatibility is needed. It can enable the usage of resources and workload across multiple cloud services.

An organisation's cloud services have to be assessed properly before selecting one or multiple could services, as sometimes the requirements are spread across multiple cloud providers to satisfy the resource needs of a particular application. However, often lack of interoperability between various cloud services is a big issue that is hampering these efforts of working across multiple cloud services. Hence, compatibility should be checked for software, scalability, redundancy, and a particular functionality available for a specific version and geographical area.

The need to integrate with different services and platforms has generated new market opportunities and such distributed IoT platforms are increasingly becoming popular. Many market leaders have emerged as the cloud API providers. Some are listed below:

- Simple Cloud
- Apache (Citrix) CloudStack
- Amazon Web Services API and Eucalyptus
- Google Compute Engine
- VMware vCloud API
- OpenStack API

Though every platform has its own benefits and challenges, some functionalities and services in them are common. For example, some common API models such as OpenStack API and AWS API are supported by the CloudStack model and VMware vCloud API. The cloud environments with secure and multiple-user support help to create a robust infrastructure that enables scalability.

11.2 INTEGRATING CLOUD COMPUTING WITH IOT

IoT systems require storage of huge volume of data as well as high computational power for processing and analysis. Cloud services can cater to such needs and can significantly increase the efficiency of many IoT tasks and provide tremendous support for IoT systems (refer to Fig. 11.4).

Cloud can also facilitate to work on collaborative tasks with several developers engaged remotely in a common cloud environment to develop applications. The big data storage facility of the cloud allows various stakeholders to access and retrieve relevant data on demand. Both established and IoT startups can leverage the pay-as-you-use model of the cloud to optimise their return on investment. Thus, the cloud can act as an important middleware between the things in the IoT and IoT based applications. The next section discusses some cloud based tools for big IoT data analytics.

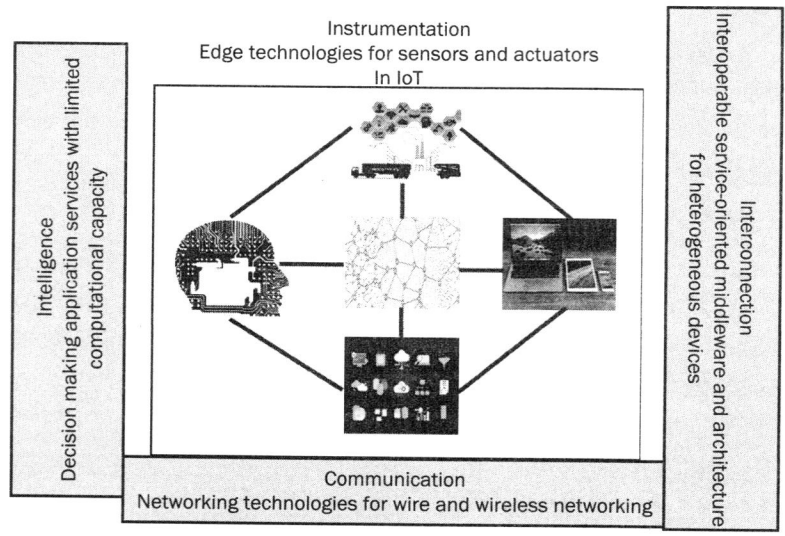

Fig. 11.4 Integration of IoT and Cloud

11.2.1 Apache Hadoop

Hadoop is an open source platform from Apache consisting of an ecosystem of tools, libraries and services. For example, it provides services for storage, NoSQL, batch as well as streaming data processing, etc. Hadoop is composed of different modules that create the Hadoop framework as mentioned below:

- Hadoop Common
- Hadoop Distributed File System (HDFS)
- Hadoop MapReduce
- Hadoop YARN

Several other modules such as Avro, Cassandra, Hive, Pig, Oozie, Flume, and Sqoop, are also useful to enhance Hadoop's power further and are useful for processing large data. Hadoop can run on commodity hardware cluster or in the cloud. The Hadoop Distributed File System (HDFS), allows access of IoT application data at high-speeds through parallelization approaches.

11.2.2 Apache Spark

Apache Spark is a general-purpose cluster computing system. It provides high-level APIs in Java, Scala, Python, and R. It also has optimized engine that supports general execution graphs. Different high level tools supported are SparkSQL for SQL and structured data processing, MLlib for machine learning, GraphX for graph processing, and Spark Streaming. Spark can also perform batch processing; however, it is used generally for streaming workloads, machine-based learning, and interactive queries. Spark possesses real-time data-processing capability and it is much faster than MapReduce's batch-processing engine. Spark has good compatibility with Hadoop and its modules. It also has a standalone mode and can work independently. Spark is a cluster-computing framework; hence, its functionality is supported by MapReduce. Spark does not have its own distributed filesystem but it uses HDFS. Spark uses Resilient Distributed Datasets (RDDs) and the MapReduce uses persistent storage. Spark is well known for its user friendly environment and good performance as it has many user friendly APIs for Spark SQL, Java, Scala (which is its native language), and Python. Spark provides an interactive mode while MapReduce does not have this feature. Hence, Spark developers as well as users can have immediate feedback for queries and other actions. Spark offers greater speed, agility, and ease of use while MapReduce provides low cost of operation. The property of real time processing makes Spark more suitable for real-time edge analytics in IoT applications.

11.3 CLOUD SERVICES

The following sections discuss the various cloud services.

11.3.1 SEaaS: Sensing-as-a-Service

SEaaS is related to cloud services that provide sensing data collected by cloud enabled sensors on demand. This data can be shared by different applications. From a business standpoint, this service model acts as a market place for sensing data, that can be bought for a price. Hence, a passive secondary source of income for a business which has already deployed IoT systems. Some areas in which this is useful include transportation, healthcare, social networking, environment/weather monitoring, etc. where the sensing data can be made available as a service either free or for a price. Several commercially available wearables also have this kind of model for sharing the sensing data. An example query such as find all people who have gone for a walk between 6 and 7 am at a particular location. Assuming that walkers having wearables are uploading data to a particular sensing-as-a-service cloud provider, it is easy to answer such questions.

11.3.2 SAaaS: Sensing and Actuator-as-a-Service

It is related to cloud-enablement of sensors and actuators through virtualisation so that they can be offered as a service. From an IoT stand point, this is vital in creating a more ubiquitous and pervasive computing model of IoT. Many innovative services can be developed that integrate clouds with sensor networks and actuators. An example scenario of the usefulness of SAaaS is forest fires monitoring. IoT sensors related to forest fires monitoring are made available as a cloud service and the alarms and notifications to fire departments as well as public are triggered based on a certain threshold of the fire intensity. These alerts and warnings could be in the form of sirens, alarms, message notifications which act as actuators and are also cloud enabled. Thus both sensors and actuators are available on demand, so developers can create new applications for authorities as well as citizens, that will help them to gain situational awareness in real-time about the disaster.

11.3.3 SEaaS: Sensor Event-as-a-Service

It is the triggered based on the events that are captured from IoT data. These could be events based on real-time sensor data such as temperature, traffic density, water levels, etc. The events could also have been generated by multiple sensors and a pattern that emerged out of their data. Chapter 12 discussed about event processing of streaming IoT data using complex event processing (CEP). The detected events can be used by a cloud-enabled service to generate messages and notifications. Further, users can register sensors for events capture and subscribe and receive the alerts based on the events. Some examples include events generated in supply chain, air quality, traffic monitoring, etc., and the subsequent notification of important alerts to the personnel/ users in these domains.

11.3.4 SenaaS: Sensor-as-a-Service

The IoT sensors, both physical and virtual (e.g., models), can be enabled through virtualisation approaches as a service that exposes the high level functions and capabilities of the sensors and hiding the complex technical aspects (e.g., communication protocols) of the sensors. The cloud middleware is responsible for the ubiquitous sensor management, authorisation, privacy, discovery of sensors that are useful for a particular task/application.

11.4 SELECTED CLOUD SERVICE PROVIDERS

When it comes to selecting cloud platforms for IoT, scalability, cost, and connectivity are the important parameters to be considered. There are many IoT cloud platforms such as Salesforce IoT Cloud, OpenIoT, Thingworx 8 IoT Platform, Microsoft Azure IoT Suite, among many others. Two open-source platforms, Kaa IoT and ThingSpeak, and two more popular platforms such as Google and Oracle Cloud are explored below.

11.4.1 Kaa IoT Platform

Kaa is an open-source, multipurpose middleware platform for end-to-end IoT application development as displayed in Fig. 11.5. Being open source, it reduces the cost, market time, and risk. For different use cases of IoT, Kaa IoT offers a variety of IoT tools.

Fig. 11.5 Kaa IoT Open-Source Cloud Computing Platform

It has many unique features such as:

- Open source
- Handles millions of devices
- Reduced development time
- Ease of implementation
- Reduced marketing time

Advantages:

- Data security
- Easy to use
- Third-party integration

Limitation Application based deployment is not possible.

11.4.2 ThingSpeak IoT Platform

ThingSpeak is an open-source platform for collecting and storing sensor data on the cloud. It provides you with apps to analyze and visualize your data in MATLAB. Arduino, Raspberry Pi, and Beaglebone boards can be used to send sensor data. In addition, a separate channel can be created to store data. Python code for client to upload data on the ThingSpeak in JSON format is shown in Box 11.1.

BOX 11.1 PYTHON CODE FOR CLIENT TO UPLOAD DATA ON THE THINGSPEAK CLOUD IN JSON FORMAT

```python
import random
import urllib.request
import requests
import threading
import json

def client_data_send():
    d = {}
    for i in range(10):
        d[i] = {}
        for j in range(10):
            d[i][j] = random.randint(0,30)

    print("Data:-")
    print(d)

    val = json.dumps(d)
    URL = "https://api.thingspeak.com/update?api_key="
    KEY = "4044IAQ2S4DUEO7G"
    HEADER ="&field1={}&field2={}".format(val,val)
    NEW_URL = URL+KEY+HEADER
    #print(NEW_URL)
    data = urllib.request.urlopen(NEW_URL)
    print(data)
    print("Data sent")


def client_data_get():
    CHANNEL_ID = 763230
    READ_API_KEY = "4044IAQ2S4DUEO7G"
    conn = urllib.request.urlopen("http://api.thingspeak.com/channels/"+str(CHANNEL_ID)+"/feeds/last.json?api_key="+str(READ_API_KEY))
    response = conn.read()
    print("http status code=%s" % (conn.getcode()))
    data = json.loads(response.decode())
    print(data["field1"])
    conn.close()

"""
client_data_send()
"""
client_data_get()
```

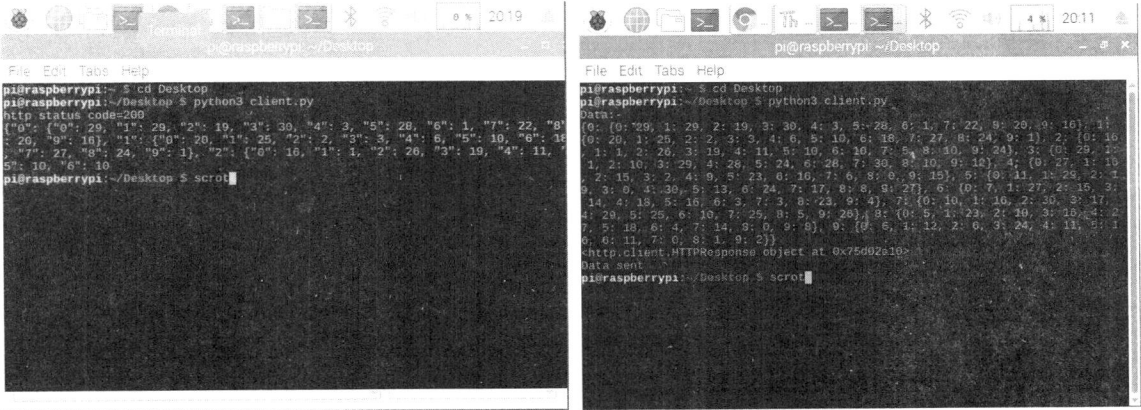

Fig. 11.6 Display of Downloaded and Saved Data from the ThingSpeak Cloud Server in JSON Format

Features of ThingSpeak

- App integration
- Collection data from private channels
- Feature supporting scheduling of event
- Visualization and analytic functionality of MATLAB

Advantages:

- Easy visualization
- Free channel hosting
- Python, Node.js, and Ruby support

11.4.3 Google Cloud

Google's cloud platform is one of the most popular cloud platforms available. Google has an end-to-end platform for IoT solutions. It facilitates easy connection, storage, and management of IoT data. Their main focus is on making smart things in an easy and fast way. Per minute use pricing is offered by Google Cloud and it is cheaper than other platforms.

Google Cloud IoT platform's main features:

- Efficient and scalable
- Very large storage capacity
- Server maintenance cost is less
- IoT data with full protection and with frequent response
- Analyses big data

Advantages:

- Lesser access time than many other platforms
- Fastest input/output
- Provides integration with other Google services

Limitations:

- Limited programming language choices
- Many components are using Google technologies

Google Cloud IoT provides many tools for edge analytics application to process, store, connect, and analyze data. This platform provides scalable cloud services managed by integrated software stack for edge computing with machine learning capabilities.

Businesses can gain by harnessing the diverse IoT cloud devices made available via Google cloud IoT. Results can be visualized with rich reports and dashboards in Google Data Studio. Various machine learning modules are integrated with Google cloud to run advanced analytics on the IoT data and gain meaningful insights. Users also take advantage of Tensor Processing Units (TPUs) to significantly increasing the computational efficiency of AI algorithms when processing big IoT data. The platform also supports many embedded operating systems.

11.4.4 Oracle Cloud

Oracle IoT platform offers real-time IoT data analysis, endpoint management, and high-speed messaging where users can get real-time notifications on their devices. Oracle IoT cloud service is a PaaS. Cloud-based offering helps in making critical business decisions.

Features offered to users:

- Real-time feedback
- Security and scalablity
- Analytics
- Reduced marketing time

Advantages:

- High-speed messaging
- Event storing capability
- Device visualization

11.5 REST-BASED WEB SERVICES FOR IOT

In resource-centric infrastructures such as IoT, REST(Representational State Transfer) style of web services are preferred due to lightweight, simple, portability, reliability and ability to directly transmit data via HTTP. The representation of the state of a IoT resource anemometer (measuring wind speed) is the value '20 mts/sec'. The interaction between client and server is stateless as opposed to Stateful web services such as those based on simple object access protocol (SOAP).

Advantages of using RESTful web services including the usage of URIs for the IoT resources (becomes web resource using URI), for example each device in a large IoT system can be given an URI, thus making it unique and universally addressable and also easy to locate because of the hyper media representation that is the use of web links that contain the metadata of the resource.

Further, the uniform interfaces enable the standard HTTP methods as applicable. Also since REST is based on Service Oriented Architecture (SOA) it inherits the basic features of loose coupling, reusability, scalability, integrity, etc. The Constrained Application Protocol (CoAP) is a specialized web transfer protocol that works with constrained nodes and constrained networks in the Internet. It is used to connect low powered devices to IoT. CoAP is based on the architectural principles of REST and runs over Universal Datagram (UDP) protocol.

THOUGHT EXERCISES

- Write a cloud client program in Embedded C for Arduino Uno and server program for Kaa IoT cloud platform to save the file in JSON format.
- Write the client program in Python language to send and store data collected in CSV format to ThingSpeak IoT cloud and write a server program on the ThingSpeak cloud server.

SUMMARY

For the real-time processing and with new emerging technologies, the need of connecting smart devices with cloud through Internet is gaining more and more importance. To work with vast number of IoT enabled gadgets there is a need for high computing facility, coupled with efficient storage infrastructure and provision of supporting software. An IoT cloud platform offers these facilities and with the added flexibility of subscription plans to suit various application domain specific requirements.

Hence, integration of cloud and IoT can bring new business opportunities and innovative smart applications. For efficient management of smart IoT applications, cloud computing provides a very good solution through its elasticity and facility to access shared resources and common infrastructure.

KEY TERMS

Cloud IoT service models, IoT Cloud platforms, ThingSpeak, SaaS, SEaaS, SenaaS, Google Cloud, Kaa IoT, Restful web API

FURTHER READING

1. https://www.edureka.co/blog/spark-tutorial/
2. GoGrid Storage Services, http://www.gogrid.com
3. iCloud, http://www.icloud
4. Amazon Web Services (AWS), http://aws.amazon.com/
5. The Pachube Feed Cloud Service, http://www.pachube.com
6. Internet of Things—ThingSpeak service, http://www.thingspeak.com

REVIEW QUESTIONS

1. List steps to set up a Hadoop cluster.
2. Compare Spark and Flink with respect to their merits and demerits.
3. Explain the benefits of integration of cloud services with IoT.

4. Write a note on Sensor as a Service (SenaaS) and Sensor Event as a Service (SEaaS).
5. Explain in short Sensing and Actuating as a Service (SAaaS) with an example.
6. Write a Python client program to connect to ThingSpeak cloud server to upload data in XML format.
7. What are the application areas of IoT where open-source Kaa IoT cloud is a suitable option?
8. What are the limitations of ThingSpeak cloud?
9. Write a note on Google Cloud and explain the best features and limitations?
10. Explain Oracle Cloud and its advantages and limitations.
11. Explain the concept of RESTful API and its use for real-time IoT applications.

REFERENCES

1. Yuriyama, M., Kushida, T. (2010), Sensor-cloud infrastructure—Physical sensor management with virtualized sensors on cloud computing. *13th International Conference on Network-Based Information Systems (NBiS)*, pp. 1–8, 14–16.
2. Shimrat, O. (2009), *Cloud Computing and Healthcare*. San Diego Physician, pp. 26–29.
3. DropBox, https://www.dropbox.com: Available online [Accessed: 20/04/2019].
4. https://www.datamation.com/data-center/hadoop-vs.-spark-the-new-age-of-big-data.html: Available online [Accessed: 20/04/2019].
5. Pithos network storage service for the Greek academic community, http://pithos.grnet.gr.
6. Rackspace cloud computing provider, http://www.rackspacke.com
7. Polar, www.polar.com: Available online [Accessed: 20/04/2019].
8. The Arduino LilyPad, http://arduino.cc/en/Main/ArduinoBoardLilyPad: Available online [last accessed: 20/04/2019].
9. Kon Kim, P. Z., Khattak, A. M., Lee, S. (2010), Chord Based Identity Management for e-Healthcare Cloud Applications, *2010 10th IEEE/IPSJ International Symposium on Applications and the Internet (SAINT)*, pp. 391–394, July 19–23, 2010.
10. Madria, S. (2018), Sensor Cloud: Sensing-as-a-Service Paradigm, 2018 19th IEEE International Conference on Mobile Data Management (MDM), Aalborg, pp. 3–6. doi:10.1109/MDM.2018.00014,
11. https://hadoop.apache.org/docs/stable/hadoop-project-dist/hadoop-common/ClusterSetup.html [Accessed: 20/04/2019].
12. Zaslavsky, A., Perera, C., Georgakopoulos, D. (2012), Sensing as a Service and Big Data. CoRR, abs/1301.0159.
13. Rohokale, V. M., Prasad, N. R., Prasad, R. (2011), A cooperative Internet of Things (IoT) for rural healthcare monitoring and control, *2nd International Conference on Wireless Communication, Vehicular Technology, Information Theory and Aerospace & Electronic Systems Technology (Wireless VITAE)*, pp. 1–6, February 28, 2011.
14. Dohr, A., Modre-Opsrian, R., Drobics, M., Hayn, D., Schreier, G. (2010), The Internet of Things for ambient assisted living, *Seventh International Conference on Information Technology: New Generations (ITNG)*, pp. 804–809, 12–14.
15. Zhang, X., Wen, Z., Wu, Y. Zou, J. (2011), The implementation and application of the Internet of Things platform based on the REST architecture, *International Conference on Business Management and Electronic Information (BMEI)*, vol. 2, pp. 43–45, 13–15.
16. Castellani, A. P., Gheda, M., Bui, N., Rossi, M., Zorzi, M. (2011), Web Services for the Internet of Things through CoAP and EXI, 2011 IEEE International Conference on Communications Workshops (ICC), pp. 1–6, 5–9.
17. https://www.edureka.co/blog/spark-tutorial/ [Accessed: 10/03/2019]

18. https://i0.wp.com/outfresh.com/wp-content/uploads/2018/06/oracl-1.jpg
19. https://www.kaaproject.org/ [Accessed: 10/03/2019]
20. S. Satpathy, B. Sahoo, A.K. Turuk Sensing and actuation as a service delivery model in cloud edge centric Internet of Things Future Gener. Comput. Syst., 86 (2018), pp. 281-296,
21. S. Alam, M. M. R. Chowdhury and J. Noll, "SenaaS: An event-driven sensor virtualization approach for Internet of Things cloud," 2010 IEEE International Conference on Networked Embedded Systems for Enterprise Applications, Suzhou, 2010, pp. 1-6, doi: 10.1109/NESEA.2010.5678060.
22. https://thingspeak.com/ [last accessed: 14/09/2020]
23. Perera, C., Barhamgi, M., De, S., Baarslag, T., Vecchio, M., & Choo, K. K. R. (2019). Designing Sensing as a Service (S2aaS) Ecosystem for Internet of Things. arXiv preprint arXiv:1904.05023.

Edge Analytics: Near Real-Time Sensor Stream Processing

CHAPTER 12

"Our minds work in real time, which begins at the Big Bang and will end, if there is a Big Crunch - which seems unlikely, now, from the latest data showing accelerating expansion. Consciousness would come to an end at a singularity."

-Stephen Hawking

OBJECTIVES

- explain the concept of stream and its characteristics and relate it in the context of IoT
- outline the fundamentals of stream processing
- explain edge analytics
- explain the concepts of Complex Event Processing (CEP)
- classify various CEP operators
- apply open source stream processing tool, (Apache Flink)
- build an IoT application that performs edge analytics for real-time decision-making

OUTCOMES

- compare and contrast real-time processing and batch processing
- summarize the attributes of real-time processing
- make use of CEP in various scenarios to enable real time warnings and alerts
- experiment with Apache Flink to develop CEP applications

REVISION

To increase your understanding of the material in this chapter, you can spend a few minutes reviewing key concepts in chapters 10 and 11

- concepts related to Big data analytics need to be reviewed
- the earlier chapter on IoT platforms described various approaches for working with data coming from IoT devices
- the chapter on IoT Protocols explained the various network and communication protocols for low powered devices. The data latency issues were also discussed.

12.1 INTRODUCTION

A variety of Internet of Things (IoT) sensor devices are enabling to gather high-frequency continuous streams of data resulting in unprecedented amounts of data. The quantity of data generated depends on the temporal resolution of the sensor and the purpose of measurement pertaining to a particular application. A weather station comprising of sensors such as temperature, relative humidity, wind speed/direction, and precipitation could generate a few kilobytes of data, if collected at an hourly rate (refer to Table 12.1). However, sensors measuring traffic for estimating traffic flow characteristics may collect gigabytes of data in few minutes. Similarly, sensor networks in industrial plants could generate multiple gigabytes of data in a second. Many other examples of continuous streams of data include the following:

- Data generated by disaster monitoring network stations. For example, water level monitoring stations for floods, seismographs for earthquakes, buoys network for Tsunamis forecast, Forest fire monitoring networks, landslides detection, etc.
- Network security monitoring and management systems.
- Healthcare systems that provide continuous status of the patients in Intensive Care Units (ICU). Remote health assistive systems that continuously monitor elderly patients.
- Home security systems that continuously monitor inside the home to detect smoke/fire and outside for detecting intruders.
- Fraud detection using behavioural patterns in financial transactions through real-time tracking and analytics.
- Companies that provide e-commerce applications track the customers' behaviour on the website, and accordingly place relevant products and advertisements at strategic locations on the webpage.
- Real-Time analysis and prediction of stock market.
- Industrial IoT applications where there is a need to react to a process based on its status- and trigger-related processes.

The aforementioned applications require real-time or online processing (the gap between the data generation and processing is minimal), also known as low latency and high throughput requirement. In reality, however, this is very challenging to achieve. An end-to-end stream processing system should have the capabilities to ingest big data sets in an optimal way. In addition, transformation, processing, querying, and analysis are other important attributes of such a system.

Table 12.1 Data from an IoT Device Measuring Various Weather Parameters

Time Stamp	Temperature (°C)	Humidity (%)	Precipitation (mm)	Wind Speed (km/h)
9:00	26.4	53	10.2	17.7
9:02	26.3	52	10.4	17.6
Similar to above, thousands of records arriving at tremendous velocity				
10:15	26	50	10.9	17.5

12.1.1 Stream Processing Workflow

IoT data ingestion The incoming data from IoT devices arrive at the data ingestion layer. The capabilities of this layer depend upon how the data is produced. For example, data coming from a traffic flow monitoring sensor may come at a high rate, and in addition to gathering this data, it is also required to provide specialized services (by a middleware application) that enables to warn the users of an imminent traffic jam. Since the data produced is at a very high rate, and the decisions also have to be taken in real time based on the incoming data, there is a requirement for new ways for ingestion of the time-series data. Hence, this layer is devised to acquire and preprocess the data as it arrives and pass it on for further analytics. The data that is once passed on will no longer be available, that is, there is no persistence in the data ingestion layer.

Preprocessing and transformation The incoming data from the IoT devices are in a variety of syntactical and structural models, and also may have noise (due to disturbing events close to the sensors) associated with them. It is necessary to preprocess these data streams to make them amenable for consumption by other layers of IoT. For example, the data may need to be converted to a format that is acceptable to a particular application in the processing layer. Recently, messaging systems such as Apache Flume (Apache Flume, 2018) and Apache Kafka (Apache Kafka, 2018) are able to convert data in a form that is easily consumed by the various stream processing platforms. In addition, the data may need to be normalized, to remove variability in the ranges of values coming from different sensors. Further, sometimes it is necessary to add additional information to the data stream to make it more context specific such as adding the geographic coordinates (i.e., Latitude and Longitude) to give the data value a location (see Fig. 12.1).

Stream processing This layer consumes the streaming data either directly or buffered in between by the ingestion and preprocessing layers, and sends the output or intermediate results to the storage layer. The heart of a stream processing system is this layer, where a variety of processing approaches can be applied on the data stream in real time. It facilitates the capture of specific predetermined events or patterns of events coming from diverse IoT streaming data sources, which are actionable immediately.

Storage At this layer, persistent storage of the data occurs. The data that is stored could be either selected time windows of data from the intermediate buffer for long-term archival purpose or the captured events that will be analysed or used again for a different purpose such as understanding the

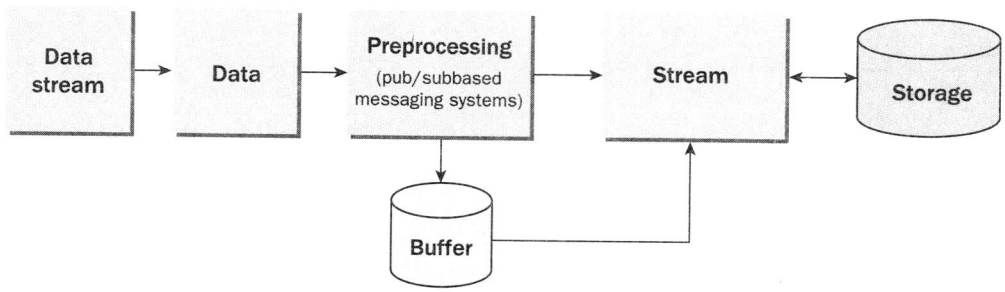

Fig. 12.1 A Typical Workflow of a Stream Processing System

limitations, faults, or combining them with other types of data. The archived data is generally used in a mini batch-processing mode for applying various techniques such as Machine Learning (ML)-based approaches for clustering and classification of the events. This topic is covered in Chapter 10 on Big IoT Data Science.

12.2 WHAT IS STREAMING DATA?

Data that resides persistently somewhere is no longer interesting than data that is in perpetual motion. The value of a data can decrease over time, especially those kinds of data that is used for real-time understanding of a phenomenon. For example, disaster monitoring requires continuously updated information to provide rapid response services, which can mitigate the loss of life and property. Some of the data that is used in such scenarios is related to weather conditions provided by a variety of meteorological sensors. The usefulness of a particular weather prediction for the next couple of hours expires as soon as that period has passed. Therefore, the information is useful only in that time window. Several such examples exist in other domains such as Traffic monitoring, stock markets analysis, and industrial IoT.

A *stream* can be defined as: 'a real-time, continuous, ordered (implicitly by arrival time or explicitly by time stamp) sequence of items. It is impossible to control the order in which items arrive, nor is feasible to locally store a stream in its entirety (Lukasz and Özsu, 2003).'

Typical characteristics of a data stream are as follows:

Unbounded data The data is arriving continuously and unbounded, that is, possibly an infinite stream.

Unordered data The data is coming in haphazard fashion without any particular order. This could be due to data buffering at the device level/gateway or coming from multiple devices and each device having its own frequency of sending the data. This results in a stream whose time stamps are not in a sequence, resulting in disparities between data acquisition time and data processing time.

Unsaved data Data is usually discarded after being processed for certain events. The extracted events may be stored for future use.

Data deviation The data distribution can deviate from the original after some time due to drift in the phenomenon being measured (e.g., rapidly changing weather), device issues and new requirements for acquisition resulting in a noisy data stream.

12.2.1 Bounded vs Unbounded Data

The general notion of streaming versus batch processing is confusing because there are systems that perform mini batch processing to mimic stream processing. Ideally, such systems are batch processors with an ability to perform very fine-grained batch operations that look like a stream process. Hence, to overcome such confusion, it is better to think in terms of bounded and unbounded data.

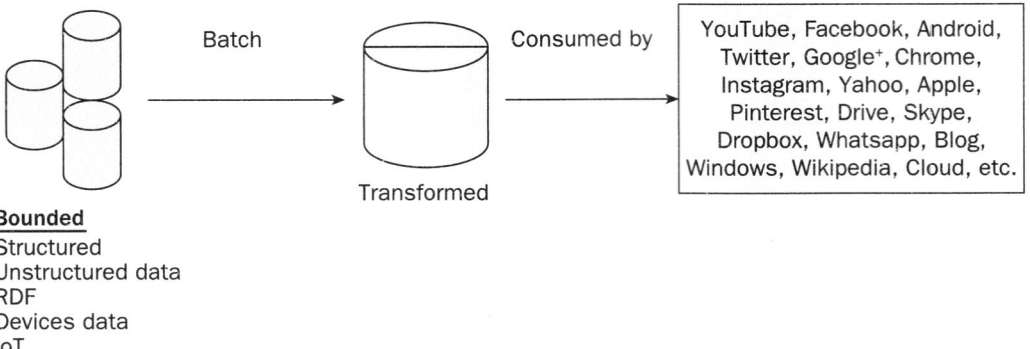

Fig. 12.2 Batch Processing on Bounded Data

12.2.1.1 Bounded Data

When data possesses distinctive starting and end points, that is, in terms of its time stamp, it is called as a bounded data set. The processing on bounded data set usually is in the batch mode (batch processing). In this approach (Fig. 12.2), a dataset in a repository (stored data), which could be in various formats (structured, unstructured, RDF triples, etc.) is processed in chunks (chunking is done based on some predefined criteria) and given to a batch-processing engine. The data transforms into a structured form at the end of the batch processing, which can be consumed by various applications.

The performance of a batch processing system can be measured in terms of *throughput* and *latency*. Theoretically, *throughput* is the amount of data that can be processed in a unit time over a known bandwidth; however, in reality this varies due to various hurdles in the network connection such as transmission and processing delays. *Latency* is the delay that occurred in processing over a network, which directly affects the *throughput*.

12.2.1.2 Unbounded Data

Unbounded data is data that is unending (infinite) and coming continuously in some ordered or unordered fashion (Fig. 12.3).

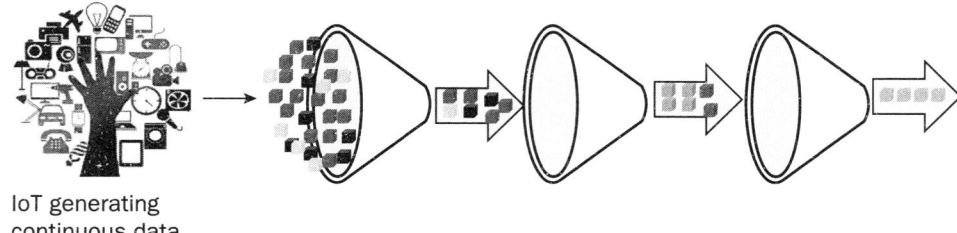

Fig. 12.3 Unbounded Data Streams from a Variety of IoT Sensors (High speed and volume streams are reduced by applying filters designed to capture specific events or patterns)

12.2.2 Time-bound Processing of Streaming Data

Streaming data processing capability is measured by time in terms of latency and throughput. It is useful to differentiate between two types of time measures, that is, event time and processing time.

12.2.2.1 Event Time

This is when the actual event has occurred. For example, if a sensor measured temperature at 15:30 Hours, the event time is the time of measurement of the phenomenon. It has a time stamp and a value associated with it.

12.2.2.2 Processing Time

This is time at which the event has arrived at the event stream-processing platform and is one of the events out a stream of events coming in sequentially.

It is quite possible that the time of processing (system time of the machine-based on the system clock) of the event and the time of the actual event happening are different. This could result in the disruption of the time-synchronized arrival of the incoming streams. Hence, it is important to keep a check on the order of the arrival of events.

This discrepancy of event time and processing time is crucial for certain applications. In the context of IoT, this is a very important consideration if there are time critical events that are being detected and acted upon.

For example, in a real time disaster application such as floods, the precipitation measurements at various geographically distributed measuring stations have an event timestamp associated with each precipitation measurement. But when some of these measurements are unable to reach the processing engine due to connectivity issues and are queued and sent later, it leads to latency issues. The processing engine meanwhile processes the other available measurements from other stations and they have a different processing time stamp than those measurements that are subsequently processed from the delayed stream of data. This can lead to a disruption in the right sequence of processing of the precipitation measurements, which are used in a model for predicting possible inundation area.

12.3 DATA STREAM MANAGEMENT SYSTEMS

Data Stream Management Systems (DSMS) are specialized systems that deal with continuously arriving data streams as against Database Management Systems (DBMS), which deal with stored data (Babcock, 2002). As shown in Fig. 12.4, the data streams are processed as they arrive, and optionally the incoming streams may be buffered in an intermediate storage (at the IoT gateway) and formatted in such as a way that is suitable for processing in the stream processing module. DSMS normally store the important events that were derived from the data streams for further analysis and also for combining them with other sources of information.

The data is stored first and then analysed in the normal data processing approaches. The data stream is immediately processed as soon as it arrives and the intermediate results are stored in a buffer for further processing.

The main differences between a Database Management System (DBMS) and Data Stream Management System (DSMS) at various levels in data processing pipeline are shown in Table 12.2.

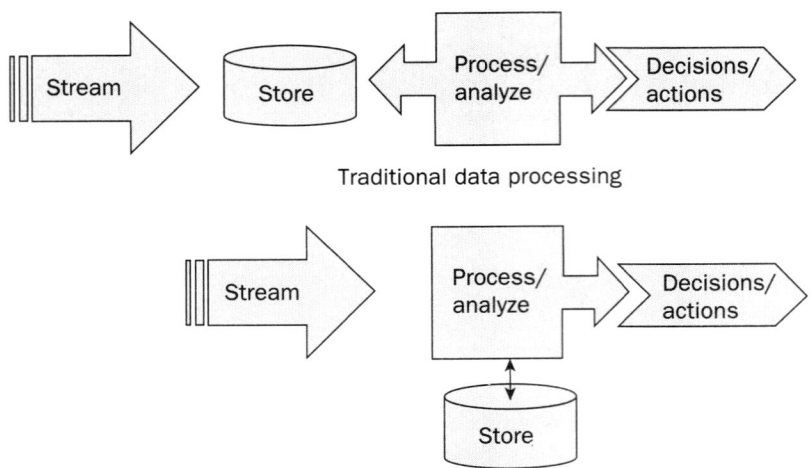

Fig. 12.4 Traditional Data Processing vs Stream Data Processing

Table 12.2 Differences between Database Management System (DBMS) and Data Stream Management Systems (DSMS)

Database Management Systems (DBMS)	Data Stream Management Systems (DSMS)
Data level	
Static/stored data, time of capture or storage of data is unimportant	Continuously changing data, time of event capture and time of processing are important
Access to the data can be either sequential or random	Data access is sequential and is usually based on the timestamp of the incoming events
Data updation is relatively slow, usually in relatively small increments	High frequency and volume of data updation
Data is consistent and has high precision	Data is noisy due to imperfections in the data capturing process
Processing level	
Processing on data available currently in the database	Processing on current as well as historical data, which could be data that arrived few seconds, hours, or days before.
Asynchronous data processing (e.g., batch processing), no need to process or deliver results in real time	Synchronous, real-time processing of data. Requirement for delivery of results rapidly
Processing on relatively large portions of data	Incremental processing approach
Data value remains consistent over time	Data can become stale and no longer be usable after a set period of time

(Contd)

Table 12.2 *(Contd)*

Database Management Systems (DBMS)	Data Stream Management Systems (DSMS)
Query level	
Queries can be dynamic (i.e., querying whenever the situation demands) and complex	Queries are pre-determined and run on time varying data. Complexity is in the capturing and processing of event patterns.
Queries are precise	Queries can be approximate and can return approximate results
Multiple rounds of data access may be done to answer a query	One time access to data, after which the data is no longer available

12.3.1 Background of DSMS Development

Various DSMSs were developed during the last decade. Here a few selected DSMS are briefly reviewed to understand the progress in the development of more sophisticated systems that are available in today's market.

Gigascope It is based on an SQL-like language, called GSQL. It was developed specifically for network domain applications such as intrusion detection and traffic monitoring (Cranor et al., 2003).

TelegraphCQ It is a system that can enable continuous querying over big streams that change over time. It is based on SQL-based language called StreaQuel. It can work on clusters (Chandrasekaran et al., 2003).

Aurora It is based on a language called SQuAl, which can be used to visually define various rules with the help of various GUI widgets (Abadi et al., 2003).

Borealis It is the successor to Aurora and a second-generation stream processing engine. It addresses two important areas of Stream processing such as dynamic revision of query results, which enables to process the data that was corrected and re-injected into the stream. If such ability is missing then the results will be imprecise. The second functionality of the system is that it enables to change the query attributes at runtime (Abadi et al., 2005).

TESLA/T-Rex T-Rex system performs events processing incrementally whenever events incoming event streams enter the system. Detection automata based algorithm is developed to perform such incremental processing (Cugola & Margara, 2010a).

Further, several other stream processing engines such as Stream Mill (Bai et al., 2006), STREAM (Arasu et al., 2003), StreaMon (Babu & Widom, 2004), Tibco-StreamBase (Tibco-Streambase, 2018), OracleCEP (OrcaleCEP, 2018), Esper (Esper, 2018), IBM WebSphere (IBM WebSphere, 2018) are available. However, some of these systems have challenges in satisfying the current big data requirements of volume and velocity. Scalability implies that, based on the requirement of the processing task the number of worker nodes (or processing units) can be increased without any damage to the system.

> **BOX 12.1: EIGHT REQUIREMENTS OF A STREAM PROCESSING SYSTEM**
>
> Strohbahach, M., et al., 2005, provided eight requirements that an ideal stream processing system should adhere to:
> 1. Keep the data moving
> 2. Query using SQL on streams (StreamSQL)
> 3. Handle stream imperfections (delayed, missing, and out-of-order data)
> 4. Generate predictable outcomes
> 5. Integrate stored and streaming data
> 6. Guarantee data safety and availability
> 7. Partition and scale applications automatically
> 8. Process and respond instantaneously

Eight requirements of stream processing systems are shown in Box 12.1. Recently, several streaming platforms have been developed that are highly scalable and have the attributes of low latency and high throughput. These platforms have the ability to run on High Performance Computing (HPC) systems so that real-time processing can be achieved.

12.3.2 Stream Processing Platforms

Recently, several stream processing platforms were developed to support large-scale applications. Among others, these systems differ in their delivery semantics as shown in Box 12.2.

In this section, a brief review of the most popular platforms is presented.

Apache Storm It is a stream processing platform that has proven to process a million records in the fraction of a second. The architecture is based on the concept of Directed Acyclic Graph (DAG), where the vertices represent either a data source or a computational unit, this form of representation is referred to as a topology in storm. Storm carries out stream processing using micro-batches of the incoming events, so a latency of a few milliseconds can happen. It supports at least once and almost once semantics (Toshniwal et al., 2014).

> **BOX 12.2: DELIVERY SEMANTICS OF IOT EDGE ANALYTICS PLATFORMS**
>
> **At-most-once:** The events are dropped if they are not processed correctly; here there is a possibility for data loss.
> **At-least-once:** In this case, each input event is monitored to see if the processing is successful within a time window. This is achieved by keeping a record in-memory. In case the event was not processed successfully, it is resent again for processing. Therefore, here the data loss issue is resolved; however, there is a possibility of having duplicates.
> **Exactly once:** Events are processed at-least once and the duplicates are detected and discarded.

MillWheel Developed at Google, MillWheel is a streaming system that uses the concept of DAG processing. The nodes of the DAG are computational units as well as persistent storage, while the vertices carry the messages. In MillWheel, it is possible to enforce a time-based watermark that makes sure that all the events data before a certain time (called the *low watermark*) is processed by the system, irrespective of the order of their arrival. This ensures that all data within a particular range of time (time stamps) are guaranteed to be processed. It supports exactly once semantics (Akidau et al., 2013).

Apache Samza Samza uses Kafka for handing the streams. In Kafka a stream of data is treated as a topic, which is a stream of related events and can be subscribed by a user. Samza can store a state as a local key-value store and supports at-least-once delivery semantics (Apache Samza, 2018).

Apache Spark Spark is a hybrid stream processing system, which can handle both steam and batch processing. Spark's streaming module is based on stream buffering at very small intervals (milliseconds) and uses them in the batch mode for processing. Due to the buffering mechanism used in Spark, there is a need to flush it in between, which can lead to latency issues. It supports exactly once delivery semantics (Apache Spark, 2018).

Apache Flink It is a hybrid stream processing approach based on the Kappa architecture, where streams are first class citizens, and are used for all kinds of processing (both batch and streams). The stream-first philosophy of Flink results in high throughput and low latency. In Flink, the *event time*, that is, when an event has actually occurred can be used to guarantee ordered streams. It guarantees exactly once record delivery semantics (Apache Flink, 2018).

The edge analytics (filters, rules, triggers, warning, etc.) are performed on live stream of data as it arrives. Complex event processing (CEP) techniques are applied to these types of event streams. The cold analytics are performed on data streams that are in a buffer or in a persistent storage; stream data mining approaches are relevant in this mode.

12.4 EDGE ANALYTICS

Edge analytics are performed at the location (or close to) of the devices from which the data is collected. It is an approach, where the incoming data is processed and analysed as it arrives, in contrast to approaches, which rely on the analysing data that is stored in a repository. Edge analytics assume a prime importance in the context of IoT because it allows capturing those events that are interesting and important to a particular task and which has a time constraint for delivering the results. The recent explosion in the volume, velocity, and variety (3 vs of Big data) demands for approaches that are able to make sense of the data in real time, not only for real-time response activities, but also for storing only those events that are interesting and discarding the rest. Some examples that tremendously benefit from edge analytics are mentioned in Section 12.1. The ability to perform real-time analytics is possible due to the techniques, methods, and tools that are developed specifically for stream processing. In general, there are two major approaches for performing analytics on IoT data streams. As described in Box 12.3, the cold analytics approach is applicable when the data is stored in some buffer or in persistent storage. Machine Learning (ML) approaches are relevant in this module. The next chapter (Chapter 10) on IoT

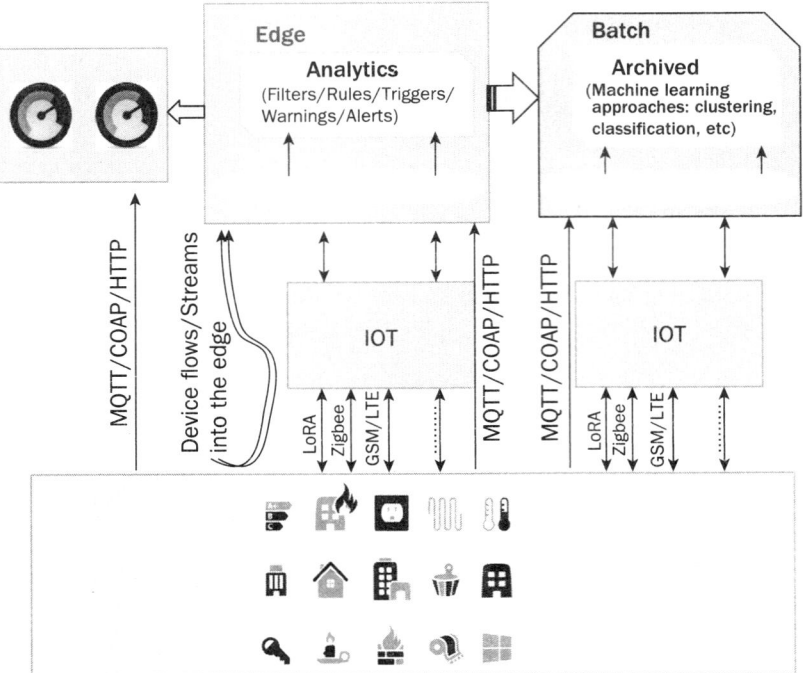

Fig. 12.5 Framework for Analytics in IoT

Data Science covers topics relevant to ML-based techniques. The analytics covered in this chapter are geared towards techniques that are applied on the fly in real time (see Fig. 12.5); hence, they are called hot analytics, which can facilitate rapid analysis to gain situational awareness.

Complex event processing is one of the major techniques to harness multiple streams of data coming from IoT sensors, which is described in Section 12.4.2.

BOX 12.3: TYPES OF IOT ANALYTICS

Cold analytics approach: In the cold analytics approach, the incoming data stream is archived first and then processed usually in a batch mode. The amount and duration of data that is processed is predetermined. This is discussed in the next chapter on data stream mining, which covers various IoT stream data mining methods such as stream learners for classification, regression, clustering, and frequent pattern mining.

Hot analytics approach: A hot analytics approach (see Fig. 12.6) which requires the stream to be processed as and when they arrive and characterized based on a predefined criteria. Stream processing and CEP approaches belong to the hot analytics approach, where the incoming data streams are continuously matched against a pattern(s) so as to capture the essence of the data stream and gain useful insights. The events that are detected are called complex event patterns.

12.4.1 Event Processing

Event An event is a record of the change of state of an entity at a given point of time. It is usually something that is of interest. A reading from an IoT sensor is an example of an event.

Atomic event An atomic event is an event that happens at a specific point in time having a time stamp and carries unprocessed information. It may have a state and value corresponding to phenomenon that is measured. Raw readings from a sensor are an example of atomic event streams and are processed in a stream processing engine; its goal is to dynamically process the data streams by some mathematical transformations.

Complex event Also called as a composite event which is based on the composition of atomic events in some predetermined form (Figs 12.6 and 12.7). It could be based on various operators that are applied on a single or multiple events to form more complex set of events. For example, the change in the air quality from good to worse, which is based on streams of events coming from different air quality measuring parameters. CEP goes beyond simple aggregation of events; it is designed to obtain insights into the relationships between streams.

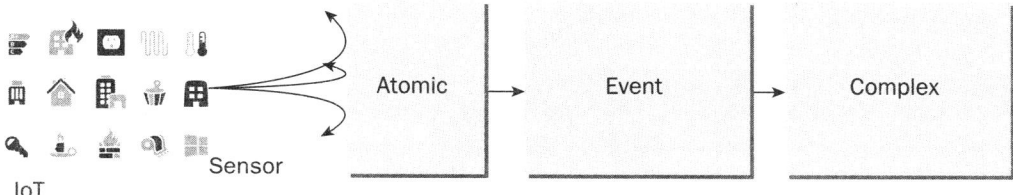

Fig. 12.6 Relation between Atomic Events, Event Streams, and Complex Events

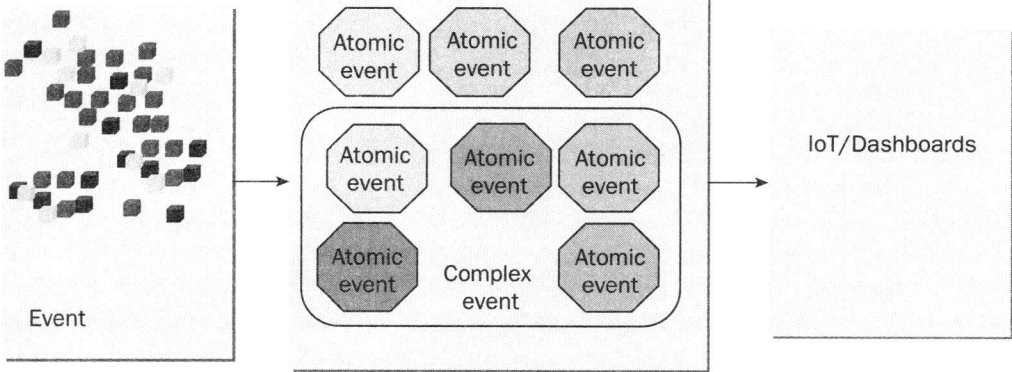

Fig. 12.7 Illustration of Atomic and Complex Events

Event pattern   An event pattern captures an event's properties and relationships (if applicable) between different (possible from multiple sources) events of a certain type. An event instance is a realization of an event pattern. Examples of such event patterns are: temporal pattern of an event such as traffic jam, weather front, and stock market. Various complex event patterns are discussed in Section 12.4.2.1.

Event stream processing (ESP)   The goal of ESP is to process big event streams in a continuous fashion. In ESP, the order of arrival of the events is not important. The earlier version of DSMS systems are based on the ESP concept. ESP is a subset of CEP.

12.4.2 Complex Event Processing

Complex event processing enables to understand, detect, correlate, and process the relationship between events. It is the principal technology solution for processing real-time data streams (Suhothayan et al., 2011). CEP was first introduced by Luckham (2002). Several authors have defined CEP in various terms such as:

Luckham (2007)   'CEP consists of principles for processing clouds of events to extract information, together with technologies to implement those principles.'

Eckert and Bry (2009)   'A technology which encompasses methods, techniques, and tools for processing events while they occur, i.e., in a continuous and timely fashion.'

BOX 12.4: DIFFERENCES BETWEEN DSMS AND CEP

DSMS were designed specifically for querying continuously varying time series of data and produce a result to the query at any point of time. However, the order of the arrival of the events has not been dealt with in these systems. Newer variants of DSMS, address this issue. In general, they are not capable of working with multiple data streams.

CEP is focused on the processing of multiple related events coming from a variety of sensors belonging to a particular domain in order to detect interesting time varying events and send continuous alerts (notifications) related to the complex patterns. The patterns are similar to those described in Section 12.4.1.2, which are usually a composition of the simple patterns to form a composite or complex pattern to deal with a more complicated scenario. The ordering of the events is important. It is possible to capture a set of complex patterns and the results may be converted to a stream of events, which can then be combined with another set of complex events to answer an advanced query. For example, warnings from a stream of events can be converted to set of event streams and another pattern can be created to capture those critical warnings (e.g., consecutive warnings of the same type, within a particular time window) that should be treated as alerts and notified to the user.

Many current systems are a hybrid of the aforementioned systems.

CEP has taken the DSMS systems to the next level, the key differences between CEP and DSMS are shown in Box 12.4.

A CEP processor captures the state change of the events, and uses such information to carry out analytics, which can predict future states. Thus, events and their state are what triggers a CEP system. Events form components which are composed together to form higher-level complex events (Fig. 12.8). The way the components are combined is based on which CEP operators (see Section 12.4.2.1) are used in the sequence to derive a query that is pertinent to a particular situation.

CEP is now being quickly adopted in the IoT systems as they are designed to respond and provide solutions in real-time to enable predicting events, obtain awareness about critical situations, conditions, and imminent threats. Some of the main reasons for developing CEP systems for IoT are mentioned in Box 12.5.

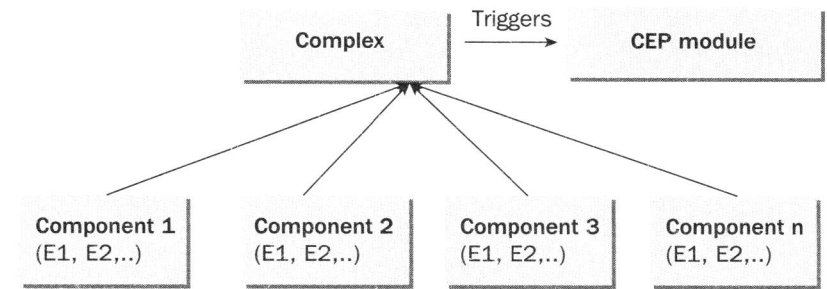

Fig. 12.8 Components Consist of Events and Encapsulated into a Higher-level Complex Event

---

BOX 12.5: MAIN REASONS FOR ADOPTION OF COMPLEX EVENT PROCESSING FOR IOT APPLICATIONS

Complex event processing technologies are becoming quite popular for IoT use cases, the main reasons are as:
1. Ability to provide situational awareness for events that are happening in a particular domain: This is a crucial requirement in IoT applications as they are designed to provide feedback or response rapidly, so that the user is aware of the current situation and status of a particular scenario.
2. Ability to capture and process high throughput big data stream coming from IoT sensors.
3. Ability to handle time varying IoT events in various forms (ordered, unordered, drifting, etc.).
4. Ability to integrate and gain understanding of complex interactions between event streams coming from a variety of sources, through various forms of filtering on the time series, and developing a variety of complex patterns.
5. Ability to obtain approximate answers to queries when time is of essence.

12.4.2.1 CEP Operators

The complex event processing engine is capable of processing multiple streams of events and understand the patterns and relationships between streams of a certain type (also called as keyed streams, e.g., all streams that originated from a station based on its stationID), but also between event streams that are independent. To enable an intuitive way of expressing the behaviour of the events, most of the currently available CEP engines allow representing events in a declarative language similar to SQL. Many stream query languages were developed, the structure of these languages are similar to SQL but they are extended with special operators for continuous stream processing (Lukasz and Özsu, 2003; Gyllstrom et al., 2007; Wu et al., 2006; Sqlstream, 2018; Arasu et al., 2006).

Below are the most often used fundamental operators (Cugola and Margara, 2010). In general, the CEP patterns are based on a combination of the below mentioned operators. Usually the pattern is in a nested form containing a sequence of the basic operators.

12.4.2.2 Single-item Operators

Selection The selection operators are similar to filtering, in which a specific condition or criteria is tested. The conditions are based on the values of the event (e.g., a value measured by a sensor). The most common criteria is a threshold. As an example, consider the following pattern, which selects the events from a ground level ozone sensor, which are between 90 and 130 parts per billion (PPB).

Select OzoneSensor (Ozone>= 90 and Ozone<=130)
From OzoneDataStream

Elaboration operators These operators are used for transformation of events. Projection and renaming are elaboration operators.

Projection Extracts a part of the attributes and processes the events related to it. For example, the location and height at which a measurement is made is extracted. Only those events that match these criteria are further examined.

Select OzoneSensor (Height, Location (Lat, Long))
From OzoneDataStream

Renaming operators These operators are used to change the name of the property of a certain event.

Select OzoneSensor ("Measurement")
From OzoneDataStream
Rename ("Ozone ground level measurement")

12.4.2.3 Logical Operators

Conjunction A conjunction of events EV1, EV2, ..., EVn implies that all of the events EV1, EV2, ..., EVn have occurred. It is applicable to two or more events occurring together. For example, it can be used to capture events related to air pollution where both Particulate Matter (PM) events and ozone at ground level events are notified within a time window of 30 min.

OzoneSensor(Ozone>130) AND PMSensor(Particulate Matter > 75)
From AirqualityStationData
(Within 30m)

Disjunction In a predefined window, the occurrence of either of the selected events.

OzoneSensor(Ozone>130) OR PMSensor(Particulate Matter > 75)
From AirqualityStationData
(Within 30m)

Repetition This pattern is useful to detect repeat occurrence of an event. The repetition can be predefined. For example, it would be useful to know how many times the air quality has deteriorated to poor quality in the last 8 h. In addition, the same event can repeat between two time periods (m, n)

Select PMSensor (Particulate Matter > 85) as PM AND
Select OzoneSensor (Ozone > 125) as OZ
From AirQualtiyData
Where count (PM and OZ) > 3

Aggregation The aggregate values from a particular event are subjected to a condition such as min, max, average, and std. For example, the 8 h average of the ozone value is used in the calculation of air quality index.

Select average (ozonesensor.Ozone)
From AirqualityData
(Within 8 Hrs)

Negation operator A negation of event EV means that the event E has not occurred. For example, it is safe to drive if:

PMSensor(PM <33) and OzoneSensor(Ozone<60) and NOT Dusty().

Sequence operator The sequence of occurrence of events is captured by the sequence operator. The order of the events (e.g., the sequence in which a measurement is made over a time interval) is important.

Quantification It is a measure of the occurrence of a number of events (n) of a particular type.

12.4.2.4 Iteration

Iterations are conditional and the sequence of events must conform to the iteration condition.

Typical steps involved in building a pattern query is shown in Box 12.6. These steps can also be compared with those from the example given in Section 12.5.

12.4.2.5 Windowing

Windows are useful to make some boundaries on the unbounded data streams, so that only a portion of the stream of events can be processed correctly in a predefined time interval or a set of events. The various operators as discussed earlier are used with the windows.

> **BOX 12.6: TYPICAL STEPS IN BUILDING A COMPLEX PATTERN QUERY**
>
> 1. **Begin:** Starting of a pattern definition:
>   `Pattern<TrafficEvent, ?> pattern = Pattern.<TrafficEvent>begin("start")`. Here we have begun a pattern definition for capturing events from traffic data
> 2. **Next:** New pattern that matches the previous matching pattern
>   `Pattern<TrafficEvent, ?> next = start.next("next");`
> 3. **Followed by:** Appends a new pattern state, but here other events can occur between two matching events: `Pattern<TrafficEvent, ?> followedBy = start.followedBy ("next");`
> 4. **Where:** Filter condition:
>    ```
>    start..where(new FilterFunction <TrafficEvent>() {
>      @override
>        public boolean filter(TrafficEvent value) throws Exception
>         {
>            return ... // some condition
>         }
>    });
>    ```
> 5. **Or:** Add new filter condition with an existing one. Example is using two where conditions with an OR in between them.
> 6. **Within:** Time interval for matching the pattern: `patternState.within(Time.minutes(5));`
>
> Note: The example complex event patterns show above are based on the representation using Apache Flink and assuming event streams from a traffic IoT sensor.

Tumbling window In these windows, the upper and lower bounds are predetermined and they remain constant. These windows do not overlap and are adjacent to each other. This creates non-overlapping adjacent windows in a stream. The tumbling windows are bounded by either time (e.g., all traffic related events that are in a fixed interval of time, i.e., 15:00 to 15:30 Hours) or by the number of events that will be aggregated together before doing some analysis on it (e.g., five traffic events (e.g., traffic jam) on particular road, aggregated, and then analysed (refer to Fig. 12.9).

Sliding window Most commonly used windows, that are useful for setting an upper and lower bound and both of them move with the same frequency. As shown in Fig. 12.10, the windows can overlap similar to the tumbling windows but here the windows can overlap. We can use it in scenarios where we need to quantify or summarize the events in a particular time frame and at the same time send the results in another time frame. For example, if we want to know the traffic density every 10 min, it should contain that information for the last 30 min.

Windows can overlap and have a predefined upper and lower bound when can be different. Each stream can be identified by its key value.

Session window It is based on how long events are occurring in close proximity to each other (refer to Fig. 12.11). A session gap is predefined, which tells how long the activity should occur together, and

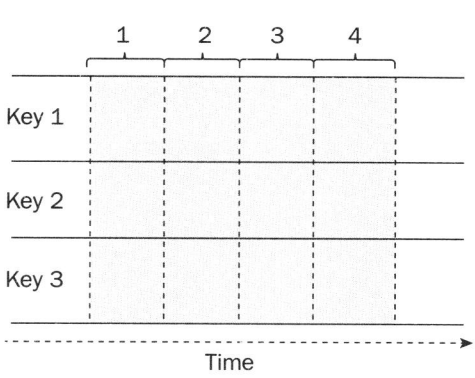

Fig. 12.9 Tumbling Windows are Non-overlapping and Their Size is Predetermined Based on Some Understanding of the Phenomenon Being Studied

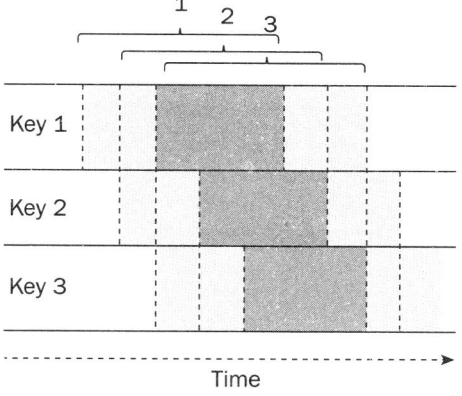

Fig. 12.10 Sliding Window Approach

how wide a gap of inactivity can be tolerated. This kind of processing is useful in situations where we are expecting activity in a particular order with an approximate time gap between them, but due to some other influence this session gap has become wider, which needs to be flagged.

For example, the peak traffic monitoring is based on sessions, i.e. morning session when the traffic is very high during office time, then again in the evening session when the traffic is at its peak from

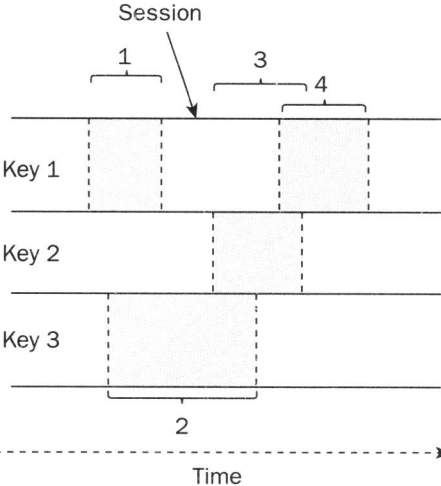

Fig. 12.11 Session Windows Capture the Activity of Events that are in Close Proximity and are Occurring in a Certain Time Period. If There is No Activity Happening for a Time Period, which is More Than What is Predefined, the Session May Be Closed.

returning office goers and in between there is an approximate time gap. Although this is a usual phenomenon, sometimes it could so happen that the people returning from office may come back at an unusual time than their regular time. This could be due to unusual traffic because of some procession or other road blockages. The session window is useful in such scenarios to flag the unusual gap between the peak traffic in the morning session and the peak traffic in the evening session.

Global window A global window can be applied when we need to process the events in their entirety. So all the events are enclosed in a global window and some analysis is done (e.g., statistical operators such as min/max and average) and then a trigger may be used to flag any anomaly.

For example, the traffic data for the whole day between 8 am to 10 pm can be processed in their entirety, so that all the events (e.g. accidents pattern, traffic congestion patterns, etc.) can be analysed.

12.5 EDGE ANALYTICS WALKTHROUGH

Imagine that you are on a road trip and read in the newspaper that yesterday the haze and smog levels in the city are alarmingly high. Which lead you to think, what should I do to avoid exposure to this pollution as I travel to work today? I need to stay away from:

- Areas and roads having pollution levels, which are classified as "Poor Air Quality"

Thankfully, the roads that you need to travel have a network of IoT sensors that are measuring the air pollution *parameters* such as:

- ground level Ozone (O3)
- particle pollution (PM10)
- carbon monoxide (CO)
- sulphur dioxide (SO_2)

Assuming the standard pollutant level for each of these pollutants are: Ozone = 100 ppb, NO_2 = 120 ppb, sulphur dioxide = 200 ppb, carbon monoxide = 9 ppm, PM10 = 50 µg/m³

(Note: Values are based on the information obtained from this site: http://www.epa.vic.gov.au/your-environment/air/air-pollution/air-quality-index/calculating-a-station-air-quality-index)

$$AQIndex = \frac{\text{Observed value of the parameter}}{\text{Standard value of the parameter}} \times 100$$

Suppose there is monitoring station whose AQI is as below:

PM10 particles	Ozone
33	56

Then the AQI summary for that station at that time would be 56, which corresponds to the 'Good' category (refer to Table 12.3). (Note: For the sake of illustration only two parameters are used in this example.)

Table 12.3 Air Quality Category Based on the Index

Air Quality Category	Index Range
Very good (VG)	0–33
Good (G)	34–66
Fair (F)	67–99
Poor (P)	100–149
Very poor (VP)	150 or greater

Adapted from www.epa.vic.gov.au; www.epa.sa.gov.au; www.soe.environment.gov.au

Now let us develop an IoT application that is able to provide air quality-related information in real time.

12.5.1 Problem Background

This example program generates a stream of monitoring events, which are analysed using Flink's CEP library. More details about Flink is shown in Box 12.6.

12.5.1.1 Scenario

Consider that there are a number of IoT-enabled air quality monitoring stations along the road network that you are travelling. For each of these stations, among different quality parameters that are being measured, let us take two of them, that is, NO_2 and PM10. These are measured every 1 h, which means two events (NO_2 and PM10) are generated. This will be a continuous stream and based on it we can detect on which roads the air quality is becoming poor. Knowing such information in real time, you can plan to reroute the travel so as to avoid those places which are highly polluted.

12.5.1.2 Goal

The goal is to detect when the status of the air quality has changed. To accomplish this goal, we will first keep track of NO_2 and PM10 events (refer to Fig.12.12).

We create a CEP pattern which generates a NO_2 and PM10 warning whenever it sees two consecutive NO_2 and PM10 events in a given time interval whose values are higher than a given threshold value. A warning itself is not critical but if we see two warnings for the same station whose NO_2 or PM10 values are rising, we want to generate an alert. This is achieved by defining another CEP pattern, which analyses the stream of generated NO_2 and PM10 warnings.

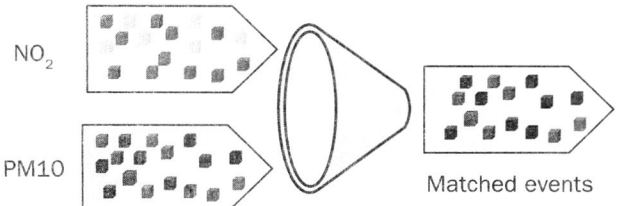

Fig. 12.12 Conceptual Map of Stream of Events that are Interesting or Useful

> **BOX 12.7: ARCHITECTURE OF STREAM PROCESSING USING APACHE FLINK**
>
> In the hands-on exercise in this chapter, we will use Apache Flink. It has hybrid architecture as it has both stream processing and batch processing. In Flink, streams are used for both stream processing as well as batch processing. As shown in the Fig. 12.13, it is useful for developing distributed, high-performing, always-available, and accurate data streaming applications. In this hands-on exercise, we will use the CEP library of Flink, which is capable of detecting event patterns in an unending stream of events and capture those events that are useful and interesting to a particular application that are useful and interesting to us.
>
>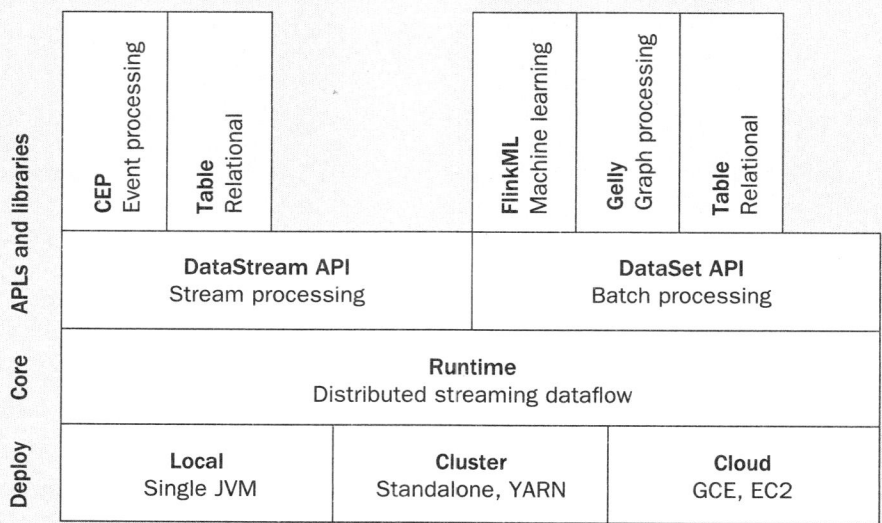
>
> **Fig. 12.13** Architecture of Flink
> *Adapted from www.ci.apache.org; www.oreilly.com; www.data-flair.training.com*

For the purpose of this walkthrough, the input event stream consists of simulated NO_2 and PM10 measurements that are used to assess the air quality at a place. These are continuous measurements and the data is received at the IoT gateway, which are then processed by the stream processing engine.

The hands-on example is based on Apache Flink 1.4.0. A brief description of the architecture is shown in Box 12.7.

12.5.2 Steps to Develop the Air Quality Monitoring Applications

1. Create the sources of stream data for both NO_2 and PM10. In this example, we will create synthetic data streams for both of these pollutants, that is, simulate stream as if they were coming from a real IoT sensor measurement.

```
public void run(SourceContext<NO2_PM10_MonitoringEvent> sourceContext) throws Exception
{
    while (running) {NO2_PM10_MonitoringEvent NO2_PM10_monitoringEvent;
  while (random.nextDouble() >= 0.5)
    {
      /* consider the Mean and Standard Deviation of for each of the sensor measurements,
      and assume a Gaussian distribution of the values that are measured */
      NO2 = random.nextGaussian() * NO2Std + NO2Mean;
      PM10 = random.nextGaussian() * PM10Std + PM10Mean;
        NO2_PM10_monitoringEvent = new NO2_PM10_Event(stationId, NO2,PM10);
    }
    sourceContext.collect(NO2_PM10_monitoringEvent);
    Thread.sleep(pause);
  }
}
```

> **CONSIDER THIS...**
>
> In order to simulate the IoT data, you may wish to use Apache Kafka, specifically Kafka producers for producing a stream of events. More information on Kafka producers is available here:
> https://kafka.apache.org/0100/javadoc/org/apache/kafka/clients/producer/KafkaProducer.htm

2. Create an input stream of monitoring events. Here, a *sliding window* is used to get every 10 min a window that contains the events that arrived during the last 30 min.

```
// Input stream of monitoring events
  DataStream<NO2_PM10_MonitoringEvent> inputEventStream = env
    addSource(new NO2_PM10_MonitoringEventSource(
      SENSOR_ID,
      PAUSE,
      NO2_MEAN,
      NO2_STD,
      NO2_RATIO,
      PM10_MEAN,
      PM10_STD,
      PM10_RATIO
      ))
    assignTimestampsAndWatermarks(new IngestionTimeExtractor<>());
  inputEventStream
  keyBy("stationID")
  window(SlidingEventTimeWindows.of(Time.minutes(30), Time.minutes(10)));
```

In the aforementioned code, "keyBy" is used to access the items with the same key. In this example, we are accessing items based on the StationID (we have a total of 10 stations). This helps to generate warnings for each station. More about keyed and non-keyed streams is shown in Box 12.8.

> **BOX 12.8: KEYED AND NON-KEYED STREAMS IN APACHE FLINK**
>
> - **Keyed stream:** Partitions a single stream into multiple independent streams by a key (e.g., StationID of the generating event stream).
> - **Non-keyed stream:** In this case, all elements in the stream will be processed together and our user-defined function will have access to all elements in a stream.
>
> For more information, see:
> https://ci.apache.org/projects/flink/flink-docs-release-1.4/dev/stream/operators/windows.html.

3. Create a warning pattern for our streams

```
Pattern<NO2_PM10_MonitoringEvent, ?> warningPattern = Pattern.<NO2_PM10_
MonitoringEvent>begin("first")
  subtype(NO2_PM10_Event.class)
  where(new IterativeCondition<NO2_PM10_Event>() {
    private static final long serialVersionUID = 3017L;
    @Override
    public boolean filter(NO2_PM10_Event value, Context<NO2_PM10_Event> ctx) throws Exception {
      return value.getNO2() >= NO2_THRESHOLD;
    }
  })
  next("second")
  subtype(NO2_PM10_Event.class)
  where(new IterativeCondition<NO2_PM10_Event>()
  {
    private static final long serialVersionUID = 1392L;

    @Override
    public boolean filter(NO2_PM10_Event value, Context<NO2_PM10_Event> ctx) throws Exception {
      return value.getNO2() >= NO2_THRESHOLD;
    }
  })
  followedBy("third")
  subtype(NO2_PM10_Event.class)
  where(new IterativeCondition<NO2_PM10_Event>() {
    private static final long serialVersionUID = 1239L;
    @Override
    public boolean filter(NO2_PM10_Event value, Context<NO2_PM10_Event> ctx) throws Exception
```

```
      {
        return value.getPM10() >= PM10_THRESHOLD;
      }
  })
    followedBy("fourth")
    subtype(NO2_PM10_Event.class)
    where(new IterativeCondition<NO2_PM10_Event>() {
      private static final long serialVersionUID = 928L;
      @Override
      public boolean filter(NO2_PM10_Event value, Context<NO2_PM10_Event> ctx) throws Exception
      {
        return value.getPM10() >= PM10_THRESHOLD;
      }
  })
within(Time.minutes(30));
```

4. Create a pattern stream from our warning pattern.

```
// Create a pattern stream from our warning pattern
  PatternStream<NO2_PM10_MonitoringEvent> NO2_PM10_PatternStream = CEP.pattern(
    inputEventStream.keyBy("stationID"),
    warningPattern);
```

5. Air quality above predefined limits as set by the user. In this example, the values of NO_2 and PM10 were set at 120 and 50, respectively.

```
//AirQuality Warnings for each matched warning pattern

  AQwarning = NO2_PM10_PatternStream.select(
  (Map<String, List<NO2_PM10_MonitoringEvent>> pattern) ->
  {
    NO2_PM10_Event first = (NO2_PM10_Event) pattern.get("first").get(0);
    NO2_PM10_Event second = (NO2_PM10_Event) pattern.get("second").get(0);
    NO2_PM10_Event third = (NO2_PM10_Event) pattern.get("third").get(0);
    NO2_PM10_Event fourth = (NO2_PM10_Event) pattern.get("fourth").get(0);

    NO2_PM10_Warning=new NO2_PM10_Warning(first.getStationID(), (first.getNO2() + second.
    getNO2()) / 2,(third.getPM10()+fourth.getPM10()/2));
    System.out.println("NO2 and PM10  Above Limits:"+NO2_PM10_Warning.toString());

    return  NO2_PM10_Warning
  }

  ).returns(NO2_PM10_Warning.class);
```

6. The results from the above matched warning pattern for NO_2 and PM10 are shown in the following text.

```
Markers  Properties  Servers  Data Source Explorer  Snippets  Console ⊠  Progress
<terminated> AirQualityMonitoring [Java Application] /Library/Java/JavaVirtualMachines/jdk1.8.0_31.jdk/Contents/
NO2 and PM10   Above Limits:3, 130.49456738827152,101.98723721245216
NO2 and PM10   Above Limits:7, 142.96069013050297,148.81254351969622
NO2 and PM10   Above Limits:2, 146.4456842158728,135.85624582363292
NO2 and PM10   Above Limits:2, 140.4763391754108,135.85624582363292
NO2 and PM10   Above Limits:9, 127.72804489846456,128.1906625010381
NO2 and PM10   Above Limits:5, 143.872038157942,157.48167538371143
NO2 and PM10   Above Limits:6, 123.63119986959003,88.05480419078972
NO2 and PM10   Above Limits:9, 129.8773930677391,114.99696644147863
NO2 and PM10   Above Limits:5, 134.05813397472497,129.6496646461116
NO2 and PM10   Above Limits:9, 121.15375929476755,99.81908927777368
NO2 and PM10   Above Limits:1, 144.19683551531753,128.73453926442707
NO2 and PM10   Above Limits:5, 155.07476393205684,79.75698130110479
NO2 and PM10   Above Limits:3, 127.93187441887719,90.58918518614776
NO2 and PM10   Above Limits:7, 121.99126328102957,120.09088663412949
NO2 and PM10   Above Limits:2, 149.88836730085944,113.30487368270528
NO2 and PM10   Above Limits:8, 126.33147097498096,109.98778955814089
NO2 and PM10   Above Limits:8, 133.58944304296432,109.98778955814089
NO2 and PM10   Above Limits:8, 125.21796537003135,109.98778955814089
NO2 and PM10   Above Limits:9, 138.20053257318295,120.34599576395033
NO2 and PM10   Above Limits:3, 125.13851510558332,121.15374039993435
NO2 and PM10   Above Limits:9, 139.96537993728202,103.5274614287112
```

7. Now let us do it for air quality monitoring based on Air Quality Index, which was defined earlier. Next shown is the inclusion of Air Quality Index calculator.

```
//AirQuality Warnings for each matched warning pattern

  AQwarning = NO2_PM10_PatternStream.select(
  (Map<String, List<NO2_PM10_MonitoringEvent>> pattern) ->
    {
      NO2_PM10_Event first = (NO2_PM10_Event) pattern.get("first").get(0);
      NO2_PM10_Event second = (NO2_PM10_Event) pattern.get("second").get(0);
      NO2_PM10_Event third = (NO2_PM10_Event) pattern.get("third").get(0);
      NO2_PM10_Event fourth = (NO2_PM10_Event) pattern.get("fourth").get(0);

      NO2_PM10_Warning=new NO2_PM10_Warning(first.getStationID(), (first.getNO2() + second.
      getNO2()) / 2,(third.getPM10()+fourth.getPM10()/2));

      double AQINO2=((((first.getNO2() + second.getNO2()) / 2)/120))*100;
      double AQIPM10=((((third.getPM10() + fourth.getPM10()) / 2)/50))*100;
      double AQIvalue=Math.max(AQINO2,AQIPM10 );

      if(AQIvalue >=0  &&   AQIvalue<=33){
         System.out.println(NO2_PM10_Warning.toString()+"="+"Very good (VG) air quality");
    }
```

```
    if(AQIvalue >33 &&   AQIvalue<=66){
       System.out.println(NO2_PM10_Warning.toString()+"="+"Good (G) air quality");
    }

    if(AQIvalue >66 &&   AQIvalue<=99){
       System.out.println(NO2_PM10_Warning.toString()+"="+"Fair (F) air quality");
    }

    if(AQIvalue >99 &&   AQIvalue<=149) {
       System.out.println(NO2_PM10_Warning.toString()+"="+"Poor (P) air quality");
    }

    if(AQIvalue >149  ) {
       System.out.println(NO2_PM10_Warning.toString()+"="+"Very poor (VP) air quality");
    }
       return  NO2_PM10_Warning;
       }
       ).returns(NO2_PM10_Warning.class);
       env.execute("Air Quality Monitoring Job");
    }
```

> **CONSIDER THIS…**
>
> Usually event processing is done on huge unending streams of events, but only a small percent of those events are really useful or of interest. Find out what is interesting that you want to capture in the domain of your choice and make a conceptual map of it before beginning to write the code.

8. The results based on the Air Quality Index for each station are given as follows:

```
<terminated> AirQualityMonitoring [Java Application] /Library/Java/JavaVirtualMachines/jdk1.8.0_31.jdk/Contents/H
Air Quality at Station 5=Fair (F) air quality
Air Quality at Station 4=Fair (F) air quality
Air Quality at Station 1=Very poor (VP) air quality
Air Quality at Station 4=Poor (P) air quality
Air Quality at Station 7=Poor (P) air quality
Air Quality at Station 5=Very poor (VP) air quality
Air Quality at Station 8=Fair (F) air quality
Air Quality at Station 1=Poor (P) air quality
Air Quality at Station 1=Fair (F) air quality
Air Quality at Station 0=Fair (F) air quality
Air Quality at Station 7=Fair (F) air quality
Air Quality at Station 2=Good (G) air quality
Air Quality at Station 2=Good (G) air quality
```

SUMMARY

Edge analytics is the key for developing real time applications by performing a part of the analytics at the IoT system endpoint before sending the data stream for further complex analytics, to achieve low latency and high throughput. The emergence of IoT has hastened the growth of new sophisticated stream processing platforms that cater to the specific needs of IoT systems. Complex event processing has re-emerged as one of the prime technologies that are driving this progress in event processing platforms. This chapter has introduced the fundamental aspects of streaming data and its processing techniques. Further, hands-on approach for developing an application using one of the most recent stream processing engine, that is, Apache Flink is discussed. It is envisaged that the domain of edge analytics is going to play a vital role in enabling the smartness of IoT systems.

PRACTICAL EXERCISE

Based on the air quality example mentioned earlier, develop a visualization module that will have a dashboard, which can display the data streams as well as the warning pattern as shown in the two results. The display should be on a map (e.g., Google maps, Bing maps, Openstreet maps, etc.) showing live updates.

To accomplish the aforementioned, it is suggested to connect the event streams from Flink with Elasticsearch and visualize it in Kibana.

REVIEW QUESTIONS

1. What insights can you gain by processing a stream of data, rather than a stored form of the same data?
2. What are the challenges in stream processing?
3. How important is stream processing in IoT? What are some typical applications that would benefit from stream processing?
4. What is an atomic event?
5. What is the difference between event stream processing and Complex event processing?
6. What is the distinction between a Database Management System (DBMS) and Data Stream Management System (DSMS)?
7. What is a complex event and how do you capture it?
8. How is complex event processing useful in IoT applications? Give some examples.
9. What are the different operators involved in complex event pattern analysis?
10. Explain various event stream operators. Relate each of the operators with a real world IoT use case.
11. What are tumbling windows? Give an example of its application.

REFERENCES

1. Apache Kafka. https://kafka.apache.org/ [last accessed: 12/2/2018]
2. Apache Flume. https://flume.apache.org/ [last accessed: 12/2/2018]
3. Foundations of Complex Event Processing
4. Lukasz, G., Özsu, M.T. (2003, Jun), Issues in data stream management, *SIGMOD Rec.* 32(2): 5–14. DOI = http://dx.doi.org/10.1145/776985.776986
5. Jenő Fülöp, L., Tóth, G., Rácz, R., Pánczél, J., Gergely, T., Beszédes, A. *Survey on Complex Event Processing and Predictive Analytics*.
6. de Carvalho, O.M., Roloff, E., Navaux, P.O.A. (2013), A survey of the state of the art in event

processing, *11th Workshop on Parallel and Distributed Processing (WSPPD)*.

7. Zhao, A., Garg, S., Queiroz, C., Buyya, R. A taxonomy and survey of stream processing systems, *Software Architecture for Big Data and the Cloud*.

8. Lan A.N., Haugen, O. (2016), *Complex Event Processing in ThingML*, J. GArbowski and S. Herbold (Eds.), LNCS 9959, pp. 20–35.

9. Meehan, J., Aslantas, C., Zdonik, S., Tatbul, N., Du, J. (2017), Data ingestion for the connected world, *CIDR'17*, Chaminade, CA.

10. Panigati, E., Schreiber, F.A., Zaniolo, C. Data streams and data stream management systems and languages, F. Colace et al. (Eds.), *Data Management in Pervasive Systems, Data-Centric Systems and Applications*, DOI 10.1007/978-3-319-20062-0_5

11. Cranor, C., Johnson, T., Spataschek, O., Shkapenyuk, V. (2003), Gigascope: a stream database for network applications, In: *Proceedings of the 2003 ACM SIGMOD International Conference on Management of Data*, pp. 647–651. ACM, New York, NY.

12. Chandrasekaran, S., Cooper, O., Deshpande, A., Franklin, M.J., Hellerstein, J.M., Hong, W., Krishnamurthy, S., Madden, S.R., Reiss, F., Shah, M.A. Telegraphcq: continuous dataflow processing, In: *Proceedings of the 2003 ACM SIGMOD*.

13. Abadi, D.J., Carney, D., Cetintemel, U., Cherniack, M., Convey, C., Erwin, C., Galvez, E., Hatoun, M., Maskey, A., Rasin, A., et al. (2003), Aurora: a data stream management system. In: *Proceedings of the 2003 ACM SIGMOD International Conference on Management of Data*, p. 666. ACM, New York, NY.

14. Abadi, D.J., Ahmad, Y., Balazinska, M., Cetintemel, U., Cherniack, M., Hwang, J.H., Lindner, W., Maskey, A., Rasin, A., Ryvkina, E., et al. (2005), The design of the borealis stream processing engine. In: *CIDR*, vol. 5, pp. 277–289.

15. Bai, Y., Thakkar, H., Wang, H., Luo, C., Zaniolo, C. (2006), A data stream language and system designed for power and extensibility, In: *Proceedings of the 15th ACM International Conference on Information and Knowledge Management*, pp. 337–346. ACM, New York, NY.

16. Arasu, A., Babcock, B., Babu, S., Datar, M., Ito, K., Nishizawa, I., Rosenstein, J., Widom, J. (2003), STREAM: The stanford stream data manager (demonstration description), In: *Proceedings of the 2003 ACM SIGMOD International Conference on Management of Data*, pp. 665–665.

17. Babu, S., Widom, J. (2004), StreaMon: an adaptive engine for stream query processing, In: *Proceedings of the 2004 ACM SIGMOD international conference on Management of data (SIGMOD '04)*, pp. 931–932, ACM, New York, NY. DOI=http://dx.doi.org/10.1145/1007568.1007702

18. Stonebreaker, M., Centintemel, U., Zdonik, S. (2005), The 8 requirements of real-time stream processing, *SIGMOD Rec*. 34(4), 2005.

19. Strohbach, M., Ziekow, H., Gaziz, V., Akiva, N., (2015), Towards a big data analytics framework for IoT and Smart city applications, In: *Modeling and Processing for Next-Generation Big Data Technologies*, pp. 257–282.

20. Luckham, D. (2002), *The Power of Events: An Introduction to Complex Event Processing in Distributed Enterprise Systems Addison*, Wesley.

21. Luckham, D. (2007), *A Short History of Complex Event Processing, Article on the development of Complex Event Processing*.

22. Eckert, M. Bry, F. (2009), *Complex Event Processing (CEP), Article on Complex Event Processing*, Informatik-Spektrum, Springer.

23. Cugola, G. Margara, A. (2012), Processing flows of information: From data stream to complex event processing, *ACM Computing Surveys (CSUR)*, 44(3): 15.

24. Babcock, B., Babu, S., Datar, M., Motwani, R., Widom, J. (2002), "Models and issues in data stream systems", In: *PODS '02: Proceedings of the Twenty-First ACM SIGMOD-SIGACTSIGART Symposium on Principles of Database Systems*, ACM, New York, NY, pp. 1–16.

25. Cugola, G., Margara, A. (2010a), Complex event processing with t-rex. Tech. rep., Politecnico di Milano.

26. Tibco-Streambase: https://www.tibco.com/products/tibco-streambase, [last accessed:12/2/2018]

27. OrcaleCEP: http://www.oracle.com/technetwork/middleware/complex-event-processing/overview/index.html [last accessed:12/2/2018]
28. Esper: http://www.espertech.com/esper/ [last accessed:12/2/2018]
29. IBM WebSphere: https://www.ibm.com/cloud/streaming-analytics [last accessed:12/2/2018]
30. Gyllstrom, D., Wu, E., Chae, H-J., Diao, Y., Stahlberg, P., Anderson, G. (2007), *SASE: Complex Event Processing Over Streams*, CIDR.
31. Wu, E., Diao, Y., Rizvi, S. (2006), High-performance complex event processing over streams, *SIGMOD*, pp. 407–418.
32. Sqlstream: http://sqlstream.com/ [last accessed: 12/2/2018]
33. Arasu, A., Babu, S., Widom, J. (2006). The CQL continuous query language: semantic foundations and query execution, *VLDB Journal* 15(2): 121–142.
30. Yasumoto, L., Yamaguchi, H., Shiegeno, H. (2016), Survey of real-time processing technologies of IoT data streams, *Journal of Information Processing*, 24(2): 195–202.
31. Suhothayan, S., Gajasinghe, K., Loku Narangoda, I., Chaturanga, S., Perera, S., Nanayakkara, V. (2011), Siddhi: a second look at complex event processing architectures, In: *Proceedings of the 2011 ACM Workshop on Gateway Computing Environments, GCE 2011*, pp. 43–50. ACM, New York, NY. http://doi.acm.org/10.1145/ 2110486.2110493
32. Flouris, I., Giatrakos, N., Deligiannakis, A., Garofalakis, M., Kamp, M., Mock, M. (2017), Issues in complex event processing: Status and prospects in the Big Data era, *Journal of Systems and Software* 127: 217–236.
33. Toshniwal, A., Taneja, S., Shukla, A., Ramasamy, K., Patel, J.M., Kulkarni, S., Jackson, J., Gade, K., Fu, M., Donham, J., Bhagat, N., Mittal, S., Ryaboy, D. (2014), Storm @ twitter, In: *Proceedings of the 2014 ACM SIGMOD International Conference on Management of Data*, pp. 147–156, Snowbird, UT. https://storm.apache.org/.
34. Akidau, T., Balikov, A., Bekiroǧlu, K., Chernyak, S., Haberman, J., Lax, R., McVeety, S., Mills, D., Nordstrom, P., Whittle, S. (2013, Aug), Millwheel: Fault-tolerant stream processing at internet scale, *Proceedings of the VLDB Endowment*, 6(11): 1033–1044.
35. Apache Samza. https://samza.apache.org/ [last accessed: 12/2/2018]
36. Apache Spark. https://spark.apache.org/ [last accessed: 12/2/2018]
37. Apache Flink. https://flink.apache.org/ [last accessed: 12/2/2018]

Where to go from here…

Following are some suggested paths to explore and gain more knowledge about edge analytics, and in particular event stream processing for IoT:
- Look at various streams of data coming from a real IoT sensor-suggested way is to interface a temperature, humidity, or any weather-related sensor with open source hardware such as Arduino or Raspberry PI. To gain a thorough understanding on how to work with these hardware and related software, it is suggested to refer to Chapter 5 (Sensors and Actuators in IoT), Chapter 6 (Open Hardware in IoT), and Chapter 9 (Prototyping IoT Applications).
- Explore the wide gamut of CEP operators available in Apache Flink. Develop a real world application with data coming from IoT sensor (e.g., develop your own using Raspberry Pi and a temperature sensor), integrate the edge analytics using Flink, and visualize with elasticsearch (https://www.elastic.co/) and Kibana (https://www.elastic.co/products/kibana)
- Look at the latest stream processing framework from Google called "Beam", which is now part of the Apache project (refer to Fig. 12.14):

(Contd)

(Contd)

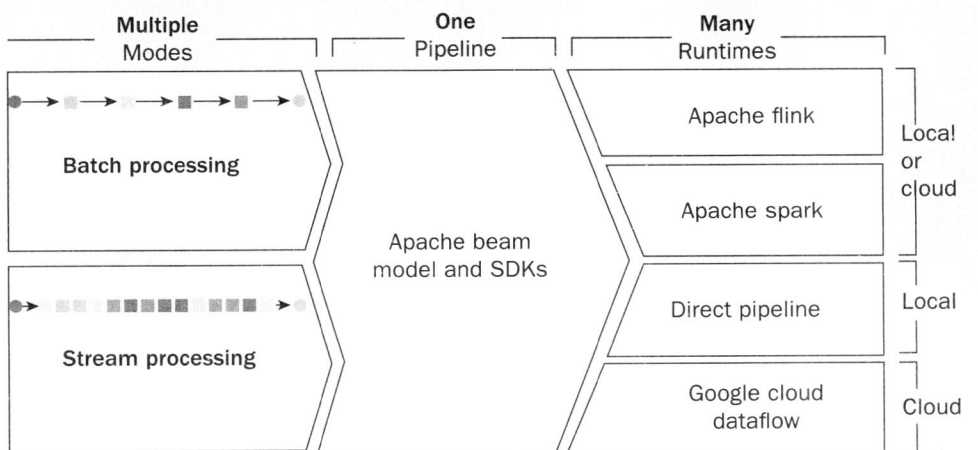

Fig. 12.14 Apache Beam

It is a unified programming model for both batch and streaming data-parallel processing pipelines. BeakSDK allow you to define pipelines for your applications. The pipelines can be executed by one of Beam's supported distributed processing back-ends, such as Apache Spark, Apache Flink, Apache Apex, and Google Cloud Dataflow.

Embedded High Performance Computing (HPC) for IoT

CHAPTER 13

"There is an entirely new class of users who do not know they are using HPC. We call it 'implicit HPC.'"
— Raj Hasrah, corporate VP and GM, Intel Corporation

OBJECTIVES

- introduce the High Performance Computing (HPC)
- describe the need for HPC in IoT
- explain various forms of HPC and parallel computing
- introduce Embedded High Performance Computing (EHPC) and its role in IoT
- describe Graphics Processing Units (GPUs)
- explain the Compute Unified Device Architecture (CUDA) for programming GPUs
- compare CPU and GPU acceleration
- describe GPU-based EHPC platforms
- explain the role of EHPC in edge computing
- understand various IoT domains in which EHPC is used

OUTCOMES

- understand HPC
- distinguish between CPU and GPU
- assess the need for using EHPC for IoT
- gain an understanding of how parallel computing is different from sequential computing
- describe various GPU-based EHPC platforms and their characteristics
- summarize some applications of EHPC in IoT

REVISION

Edge computing in Internet of Things (IoT) as described in Chapter 12 is gaining increasing attention due to the requirement of rapid and real-time processing of IoT device data for near instant feedback. However, the edge devices are not equipped with enough computational power to process high volume and velocity of streaming data from IoT devices. Hence, there is a need to integrate HPC into the edge devices to significantly reduce data processing time, and at the same time have low power consumption. Chapter 10 on BigIoT data science described the end-to-end process for processing IoT big data using machine-learning approaches. However, these machine learning techniques require heavy computations and are normally suited to work on the cloud infrastructure. Further, incorporating such computationally heavy workloads on the edge devices is highly challenging. This chapter addresses these issues and provides a background on the application and integration of HPC with IoT systems.

13.1 INTRODUCTION TO HIGH PERFORMANCE COMPUTING

Internet of Things (IoT) devices are becoming a major source of large amounts of data. This data has big data characteristics such as volume, velocity, variety, and veracity. The processing of this data is highly challenging and requires High Performance Computing (HPC) systems. Consequently, HPC is now no longer solely used in scientific areas such as climate, hydrological processes, environmental studies, and many branches of science and engineering, but is increasingly gaining importance in many industrial, business, defence applications, etc. The need for rapid decision-making in many compute intensive real-time applications is the main driver for the recent surge of commercial HPC solutions. The integration of cloud with HPC is a relatively new development and various forms of HPC are being offered as a cloud service.

From an IoT-specific view, HPC is useful for accelerating computations at IoT device level, edge computing as well as cloud-based big data analytics. This requires two variants of HPC (see Fig. 13.1):

- Embedded HPC (eHPC) for real-time edge analytics using computing devices has compact modules that can perform large number of computations. These HPC devices could be integrated with gateways or custom edge or fog infrastructure that are situated near the IoT-sensing devices and are capable of performing real-time streaming analytics.
- Cloud HPC is an integration of cloud infrastructure with parallel HPC modules. These are more sophisticated systems that are usually available in the form of clusters and highly distributed in nature. These kinds of systems are capable of processing extremely large volumes of data in a relatively short time. The BigIoT data that is sent to the cloud can be processed rapidly using the HPC infrastructure.

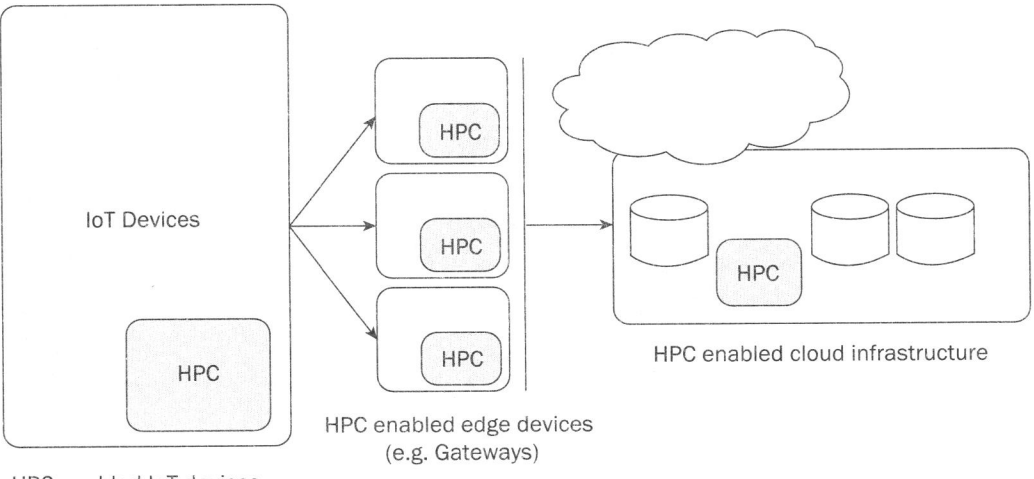

Fig. 13.1 High Performance Computing (HPC) at the Device, Edge and Cloud

13.1.1 Parallel Computing

Most conventional software is written to process instructions in a sequential form, that is, the instructions are processed as smaller subproblems and executed on a central processing unit (CPU) one after the other in a sequence. In contrast, parallel computing is a computational approach in which many calculations are carried out simultaneously (Fig. 13.2).

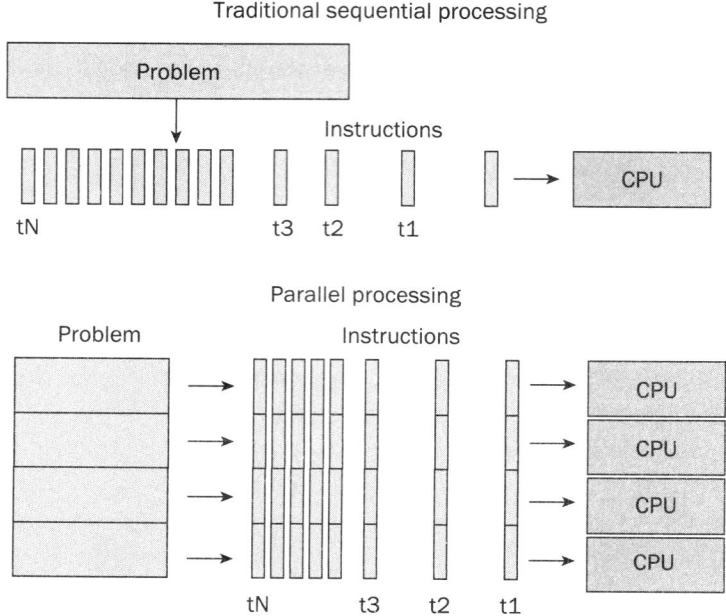

Fig. 13.2 Comparison of Serial and Parallel Computing Approaches

It is accomplished by dividing a given task/problem into subproblems, which are independent in themselves. These subproblems are then assigned to different processors and executed independently. If they need to interact between themselves, communication is enabled. The solutions to all subproblems are then aggregated and the final output is generated. In essence, several computational nodes are used to execute pieces of code in parallel to optimize the computing resources and solve the problem. The main advantages of using a parallel computing approach are: computational power (it refers to the speed with which a processor can perform an operation or instructions), fault tolerance, and large memory.

13.2 EMBEDDED HIGH PERFORMANCE COMPUTING (EHPC)

An embedded system is a computer hardware system having software embedded in it. It is usually a stand-alone system having specific functionality, but can also be one module of a larger system. A microcontroller or microprocessor is the heart of embedded systems. The major components of an embedded system are hardware, software, and operating system (OS).

Recently, the embedded systems that are being used in IoT systems are increasingly seeking more computational power to cater to the demands of real-time online processing. Edge computing is one such example where AI can be applied at the edge in real time, i.e., AI on the fly.

Due to these real-time and low-power requirements, current single processor systems fail to cater to such needs (e.g. rapid processing of device data in areas such as medical, defence, and aerospace). Hence, dedicated hardware that can significantly improve the computational aspects needs to be integrated with embedded systems. Hence, high performance embedded computing systems have recently emerged that integrate a large number of distributed processors, I/O, software stacks, and all connected by a low latency infrastructure.

The desired characteristics of embedded systems specifically useful for IoT are:

- High computational capability
- Seamless integration with Internet
- Low latency
- Low-energy consumption
- Enable development of real-time applications

The next section discusses the General Purpose Graphics Processing Units (GPGPUs) that are now becoming very popular for developing embedded HPC applications.

13.3 GRAPHICS PROCESSING UNITS (GPU)

Graphics processing units are designed to work with CPU to accelerate general purpose highly computationally expensive applications which are very common in many scientific applications. GPUs can be programmed to work in parallel and hence are significantly faster than CPUs. The GPU is based on many-core architecture that is based on threads to execute parallel tasks, which is in contrast to the CPU with a limited number of cores and is more suitable for serial processing (see Fig. 13.3). However, recent multicore CPUs are capable of doing parallel processing, albeit in a limited way as compared to GPU. Table 13.1 lists the major differences between a CPU and GPU.

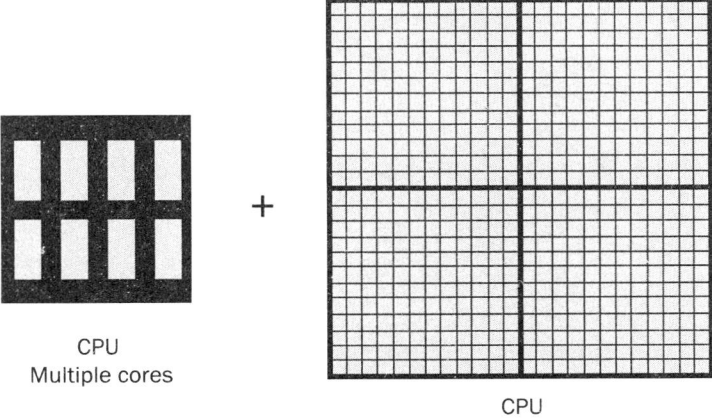

Fig. 13.3 CPU vs GPU

Table 13.1 Difference Between CPU and GPU

CPU	GPU
Number of cores are few but have complex functionality, i.e., density of computation is low	A large number (usually in hundreds to thousands) of simple cores providing high density of computation
Throughput is low	Throughput in high
Not useful for carrying parallel operations. New breed of CPUs can perform parallel operations but in a limited way	Specifically built for parallel operations
Optimization of few threads for high performance	Thousands of concurrent threads are spawned for processing in parallel
Large amount of common cache is available	Large number of small individual caches. Performance is improved using multithreading

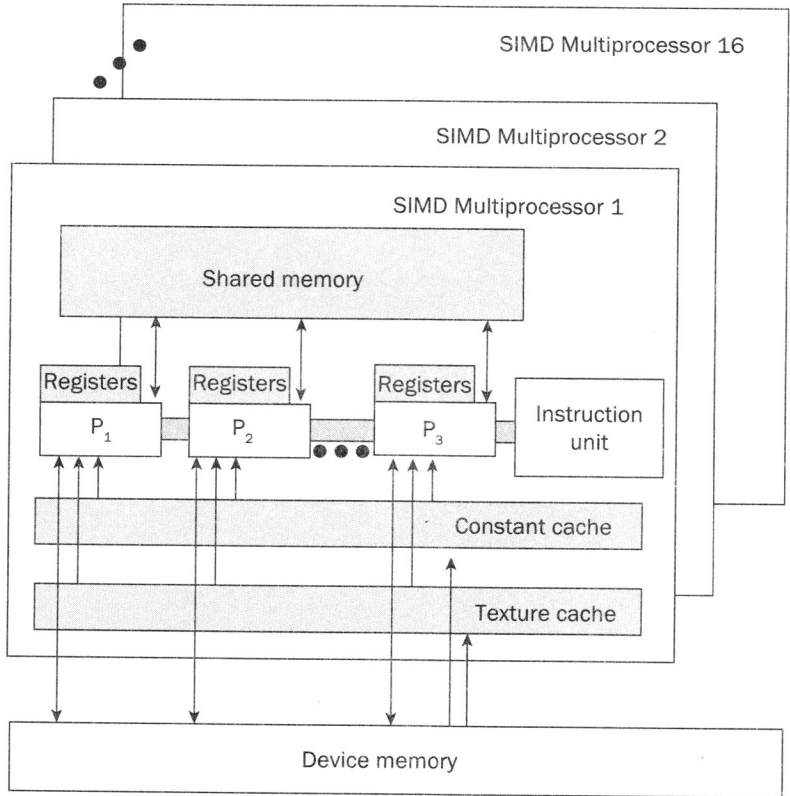

Fig. 13.4 GPU Architecture

13.3.1 General Architecture of GPU

The architecture of the graphical processing unit is shown in Fig. 13.4. It consists of the following components.

13.3.1.1 Multiprocessors

The core of GPU consists of a number of multiprocessors and they in turn consist of parallel processors called threads. The Single Instruction Multiple Thread (SIMT) approach is used by these threads to execute in parallel the same piece of code/program on different data sets.

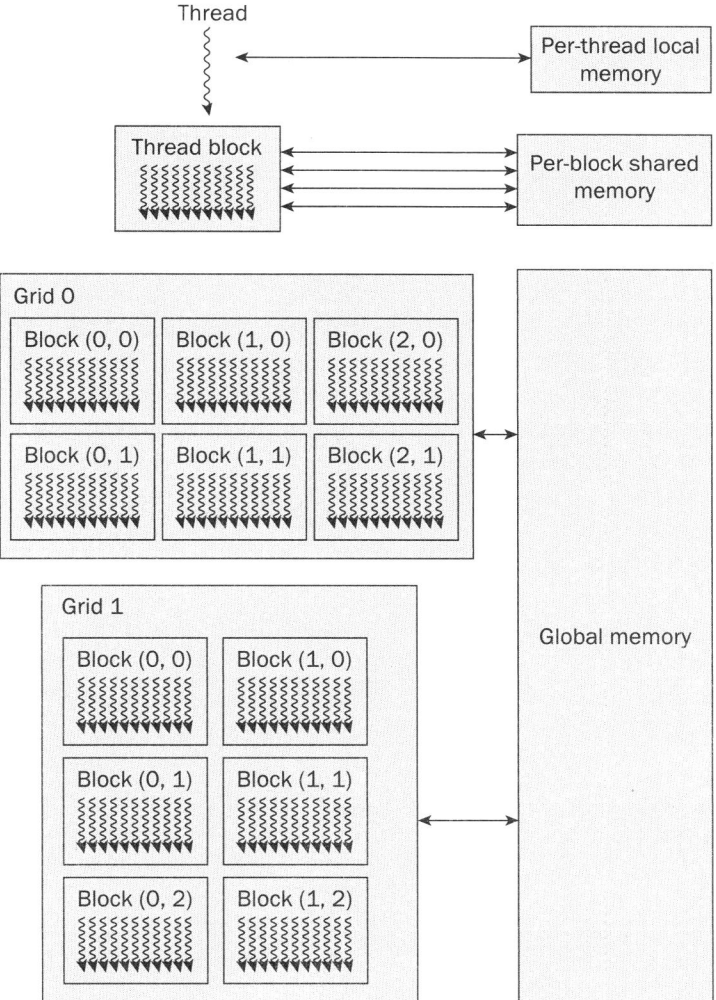

Fig. 13.5 Hierarchical Memory Pattern of GPU

13.3.1.2 Memory

The GPU also called as device in this context has its own memory called the device memory. The memory pattern of GPU is hierarchical in nature. As shown in Fig. 13.5, each thread processor has a local memory, which means that a block of threads can use a shared memory and global memory is available to all the grids (comprising several blocks of threads). This kind of memory management makes the GPU to perform better and also helps in the streaming access and processing of large datasets.

13.3.1.3 Parallelism

The GPU uses a multithreading approach as against using large caches for performance improvement. The thread processors are always kept busy in either processing a task or fetching data from memory. While the memory operation is in progress for a particular thread, the memory is blocked and once it fetches the required value, the other thread is allowed to access the memory, but in the meanwhile, other threads are executing and doing their assigned operation (e.g., arithmetic operation). In this way, the SIMT architecture (same program or operation is executed on each data element) of GPU can achieve a high degree of parallelism. This is in contrast to the CPU, where the frequent memory accesses causes it to slow down.

13.3.1.4 Programming Model

The GPUs need to be programmed using programming APIs specifically developed to take advantage of the parallel computing capabilities of GPU.

Compute Unified Device Architecture (CUDA) is a parallel computing platform and programming model that can be used in a software environment to develop code that is suited to run on a GPU. Using C as a high-level programming language, efficient parallel algorithms can be coded. In addition, wrappers to CUDA (hide the complexity and make it accessible) in various other programming languages such as C++, JAVA (e.g., JCUDA), and Python (e.g., PyCUDA) are available.

A crucial requirement of designing CUDA applications is to organize threads, thread blocks, and grids in an optimal way. CUDA defines three core abstractions which can be used by the programmer. They are groups of threads in the form of hierarchy, shared memories, and barrier synchronization. As shown in Fig. 13.6, the CUDA model is based on hierarchy structure with each thread having its own local memory and registers. Further, a block consists of a group of threads, which are executed on multiprocessors.

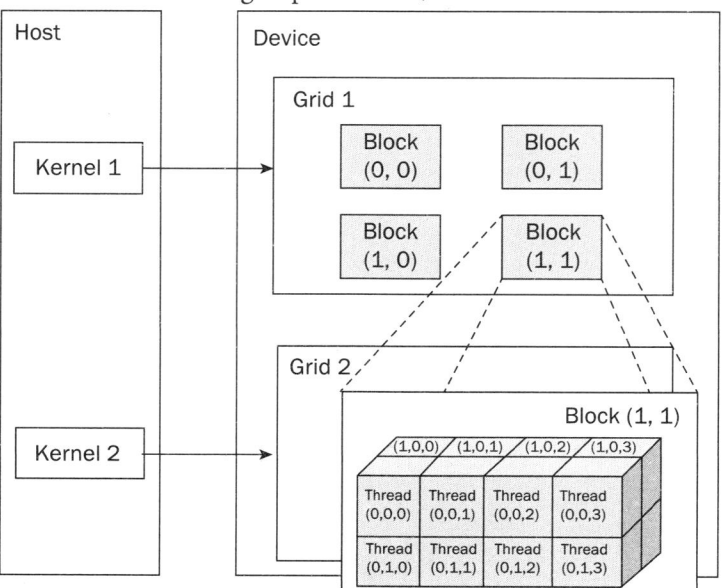

Fig. 13.6 CUDA Programming Model

The group of threads together builds a thread block and thread blocks are executed on multiprocessors. Threads in the thread block have access to the shared memory of the block (Fig. 13.6). Many thread blocks are allowed to reside on a multiprocessor, which is limited only by the resources available to the multiprocessor.

The host executes the kernel, which in turn launches the grid, which comprises of several thread blocks (see Fig. 13.6). However, only a single kernel is allowed to execute on each device at a time and also can access only the dedicated memory available on the GPU. The steps to execute a CUDA program are shown in Box 13.1.

BOX 13.1: BASIC STEPS TO RUN A CUDA PROGRAM

Steps to run a CUDA program
The following are the basic steps for running a CUDA program:
1. Allocate memory space on GPU device for data
2. Allocate memory on host CPU
3. Copy data to GPU from host memory (CPU) to GPU device memory
4. Call kernel to run on the GPU cores to compute predefined function on the data
5. Transfer the GPU output data from device memory back to host memory
6. Free the device memory
7. Free host memory

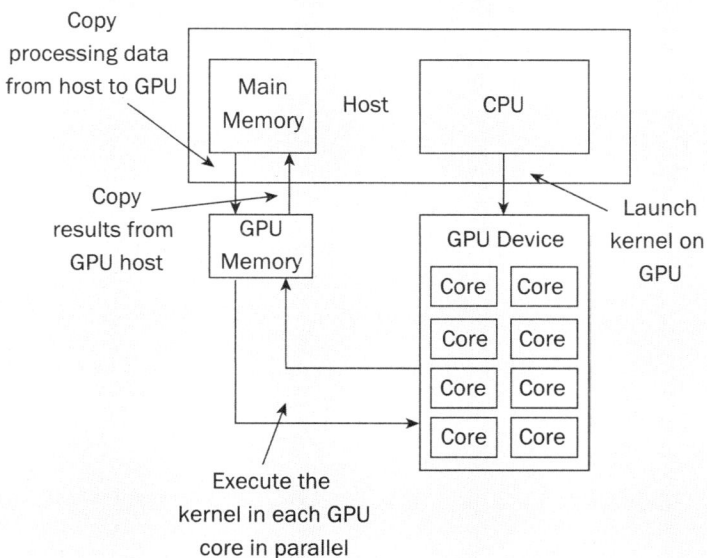

13.3.1.5 CUDA Toolkit

A CUDA toolkit consists of a compiler, debugging and optimization tools, libraries (e.g., cuBLAS, cuRAND, cuSOLVER, cuFFT, etc.), application deployment tools, etc. It facilitates the coding of parallel algorithms and development of applications based on deep learning, signal processing, etc. CUDA runs on all the NVIDIA GPU families such as QUADRO, TESLA, GEFORCE, TEGRA, etc.

13.4 NEED FOR EMBEDDED HPC EDGE DEVICES

Currently, IoT data at the edge is gaining increasing importance due to the requirement of real-time applications that need rapid processing of data from IoT devices at the edge itself instead of sending it to cloud-based processing. However, these edge devices currently have limited computing power that can be harnessed to process high-volume and high-speed IoT device data. Due to these limitations, the edge devices are unable to support the use of machine-learning/deep-learning-based models that require sufficient computational capability to execute on the edge.

Thus, there is a need to have high computational power available on the edge devices that use local computing infrastructure that has minimum latency to deliver results in near real time.

13.5 EMBEDDED HPC PLATFORMS

To support the use of HPC in IoT, embedded HPC platforms play an important role. These come in several forms such as CPU and Field Programmable Gate Array (FPGA) integrated on the same board and in some platforms on the same chip. For example, Aldec's TySOM boards integrate ARM programmable system and FPGA. The below discussion is focused on GPU-based embedded HPC platforms from NVIDA, which are currently the leading HPC platforms in the market.

13.5.1 NVIDIA's Jetson TX1, TX2, and Nano Embedded HPC Platforms

The embedded computing devices Jetson TX1 consist of 256-core NVIDIA Maxwell-based GPU and Jetson TX2 development boards have 256-core NVIDIA Pascal-based GPU and ARM CPU.

Table 13.2 Technical specifications of Jetson TX2 and Nano

Hardware/Component	Jetson Nano	Jetson TX2
CPU (ARM)	4-core ARM A57 @ 1.43 GHz	4-core ARM Cortex-A57 @ 2 GHz, 2-core Denver2 @ 2 GHz
GPU	128-core Maxwell @ 921 MHz	256-core Pascal @ 1.3 GHz
Memory	4 GB LPDDR4, 25.6 GB/s	8 GB 128-bit LPDDR4, 58.3 GB/s
Storage	MicroSD	32 GB eMMC 5.1
Video	Encode: 4K @ 30 (H.264/H.265) Decode: 4K @ 60 (H.264/H.265)	Encode: 4K × 2K 60 Hz (HEVC) Decode: 4K × 2K 60 Hz (12-bit support)
Connectivity	Gigabit Ethernet	Gigabit Ethernet, WiFi, Bluetooth
PCIE	Gen 2 | 1×4	Gen 2 | 1×4 + 1×1 OR 2×1 + 1×2
Power	5W / 10W	7.5W / 15W
AI Performance	472 GFLOPs	1.3 TFLOPs

As shown in Table 13.2, the Jetson TX2 is a supercomputer-on-module having a 256-core pascal-based GPU and very good power efficiency. The CPU consists of a Quad ARM A57. It has a memory of 8 GB 128-bit LPDDR4. The on-board storage capacity is 32 GB eMMC. Furthermore, it has Bluetooth connectivity, 4K video two times over at 60 frames-per-second encode and decode. Jetson TX2 (see Fig. 13.7) is supported by Nvidia's Parker system-on-a-chip (SOC). It also contains a variety of standard hardware interfaces, which make it a highly flexible and extensible platform for developing a wide variety of embedded applications.

TX2 developer kit enables fast and easy ways to develop hardware and software for the Jetson TX2 board.

Fig. 13.7 NVIDIA's Jetson TX2 and the Developer kit

Fig. 13.8 NVIDIA's Jetson Nano

Jetson Nano (Fig. 13.8) is available as a developer kit that is specifically designed to run Deep learning (Neural Networks) based applications. Table 13.2 shows the specifications of Jetson Nano in comparison with Jetson TX2. Nano has a 128 CUDA core Maxwell GPU and quad-core ARM A57 CPU running at 1.43 GHz and 4GB of LPDDR4 memory. The Jetson development kit provides a Linux environment called L4T. Also, it provides design guides and documentation. The developer kit comes pre-flashed with a Linux development environment and has support for NVIDIA Jetpack SDK, which comes bundled with board support package (BSP), libraries for deep learning, computer vision (OpenCV), GPU computing, multimedia processing, TensorFlow Models (Tensor RT), etc. For example, it contains cuDNN (CUDA Deep Neural Networks), which is a library for building deep neural networks. CuDNN provides implementations of the routines that arise frequently in deep-learning applications. It works across the full range of NVIDIA GPUs. The user can also install popular open source Machine Learning (ML) frameworks such as TensorFlow, PyTorch, Caffe, etc. Nano delivers 472 GFLOPS for running modern AI algorithms.

13.6 IOT APPLICATIONS DEVELOPMENT USING EMBEDDED HPC

The embedded HPC platforms are being increasingly adopted in many IoT application areas such as face recognition, assistive technologies for the visually impaired, autonomous underwater navigation, and surveillance applications. Below is a brief description of some applications in two domains.

13.6.1 Transportation

- Jetson TX1-based system was developed to automatically detect and recognize the traffic sign using convolutional neural networks. In this system, a USB webcam is integrated with Jetson TX1 to capture video frames, which are analysed in real time to detect the traffic sign and its type.
- The detection of lanes on the road for autonomous navigation using deep learning. Jetson TX1-based system was developed using an imaging system to capture video and run the models.
- Analysing traffic patterns at intersections helps to detect congestion and better manage the traffic. A Jetson TX2-based system was developed to capture video through a camera placed at the intersection. Subsequently, key frames are extracted, which are then used to run deep-learning models to detect the vehicles that are entering or exiting a lane.
- Locating a vacant parking spot is a typical IoT application. Using overhead as well as ground cameras, it is possible to guide a vehicle to a vacant parking spot and subsequently charge them accordingly. However, this requires the acquisition of data from multiple cameras and analysing them in real time. Although the cameras may be connected to light-weight microcontrollers such as Raspberry Pi, the real-time processing of the video data requires HPC such as the Jetson TX2.

13.6.2 Healthcare

- Analysis of tissue biopsies using AI can significantly improve the classification of various skin-related diseases.

- Predictive health applications such as those that can detect risk factors early are also emerging recently. These systems incorporate the knowledge gleaned from thousands of health records to develop predictive models based on AI. Increasingly, these applications are pushed on mobile platforms and embedded HPC platforms are being used for this purpose.
- The integration of edge computing with wearables technology is enabling the development of a large number of applications that are specifically targeted at facilitating assisted living environments for the elderly. These are already being well adopted and are leveraged by the aging population to live healthier lives and continuously be able to track various health-related parameters.
- Telemedicine is another area that is going to be enormously benefitted by embedded HPC devices, as they can be used to do the computation at the edge. For example, several telemedicine kiosks can have a common embedded HPC-based system that can perform various analysis there itself, and send back the results instead of telemetry of the data from the sensing devices attached to the patient to remote locations that may have poor connectivity.

Box 13.2 describes an example of interfacing Jetson Nano with webcam to rapidly process image data by applying an image processing algorithm.

BOX 13.2: INTERFACING JETSON NANO WITH A WEBCAM

In this hands-on example, a webcam is connected to the Jetson Nano and is used to capture an image. The image is read back by the device and used to perform the sobel edge detection operation that is specifically coded using CUDA to run on a GPU. It is compared with the CPU version of the sobel edge detector to understand the speedup gained by using an HPC device.

Figure 13.9 shows the connection of Jetson Nano with a webcam.

Fig. 13.9 Connection of Webcam with Jetson Nano via USB

(Contd)

Box 13.2 *(Contd)*

Mean Shift Algorithm:

The mean shift is an unsupervised algorithm clustering algorithm. The objective of the mean shift algorithm is to find the densest region. To achieve it, meanshift defines a window of predefined size around the data points and computes the mean (e.g., it could be mean of a feature such as color) and the centroid of the window.

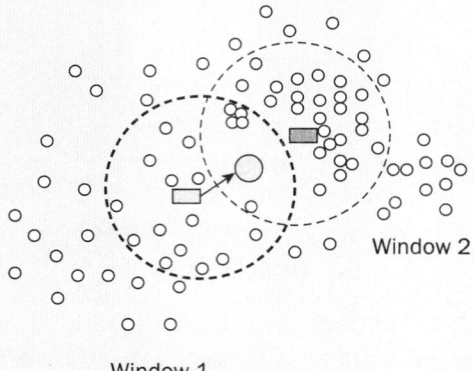

Fig. 13.10 Mean Shift Approach of Finding the Densest Region by Shifting a Window

As shown in Fig. 13.10, in the initial window, the mean and the centroid (high density of data points) do not coincide. Hence, the window is shifted such that the centroid becomes the new windows center. This process of moving the window to a more denser region continues until convergence; where the distance between the mean and centroid is less than a predefined value (i.e. threshold). The final window contains dense or maximum data distribution.

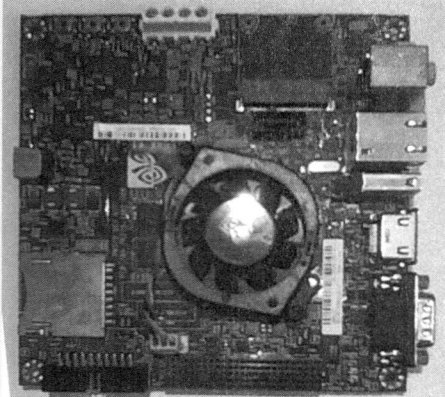

Fig. 13.11 Original Image used for Performing Mean Shift Operations on Jetson Nano

The Mean Shift algorithm can be used for both edge-preserving smoothing (filtering) and clustering/segmentation. Figure 13.11 shows a sample image used for performing filtering and segmentation using OpenCV and the embedded HPC device Jetson Nano. Box 13.3 shows the steps for executing these two operations (i.e., mean shift filtering and segmentation). Listings 13.1 and 13.2 provide the code to run on Jetson Nano. The results of filtering and segmentation are shown in Figs 13. 12 and 13.14, respectively.

(Contd)

Box 13.2 *(Contd)*

Fig. 13.12 Image Obtained after Performing Mean Shift Filtering (Smoothing) on Jetson Nano Image

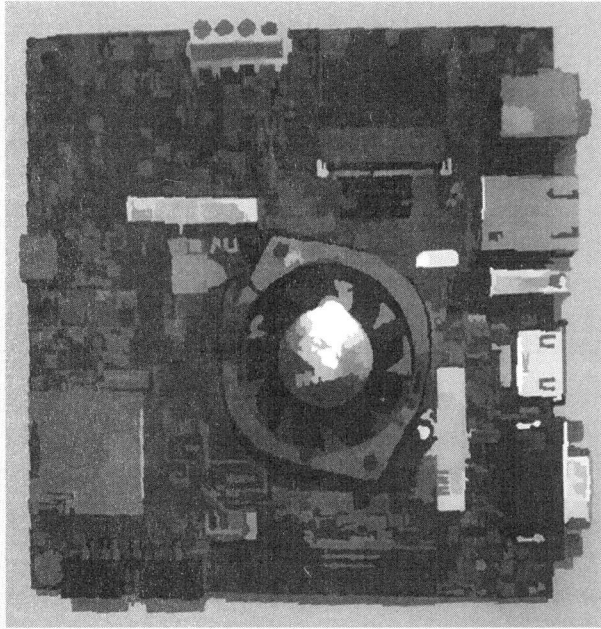

Fig. 13. 13 Image Obtained After Performing the Mean Shift Segmentation Operation on Jetson Nano Image (notice tha various regions on the image obtained by segmentation)

BOX 13.3: STEPS TO PERFORM MEAN SHIFT FILTERING AND MEAN SHIFT SEGMENTATION OPERATIONS ON JETSON NANO IMAGE

Directory Structure:
```
|- data
        |- The image captured in imageCapture operation would be stored here. The
           outputs of meanShiftFiltering operation would also be stored in this folder.
|- imageCapture
        |- Operation for capturing an image from webcam using OpenCV and Python.
                |- Python
                |- OpenCV
                |- Webcam connected to nVIDIA Jetson Nano via USB
        |- meanShiftFiltering
                |- Operation for performing CUDA accelerated Mean Shift Filtering
                   on the captured image
|- meanShiftSegmentation
        |- Operation for performing CUDA accelerated Mean Shift Segmentation on the
           captured image
```

Prerequisite: If the nVIDIA Jetson Nano has been flashed using the official nVIDIA Jetpack, then no prerequisites are required for this section.

****

In this section, we are going to cover two operations on an embedded supercomputing platform - nVIDIA Jetson Nano. Open a terminal using Ctrl+Alt+T.

Following steps should be followed for performing the Operations (1. Meanshift filtering 2. Meanshift segmentation):

Step 1: Capturing image from webcam using OpenCV and Python.
    1.1. Enter the imageCapture directory and execute openCvWebCamImageCapture.py by "python openCvWebCamImageCapture.py".
    This will open a window for webcam. After pressing "SPACE" on the keyboard, the current frame would be stored in data folder of the directory as "capturedColorImage.png".

Step 2: Performing CUDA Accelerated Mean Shift Filtering operation
    2.1. Checking if the nVIDIA CUDA Complier (NVCC) is in PATH.
        2.1.1 Execute - "nvcc --version" to check the version of NVCC. If the command returns an error then continue otherwise skip to 2.2.
        2.1.2 Execute - "export PATH=${PATH}:/usr/local/cuda/bin && nvcc --version". This command will set the PATH for CUDA and will return the version of NVCC.
    2.2. Enter the meanShiftFiltering directory.
        2.2.1 Creating the executable for CUDA accelerated mean shift filtering script.
        - Execute "g++ meanShiftFiltering.cpp -I/usr/local/include/opencv4/ -L/usr/local/include/opencv4/opencv2 -lopencv_objdetect -lopencv_imgproc -lopencv_core -lopencv_highgui -lopencv_imgcodecs -lopencv_videoio -lopencv_cudaobjdetect -lopencv_cudaimgproc -lopencv_cudawarping -o meanShiftFilter".

(Contd)

Box 13.3 *(Contd)*

- The execution of the above command will create an executable file with the name "meanShiftFilter".
2.2.2 Executing the mean shift filtering operation using the executable.
- Execute "./meanShiftFilter".
- The results of mean shift filtering operation - "meanShiftFilter.png" would be stored in the data folder. The time required for executing mean shift filter operation using CPU and GPU would be displayed on terminal.

Step 3: Performing CUDA Accelerated Mean Shift Segmentation operation
3.1. Checking if the nVIDIA CUDA Complier (NVCC) is in PATH.
3.1.1 Execute - "nvcc --version" to check the version of NVCC. If the command returns an error then continue otherwise skip to 2.2.
3.1.2 Execute - "export PATH=${PATH}:/usr/local/cuda/bin && nvcc --version". This command will set the PATH for CUDA and will return the version of NVCC.
3.2. Enter the meanShiftSegmentation directory.
3.2.1 Creating the executable for CUDA accelerated mean shift segmentation script.
- Execute "g++ meanShiftSegmentation.cpp -I/usr/local/include/opencv4/ -L/usr/local/include/opencv4/opencv2 -lopencv_objdetect -lopencv_imgproc -lopencv_core -lopencv_highgui -lopencv_imgcodecs -lopencv_videoio -lopencv_cudaobjdetect -lopencv_cudaimgproc -lopencv_cudawarping -o meanShiftSeg".
- The execution of the above command will create an executable file with the name "meanShiftSeg".
3.2.2 Executing the mean shift segmentation operation using the executable.
- Execute "./meanShiftSeg".
- The results of mean shift Segmentation operation - "meanShiftSegmentation.png" would be stored in the data folder. The time required for executing mean shift filter operation using CPU and GPU would be displayed on terminal.

****

Note: Parameters used in implementation
1.1. sp - Spatial window radius = 60, sr - Color window radius = 60.
1.2. cv::cuda::meanShiftFiltering(InputArray   src,
                                  OutputArray dst,
                                  int   sp,
                                  int   sr)
2.1. sp - Spatial window radius = 20, sr - Color window radius = 20, minSize - Minimum segment size = 50, outputArray dst is host memory array.
2.2. cv::cuda::meanShiftSegmentation(InputArray   src,
                                     OutputArray dst,
                                     int   sp,
                                     int   sr,
                                     int   minsize)

****

(Contd)

Box 13.3 *(Contd)*

```
Appendix:
nano@nano:~$ nvcc --version
bash: nvcc: command not found
nano@nano:~$ export PATH=${PATH}:/usr/local/cuda/bin
nano@nano:~$ nvcc --version
nvcc: NVIDIA (R) Cuda compiler driver
Copyright (c) 2005-2018 NVIDIA Corporation
Built on Sun_Sep_30_21:09:22_CDT_2018
Cuda compilation tools, release 10.0, V10.0.166
```

LISTING 13.1: CODE FOR MEANSHIFT FILTERING ON JETSON NANO IMAGE

```cpp
#include <time.h>
#include </usr/local/include/opencv4/opencv2/opencv.hpp>
#include </usr/local/include/opencv4/opencv2/opencv_modules.hpp>
#include </usr/local/include/opencv4/opencv2/core/cuda.hpp>
#include </usr/local/include/opencv4/opencv2/cudaimgproc.hpp>
#include </usr/local/include/opencv4/opencv2/cudaarithm.hpp>
#include </usr/local/include/opencv4/opencv2/imgproc.hpp>
#include </usr/local/include/opencv4/opencv2/imgcodecs.hpp>
#include </usr/local/include/opencv4/opencv2/highgui.hpp>
#include <string.h>
#include <stdio.h>

using namespace cv;

int main()
{
        unsigned long startTimeCPU, startTimeGPU=0;
        unsigned long endTimeCPU, endTimeGPU=0;
        float secCPU, secGPU;

        //load image
        Mat img = cv::imread("../data/capturedColorImage.png");
        Mat outImgCPU, outImgGPU;

        //Meanshift Filtering using CPU
        startTimeCPU = getTickCount();
        pyrMeanShiftFiltering(img, outImgCPU, 60, 60);
        endTimeCPU = getTickCount();
        secCPU = (endTimeCPU - startTimeCPU)/getTickFrequency();

        //Meanshift Filtering using GPU
        cv::cuda::GpuMat downImgGPU, imgGPU, upImgGPU;
        startTimeGPU = getTickCount();
        upImgGPU.upload(img);
```

(Contd)

Listing 13.1 *(Contd)*

```
        //Currently, only CV_8UC4 images are supported by GPU mean-shift filtering
        cuda::cvtColor(upImgGPU, imgGPU, COLOR_BGR2BGRA);
        cuda::meanShiftFiltering(imgGPU, downImgGPU, 60, 60);
        downImgGPU.download(outImgGPU);
        endTimeGPU = getTickCount();
        secGPU = (endTimeGPU - startTimeGPU)/getTickFrequency();
//Timing Analysis
printf("CPU %.4lf(sec)", secCPU);
printf("GPU %.4lf(sec)", secGPU);

//Save Outputs
cv::imwrite("../data/meanShiftFilter.png", outImgGPU);

//Display Outputs
cv::imshow("Original Image", img);
cv::imshow("Meanshift Filter Output", outImgGPU);

cv::waitKey();

return 0;

}
```

LISTING 13.2: CODE FOR MEANSHIFT SEGMENTATION ON JETSON NANO IMAGE

```
#include <time.h>
#include </usr/local/include/opencv4/opencv2/opencv.hpp>
#include </usr/local/include/opencv4/opencv2/opencv_modules.hpp>
#include </usr/local/include/opencv4/opencv2/core/cuda.hpp>
#include </usr/local/include/opencv4/opencv2/cudaimgproc.hpp>
#include </usr/local/include/opencv4/opencv2/cudaarithm.hpp>
#include </usr/local/include/opencv4/opencv2/imgproc.hpp>
#include </usr/local/include/opencv4/opencv2/imgcodecs.hpp>
#include </usr/local/include/opencv4/opencv2/highgui.hpp>
#include <string.h>
#include <stdio.h>

using namespace cv;

int main()
{
        unsigned long startTimeGPU=0;
        unsigned long endTimeGPU=0;
        float secGPU;

        //load image
        Mat img = cv::imread("../data/capturedColorImage.png");
```

(Contd)

Listing 13.2 *(Contd)*

```
        Mat outImgCPU, outImgGPU;

        cv::cuda::GpuMat imgGPU, upImgGPU;
        startTimeGPU = getTickCount();
        upImgGPU.upload(img);

        //Currently, only CV_8UC4 images are supported by GPU mean-shift filtering

        cuda::cvtColor(upImgGPU, imgGPU, COLOR_BGR2BGRA);
        cuda::meanShiftSegmentation(imgGPU, outImgGPU, 20, 20, 50);

        //downImgGPU.download(outImgGPU);
        endTimeGPU = getTickCount();
        secGPU = (endTimeGPU - startTimeGPU)/getTickFrequency();

        //Timing Analysis
        printf("GPU %.4lf(sec)", secGPU);

        //Save Outputs
        cv::imwrite("../data/meanShiftSegmentation.png", outImgGPU);

        //Display Outputs
        cv::imshow("Original Image", img);
        cv::imshow("Mean Shift Segmentation Output", outImgGPU);

        cv::waitKey();

    return 0;
}
```

SUMMARY

The need for high performance computing in IoT has long been recognized due to the real-time requirement of various IoT applications. The low-power requirement of IoT devices further complicates the integration of HPC. Recent advances in computational hardware are enabling the development of low-power devices that have significant computational capabilities. The advent of GPUs for general purpose computing revolutionized the development of light weight, low-powered, and high computational powered device, which is packed in a small form factor. These can be integrated with IoT devices where high computations are required such as the IoT edge devices and sensing systems. This chapter provides the background for developing parallel computing applications using GPUs. Further, the emerging EHPC platforms such as those from NVIDIA and various IoT application domains in which these embedded devices can be used are also discussed.

REVIEW QUESTIONS

1. What is high performance computing?
2. Explain parallel computing with a diagram. How is it different from sequential computing?
3. What is embedded HPC?
4. Explain how embedded HPC is useful for IoT.
5. What is the need for EHPC in edge computing?

6. Describe graphics processing units (GPUs).
7. Compare CPU and GPU.
8. Describe the hierarchical memory pattern of a GPU.
9. Explain the CUDA programming model.
10. What are the steps involved in executing a CUDA program?
11. Explain the architectures of Jetson TX2 and Jetson Nano.
12. Describe two application areas of EHPC in IoT.

REFERENCES

1. Hosseinabady, M., Amiruddin Bin Zainol, M., Nunez-Yanez, J., Heterogeneous FPGA + GPU embedded systems: Challenges and opportunities. arXiv:1901.06331 [cs.DC].
2. NVIDIA embedded devices: https://www.nvidia.com/en-us/autonomous-machines/embedded-systems/ [last visited: 10/6/2019].
3. NVIDIA Jetson TX2 https://www.nvidia.com/en-us/autonomous-machines/embedded-systems/jetson-tx2/ [last visited: 10/6/2019].
4. NVIDIA Jetson Nano https://developer.nvidia.com/embedded/jetson-nano-developer-kit
5. NVIDIA Pascal GPU architecture: https://www.nvidia.com/en-us/data-center/pascal-gpu-architecture/ [last visited: 10/6/2019].
6. Embedded HPC: https://www.aldec.com/en/solutions/hpc/embedded_hpc [last visited: 10/6/2019].
7. Han, Y., Oruklu, E. (2017), Traffic sign recognition based on the NVIDIA Jetson TX1 embedded system using convolutional neural networks. pp.184–187. 10.1109/MWSCAS.2017.8052891.
8. Wang, Z., Ren, W., Qiu, Q. (2018), Lanenet: Real-time lane detection networks for autonomous driving, arXiv:1807.01726.
9. Sreekumar, U. K., Devaraj, R., Li, Q., Liu, K., TPCAM: Real-time traffic pattern collection and analysis model based on deep learning, in: IEEE SmartWorld/SCALCOM/UIC/ATC/CBDCom/IOP/SCI, 2017, pp. 1–4.
10. Bura, H., Lin, N., Kumar, N., Malekar, S., Nagaraj, S., Liu, K. (2018), An edge based smart parking solution using camera networks and deep learning, in: 2018 IEEE International Conference on Cognitive Computing (ICCC), IEEE, 2018, pp. 17–24.
11. Comaniciu, D and Meer, P (2002), "Mean Shift: A robust approach toward feature space analysis". IEEE Transactions on Pattern Analysis and Machine Intelligence. pp. 603-619.
12. OpenCV and GPU: https://docs.opencv.org/2.4/modules/gpu/doc/gpu.html [last visited: 28/01/2020]

PART IV: DATA MANAGEMENT IN IOT

Chapter 14: Interoperability in the IoT Ecosystem

Chapter 15: CyberSecurity and Privacy

Chapter 16: IoT and Business Processes Management

Interoperability in the IoT Ecosystem

CHAPTER 14

"The Achilles' heel of emergency management is lack of interoperability."

-Mark Hammond

OBJECTIVES

- explain the need for a reference model and architecture
- outline various reference models
- illustrate with examples where the reference model is useful
- explain the principles of reference architecture
- explain the concept of interoperability
- outline the various issues of interoperability in IoT systems
- show the emergence of Web of Things (WoT)
- explain the various layers of IoT where semantics are necessary
- summarize various initiatives of world wide web for semantic integration
- outline the main concepts of semantic sensor network ontology

OUTCOMES

- analyze IoT reference models and architectures
- evaluate some well-known IoT reference architectures
- develop own reference architecture for a specific application
- assess data interoperability issues
- differentiate between syntactic and semantic interoperability
- assess syntactic and semantic approaches for interoperability

REVISION

The concept of interoperability is envisioned as one of the key requirements of Internet of Things (IoT). Interoperability is also emphasized as one of the key technological challenges for the further evolution of IoT. The need for standardization at various layers of IoT is highlighted and various organizations involved in standardization efforts are also briefly presented. Chapter 1 highlighted the interoperability issues and described it as one of the key challenges for the future proliferation of IoT. Chapter 4 dealt with IoT standards and various protocols in a more comprehensive manner, which has addressed to a large extent the interoperability issues related to network and connectivity. It is suggested to go through these two chapters to gain basic understanding about interoperability and how it is being addressed at various levels of an IoT system. This chapter is more focused on the interoperability aspects beginning with an IoT reference model and

> architecture, which is seen as a fundamental way of developing interoperable IoT systems. Secondly, at the data management level, that is, the issues surrounding the seamless and unambiguous access of data and application services between various interconnected IoT networks having a variety of data representations and configurations requires the use of syntactic and semantic technologies to overcome these heterogeneities.

14.1 NEED FOR INTEROPERABILITY IN IOT SYSTEMS

The emerging Internet of Things (IoT) is leading to an unprecedented number of things being connected to the Internet. The amount of data that needs to be processed and managed is posing a huge challenge, not only due to their number but also due to the diverse nature of IoT such as:

- Low-power versus high-power devices, both existing in the same ecosystem
- Interconnected networks having varied network and communication protocols (6LoWPAN, ZigBee, etc.)
- Diverse services
- Variety of data representations and models

Due to such heterogeneity, it is becoming difficult to integrate devices, data, services, and applications in the IoT ecosystem. The way to achieve this seamless integration is called 'interoperability.' A few definitions of interoperability are discussed in the next section.

14.1.1 Various Definitions of Interoperability

Several organizations have taken up the task of developing standards in a variety of domains to address various issues of interoperability in those areas. Below are some selected definitions of interoperability as put forth by these organizations.

14.1.1.1 IEEE
Interoperability is defined as the 'ability of two or more systems or components to exchange information and to use the information that has been exchanged' [IEEE, 1991].

14.1.1.2 European Telecommunications Standards Institute (ETSI) Project TIPHON
'Interoperability is the ability of two systems to interoperate using the same communication protocol.'

14.1.1.3 ETSI Project Technical Committee TISPAN
'Interoperability is the ability of equipment from different manufacturers (or different systems) to communicate together on the same infrastructure (same system), or on another while roaming.'

14.1.1.4 Webopedia
'The ability of software and hardware on different machines from different vendors to share data.'

14.1.1.5 Healthcare Information Management Systems Society (HIMMS)

'Interoperability describes the extent to which systems and devices can exchange data, and interpret that shared data. For two systems to be interoperable, they must be able to exchange data and subsequently present that data such that it can be understood by a user.'

14.1.1.6 Army Information Technology Implementation Instructions (2013) by the United States Army

'The exchange of information that preserves the meaning and relationships of the data exchanged.'

14.1.2 Current IoT Systems are in Silos

The IoT technology is applied in many domains such as traffic monitoring, water quality, waste management, and air-quality monitoring to name a few. These applications are thought of as verticals, that is, their growth in terms of functionality, features, and applications is confined to the specific domain and the opportunities are for products that cater to that specific area. IoT solutions providers (public/private) tend to develop the solutions keeping in mind the requirements for that specific domain and offer their products, that is, in effect they tend to be self-contained. It is possible that in a single domain/area of interest many vendors may have provided their products and these tend to resemble a silo. Each of these IoT-based products/solutions for a specific domain is built around a particular architecture and hence it is possible that they cannot be integrated across domains.

Overcoming interoperability challenges is the single biggest challenge for IoT for mass adoption as the benefits from such seamless access are numerous. The hurdles related to multiple vendors, heterogeneous devices, services, data models, systems, etc. are leading to non-interoperability and silos as shown in Fig. 14.1, which means that the users are tied to certain types of IoT systems

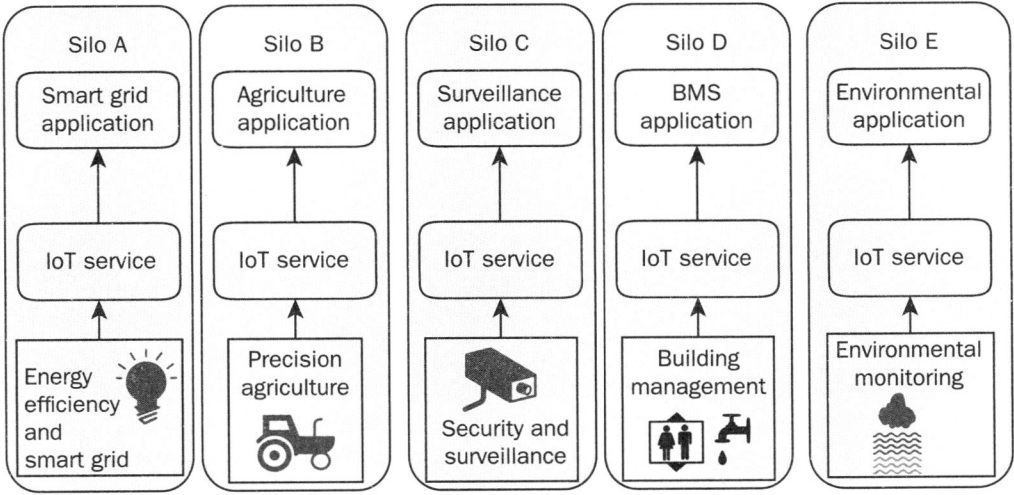

Fig. 14.1 IoT Systems are Currently Fragmented and Live in Silos Leading to Non-interoperability

and cannot in the future be able to use cross domain data and applications. This inflexibility, coupled with vendor-specific requirements for management of the IoT system puts a lot of constraints on the user. Hence, it is important to develop models that enable to describe the things, their interactions, and applications in a more generalized form so that ad-hoc interactions between things and applications can be enabled. The granularity at which a user can interact with the things (for example, single, small group or large group of things) and services and applications should be facilitated, which can lead to the development of numerous innovative domain-specific mashups and applications. An example scenario that shows the need for interoperability is shown in Box 14.1.

The advantages of interoperability are:

- Once the IoT system is made interoperable, new things and related applications can be integrated easily due to the standardized models that are already available
- Lower upfront cost and maintenance
- It is vendor neutral

BOX 14.1: EXAMPLE SCENARIO FOR INTEROPERABILITY

Imagine IoT systems that were deployed for two different applications such as surveillance and environmental monitoring. The IoT device involved in the surveillance application could be networked IP cameras, motion detection sensors, etc. The sensors in the environmental monitoring applications could be air pollution monitoring sensors (PM2.5, Ozone, NO_2, CO, etc.) and assuming that these air-quality monitoring stations are deployed along the transportation network to monitor the pollution from vehicles. These two applications are doing their job for the intended applications. Tomorrow, it is felt that it would be good if there is a way to capture those vehicles that are polluting more, which is visible by the amount of exhaust from the vehicle. Since, the cameras are already there capturing the movement on the roads, someone can ask: How can we use those cameras and then capture those vehicles that are responsible for more pollution? Suppose, if the camera captured 50 vehicles during a day with excessive exhaust coming from their vehicles at a location, it is possible to look at the air-quality monitoring station and see how much more was the pollution that day, and can be compared with the day before and several more statistical analysis could be done. Therefore, to make all this happen, we need to combine information coming from surveillance cameras with air-quality monitoring sensors and in real time able to provide the status of that particular place as far as air quality is concerned. The law enforcement can quickly react and put a checkpoint to monitor the pollution from vehicles and also of a particular type, which are causing more pollution. They can divert the traffic of vehicles of a certain kind so as to reduce the pollution load on that route. All these cannot happen unless there is a way to seamless access and combine data from two different sets of IoT devices and applications, which were not originally meant to be combined. However, if the devices and their data and applications follow certain standards, it is easy to integrate information from both of them in real-time and hence achieve interoperability.

14.2 TYPES OF INTEROPERABILITY

Various types of interoperability relevant to IoT are (see Fig. 14.2) discussed in further sections.

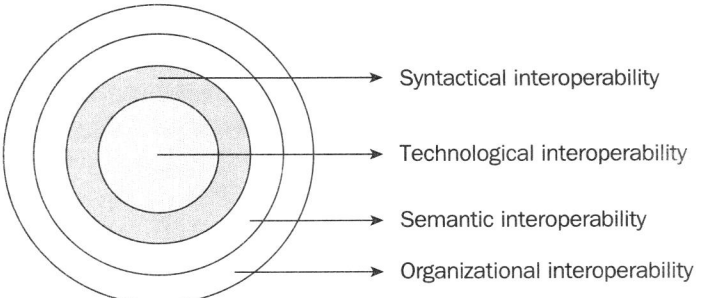

Fig. 14.2 Types of Interoperability

14.2.1 Device or Technological Interoperability

According to ETSI, technical interoperability is 'centered on (communication) protocols and the infrastructure needed for those protocols to operate.'

The device-level interoperability refers to the seamless access to a variety of IoT devices without the need to make special efforts to understand the underlying physical hardware. Following are the desirable characteristics of device or technological interoperability:

- Enable real-time applications to access and use these various IoT devices by allowing anytime and anyway ad-hoc connections.
- Facilitate the discovery and access of IoT devices that are distributed in various relevant domains so that they can be integrated to create solutions for cross-domain problems.

14.2.2 Syntactic Interoperability

This refers to the data structure or model in which the messages are encoded and then exchanged between various IoT devices, systems, and applications. These are highly dependent on syntax, which is pre-agreed upon by organizations, communities, and people who are interested to develop interoperable systems.

ETSI defines syntactic interoperability as a representation that 'deals with the format and structure of the encoding of the information exchanged among Things. It includes the middleware layer of TCP/IP stack.'

These are usually based on Extensible Markup Language (XML) and many of its variants such as Javascript Object Notation (JSON), JSON for Linked Data JSON-LD), etc. These are mainly used with web services that are designed to standardize the requests from client software and responses from the server (web service). XML is the de facto standard for such exchanges. In case of IoT, the device messages need to be exchanged, so there is a need for a syntax that could be well understood across various devices. This ensures that the communication problems between devices are minimized while receiving, sending, or consuming different pieces of information.

14.2.3 Semantic Interoperability

It is the interoperability that is required when different IoT devices, systems, and applications use varied concepts/vocabulary to describe discovery, access, and understanding of the information from them. This kind of interoperability is highly severe when the IoT systems are developed in isolation without regard to existing standards, and also minimal understanding of the commonly used terminology in a particular domain.

ETSI defines semantic interoperability as:

'The capability of two components to interpret exchanged data identically and share a common understanding of it.' In other words, understanding the meaning of the common terms (vocabulary) shared in messages that are common between IoT systems and unambiguously using these terms while performing a certain task.

14.2.4 Organizational Interoperability

Organizational interoperability is achievable when business processes and related information can be seamlessly coordinated and exchanged between organizations without any conflict. Standards play an important role in minimizing the efforts required to enable meaningful sharing of data and information where the organizations are highly diverse in nature having different information technology (IT) infrastructures, information models, and may even be geographically distributed. Ensuring organizational interoperability allows reduction in operating expenses, time, with consistent and better usability of services by the users. As more and more organizations are adopting IoT technologies, organizational interoperability will play a key role in ensuring IoT assets and services to be available across multiple organizations/entities without the need of extra developmental efforts to integrate with their own business processes.

14.2.5 Approaches for Interoperability

There are three very broad approaches to address interoperability in the IoT ecosystem:

- Use a comprehensive architectural reference model as the basic foundation that provides extensive guidelines for designing the protocols, interfaces and across all functional groups (FGs) and communication layers of the IoT systems. Therefore, systems built using (as a blueprint) this reference model and architecture ensure interoperability between each other. This type of interoperability approach is discussed in Section 14.3.
- The second type of approaches are based on the standardization at various levels of IoT stack such as Internet protocols for IoT, mobile communication standards, standards for low-power wide area network, wireless standards supporting IoT, etc. These concepts are described in more details in Chapter 4.
- The above-mentioned protocols can facilitate the integration of smart things at the network layer. However, at the application layer due to platform incompatibilities, there exist interoperability issues. Therefore, the third type of approach addresses the issue of integrating existing heterogeneous systems and platforms at the data and application layers using syntactic and semantic interoperability approaches. These are described in Section 14.6.

14.3 IOT REFERENCE MODEL AND ARCHITECTURE

As discussed in Section 14.1.2, a situation where horizontal integration, that is, between domains becomes increasingly difficult. Hence, there is a need for a common understanding of IoT domains and their specific requirements. These can then be synthesized into a model that captures their core aspects and incorporated into the overall IoT systems in general. This is captured in the form of a reference model hereafter referred as the Architecture Reference Model (ARM).

Further, there is a need to give developers an architecture that is firmly grounded on the reference model and that captures the high-level concepts of the IoT systems and general enough to instantiate IoT architectures based on the requirement of a certain domain. This is termed as the reference architecture and discussed in more detail in Section 14.5.

14.4 ARCHITECTURE REFERENCE MODEL

An architecture reference model (ARM) consists of: (i) reference model to promote a common understanding of the domain and (ii) reference architecture that describes essential components and design choices to overcome conflicting requirements.

An ARM is useful for (Bauer and Walewsk, 2013):

- Cognitive aid: ARM forms the basis for enabling anyone to use the commonly understood language or the concepts involved in a system so that everyone in a community can get an overall understanding of the domain of discourse in a better way.
- Common grounding
- Generation of architectures
- Identify differences in derived architectures
- Interoperability
- System road maps and product life cycles
- Benchmarking

14.4.1 Reference Model

A reference model is developed to promote common understanding of a domain. It helps to resolve conflicts in representation of the domain concepts and provide a common platform to derive more specific architectures.

The definition of a reference model is provided by the OASIS organization as below (SOA-RM):

'A reference model is an abstract framework for understanding significant relationships among the entities of some environment. It enables the development of specific reference or concrete architectures using consistent standards or specifications supporting that environment.'

In addition, a reference model consists of 'a minimal set of unifying concepts, axioms, and relationships within a particular problem domain, and is independent of specific standards, technologies, implementations, or other concrete details.'

14.4.2 IoT Reference Model

The IoT reference model provides the highest abstraction level for the definition of the IoT. An architectural reference model (ARM) describes the immutable components of IoT domain, that is, those aspects that remain constant. The above definition of a reference model is very generic in nature. To apply it to the IoT domain, the IoT reference model (IoT-RM) is developed, which can be useful to identify and understand the most fundamental concepts and relationships among the various entities involved in IoT. It is a high-level abstract description and does not depend on:

- Any particular technology (e.g., sensors technology, connectivity technology, middleware, etc.)
- Any standards such as standards IPV6, 6LOWPAN, LORA, etc.
- Any implementations such as various IoT frameworks, IoT Platforms, or IoT applications
- Any concrete details that describe a specific component of an IoT system, for example, the sensors/actuators that are used in a particular application, the specific cloud solution that is integrated, etc.

14.4.2.1 IoT-A Reference Model

The IoT-A reference model is currently developed through a project of the European FP7 Research Project IoT-A. It is now a widely adopted IoT reference model. It consists of several submodels such as (see Fig. 14.3):

- Domain model
- Functional model
- Information model
- Communication model
- Trust, security, and privacy model

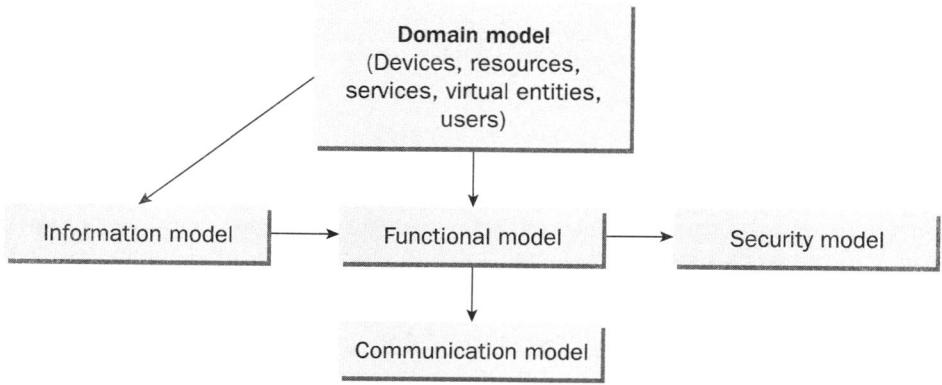

Fig. 14.3 The Various Components of the IoT-A Reference Model; The Primary Model is the Domain Model from Which Other Models Emerge

The IoT domain model is the key model in this reference model, which is mandatory to be used for developing any reference architecture based on this reference model. All the other submodels can be used as per the specific requirement of the domain application.

Below is a brief description of each of these models:

Domain model The domain model represents the concepts that are used in the IoT systems. It describes the domain in terms of concepts and their relationships.

Currently, in the IoT domain there are very heterogeneous and inconsistent terminologies being used leading to confusion in understanding the meaning of many core terms of the domain (Haller, 2010).

The domain model makes a distinction between what changes and what does not over a period of time. Below are some examples of concepts that may not vary over time:

Device The concept of *device* could remain the same in the foreseeable future, but the type of devices may change for a particular application. For instance, there may be several kinds of devices that can be used for home automation, depending on the requirement, many types of devices can be used, for example, temperature control, locking systems, light control, etc. The specific device that could be used to perform these tasks could change based on the technology at that point of time, but the need for smart device remains the same. Therefore, the device concept may not change in the future. The devices can basically take three forms, that is, sensors, actuators, and tags.

Resource The resource concept is used in the reference model because it is general enough to encompass a wide variety of resources such as network resources, device resources, etc. Although specific instantiations of these resources, for example, the network resources could comprise of data, information, and hardware devices that can be accessed by a group of computers via a shared connection. There are many types of data, hardware devices that are used currently, and many other forms of these can emerge in the future; however, the overall concept of *resource* to denote all these remains the same.

Physical entity It defines various entities that exist in a physical form. The physical entity could be a room in a home that is monitored using various sensors such as temperature, lighting condition, and air quality. Here the 'room' is a physical entity that exists in the real world and many kinds of physical entities can occur depending on the application of the IoT system, but the general concept of 'physical entity' remains the same. Hence, this is one of the core concepts in the reference model. Further, as shown in Fig. 14.4, the relationships *Sensors (temperature and humidity sensors) Monitors Physical Entity* and Sensor *isAttachedTo Device* are defined in the reference model. From an IoT perspective, the physical entities are usually interacted by calling a *service*, which usually gives more information about that physical entity and also can perform a specific action (i.e., controllable). This type of interaction with a physical entity through a service is performed by a software user interface.

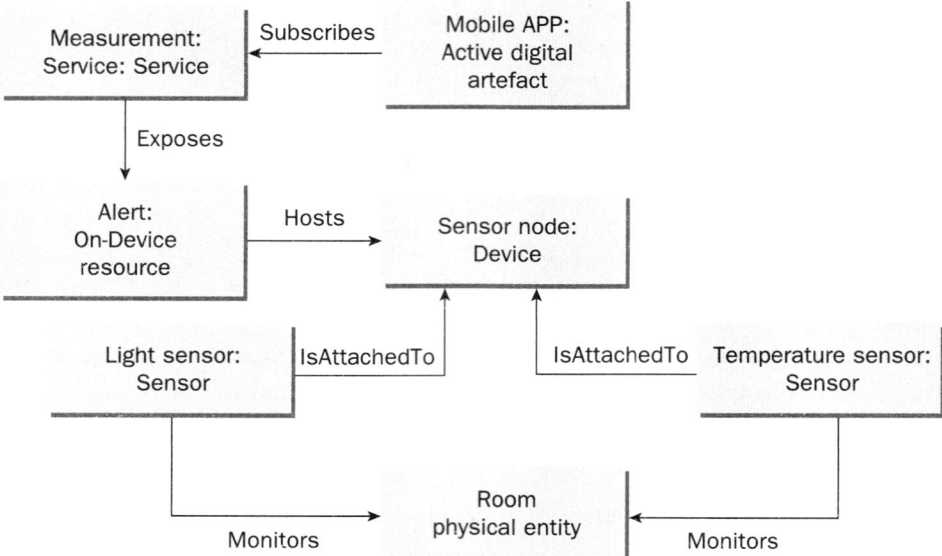

Fig. 14.4 Instantiation of the IoT-A Domain Model

Virtual entity In the digital world, the physical entities are represented as virtual entities. A virtual entity can be thought of as a digital artifact and can be classified into: (i) Active Digital Artifact (ADA) that represents software applications, agents, or services that may access other services or resources and (ii) Passive Digital Artifacts (PDA) that represent passive elements of a software such as database entries that act as representatives of the actual physical entity. These artifacts enable interaction with the real-world physical entities, for example, the change of state of a particular device. For instance, a surveillance camera can be panned to acquire new information in a different direction. The panning is triggered from a software where the Pan component of the user interface of the software is given a value (e.g., 180° of panning).

Augmented entity The concept of augmented entity denotes the composition of a physical entity with the corresponding virtual entity. In the IoT context, these two usually occur together to form the *Thing* in IoT and make it smart. For example, a surveillance camera (physical entity) is combined with an ADA (a part of the virtual entity), that is, a software to remotely control the camera. These two entities together form the augmented entity.

Human user The human user is the one that is interacting with the physical entities. It is also possible to think about it as machines that are interacting with each other. The concept of ADA is relevant here as it can be thought as a software, which is interacting with other machine, that is, a device.

The domain model can be instantiated to represent a real-world use case as shown in Fig. 14.4. It is represented in Unified Modeling Language (UML). It can be see that a *room* is an instance of a domain concept called *Physical Entity* (reference model) and sensors such as light and temperature *Monitor* it.

Functional model The functional model is defined as (IoT-A): 'the functional model is an abstract framework for understanding the main FGs and their interactions. This framework defines the common semantics of the main functionalities and will be used for the development of IoT-A compliant functional views.'

In the above definition, the concept *abstract* refers to a functional model that is independent of any specific technology, implementation, or application domain. It is necessary to think about the FGs in terms of their interactions and not independently. The functional views are related to the runtime aspects of each of the functional components.

The functional model consists of the following FGs.

IoT process management This FG is focused on those functional concepts that enable the integration of the business process management (BPM) systems with the IoT ARM at the conceptual level. The advantage of developing these kinds of relationships is that it can allow various systems and subsystems of IoT to conform to various standards and best practices that are prevalent in the BPM systems. This will make it easy for the IoT systems to gain wider acceptance and reduce proprietary kind of solutions.

Service organization This FG provides the necessary glue or hub for other functionality groups. Its function is to link service request from other FGs, external applications, resource servers and associate them with virtual entities to properly address a request. To achieve this, service orchestration is used, which involves service composition. It allows various primitive-level services to be combined to allow a higher-level request to be responded. For example, combining temperature from a Temperature service with wind speed from a WindSpeed service will derive wind chill factor.

Virtual entity and IoT service The meaning of virtual entity is described earlier in the domain model. Here in the functional model, the various FGs of the virtual entity are responsible for providing functionalities such as search and discovery of those services that provide relevant information about the virtual entities so that various *interactions* between the virtual entities and the services can take place such as 'Get the rainfall in the last 24 h from RaniGauge with ID X' or 'Start the Water pump (using an actuator).' Both these are IoT service-level requests. In these type of *interactions*, there is a need to explicitly link the rain gauge with the SmartFarm. As soon as the rainfall value is retrieved, it needs to be linked with virtual entity, that is, SmartFarm (see Fig. 14.5), this can happen only when these connections are predefined/programmed. Here, the SmartFarm is a virtual entity that is interacting with rain service that is built for the rain gauge sensor. In addition, the discovery of services can happen when at the virtual entity a higher-level modeling is performed, which can enable the use of a service based on the context. Similarly, there could be an *association* of sensor service with the SmartFarm virtual entity to perform a certain task. Hence, virtual entity service requests could be 'Give me the rainfall at the SamrtFarm' or 'Open the water pump at the SmartFarm.' In these cases, there needs to be an understanding that the rainfall value that is obtained is from a particular Sensor service belongs to the SmartFarm.

Further, discovery of services implies the association of service which is designed for a particular domain/task can be used to accomplish another task and also usually in real-time. For example, a weather station can be used to give the temperature, humidity, wind speed, etc., to enable humans to adjust to the outside temperature, these readings can also be used in another context for air-quality monitoring. Here is the semantics play a vital role in understanding the context. Therefore, the virtual entity and IoT service *associations* (see Fig. 14.5) can provide such higher-level discovery functionality. Thus, the virtual entity contains the necessary FGs to ensure the proper management of the interactions and associations.

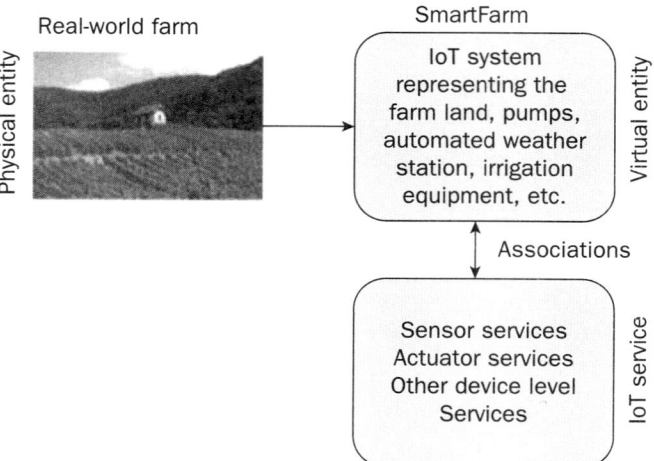

Fig. 14.5 Abstraction of Virtual Entity and IoT Service

IoT communication This FG enables the management of high-level information flow from various IoT systems and facilitates the interaction with the IoT service FG. To achieve the communication between various IoT systems, various protocol translation functionalities are described. The various security mechanisms based on various signature and encryption schemes are also enforced here.

Device and application These FGs are more generic and they are not just specific to the functional model but also applicable in other components of the reference model.

Management This FG provides the necessary functionalities to address high-level goals.

Security All security-related functions of the IoT system are described in this FG. Security features such as client registration to the IoT system, protecting unauthorized access of the private details of the users, and other identity management and privacy tasks are handled in this FG. Further, peer group authentication, trust, integrity, confidentiality and secure communication, etc. is ensured.

Information model The information model component of the IoT-A reference model defines the relations, attributes/characteristics, and services of the information pertaining to virtual entities. It is a high-level conceptual description and avoids the specific details about the representation aspects such as whether the information is represented in the form of CSV, ASCII, XML, RDF, JSON, JSON-LD, etc. These specific details are beyond the scope of the information model, its purpose is only to define the fundamental structure of information.

The core elements are: *Virtual Entity* that acts as a representative of a physical entity, that is, it models the *Physical Entity*. Further, a service provides information about a physical entity and a description about that service is provided by the *Service Description*.

The attribute is represented by an attributeName (hasWindspeed) and attributeType. A class called VirtualEntity (e.g., anemometer measurement) has an entityType (WindSpeed), which is usually a concept that has a formal definition and is part of a well-defined vocabulary pertaining to a domain. These can also be pointed to a class defined in domain ontology (a shared conceptualization of a domain (Gruber, 1995)).

Example of information model A smart agriculture farm can be monitored with an automated weather station having various sensors such as temperature, relative humidity, wind speed, wind direction, and rainfall. These measurements will help to assist in various farm-related activities such as irrigation, pest/disease, and productivity. For example, a particular range of temperature, humidity, and wind speed, can trigger the onset of a pest in the farm. Therefore, agro-meteorological IoT platforms are now being used to continuously monitor the farms and give real-time advisory. In order to model the information aspects of the above scenario, it is necessary to identify various components of the information model such as virtual entity, service description. The illustrative example that models the above smart farm is shown in Fig. 14.6. It can be seen that the SmartFarm is represented as an instance of virtual entity (a virtual representation of the actual physical farm, i.e., PhysicalEntity).

The *MeasurementRelativeHumidity* is an attribute that denotes attribute Name, which is measured at the SmartFarm. The relative humidity measurement is not directly sent to the user, but rather a service is made available (e.g., SmartFarm service), which can be queried by the user by sending a request such as getRelativeHumidity. This service description provides more information about the capabilities of the service, that is, at a minimum all the parameters that it can give. To finally get the actual value of the relative humidity, the association class of the information model is used which provides the connection between the attribute hasMeasurementRelativeHumidity and the SmartFarm service.

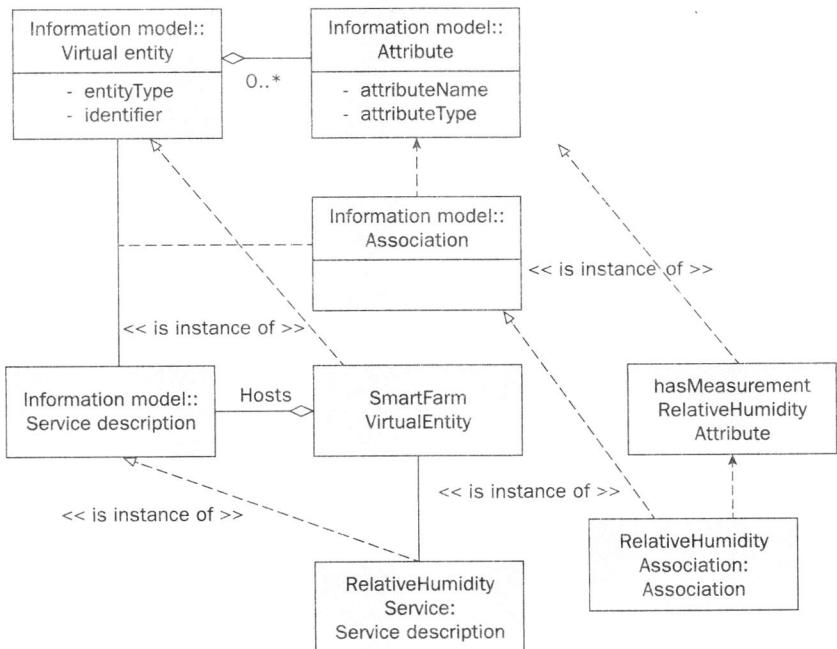

Fig. 14.6 Example of an Information Model

Communication model   The IoT communication model describes:

- The core communication functionality for connecting various components of the IoT domain model such as the device, service, active digital artifact, and human user.
- Interoperability aspects of the communication describe a set of rules that can be used as reference for building interoperable stacks. The ISO OSI 7 layer model for networks is taken as a reference for distinguishing the various requirements for interoperability between the various layers.

Due to the unique way in which networks are usually formed in IoT, that is, network of devices that are constrained by power and having a variety of protocols, and network of gateways, resulting in the adoption of different strategies for optimal communication between various IoT networks.

Security model   In the security model of IoT, the core properties such as trust, security, privacy, and reliability are defined. These are necessary in the IoT systems as they integrate a wide variety of objects, data, and computing devices to form large information networks.

14.4.3 ITU-T Reference Model

The International Telecommunication Union (ITU) IoT reference model consists of various layers that capture the essential functions and capabilities of IoT architecture. One of the goals of reference model is to enable the development of interoperable IoT systems.

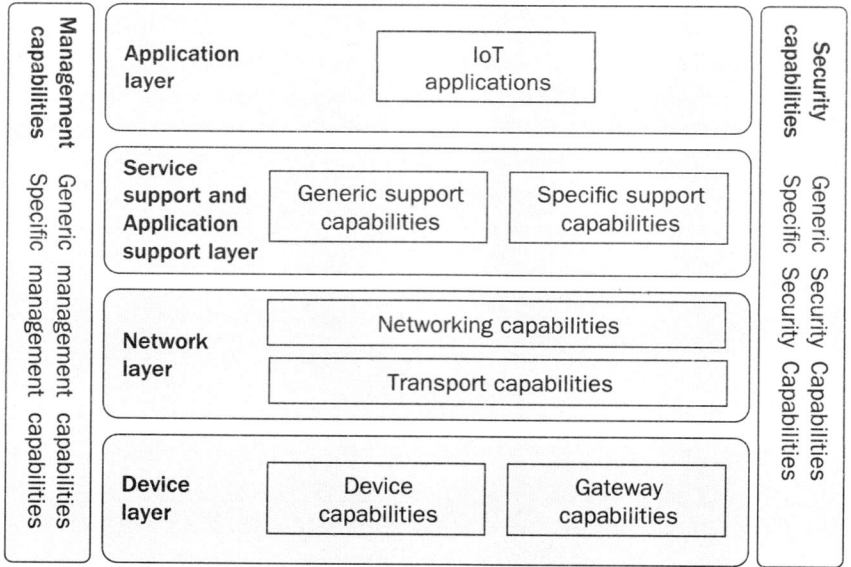

Fig. 14.7   ITU-T Reference Model

(Source credit: ITU-T Recommendation Y.4000/Y.2060 (06/12) https://www.itu.int/rec/T-REC-Y.2060-201206-I)

This layered reference model essentially consists of four layers that are supported by management and security functions (see Fig. 14.7).

14.4.3.1 Device Layer

The *device layer* consists of the *device capabilities* and *gateway capabilities*. The device capabilities include direct and indirect interactions with the communication network, ad-hoc networking, sleeping, and waking-up functions. These allow the things to interact with the network or gateway in various ways. Further, the gateway capabilities support multiple interfaces including support for devices connected through various wired or wireless technologies, also support heterogeneous communication technologies such as 4G, LTE, and DSL. The device layer also facilitates protocol conversion, for example, when the device layer and network layer are using different protocols (device layer uses Zigbee and network layer uses 4G) it becomes challenging to communicate.

14.4.3.2 Network Layer

The *network* layer also has two groups of capabilities, that is, networking and transport. The connecting of *Things* to networks (based on various protocols) and ensuring sustained connection to that network is one of the prime functions of *networking capabilities*. This layer also obtains the support of management and security capabilities (applicable to all the four layers of the IoT-T architecture) to enable various IoT security features.

14.4.3.3 Service and Application Support Layer

The *service and application support layer* contains two broad components, that is, the *generic support capabilities* and *application-specific support capabilities*. The generic support capabilities are common capabilities, which can be used across many IoT applications and are very general in nature. However, the other component of this layer, that is, the application-specific capabilities are intended to have particular characteristics to serve the needs of specific applications. These are tailor-made capabilities for particular IoT applications and are not applicable to the IoT system wide.

14.4.3.4 Application Layer

The *application layer* consists of various IoT applications, for example, SmartFarm, Smart Homes, e-waste management, etc.

14.4.3.5 Management and Security Capabilities

The *management and security capabilities* comprise of generic and specific capabilities. The generic management capabilities include device management functions such as remote activation or deactivation of the device, various diagnostics functions, capability to access and control the device, obtaining the current status and health of the device, automatic remote software updates, network topology management, and various network management functions such as overflow detection, traffic, and congestion control, resource queuing system to make the device available based on certain priorities. The generic security capabilities are based on the layer at which they are applicable. These include the application layer, where the authorization, authentication, application-specific data confidentiality, data and signaling integrity checks and protection, privacy protection, etc. are important. At the network layer, authentication, authorization, device integrity validation, data access and control, and integrity protection are the desired capabilities.

Having understood the IoT reference models, the next section (refer Section 14.5) provides details about the IoT reference architectures. This section in particular focuses on the IoT-A reference architecture.

14.5 IOT REFERENCE ARCHITECTURES

A reference architecture provides guidelines and best practices which can be used to develop concrete real world architecture in a particular domain.

14.5.1 Need for a Reference Architecture

The building of real-world IoT systems requires a thorough understanding of the many facets of its various components and their constraints. IoT systems can become very large based on the domain of application. For example, IoT systems designed for smart cities' applications usually can have hundreds of devices deployed to make a particular task smart; it could be waste disposal, traffic management, air-quality updates, commuter services, etc. To develop such large IoT systems, there is a need for architectures to help in designing, building, and testing these real-world systems.

A reference architecture can be developed by understanding the usage of various components in existing architectures such as standards that were used to build those architectures; then take these essential ingredients and develop a more general architecture called the reference architecture. One of the most important functions of the reference architecture is to provide guidance in the form of best practices so that new architecture for specific application domains/scenarios can be developed. This will help to resolve conflicts related to functionality requirements, performance, deployment, and security needs.

IoT systems that were built based on the same reference architecture are interoperable, compliant, and can have similar core components, which provides homogeneity and better way to integrate cross-domain IoT systems.

In the next section, a top-level architecture of IoT is described to emphasize the essential layers in it.

14.5.2 Simplified Outline of IoT Architecture

The physical sensing layer contains embedded devices that make use of sensors to gather real-world data. The gateway layer provides the mechanism and protocols for devices to expose their sensed data to the Internet (e.g., Wi-Fi, Ethernet, GSM, etc.). The middleware layer facilitates and manages the communication between the real-world-sensed activities and the application layer. The application layer maps onto applications that can be used by the consumer to send commands to real-word objects over the Internet via mobile applications, web apps, etc. (see Fig. 14.8).

14.5.2.1 Definition of Reference Architecture

'A reference architecture is an architectural design pattern that indicates how an abstract set of relationships realizes a set of requirements. The main purpose of reference architecture is to provide guidance for the development of concrete architectures. More reference architectures may be derived from a common reference model.'

Fig. 14.8 Simplified Outline of IoT Architecture

The above definition essentially means that reference architecture is the first thing that an IoT systems developer(s) should consult to obtain suggestions for best practices in terms of the functionalities, protocols, information models, etc. It also provides synoptic/top-level views and perspectives to develop new IoT systems.

14.5.3 IoT-A Reference Architecture

To enable the development of a robust IoT system, the IoT-A reference architecture provides high-level views that provide various angles of the reference architecture, by using which a proposed IoT architecture can be developed. In addition, perspectives are provided so that certain level of adherence is maintained in the various tasks, approaches, and designing of the concrete or real-world IoT system (see Fig. 14.9).

Next section is a brief description of IOT-A architectural views and perspectives.

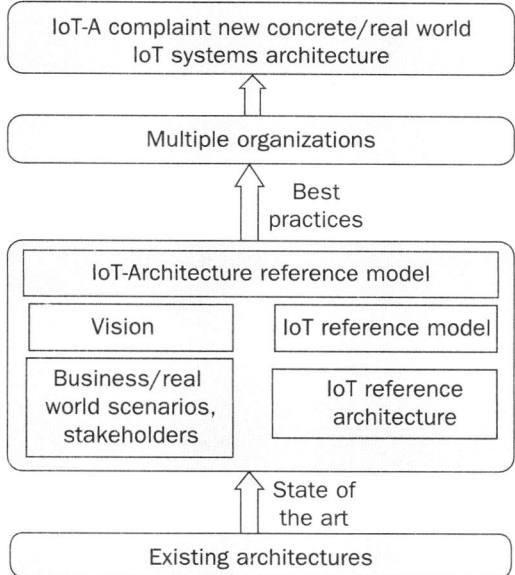

Fig. 14.9 Main Components of the IoT-A Reference Architecture

14.5.3.1 Architectural Views

Functional view It describes the functional building blocks of the architecture, specifically the runtime functional components of the IoT system as well as their default functionality, interfaces, and basic interactions. The functional view is derived by functional decomposition as described in Section 14.4.2.1. Two important concepts in the functional view are:

- 'Unified requirements,' which can be thought of as the understanding and capture of requirements in terms of their function from various business/real world use case scenarios, existing architectures, and expectations and requirements of the stakeholders. All these put together leads to a set of unified requirements.
- IoT functional model describing the main functionality groups (FG) (refer Section 3.2.1.1) (see Fig. 14.10) and their interactions. The common semantics of the main functionalities are captured and are used for the development of IoT-A compliant functional views.

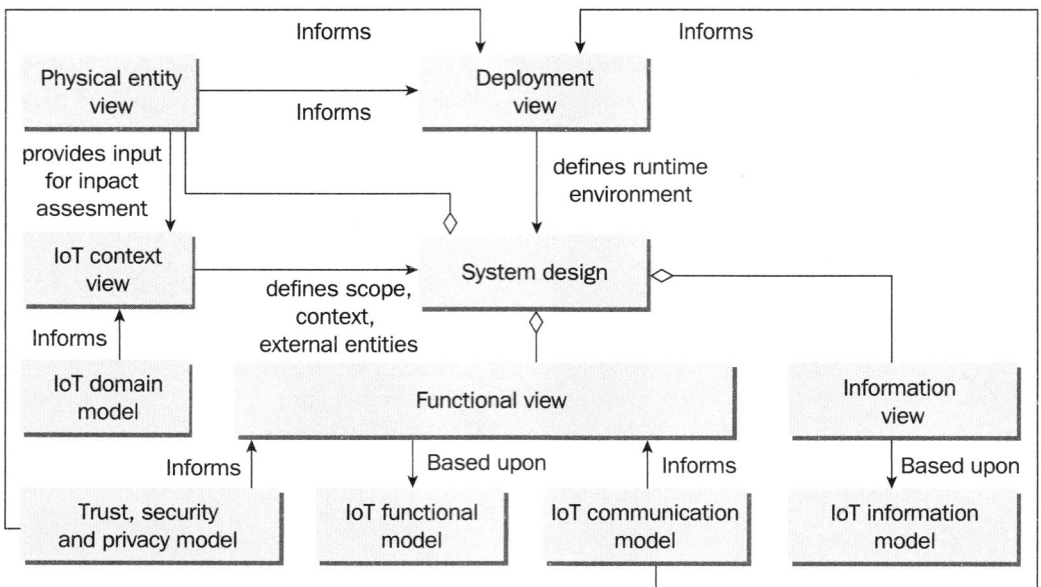

Fig. 14.10 Linkages of the Architectural Views with the IoT-A Reference Model

(Source credit: INSTICC)

Information view The information view describes the representation of two components in the IoT system, that is, (i) the static information, which is represented by virtual entities and in terms of hierarchies and the associated semantics (refer to Section 14.4.2.1 for a description of virtual entities and various viewpoints), (ii) dynamic information flow depicting the details of the information processing and storage. The information view captures actual phenomenon being measured by the sensors such as 'relative humidity' of a farm.

Deployment and operation view Provides some guidelines to enable the user to optimally select technologies for deployment (based on the reference model) for deployment. The deployment and operation view enables such guidance for: (i) How to go beyond the service description and identify the various functional elements to actually do the implementation of the service, (ii) How to select the best technologies for a particular component of the IoT system out of many available technologies such as sensor and actuator networks; RFIDs and smart tags; Wi-fi or other unconstrained technologies; and cellular networks.

From these groups of technologies, the deployment and operations view guides the users with selecting specific technologies from each group that will fit to the needs of their specific IoT system.

14.5.3.2 IoT-A Perspectives

An architectural perspective is defined as (Woods and Rozanski, 2005) 'a collection of activities, tactics, and guidelines that are used to ensure that a system exhibits a particular set of related quality properties that require consideration across a number of the system's architectural views.'

Often the reference architecture and its components may not be fully able to capture the aspirations of the stakeholder as the various views that the reference architecture provides may not address the nonfunctional or quality properties as these properties may span across multiple views. These kind of qualitative requirements (e.g., performance, security, or scalability) of the stakeholders are captured in the perspectives. IoT-A identified four important perspectives that are essential for IoT systems (refer Fig. 14.9).

Evolution and interoperability It addresses the stakeholders concern that a particular technology that is being adopted today can quickly become obsolete in the near future. Hence, the software should be able to adapt and interoperate to the later technologies. Since IoT is still emerging, there are many technologies that have not matured yet and no guarantee that a particular technology will become successful. Therefore, the evolution of the technology needs to be taken into account so that the underlying software is able to evolve in tandem with the changing technology.

Performance and scalability Due to the highly distributed nature of IoT, it is difficult to not only evaluate the performance (quality property) of an IoT system but also to build systems that are highly scalable (quality property).

Trust, security, and privacy The security features that are enabled in an IoT system dictate the quality of the security that it provides, which in turn form the prerequisites for trust and privacy. These are very challenging to obtain, as they are dependent on the various performance aspects of the IoT system such as computation and communication on low-power constrained devices.

Availability and resilience These qualitative properties refer to the availability of an IoT system as anticipated by the stakeholder, that is, a specified up time. Since IoT systems can be huge, maintaining such availability is challenging. Even after an unscheduled down time, the stakeholder can expect the system to quickly recover from the failure and return to normal operation thus showing the property of resiliency.

14.6 INTEROPERABILITY USING SYNTACTIC AND SEMANTIC APPROACHES

To ensure interoperability in the IoT ecosystem, there is a need to standardize the way data and information is exchanged between various IoT systems in an unambiguous way. Syntactic interoperability is possible by using pre-agreed terminology and structure by all the systems that are involved, which enable IoT applications to automatically parse it. Further, understanding the meaning (semantic) of the vocabulary (or common terms) used in various IoT domains allows IoT systems to exchange information in a more meaningful way, enabling the context to be understood, thus making it easier to discover and access relevant information from diverse IoT systems.

14.6.1 Interoperability at Various Layers of IoT

IoT systems are highly heterogeneous in nature with a variety of terminologies and technologies used at the various layers of the IoT stack. Standards at these layers ensure that IoT systems do not remain in silos but have the capability to connect with each other when required and seamlessly exchange information.

14.6.1.1 Device Layer

As shown in Fig. 14.11, the various protocols that are available at the device level and connectivity level (link, network, and transport layers) need to be compatible with each other so as to minimize hindrance in using them.

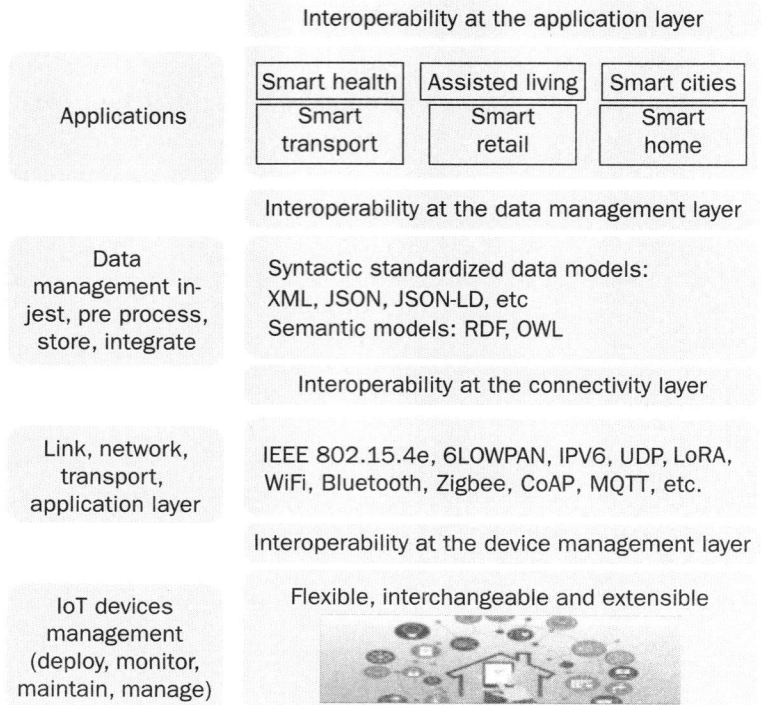

Fig. 14.11 Interoperability at Various Layers of IoT

The key to incorporate these characteristics is through standards. Several such efforts for standardization are already ongoing; please refer to Fig. 1.12 (Chapter 1) showing a number of standard protocols that are currently available for IoT at various layers such as datalink, network, and session. More comprehensive discussion on these aspects is presented in Chapter 4. Despite the various efforts for standardization, the problem of interoperability still persists due to the incompatibility of the standards. As a large number of these standards are emerging, further harmonization of these is becoming challenging. In addition, many products (devices, platforms) from commercial entities are emerging in the market with their own version of protocols, communication technologies, and data models, which is further making it more challenging to integrate them in both within the same as well as cross-domain applications.

14.6.1.2 Network Layer

The network stack includes several standardized protocols such as IEEE 802.15.4e, 6LOWPAN, IPV6, UDP, LoRA, Wi-fi, bluetooth, Zigbee, Constrained Application Protocol (CoAP), MQTT at various layers such as Medium Access Control (MAC) layer, network layer, and session layer. Considering the large variety of these protocols that are available and more being added frequently, there arises an interoperability challenge if IoT systems are developed with heterogeneous protocols.

14.6.1.3 Data Management Layer

The data management layer facilitates and manages the communication between the real-world-sensed activities and the application layer. The approaches for integrating various IoT platforms and applications at this layer are based on syntactic and semantic approaches. These are further described in Sections 14.6.2 and 14.6.3.

14.6.1.4 Application Services Layer

The application layer consists of applications through which the user interacts with the IoT devices via the Internet using most commonly a mobile app, web app, etc. The interoperability issues could arise as one application may be specifically configured to use a particular protocol (e.g., MQTT) to interact with a particular device, but when it may need to access other remote IoT devices configured with another type of protocol such as CoAP, the application will not be able to interact with these devices.

Thus, there is a requirement of middleware that will support multiple protocols and able to translate between each other (see Chapter 7 for more details). Further, the heterogeneity of applications at this layer with each of them specifically developed for a certain domain of interest makes them monolithic and locked-in with a particular vendor and non-interoperable. For example, the data from a smart health app may not work with an assisted living app used by elderly; each one works on its own and application interoperability is rarely supported.

14.6.2 Syntactic Interoperability Approaches

Web services based on service oriented architecture (SOA) are a popular way to ensure syntactic interoperability. They are either based on the simple object access protocol (SOAP) or representational state transfer (REST) based web services. In both of these web services, a pre-agreed set of vocabulary is used to ensure that different systems using them are interoperable. The standardization happens in the form of XML schemas that have a set of XML elements and their structuring in the schema document.

In the IoT domain, an example of syntactical interoperability standard is the recently introduced networking protocol 6LoWPAN that can be used for connecting low-power wireless embedded devices. It is able to interoperate with traditional computing infrastructure (devices on any other IP network link). At the application level, it uses the well-known and used data models and services based on HTTP, XML, SOAP, and REST. Another example is CoAP that allows IoT devices to communicate and publish data on the Web. It is similar to HTTP for low-powered devices and enables REST services at the sensor level; hence, IoT systems implementing CoAP are syntactically interoperable. Similarly, other syntactic open standards are WirelessHART, Z-Wave, etc.

The Sensor Web Enablement (SWE) framework developed by the Open Geospatial Consortium (OGC) consists of a set of standard web service interfaces for seamless access and sharing sensor data.

The OGC SensorThings API is a specifically designed framework for IoT and lightweight as compared to SWE. It provides an open, geospatial-enabled, and unified way to interconnect the IoT devices, data, and applications over the Web. The standard has been developed specifically for low-powered internet connected devices.

The silos nature of the IoT platforms is addressed by the Web of Things (WoT) technology, which is now being actively developed by the World Wide Web consortium (W3C) through a working group.

14.6.2.1 Web of Things (WoT)

According to W3C, 'WoT is intended to enable interoperability across IoT platforms and application domains. Primarily, it provides mechanisms to formally describe IoT interfaces to allow IoT devices and services to communicate with each other, independent of their underlying implementation, and across multiple networking protocols. Secondarily, it provides a standardized way to define and program IoT behavior.'

While the IoT is concerned about connecting things to the Internet, WoT connects things and applications to the internet by using RESTful interfaces. Its primary focus is to reduce the silo architecture (see Fig. 14.1) and increase the interoperability between the IoT platforms. It further reduces the conflicts arising from multiple standards and provides an easy way to discover relevant devices for a particular need. Some of the emerging WoT platforms include ThingWorx, Socrades, EvryThng, SpitFire Open.Sen.se, WoTKit, and Xively.

14.6.3 Semantic Interoperability Approaches

Semantic interoperability of IoT systems implies the ability to exchange data between them in an unambiguous manner. The interoperability is achieved by sharing common vocabularies or shared representation of a domain.

14.6.3.1 Semantic Technologies

There are various semantic technologies that are widely used for semantic interoperability. These are based on semantic web concepts. The semantic web is an extension of the current Web in which data in web pages is structured and tagged in such a way that it can be read directly by computers. Various semantic technologies include Resource Description Framework (RDF) and RDF Schema, JSON-LD, Web Ontology Language (OWL), Description Logics, and SPARQL Query Language.

14.6.3.2 Semantic Data Integration

As shown in Fig. 14.12, an ontology (see Section 14.6.3.1 for more details), which is a shared representation of concepts/vocabulary of a domain is used to represent the data model. The integration of two different IoT data models is achieved by mapping the corresponding concepts called semantic mapping.

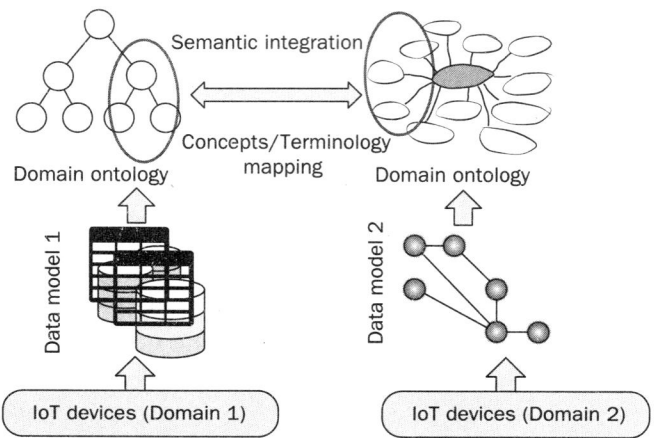

Fig. 14.12 Integration of Two Different IoT Data Models Using Ontologies to Achieve Semantic Interoperability

Semantic Sensor Network (SSN) and Sensor, Observation, Sample, and Actuator (SOSA) ontologies According to W3C, SSN and SOSA ontologies 'provide flexible but coherent perspectives for representing the entities, relations, and activities involved in sensing, sampling, and actuation.' Using the SSN ontology, an example of how to represent air temperature is described further.

An Automated Weather Station (AWS) can measure the temperature and call it 'air temperature,' similarly an air-quality monitoring station can also measure temperature and call it 'ambient temperature.' Unless we map manually, i.e. *air temperature* is equivalent to *ambient temperature*, it will be difficult for the computer to automatically do this mapping. Instead, we can represent *Air Temperature* as shown in Fig. 14.13.

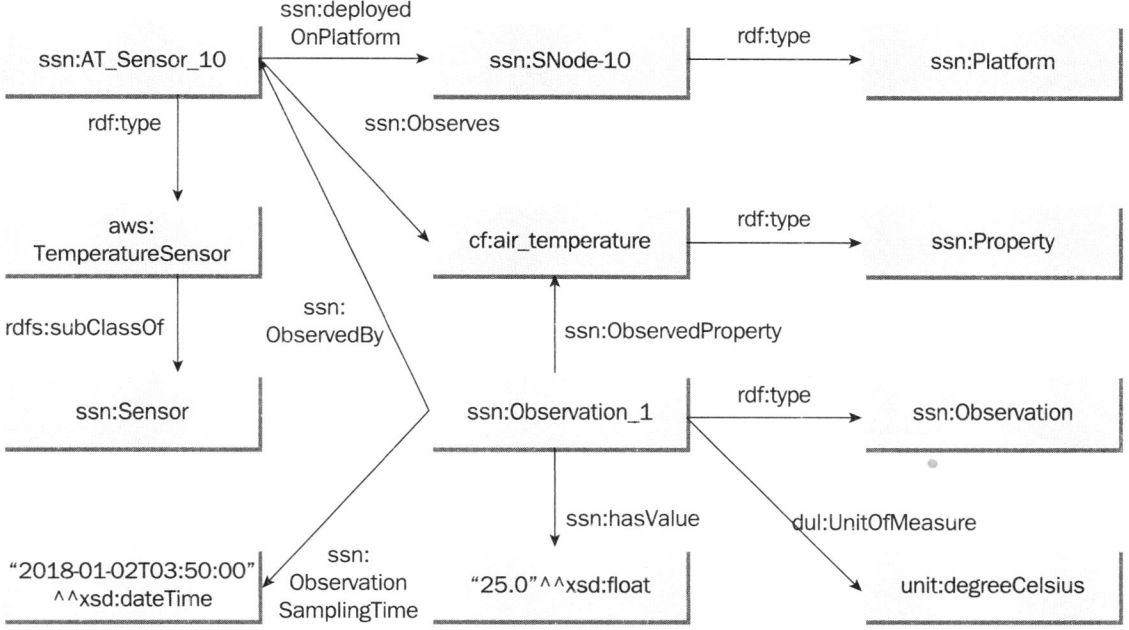

Fig. 14.13 Ontological Representation of the Concept Called Air Temperature in Terms of Class/Subclass, Object Property, and Data-type Property and their Relationships

The concept *air temperature* is an object property *Observes* of the class *Sensor_AT_1*, which is a subconcept of the class *TemperatureSensor* and which in turn is a subconcept of *Sensor*. The concept *Sensor* is represented in a different ontology called SSN as shown in Fig. 14.14. The SSN ontology describes sensors and observations, and related concepts. In SSN, an *observation* (called as an object property, here the object is the sensing device) is made by a *sensing device*. Further, the *sensing device* has *location*, measures a set measurement property called *ObservedProperty* and given in a *UnitofMeasure*. All are represented as Uniform Resource Indicator (URIs); hence users can find detailed explanations of the concepts involved.

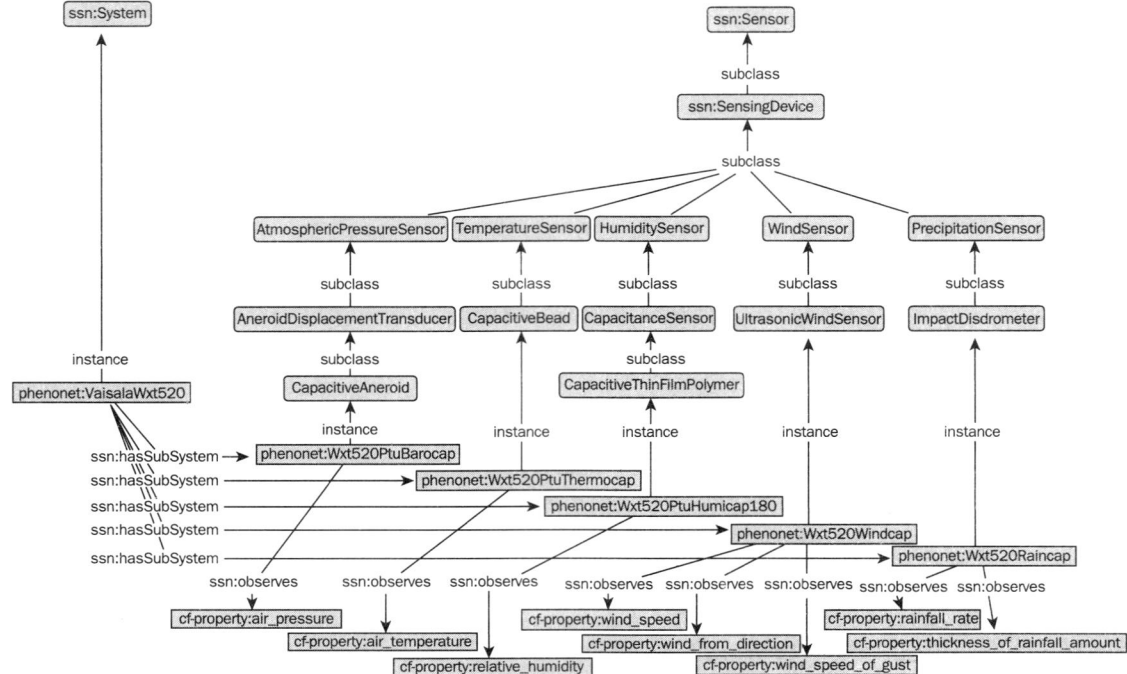

Fig. 14.14 An Example of Representing an Automated Weather Station Using SSN Ontology

(Source credit: Copyright © [1-February-2015] World Wide Web Consortium, (MIT, ERCIM, Keio, Beihang). http://www.w3.org/Consortium/Legal/2015/doc-license)

Based on this type of representation of the IoT data models in standardized and shared representation such as the SSN ontology, it is possible to easily integrate diverse IoT data models and hence achieve semantic interoperability (see Fig. 14.15).

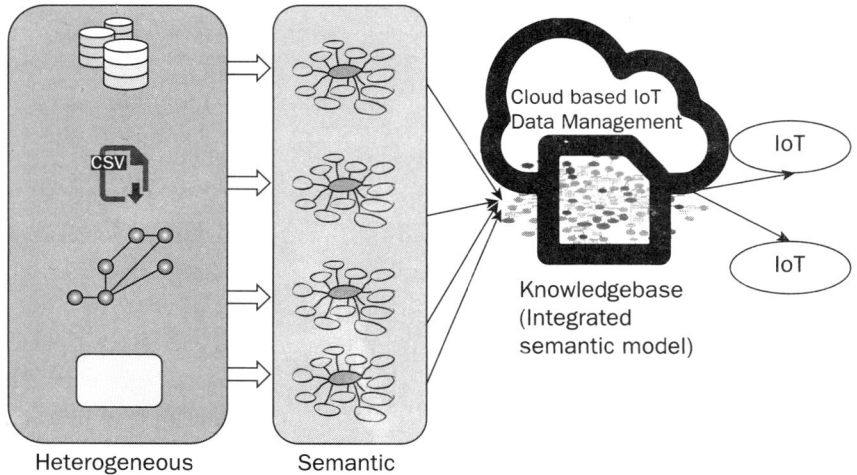

Fig. 14.15 Semantic Data Integration Applied at the Cloud Level to Harmonize Various Data Models to Enable Seamless Access to Multiple IoT Data Sources, which are in Different Data Models

SUMMARY

This chapter described the fundamental aspects for building IoT systems. It highlighted the need for a reference model that abstracts the significant relationships among the entities of some environment and is independent of specific standards, technologies, or implementations. It enables deriving very specific reference or concrete architectures using consistent standards or specifications that are valid in that environment. This concept is applied for IoT systems and the result is the development of an ARM focusing on the immutable components of IoT domain, that is, those aspects that remain constant. The various submodels of IoT-A were described along with their instantiations of real-world scenarios to help understand how an IoT reference model is actually useful. A related reference model from the International Telecommunication Union (ITU-T) is also described to gain a different perspective of the reference model. The IoT-A reference architecture can be used for the development of robust IoT systems, as it provides high-level views that provides various angles of the reference architecture.

Further, various types of IoT interoperability is described and in particular focused on the interoperability at the data and application layers of the IoT stack. The interoperability at these layers is explained in terms of syntactic- and semantic-based techniques. The recent emergence of WoT which is enabling interoperability by connecting things and applications to the Internet using emerging syntactic methods. The role of W3C in developing and promoting standards related to sensor networks and IoT is also presented with some examples.

REVIEW QUESTIONS

1. Explain the need for an IoT reference model.
2. What is an architecture reference model?
3. Describe the basic components of IoT-A reference model.
4. How do the various submodels of the IoT-reference model interact? Explain with an interaction diagram.
5. Explain in the domain model of IoT-A reference model.
6. How can the domain model be instantiated? Describe with a real-world example.
7. What is an augmented entity? Given an example.
8. Differentiate between physical entity and virtual entity.
9. Define functional model.
10. Explain the seven functional groups of the functional model with a block diagram.
11. How is the virtual entity and IoT service abstracted in the functional model. Give an example.
12. What is the need for an IoT information model?
13. Given an example of a real-world IoT information model. Show the interactions in an interaction diagram.
14. Explain the various layers of the ITU-T reference model.
15. Define reference architecture.
16. What is the need for reference architecture?
17. Give a simplified high-level outline of IoT architecture.
18. What are the main components of IoT-A reference architecture?
19. What is the purpose of architectural views and perspectives?
20. Explain IoT-A architecture views.
21. What is the role of perspectives in the IoT-A reference architecture?
22. Why is interoperability important in IoT?
23. Explain interoperability at different layers of IoT.
24. Explain different types of interoperability.
25. Explain syntactic interoperability with an example.
26. Describe Web of Things? Does it help in IoT interoperability?
27. What is semantic interoperability? Why do we need it?

REFERENCES

1. Bassi, A., Bauer, M., Fiedler, M., Kramp, T., Kranenburg, R. V., Lange, S., Meissner, S. (2013), *Enabling Things to Talk, Designing IoT Solutions with the IoT Architectural Reference Model*, Springer, Berlin, Heidelberg.
2. Bauer M., Walewski, J. W. (2013), In: Bassi, A. et al. (eds.), *Enabling Things to Talk, The IoT Architectural Reference Model as Enabler*. Springer, Berlin, Heidelberg.
3. Fremantle, P. (2015), a Reference Architecture for the Internet of Things, WSO2. [online] https://wso2.com/wso2_resources/wso2_whitepaper_a-reference-architecture-for-the-internet-of-things.pdf
4. Weyrich, M, Ebert, C. (2016), Reference Architectures for the Internet of Things, IEEE computer society, OASIS [Available online]: http://docs.oasis-open.org/soa-rm/soa-ra/v1.0/soa-rapr-01.pdf
5. Carrez, F., Elsaleh, T., Gomez, D., Sánchez, L., Lanza, J., Grace, P. (2017), A Reference Architecture for Federating IoT Infrastructures Supporting Semantic Interoperability, *European Conference on Networks and Communications (EuCNC)*.
6. Gruber, T. R. (1995), Toward principles for the design of ontologies used for knowledge sharing, *International Journal Human-Computer Studies*, 43(5-6): 907-928.
7. Kafle, V. P., Fukushima, Y., Harai, H. (2016). Internet of Things standardization in ITU and prospective networking technologies, IEEE Communications Magazine.
8. IoT-A FP7 Project (2012) Terminology – IOT-A: internet of things architecture, http://www.iot-a.eu/public/terminology
9. IoT-A FP7 Project (2013) Requirements – IoT-A: internet of things architecture, http://www.iot-a.eu/public/requirements
10. ITU-T Y.2060, Series Y: Global Information Infrastructure, Internet Protocol Aspects and Next-generation Networks. Next generation networks – Frameworks and functional architecture models.
11. Rozanski, N. (2013), The context viewpoint, http://www.viewpoints-and-perspectives.info/home/viewpoints/context/
12. Rozanski, N., Wodds, E. (2005), *Applying Viewpoints and Views to Software Architecture* [online] http://www.viewpoints-and-perspectives.info/vpandp/wp-content/themes/secondedition/doc/VPandV_WhitePaper.pdf.
13. Rozanski, N., Woods, E. (2011), *Software Systems Architecture: Working with Stakeholders using Viewpoints and Perspectives*. Addison Wesley, Boston.
14. Stravoskoufos, K., Sotiriadis, S., Petrakis, E. G. M. (2016), IoT-A and FIWARE: Bridging the barriers between the cloud and IoT systems design and implementation, *6th International Conference on Cloud Computing and Services Science*, CLOSER, DOI: 10.5220/0005912001460153.
15. SOA-RM: http://docs.oasis-open.org/soa-rm/v1.0/soa-rm.pdf [last accessed: 05/04/2019].
16. Web of Things (WoT): https://www.w3.org/TR/wot-architecture/[last accessed: 05/04/2019].
17. Guinard, D., Trifa, V., Wilde, E. (2010), A resource oriented architecture for the Web of Things. *2010 IoT*, pp. 1–8.
18. Semantic Sensor Network (SSN): https://www.w3.org/2005/Incubator/ssn/wiki/Report_Work_on_the_SSN_ontology [last accessed: 05/04/2019].
19. SSN Ontology: https://www.w3.org/2005/Incubator/ssn/ssnx/ssn [last accessed: 05/04/2019]. Gao, L., Bruenig, M., Hunter, J. (2014), Estimating fire weather indices via semantic reasoning over wireless sensor network data streams, *International Journal of Web & Semantic Technology (IJWesT)*, 5(4).
20. SSN and SOSA: https://www.w3.org/TR/2017/REC-vocab-ssn-20171019/ [last accessed: 05/04/2019].

21. IEEE (1991), IEEE Standard Computer Dictionary: A Compilation of IEEE Standard Computer Glossaries, IEEE Std 610, pp. 1–217.
22. Xiao, G., Guo, J., Xu, L. D., Gong, Z. (2014), User interoperability with heterogeneous IoT devices through transformation, *IEEE Transactions on Industrial Informatics*, 10(2).
23. Kiljander, J., D'elia, A., Morandi, F., Hyttinen, P., Takalo-Mattila, J., Ylisaukko-Oja, A., Soininen, J. P., Cinotti, T. S. (2014), Semantic interoperability architecture for pervasive computing and internet of things. *IEEE Access*, 2: 856–873. doi:10.1109/ACCESS.2014.2347992.
24. Conference Proceedings, 2003. [22] S. Haller, "The things in the internet of things," Poster at the (IoT 2010). Tokyo, Japan, November, vol. 5, 2010.

FURTHER READING

1. Noura, M., Atiquzzaman, M. & Gaedke, M. Interoperability in Internet of Things: Taxonomies and Open Challenges. Mobile Netw Appl 24, 796–809 (2019). https://doi.org/10.1007/s11036-018-1089-9
2. https://iot-epi.eu/wp-content/uploads/2018/07/Advancing-IoT-Platform-Interoperability-2018-IoT-EPI.pdf
3. eWoT: A Semantic Interoperability Approach for Heterogeneous IoT Ecosystems Based on the Web of Things (https://www.mdpi.com/1424-8220/20/3/822/htm)
4. Semantic Interoperability in IoT: Extending the Web of Things Architecture. https://research.aalto.fi/en/journals/acm-transactions-on-internet-of-things(513500d3-67c0-466b-b1f9-a962c7619897)/publications.html

CyberSecurity and Privacy

CHAPTER 15

"The good we secure for ourselves is precarious and uncertain, until it is secured for all of us and incorporated into our common life."

— Jane Addams

OBJECTIVES
- understand the introduction to IoT security challenges and security issues, privacy preservation, and security architecture in the various layers of IoT stack
- gain knowledge of various types of attacks on IoT devices pertaining to different layers, which affect the confidentiality, integrity, and availability (CIA) aims of IoT security
- understand different control methods to avoid security threats
- explore selected IoT case studies focussing on the security aspects and best practices for developing IoT systems

OUTCOMES
- assess security issues for a given IoT system application
- design IoT system with security controls for protecting CIA principles
- apply lightweight elliptic-curve cryptography (ECC) for data confidentiality and integrity in the IoT system application
- use best practices for IoT system security

REVISION

To increase your understanding of the material in this chapter, you can spend a few minutes reviewing key concepts in the following chapters:

Chapter 3: Concept and characteristics of sensors
Chapter 6: Open Hardware
Chapter 5: Understand the general framework for IoT platforms
Chapter 6: Understand the low-power IPv6 stack and related protocols
Chapter 7: Review the section on WSN communication patterns

15.1 INTRODUCTION

Internet of Things (IoT) technology is opening opportunities in various application domains. Billions of smart things will be connected in near future for data sharing, data analysis, and information retrieval. A huge amount of data will be generated and shared by different IoT devices, containing private and sensitive information. Hence, data privacy and security has prime importance in an IoT system. An IoT can be a physical thing, or software, or any virtual object that has the ability to communicate with the outside world through the Internet to provide a smart service. In addition to data security, to develop a reliable application suitable for any business process, which is protected from all kinds of threats (e.g., interruption, interception, modification, and fabrication), it is necessary to implement hardware, software, and network security at different network communication layers. The major cause of the ever-growing security risks to IoT devices is due to the diversity of new IoT applications that are being developed in a variety of domains.

Three main classes of IoT systems are as follows:

Customer friendly These devices are sold to customer. Any special expertise is not needed to avail the service from these devices. For example: IoT based Smart Bulb, Smart cooking appliances, etc.

Always live These devices are connected to the Internet permanently and are always on. Example: Surveillance devices.

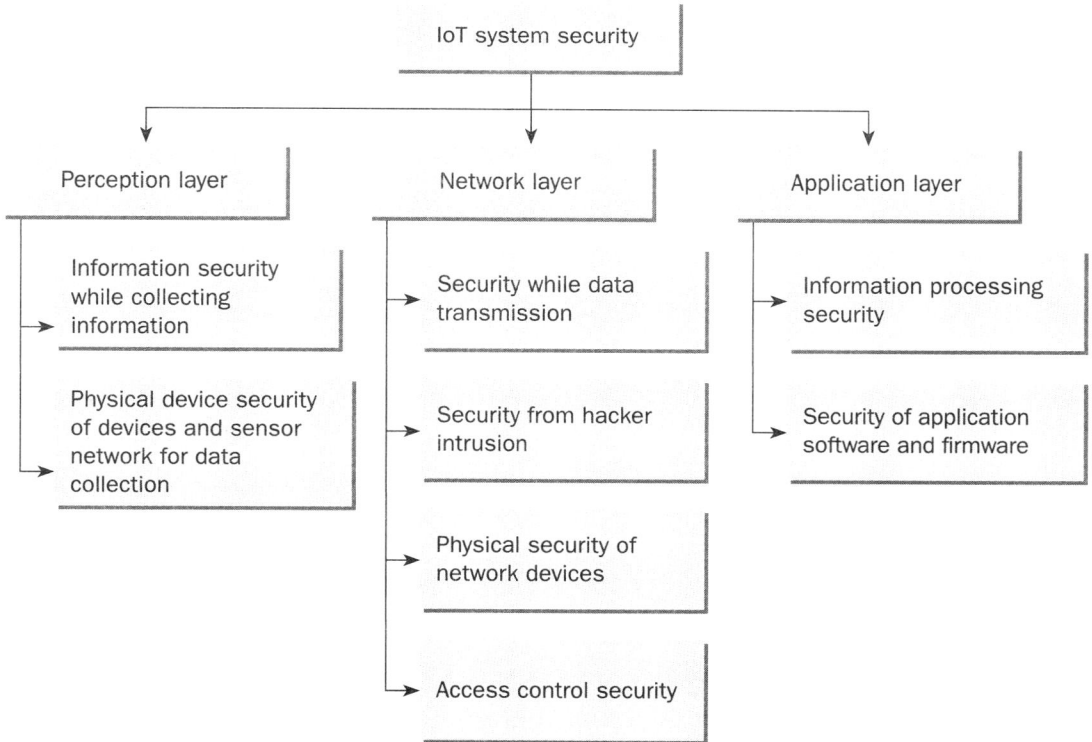

Fig. 15.1 IoT System Security Architecture

Devices interacting with the physical environment These devices have the capability to measure various phenomenon on Earth using specialized sensors to run models and make predictive analysis. For example: IoT-based weather station, water level monitoring stations, etc.

Each of the above class of IoT systems has different types of security requirements. While considering security measures for these IoT devices, there is a need to incorporate best practices so that the threats can be minimized. There are unique security challenges for IoT devices specifically as their characteristics deviate from normal devices. Figure 15.1 depicts the high level architecture for IoT system security in three different layers such as Perception layer, Network layer, and Application layer.

15.1.1 IoT Security Challenges

Device size and processing power IoT devices are small in size with limited CPU power for providing efficient security enforcing computations. As these devices have limited processing power, it is necessary to design lightweight encryption techniques.

Power consumption In general, various sensors in IoT system need to measure an environmental phenomenon with a certain temporal frequency, specific to the application, which can consume power constantly.

Hence, another challenge is to provide uninterruptible power supply for considerably long duration to keep the sensors working to enable continuous measurements, and at the same time ensure that malicious attacks do not artificially increase the power consumption.

Access control Development of key exchange management and identity management for providing authorized access control for securing confidentiality for a variety of IoT devices is challenging. Unless this is accomplished in a robust way, various IoT applications based on these devices are very vulnerable for attacks.

Edge security Endpoint device security is another challenge for securing various new IoT devices such as new firmware, new embedded software, and OS.

Exploding network traffic As a large number of IoT devices are expected to be connected through the Internet in the next few years, issues related to huge network traffic are required to be addressed. As network security is complex, increased network traffic will make it more complex while solving traffic issues and the traffic analysis will become a challenging task.

Based on the aforementioned text (see also Fig. 15.2), it is also important to understand the security aspects from a domain perspective. It will enable to clearly highlight the various issues in a particular domain and the remedial measures that are required to address them.

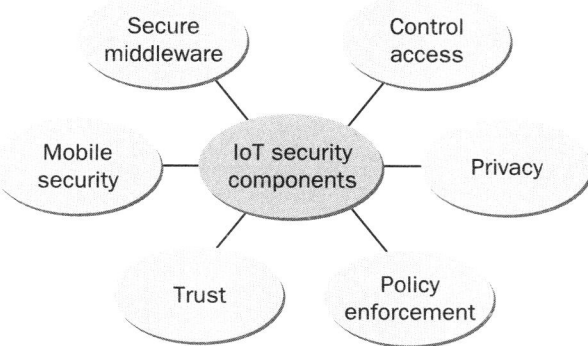

Fig. 15.2 Security Components in IoT Systems

15.1.2 IoT System Security Domains

IoT system security is required in the following security domains:

Information security Implemented by end-to-end encryption, secure network protocols, network access control to authentic users.

Physical security Enabled by providing proper casing of the hardware, controlling physical device access to legitimate users, etc.

Information technology security Ensuring authentic softwares with proper certification of authenticity with less vulnerability to avoid attacks.

Operational security Enforced through the development of secured software with layered security to avoid backdoors.

It is envisaged that an IoT system will combine all these domains; hence, an integrated approach is necessary to detect the issues and provide countermeasures. In addition, as IoT systems are going to massively invade the private space both of an individual and organizations; there is a lot of interest in developing ways to handle privacy issues. For example, intruders gaining access to homes through IoT-enabled home security systems, baby monitors, accessing healthcare-related information through smart medical devices, intruding into industrial process that are managed by IoT-enabled devices, etc.

15.2 SECURITY ISSUES IN IOT SYSTEMS AND PRIVACY PRESERVATION

Privacy is a very sensitive issue while providing IoT services. Through IoT devices, which generate large amount of data, users are gaining access to many personalized services and data. Few examples of IoT services are energy consumption control, smart parking, remote-monitoring of patients, production chain, and inventory management. In all these services, users need protection of their personal data related to their movement, habits, and interaction with other people. Figure 15.3 shows the various

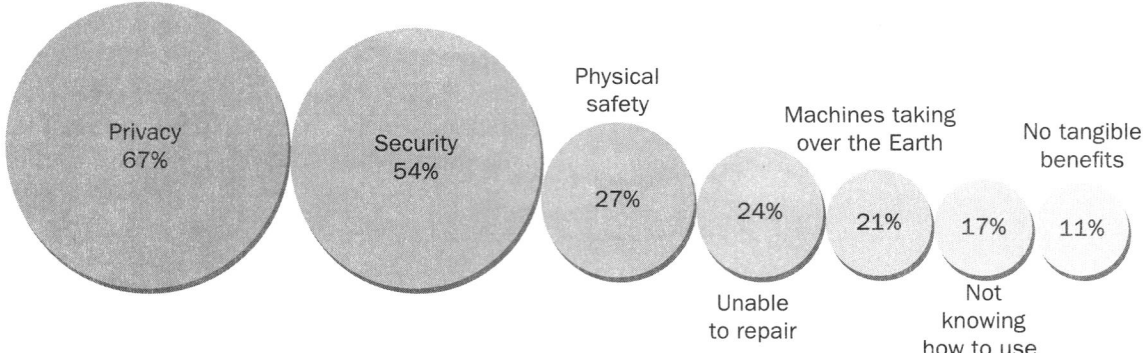

Fig. 15.3 Various Concerns While Adapting IoT Services

(Source credit: Ericsson White papers, 2017)

concerns that users of IoT-based applications face. It is clear that privacy is of utmost concern and needs to be incorporated in most of the IoT services.

Further, the wide usage or adaption of an IoT service depends on how secure it is from various perspectives. To further understand these aspects, it is pertinent to look at the three-layered IoT architecture and the detailed functionality of each of its components. Box 15.1 explains the RFID technology.

BOX 15.1: RFID TECHNOLOGY

Radio Frequency Identification (RFID) technology is used in information tags for automatic communication with each other. In a RFID tag an antenna is embedded in a microchip. The RFID tag also consists of a memory chip which embeds a unique identifier known as Electronic Device Code (EDC).

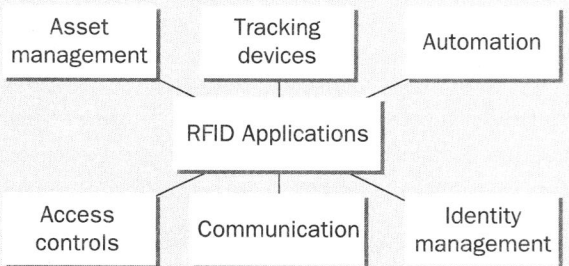

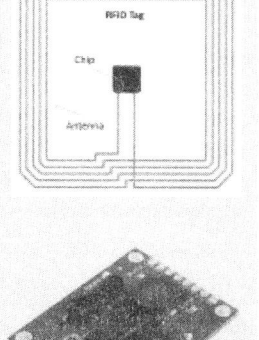

Different types of RFID tags are:

Active tag These types of tags have in-built battery for sensing the information from a limited distance.

Passive tag In this type of tag the information is read from this tag by activation of the tag by a transceiver from a specific distance. No internal battery is present in this type of tag.

Radio transceiver (RFID reader) RFID reader interacts with RFID tags to read the information by using unique identifier of the tag under scan using its Electronic Product Code (EPC) as shown below. The products with EPC can capture unique identifiers at very high rates using radio frequencies, without the need for line of sight. A distance of 10 meters is usually preferable.

Header	EPC manager number	Object class	Serial no.

15.2.1 Three-layer IoT Architecture and Security Issues in Each Layer

IoT system architecture has three main layers, which are as follows:

- Perception layer
- Network layer
- Application layer

15.2.1.1 Perception Layer

Main functionality of the perception layer in the IoT system is collection of information using different devices such as Smart card, RFID tag, and other sensors in domains such as healthcare, transportation, retail, and industrial IoT. The main security issues in perception layer are terminal security, sensor network security by proper authentication and access control mechanism to ensure confidentiality, and availability of IoT device services to the legitimate users. Figure 15.4 shows specific security issues that are related to the perception layer. Node capture, fake node and malicious data, denial of service attack, timing attack, routing threats, and replay attacks are some of the threats in this layer. More details of these threats are given in Section 15.3.

15.2.1.2 Network Layer

Various components of wireless and wired network components in the network layer of the IoT system need protection from threats due to different vulnerabilities present in the network components. Main functionality of the network layer of an IoT system is the transmission of data while preserving the confidentiality and integrity of the data. In the network layer, many vulnerabilities are present at the entry points and can be exploited by attackers such as eavesdropping, tampering the data by modification, insertion, or fabrication. Physical security of network layer devices, such as interfacing devices, is important to deliver uninterrupted service of IoT applications. By ensuring data encryption method suitable for IoT applications and access control to the networking devices, security goals can be achieved.

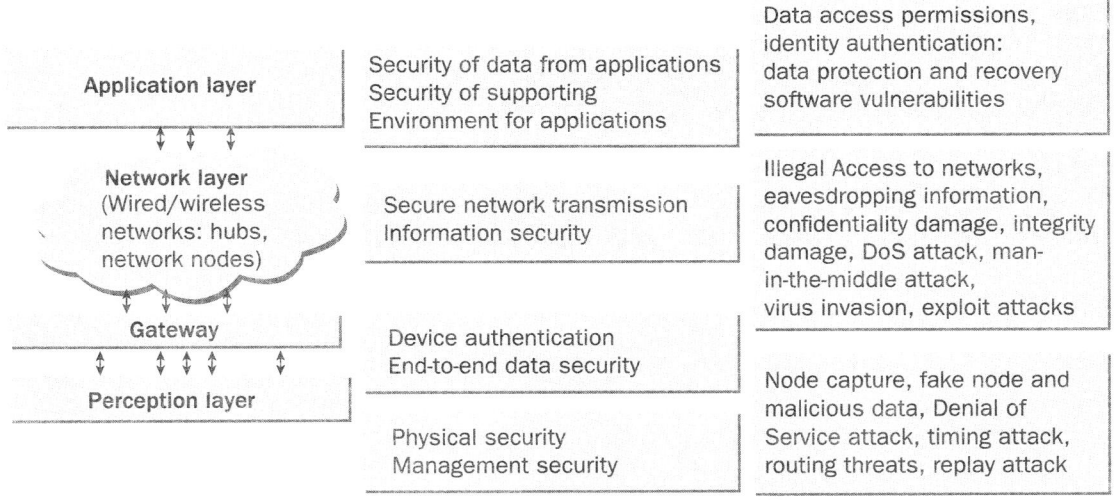

Fig. 15.4 Three-layer Architecture of IoT and Corresponding Security Aspects

15.2.1.3 Application Layer

The application layer, sometimes known as processing layer of the IoT system, has intelligent devices performing the data analysis task for information retrieval and for deriving inferences to support the decision making for further control. It provides a user interface for interacting with the IoT system. Intelligent computing technologies are used to process the information to control different objects and devices. These smart controls decide, what, when, and how to accomplish it. The main security goal that is to be achieved in this layer is privacy while processing and transmitting the data, which can be obtained by implementing end-to-end encryption.

15.3 IOT SECURITY REQUIREMENTS BASED ON CIA PRINCIPLES

IoT system security has to address basic security goals as defined by CIA (Confidentiality, Integrity, and Availability). It has to incorporate security parameters such as privacy and authentication that supports the security goals, confidentiality, and availability.

Confidentiality Any sensitive information should not be leaked to illegitimate users through the data reading devices. Confidentiality must be maintained while collecting, processing, transmitting, and storing the information.

Integrity While transferring the information from the IoT device to IoT application through various layers, ensuring the data security is necessary to focus on threats such as interruption, interception, modification, and fabrication so as to avoid leakage and tampering of the information, and also to ensure the availability of the data to the legitimate user.

Availability Availability and access to different kinds of IoT enabled smart devices to legitimate users is a primary goal in IoT security. Balancing is needed while achieving two goals, that is, confidentiality and availability. As while securing confidentiality, availability of services to legitimate users and objects, may get affected.

Section 15.3.1 describes various attacks that are possible on IoT systems.

15.3.1 Denial of Service (DoS) Attacks in Physical Layer

In this layer, the actual transmission and reception of the data is carried out with selection and generation of carrier frequency signals, modulation and demodulation, encryption, and decryption techniques. Various attacks that are possible in this context are as follows:

Jamming In this DoS attack, the intruder exhausts the bandwidth of the channel by creating fake traffic to prevent the nodes of WSN from communicating with each other.

Node tampering In this attack, the WSN node is tampered with by eavesdropping to steal and tamper some important information. Thus, the availability of correct information is affected.

Additional security goals are listed in Box 15.2.

> **BOX 15.2: ADDITIONAL SECURITY GOALS**
>
> In addition to the CIA-based security measures, IoT systems need four more such as:
>
> **Authenticity:** For preserving confidentiality, the information reading devices should receive information from legitimate users, and the processed information should reach to the authentic concerned person to preserve privacy of information and to ensure non-repudiation.
>
> **Reliability:** It refers to the ability to provide continuous service to the end user without interruption and on demand. In addition, service is trustworthy, precise, and meets the users' requirements.
>
> **Resilience:** The IoT system should be able to quickly recover from any attacks, accidents, and other kinds of incidents, adapt to continuously changing environmental conditions, resist perturbations, and get back to normalcy within a tolerance limit. An example is the recovery of a communication system after a disaster and it continues to operate on other modes albeit in a limited fashion.
>
> **Safety:** Absence of conditions that could cause physical damage to people and property. The IoT system should not pose any risk to the physical well-being of a person(s) who interact with it on a daily basis. A typical example of such an environment is Industrial IoT.

15.3.2 DoS Attacks in Link Layer

Various data streams are multiplexed in the Link layer of IoT system. The data frame detection and error control and medium access control functionalities are also provided by Link layer. Some of the attacks on Link layer are as follows:

Collision When two packets are transmitted on the same frequency, the collision of the packets happens due to sharing the transmission medium simultaneously and the data packets are corrupted due to the collision. Hence, retransmission of the data packets is required to remove the error.

Battery exhaustion When a DoS attack generates large amount of data traffic, the transmission channel is available only for a few devices in an IoT network; hence, large number of requests (request to send) are sent by many other devices for data transmission continuously, which ends up in exhausting the battery of some of the IoT devices.

15.3.3 DoS Attacks in Network Layer

While routing the packets in WSN, some specific attacks take place such as the following:

Spoofing Replaying and misdirection of the traffic is done in this attack by sending useless messages to exhaust the bandwidth of the channel to affect the network availability of a legitimate user.

Selective forwarding In this attack, the compromised node is used for forwarding the messages to only selected nodes to enable the intention of the attacker to perform the malicious activity (Fig. 15.5).

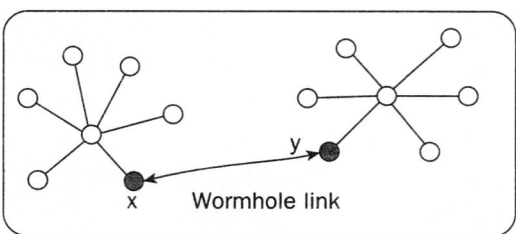

Fig. 15.6 Wormhole Attack

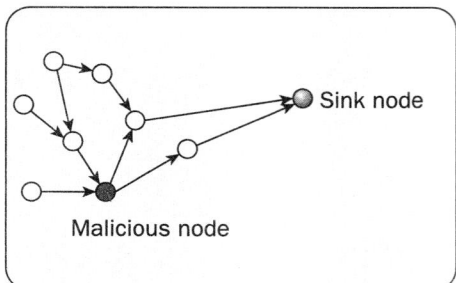

Fig. 15.5 Malicious Node in the IoT Network Performs Selective Forwarding to Divert the Traffic for Some Attack

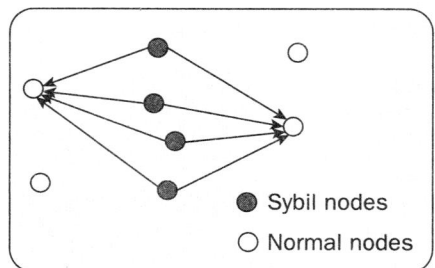

Fig. 15.7 Malicious Node with Multiple Identities

Homing In this attack, search is done in the traffic to find out nodes, which do key management and search cluster heads for taking control for malicious activities.

Wormhole In this attack (Fig. 15.6), through tunnelling of bits of data on a low latency link, a relocation of the data packet is carried out by changing the data position on the network.

Sybil An attacker replicates a single node with multiple identities to other nodes in the Sybil attack (Fig. 15.7).

Acknowledgement flooding In this attack, intruder spoofs the wrong acknowledgment to the sensor network node.

15.3.4 DoS Attacks in Transport Layer

Transport layer of WSN due to its architecture avoids congestion by reducing traffic and provides reliable transmission. The attacks on this layer are as follows.

Desynchronizing In this attack, fake messages are generated at endpoint nodes asking for retransmission of message, though no error exists in the message. Such messages increase traffic and consume battery power at node to execute the additional frequent instructions for retransmission.

Flooding In this attack, traffic is generated by useless messages to create congestion for affecting availability of transmission facility to authentic user.

15.3.5 DoS Attacks in Application Layer

In application layer of IoT, while carrying out software services, this layer also provides traffic management service. Path-based DoS attacks are dominant in this layer by simulating the IoT sensor nodes for creating huge traffic towards the IoT gateway.

Some other DoS attacks are node subversion, node outage, node malfunction, false node, message corruption, neglect and greed, black holes, and interrogation.

15.4 SECURITY TECHNOLOGIES

For secure communication between IoT devices to avoid open inbound network ports, various network connectivity technologies are needed as shown in Table 15.1.

Table 15.1 IoT System Layers and its Specifications for Security Controls

IoT Layer	Components	Working of Layer	Security Issues	Security Parameters	Counter-measures
Perception layer	Smart card, RFID tag, sensors	Collection of information	Terminal security, sensor network security	Authentication, confidentiality	Certification and access control
Network layer	Wireless or wired network, computer, components	Transmission of information	Information transmission security	Integrity, availability, confidentiality	Hop-by-hop data encryption
Application layer	Intelligent devices	Analysis of information, control decision-making	Information processing	Safety of IoT, privacy	End-to-end encryption

15.4.1 Network Connectivity Technologies and IoT Device Security Issues

To take care of different security issues, a well-planned and designed security model is needed for implementing IoT systems. Internet connectivity is a primary requirement for IoT devices. Hence, best practices for IoT devices are discussed in this section, considering network security as primary concern.

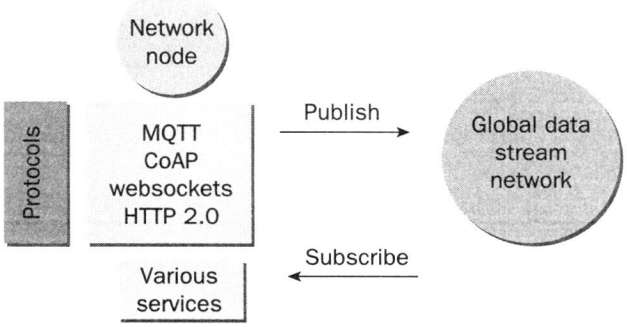

Fig. 15.8 Connectivity Technologies

Protocols for secure and reliable communication For secure and reliable communications protocols for low powered devices such as, MQTT, CoAP, Web Socket, and HTTP 2.0 facilitates Publish-Subscribe secure communication between IoT devices with no open ports (see Fig. 15.8). To cater to the needs of IoT scale, distributed high-performance servers replicated at multiple points are needed to handle data streams.

Table 15.2 lists various IETF standards designed specifically for low-powered devices such as those that are usually implemented in IoT systems.

Table 15.2 IETF Standards that are Useful in Implementing the IoT System

Standard	Purpose	URL
6LowPAN	IP connectivity	http://datatracker.ietf.org/wg/6lowpan/
ROLL	IP connectivity	http://datatracker.ietf.org/wg/roll/
CoAP	Generic web protocol definition	http://datatracker.ietf.org/wg/core/
CoRE	Lightweight REST web service architecture	http://datatracker.ietf.org/wg/core/

Further, various security aspects of these standards based protocols are compared in Table 15.3.

Table 15.3 Comparison of Security Aspects in Various Application Layer Protocols

Protocol	Security Goal	Purpose	Features	Application Area
Message Queue Telemetry Transport (MQTT)	Confidentiality, data integrity	Machine-to-machine communication	Small footprint and minimal bandwidth consumption	Mobile applications and useful for connection with remote location
Constrained Application Protocol CoAP	Confidentiality, data integrity	Multiplexing responses for sending parallel responses	Simple, low overhead and multicasting capability	Resource constraint, Internet devices such as wireless sensor node
Web socket	Integrity, confidentiality	Monitoring systems and for quick and/or constant updates	Bidirectional transactions	Secure financial transactions
HTTP 2.0	Data integrity, confidentiality, and availability	Data streaming protocol intended to speed up browser-side and server-side transactions	Bidirectional and full duplex messaging, compact transmissions and low overhead	Realtime bidirectional transactions
Low-Power Wireless Personal Area Networks (6LoWPAN)	Integrity, confidentiality	Low-power devices with limited processing capabilities	Low-power consumption	Home, office, factory

15.5 IOT SYSTEM SECURITY CONTROLS

CIA goals for data security in an IoT system are described in this section.

15.5.1 IoT Security for Data Access, Integrity, Availability, and Data Communication

15.5.1.1 Data Confidentiality

As in the sensor network, many hops of data through intermediate nodes take place. Hence, there is a high threat of data leakage. For securing the data while data transmission, data is encrypted and only recipient can decrypt the data.

15.5.1.2 Data Integrity

The data received by receiver should be in its original form without any alteration through modification or fabrication is called as data integrity. Intruders change the original data for some malicious purpose affecting data integrity.

Secure and reliable communication requirements

Strong encryption and secure protocols   In IoT systems, while transmitting the data over the network different encryption techniques are used to achieve data integrity. Various attacks on data integrity such as modification and fabrication can be avoided with strong encryption techniques.

End-to-end encryption   Transportation Layer Security (TLS) is an industry standard layer for communication to send encrypted data over wide area network (see Fig. 15.9). Added layer security is given with AES encryption to provide end-to-end encryption. TLS/SSL protects the data streaming at top level. Advanced Encryption Standard (AES) is used for data encryption. AES is paired with TLS for key management. The message body is encrypted with AES, while the envelope that holds the key (has to be used at midstream) is encrypted at the endpoint with TLS to provide true end-to-end encryption in IoT systems.

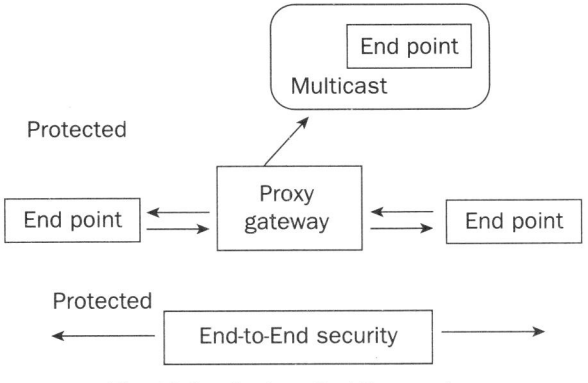

Fig. 15.9 End-to-End Encryption

Lightweight cryptography   It is challenging to implement cryptographic functions in a constrained computation environment. A lightweight cryptography algorithm is tailored to work in a constrained environment, which is useful for hardware devices, which are having limitations in RAM size, energy consumption, and chip size (e.g., RFID tags, different kinds of sensors, contactless smart card healthcare devices, etc.). Lightweight cryptography provides adequate security, though it is not always good to exploit the trade-off between security and efficiency.

Symmetric-key cryptography Broadly, there are two kinds of cryptographic systems— symmetric-key and public key cryptosystems. In symmetric-key schemes, the communicating entities first agree upon keying material that is both secret and authentic. Subsequently, they may use a symmetric-key encryption scheme such as the Data Encryption Standard (DES), RC4, and Advanced Encryption Standard (AES), etc. The major advantage of symmetric-key cryptography is its high efficiency; however, there are significant drawbacks to these systems. The major drawback is the key distribution problem, i.e. the need for a channel that is both secret and authenticated for the distribution of keying material.

Block cipher In AES, many block ciphers with lightweight properties such as CLEFIA and PRESENT are proposed. These ciphers are ready for practical use.

Stream cipher ECRYPT II eSTREAM project held from 2004 to 2008 selected a set of effective new stream ciphers.

Hash function NIST's new cryptographic hash algorithm 'SHA-3' is one of the popular hash algorithms as a general purpose hash algorithm, but most of its versions do not have lightweight properties. Research on lightweight dedicated hash functions based on lightweight block ciphers is an ongoing effort.

Public key cryptography For key management, lightweight public key cryptographic protocols are preferred in the IoT network system. The resources requirement for public key primitives is much larger than that of symmetric key primitives. There are no trustable primitives, which can meet the balance between security and efficiency; however, if the focus is on lightweight properties (as compared to RSA), some public key primitives (e.g., ECC) can be implemented with relatively small footprint.

15.5.2 Need for Lightweight Cryptography for IoT Systems

To achieve end-to-end security and secure and efficient end-to-end communication where end node-points perform processing, implementation of symmetric key algorithm can be done. However, for IoT devices with constraints on the resources, cryptographic solutions having less energy consumption is needed. In such applications, lightweight cryptographic algorithms are suitable.

Lightweight cryptographic solutions having smaller footprint when used for secure communication consume less bandwidth to provide optimum use of network resources for more IoT devices.

15.5.2.1 Elliptic Curve Cryptography (ECC)

Elliptical Curve Cryptography (ECC) is used as a lightweight cryptosystem. Certain criteria are needed to be considered, while choosing public key cryptosystem for specific applications, such as capability of the public key cryptosystem, security provided by the crypto system protocols and performance objectives of public key cryptosystem method to meet the required level of security (refer to Box 15.3).

> **BOX 15.3: ELLIPTIC CURVE KEY GENERATION**
>
> The equation of an elliptic curve is:
> $$y^2 = x^3 + ax + b$$
>
> - Let E be an Elliptic Curve defined for a finite field F.
> - If P is a point on this elliptic curve and if the prime order of point P is n then the cyclic subgroup of the elliptic curve over the finite field F generated by P is $|p| = \{\infty, P, 2P, 3P, \ldots, (n-1)P\}$.
> - The elliptic curve E, the point P and its order n, the prime p, are the parameters for the public domain.
> - A private key is an integer d and it is selected from the interval $[1, n-1]$ randomly and the corresponding public key is $Q = dP$.
> - Using elliptic curve discrete logarithm (ECDL), d is determined when the domain parameters and Q are given.
>
>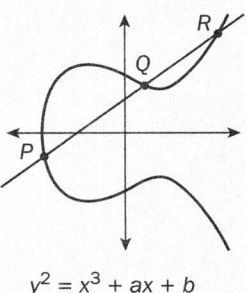
>
> Advantages of using ECC for IoT systems:
>
> - Achieving a certain level of security with shorter keys. Thus, making it a lightweight cryptosystem, which is useful for the IoT systems that are resource constrained to handle computational complexity.
> - Very few attacks are developed so far for ECC cryptosystems due to the unexplored mathematics of arithmetic operations to form Abelian groups to add points on the elliptical curve.

ECC is based on mapping plain text as points on an elliptic curve, which also adopts the idea of public key cryptosystem for key management as well as providing security in the process of key transmission and management.

15.5.2.2 Elliptical Curve Groups

Consider the example, where p is a prime number and let F_p be the field of integers modulo p. The elliptical curve $E(F_p)$ is defined by an equation of the form

$$y^2 = x^3 + ax + b \qquad 15.1$$

Where, $a, b \in F_p$ satisfy $4a^3 + 27b^2 \equiv 0 \pmod{p}$. A point $P(x, y)$, where $P(x,y) \in F_p$ is a point on the elliptical curve if $P(x, y)$ satisfies Equation 15.1.

Let us consider a field for prime number $p = 7$. Let $E(F_p)$ is the elliptical curve over field $F_p = F_7$. For example, let the elliptical curve has defining equation,

$$y^2 = x^3 + 2x + 4 \qquad 15.2$$

Then the points (as shown below) that are on the elliptical curve are:

$E(F_7) = \{\infty, (0, 2), (0, 5), (1, 0), (2, 3), (3, 3), (3, 4), (6, 1)\}$

Let $P(x, y) = P(0, 2)$

$x = 0$ and $y = 2$ satisfy the elliptical curve Equation 15.2.
$$x^3 + 2x + 4 \equiv 4 \bmod 7 = 4$$
$$y^2 \equiv 4 \bmod 7 = 4$$

Hence point $P(0, 2)$ is on the elliptical curve $E(F_7)$, and satisfies the Elliptical curve Equation 15.2.

15.5.2.3 Elliptic Curve Key Pair Generation

Elliptic curve encryption method Here a procedure for the elliptical curve encryption and decryption scheme is explained using the basic ElGamal encryption scheme. A plain text m is presented by a point M and this point is encrypted by adding it to kQ, where k is an integer selected randomly and Q is a public key for the recipient of the message. The sender transmits the encrypted ciphertext {C1, C2} where, C1 = kP. P is a point on the elliptical curve to be made public to the recipient for key generation and C1 = kP who decrypt the received ciphertext using the private key d, to compute $dC1 = d(kP) = k(dP) = kQ$ and then M is computed by the equation $M = C2 - kQ$. An eavesdropper who is listening to the transmission and wish to recover M must know kQ. The computation of kQ using the domain parameters Q and C1 = kP is the elliptical curve analogue of Diffie-Hellman key exchange algorithm.

Pseudocode

Input: Elliptic curve domain parameters (p, E, P, n)
Output: Public key Q and private key d generated from the public point P
    Select d ∈ R [1, n-1]
    Compute Q = dP
    Return(Q, d)

15.5.2.4 Basic ElGamal Elliptic Curve Encryption

The basic ElGamal is public-key cryptography which uses an asymmetric key encryption algorithm based on the Diffie–Hellman key exchange. ElGamal encryption consists of three steps namely the key generator, the encryption algorithm, and the decryption algorithm.

Pseudocode

Input: Elliptic Curve domain public key Q, plaintext m, and parameters (p, E, P, n)
Output: Cipher text (C1, C2).
Represent the message m as a point M in E(F).
    Select k ∈ R [1, n-1]
    Compute C1 = kP
    Compute C2 = M + kQ
    Return (C1, C2)

15.5.2.5 Basic ElGamal Elliptic Curve Decryption

Pseudocode

Input: Domain parameters (p, E, P, n), private key d, cipher text (C1, C2)
Output: Plaintext m
    Compute M = C2 - dC1, and extract m from M
    Return (m)

Solved Exercise

Exercise: If some plaintext m is representing a point $M(3, 3)$ on an Elliptical curve, $E(F_7)$, with equation, $y^2 = x^3 + 2x + 4$, then using Elliptical Curve Cryptographic method generate the public and private keys using public point $P(2, 3)$. Using these keys find the ciphertext, using ECC encryption algorithm. Apply ECC decryption algorithm to recover the point M. Given prime number p with prime order $n = 101$.

Solution
Elliptical curve key pair generation

Given: In the Elliptical curve $E(F_7)$, where, the prime number $p = 7$, Public key Q, private key d.
Given prime order $n = 101$
Primary key is an integer d randomly selected from the interval $[1, …, (n-1)]$
In this case, the range is $[1, 100]$ as $n = 101$
Let private key, $d = 99$
Public key $Q = dP$, where P is the point on the elliptical curve which is public and to be used for key generation.
Here P is $P(x, y) = P(2, 3)$ and elliptical curve is $E(Fp) = E(F_7)$
Public key $Q = (2d, 3d)$
$Q = (2 \times 99, 3 \times 99)$
$Q = (q_1, q_2) = (198, 297)$

ECC encryption

Given (p, P, d, Q)
$p = 7$, Message point: Plaintext point: $M(3, 3)$, $d = 99$, $Q(198, 297)$
Let $k = 10$, be a randomly chosen integer
$C_1 = kP = \{10 \times 2, 10 \times 3\} = \{20, 30\}$ // P is a public point
$C_2 = M + kQ$
$C_2 = \{3 + kq_1, 3 + kq_2\}$
$C_2 = \{3 + (10 \times 198), 3 + (10 \times 297)\}$
$C_2 = \{1983, 2973\}$

ECC decryption

Given $C_2 = \{1983, 2973]$, $d = 99$, $C_1 = \{20, 30\}$
$dC_1 = \{99 \times 20, 99 \times 30\}$
$dC_1 = \{1980, 2970\}$
$M = C_2 - dC_1$
$M = \{(1983 - 1980), (2973 - 2970)\}$
$M = (3, 3)$
Hence point M is decyphered from the encrypted cyphertext as $M(3, 3)$.

15.5.4 Token-based Access Control

Though AES and TLS/SSL are used for data encryption, even fine-grained access control, over what to be transmitted and to whom it should be sent is required and it is quite challenging to implement fine-grained access control.

Token can be distributed to devices for granting access in publish/subscribe structure. A fine-grained control on the access of data is achieved in this paradigm and centralized control can be established for revoking the access permissions of the devices. In this way, network security architecture gains capability to manage the devices speaking to and listening to specific devices, which have the required token for the access.

15.5.5 Device Status Monitoring

It is difficult to monitor online and offline status of the IoT devices of various applications. When a device stops sending and receiving data, the reason could be local tampering or it may be due to Internet or power outage.

A separate devoted channel is needed for sending the data streams to easily track the IoT metadata such as the online/offline status of the device in IoT systems. Such a dedicated channel is useful for sending an alert to the owner about the change in the lock status if the owner's phone is not in the decided range when the lock will be opened. If a sensor network goes offline, a maintenance person can be sent to the site immediately to take the appropriate action.

Real-time and highly reliable IoT applications will gain the confidence of both consumers as well as manufacturers. As per predictions, 50 billion new IoT devices will be there in next 5 years. Without the trust in the system devices, their adoption will be difficult.

15.5.6 User-friendly Set-up and Upgrades

For IoT devices to be up in the working state always, it is necessary to keep them updated by upgrading the software and the firmware of the devices.

Most of the times instead of receiving reliable service from the vendor for the IoT device, the customer is held responsible for failure of service due to some IoT device set up. For example, a Wi-Fi-enabled camera used as a part of the IoT system for house security is held responsible for blocking their home firewall or broadcasting the packets to the wrong port. Hence, a user-friendly set-up is an important factor for success of any IoT system.

15.5.7 Access Control for Availability

Fine-grained access control is an essential requirement for IoT devices. As in near future, billions of devices will be trying to listen from the assigned port, it is insecure and inefficient to filter out unwanted messages at the endpoint device for listening the correct one. Instead, the network should carry out the bulk of the task.

A token-based access control can be used under publish/subscribe paradigm. In this approach, the end IoT devices will be given access to certain ports based on the token distributed to them with specific grant permission for the data use. This fine-grained control will assign permissions to the end devices to access for listening and speaking to specific ports on the network.

15.5.8 IoT Security Controls for Middleware Platforms

In IoT paradigm, various heterogeneous technologies are present at different layers of the IoT system architecture. Several types of middleware layers are developed for providing integration and security to the devices. Different middleware platforms during communication, must respect the security of IoT devices. Hence, for communication between different middleware technologies, different communication mediums need to be considered in the design, development, and deployment of IoT systems.

15.6 OTHER SECURITY CONTROLS FOR IOT SYSTEMS

Few more security controls for IoT systems are discussed below.

15.6.1 Fault Tolerance

As billions of smart objects will be added through IoT systems to Internet, many vulnerabilities will be introduced which will help to perpetrate attacks. Hence, fault tolerance is extremely important to provide reliable IoT services. To achieve fault tolerance, cooperative efforts are needed. All objects must be made secure from different threats by default. Development of secure protocols and high-quality software is of prime importance, to reduce the software patch requirement to upgrade the software to remove bugs and loopholes.

IoT objects should be designed to provide capability to know network status and should be able to give feedback to the network and also should be able to defend themselves from network failures and attacks.

15.6.2 Privacy Preservation Methods

Privacy by design This is one way for providing privacy where design of the system is such that it incorporates certain tools, which facilitates the users to protect and manage their own data. Whenever user produces some data fragment, control access is given to outside world through some dynamic consent tools.

Data management It is very important who manages the data and how the secrecy and access control tools are deployed. It is not feasible for some systems to incorporate encryption and access control mechanism. In such scenarios, establishment of data management policy is mandatory.

Transparency Users must know which objects are managing their data, when and for what purpose that data is used. Hence, transparency is necessary. Stakeholders such as service providers should execute licence agreement for the data usage by considering duration and usage type for different functionalities.

15.6.3 Identity Management

Considering variety of identities and different relationships associated with those identities of various objects, in IoT system, identity management is required. According to object identity principles,

- An object can have a main identity and many other temporary identities
- An object identity can be different than the identity of the underlying mechanism
- An object can be identified using its identity or by using its specific feature
- Objects know the identity of the owner

Identity management in IoT offers both challenges and opportunities in practical use of security.

15.6.4 Trust and Governance

The term 'Trust' is used in different contexts with various connotations. Here, while mentioning trust in IoT devices, as most of the smart objects/devices are human-operated, malicious nodes try to attack basic functionality of IoT by trust-related attacks such as self-promoting, bad mouthing, good mouthing, and so on. For trust evaluation, various parameters that are judged are: honesty, cooperativeness, and community interest. These attributes are useful to develop trust management protocols to cope with the need of the changing environment and also to adapt to the changes in the trust parameters.

Trust management system for IoT has ability to assess truth level of a node from its behavioural patterns based on various cooperative services. Various trust models are suggested in the literature to develop trust management system for IoT. However, following issues related to trust management are yet to be explored for further advancement of trust management systems for IoT:

- Supporting semantic interoperability in IoT context, for introducing well-defined trust negotiation language
- Defining smart objects or devices management systems
- Developing models for trust negotiation mechanism for controlling data stream access

Governance helps in strengthening trust in the IoT system. A proper governance mechanism and a good framework can reduce liability. Yet, there are many challenges while implementing governance for IoT system.

> **THOUGHT EXERCISES**
>
> - Design a suitable IoT system security model for assuring best practices for automated transportation of goods.
> - Design the layer-wise security technologies using layer model of IoT system for healthcare monitoring.
> - Design an IoT-based network considering both the CIA principles of security and also IoT-specific security measures for air quality monitoring considering the parameters such as humidity, temperature, particulate matter, and ozone.

15.7 BEST PRACTICES FOR SECURING IOT DEVICES

Some best practices for securing IoT systems are listed as follows.

15.7.1 Tamper-resistant Hardware

The IoT devices should be kept in isolation and only designated persons should get the physical access of the IoT devices, especially for the devices, which are unattended continuously. This provides safety to such devices and makes them tamper resistant.

Physical endpoint security can be ensured by camera covers, small plastic devices, port locks to provide secure cover to webcams, USB, and Ethernet ports. Implementing strong boot password for hardware/software is one of the best practices for device security. TCP/UDP ports, places for code injections such as web servers, communications without encryption, open serial ports, and open password prompts are the open vulnerabilities susceptible for attacks very often. Such known vulnerabilities should be protected.

15.7.2 Firmware Updates/Patch Updates

Even after taking care of known vulnerabilities to provide security measures, some vulnerabilities still remain, which can be exploited by attackers. Hence, firmware-upgrading patches are needed to be developed from time to time to upgrade the firmware to remove the loop holes. This maintenance service enables the IoT systems to be more efficient and reliable.

At present, most of the IoT devices are not developed to support the patch updates by OTA (Over the Air). Hence, most of the IoT devices are vulnerable to attacks. There is a need by manufacturers and vendors to supply the information of potential risks, and details about patches and upgrades and information, related to policy and functionality in a transparent way to the user of the IoT system.

15.7.3 Dynamic Testing

For assigning minimum baseline security, testing of IoT system devices is essential. Static testing is not useful to find vulnerabilities in the off-the-shelves products. Dynamic testing is useful for finding vulnerabilities in the code as well as weakness in the hardware, which is not visible with static testing. For checking the hardware and software items, used in the IoT systems, manufacturers should perform dynamic testing.

15.7.4 Strong Authentication Technique Practices

Strong username and passwords credentials should be used by IoT devices for authentication purpose. Default credentials that are generally used by multiple devices are big threats as attackers may try these common credentials for unauthorized access. Unique username/password should be maintained by each IoT device and the password should follow the strong password rules so as to deter the attacker from guessing the password.

Even the IoT system is recommended for opting, two-factor authentication where one more level of security is provided by another authentication technique such as OTP code through SMS is employed.

For IoT applications, even adaptive authentication such as context-aware authentication (CAA) is advised in which a background machine-learning algorithm is constantly checking the contextual information, to avoid illegitimate use of IoT devices.

15.7.5 Use of Secure Protocols and Encryption

Though strong authentication is provided for access control through password, still IoT systems can be hacked. In the heterogeneous environment of the IoT systems, many protocols are used such as Zigbee, Z-Wave, 6LoWPAN, NFC, Wi-Fi, Cellular, Neul, Sigfox, and Bluetooth. Depending upon the kind of protocol and the device computation capability, the use of encryption technique is enforced before data transmission. Hence, strength of encrypted data to resist the attacker is doubtful.

15.7.6 Network Division into Segments

Division of a larger network into domain specific smaller networks using VLANs, IP address ranges, or a combination of them should be promoted. Such division of the network creates different security zones with different security policies for each zone. This can be established based on the kind of application, information, and threat level, resulting in preventing internal and external unauthorized access.

15.7.7 Sensitive Information Protection

IoT smart devices provide services that are discoverable by other devices. In addition, most of the protocols leak personally identifiable information (PII). This information can be used by other information sources for targeting some attacks.

15.7.8 Encouraging Ethical Hacking and Discouraging Safe Harbour for Unethical Practices

Legislation should be useful for promoting safe IoT ecosystems for everyone. The offenders should be punished by the law, and strongly discourage safe harbours for harmful activities. Provisions in legislation should be made for ethical hacking. Some check and bounds for manufacturers should be in place, which will deter manufacturing of harmful and insecure products for some financial gain.

15.7.9 Need for IoT Security and Privacy Certification Board

There is need for professional bodies/organisations to proactively develop and provide professional certification programs for designers, manufacturers, and providers of IoT technologies for guiding in the creation of new devices. There should be some oversight to verify whether recommended engineering practices are adhered to while providing the new products.

15.8 IOT SECURITY WITH BEST PRACTICES FOR HOME AUTOMATION APPLICATION

Following is a list of best practices tailored for a smart home application (see Fig. 15.10):

- Tamper resistant hardware by providing proper casing, covers for webcams, Ethernet port locks.
- Wi-Fi Internet connectivity for firmware updates for the smart objects such as smart door lock, fridge, and air conditioners.

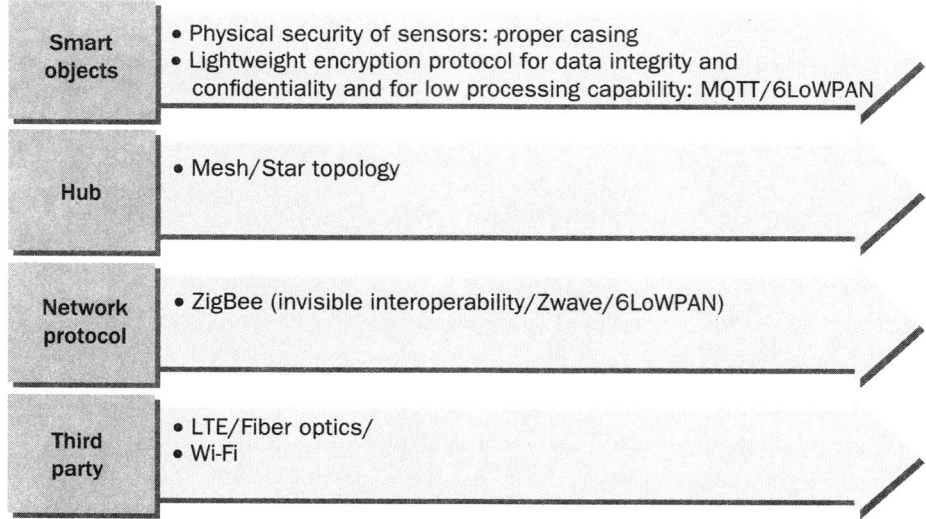

Fig. 15.10 Secured Smart Home Management

- Dynamic testing before adding new smart object for checking interoperability, data privacy, and access control.
- Secure network protocols selection for data communication to third party and for data encryption.
- Smart objects maintenance contract with the IoT system provider for regular maintenance to remove security flaws.
- Two level strong authentication for access control.
- Network segmentation to isolate private smart home network from third party to provide access control through isolation.
- Secure data disposal from server when the smart object is discarded or changed.
- Manufacturer should provide security certification for ensuring best practices implementation while designing manufacturing and deploying the smart home system for privacy preservation and trust building.

SUMMARY

In the Internet of Things, every physical object has a virtual component, which produces and/or consumes the service. Novel approaches must be used to provide secure and trustable IoT systems, which can be easily adopted by consumers for the safe and ethical use. The manufacturers gain reputation by providing such trustworthy IoT devices.

For strengthening the security, strong security enforcement is needed at in-house, device-by-device, and for the complete lifecycle of every product. Different security threats, issues, and attacks in different layers of IoT system architecture are to be considered while designing, developing, and deploying the security controls to IoT devices to create an innovative, reliable, and user-friendly environment which will enforce the fundamental tenets of security.

KEYWORDS

IoT system security architecture, IoT system layers, Security issues in IoT system, Vulnerabilities, Security threats, Attacks, Security controls, WSN security, Best practices

REVIEW QUESTIONS

1. Design a IoT-driven network for monitoring atmospheric conditions such as temperature, humidity, solar index, and soil parameters such as moisture content to analyse the need for watering the plants of a garden with sprinkle irrigation.
2. If a plain text message character is mapped to Elliptic Curve Point is $M(6, 1)$, for the elliptical curve defined by equation $y^2 = x^3 + 2x + 4$. Find the public and private key using public point $P(2, 3)$ and encrypt the message to find ciphertext $(C1, C2)$ and decrypt the ciphertext using the keys to recover the message point M, using ECC with elliptical curve of the field $F_p = F_7$ for prime number $p = 7$.
   Given: $d = 199$ for prime order
   $n = 201, k = 10$
3. What are the advantages of elliptical curve cryptosystem? Explain with reference to some IoT system considering the resource constraints of that system.
4. Select a suitable application layer protocol for the smart energy grid IoT system to protect CIA principles of security. Justify your selection.

5. Explain IoT security issues in perception layer of IoT system.
6. What are the challenges to provide security for IoT system?
7. Why data privacy is of prime importance in IoT systems?
8. Why lightweight cryptography is needed for IoT systems?
9. Explain two IoT security controls for middleware platform.
10. Explain best practices for IoT system security.

REFERENCES

1. Liwei, R., Trend, M. (2015, Sep), IoT security: problems, challenges and solutions, *Data Storage Security Summit*, Santa Clara, CA.
2. Roman, R., Najera, P., Lopez, J. (2011), Securing the internet of Things, *IEEE Computer*, 44: 51–58.
3. Internet of Things (IoT) Security Best Practices, *IEEE Internet Technology Policy Community White Paper*, February 2017.
4. Ericsson White paper, 284 23–3302 Uen, February 2017.
5. A New Approach to IoT Security, 5 Key Requirements to Securing IoT Communications, PubNub, San Francisco, 2009–2015.
6. Tackling Data Security and Privacy Challenges for the Internet of Things, Dave R., W3C, June 2016, IoT TechExpo, Berlin.
7. Jitender, G., Shikha, S. (2016), Security issues in wireless sensor network – a review, *5th International Conference on Reliability, Infocom Technologies and Optimization*, Noida, India.
8. Darrel, H., Alfred, M., Scott, V. (2003), *Guide to Elliptic Curve Cryptography*, Springer, New York, NY, pp. 1–147.
9. Website: http://www.cse.wustl.edu/~jain/cse570-15/ftp/iot_sec/index.html [last accessed: 22/01/2018].
10. Website: https://www.comsys.rwth-aachen.de/fileadmin/papers/2011/2011-heer-iot-challenges.pdf [last accessed: 24/01/2018].
11. Russell, B., Garlati, C., Lingenfelter, D. (2015, Apr), *Security Guidance for Early Adopters of the Mobile Working Group*, website: https://downloads.cloudsecurityalliance.org/whitepapers/Security_Guidance_for_Early_Adopter [last accessed: 27/01/2018].
12. Vucinic, M., Tourancheau, B., Rousseau, Duda, A., Damon, L., Robert. (2014), Security architecture for the Internet of Things, *Proceedings of WoWMoM, IEEE*, website: https://cryptome.org/2014/05/oscar-iot.pdf [last accessed: 24/01/2018].
13. Escribano, B. Privacy and security in the Internet of Things: challenge or opportunity, OIs, website: http://www.olswang.com/media/48315339/privacy_and_security_in_the_iot.pdf [last accessed: 25/01/2018].
14. Shahid, R. (2014), *Lightweight Security Solutions for the Internet of Things*, Doctoral thesis, Mlard, http://soda.swedish-ict.se/5548/1/thesis.pdf [Kim14] "Kim Rowe", 2014. Website: http://embedded-computing.com/articles/internet-things-requirements-protocols/ [last accessed: 26/01/2018].
15. Baldini, G., Peirce, T., Tallachini, M.C. (2014, Jan), Internet of Things: IoT Governance European Research Cluster on the Internet of Things, website: http://www.internet-of-things-research.eu/pdf/ [last accessed: 23/01/2018].
16. Fremantle, P., Scott, P. A security survey of middleware for the Internet of Things, Peer, https://peerj.com/preprints/1241v1.pdf
17. Whitehouse, O. (2014, Apr), Security of Things: An Implementers Guide to Cyber-Security for Internet of NCC Group Publications, website access date 24 Jan 2018: https://www.nccgroup.trust/globalassets/our-research/uk/whitepapers/2014-04-09
18. Jha, A., Sunil M.C. Security considerations for Internet of Things, whitepaper, L and T Techn, http://www.lnttechservices.com/media/30090/

19. Oltsik, J. (2014, Oct), The Internet of Things: A CISO and Network Security Perspective, *ESG White Pap Systems*, website: https://www.cisco.com/web/strategy/docs/energy/network-security-perspective.pdf [last accessed: 26/01/2018].
20. Roman, R., Najera, P., Lopez, J. (2011, Sep), Securing the Internet of Things, *Computer Society* 58, website access date 18 jan 2018: https://www.nics.uma.es/sites/default/files/papers/1633.pdf [last accessed: 28/01/2018].
21. Heer, T., Garcia-Morchon, O., Hummen, R., Keoh, S.L., Kumar, S.S., Klau. (2011, Dec), in the IP-based Internet of Things, *Wireless Personal Communications: An International Journal*.
22. Akishita, T., Hiwatari, H. (2011), Compact hardware implementations of the 128-bit blockcipher CLEFIA, In: *Proceedings of Symposium on Cryptography and Information Security –SCIS 2011* (in Japanese).
23. Bogdanov, A., Knudsen, L.R., Leander, G., Paar, C., Poschmann, A., Robshaw, M.J.B, Seurin, Y., Vikkelsoe, C. (2007), PRESENT: an ultra-lightweight block cipher, In: *CHES 2007*, no. 4727 in LNCS, pp. 450–466, Springer-Verlag.
24. Poschmann, A. (2009), Lightweight Cryptography – Cryptographic Engineering for a Pervasive World, in IACR ePrint archive 2009/516.
25. Broadband Internet Technical Advisory Group. (2016), Internet of Things (IoT) Security and Privacy Recommendations. Retrieved from BITAG website:https://www.bitag.org/documents/BITAG_Report_Internet_of_Things_(IoT)_Security_and_Privacy_Recommendations.pdf
26. US Department of Homeland Security. (2016), Strategic Principles for Securing the Internet of Things (IoT), https://www.dhs.gov/sites/default/files/publications/Strategic_Principles_for_Securing_the_Internet_of_Things-2016-1115-FINAL
27. Guide, R. Elliptical Curve Cryptography (ECC). Available online: http://www.sysax.com/ftblog/windows-ftp/elliptic-curve-cryptography-ecc/

IoT and Business Process Management

CHAPTER **16**

"The service-led IoT economy needs orchestration, collaboration and continuous optimisation for efficiency-this is where the role of BPM comes in."

-Chloe Green

OBJECTIVES
- define a business process
- explain business process in various domains
- describe business process management (BPM)
- introduce concepts of integration of Internet of Things (IoT) technologies and BPM
- introduce business process modeling and notation (BPMN) and its extension to IoT
- describe various IoT-centric business processes

OUTCOMES
- understand the concept of business process
- relate business process with IoT and understand their complementary nature
- give examples of business processes that are benefited by IoT
- use business process notation to describe a business process
- use BPMN to describe IoT driven business processes

REVISION

Chapter 14 on interoperability in IoT ecosystem described IoT reference model and architecture, which is fundamental in developing interoperable IoT systems. IoT business process management is described as one of the seven functional groups of the IoT-based functional model. This chapter is focussed on business process management and its integration with IoT.

16.1 BUSINESS PROCESS

A business process consists of a set of logically related tasks and activities that result in the delivery of a specific service or product to a client. The end result of this process is to enable organizations to meet their goals in a more optimized way and also to enable new innovations in the delivery of a service/

product and stay competitive in the market. A business process is usually depicted in the form of a flow chart to enable easy understanding of a complex process.

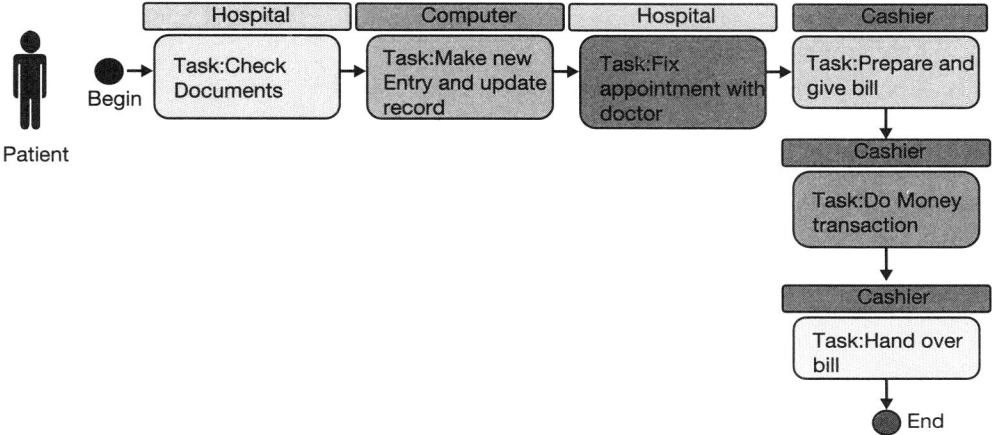

Fig. 16.1 Business Process in Healthcare

Figure 16.1 shows the example of a business process in the healthcare industry. It consists of several tasks each of which is handled by different persons and entities. For example, the task 'check documents' is handled by the hospital personnel, whereas making entry and updating record is made by a computer. A cashier is involved in the task of preparing and delivering bills. As shown in Fig. 16.1, there are multiple tasks and activities involved in the business process of admitting a patient. Several such business processes are integrated at various levels in a hospital, and some of those processes are not apparent and maybe hidden from the end user, but address important business functions and guide the overall business. Similarly, business processes (BPs) exist in many business areas as shown in Box 16.1.

> **BOX 16.1: BUSINESS PROCESS IN VARIOUS DOMAINS**
>
> Business processes form an important building block that enables an organization to optimally take decisions regarding processes, information, and technologies of that business. Once the business process is well defined and tested (see section 16.2.1), it can automate many tasks of the business. Some business processes in various domains are shown below. Each of these processes is modelled using standardised notation elements as described in section 16.3.
>
> | Domain | Business Process |
> |---|---|
> | Human resources (HR) | Recruitment of new employees
Annual assessment of employees
Salary increments
Training employees |

(Contd)

Box 16.1 *(Contd)*

Accounts & financial	Managing salaries of the employees
	Financial transactions of the business
	Income tax related functions
	Managing bank transactions
	Annual financial report
Marketing and sales	Selecting potential areas for product launch
	Advertisement of the product
	Making a sale of the product
Manufacturing	Product specifications
	Product assembly pipeline creation
	Quality control

16.2 BUSINESS PROCESS MANAGEMENT

An end-to-end understanding and improvement of the business processes by various approaches such as analysis, modeling its performance in various scenarios, optimizing the execution of the business processes, and continuous monitoring of the flow of the improved processes is termed as business process management (BPM).

According to August-Wilhelm Scheer, "Business process management (BPM) is a discipline involving any combination of modeling, automation, execution, control, measurement and optimization of business flow activities, in support of enterprise goals, spanning systems, employees, customers and partners within and beyond the enterprise boundaries". Various people and tools are involved at different stages of a business process management system (BPMS).

As shown in Fig.16.2, the first stage is to define the business process conceptually. This is done by business analysts and domain experts, and it provides the fundamental basis on which the rest of the components of the management are built. This stage captures the experience and field knowledge/research, organization profile, and understanding of key performance indicators of the business. Once the definition of the processes is done, it needs to be represented in a formal manner, which is termed as process modeling. To enable ease of representation, visual modeling tools and languages are used to develop flow diagrams that will unambiguously capture various tasks and activities of the process. In consultation with domain experts, software architects develop these process models. These models can be executed as the process steps through various tasks; the software developers enable the development of executable business processes and most often these executable pieces of software are either embedded within the core business software or as standalone web services which can be called on demand. These business processes are continuously monitored and tweaked to make sure that they are properly aligned with the end business goals. The complete BPM lifecycle is described in the next section.

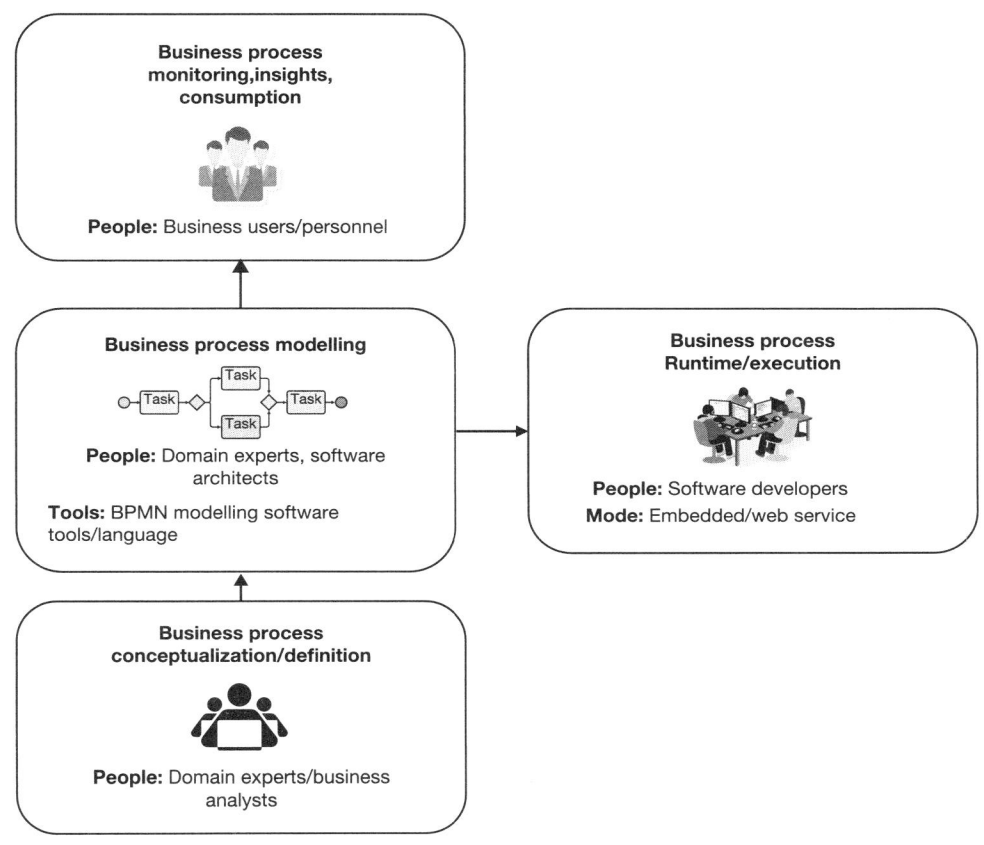

Fig. 16.2 End-to-end Components of Business Process Management

16.2.1 BPM Lifecycle

BPM consists of various steps which are often called as its lifecycle. It is able to capture business related information in a formal and structured way. These stages of the process go through a cycle as long as the process is active and allows continuous process improvement. As shown in Fig. 16.3, it consists of various states as described below.

16.2.1.1 Design

It involves determining the requirements of existing processes and future envisaged processes. Various tools are used to develop the design such as flow charts, simulation software, etc.

16.2.1.2 Model

Modeling is capturing conceptually at a very high level the business processes involved in a domain. Domain knowledge plays an important role in this process. The focus here is to obtain all the parameters/variables and their combinations correctly that are required to build a model. Several assistive software tools such as business processing modeling & notation (BPMN) can aid in the visual development of the models.

16.2.1.3 Execution

Various tasks/activities involved in the business processes are launched either in a human-in-the-loop mode (semi-automated) or in an automated mode.

16.2.1.4 Monitoring

It involves the continuous understanding and tracking the performance of the activities involved in the processes. This includes obtaining various key performance indicators (KPIs) and also related statistical information, which allows assessment of particular activity in a more realistic way.

16.2.1.5 Optimization

It is focused on improving the business process by understanding the underperformance of the activities in the processes and tweaking them so that their performance meets the KPIs. The outputs from the monitoring and modeling phases are used in the optimization phase.

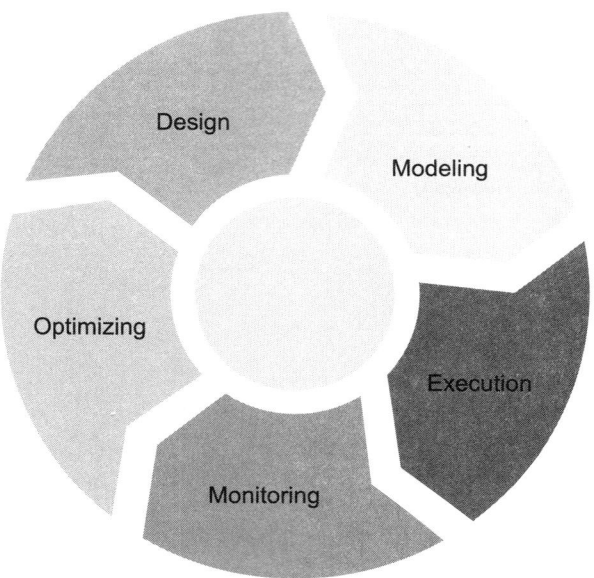

Fig. 16.3 Lifecycle of Business Process Management

16.3 BUSINESS PROCESS MODELING & NOTATION

Business process modeling & notation (BPMN) is a standardized way to develop models for business processes using a specific type of notation in a graphical format. It is easy for business users, managers and analysts to understand and to create and design models for the business processes.

BPMN is also useful for technical developers for implementing the technology that executes those processes. BPMN supports XML languages designed for the execution of business processes such as Business Process Execution Language Process Execution Language for Web Services (BPEL4WS), etc.

BPMN provides certain groups of elements that can be used to develop the graphical representation of the business processes. These are symbols that are categorized into: flows, connections, swimlanes/pools and artifacts (Fig. 16.4).

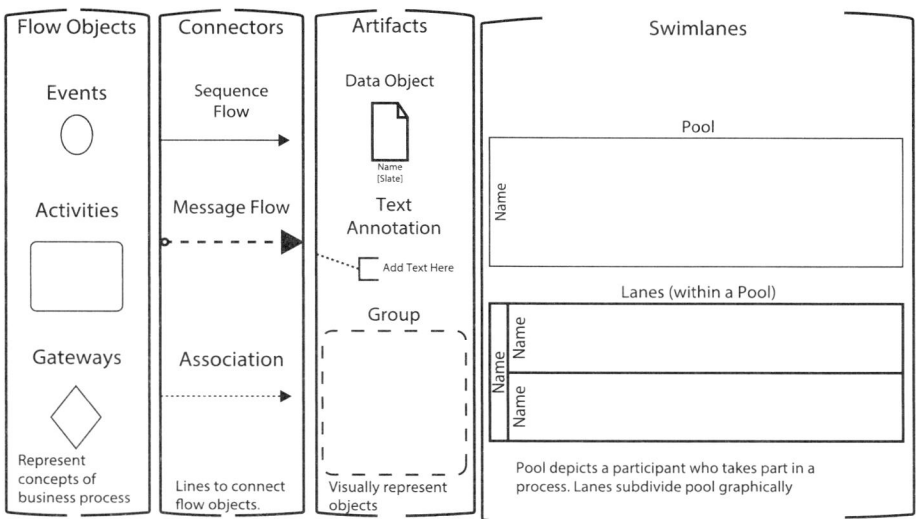

Fig. 16.4 BPMN Elements used for Graphical Representation of Business Processes

Flow objects Flow objects consist of events, activities, and gateways. Events are those that have an effect on the business process in some way. These are normally represented by circles (Fig. 16.4) and can be used to depict a start event, intermediate event, and end event. A business process consists of activities as represented by round rectangles, which are further divided into tasks (Fig. 16.1) and subprocesses. Gateways are decision making places where the process is controlled based on the process data. An example of a gateway is shown in Fig. 16.4, where the decision is made to send an alert or not based on the process data, that is, air quality level obtained by calculating the air quality index.

Connectors Connectors are elements that connect different flow objects. These include sequence flows which are used to connect flow elements (Fig. 16.4). Message flows are used to connect between pools (Fig. 16.4). Data objects are used to model data which could be data input, output, and storing data.

Swimlanes Swimlanes are represented by rectangular boxes and are used for showing the different entities involved in a business process. Flow objects used within lanes of the pool are used to represent business process. Each lane is based on a specific role within the process, and job sharing and responsibilities are possible between the lanes of the pool.

16.4 IOT AND BUSINESS PROCESS MANAGEMENT

Business process involves a set of tasks and activities executed in some logical way and over a period of time to achieve a business goal. Many applications are emerging by integrating business process management so that the various processes involved in IoT systems are managed in a more systematic (controlled execution of steps or flow of a process) and autonomous way (ability to react to runtime events in the IoT system independently). It enables high-level interaction with BPM integrated IoT system where users need not worry about the complexity of implementation. Hence, the focus of such systems is mainly process modeling (developing a BPM Model) and understanding various behaviours, rather than the application code, which is taken care by the BPM tools.

The integration of IoT with Business Process Management Systems (BPMS) requires modeling the IoT components or entities in a way that can be used with processes in BPM. As shown in Fig. 16.5, to enable true integration of IoT with BPM, each stage of BPM needs to be augmented with IoT specific technologies so that at the business process level, IoT data makes considerable value addition. Thus, the real-time data capture from IoT devices and using it in BPM gives businesses considerable cost savings, optimization, and efficiency.

At design and modeling stage of BPM (Fig. 16.5), new IoT process models need to be developed that contain IoT specific tasks and services. The introduction of new notation elements in BPMN will allow IoT specific visual modeling and combine with other regular business process notations that are already available in BPMN.

IoT integration at the execution stage of BPM requires the BPM engine to have the ability to consume data from the sensors and actuators while executing a particular process.

The monitoring stage of BPM should allow for new forms of querying and visualization as the data is in real time from IoT. The BPM systems are also expected to track the performance of the IoT related tasks in addition to their normal functions.

The analysis stage of BPM relates to mining the event logs and further deeply assessing the performance of the processes so that tweaking in the processes can be suggested. Due to the integration of IoT data, the big data perspective is required in BPM to enable it to be processed in high volume, high velocity data and use the insights gained from big data analytics.

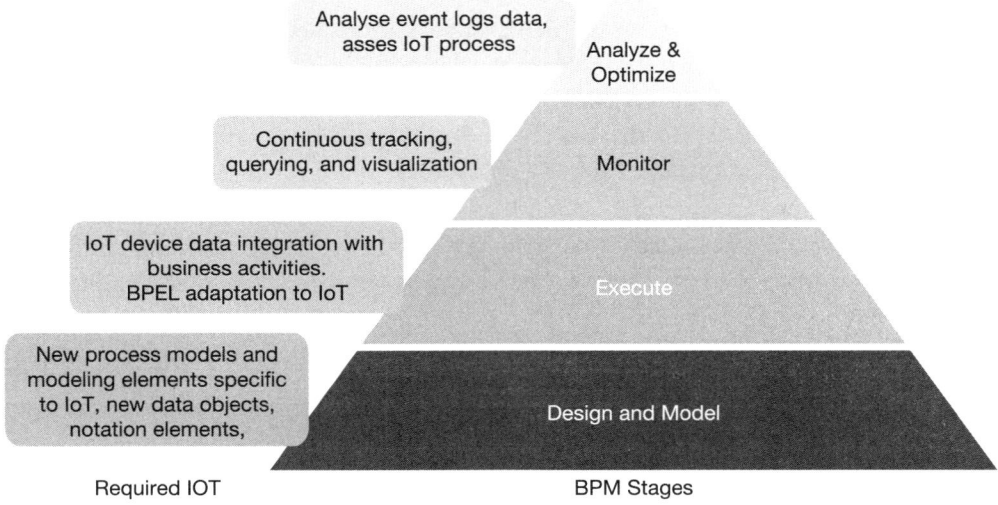

Fig. 16.5 IoT Technological Extensions that Need to be Integrated at Various Stages of BPM

Two possible approaches for integrating IoT with BPM are as follows:
- Provisioning IoT devices as web services and making them available over the internet. These web services (e.g. SOAP-based or REST-based web services) can be interacted through standard requests/responses. By using IoT devices in this way, the existing BPMS need not be modified, and they can be assessed on the requirement of a particular task in the process to obtain data from an IoT device or to change through an actuator which is also available as a web service. This service-based approach enables interoperability and can easily consume data from multiple heterogeneous IoT devices, communication protocols, and data models.
- Developing new elements and extending BPMS to accommodate the IoT devices is another approach. A new set of BPMN elements are added to specifically enable the use of IoT devices in BPMS (Fig. 16.6). This approach is useful when IoT devices are not available as a web service and cannot be accessed via a network.

The IoT modeling elements for BPM are those that are specifically developed for representing IoT processes. The existing BPM systems do not possess such capabilities. Figure. 16.6 is an example of a suggested IoT extension for BPMN.

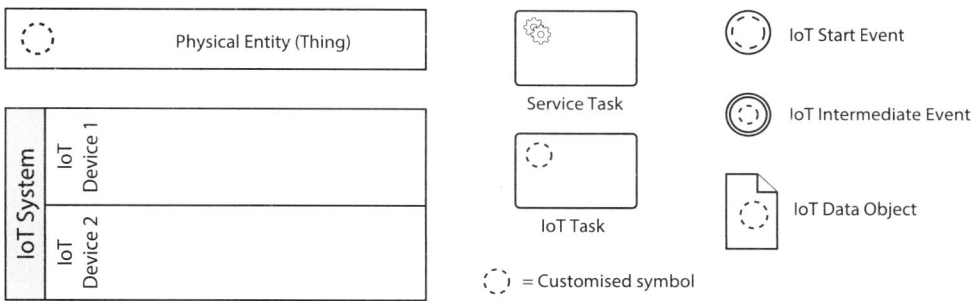

Fig. 16.6 Extension of BPMN to Include IoT Elements

(Source credit: Chang et al, 2017)

The IoT process is represented as a pool (separate from the pools of business processes) with lanes depicting activities of different IoT devices. The IoT data object represents data that is being continuously collected, that is, streaming data which is moved down the pipeline in periodic intervals. This is in contrast to the normal BPM where data is collected once and tends to remain static. The IoT task and service tasks are new notational elements that are shown with specific symbols related to IoT. The IoT start and intermediate events signify the start of an event specifically when an actuator is triggered and its status as the event progresses.

Figure 16.7 shows an example of BPMN elements that were extended with IoT related activities. The two swimlanes show two different IoT processes, i.e., air quality monitoring and traffic monitoring. The air quality monitoring information is used to generate alerts, which are subsequently used by the traffic monitoring system to divert traffic from those roads which have the worst air pollution.

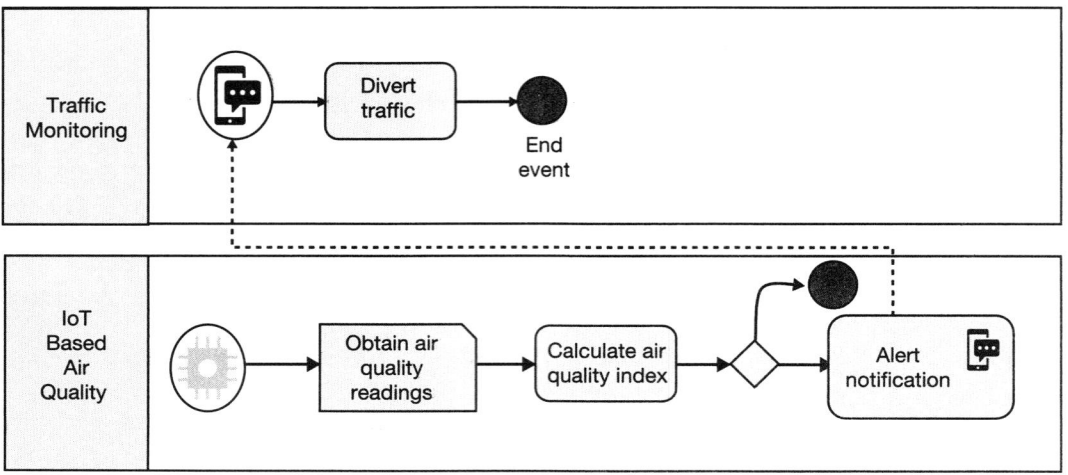

Fig.16.7 Extending BPMN with IoT Specific Modeling Elements

16.4.1 IoT-based Business Processes

Recently, IoT and business processes have been combined in several domains such as smart buildings, logistics, healthcare, and assisted living for the elderly. Box 16.2 shows some of these applications.

BOX 16.2: IOT-CENTRIC BUSINESS PROCESSES

IoT centric business processes are those that use IoT data to drive a business process. Data from IOT, which is streaming in nature, enables the business process to provide real time analysis and insights. Several domains and their corresponding business process which have some component of IoT involved in them are shown below.

Domain	Business Process
Agriculture	IoT-driven precision fertilizer delivery, irrigation, monitoring, pumps, water meters, etc. Sorting and packaging of vegetables/fruits, and managing delivery centers
	Sorting and packaging of vegetables/fruits, and managing delivery centers
Warehouses	Intrusion detection, product quality assessment, and product tracking
Banking	Smart IoT driven personalised services, predicting fraud in debit/credit card related transactions, IoT devices-based digital payments
Heating, ventilating, and air conditioning (HVAC) systems used in the modern buildings	Measuring the usage of electricity and heating system, and billing customer based on actual usage Smart home
Smart home	IoT-based indoor monitoring devices can track home environment, and alert remotely for events

16.5 IOT AND BUSINESS PROCESS EXECUTION LANGUAGE

Business Process Execution Language (BPEL) is an XML-based language for defining business processes of the enterprises within web services. Business process flow is defined in a unique way by every enterprise. The major task of BPEL is to standardize the format or definition of business process flow so as to get seamless integration of services by different enterprises using web services. BPEL also supports business transactions through interaction using web implemented services. Web services use XML documents in a standardised manner that is compatible on any platform or product that supports BPEL specification.

BPMN maps directly to BPEL (Fig. 16.8). BPEL software usually provides rich and comprehensive support for BPMN. It supports export of live workflows for BPMN or BPEL files and provides an activation layer for generating applications using BPMN and BPEL concepts.

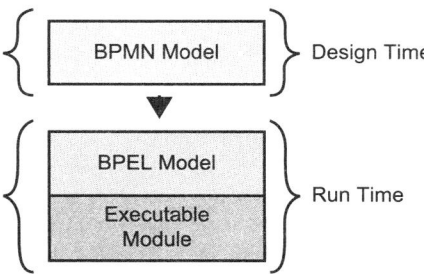

Fig. 16.8 BPMN and BPEL

BPEL supports two different business processes:

Executable processes Actual behaviour of participants is modelled in a business interaction by these processes.

Abstract processes Manually perceivable behaviour uses process description for message exchange between the participants involved in the protocol, without revealing their internal behavioural pattern. BPEL is used to model both executable and abstract processes.

Web services business process execution language (WS-BPEL) is a standard from OASIS foundation. The business process can be defined as an orchestration of web services and can be used for obtaining information from sensors. However, information from IoT devices is difficult to incorporate into WS-BPEL without modification as the process definitions have to be changed/programmed so that the process can use either periodic information or information based on unusual or interesting events from the IoT devices. Some extensions to WS-BPEL were developed to overcome these issues, but are still an active area of development.

16.6 BPM AND IOT CASE STUDY: SUPPLY CHAIN MANAGEMENT

Supply chain management is related to handling activities and business processes such as procurement of raw materials, management of manufacturing, storage of raw as well as finished products, inventory management, finances, and transport of finished product to the place of consumption. In a nutshell, it tracks the complete lifecycle of a product from its inception to the final destination (see Fig. 16.9).

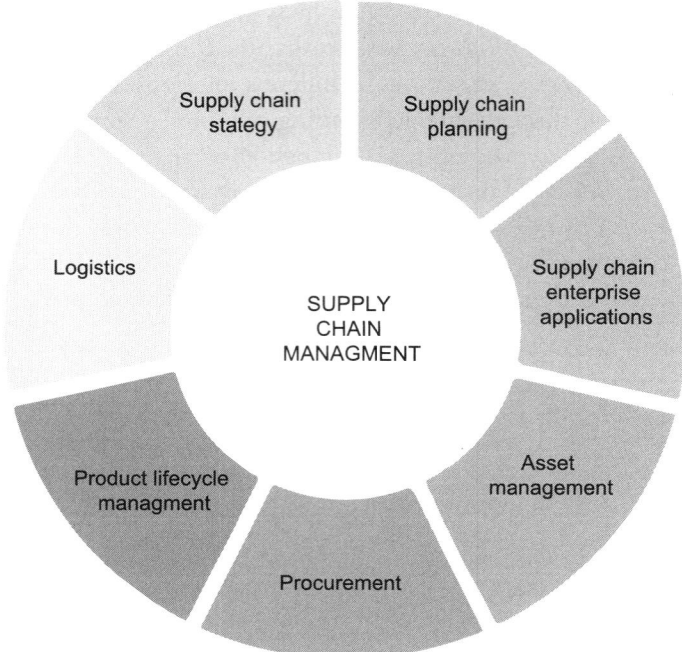

Fig. 16.9 Life Cycle of a Supply Chain Management

IoT has made a huge impact on supply chain management. There are many entities such as suppliers, manufacturers, transportation companies, and distributors involved in a supply chain. Hence, it requires coordination between various links to enable the smooth flow of goods. IoT is enabling the automation of these networks and making it reliable and efficient. IoT is useful at the product manufacturing stage (e.g. Industrial IoT), procurement, real-time tracking of goods, understand the condition of the goods (either in a warehouse or in the transit) and also give information about the expected time of delivery at a particular location. Below is an example that shows the integration of BPM with IoT.

Example A company dealing with Oranges has several activities and processes in its supply chain management system. The following processes are involved (only some selected processes are described below) (see Fig. 16.10):

Procurement of oranges This process is usually based on a pre-agreed contract between the farmer(s) and the company. The IoT device involved in this process is a weighing device that can transmit the data to the cloud, so that various personnel from the company can simultaneously procure the oranges from the farmers at various locations. This will allow you to calculate in real time the amount of oranges that are procured and accordingly adjust till it meets the requirements of the company. The company can take these raw goods (oranges) and transport them to a location where further processing is carried out.

IoT and Business Process Management

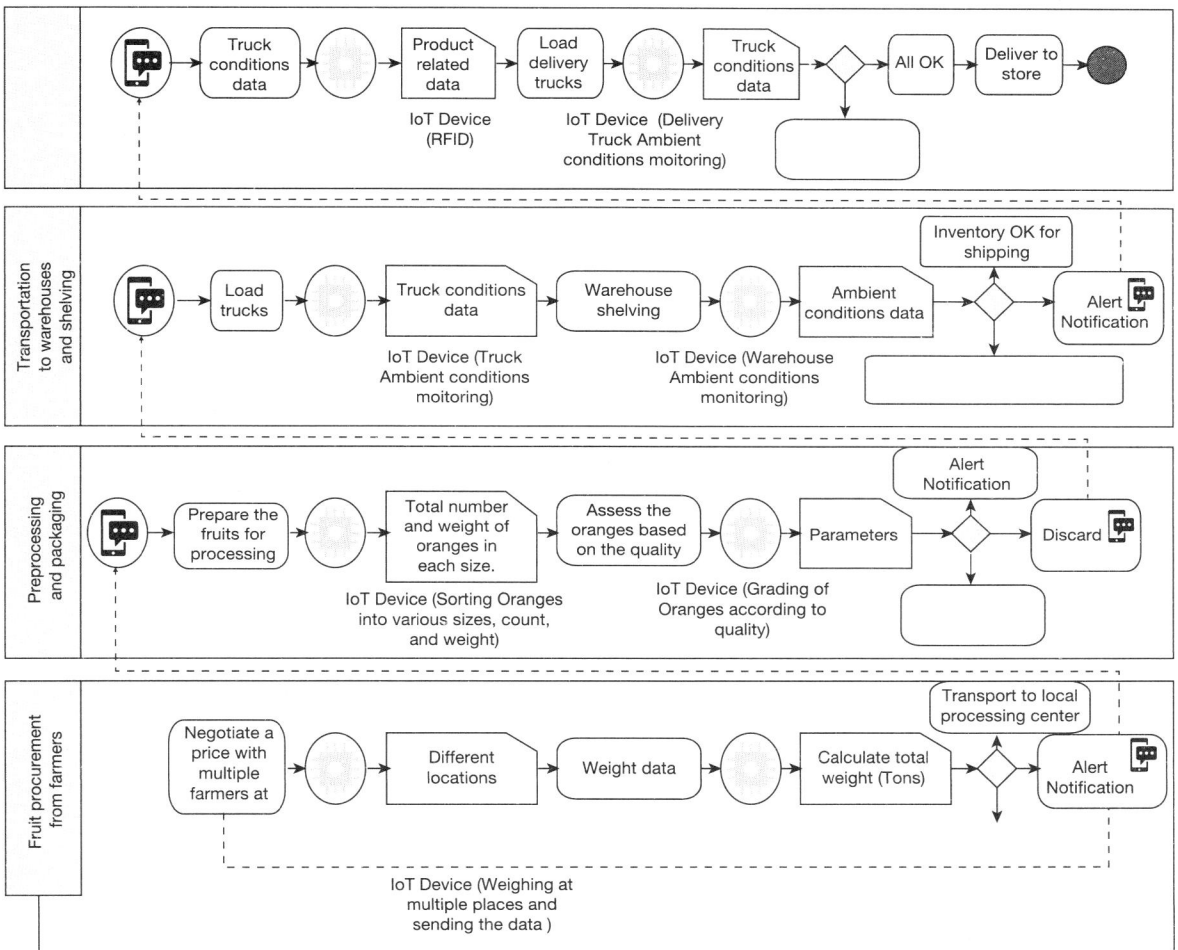

Fig. 16.10 BPMN with IoT Depicting a Supply Chain Scenario

Preprocessing and packaging The procured oranges need to be subjected to various pre-processing operations such as sorting, grading, polishing, etc. The IoT devices involved in this process could be a sorting device that automatically sorts the oranges based on size and also counts and weighs them. This information can be used next in grading the oranges according to the quality (e.g., cuts, misshape, punctured skin, bruising, rottening, rusting, etc). Some new kinds of IoT devices that are capable of measuring such quality parameters are available in the market. After the grading process, the oranges are packed and moved to a warehouse.

Transportation to warehouses and shelving The packed oranges are loaded into trucks and moved to warehouses. In this process, to ensure the quality of the oranges, the truck is continuously monitored for its ambient conditions. The IoT devices include those that can measure temperature, humidity, air pressure, etc. In addition, IoT devices that can measure vibration are also employed to ensure that the oranges are transported in a proper way. Further, IoT sensors for security (e.g. locking system), and tracking (e.g., GPS) are also used to protect and track the product until it reaches the warehouse. The product is then shelved in the warehouse but is continuously monitored for quality parameters and the warehouse conditions are automatically adjusted based on IoT devices to provide a conducive environment for the oranges to remain fresh.

Delivery to retail stores   Based on the orders received from the retail stores, the oranges are removed from the warehouse and loaded into a truck. The process of moving these goods again involves continuous monitoring of the ambient conditions, vibration, security, and other related aspects. Hence, IoT devices are used to obtain data in real-time and dynamically adjust the truck conditions as it passes through different outside temperatures and driving conditions till it reaches the destination (a retail store).

The above example illustrates the need for IoT integration with BPM to enable more insights into the end-to-end process of supply chain management.

SUMMARY

Integrating IoT aspects into various stages of BPM and related tools enables to overcome many challenges for wider deployment of IoT technologies. There is a need to support business process by developing new IoT-specific elements. Further, issues related to security and privacy in business processes of an organisation can be addressed by implementing relevant IoT technologies. Enabling secure communication between the two domains i.e. IoT and BPM with corresponding privacy/security levels and policies is important. Further, there are various conceptual and technological challenges that need to be addressed to deeply integrate IoT with BPM at each stage of the BPM lifecycle.

REVIEW QUESTIONS

1. What is a business process? Explain with a diagram.
2. Give some examples of business process in various domains.
3. What is business process management?
4. Explain the end-to-end components of BPM.
5. Describe the lifecycle of BPM.
6. What is business process modeling & notation (BPMN)?
7. Explain various BPMN notations with a diagram.
8. Describe how BPM and IoT can be integrated.
9. Describe various technological extensions that need to be developed at each stage of BPM with a diagram.
10. Explain two basic ways in which IoT and BPM can be integrated.
11. Explain with examples IoT centric business processes.
12. Describe BPEL. What is the relation between BPEL and BPMN?
13. What are the limitations of current BPEL standard for use with IoT? How can it be used with IoT?
14. List some mutual benefits of integrating IoT and BPM

REFERENCES

1. Dumas, M., La Rosa, M., Mendling, J., Reijers, H. A (2013), Fundamentals of business process management. Berlin:Springer.
2. Gubbia, J., Buyyab, R., Marusica, S., Palaniswamia, M. (2013), Internet of things (Iot): A vision, architectural elements, and future directions. Future Generation Computer Systems, 29(7):1645–1660.
3. Cherrier, S., Deshpande, V. (2017), From BPM to IoT. International Conference on Business Process Management, pp.310-318, Sep 2017, Barcelona, Spain.ff10.1007/978-3-319-74030-0_23ff. ffhal01613738v2
4. Kannengiesser, U., Neubauer, M., Heininger, R. (2015), Subject-oriented bpm as the glue for integrating enterprise processes in smart factories. OTM Workshops, 2015, pp. 77–86.
   BPMN: http://www.bpmn.org/
   BPMN Examples: http://www.omg.org/spec/BPMN/2.0/examples/PDF
5. Meyer, A., Magerkurth, R.C. (2013), Advanced Information Systems Engineering: 25th International Conference, CAiSE 2013, Valencia, Spain, June 17-21, 2013. Proceedings, Springer Berlin Heidelberg, Berlin, Heidelberg, 2013, Ch. Internet of Things-aware process modeling: Integrating IoT devices as business process resources, pp. 84–98.
6. Sungur, C. T., Spiess, P., Oertel, N., Kopp O. (2013), Extending bpmn for wire-less sensor networks, in: Proceedings of the 15th. IEEE Conference on Business Informatics (CBI '13), IEEE, Vienna, 2013, pp. 109–116.
7. Tranquillini, S., Spieß, P., Daniel, F., Karnouskos, S., Casati, F., Oertel, N., Mottola, L., Oppermann, F. J., Picco, G. P.,omer K. R, et al. (2012), Process-based design and integration of wireless sensor network applications, in: Business Process Management, Springer, Berlin Heidelberg, 2012, pp. 134–149.
8. Chang, C., Srirama, S.N., Rajkumar Buyya R. (2016), Mobile cloud business process management system for the Internet of Things: A Survey. ACM Comput. Surv. 49, 4, Article 70 (December 2016), 42 pages. DOI: https://doi.org/10.1145/3012000
9. Domingos, D., Martins, F., Cândido, C., Martinho, R. (2014). Internet of Things aware WS-BPEL business processes context variables and expected exceptions. J. UCS, 20, 1109–1129.
   [OASIS, 2007] https://www.oasis-open.org/standards.

PART V: COMPELLING USE CASES OF IOT

Chapter 17: IoT Use Cases

Chapter 18: Future Outlook

IoT Use Cases

CHAPTER 17

"Smart homes and other connected products won't just be aimed at home life. They'll also have a major impact on business."

— Jared Newman

OBJECTIVES
- introduction to use cases of IoT applications from various domains
- explain the use cases, smart home, smart goods transportation and smart agriculture, along with hands-on examples

OUTCOMES
- elucidate various use cases in different IoT disciplines of IoT applications
- understand the requirements and constraints for a given application

REVISION
In chapters 3, 4, 5, 6, 7 and 8, various IoT enabling hardware and software technologies are covered. In chapter 9, different steps of physical working prototyping are explored with some IoT application examples. In this chapter, various IoT use cases are presented with step by step details on design and development.

17.1 INTRODUCTION

IoT is a highly disruptive and game changing technology that can impact businesses and provide new opportunities to develop applications that can possess the ability of connecting anything, anytime, anyplace, anyone, any service, and any network. IoT provides appropriate solutions for a wide range of applications such as waste management, smart cities, traffic congestion, healthcare, logistics, retails, emergency services, industrial control (see Fig.1.11 (chapter 1)).

17.2 USE CASE FOR HOME AUTOMATION USING SMART HOME APPLIANCES

In this section we will explore the use case Smart home using IoT technologies. The home appliances Fan, Light and Door lock are explored in detail. Energy conservation and management using smart home appliances is explained further.

17.2.1 Overview

Traditional home appliances such as light, fan, refrigerator, exhaust fan, air conditioners can be operated manually by switching on and off. IoT technology is changing this scenario drastically for operation and control of home appliances. In existing systems, remote control devices are used to operate the appliances without pressing the button on the switch. The remote is now replaced by smartphones, where an android application can be used to control the home appliances. For example, the fan can be switched on and off using the android application without pressing the button of the switch board. Also, the user can control and track the status of the speed of the fan at low, medium and high state.

Considering existing systems that have been developed for controlling the home appliances, the goal is to develop a system that works in automatic mode completely without other device intervention. Such smart systems can be developed in such a way that efficient energy management can be achieved.

17.2.2 Existing Home Automation Systems

Various existing home automation systems are listed below.

Bluetooth-based home automation system The Home Automation System can be controlled by mobile application in which devices and components can be connected using Bluetooth Module. The Bluetooth Module allows the user to operate the devices within specific range. This system is similar to switching the appliances turning on and off using button on the switch board. The buttons on the switch are replaced using mobile application.

WiFi-based home automation system The Home Automation System developed using WiFi Module, can control the home devices with the android application or a website or a desktop application. This system is similar to the Bluetooth based home automation system. This system requires an internet connection so as to connect an Automation system with the devices.

Remote-based home automation system The IR Remote Control can be used to control the home appliances. The light, fan, TV and other appliances can be turned on and off using remote control.

Mobile-based home automation system using GSM module This system displays the status of the home appliances in the mobile application using GSM. The commands can be used for controlling the appliances. The commands can send SMS to turn on and off the devices.

17.2.3 Problem Statement for the Use Case Home Automation using IoT: A Novel Approach

Automation of home appliances such as light, fan and door lock using Internet of Things technologies. The home appliances can be operated in default(manual) or smart automatic mode. Generally, it operates in smart mode. But, can be switched to manual.

Objectives

- In default mode, the light is operated manually ON/OFF. If default mode is selected it overrides smart automatic mode.
- In default mode, the fan is operated manually and default mode ON / OFF and in ON mode a specific fan speed. This mode if selected overrides smart automatic mode.
- In smart mode, the light is made ON or OFF based on logic with inputs as natural light present in the room and human existence in the room.
- In the smart mode, fan is controlled using a fuzzy logic controller with inputs of temperature and humidity of the room
- Design of a smart lock
- Energy management and saving using smart appliances

The smart light can be switched ON and OFF based on the presence or absence of a person in the room. The smart fan can be switched ON or OFF based on the presence or absence of a person in the room as well as considering temperature and humidity parameters. The smart door lock is also operated in two modes

Default mode In this mode the smart lock is disabled and the door can be opened manually using key.

Smart mode In this mode the door can be opened with face recognition of an authorized person of the house with a two level security.

First level The smart door lock is opened based on face recognition of an authorized person.

Second level The door is opened manually with the key, when the key is given to third person.
Internet of Things technologies are used to develop the system for automation of home appliances. In this the sensors and actuators are connected with the microcontroller board. The microcontroller board takes input from the sensors and instructs the actuators to work. The complete system is automatic and beneficial for reducing energy consumption and saves energy.

Energy management system A smart home energy management system is developed using Internet of Things. Large amounts of data that are collected from the sensors are analyzed using big data analytics and sometimes predictive analysis approach is used to analyze the data. The variations in the voltage and changes can be tracked using various sensors and actuators. Such voltage fluctuations are the cause of damage of some electrical appliances. In such scenario of voltage fluctuations smart voltage regulators can be given as a solution, an android application allows users to operate the home appliances.

A network is developed consisting of hubs of sensors and actuators and other devices through which home appliances can be monitored and controlled. A virtual connection is created between the hubs and device using Internet of Things.

17.2.4 Block Diagram

The home appliances can be operated automatically using IoT. This system requires microcontroller board to instruct the sensors and actuators. The Arduino Uno ATmega 328P microcontroller takes information from the sensor and analyzes it to provide an output. The light can be switched on and off using sensor input values and fuzzy logic based on mode of operation.

The PIR Sensor Module takes the human motion as an input. If the motion is detected then the light is switched on otherwise it will remain off. The LDR Sensor Module checks whether there is enough light present in the room. If the room has enough brightness then the light will not be turned ON else it will be ON if the room is dark.

The block diagram for smart light is given in Fig. 17.1.

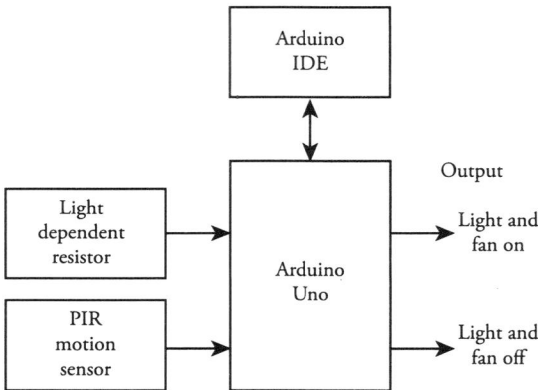

Fig. 17.1 Block Diagram of Smart Light

17.2.5 Hardware Components Used

In this system, various sensors and actuators are used to develop the home automation system. These sensors and actuators can be interconnected through the microcontroller board that generate an output which controls the home appliances such as light and fan. The following are the components of general block diagram for smart light as shown in Fig 17.1.

17.2.5.1 Arduino Uno

Arduino Uno is an open source microcontroller board which is based on microchip ATmega328P microcontroller. It has 8-bit microchip AVR CPU. It has Static Random Access Memory (SRAM) and EEPROM storage. This board consist of 6 analog input pins and 14 digital input/output pins and from these digital pin 6 pins are used as an output pins. It also consists of 16 MHz quartz crystal, USB connection, power jack, ICSP header and a reset button.

17.2.5.2 Arduino Software

The Arduino software is an open source Arduino IDE which is used to write code in 'Embedded C' programming language. The code is then uploaded to the Arduino Uno board. The set of instructions are written in the code which includes variables, functions and methods that allows the components which are connected to the microcontroller board to work accordingly. The Arduino Desktop IDE can be installed on Windows, Mac OS, and Linux. The Arduino Web Editor is useful to write the code online.

17.2.5.3 Other Components

Breadboard A breadboard is a device that is used for building the prototype of the electronic circuit and it is also used for testing the electronic circuit. The capacitors, inductors, resistors and other components can be connected with the breadboard to build the circuit. Breadboard is made up of perforated plastic blocks. This is plated with phosphor bronze silver alloy clips. There are free holes that allows resistors, capacitors and inductors to get inserted into it.

Jumper wires The jumper wires are electronic wires that are used to interconnect the components within a circuit. The components are connected to the microcontroller board and breadboard using jumper wires. There are various kinds of connectors provided at the end of jumper wires. The connectors can be RCA connectors, RF connectors solid tips, crocodile clips, banana connectors, registered jack etc. In this system male to male jumper wires, female to female jumper wires and female to male jumper wires are used for the connection of the circuit.

Resistor Resistor is a passive electronic component. It controls the flow of currents in the electronic circuit. It is also used to adjust signal levels and to divide the voltages. There are different types of resistor such as variable resistors, fixed resistors and high-power resistors. The resistor value can be calculated using the color band code on it using Resistor Colour Code System.

17.2.6 Sensors

Photoresistor Photoresistors are light dependent resistors (LDR). The surrounding light intensity can be measured using photoresistor. It is used to compute whether there is a brightness or darkness present in the room. The resistance is high when there is darkness present and the resistance is low when there is presence of brightness. The threshold can be set and accordingly the light source can be turned ON and OFF. If the analog value of the photoresistor is greater than the threshold then there is brightness in the room, and if the analog value of the photoresistor is less than the threshold then there is darkness present in the room.

Light dependent resistor Light Dependent Resistor Module is a sensor module that detect the light intensity. It can read analog value as well as digital value. The resistance can be high when the light intensity is low and it can be low when the light intensity is more. The specifications and pin description are provided in Tables 17.1 and 17.2, respectively.

Table 17.1 Specifications of LDR Module

S. no.	Specifications	Details
1.	Operating Voltage	3.3 V to 5 V DC
2.	Operating Current	15 mA
3.	LEDs	Indicates output and power
4.	LM 393 based design	
5.	Output Digital	0 V to 5 V, Adjustable trigger level from preset
6.	Output Analog	0 V to 5 V. It depends on light fall on its photoresistor
7.	PCB Size	3.2 cm * 1.4 cm

Table 17.2 Pin Description of LDR Module

S. no.	Pin Name	Pin Details
1.	Input Voltage	3.3 V to 5 V DC
2.	Output pin	Analog and Digital
3.	GND pin	Ground pin

17.2.7 PIR Motion Sensor Module

A Passive Infrared Sensor (PIR) is a sensor that is used to detect the motion of a human body. When a person is passed across the sensor at some angle, the motion is detected. This sensor can be used as an input to operate other things. It has the detection range up to 10m. The specifications and pin configuration are provided in Tables 17.3 and 17.4, respectively.

Table 17.3 Specifications of PIR Sensor Module

S. no.	Specifications	Details
1.	Voltage	4.5 V to 20 V
2.	Output	High at 3.3 V and Low at 0 V
3.	Detection Angle	120 degrees
4.	Range	Adjustable, up to 7 m
5.	Trigger modes	Default is high at repeatable trigger, low at unrepeatable trigger
6.	PCB Dimensions	33 * 25 mm
7.	Lens	11 mm high, 23 mm diameter
8.	Weight	6 g

Table 17.4 Pin Description of PIR Motion Sensor Module

S. no.	Pin Name	Pin Details
1.	Input Voltage	3.3 V to 5 V DC
2.	OUT pin	Output pin
3.	GND pin	Ground pin

17.2.9 Actuators

LED LED is an electric light source. It is a semiconductor light that emits light when the current flows through it. It has two leads anode and cathode.

Relay It is an electrically operated switch. It can control the flow of current flowing through the appliances. Pin description of the Relay module is provided in Table 17.5.

Table 17.5 Pin Description of Relay Module

S. no.	Pin Name	Description
1.	Input Voltage	3.3 V to 5 V
2.	IN pin	Input pin
3.	GND pin	Ground pin
4.	Normally Close (NC)	It is used to stop the current
5.	Common pin (COM)	Common pin
6.	Normally Closed (NO)	It is used to flow the current

The block diagram for fan speed control based on temperature and humidity using Fuzzy logic is shown in Fig. 17.2.

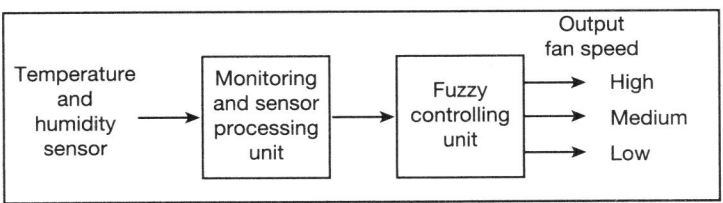

Fig. 17.2 Block Diagram of Fan Speed Control based on Temperature and Humidity using Fuzzy Logic

17.2.10 Software Design: UML Diagrams

Class diagram, sequence diagram, and use case diagram are provided in Figures 17.3, 17.4, and 17.5, respectively.

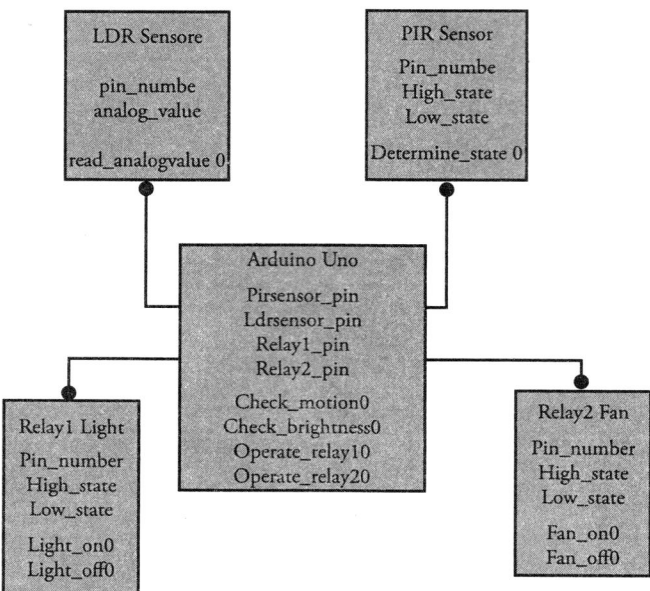

Fig. 17.3 Class Diagram for Smart Light and Fan Appliances

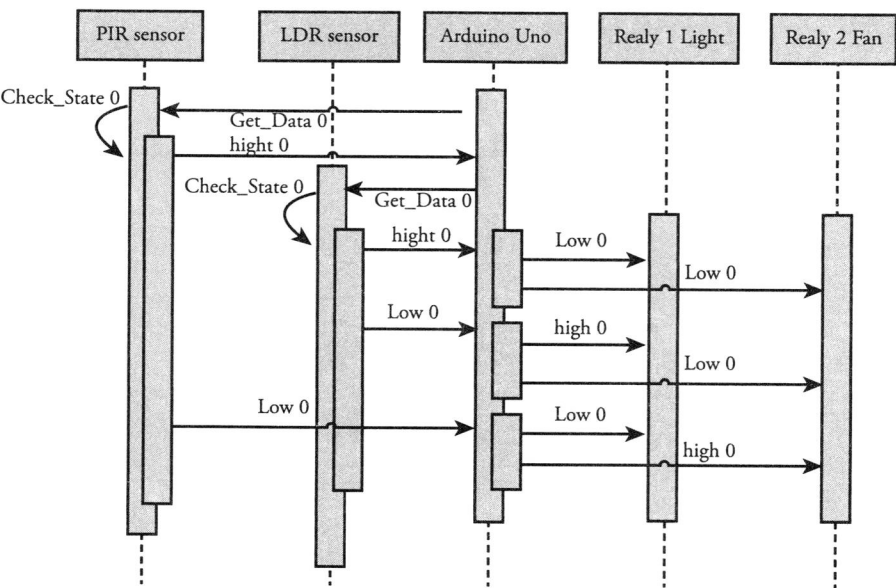

Fig. 17.4 Sequence Diagram for Smart Light and Fan Appliances

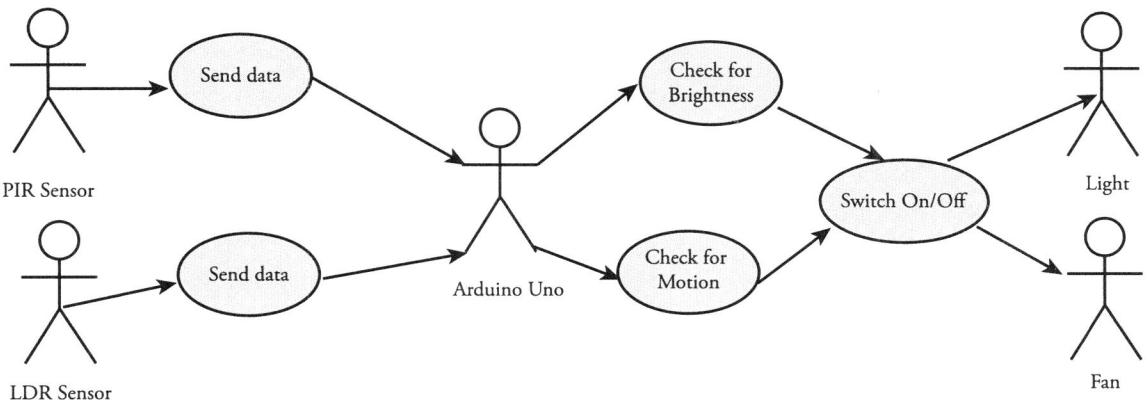

Fig. 17.5 Use Case Diagram for Smart Light and Fan Appliances

17.2.11 Pseudocode

Fuzzy logic controller for fan speed control based on temperature and humidity as inputs is presented as below:

Step 1: Define input and output parameters and their linguistic variables.

The inputs parameters are 'temperature' and 'humidity'. The temperature is measured in degree Celsius and humidity is measured in percentage. The output is fan 'speed' measured in rotation per minutes (rpm). Three linguistic variables are used for each input and output variables.

Linguistic variables for temperature are as below:

LT – Low Temperature
MT – Medium Temperature
HT – High Temperature

Linguistic variables for humidity are as below:

LH – Low Humidity
MH – Medium Humidity
HH – High Humidity

Linguistic variables for fan speed are as below:

LS – Low Speed
MH – Medium Speed
HS – High Speed

Step 2: Define membership functions for each input and output.

The triangular membership functions for temperature and humidity and speed are as shown in Figures 17.6 and 17.7, respectively.

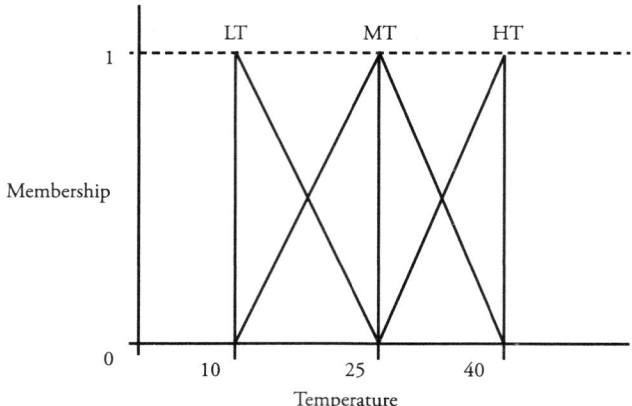

Fig. 17.6 Membership Function for Temperature

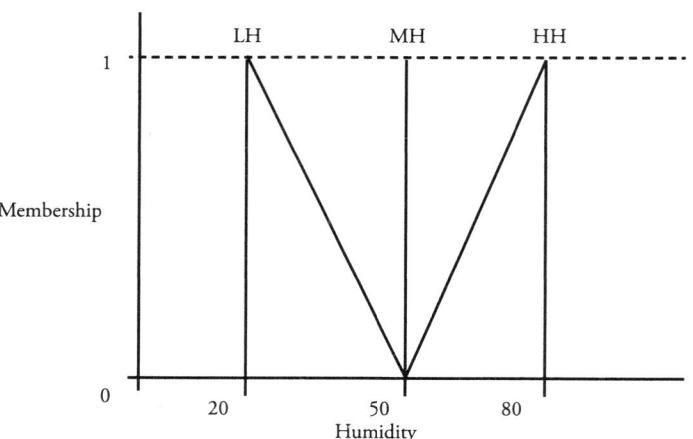

Fig. 17.7 Membership Function for Humidity

Membership function for the output fan speed is shown in Fig. 17.8.

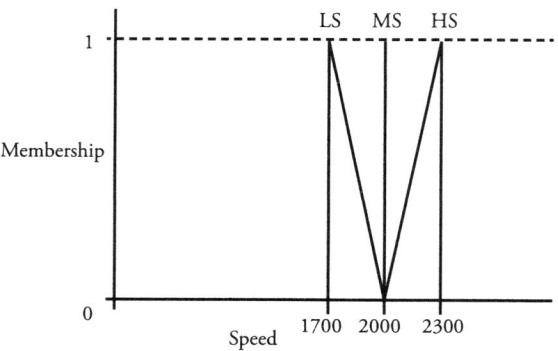

Fig. 17.8 Membership Function for the Output Fan Speed

Step 3: The Rule Base is designed using Logic as per Fig. 17.9 for the temperature and humidity inputs and nine 'if---then' rules are defined.

	Low Humidity	Medium Humidity	High Humidity
Low Temperature	Low Speed	Low Speed	Medium Speed
Medium Temperature	Medium Speed	Medium Speed	High Speed
High Temperature	Medium Speed	High Speed	High Speed

Fig. 17.9 Decision Rule Table

Step 4: Rule Evaluation is done as per the rule base and membership functions and fuzzification rules
Step 5: Defuzzification to get crisp control output using 'Mean of Max' defuzzification.

17.2.12 Smart Door Lock System

The Smart Door Lock System provides a smart security system for opening the door lock. In this system, two level security is developed. With the first level security, only the authorized person can be able to open the lock after face recognition. The second level security is a manual mode and the door can be open using key. If the key is given to a person who is not authorised with face registration then the person who cannot open the lock. Figure 17.10 shows the block diagram of Smart Door Lock System.

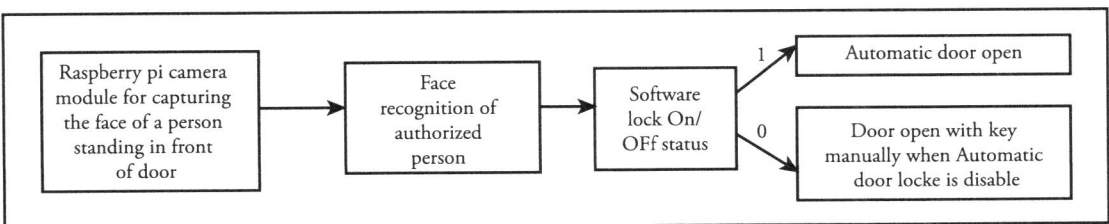

Fig. 17.10 Block Diagram of Smart Door Lock System

The different modules of the above block diagram are as below:

Raspberry Pi camera module for capturing the face of a person standing in front of door The Raspberry Pi camera module is used to capture the face of a person when standing in front of door. This is the input for face recognition module.

Face recognition of authorized person The image data is analyzed which is collected from Raspberry Pi camera module. If a person is authenticated with its face recognition as an authorized person of the house then the person is allowed to open the door by opening smart lock. Then the person can open the door also using the key.

Software lock on/off status The on and off manual mode is provided that decides whether the door lock should be in manual mode or by smart lock mode with face recognition. For manual mode the smart lock security is disabled by the authorized person remotely for providing access to a person whose registration is not done for smart lock mode and then the person can open the door manually with the key.

17.2.13 Component List

Table 17.6 shows list of components required for development of the circuit for these three smart appliances. Tables 17.7 and 17.8 show the list of sensors and list of actuators, respectively.

Table 17.6 List of Components

S. no.	Component Name	Description	Image
1.	Arduino Uno	• open source microcontroller board. • based on microchip ATmega 328P microcontroller.	
2.	Connector Cable	• USB A to USB B connector cable. • Arduino Uno to Laptop.	
3.	Breadboard	• used for building the prototype of an electronic circuit.	
4.	Jumper Wires	• These are electronic wires that are used to interconnect the components within a circuit. • The male to male, female to female and female to male jumper wires are used.	
5.	Resistors	• It is a passive electronic component. • It controls the flow of current in the electronic circuit.	

Table 17.7 List of Sensors

S. no.	Sensor Name	Model Name	Specifications	Image
1.	LDR Sensor Module	LDR Light Sensor	• Working Voltage: 3.3V – 5V. • LM393 chip is used. • On board sensitivity adjustment.	
2.	PIR Motion Sensor	Big Dome PIR	• Input Voltage: 5V DC. • Sending angle: 110 degrees. • Range: 3 to 5 meter.	

Table 17.8 List of Actuators

S. no.	Component Name	Description	Image
1.	LED	• Electric light source. • Semiconductor light that emits light when the current flows through it.	
2.	Relay Module	• Electrically operated switch. • To control the flow of current flowing through the appliance.	
3.	Bulb	• Night lamp	
4.	Fan	• 12 V DC fan.	

17.2.13.1 Connection Details

- Connect A0 pin of LDR Module to the A0 pin of Arduino Uno. Connect D0 pin of LDR Module to the digital pin 7 of Arduino Uno. Connect Vcc pin of LDR Module to the 5V pin of Arduino Uno. Connect GND pin of LDR Module to the GND pin of Arduino Uno (see Fig. 17.11).
- Connect Vcc pin of PIR Sensor to the 5V pin Arduino Uno. Connect OUT pin of PIR Sensor to the digital pin 5 of Arduino Uno. Connect GND pin of PIR Sensor to the GND pin of Arduino Uno.
- Connect positive end of LED to the resistor and another end of resistor is connected to digital pin 13 of the Arduino Uno. Connect negative end of LED to the GND pin of Arduino Uno.
- Connect IN pin of relay module to the digital pin 9 of Arduino Uno. Connect GND pin of relay module 1 to the GND pin of Arduino Uno. Connect Vcc pin of relay module to the 5 V pin of Arduino Uno. Connect bulb and its supply pin to the NC and COM connection port of relay module.
- Connect IN pin of relay module to the digital pin 9 of Arduino Uno. Connect GND pin of relay module 1 to the GND pin of Arduino Uno. Connect Vcc pin of relay module to the 5 V pin of Arduino Uno. Connect fan and its supply pin to the NC and COM connection port of relay module.

17.2.13.2 Circuit Diagram

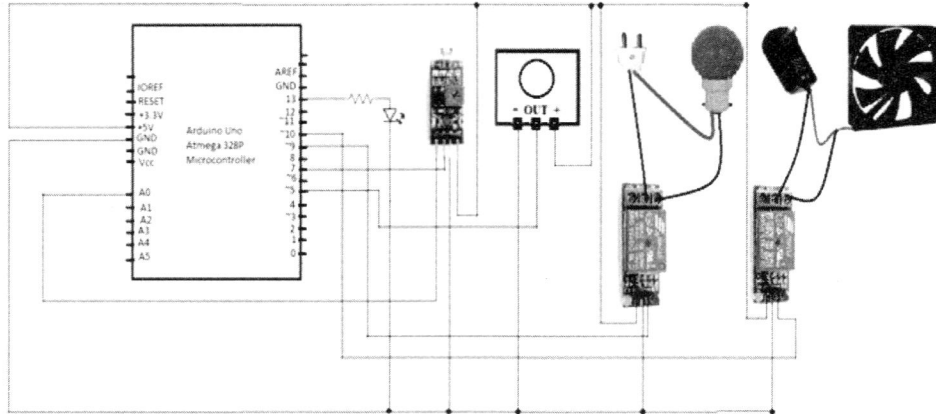

Fig. 17.11 Circuit Diagram of Smart Light and Smart Fan with Fuzzy Logic Controller

Test cases
- Case 1: When person enters the room, the motion is detected and if enough natural light is present in the room then fan turns on but bulb remains off.
- Case 2: When person enters the room and motion is detected but there is darkness in the room then bulb and fan both devices are turned on.
- Case 3: When there is no person present in the room the bulb and fan are switched off.

17.2.14 Sample Source Code in Embedded C for Arduino Uno Board

Figure 17.12 shows the sample embedded C code for smart devices light and fan.

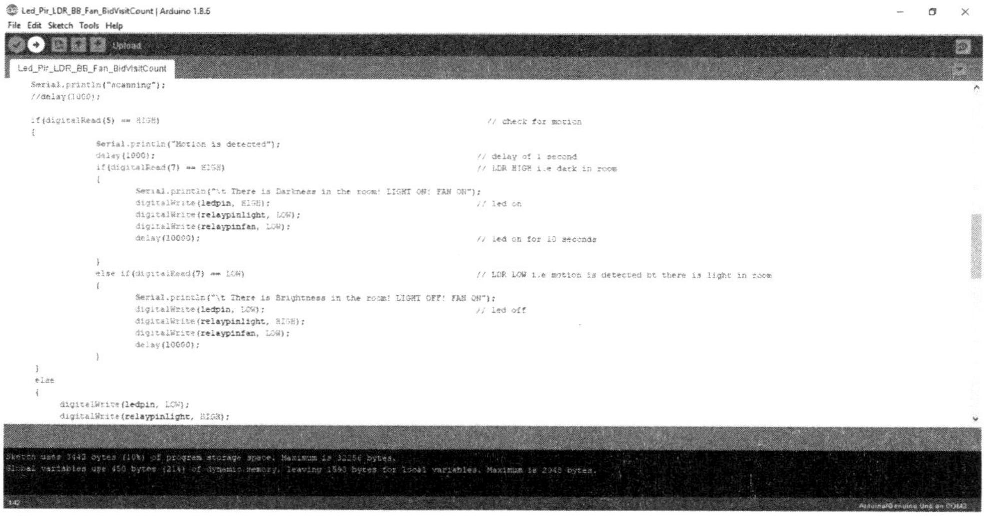

Fig. 17.12 Sample Embedded C Code for Smart Devices Light and Fan

17.2.15 Output

The embedded C code output for the code in Fig. 17.12 for smart devices, Light and Fan, is shown in Fig. 17.13.

Fig. 17.13 Embedded C Code Output for the Code in Fig. 17.12 for Smart Devices, Light and Fan

The fan speed can be controlled depending on the temperature and humidity parameters as inputs. The fan speed can be stated as high, medium and low. The fan speed control is obtained using fuzzy logic. The inputs are temperature and humidity. The temperature is measured in degree Celsius and humidity is measured in percentage. The output is fan speed measured in rpm.

Few steps of the python code are presented below, for implementation of fuzzy logic for fan speed control based on temperature and humidity

High level APIs such as numpy module, skfuzzy module and control module from the skfuzzy module are imported.

```
import numpy as np
import skfuzzy as fuzz
from skfuzzy import control as ctrl
```

Temperature and humidity are the inputs to control the fan speed as an output. Antecedent and consequent holds the universe variable and membership functions for temperature, humidity and speed.

```
temperature = ctrl.Antecedent(np.arange(0, 41, 1), 'temperature')
humidity = ctrl.Antecedent(np.arange(0, 81, 1), 'humidity')
speed = ctrl.Consequent(np.arange(0, 2500, 1), 'speed')
```

The descriptors for input and output variables are defined using triangular membership function. The descriptors for temperature are given the linguistic variable as low, medium and high. The descriptors for humidity are given the linguistic variables as less, medium and high. The descriptors for speed of fan as output are defined with linguistic variables as low, medium and high.

```
temperature['low'] = fuzz.trimf(temperature.universe, [10, 10, 25])
temperature['medium'] = fuzz.trimf(temperature.universe, [10, 25, 40])
temperature['high'] = fuzz.trimf(temperature.universe, [25, 40, 40])

humidity['less'] = fuzz.trimf(humidity.universe, [20, 20, 50])
humidity['medium'] = fuzz.trimf(humidity.universe, [20, 50, 80])
humidity['high'] = fuzz.trimf(humidity.universe, [50, 80, 80])

speed['low'] = fuzz.trimf(speed.universe, [1700, 1700, 2000])
speed['medium'] = fuzz.trimf(speed.universe, [1700, 2000, 2300])
speed['high'] = fuzz.trimf(speed.universe, [2000, 2300, 2300])
```

To view the membership function of temperature variable following function is called.

```
temperature.view()
```

To view the membership function of humidity variable following function is called.

```
humidity.view()
```

Figures 17.14 (a) and (b) show the triangular membership function plot for the parameters temperature and humidity.

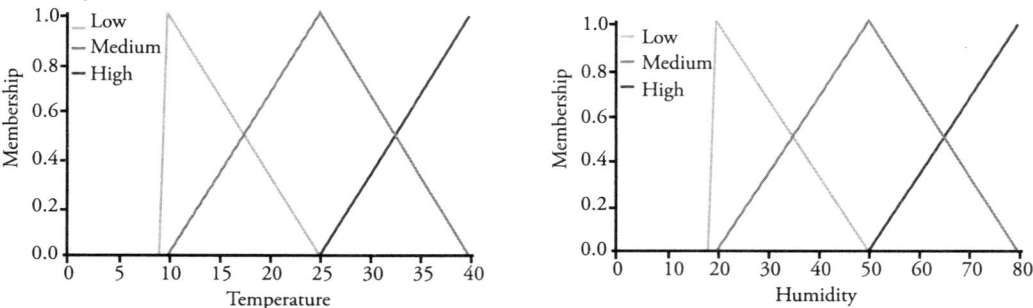

Fig. 17.14 Triangular Membership Function Plot for the Parameters (a) Temperature and (b) Humidity

To view the membership function of speed, following function is called.

```
speed.view()
```

The triangular membership f=unction plot for the output fan speed is shown in Fig. 17.15.

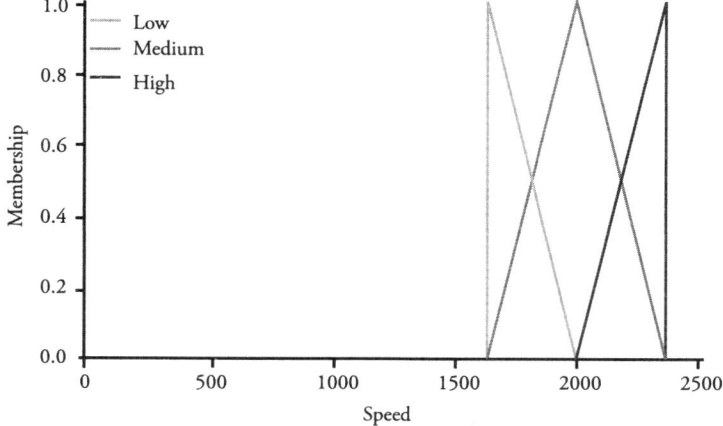

Fig. 17.15 Triangular Membership Function Plot for the Output Fan Speed

Then, the rules are formed to apply fuzzification.

```
rule1 = ctrl.Rule(temperature['low'] | humidity['less'], speed['low'])
rule2 = ctrl.Rule(temperature['low'] | humidity['medium'], speed['low'])
rule3 = ctrl.Rule(temperature['low'] | humidity['high'], speed['medium'])

rule4 = ctrl.Rule(temperature['medium'] | humidity['less'], speed['medium'])
rule5 = ctrl.Rule(temperature['medium'] | humidity['medium'], speed['medium'])
rule6 = ctrl.Rule(temperature['medium'] | humidity['high'], speed['high'])

rule7 = ctrl.Rule(temperature['high'] | humidity['less'], speed['medium'])
rule8 = ctrl.Rule(temperature['high'] | humidity['medium'], speed['high'])
rule9 = ctrl.Rule(temperature['high'] | humidity['high'], speed['high'])
```

The rules are evaluated the function ControlSystemSimulation.

```
temp1 = ctrl.ControlSystem([rule1, rule2, rule3, rule4, rule5, rule5, rule6, rule7, rule8, rule9])
temp2 = ctrl.ControlSystemSimulation(temp1)
```

For example, If temperature = 30 °C and humidity = 55 %
Then after computing above rules the following output is displayed.

```
[10]: temp2.input['temperature'] = 30
      temp2.input['humidity'] = 55
      temp2.compute()

      print(temp2.output['speed'])
      speed.view(sim=temp2)
```

The output value for the fan speed on the membership function is shown in Fig. 17.16.

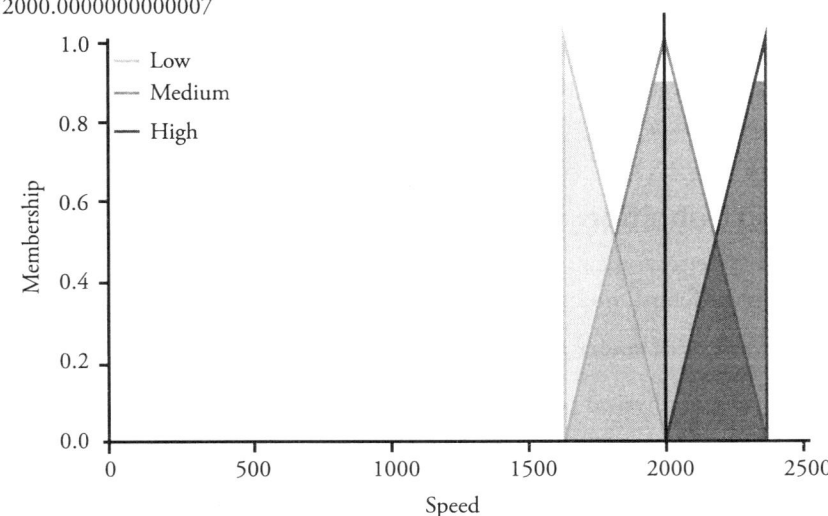

Fig. 17.16 Output Value for the Fan Speed Shown on Membership Function

At temperature at 30 degree Celsius and humidity at 55%, the fan speed is at 2000 rpm. When the temperature is medium and humidity is medium then the fan speed is medium at 2000 rpm.

17.2.16 Energy Saving and Management using Smart Home Appliances

Home Automation for smart home appliances such as lights, fans, refrigerator, air conditioner will save considerable electrical energy per home. For example a smart home with minimum 1000 watts appliances will save electrical energy of 0.5 unit per day, if smart appliances are switched off efficiently when not in use. Thus 15 units of electrical energy will be saved by a house with 1000 watts of electrical appliances and 30 minutes of less use of each of these appliances. Cumulatively thousands of smart houses will save large amount of electrical energy.

17.3 USE CASE: SMART GOODS TRANSPORTATION

This use case focuses on the development of an IoT based application that can assist in the easy hiring and transport of goods using commercial heavy transportation vehicles.

17.3.1 Overview

This use case application has similar functionality like Uber transport but this is Goods Transport system while Uber is a taxi service for customer travel while this smart IoT application is useful for transporting goods. Goods transportation is important for businesses. However, the traffic congestion is a major constraint while delivering the goods in time. Many other motivating factors to develop this smart application are scarcity of loading/unloading areas, road conditions and idle return of vehicles and poor utilization of vehicle resources causing increase in per trip cost. The safety risks are also major concern for transport of dangerous goods like inflammable material. The proposed system will make goods transportation smarter, more efficient, environmentally friendly and safe.

A major issue which the goods transportation system may have is the under utilisation of the vehicle resources such as movement of under capacity or unloaded truck due to lack of orders or in time order or booking. Currently, goods transportation system suffers from lack of bookings because unavailability of smart searching option. Another problem that arises in the goods transportation system is that some goods may get damaged while some goods are perishable.

17.3.2 Problem Definition

Smart transportation system can be used for transporting the goods from one place to another. In goods transportation system, different modules can be incorporated as below.

Modules for development of smart goods transportation system

- Design and develop a physical prototype for Smart Goods Transportation
- Design and develop front-end and back-end of software system

This use case presents an application which will be help to book one of our various vehicle types. As this is an on-demand system, our servers will locate the drivers nearest to the customer and assign him to the customer. Thus, no vehicles will go under-capacity.

17.3.3 Hardware and Software Requirements

Hardware Requirements:

- A computer/laptop for coding with IDE (android and Arduino Uno Board)

Minimum requirements to be met:
- Intel i5 processor
- 8 GB RAM
- Running Windows 10
- Android phone for development and testing purposes
- Running Android 5.0 +
- 2 GB RAM
- Arduino Uno Wifi integrated
- Sensors (MQ135)

Software Requirements for development:
- Arduino IDE for pushing code onto board.
- Jupyter Notebook for Python code development
- Thingspeak cloud platform for storing data.
- Firebase Google cloud platform
- Android Studio to develop the applications
- Windows OS
- Raspberry Pi, Pycharm, Android Studio and other software.

Hardware Requirements for implementation:
- Mobile phones to run the applications
- Minimum requirements to be met:
- Android version 5.0 and Above
- 4 GB Ram
- Internet connection

17.3.4 Block Diagram of the System Model

Figure 17.17 shows the block diagram of the system model.

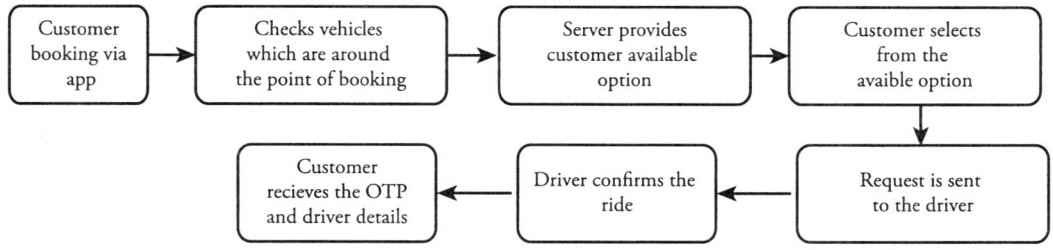

Fig. 17.17 Block Diagram

17.3.5 Software and User Interfaces of the Smart Goods Transportation System

- Real Time database on open-source cloud server platform named Firebase
- Cloud Server software module to manage real time requests and responses
- User interfaces

Mobile apps
- Customer
- Vehicle Driver
- Owner

17.3.6 Pseudocode of the Workflow

- Customer registers with the customer app to the smart goods transportation system and registration details are saved on real-time cloud server
- Customer creates Login credentials which are saved on backend real-time cloud server
- Customer provides source and destination and type of goods to book a vehicle and this request backend real-time cloud server
- Available and suitable vehicles are sent to the customer app
- Customer selects a vehicle from the given option and click confirm option on the app
- This request is sent to the backend server
- Server reserves vehicle for this customer and generates and send 4 digit OTP encrypted with ECC encryption to the customer app and the source details to the driver app
- Customer app decrypts the OTP using ECC decryption and the key
- Driver reaches to the source with the vehicle booked by the customer
- Customer enters the OTP and these authentication credentials are sent to backend server for authentication of the customer and then the journey starts
- The journey and vehicle and driver details are sent to customer and owner app

The cost of trip is computed based on following factors:
- Distance between source and destination
- Diesel Price
- Mileage of the Vehicle
- Toll and other taxes
- Cost of vehicle according to the type of goods
- Agent commission
- Trip and goods insurance cost

Cost of the trip is calculated as below:

Cost of the trip = (Distance/Mileage)*Diesel Price + Cost of vehicle + Toll prices + Insurance

Total amount = Cost of the trip + (Cost of the trip * agent's percentage commission)

17.3.7 Major Functionalities of the Back-end Server System

- Real-time Database storage and management of Customer registration and Login credentials
- Real-time Database storage and management of vehicles and owners registered with the system
- OTP generation and ECC encryption
- Customer authentication
- Vehicle allocation
- Information notification and management of customer, driver app and owner app
- Calculation the trip cost accurately
- Best route finding by time series data analysis

17.3.8 Performance Requirements

- Reliability: The system must give accurate prediction and right vehicle allocation and security to the goods while in transport
- Scalability: System should expandable to accommodate heavy customer load and enable to cover wider geographical area
- Capacity: System should be capable for storage requirements and heavy load of request response and management
- Response time: Being a near real-time system the response to the request should be in near real-time for information and processing

17.3.9 Software Design (UML Diagrams)

Software design is done using the unified Modelling Language (UML diagrams). Figures 17.18, 17.19 and 17.20 are showcasing Class diagram, Sequence diagram and Use case diagram, respectively.

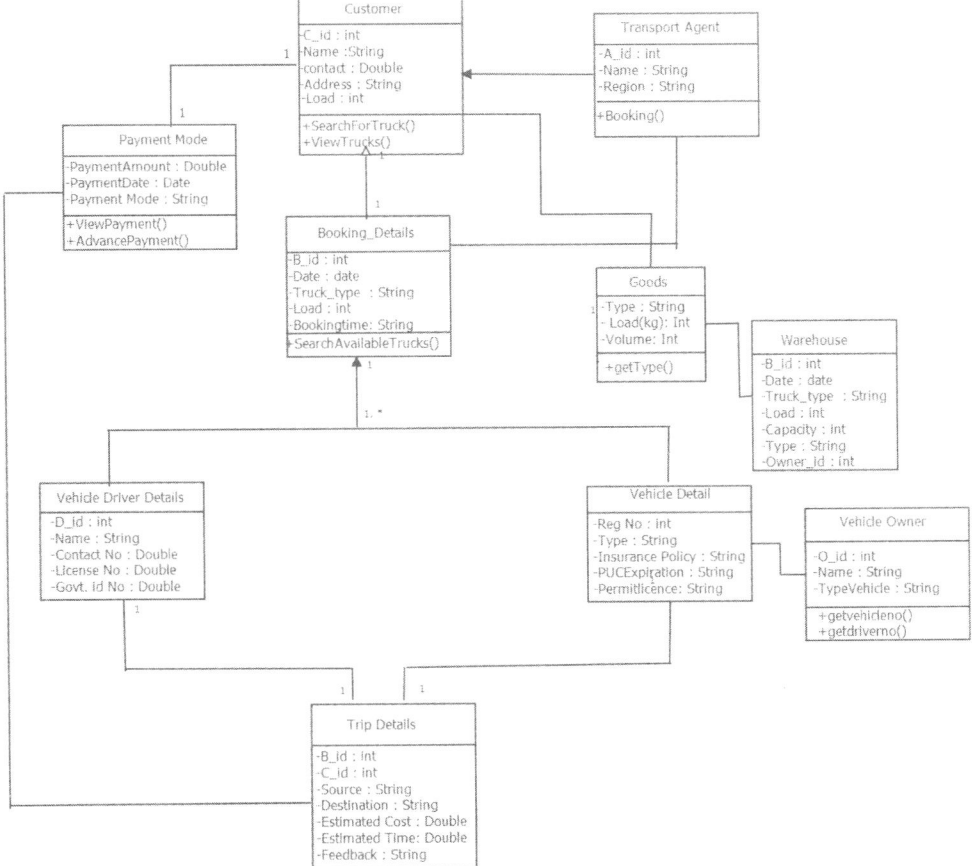

Fig. 17.18 Class Diagram for Smart Good Transportation

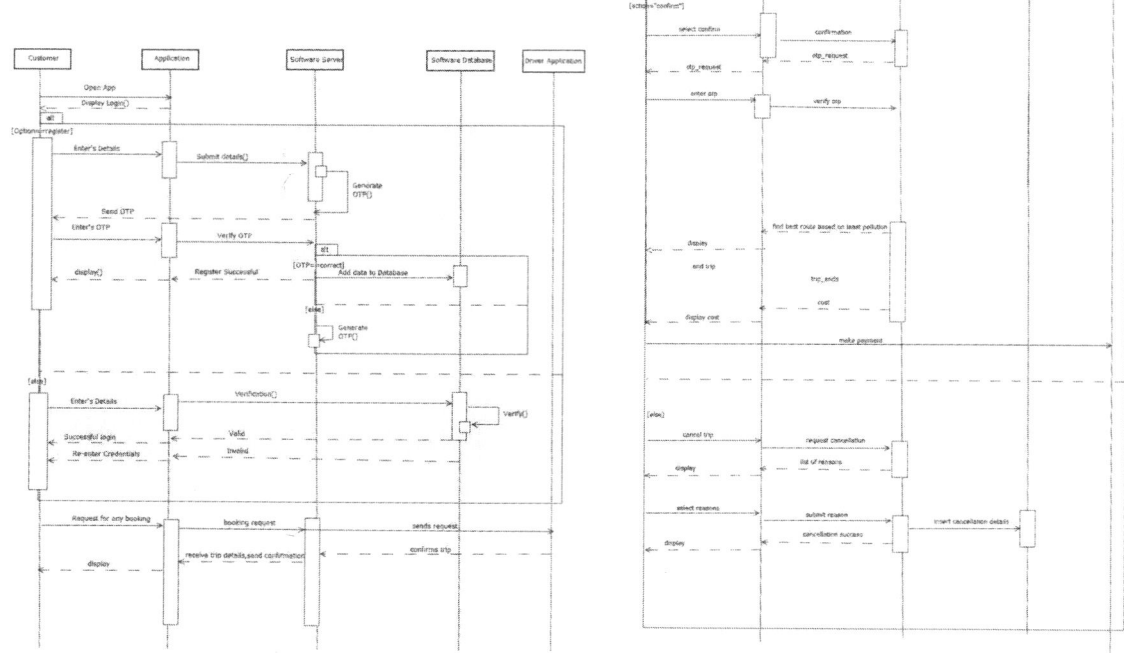

Fig. 17.19 Sequence Diagram for Smart Good Transportation

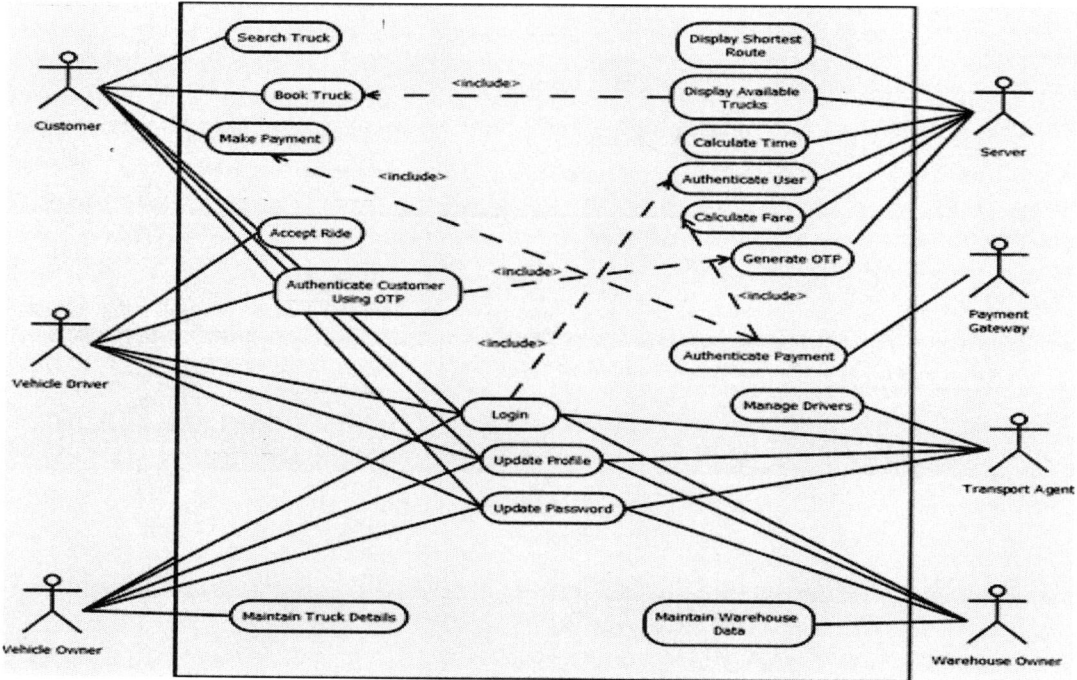

Fig. 17.20 Use Case Diagram for Smart Good Transportation

Figure 17.21 shows the user interface customer app, registration, login and vehicle booking screen; and Fig. 17.22 displays the customer app screens.

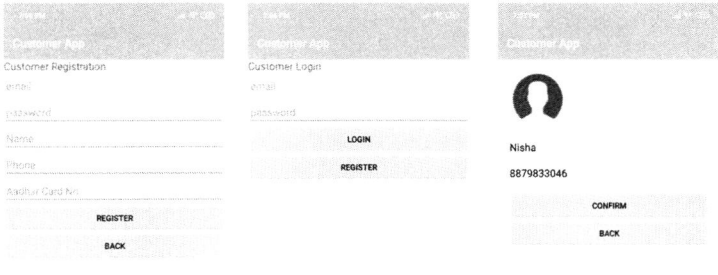

Fig. 17.21 User Interface Customer App, Registration, Login and Vehicle Booking Screen

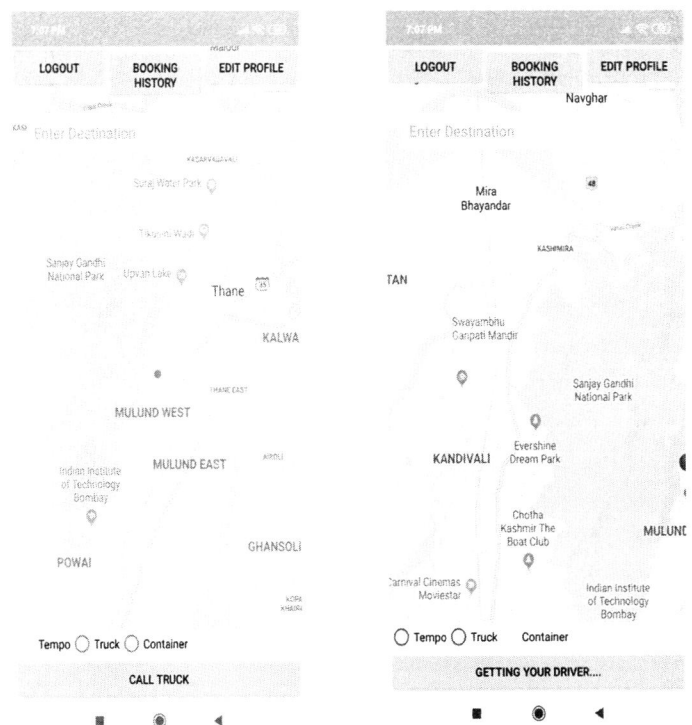

Fig. 17.22 Customer App Screens

17.4 HEALTHCARE USE CASE: IoT FOR HEALTHCARE DEVICES AND CHALLENGES

IoT has a great potential to work through edge analytics processing of healthcare data of collected patients. It can be useful to a physician as support system for data collection, edge processing and analytics, report generation, GUI application for end user, etc. Many challenges and limitations are faced while handling healthcare data of a patient due to the requirements of privacy and confidentiality of the data. Some of those challenges are discussed in the following sections.

Security of personal health information   Security of sensitive personal health information of patients is essential. Hence many organisations such as hospitals, clinical laboratories store the personal health information in encrypted format to avoid confidentiality breach.

Filtered data collection from huge available data   Right data collection from available large volume of healthcare data is a challenging task. A good domain knowledge and technology expertise is needed to extract and process the correct information needed as per the health issues of the patients. This data is collected from multiple devices.

Data integration   Data collection is needed from multiple sensor devices for developing healthcare solutions. Integration of this sensors data, and pre-processing is needed to transform the data into information. Due to different formats of the data from different kind of devices the integration task is challenging. The diverse data formats and protocols is one of the biggest hurdles in the development of healthcare solutions using IoT technology.

17.4.1 Teleradiology Platform for Screening Covid19 Patients and Remote Diagnosis using IoT Technologies

In the present worrisome scenario of COVID 19, it is generally accepted that social distancing screening and testing for covid19 infected people, quarantine them for minimum 14 days and treating them the best possible way is the only solution at present (with no guarantee of 100% cure as it depends on individual's immunity). Hence, speedy screening and quarantine of COVID 19 infected people is the best option for reducing further spread.

Current screening methods

At present predominantly two method are used for COVID 19 patient rapid screening

1. Symptomatic: By checking temperature and if the person is having temperature/ if the person is coughing, then throat and nasal swab test and blood test, and X-ray and then decide treatment protocol
2. By CT scan diagnosis

Constraints to use present screening/testing methods

Many constraints are faced when CT scanning is used for fast screening of COVID 19 patients. Some are as below:

1. Due to the lack of enough number of machines and then difficulty in sanitizing the CT machine after CT scan of every individual in this COVID 19 situation, at present in India this is a very slow, difficult method.
2. Blood test is little time consuming and even X-Rays are needed for further treatment to diagnose its spread in lung

17.4.2 A Tele-Radiology Platform Solution for Screening with X-Ray AI Module for Screening/Testing Protocol for Diagnosis and Further Treatment

Tele radiology platform for fast screening of COVID 19 patients is effective due to various reasons. As of today, no screening method can screen COVID 19 infected people with 100% accuracy. Any present screening method need to be supported with other information through blood test/ CT scan etc. Though X-Ray shows COVID 19 infection in a person from day 4 onwards from the infection day (and for good immunity person it does not even show at all) Many that are not detected as COVID19 infected, can be detected as the outcome of this Tele-radiology X-Ray screening in a short time. Many of the infected people might get their screening done only on 4th or 5th day onward as currently screening facilities are limited.

X-Ray screening with AI module can be effective as currently technical literature talks about achieving 97% accuracy and some already existing Tele-Radiology platforms in India are reporting 95% recall accuracy for their X-Ray AI module. Tele-radiology platform integrated with X-Ray AI module can be a good option for mass screening and for further investigation of COVID19 infected people. Through Tele radiology the AI module output can be examined further by radiologist and may be with additional blood test parameters the testing/treatment guidelines can be established in near real time of about maximum 45 to 60 minutes till final report generation.

X-Ray machines have huge screening capacity as one machine can run for 18 hours in a day and per hour imaging capacity is 15 images/hour hence total scanning capacity is 18 x15 per day. For example, 1000 X-Ray machines can scan 1000 x 270 = 270000 images in one day. For example if 800 radiologists working for 9 hours and can check 30 X-Ray images then Tele-radiology platform with associated centres and radiologist can screen, till final report 800 x 250 = 200000, X-Ray images per day and in the current scenario mass screening can be is achieved in reduced time to screen COVID 19 infected patients. These Tele-radiology platforms are scalable with proper hardware software enhancement.

Storage and privacy of patient images can be taken care by saving the image in lossless compressed format for the region of interest cropped images. Cloud storage or dedicated storage servers can take care of needed large storage capacity. These Tele-radiology platforms will be also useful for diagnosis and treatment of various diseases related to lung other than COVID 19 such as pneumonia, Tuberculosis (TB) and in future a nationwide large Tel- radiology platform for healthcare solution be established. The block diagram for the IoT based teleradiology platform for screening COVID 19 patients is shown in Fig. 17.23.

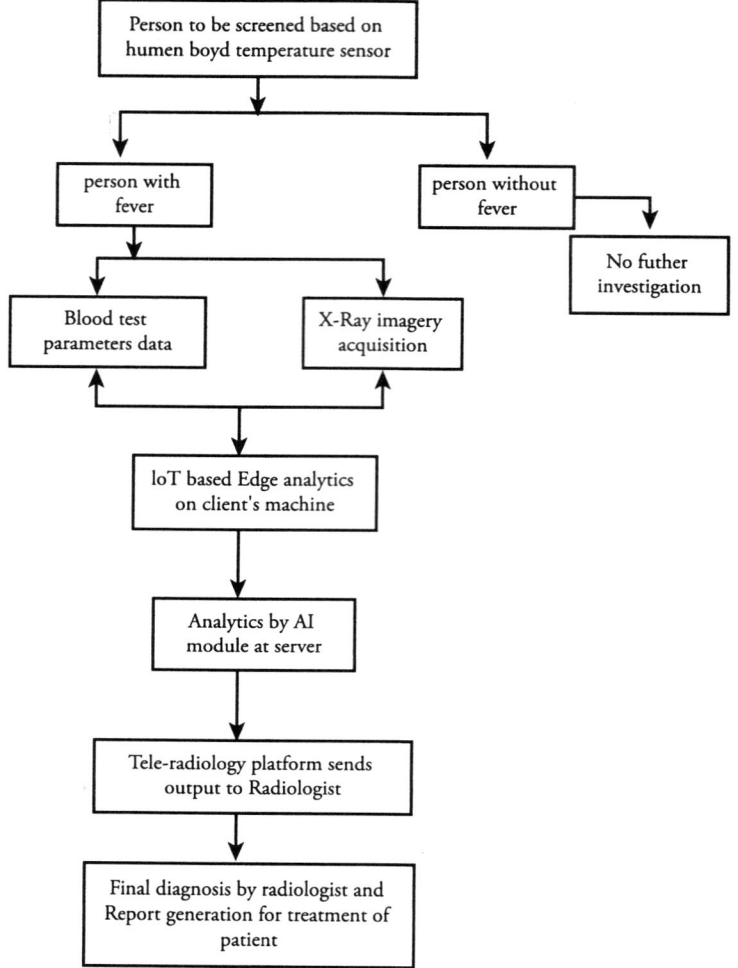

Fig. 17. 23 Overall Block Diagram: IoT-based Teleradiology Platform for Screening COVID 19 Patients

17.4.3 Hardware Requirements

1. Hardware server platforms
2. Cloud storage platform for secure storage and management of patients' health data for preserving privacy
3. Hardware client machines for collecting the data and for loading the client software
4. IoT Hardware and fast network connectivity to remotely placed radiologists, hospitals and laboratories for collecting data and sending to local server and then to cloud server for processing in AI module

17.4.4 Software Requirements

1. Local Server software for temporary data storage and management
2. Cloud storage and management software
3. Client software at end user machine at hospital or remote radiologist or laboratory for edge analytics and temporary data storage and transfer
4. Network and data Security infrastructure for information security

17.4.5 Methodologies

Some Pre-processing techniques that are to be carried out before the data to be submitted to the AI module are listed below.

X-Ray spatial enhancement Before finding high level features the X-Ray image spatial enhancement needs to be after cropping the image for Region of Interest (RoI). Few Spatial enhancement techniques are mentioned below that can be tried/carried out for pre-processing X-Ray image for extracting different features

- Feature extraction: Design of new auto encoder is useful to extract features of interest.
- Feature selection: It is a good strategy to find discriminating features, through various feature selection methods, which can then be passed on to a deep learning module.

Box 17.1 shows the pseudocode for the teleradiology platform for screening COVID 19 patients.

BOX 17.1 PSEUDO CODE: IOT BASED TELERADIOLOGY PLATFORM FOR SCREENING AND DIAGNOSIS OF COVID 19

Screen patient with temperature sensor by measuring Human body temperature.

1. If Sensed Temperature above normal
    i. swab data extraction from collected swab test
    ii. Xray imagery data collection
    iii. X-Ray Image analysis
1. Feature Extraction
2. Teleradiology AI module for classification as COVID 19 positive or COVID 19 Negative
    iv. If patient screened positive in the AI module, then the data is transferred to a radiologist using IoT cloud platform for doctor's diagnosis at remotely place using IoT based Teleradiology platform
    v. If reported positive also by radiologist, then report sent to the hospital
    vi. RTPCR test result parameters sent to IoT and cloud-based AI module for deciding COVID positive screening accuracy to decide treatment protocol
2. Else
   No further investigation of that patient

17.5 AGRICULTURE USE CASE: IOT-BASED SMART IRRIGATION

IoT has shown to have significant potential in agricultural applications. There are various areas within agriculture domain such as:

- Smart irrigation systems that can significantly reduce water usage, this is especially crucial for ard. semi- arid areas and crops that require more water such as sugarcane. Also, this can help in those areas where groundwater is a major source of water for irrigation.
- Pest and disease monitoring using in situ as well as remote sensors for near real-time monitoring of crop health.
- IoT integrated Agro-meteorological and remote sensing platforms to understand crop growth, disease, and yield aspects.
- Greenhouses are mostly migrating to automatically maintain various parameters, such as temperature, humidity, light conditions, etc., based on IoT technology
- IoT driven field-to market applications that track the farm produce till the last mile delivery for parameters, such as quality parameters (e.g. freshness), inventory status, etc. using IoT sensors with data anal;ytics performed and visualized on Dashboards.
- Applications that use IoT sensors to manage livestock (e.g cattle) are also gaining a lot of attention. For example, IoT sensors put around the cattle neck are used to monitor the cattle health continuously.

17.5.1 Development of IoT Based Irrigation System

This use case describes the development of a smart irrigation system that can automatically sense the water requirement in a farm based on soil moisture measurements, using a soil moisture sensor. A drip irrigation system is activated (triggers an actuator automatically) based on the soil moisture levels so that optimal water is put in the farm.

The following discussion provides a walkthrough in the development process

Pre-requisites
- Arduino IDE

List of hardware and pinouts

The components required are shown in Figures 17.24, 25, 26, and 27.

- Arduino Uno

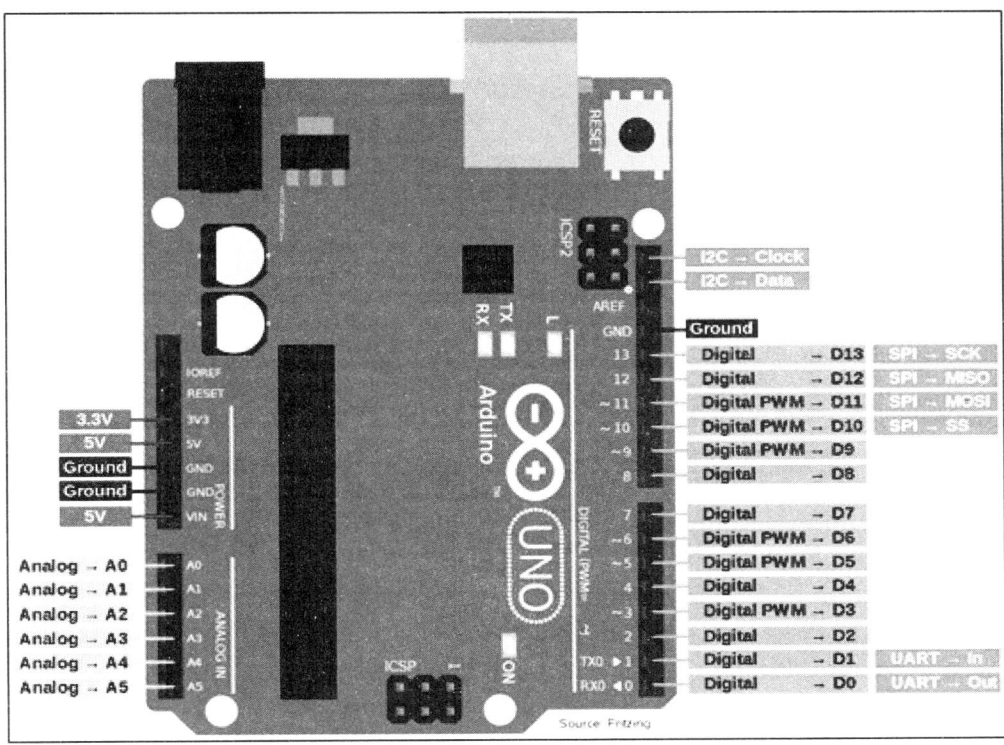

Fig. 17.24 Arduino Board

- Capacitive Soil Moisture Sensor

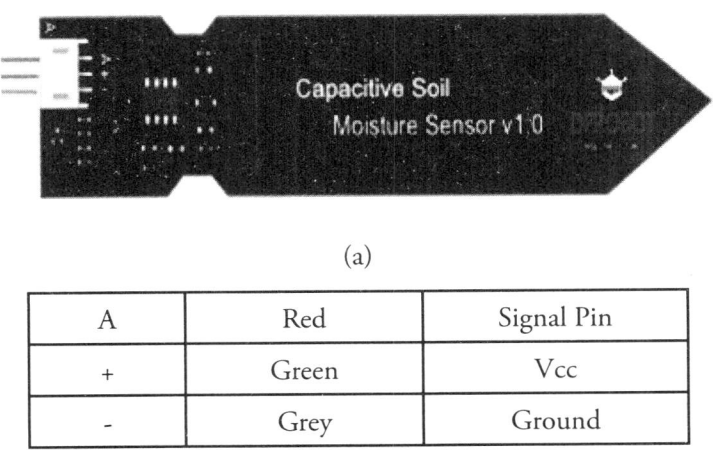

(a)

A	Red	Signal Pin
+	Green	Vcc
-	Grey	Ground

(b)

Fig. 17.25 (a) Capacitive Soil Moisture Sensor (b) Pin Details

- DC Motor

Fig. 17.26 DC Motor

- Waterproof DS18B20 Digital temperature sensor

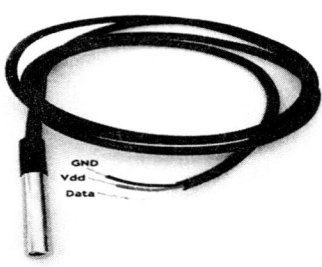

Fig. 17.27 Digital Temperature Sensor

17.5.1.1 Measurement of Soil Moisture

- Pinout:
    - Data wire of Soil Temperature Sensor - Pin 2 of Arduino
    - Signal Pin of Soil Moisture Sensor - Pin A0 of Arduino
- Concept: Checks every 1s for Soil Moisture value

LISTING 17.1: MEASUREMENT OF SOIL MOISTURE

```
#include <OneWire.h>
#include <DallasTemperature.h>
#define ONE_WIRE_BUS 2 // Data wire is plugged into pin 2 on the Arduino

OneWire oneWire(ONE_WIRE_BUS);

DallasTemperature sensors(&oneWire);

unsigned long lastSend;
float SMpin = A0;

void setup()
{
```

(Contd)

Listing 17.1 *(Contd)*

```
  Serial.begin(115200);

  sensors.begin();
  delay(10);
  lastSend = 0;
}
void loop()
{
  if ( millis() - lastSend > 1000 ) { // Update and send only after 1 seconds
    getSoilTemperatureAndMoistureData();
    lastSend = millis();
  }
}

void getSoilTemperatureAndMoistureData()
{
  Serial.println("Collecting Moisture Percentage");

  float moisture_percentage;

  moisture_percentage = ( 100.00 - ( (analogRead(SMpin)/1023.00) * 100.00 ) );

  // Check if any reads failed and exit early (to try again).
  if (isnan(moisture_percentage)) {
    Serial.println("Failed to read Soil Moisture value!");
    return;
  }
  Serial.print("Soil Moisture: ");
  Serial.print(moisture_percentage);
  Serial.print(" %\t");
}
```

17.5.1.2 Controlled Irrigation using Single Actuator (Motor) depending on Soil Moisture

- Pinout:
  - Data wire of Soil Temperature Sensor - Pin 2 of Arduino
  - Signal Pin of Soil Moisture Sensor - Pin A0 of Arduino
  - DC motor Positive Supply - Pin 13 of Arduino
- Concept: Checks with a frequency of every 1 second for Soil Moisture value and starts the motor if the soil moisture percentage is less than smThres = 75%.

LISTING 17.2: TRIGGERS AN ACTUATOR(MOTOR) BASED ON THE SOIL MOISTURE VALUE

```
#include <OneWire.h>
#include <DallasTemperature.h>
#define ONE_WIRE_BUS 2 // Data wire is plugged into pin 2 on the Arduino
OneWire oneWire(ONE_WIRE_BUS);
DallasTemperature sensors(&oneWire);
unsigned long lastSend;
float SMpin = A0;
int actPin = 13; //Actuator(motor) connected to pin 13
float smThres = 75.0; //Threshold for triggering actuator - 75%
float moisPercent; //Current Soil Moisture value in percentage
float moisture_percentage=0; //Initial moisture percentage value as 0
void setup()
{
  Serial.begin(115200);
  pinMode(13,OUTPUT); //Set pin 13 as OUTPUT pin
  sensors.begin();
  delay(10);
  lastSend = 0;
}
void loop()
{
  if ( millis() - lastSend > 1000 ) { // Update and send only after 1 seconds
    moisPercent = getSoilTemperatureAndMoistureData();
    if (moisPercent <=smThres){
      digitalWrite(actPin, HIGH);// turns on the motor
    }
    else {
      digitalWrite(actPin, LOW);// turns on the motor
    }
    lastSend = millis();
  }
}

float getSoilTemperatureAndMoistureData()
{
  Serial.println("Collecting Moisture Percentage");

  moisture_percentage = ( 100.00 - ( (analogRead(SMpin)/1023.00) * 100.00 ) );

  // Check if any reads failed and exit early (to try again).
  if (isnan(moisture_percentage)) {
    Serial.println("Failed to read Soil Moisture value!");
    return 999;
  }
  Serial.print("Soil Moisture: ");
  Serial.print(moisture_percentage);
  Serial.print(" %\t");
  return moisture_percentage;
}
```

17.5.1.3 Controlled Irrigation using Single Actuator (Motor) depending on Soil Moisture with Setting User-defined Speed

- Pinout:
  - Data wire of Soil Temperature Sensor - Pin 2 of Arduino
  - Signal Pin of Soil Moisture Sensor - Pin A0 of Arduino
  - DC motor Positive Supply - Pin 13 of Arduino
- Concept: Checks with a frequency of every 1 second for Soil Moisture value and starts the motor if the soil moisture percentage is less than 75%. The speed of the motor can be selected by defining the spMotor variable in the code.

LISTING 17.3: TRIGGERS AN ACTUATOR (MOTOR) BASED ON THE SOIL MOISTURE VALUE BUT WITH USER-DEFINED SPEED OF THE MOTOR

```
#include <OneWire.h>
#include <DallasTemperature.h>
#define ONE_WIRE_BUS 2 // Data wire is plugged into pin 2 on the Arduino

OneWire oneWire(ONE_WIRE_BUS);
DallasTemperature sensors(&oneWire);
unsigned long lastSend;
float SMpin = A0;
int actPin = 13; //Actuator(motor) connected to pin 13
float smThres = 75.0; //Threshold for triggering actuator - 75%
int spMotor = 180; //Predefined speed of motor for dc motor
float moisPercent; //Current Soil Moisture value in percentage
float moisture_percentage=0; //Initial moisture percentage value as 0

void setup()
{
  Serial.begin(115200);
  pinMode(13,OUTPUT); //Set pin 13 as OUTPUT pin
  sensors.begin();
  delay(10);
  lastSend = 0;
}

void loop()
{
  if ( millis() - lastSend > 1000 ) { // Update and send only after 1 seconds
    moisPercent = getSoilTemperatureAndMoistureData();
    if (moisPercent <=smThres){
      analogWrite(actPin, spMotor);// turns on the motor
    }
    else {
      analogWrite(actPin, spMotor);// turns on the motor
    }
```

(Contd)

Listing 17.3 *(Contd)*

```
    lastSend = millis();
  }
}

float getSoilTemperatureAndMoistureData()
{
  Serial.println("Collecting Moisture Percentage");

  float moisture_percentage;

  moisture_percentage = ( 100.00 - ( (analogRead(SMpin)/1023.00) * 100.00 ) );

  // Check if any reads failed and exit early (to try again).
  if (isnan(moisture_percentage)) {
    Serial.println("Failed to read Soil Moisture value!");
    return 999;
  }

  Serial.print("Soil Moisture: ");
  Serial.print(moisture_percentage);
  Serial.print(" %\t");
  return moisture_percentage;
```

SUMMARY

The Internet of Things (IoT) opens up tremendous opportunities for development of smart pervasive frameworks. As of now, many application domains, including smart home, smart cities, smart transportation, smart healthcare, smart energy management etc., are seeing impactful transformations. IoT is modernizing healthcare with promising technological, economic and social benefits. In this chapter the use cases for smart home appliances for home automation smart good transportation, and smart agriculture are explored in detail.

KEY TERMS

Smart Home, Smart Goods Transportation, Smart healthcare, Smart Agriculture

REVIEW QUESTIONS

1. Design a smart fridge using IoT technologies.
2. List the software and hardware for any smart healthcare application
3. Draw UML diagrams for smart farming application.
4. Write an Embedded C program for a smart Air conditioner.
5. List the required sensors for smart farming.
6. Write a note on smart city with respect to challenges, requirements and constraints.

7. Write design steps for smart supply chain application.

8. Explain the various areas in the agriculture domain that IoT is making an impact.

REFERENCES

1. Dennis Pfisterer et al. SPITFIRE: toward a semantic web of things. IEEE Communications Magazine, 49(11):40–48, 2011.
2. Freddy L'ecu'e et al. Smart traffic analytics in the semantic web with STAR-CITY: Scenarios, system and lessons learned in Dublin City. Web Semantics: Science, Services and Agents on the World Wide Web, 27:26– 33, 2014.
3. CityPulse EU FP7 Project, 2016. http://www.ict-citypulse.eu/page/.
4. Roland St¨uhmer et al. PLAY: Semantics-based Event Marketplace. In Collaborative Systems for Reindustrialization, pages 699–707. 2013.
5. SenseFly SA, 2016. https://www.sensefly.com/.
6. Duan Yan-e. Design of intelligent agriculture management information system based on IoT. In Proc. of ICICTA, pages 1045–1049, 2011
7. Sosa, J., Joglekar. J., 2019, Smart Home Automation using Fuzzy Logic and Internet of Things Technologies" in Lecture Notes in Network and Systems, vol. 57, Proceedings by Springer.
8. Joglekar, J., Bhutani, S., Patel, N., Soman, P., 2020, "'Lightweight Elliptical Curve Cryptography (ECC) for Data Integrity and User Authentication in Smart Transportation IoT system", Book Chapter, Lecture Notes on Data Engineering and Communications Technologies, ISBN 978-3-030-34514-3, Springer Nature Switzerland AG 2020
9. Abdul-rahman Al-Ali, Abdul Khaliq and Muhammad Arshad, "GSM-Based Distribution Transformer Monitoring System", IEEE MELECON, 2004, pp. 999 -1002.
10. Bernd Karl, Stanley Finkelstein, and William Robiner, "The Design of an Internet-Based System to Maintain Home Monitoring Adherence by Lung Transplant Recipients", IEEE Transactions on Infomartion Technology in Biomedicine, Vol 10, No. 1, 2006, pp. 66-76. Figure 8. Set a speed for Fan.
11. Jan L., Suomalainen, J., Ventola, P., "Implementing Mobile Access to Heterogeneous Home Environment", Home Oriented Informatics and Telemetric, California, USA, 2003.
12. Sosa, J., Automation of Home Appliances using Internet of Things Technologies, M.Tech Project Thesis, 2019
13. Juha Koivisto , "Wireless Home Network Architecture and Concepts for User Interactions", VTT (Technical Research Center of Finland) Research Notes, Information Technology, 2002.
14. Jan Lucenius, Jani Suomalainen, Piia Ventola, "Implementing Mobile Access to Heterogeneous Home Environment", Home Oriented Informatics and Telemetric, California, USA, 2003.
15. Bhutani S., Patel, N., 2019, , Smarts Goods Transportation, B.Tech Project Thesis, KJSCE.
16. Juha Koivisto , "Wireless Home Network Architecture and Concepts for User Interactions", VTT (Technical Research Center of Finland) Research Notes, Information Technology, 2002.
17. Abdul-Rahman Al-Ali, Abdul Khaliq and Muhammad Arshad, "GSM-Based Distribution Transformer Monitoring System", IEEE MELECON, 2004, pp. 999 -1002.
18. Bernd Karl, Stanley Finkelstein, and William Robiner, "The Design of an Internet-Based System to Maintain Home Monitoring Adherence by Lung Transplant Recipients", IEEE Transactions on Information Technology in Biomedicine, Vol 10, No. 1, 2006, pp. 66-76.
19. https://create.arduino.cc/projecthub/electronicprojects/smart-irrigation-system-using-arduino-uno-afcb31[last accessed: 16/09/2020]

Future Outlook

CHAPTER 18

"The Internet will disappear. There will be so many IP addresses, so many devices, sensors, things that you are wearing, things that you are interacting with, that you won't even sense it. It will be part of your presence all the time. Imagine you walk into a room, and the room is dynamic. And with your permission and all of that, you are interacting with the things going on in the room."

— Eric Schmidt, Google chairman, on a panel at the World Economic Forum

OBJECTIVES
- introduce the major areas that will impact the future of IoT
- explain the future of the technologies in each layer of IoT
- discuss futuristic IoT use cases

OUTCOMES
- understand the future of IoT technologies
- relate the current technologies and how they are evolving and their future directions
- summarize the future scope of IoT

REVISION

This chapter brings together the various IoT technologies discussed in the earlier chapters and gives a futuristic outlook of them. The layered architecture of IoT as discussed in Chapter 1, the discussion in Chapter 4 on the various IoT standards and protocols, Chapters 5 and 6 on sensors and hardware, and cloud computing and analytics are looked at from a future perspective. How these are evolving and could lead to major innovations and emergence of disruptive technologies in various IoT domains is discussed in this chapter.

18.1 FUTURE ROADMAP

IoT technology has emerged as a highly disruptive technology that is permeating in many walks of life. It has brought in high-end technology and has become a key enabler of digital business transformation. It has also triggered numerous startup opportunities, which are increasing by the day. The scope of IoT has expanded significantly and is impacting many business models. This is due to the way the processed data (aka analytics) from connected devices and sensors is being delivered in a timely and customized fashion that enables businesses to gain useful insights.

These emerging technologies are defining new ways of access to information and put significant emphasis on data protection and privacy controls, so that a connected things world with high autonomy can work to make our lives smarter, more comfortable, and transform the global economy.

The continued and sustained success of IoT will greatly depend on new technology and innovations in all the layers of the IoT model. Below discussion provides the emerging trends in each of the levels of the IoT layer, that is, device, network, platform, and service.

18.1.1 Device

Innovations in the device (a thing with an onboard chip to collect and communicate data over the network) space are gaining a lot of attention recently.

18.1.1.1 Sensors and Actuators

At the sensors and actuators level, the advances in micro-electrical-mechanical systems (MEMS) are enabling numerous IoT hardware innovations. This is due to their portability in terms of small form factor (between 1 μm and 1 mm), low power consumption, low cost, and high performance. The transducers (device that converts energy from one form to the other) in MEMS sensors and actuators are getting more intelligent by being able to act in an autonomous manner and the actuator is able to take a decision with little or no human input.

Examples of innovations relevant to IoT include, vibration-based energy harvesting, graphene FET sensors for gas sensing, smart dust comprising of microcomputers the size of a sand grain, which can be sprinkled in a field for very fine-grained sensing (e.g., soil nutrients/temperature sensing for crop yield predictions, factory monitoring, inventory, etc.), paper-based devices, navigation devices such as gyroscopes and biodegradable sensors. Further, MEMS are revolutionizing the consumer segment in the wearables, smart cars, devices for medical diagnostics, etc.

18.1.1.2 Device Security

In IoT it is necessary to keep track of the device behaviour over time, so that anything that is out of normal can be detected quickly and remedial actions can be initiated. For example, IoT device resources are being excessively used by some application/device, while others are kept waiting and are being unfairly delayed or denied. This inhomogeneous usage of device resources needs to be quickly identified and remedial actions are initiated. One of the future technologies for device security that is highly recommended is the blockchain technology.

The blockchain technology is based on a data structure, which is composed of several data blocks, where each of these blocks is linked with the previous one by a hash of the former's contents. A distributed database composed of several nodes holds this data structure. Due to the key property of these databases, it is highly challenging to modify the database by a few participants (minority) in the system.

Further, light-weight device security architectures for trust establishment are continually being developed to address the low power constraint of the IoT devices, but the sheer variety of IoT devices that are available in the market makes it challenging to develop generic solutions. Although security is described from a device point of view here, the security aspects are equally applicable in all the layers of the IoT stack and will be a major focus in the future.

18.1.1.3 Device Interoperability

Several protocols such as light-weight Machine 2 Machine (LWM2M) from Open Mobile Alliance (OMA) device management protocols are gaining importance as they will enable standardized communication protocols for device management (see Chapter 15 for more details). In absence of such protocols, interoperability is hindered. For example, adding a new smart thing in your home should not be too difficult and should be able to work with your existing IoT setup (e.g., via existing gateway) for home automation. However, this is difficult to achieve in reality, further, making the device understand the personal identity of the person for securely managing that device is not easy. Hence, device interoperability is a major focus area in the future IoT systems.

Some smart devices of the future include smart refrigerators, autonomous cars, smart toothbrushes, delivery drones, physiological monitors, wearables, diagnostic equipment, etc.

18.1.2 Network

Network scalability is one of the top priorities of future IoT systems, which will help in its growth in the long run. The physical infrastructure of IoT network systems is increasingly becoming highly heterogeneous and complex. Hence, managing such an infrastructure requires more efficient ways and also able to do it in real-time or dynamically. To address these issues, virtualization is now widely used for using resources irrespective of its location, size, format, etc.

18.1.2.1 Virtualization

According to Rick F. Van der Lans, 'Virtualization means that applications can use a resource without any concern for where it resides, what the technical interface is, how it has been implemented, which platform it uses, and how much of it is available.'

Virtualization is possible through software implementation of the logical abstraction of the hardware that resides in a network. Thus, through a software interface, a resource can be easily managed and various tasks such as modification, upgradation, etc. can be accomplished. This concept when applied to network infrastructure takes the form of network virtualization. It is a mechanism where software, hardware, and network functionality are abstracted into a logically configured software also called as the virtual network. In the recent past, much work in the area of network virtualization has been done. A discussion on two important techniques, that is, software-defined networks (SDN) and network function virtualization (NFV) which are going to be key drivers in future of IoT networking are described below. It is also the technology adopted by cloud providers to reduce hardware, cost, and also to enable energy savings.

18.1.2.2 Software-Defined Network (SDN)

Software Defined Network (SDN) technology is based on the concept of separating the hardware in a network and the controllers that instruct the router switches about packet forwarding. The controller is responsible for managing the network hardware. As shown in Fig. 18.1, the three components of SDN are:

Infrastructure layer This layer can also be called as the networking devices layer. It consists of the networking hardware (e.g., switches) that have predefined set of instructions such as forwarding incoming packets to ports, controller, etc.

Control layer It is a logical entity that is separated from the devices layer and is capable of acting upon instructions that it receives from the application layers. In addition to the high-level global view of the network in the abstract form, it can also send several pieces of information about the network related to its state in the form of summary statistics and event notifications. This separation of the control from the device layers has the advantage that it can exist anywhere geographically. Hence, it is available either as a centralized system or in the distributed model.

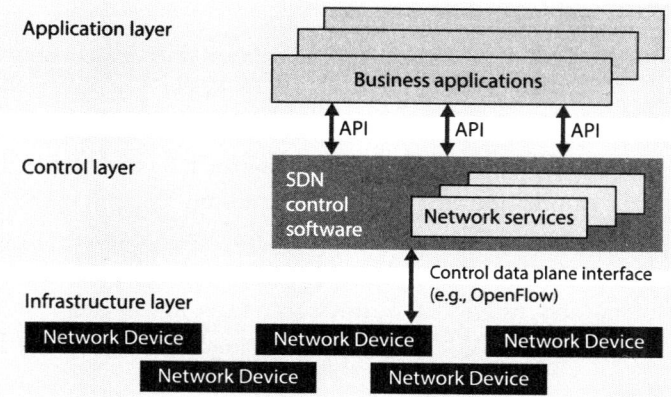

Fig. 18.1 Architecture of Software-Defined Network (SDN)

Application layer This layer, also called as the management layer, can be used to interact with the hardware and monitor them via the control layer. Several types of applications are being developed in this layer that are focused to address a particular aspect of the network such as load balancing, network security, analytics, and business applications.

18.1.2.3 Network Functions Virtualization (NFV)

This approach enables to separate the various network functions which are usually tightly integrated with the hardware and mostly proprietary in nature. The decoupling of these functions and implementation in software running on standardized hardware gives more flexibility in terms of creating and offering network services, on-demand service, scalability, cost reduction, space, energy savings, etc. Thus, any infrastructure can be enabled with networking components such as storage, network, and computing. Examples of functions that are virtualized, also called virtualized network functions (VNFs), include firewalls, switching functions, intrusion detectors, load balancing functions, etc. Figure 18.2 shows the architecture of NFV.

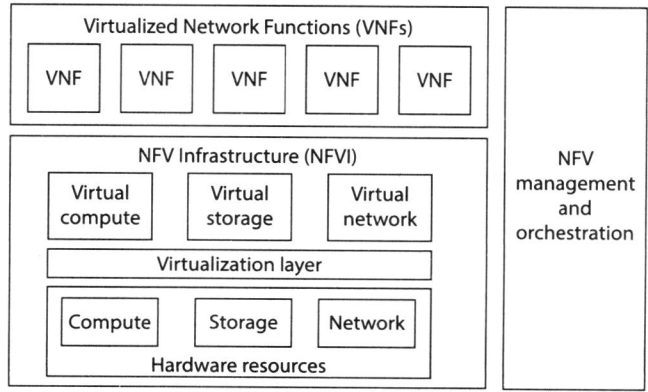

Fig. 18.2 Architecture of Network Functions Virtualization

From an IoT perspective, device and sensor virtualization are also emerging technologies.

18.1.3 Platform

The IoT platform provides various management functions related to device, network connections, and data so that the users can focus on the domain specific problem and leave these core tasks to a software platform. It is envisaged that IoT platforms will play a key role in the future not only in terms of making IoT solutions easier to deploy but will also be one of the major revenue generators. Industry 4.0 is the next wave of industry automation that is being built around technologies such as IoT, cloud, and cognitive computing. The platform will be one of its core pillars and will permeate into the industrial ecosystem. Deep integration of AI and machine learning into cloud-based IoT platforms will enable powerful analytics providing rich insights for businesses to react in real time.

18.1.4 Service

IoT services at the edge are becoming increasingly sophisticated and able to process huge amounts of streaming data from IoT devices and provide intelligence at massive scale. The other kind of IoT services are enabled at the cloud. However, the increasing complexity of these services is leading to maintenance, reliability, and security issues. Hence, there is a need to integrate the edge and cloud services. This process is termed as orchestration (Fig. 18.3). It facilitates gaining more control over the entire data stack so that relevant data can be moved between edge and cloud based on specific requirements and further integrated with an organization's enterprise software. The future IoT services are envisaged to have high orchestration capabilities.

The service orchestration is generally a centralized node, which has the capability to control all the services. However, one disadvantage of such an approach is that all the control is concentrated from one centralized place or organization. It is recommended that distribution of this functionality enables better usage of resources and management. Hence, the concept of choreography emerged. It is a distributed version of orchestration, which makes the accessibility to data and other services easier, thus enabling to perform quick analytics.

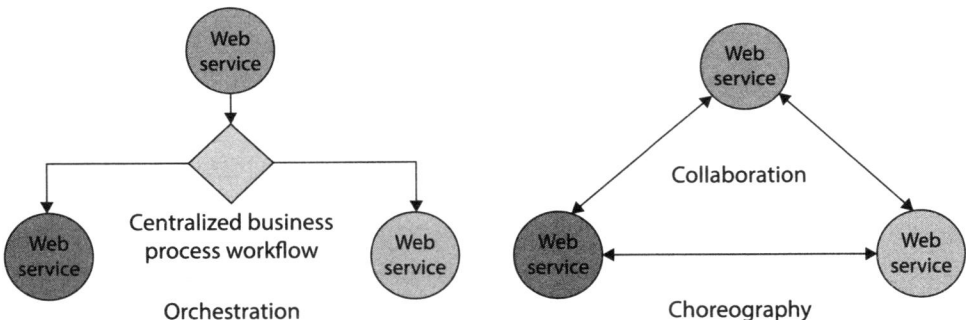

Fig. 18.3 Service Orchestration vs Choreography

Large-scale IoT services immensely benefit from service choreography where each service can react and respond in an independent way. However, these kinds of IoT service solutions need to be carefully designed so that they can process multiple services requests seamlessly. Future IoT systems will take advantage of both these service models, that is, orchestration and choreography and develop hybrid approaches that will work across the wide gamut of IoT applications.

18.2 EXPANDED OPPORTUNITIES FOR IOT APPLICATIONS

The highly accelerated innovations that are taking place in IoT are expected to expand opportunities in several application areas. One such area where IoT is making a huge difference is the area of assisted living.

18.2.1 Home Automation

Home products are becoming smarter and more energy efficient and are called green products. This is going to be a key game changer; achieving overall energy efficiency will be a driving force for home automation. The user is kept in the loop and can make informed decisions based on the feedback from home appliances for conserving energy. These are possible by the integration of machine-learning-based analytics, which will track the interaction pattern with appliances at home and able to make future projections and hence provide the consumer with early knowledge about what is going to happen in the immediate future. The appliances (refrigerators, thermostats, washing machines, microwaves, coffee machines, etc.) will have the potential of having independent control, self-diagnosing capability, and able to interact with other devices. Device manufacturers will build in interoperable frameworks where devices from one vendor can communicate with a device from other vendors seamlessly.

18.2.2 Ambient-Assisted Living (AAL)

Ambient-assisted living provides personalized care to the elderly in their own homes by understanding the home environment and their activities, enabling them to live independently.

Advances in ambient sensing, ambient intelligence, and ambient localization are going to provide new kinds of applications for care-based institutions and families in this area. Figure 18.4 shows the growing elderly population, which reflects the urgent need for more applications that are highly contextual in nature and fit to the needs of the individual.

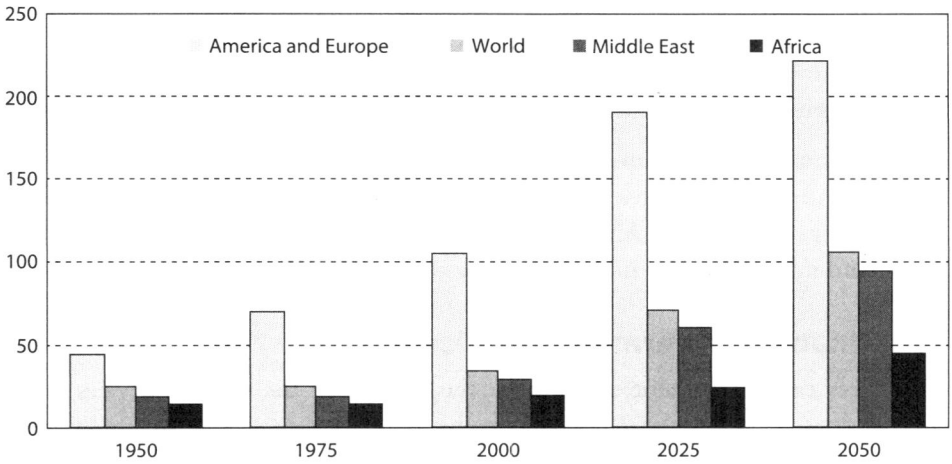

Fig. 18.4 Statistics of Ageing Population Showing Number of Persons Aged 65 Years or Over, Per 100 Children Under 15 Years

(Source credit: From United Nations, Department of Economic and Social Affairs, Population Division (2013).World Population Ageing 2013. ST/ESA/SER.A/348. Copyright © United Nations, 2013. Used with the permission of the United Nations)

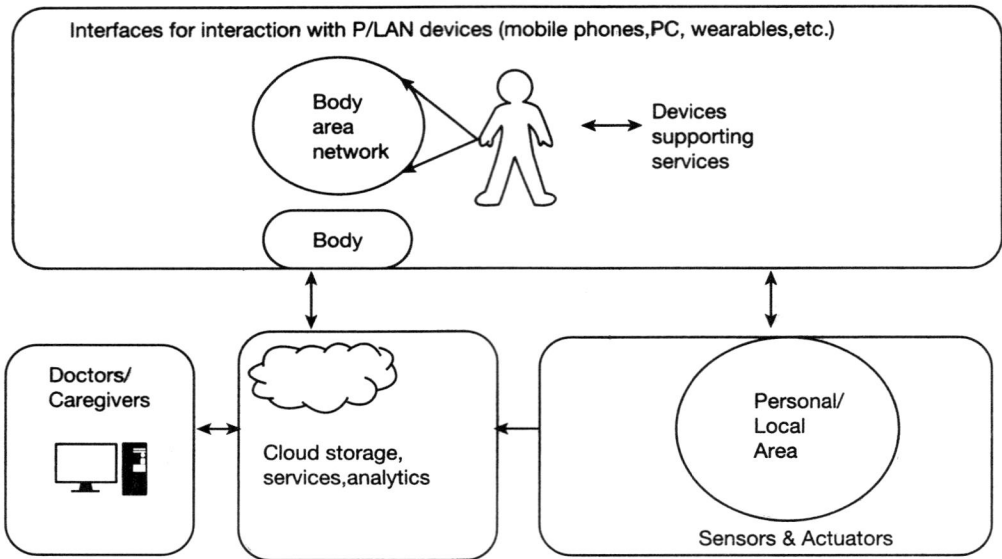

Fig. 18.5 Ambient-assisted Living

IoT-based solutions enable to continuously monitor the living space of the individual and in real time are able to react and provide assistance based on the events that happen in that space. This requires a number of IoT devices to measure various parameters in the indoor environment from different perspectives, as well as the individual health-related indicators to provide situational awareness (Fig. 18.5). Some examples of sensors and actuators that are used for this purpose are:

- Magnetic switch for opening/closing of doors, windows, cabinets, etc.
- Infrared motion sensors for detecting movement of the elderly person
- Force sensor for detecting falls
- Measuring illuminance level with photo sensors
- Temperature sensors for ambient, water, objects temperature

The ALLIANCE organization is a European next generation ambient-assisted living innovation alliance that is providing impetus in this area. According to it 'Standardization and interoperability are key market factors for the success of AAL solutions.' Refer to Chapter 14 for a detailed discussion on standardization and interoperability in the IoT ecosystem.

18.2.3 IoT-enabled Government Services

Public IoT services can create value addition to the citizens in the various services offered by the government and also (a) increase the efficiency of using public facilities and resources by the citizens (b) to optimize the various processes/procedures by the government. This could also enable more citizen participation and contribute to the growth of healthy communities.

IoT-enabled services are beginning to make an impact in improving government operations in several public sector areas such as:

- **Urban planning and management**

The IoT systems when deployed in a judicious way can provide accurate and timely information on various urban parameters and such as smart water delivery, transportation routing, traffic events, land zoning, etc.

- **Sanitation**

Sensors embedded in toilets can capture data and are used for logging the health status of a person and primary diagnosis can be sent to a smartphone. The data can be relayed to a doctor for more complex analysis and related advice can be sent back to that person. This process can also be implemented at a community level and will help in government health officials to keep track of any disease outbreak and respond quickly. Further, basic personal hygiene maintained by people can be monitored at homes, work, and other public places to understand patterns and provide suggestive actions for better hygiene.

- **Parks and recreational areas**

Public sector entities that are responsible for the management of parks and recreation areas can integrate IoT based systems to provide better user experience at parks by providing real-time information about the parks facilities, directions, and registration to various events in the recreational facility, safety and rapid emergency response. Further, information about various modes of transportation, parking facilities can be informed to the public in a better way. The water and nutrient requirements of lawns and other vegetation in the recreational area can also be optimised by using various IoT devices.

- **Utility monitoring**

Utilities such as electricity, water, natural gas, etc, can be monitored using smart meters that can send the data to a cloud platform and various analytics can be performed on this data. The user can check the usage in real-time and accordingly adjust the usage to suit his/her daily spending limit on utilities.

- **Disaster monitoring and assessment**

Disasters monitoring requires information on a dynamically changing ground situation. Local governments are increasingly deploying IoT devices to capture the severity and extent of damage. For example, water level measuring devices can give information about the flood waters. Flood water level network is developed in the UK called the Flood Network (https://flood.network/) to send alerts about areas having high water levels. Similarly, for monitoring and management of various natural and manmade disasters, IoT technologies can play a vital role and help the local authorities in the rescue activities.

In addition to the above, several other sectors such as public safety, smart voting, cybersecurity, healthcare, smart cities, agriculture, etc also benefit from the emerging IoT technologies.

SUMMARY

The future roadmap of IoT can be thought in terms of the major innovations that are taking place in the technologies belonging to the various layers of the IoT stack. The device space is currently a hotbed of new technologies that are quickly being adapted in various applications. The MEMS-based sensors are expected to make huge strides in the IoT devices development. The network layer is also seeing the integration of many technologies and new paradigms such as software-defined networks and network function virtualization which are increasingly being adapted for IoT solutions.

The IoT platforms are at a consolidation phase currently and the competition is huge in this space. It is projected that products based on IoT platforms are going to be major revenue generators for businesses; hence huge investments and product development are happening in this area, where many big companies are involved. IoT services is another area that is gaining more attention as it is more driven by the need to manage the complexity of IoT services. Services orchestration approaches are currently popular but the services choreography approach, which is more decentralized and distributed in nature, is going to be adapted more in the future. Hybrid approaches for services are also being proposed that have both centralized and distributed services components to enable more efficient way of provisioning IoT services.

The IoT technology is here to stay and will play a transformative role in every walk of our lives in the future.

REVIEW QUESTIONS

1. Write a note on the future roadmap of IoT.
2. Explain the innovations in devices that will shape IoT.
3. What are the emerging techniques in network?
4. What is network virtualization? Why is it required?
5. Describe software-defined network.
6. Describe network functions virtualization.
7. What is service orchestration?
8. Explain service choreography.
9. Describe ambient-assisted living and how IoT can impact it.

REFERENCES

1. Lee, S. K., Bae, M., Kim, H. (2017), Future of IoT networks: a survey, *Appl. Sci.* 7: 1072. doi:10.3390/app7101072.
2. [MEMS]: https://spectrum.ieee.org/nanoclast/energy/renewables/a-mems-vibration-energy-harvester-for-the-iot [last accessed: 01/05/2019].
3. [Transducers] https://www.i-scoop.eu/internet-of-things-guide/transducers-iot-internet-things/ [last accessed: 01/05/2019].
4. Mohan, S., Asplund, M., Bloom, G., Sadeghi, A.-R., Ibrahim, A., Salajageh, N., Griffioen, P., Sinopoli, B. (2018), The future of IoT security: special session. *In Proceedings of the International Conference on Embedded Software (EMSOFT '18)*, IEEE Press, Piscataway, NJ, USA, Article 16, 7 pages.
5. Alam, I., Sharif, K., Li, F., Latif, Z., Karim, M. M., Nour, B., Biswas, S., Wang, Y. (2019), IoT virtualization: a survey of software definition and function virtualization techniques for Internet of Things, arXiv:1902.10910.
6. Van Der Lans, R. (2012). Data Virtualization for business intelligence systems: revolutionizing data integration for data warehouses. Elsevier.
7. United Nations. (2012), Changing balance between age groups. United Nations, New York.
8. Al-Shaqi, R., Mourshed, M., Rezgui, Y. (2016), Progress in ambient assisted systems for independent living by the elderly. *SpringerPlus*. 5: 624. 10.1186/s40064-016-2272-8.
9. Van Den Broek, G., Cavallo, F., Wehrmann, C. (2010), *AALIANCE Ambient Assisted Living Roadmap (Ambient Intelligence and Smart Environments)*, IOS Press: Amsterdam, The Netherlands. The publication is available at IOS Press through http://dx.doi.org
10. Dorronzoro, E., Gómez, I., Medina, A.V., Gómez, J. A. (2015), Design and implementation of a prototype with a standardized interface for transducers in ambient assisted living. *Sensors (Basel)*. 15: 2999–3022. 10.3390/s150202999.
11. [AALIANCE] http://www.aaliance.eu/ [last accessed: 01/05/2019].

About the Authors

Dr Surya S. Durbha is Professor at CSRE, Indian Institute of Technology Bombay (IITB). Before joining IITB, he worked as an Assistant Research Professor at the Centre for Advanced Vehicular Systems (CAVS), Geosystems Research Institute (GRI) and also held an adjunct faculty position with the electrical and computer engineering department at Mississippi State University (MSU).

Earlier, Dr Durbha worked as a Scientist at the Indian Institute of Remote Sensing (IIRS), ISRO, Govt of India. He received B.E. degree in Civil-environmental engineering and M.Tech degree in remote sensing both from Andhra University, India, in 1994, 1997, respectively, and Ph.D degree in computer engineering from Mississippi State University (MSU), MS, U.S.A, in 2006. At MSU, he researched and developed image information mining tools for content-based knowledge retrieval from remote sensing imagery and the retrieval of biophysical variables from multi-angle satellite data.

Dr Durbha has published over 80 peer reviewed articles, served on program committees of several international conferences including SSKI, SSTDM, and IGARSS, co-chaired sessions at various conferences, and has been an invited speaker for HPC, Geospatial technologies, and IOT training programs in various institutes. He is a manuscript reviewer for IEEE, Elsevier, Springer, and other high impact Journals. He organized the Distributed and Embedded High Performance Computing International symposium at IIT Bombay in 2016. He received the Excellence in Teaching award at IIT Bombay, and NVIDIA Innovation Award 2016 for his work in Image Information Mining and High Performance Computing (HPC). Dr Durbha also received the StatePride Faculty and Outstanding Research awards earlier at MSU.

Dr Jyoti Joglekar is Professor in the Department of Computer Engineering at K. J. Somaiya College of Engineering (KJSCE), Somaiya Vidyavihar University (SVU), Mumbai. She holds a degree in 'Master of Computer Engineering' from the University of Mumbai and a Bachelor degree in 'Electrical Engineering' from Walchand College of Engineering, Sangli. Dr Joglekar holds Ph.D. from IIT Bombay in the area of 'Stereo Image Analysis of Satellite Images'. She has presented her research work in several International conferences of repute such as the International Society of Photogrammetry and Remote Sensing (ISPRS). Dr Joglekar has over 27 publications in international journals and international conferences of repute. She is a reviewer of international journals such as IEEE Transactions on Geoscience and Remote Sensing (TGRS), IEEE letters, IEEE Access, IET, etc. She has been honoured as Fellow member of IETE (Institute of Electronics and Telecommunication Engineering) and is a Life Fellow on Computer Vision and Imaging AI at the PanIIT Institute. She is a member of Board of Studies of various eminent institutes.

She has been invited as an expert speaker in various Quality Improvement Programs (QIP), Faculty Development Programs (FDP) and Short-term Training Programs (STTP) in various institutions such as IIT Bombay and Engineering institutes of Mumbai University.

Dr Joglekar won the second prize for her poster paper presentation at INAC-4 conference by ISSE and ISRO held at SAC, ISRO, Ahmedabad in September 2019. She is an active member of the SIH Innovative Product Drive Ecosystem and has mentored students of winning teams in Smart India Hackathon (SIH) 2018 and 2019. She has over 25 years of teaching experience to undergraduate and post-graduate students. She also possesses few years of industry experience. She is an active research volunteer with IIT Alumni Council since April 2020 and is working on several cutting-edge technologies in the area of ultrasound imaging and quantum computing as social initiatives of the council. She was awarded as a Distinguished Research Fellow by IIT Alumni Council on 20 Dec 2020 for her work in Holographic Imaging and AI. She is working on some research projects funded by eminent research organisations of India.

Related Titles

DATA STRUCTURES USING PYTHON (9780190124083)

Shriram K. Vasudevan, Assistant Professor, Department of Computer Science and Engineering, Amrita Vishwa Vidyapeetham, Coimbatore, Tamil Nadu

Abhishek S. Nagarajan is working as a Data Scientist in [24]7.ai.

Karthick Nanmaran, Assistant Professor, Department of CSE, SRM Institute of Science and Technology, Chennai

Data Structures using Python provides an introduction to design, analysis, and implementation of data structures using the powerful language, Python. This book is designed for a first course on the subject. It is written for the undergraduate students of computer science, information technology, and allied disciplines.

Key Features

- Offers Simple and Lucid explanations for complex Data Structure concepts using analogies from real-world objects/systems
- Includes 170+ Codes and 190+ Figures, illustrating the concepts
- Comes with 300+ Chapter-end Exercises including multiple-choice questions, theoretical review questions, and exploratory application exercises.
- Provides 150+ 'Food for Brain' mid-chapter questions, picto puzzles, and mini projects, and 60+ Solved Examples

PYTHON PROGRAMMING: USING PROBLEM SOLVING APPROACH (9780199480173)

Reema Thareja, Assistant Professor, Department of Computer Science, Shyama Prasad Mukherji College for Women, University of Delhi

Python Programming is designed as a textbook to fulfil the requirements of the first-level course in Python programming. It is suited for undergraduate degree students of computer science engineering, information technology as well as computer applications. This book will enable students to apply the Python programming concepts in solving real-world problems.

Key Features

- Simple and lucid treatment of concepts supported with illustrations for easy understanding.
- Numerous programming examples along with their outputs to help students master the art of writing efficient Python programs.
- Notes and programming tips to highlight the important concepts and help readers avoid common programming errors.
- Strong chapter-end pedagogy including plenty of objective-type questions, review questions, programming and debugging exercises to facilitate revision and practice of concepts learnt.
- 7 Annexures and 5 appendices covering types of operating systems, differences between Python 2.x and 3.x, installing Python, debugging and testing, iterators, generators, getters, setters, Turtle graphics,

plotting graphs, multi-threading, GUI and Web Programming provided to supplement the text.
- Case studies on creating calculator, calendar, hash files, compressing strings and files, tower of Hanoi, image processing, shuffling a deck of cards, and mail merge demonstrate the application of various concepts.
- Point-wise summary and glossary of key terms to aid quick recapitulation of concepts.

PLACEMENTOR (9780199488780)

Archana Ram, Co-founder of SMART Training Resources Pvt. Ltd, Chennai.

Tests of Aptitude for Placement Readiness is designed to be an indispensable resource material for students to develop the key skills of employability, namely quantitative aptitude, logical reasoning and verbal ability. The book, by addressing the key components of campus placement tests, offers a complete package for students embarking upon their career journey from academics.

Key Features

- Addresses all key skills required for gaining success in campus recruitment tests
- Provides discussion on soft skills for employability covering topics such as body language, handling interviews, GDs, etc.
- Presents a brief overview of each topic along with examples, and plenty of exercise questions for practice with complete solutions at the end of each chapter

CYBER FORENSICS (9780199489442)

Dejey, Assistant Professor, Department of Computer Science and Engineering, Anna University, Tirunelveli Regional Centre

S. Murugan is a 1997 batch Indian Police Service (IPS) officer and currently the Inspector General (IG) of Police and Joint Director, Vigilance and Anti-corruption, Chennai.

Cyber Forensics is a textbook designed for the undergraduate engineering students of Computer Science and Information Technology programmes for the related course. The book will be equally useful as a primer for students from diverse backgrounds to help understand how cyber media is misused for committing crimes. It will also be useful for cyber forensic professionals, cybercrime investigators, and computer professionals for implementing security measures to protect their digital assets.

Key Features

- Provides a perfect balance of discussion on cybercrime, forensics, and cyber laws (both Indian and International)
- Discusses principles, processes, and case studies for a better grasp of concepts
- Introduces a fundamental chapter on computer networks and security
- Provides a model case example report as an appendix for a better understanding of how forensic examination findings are reported and documented

OTHER RELATED TITLES

Remote Sensing and GIS, 3e, Bhatta [9780199496648]
Artificial Intelligence & Intelligent Systems, N.P. Padhy [9780195671544]

Robotics: Fundamental Concepts and Analysis, Ashitava Ghosal [9780195673913]